T H E
WINSTON READER

T H E
WINSTON READER

BONNIE CARTER

CRAIG SKATES

UNIVERSITY OF SOUTHERN MISSISSIPPI

Holt, Rinehart and Winston, Inc.

Fort Worth   Chicago   San Francisco   Philadelphia
Montreal   Toronto   London   Sydney   Tokyo

Publisher   Ted Buchholz
Acquisitions Editor   Michael A. Rosenberg
Developmental Editor   Leslie Taggart/Christine Caperton
Project Editor   Steve Welch
Production Manager   Ken Dunaway
Art & Design Supervisor   Serena Barnett/Pat Bracken
Text Designer   Caliber/Phoenix Color Corp.
Cover Designer   Vicki McAlindon Horton
On the Cover   Richard Estes's *Revolving Doors,* 1968, 30 x 34 inches, oil on masonite.
Courtesy Louis K. Meisel Gallery, New York. Photo by Steve Lopez.

Library of Congress Cataloging-in-Publication Data

The Winston reader / [compiled by] Bonnie Carter, Craig Skates.
    p.   cm.
    Includes bibliographical references and index.
    ISBN 0–03–026597–5
    1. College readers.   2. English language—Rhetoric.   I. Carter,
Bonnie.   II. Skates, Craig Barnwell.
    PE1417.W55   1991   90–24912
    808′.0427—dc20   CIP

Address for Editorial Correspondence: Holt, Rinehart and Winston, Inc., 301 Commerce Street, Suite 3700, Fort Worth, TX 76102.

Address for Orders: Holt, Rinehart and Winston, Inc., 6277 Sea Harbor Drive, Orlando, FL 32887. 1-800-782-4479, or 1-800-433-0001 (in Florida).

Printed in the United States of America

1 2 3 4   090   9 8 7 6 5 4 3 2 1

Holt, Rinehart and Winston, Inc.
The Dryden Press
Saunders College Publishing

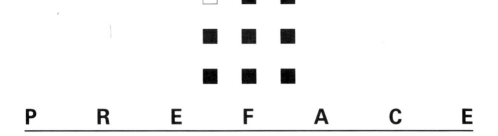

P R E F A C E

When writing an essay, Gilbert Highet advises, "Be interested and you will be interesting." But interest is not always easy to summon up. And as the teacher of composition knows, lack of interest often results in poor writing. The purpose of this text is to get students interested. It provides readings on many different subjects—some personal, some social, some academic, some scientific and technical. Throughout, the selections mix moods and styles—light and serious, broad and specific, journalistic and literary.

For example, in "Memories," Elizabeth Stone and Sallie Tisdale write seriously about how our families shape us; Russell Baker takes a humorous look at a favorite uncle; Eudora Welty creates wacky siblings in a family of eccentrics. Maya Angelou writes movingly about prejudice at her high school graduation in the South; Richard Thurman tells an entertaining tale of prejudice in a Utah grammar school; Ernesto Galarza describes his California grammar school as a "griddle" that "roasted racial hatreds out of us."

In another typical section, "Traditions," Daniel Boorstin views Christmas celebrations from the historian's point of view, while Jessica Mitford exposes the rituals of the funeral business through the eyes of the reformer. Ink Mendelsohn presents a broad picture of clothing through the ages. Roy Blount, however, takes a humorous look at specifically the hat, and Roland Sodowsky spins a strange tale about the cowboy boot. Reay Tannahill, Peter Farb, George Armelagos, and Guy Davenport look at the sociology and anthropology of food; and A. R. Gurney, Jr. writes a piece on the sophisticated dinner party.

All the sections cover a variety of terrains. In "Film and Television," Joan Didion writes a love song to John Wayne, and Roger Rosenblatt blasts Rhett Butler. In "Travel," N. Scott Momaday waxes nostalgic over his roots in New Mexico, and Manuela Hoelterhoff casts her journalist's eye on Disney World and finds it wanting. In "Plants and Animals," David Quammin mixes humor with scientific facts about crows, while Loren Eiseley mixes poetry with anthropology to explain how flowers changed the world. On computing, Tom Bodett and Kurt Vonnegut offer humorous looks; but Sherry Turkle takes a more serious attitude. On nuclear war, Lydia Dotto writes a scientifically detached essay, in contrast to Joy Kogawa, who presents a personal and tragic view.

In addition to the abundance of subjects and viewpoints, students will find a variety of voices. Of the hundred selections, fifty were written by women and fifty by men. Many of the authors belong to minorities. Some authors are famous; others, relatively unknown. Some are contemporary, and some speak from the past.

Questions at the end of each reading help students discover and consider the content of the selection and the techniques of the writer. In addition, each reading is followed by writing suggestions to stimulate ideas for student compositions. And each section ends with recommendations for combining sources in a composition so that students can practice bringing sources together—comparing, contrasting, and integrating ideas. In all, there are 547 suggestions for student papers.

Reading is one of the fastest and most productive ways to find interesting writing topics. With regular deadlines, students haven't much time to wait for inspiration; usually, they must stimulate ideas by some other means. In this text, the wealth of variety—in subject, style, and voice—stimulates the student of composition to "be interested" and thus "be interesting."

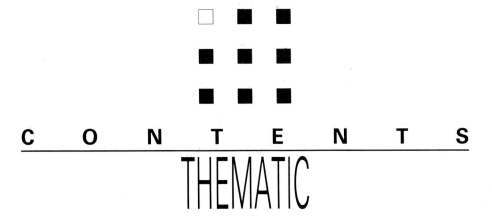

C O N T E N T S

THEMATIC

CHAPTER 1 MEMORIES

HOME AND FAMILY   1

Elizabeth Stone, "How Our Family Stories Shape Us"   **1**
   "These stories last not because they're entertaining, though they may be; they last because in ways large and small they matter."

Margaret Laurence, "Where the World Began"   **6**
   "The oddities of the place were endless."

Nikki Giovanni, "400 Mulvaney Street"   **11**
   "Something called progress killed my grandmother."

Russell Baker, "Uncle Harold"   **18**
   "In spite of his reputation for varnishing a fact, or maybe because of the outrageousness with which he did the varnishing, I found him irresistible."

James D. Houston, "How Playing Country Music Taught Me
   To Love My Dad"   **23**
   "I still love the galliards. . . . But it took me twenty years of part-time music life to discover, or rather to quit being ashamed of the fact and come right out and admit that I love San Antonio Rose *more."*

Sallie Tisdale, "Bound upon a Wheel of Fire"   **29**
   "At odd times—during dinner, late at night—the alarm would sound, and my father would leap up, knocking dogs and small children aside as he ran from the house."

Eudora Welty, "Why I Live at the P.O."   **36**
   " 'And as to where I intend to go, you seem to forget my position as postmistress of China Grove, Mississippi,' I says."

SCHOOL AND FRIENDS   47

John Updike, "Three Boys"   **47**
"He was my friend before kindergarten, he is my friend still."

Annie Dillard, "The Chase"   **51**
"I got in trouble throwing snowballs, and have seldom been happier since."

Phillip Lopate, "My Early Years at School"   **54**
"Yet even then I knew (children know it better than adults) that in telling a lie, fidelity is everything."

Ernesto Galarza, "Lincoln School"   **58**
"The school was not so much a melting pot as a griddle where Miss Hopley and her helpers warmed knowledge into us and roasted racial hatreds out of us."

Elizabeth Bishop, "Primer Class"   **64**
"Every time I see long columns of numbers, handwritten in a certain way, a strange sensation or shudder, partly aesthetic, partly painful, goes through my diaphragm."

Maya Angelou, "Graduation at Lafayette County Training School"   **70**
"I was no longer simply a member of the proud graduating class of 1940; I was a proud member of the wonderful, beautiful Negro race."

Richard Thurman, "Not Another Word"   **80**
"Because I was one of the bigger, healthier boys . . . and also one of the biggest, smoothest liars, and thus apt to set an inspiring example for the others—Miss Devron would often begin the morning's inquisition with me."

CHAPTER 2   TRADITIONS

RITUALS AND CELEBRATIONS   97

Daniel J. Boorstin, "Christmas and Other Festivals
   of Consumption"   **97**
"In a nation of consumption communities, there was a tendency for all festivals somehow to become Festivals of Consumption."

William Geist, "Megawatt Miracles of the Yuletide"   **104**
"This is a time in the suburbs for hauling out the ladder and wrapping the bushes in lights. . . ."

Michael J. Arlen, "Ode to Thanksgiving"   **107**
"It is time, at last, to speak the truth about Thanksgiving, and the truth is this. Thanksgiving is really not such a terrific holiday."

Jessica Mitford, "The American Way of Death"   **111**
"A new mythology, essential to the twentieth-century American funeral rite, has grown up . . . to justify the peculiar customs surrounding the disposal of our dead."

Pat Esslinger Carr, "The Party"   **115**

"A massive pink frosted cake with a circle of twelve pink candles in flower holders sat in the center of the table, and the whole rest of the table top was jammed with pink paper plates holding a pink snapper each and a pink nut cup stuffed with cashew nuts."

CLOTHING   122

Ink Mendelsohn, "We Were What We Wore"   **122**

"Clothing's most pervading function has been to declare status."

Alison Lurie, "The Language of White Costumes"   **132**

"Perhaps because it soils easily, or perhaps because of its long association with infancy and early childhood, all-white clothing has often suggested delicacy, and even physical infirmity or weakness, especially when the material is fragile."

Carin C. Quinn, "The Jeaning of America—and the World"   **135**

"[Blue jeans] draw no distinctions and recognize no classes; they are merely American."

Roy Blount, Jr., "On Hats"   **138**

"Nothing in this world makes a person who is not a cowboy look less like a cowboy than wearing a cowboy hat. . . ."

Roland Sodowsky, "The Origins of the Cowboy Boot"   **142**

"Many puzzled historians have noted that the Texas Occident boot resembles the contours of the human foot about as much as bandannas do bananas."

EATING   147

Peter Farb and George Armelagos, "Understanding Society and Culture Through Eating"   **147**

"With so much cultural importance attached to eating, it is no wonder that food to a large extent is what holds a society together."

Guy Davenport, "The Anthropology of Table Manners from Geophagy Onward"   **153**

"Eating is always at least two activities: consuming food and obeying a code of manners."

Reay Tannahill, "Future Eating Patterns"   **160**

"In any attempt to shape future eating habits . . . it would be important to remember just how deeply ingrained certain food traditions are."

Vernon Pizer, "BLT, Hold the Mayo"   **168**

"In the world of snack foods, America is the undisputed superpower, totally unrivaled for that position by any other nation."

Joseph Monninger, "Fast Food"   **175**

"Fast food was, and is, designed for travel, . . . for people too busy to linger over a slower-paced restaurant meal."

A. R. Gurney, Jr., "The Dinner Party"   **186**
"It all looked as sacred and mysterious as the altar at Trinity Church, where we'd go the next day if our parents weren't too tired."

CHAPTER 3   ENTERTAINMENT

FILM AND TELEVISION   **193**

Joan Didion, "John Wayne: A Love Song"   **193**
". . . when John Wayne rode through my childhood, and perhaps through yours, he determined forever the shape of certain of our dreams."

Roger Rosenblatt, "Reconsideration: *Gone with the Wind*, the Movie"   **200**
"Men would die for her, and do, not because they are spellbound by the softness of Scarlett's skin, but by her will."

Stephen King, "My Creature from the Black Lagoon"   **206**
"He might be waiting in the closet when we got back; he might be standing slumped in the blackness of the bathroom at the end of the hall, stinking of algae and swamp rot, all ready for a post-midnight snack of small boy."

Walter Karp, "Where the Media Critics Went Wrong"   **214**
"In America you cannot promote deference and successfully sell soap. You cannot promote servility and amuse a vast audience."

Marie Winn, "How Parents Survived before Television"   **220**
"Without doubt the availability of television as a child-rearing tool has reduced parents' immediate need to know their children well."

Gwen Kinkead, "Another World"   **225**
"Nowhere else in show business is there anything like the attachment between soap actors and viewers."

TRAVEL   **230**

N. Scott Momaday, "Discovering the Land of Light"   **230**
"It happens that I have traveled far and wide, and I have made my home elsewhere. But some elemental part of me remains in the hold of northern New Mexico."

Manuela Hoelterhoff, "Walt's Wonderful World Turns Out to Be Flat"   **236**
"Somehow the plastic heart of Disney didn't beat for me."

Jean Stafford, "Why I Don't Get Around Much Anymore"   **241**
"Far from broadening, travel in this unenlightened age has narrowed my mind to a hairsbreadth."

Ben Yagota, "Unfolding the Nation"   **248**
"Unfolding a state map and following a crooked line to a town called, say, Clarion, is a potent imaginative experience: it makes you ponder."

Jan Morris, "On Wateriness"   **252**

". . . our instinct leads always, wherever we are, like lemmings to the water's edge."

Bobbie Ann Mason, "The Ocean"   **256**

"The interestate highway was like the ocean. It seemed to go on forever and was a similar color."

SPORTS   270

Rheta Grimsley Johnson, "Greg Pratt Is Dead"   **270**

"Pratt's funeral delayed practice one day, but any fool believing his death might stop for one moment the actual game is green as new Astroturf."

Leonard Koppett, "Baseball's Hits and Misses"   **272**

"Baseball fans have witnessed many developments in their game of choice during the 40 years since the end of World War II, some favorable, some not so."

Donald Hall, "Basketball: The Purest Sport of Bodies"   **279**

"Professional basketball combines opposites—elegant gymnastics, ferocious ballet, gargantuan delicacy, colossal precision. . . ."

Joyce Carol Oates, "On Boxing and Pain"   **283**

"Boxing is about being hit rather than it is about hitting, just as it is about feeling pain . . . more than it is about winning."

Nikki Giovanni, "Toward Better Human Understanding"   **287**

"Men and women are different, and no matter what kind of data we uncover we will still see the differences . . . and sports proves it."

CHAPTER 4 NATURE

PLANTS AND ANIMALS   295

John Stewart Collis, "The Potato"   **295**

". . . faith is reborn whenever anyone chooses to take a good look at anything—even a potato."

Loren Eiseley, "How Flowers Changed the World"   **299**

"Flowers changed the face of the planet. Without them, the world we know . . . would never have existed."

Sally Carrighar, "The Cutthroat Trout"   **307**

"Every instinct whispers some command; for him the loudest command was always, live."

Edward Hoagland, "The Courage of Turtles"   **317**

"Turtles cough, burp, whistle, grunt and hiss, and produce social judgments."

David Quammin, "Has Success Spoiled the Crow?"   **323**

"Crows are not stupid. Far from it. They are merely underachievers."

Phyllis S. Busch, "Plants and Animals in Winter"   **327**

"It is as if thousands of actors . . . gave a rehearsed performance, finished on cue, then slowly made their exit, leaving behind a cold stillness."

Alice Walker, "Am I Blue?"   **334**

"I almost laughed (I felt too sad to cry) to think there are people who do not know that animals suffer."

HUMANS AND THE ENVIRONMENT   340

James C. Rettie, " 'But a Watch in the Night': A Scientific Fable"   **340**

"We have just arrived upon this Earth. How long will we stay?"

Marjorie Kinnan Rawlings, "Who Owns Cross Creek?"   **345**

"It seems to me that the earth may be borrowed but not bought. It may be used, but not owned."

Eleanor Perényi, "Partly Cloudy"   **348**

"No wonder the prospect of a little bad weather makes us nervous. We aren't equipped to handle it physically or—what is more important in the long run—psychologically either."

Robert Finch, "One That Got Away"   **353**

"It would be a less than graceful crossing, but it seemed so silly, so stupid, to be turned back at this point by something as trivial as a leaky boot."

Jesse Hill Ford, "To the Open Water"   **360**

"He had hunted them because he loved them then with the same passionate ache in his throat that he felt now for those creatures settled there on the open water by the thousands, their wild hearts calling his own, it seemed."

Rachel Carson, "The Obligation to Endure"   **367**

"These sprays, dusts, and aerosols are now applied almost universally to farms, gardens, forests, and homes—nonselective chemicals that have the power to kill every insect, the 'good' and the 'bad,' to still the song of birds and the leaping of fish in the streams, to coat the leaves with a deadly film, and to linger on in soil—all this though the intended target may be only a few weeds or insects."

CHAPTER 5   SCIENCE AND TECHNOLOGY

THE COMPUTER   375

Norman Cousins, "The Poet and the Computer"   **375**

"The danger is not so much that man will be controlled by the computer as that he may imitate it."

Tom Bodett, "Command Performance"   **378**

"Unlike fire, computers are what they call 'user-friendly.' Now, what I think that means is that those little boxes of microchips like you and want to hang around with you."

Craig Brod, "Childhood Lost"   **381**

  "The computer can become a refuge from the problems and conflicts of the real world, and well-rounded development and maturity can suffer."

Sherry Turkle, "The New Philosophers of Artificial Intelligence"   **394**

  "Ask different AI theorists what are the most important AI theories, and you get different answers. But what is common to all of them is an emphasis on a new way of knowing."

Kurt Vonnegut, Jr., "EPICAC"   **400**

  "You can call him a machine if you want to. He looked like a machine, but he was a whole lot less like a machine than plenty of people I could name."

NUCLEAR POWER   407

Paul Loeb, "Atomic Soap: On the Job With the Young and the Restless"   **407**

  "The operators—wearing their filtered breather masks for protection—ended up scrubbing away the contamination with soap, rags and elbow grease just like any not-so-happy housewife in any soiled suburban kitchen."

Helen Caldicott, "What You Must Know about Radiation"   **413**

  "The reason for care is that human beings are more sensitive to the effects of radiation than any other animal."

Calvin Trillin, "Nuclear War: My Position"   **424**

  "Looking for ways to ease my mind about signs that the danger of nuclear war is increasing, I stumbled across one comforting thought: maybe the Russian missiles won't work."

Lydia Dotto, "The Environmental Consequences of Nuclear War"   **427**

  "The deployment of increasing numbers of more powerful weapons since the experience of Hiroshima and Nagasaki inevitably prompts the question: What would happen if many modern nuclear weapons were to be exploded?"

Joy Kogawa, "The Letters"   **437**

  "The letter is dated simply 1949. It was sent, Sensei says, from somewhere in Nagasaki. There was no return address."

Annabel Thomas, "The Phototropic Woman"   **443**

  "She wondered what was going on outside. Was the world burnt to ashes? Were scarred people picking about through swelling corpses, twisted metal, broken glass?"

THE FUTURE   451

Isaac Asimov, "A Choice of Catastrophes"   **451**

  "With the view of the world as science has given it to us these last three centuries, can we laugh and say that the world will not, and cannot, come to an end? No. . . ."

Barbara Tuchman, "Is History a Guide to the Future?"   **462**

"History is the record of human behavior, the most fascinating subject of all, but illogical and so crammed with an unlimited number of variables that it is not susceptible of the scientific method nor of systematizing."

Holcomb B. Noble, "Beyond the Knowable: The Ultimate Exploration"   **471**

"Two bits of the present unknown that now nag persistently at the human consciousness and somehow seem more and more knowable are phenomena largely regarded in the past as quaint whimsy: extrasensory perception and extraterrestrial intelligence."

Larry Thompson, "The Eerie World of Living Heads"   **480**

"Can you imagine looking around the room, and you're just a head?"

Ursula K. Le Guin, "SQ"   **486**

". . . every month the personnel of the Psychometric Bureau got smaller, since some of them always flunked their monthly Test and were committed to Bethesda."

Vonda N. McIntyre, "Thanatos"   **494**

"All the horses, all the mammals larger and smaller than a rat, were extinct. Except for human beings."

CHAPTER 6   EDUCATION

THE STUDENT   502

Claudia H. Deutsch, "Cheating: Alive and Flourishing"   **502**

"It is a picture of cheating among top students at top schools; of habits that take root in elementary school, bud in high school and flower in college; of parents who care more about their children's success than about their moral development. . . ."

Michele Manges, "The Dead-End Kids"   **509**

"Educators . . . are beginning to wonder whether teen-age work today is not only irrelevant to future careers but even damaging to them."

Mike Royko, "Write On, Barbarians"   **512**

"But frankly, if I were an English teacher and they were my students, I'd lock the letters away where no one could see them."

Helen C. Vo-Dinh, "Excuses, Excuses"   **514**

"I'll know the public and the people who run the schools are serious about improving them the year my classes have not been shortened, delayed, canceled, interrupted or depleted for any reason short of illness, an emergency or the Second Coming."

Neil Postman, "The Classroom"   **517**

"I want merely to affirm the importance of the classroom as a special place . . . in which the uses of the intellect are given prominence in a setting of elevated language, civilized manners, and respect for social symbols."

Peter Cameron, "Homework"   **526**
  "Find the value for n *such that* n *plus everything else in your life makes you feel all right. What would* n *equal? Solve for* n.*"*

THE SYSTEM   533

Dava Sobel, "Acid Test"   **533**
  "Several times a year, approximately 40 million youngsters around the country pile into classrooms, where they hunch over their desks and spend hours blackening tiny bubbles on a piece of paper."

Robert MacNeil, "Is Television Shortening Our Attention Span?"   **536**
  "You are required, in much popular television fare, to pay attention to no concept, no situation, no scene, no character, and no problem for more than a few seconds at a time."

Grace Lichtenstein, "Playing for Money"   **543**
  "Individually and collectively, athletes are charging that college prevented them from getting their degrees, injected them with needless painkillers and even bribed them."

Mortimer J. Adler, "Paideia Proposal: The Same Course of Study for All"   **554**
  "All sidetracks, specialized courses, or elective choices must be eliminated. Allowing them will always lead a certain number of students to voluntarily downgrade their own education."

Floretta Dukes McKenzie, "The Yellow Brick Road of Education"   **563**
  "This belief, that what is best for the best is best for all, is a dangerously elitist tenet which may destroy the potential of countless young minds."

Diane Ravitch, "On Thinking About the Future"   **568**
  "Because the social and political trends of our nation are increasingly egalitarian, we will want the school in the year 2000 to provide for all children the kind of education that is available today only to those in the best private and public schools."

CHAPTER 7   OUTSIDERS

DISCRIMINATION   579

James Baldwin, "Fifth Avenue, Uptown: A Letter from Harlem"   **579**
  "Walk through the streets of Harlem and see what we, this nation, have become."

Mary Mebane, "The System"   **587**
  "The people who devised this system thought that it was going to last forever."

Roger Kahn, "A Jewish Education"   **593**
  "Rosen fought for a lot of reasons, but he had learned to fight because he was a Jew."

Virginia Woolf, "No Woman Wrote a Word"   **600**

"For it is a perennial puzzle why no woman wrote a word of that extraordinary literature when every other man, it seemed, was capable of song or sonnet."

Casey Miller and Kate Swift, "One Small Step for Genkind"   **607**

"Semantically speaking, woman is not one with the species of man, but a distinct subspecies."

POVERTY AND HOPELESSNESS   619

Don Oldenburg, "Born to Run"   **619**

"I wood like to be home and that mean not in and institution that has and iron gate that locks me in."

Elizabeth Marek, "The Lives of Teenage Mothers"   **633**

"In all their stories, I hear again and again how little volition these girls feel they have, how little control over the events of their lives."

Jonathan Kozol, "A Captive State"   **643**

"As families are compelled to choose between feeding their children or paying their rent, homelessness has taken on the characteristics of a captive state."

Marjorie Hope, "A Clean, Well-Lighted Bench"   **656**

"Franz was not a child, or a woman, or an alcoholic, or a patient with an identifiable malady. . . . He was only a homeless old man."

Gail Regier, "Users, Like Me: Membership in the Church of Drugs"   **670**

"What we had in common was drugs. Getting high bound us together against outsiders, gathered us into a common purpose."

Toni Cade Bambara, "The Lesson"   **677**

"And then she gets to the part about we all poor and live in the slums, which I don't feature."

C O N T E N T S

RHETORICAL

The selections are categorized according to overall purpose and any characteristic worthy of special note.

DESCRIPTION

Margaret Laurence, "Where the World Began"   6
Nikki Giovanni, "400 Mulvaney Street"   11
Russell Baker, "Uncle Harold"   18
James D. Houston, "How Playing Country Music Taught Me To Love My Dad"   23
Sallie Tisdale, "Bound upon a Wheel of Fire"   29
Eudora Welty, "Why I Live at the P.O."   36
Annie Dillard, "The Chase"   51
Phillip Lopate, "My Early Years at School"   54
Ernesto Galarza, "Lincoln School"   58
Elizabeth Bishop, "Primer Class"   64
Maya Angelou, "Graduation at Lafayette County Training School"   70
Richard Thurman, "Not Another Word"   80
William Geist, "Megawatt Miracles of the Yuletide"   104
Michael J. Arlen, "Ode to Thanksgiving"   107
Pat Esslinger Carr, "The Party"   115
Roland Sodowsky, "The Origins of the Cowboy Boot"   142
A. R. Gurney, Jr., "The Dinner Party"   186
Joan Didion, "John Wayne: A Love Song"   193
Roger Rosenblatt, "Reconsideration: *Gone with the Wind*, the Movie"   200
Stephen King, "My Creature from the Black Lagoon"   206
N. Scott Momaday, "Discovering the Land of Light"   230

Manuela Hoelterhoff, "Walt's Wonderful World Turns Out to Be Flat"   **236**
Bobbie Ann Mason, "The Ocean"   **256**
Donald Hall, "Basketball: The Purest Sport of Bodies"   **279**
John Stewart Collis, "The Potato"   **295**
Loren Eiseley, "How Flowers Changed the World"   **299**
Sally Carrighar, "The Cutthroat Trout"   **307**
Edward Hoagland, "The Courage of Turtles"   **317**
David Quammin, "Has Success Spoiled the Crow?"   **323**
Marjorie Kinnan Rawlings, "Who Owns Cross Creek?"   **345**
Robert Finch, "One That Got Away"   **353**
Jesse Hill Ford, "To the Open Water"   **360**
Kurt Vonnegut, Jr., "EPICAC"   **400**
Paul Loeb, "Atomic Soap: On the Job With the Young and the Restless"   **407**
Joy Kogawa, "The Letters"   **437**
Annabel Thomas, "The Phototropic Woman"   **443**
Ursula K. Le Guin, "SQ"   **486**
Vonda N. McIntyre, "Thanatos"   **494**
Peter Cameron, "Homework"   **526**
James Baldwin, "Fifth Avenue, Uptown: A Letter from Harlem"   **579**
Mary Mebane, "The System"   **587**
Gail Regier, "Users, Like Me: Membership in the Church of Drugs"   **670**
Toni Cade Bambara, "The Lesson"   **677**

NARRATION

Nikki Giovanni, "400 Mulvaney Street"   **11**
Russell Baker, "Uncle Harold"   **18**
James D. Houston, "How Playing Country Music Taught Me To Love My Dad"   **23**
Sallie Tisdale, "Bound upon a Wheel of Fire"   **29**
Eudora Welty, "Why I Live at the P.O."   **36**
Annie Dillard, "The Chase"   **51**
Phillip Lopate, "My Early Years at School"   **54**
Ernesto Galarza, "Lincoln School"   **58**
Elizabeth Bishop, "Primer Class"   **64**
Maya Angelou, "Graduation at Lafayette County Training School"   **70**
Richard Thurman, "Not Another Word"   **80**
William Geist, "Megawatt Miracles of the Yuletide"   **104**
Pat Esslinger Carr, "The Party"   **115**
Roy Blount, Jr., "On Hats"   **138**
Roland Sodowsky, "The Origins of the Cowboy Boot"   **142**

Guy Davenport, "The Anthropology of Table Manners from Geophagy
    Onward"   **153**
Joseph Monninger, "Fast Food"   **175**
A. R. Gurney, Jr., "The Dinner Party"   **186**
Joan Didion, "John Wayne: A Love Song"   **193**
Stephen King, "My Creature from the Black Lagoon"   **206**
N. Scott Momaday, "Discovering the Land of Light"   **230**
Manuela Hoelterhoff, "Walt's Wonderful World Turns Out to Be Flat"   **236**
Jean Stafford, "Why I Don't Get Around Much Anymore"   **241**
Bobbie Ann Mason, "The Ocean"   **256**
Rheta Grimsley Johnson, "Greg Pratt Is Dead"   **270**
Joyce Carol Oates, "On Boxing and Pain"   **283**
John Stewart Collis, "The Potato"   **295**
Sally Carrighar, "The Cutthroat Trout"   **307**
Edward Hoagland, "The Courage of Turtles"   **317**
Alice Walker, "Am I Blue?"   **334**
James C. Rettie, " 'But A Watch in the Night': A Scientific Fable"   **340**
Robert Finch, "One That Got Away"   **353**
Jesse Hill Ford, "To the Open Water"   **360**
Tom Bodett, "Command Performance"   **378**
Sherry Turkle, "The New Philosophers of Artificial Intelligence"   **394**
Kurt Vonnegut, Jr., "EPICAC"   **400**
Paul Loeb, "Atomic Soap: On the Job With the Young and the Restless"   **407**
Joy Kogawa, "The Letters"   **437**
Annabel Thomas, "The Phototropic Woman"   **443**
Peter Cameron, "Homework"   **526**
Diane Ravitch, "On Thinking About the Future"   **568**
Mary Mebane, "The System"   **587**
Roger Kahn, "A Jewish Education"   **593**
Don Oldenburg, "Born to Run"   **619**
Elizabeth Marek, "The Lives of Teenage Mothers"   **633**
Marjorie Hope, "A Clean, Well-Lighted Bench"   **656**
Gail Regier, "Users, Like Me: Membership in the Church of Drugs"   **670**
Toni Cade Bambara, "The Lesson"   **677**

ARGUMENT

Elizabeth Stone, "How Our Family Stories Shape Us"   **1**
Daniel J. Boorstin, "Christmas and Other Festivals of Consumption"   **97**
Michael J. Arlen, "Ode to Thanksgiving"   **107**
Jessica Mitford, "The American Way of Death"   **111**

Reay Tannahill, "Future Eating Patterns"   **160**
Roger Rosenblatt, "Reconsideration: *Gone with the Wind,* the Movie"   **200**
Jean Stafford, "Why I Don't Get Around Much Anymore"   **241**
Leonard Koppett, "Baseball's Hits and Misses"   **272**
Loren Eiseley, "How Flowers Changed the World"   **299**
Eleanor Perényi, "Partly Cloudy"   **348**
Rachel Carson, "The Obligation to Endure"   **367**
Norman Cousins, "The Poet and the Computer"   **375**
Craig Brod, "Childhood Lost"   **381**
Helen Caldicott, "What You Must Know about Radiation"   **413**
Barbara Tuchman, "Is History a Guide to the Future?"   **462**
Holcomb B. Noble, "Beyond the Knowable: The Ultimate Exploration"   **471**
Michele Manges, "The Dead-End Kids"   **509**
Helen C. Vo-Dinh, "Excuses, Excuses"   **514**
Neil Postman, "The Classroom"   **517**
Robert MacNeil, "Is Television Shortening Our Attention Span"   **536**
Grace Lichtenstein, "Playing for Money"   **543**
Mortimer J. Adler, "Paideia Proposal: The Same Course of Study for All"   **554**
Floretta Dukes McKenzie, "The Yellow Brick Road of Education"   **563**
James Baldwin, "Fifth Avenue, Uptown: A Letter from Harlem"   **579**
Roger Kahn, "A Jewish Education"   **593**
Virginia Woolf, "No Woman Wrote a Word"   **600**
Casey Miller and Kate Swift, "Onc Small Step for Genkind"   **607**
Jonathan Kozol, "A Captive State"   **643**

ENUMERATION

John Updike, "Three Boys"   **47**
Jessica Mitford, "The American Way of Death"   **111**
Alison Lurie, "The Language of White Costumes"   **132**
Vernon Pizer, "BLT, Hold the Mayo"   **168**
A. R. Gurney, Jr., "The Dinner Party"   **186**
Leonard Koppett, "Baseball's Hits and Misses"   **272**
Joyce Carol Oates, "On Boxing and Pain"   **283**
Nikki Giovanni, "Toward Better Human Understanding"   **287**
Phyllis S. Busch, "Plants and Animals in Winter"   **327**
Sherry Turkle, "The New Philosophers of Artificial Intelligence"   **394**
Lydia Dotto, "The Environmental Consequences of Nuclear War"   **427**
Isaac Asimov, "A Choice of Catastrophes"   **451**
Dava Sobel, "Acid Test"   **533**
Casey Miller and Kate Swift, "One Small Step for Genkind"   **607**
Jonathan Kozol, "A Captive State"   **643**

COMPARISON/CONTRAST

John Updike, "Three Boys"   47
Richard Thurman, "Not Another Word"   80
Ink Mendelsohn, "We Were What We Wore"   122
Reay Tannahill, "Future Eating Patterns"   160
Joseph Monninger, "Fast Food"   175
Roger Rosenblatt, "Reconsideration: *Gone with the Wind,* the Movie"   200
Marie Winn, "How Parents Survived before Television"   220
Ben Yagota, "Unfolding the Nation"   248
Donald Hall, "Basketball: The Purest Sport of Bodies"   279
Nikki Giovanni, "Toward Better Human Understanding"   287
Loren Eiseley, "How Flowers Changed the World"   299
Edward Hoagland, "The Courage of Turtles"   317
Alice Walker, "Am I Blue?"   334
Eleanor Perényi, "Partly Cloudy"   348
Norman Cousins, "The Poet and the Computer"   375
Craig Brod, "Childhood Lost"   381
Barbara Tuchman, "Is History a Guide to the Future?"   462
Roger Kahn, "A Jewish Education"   593
Virginia Woolf, "No Woman Wrote a Word"   600

CLASSIFICATION

Alison Lurie, "The Language of White Costumes"   132
Phyllis S. Busch, "Plants and Animals in Winter"   327
Craig Brod, "Childhood Lost"   381
Isaac Asimov, "A Choice of Catastrophes"   451
Mortimer J. Adler, "Paideia Proposal: The Same Course of Study for All"   554
Casey Miller and Kate Swift, "One Small Step for Genkind"   607

ILLUSTRATION

Elizabeth Stone, "How Our Family Stories Shape Us"   1
John Updike, "Three Boys"   47
Daniel J. Boorstin, "Christmas and Other Festivals of Consumption"   97
William Geist, "Megawatt Miracles of the Yuletide"   104
Michael J. Arlen, "Ode to Thanksgiving"   107
Jessica Mitford, "The American Way of Death"   111
Ink Mendelsohn, "We Were What We Wore"   122

Alison Lurie, "The Language of White Costumes"   **132**
Roy Blount, Jr., "On Hats"   **138**
Peter Farb and George Armelagos, "Understanding Society and Culture Through
    Eating"   **147**
Guy Davenport, "The Anthropology of Table Manners from Geophagy
    Onward"   **153**
Vernon Pizer, "BLT, Hold the Mayo"   **168**
Joseph Monninger, "Fast Food"   **175**
Roger Rosenblatt, "Reconsideration: *Gone with the Wind,* the Movie"   **200**
Stephen King, "My Creature from the Black Lagoon"   **206**
Walter Karp, "Where the Media Critics Went Wrong"   **214**
Jean Stafford, "Why I Don't Get Around Much Anymore"   **241**
Jan Morris, "On Wateriness"   **252**
Joyce Carol Oates, "On Boxing and Pain"   **283**
Nikki Giovanni, "Toward Better Human Understanding"   **287**
Phyllis S. Busch, "Plants and Animals in Winter"   **327**
Craig Brod, "Childhood Lost"   **381**
Barbara Tuchman, "Is History a Guide to the Future?"   **462**
Holcomb B. Noble, "Beyond the Knowable: The Ultimate Exploration"   **471**
Claudia H. Deutsch, "Cheating: Alive and Flourishing"   **502**
Michele Manges, "The Dead-End Kids"   **509**
Mike Royko, "Write On, Barbarians"   **512**
Helen C. Vo-Dinh, "Excuses, Excuses"   **514**
Grace Lichtenstein, "Playing for Money"   **543**
Roger Kahn, "A Jewish Education"   **593**
Virginia Woolf, "No Woman Wrote a Word"   **600**
Casey Miller and Kate Swift, "One Small Step for Genkind"   **607**
Don Oldenburg, "Born to Run"   **619**

DEFINITION

Gwen Kinkead, "Another World"   **225**
Joyce Carol Oates, "On Boxing and Pain"   **283**
Eleanor Perényi, "Partly Cloudy"   **348**
Casey Miller and Kate Swift, "One Small Step for Genkind"   **607**

ANALYSIS

Jessica Mitford, "The American Way of Death"   **111**
Peter Farb and George Armelagos, "Understanding Society and Culture Through
    Eating"   **147**

Roger Rosenblatt, "Reconsideration: *Gone with the Wind,* the Movie" **200**
Stephen King, "My Creature from the Black Lagoon" **206**
Gwen Kinkead, "Another World" **225**
Helen Caldicott, "What You Must Know about Radiation" **413**
Lydia Dotto, "The Environmental Consequences of Nuclear War" **427**
Dava Sobel, "Acid Test" **533**
Grace Lichtenstein, "Playing for Money" **543**
James Baldwin, "Fifth Avenue, Uptown: A Letter from Harlem" **579**
Jonathan Kozol, "A Captive State" **643**

PROBLEM/SOLUTION

Reay Tannahill, "Future Eating Patterns" **160**
Ben Yagota, "Unfolding the Nation" **248**
Nikki Giovanni, "Toward Better Human Understanding" **287**
Rachel Carson, "The Obligation to Endure" **367**
Norman Cousins, "The Poet and the Computer" **375**
Tom Bodett, "Command Performance" **378**
Craig Brod, "Childhood Lost" **381**
Helen Caldicott, "What You Must Know about Radiation" **413**
Neil Postman, "The Classroom" **517**
Robert MacNeil, "Is Television Shortening Our Attention Span?" **536**
Mortimer J. Adler, "Paideia Proposal: The Same Course of Study for All" **554**
Floretta Dukes McKenzie, "The Yellow Brick Road of Education" **563**
James Baldwin, "Fifth Avenue, Uptown: A Letter from Harlem" **579**

QUESTION/ANSWER

Walter Karp, "Where the Media Critics Went Wrong" **214**
David Quammin, "Has Success Spoiled the Crow?" **323**
Marjorie Kinnan Rawlings, "Who Owns Cross Creek?" **345**
Barbara Tuchman, "Is History a Guide to the Future?" **462**
Robert MacNeil, "Is Television Shortening Our Attention Span?" **536**
Virginia Woolf, "No Woman Wrote a Word" **600**

CAUSE/EFFECT

Elizabeth Stone, "How Our Family Stories Shape Us" **1**
James D. Houston, "How Playing Country Music Taught Me To Love My
    Dad" **23**

Sallie Tisdale, "Bound upon a Wheel of Fire"   **29**

Daniel J. Boorstin, "Christmas and Other Festivals of Consumption"   **97**

Ink Mendelsohn, "We Were What We Wore"   **122**

Alison Lurie, "The Language of White Costumes"   **132**

Carin C. Quinn, "The Jeaning of America—and the World"   **135**

Peter Farb and George Armelagos, "Understanding Society and Culture Through Eating"   **147**

Guy Davenport, "The Anthropology of Table Manners from Geophagy Onward"   **153**

Joseph Monninger, "Fast Food"   **175**

Marie Winn, "How Parents Survived before Television"   **220**

Rheta Grimsley Johnson, "Greg Pratt Is Dead"   **270**

Loren Eiseley, "How Flowers Changed the World"   **299**

David Quammin, "Has Success Spoiled the Crow?"   **323**

Alice Walker, "Am I Blue?"   **334**

Rachel Carson, "The Obligation to Endure"   **367**

Helen Caldicott, "What You Must Know about Radiation"   **413**

Lydia Dotto, "The Environmental Consequences of Nuclear War"   **427**

Larry Thompson, "The Eerie World of Living Heads"   **480**

Claudia H. Deutsch, "Cheating: Alive and Flourishing"   **502**

Michele Manges, "The Dead-End Kids"   **509**

Helen C. Vo-Dinh, "Excuses, Excuses"   **514**

Neil Postman, "The Classroom"   **517**

Dava Sobel, "Acid Test"   **533**

Robert MacNeil, "Is Television Shortening Our Attention Span?"   **536**

Grace Lichtenstein, "Playing for Money"   **543**

Mortimer J. Adler, "Paideia Proposal: The Same Course of Study for All"   **554**

Floretta Dukes McKenzie, "The Yellow Brick Road of Education"   **563**

Diane Ravitch, "On Thinking About the Future"   **568**

James Baldwin, "Fifth Avenue, Uptown: A Letter from Harlem"   **579**

Roger Kahn, "A Jewish Education"   **593**

Virginia Woolf, "No Woman Wrote a Word"   **600**

Don Oldenburg, "Born to Run"   **619**

Elizabeth Marek, "The Lives of Teenage Mothers"   **633**

Jonathan Kozol, "A Captive State"   **643**

Marjorie Hope, "A Clean, Well-Lighted Bench"   **656**

THE
WINSTON READER

C H A P T E R 1

MEMORIES

Home and Family

■ ■ ■

HOW OUR FAMILY STORIES SHAPE US

☐ **ELIZABETH STONE**

¹ In the beginning, as far back in my family as anyone could go, was my great-grandmother, and her name was Annunziata. In the next generation, it would be my grandmother's first name. In the generation after that, in its anglicized form, Nancy, it would be my aunt's first name and my mother's middle name, and in the generation after that, my sister's middle name as well. I never met that first Annunziata, but my mother often told me a family story about her which, as a child, I knew as well as I knew the story of Cinderella and loved better.

² Annunziata was the daughter of a rich landowner in Messina, Sicily, so the story went, and she fell in love with the town postman, a poor but talented man, able to play any musical instrument he laid eyes on. Her father heard about this romance and forbade them to see each other. So in the middle of one night—and then came the line I always waited for with a thrill of pleasure—she ran off with him in her shift.

³ I didn't know what a shift was and didn't want my settled version of the story disrupted by any new information. I loved the scene as I saw it: in the

1

background was a house with a telltale ladder leaning against the second-story window. In the foreground was my great-grandmother, like some pre-Raphaelite maiden dressed in a garment white and diaphanous and flowing, holding the hand of her beloved as she ran through a field at dawn, toward her future, toward me.

4   As a child, I was on very close terms with that story. I loved and admired my family—my grandmother especially—and as I saw it, her mother had been the start of us all. I never thought about any of my other great-grandparents or who they were. My grandfather, my mother's father, had died long before I was born; so I didn't think about him in any way that would bring him or his parents to life for me. As for my father, his parents had come from Austria, but he wasn't close to them, so I certainly wasn't. Nothing to build on there.

5   As a further refinement, I have to add that I paid absolutely no attention to the framed picture of my great-grandmother hanging over my grandmother's bed. That was just an old woman who, despite the fact that she happened to look like Sitting Bull, was of no interest to me. It was years before I realized that the person in the frame and the one in the story were the same. For me, it was always the stories that held the spirit and meaning of our family.

6   The first appeal of that story, then, was that it seemed to be the story of our genesis as a family. But there was a second appeal as well, and it was that my great-grandmother was everything I would have made her if I were inventing her. She was spunky, dazzlingly defiant, and, I was sure, beautiful. Later, when I understood more about class and money, I admired her for having chosen my poor but talented great-grandfather in the first place. She was principled and egalitarian, someone I wanted to be like, hoped maybe I already was a little like, and most important, felt I *could* be like. She wasn't distant like a film star or imaginary like a fairy-tale heroine. She was real. And she was my relative.

7   Other family stories stayed with me, too. Some were old and ancestral but some were new, about my mother's generation or mine. None was elaborately plotted; some relied only on a well-developed scene—like the one in which my great-grandfather and his half-dozen sons were playing music after dinner in the courtyard as people came "from miles around" to listen. And still others were simply characterizations of people—"you had one ancestor who was a court musician" or "you had another ancestor who was an aide to Garibaldi." These qualified as stories in the way haiku qualify as poems. Almost any bit of lore about a family member, living or dead, qualifies as a family story—as long as it's significant, as long as it has worked its way into the family canon to be told and retold.

8   These stories last not because they're entertaining, though they may be; they last because in ways large and small they matter. They provide the family with esteem because they often show family members in an attractive light or define the family in a flattering way. They also give messages and instructions;

they offer blueprints and ideals; they issue warnings and prohibitions. And when they no longer serve, they disappear.

9   I first began to realize how much these stories mattered in my own family when I was doing an article on growing up Italian-American for *The New York Times Magazine.* My grandparents had both been immigrants who came here from Sicily near the turn of the century—my grandfather in the late 1880s, my grandmother in 1905. They could both read—my grandmother was eager to learn English and get a library card—but other than that there was nothing to distinguish them from the millions of Southern Italians who had come when they did. But their six children and their children's children hadn't turned out at all the way, demographically speaking, they might have been expected to.

10   It wasn't at all "typical" that one uncle would want to become a writer and would succeed at getting several of his novels published, nor that my mother would go on to Hunter College or end up playing in a Strindberg production on Broadway. All six of my grandparents' children read too much poetry, listened to too much opera, cared too much about getting rid of their Brooklyn accents and too little (with one exception) about improving their finances. My generation wasn't typical either—too many people with artistic inclinations, advanced degrees, and galloping exogamy.

11   When I tried to understand what had lured us off the demographic tack, the only thing I could find were our family stories. In the canon were the proud or inspirational or defiant stories my grandmother had told to her children (including the one about going to night school at the age of fifteen to learn English). Added to them were the stories that the children themselves, my aunts and uncles, had contributed over their lives. School stories, friendship stories, Sacco and Vanzetti stories, Depression stories, at-home stories, love stories, almost all of them nudging and pushing us in the direction of assimilation. A single surviving story about a long-dead pair of family cats named Abraham Lincoln and George Washington wouldn't have meant anything if it had not been surrounded (as it was) by a host of other stories that, all together, gave the big picture.

12   These stories seemed at once to sponsor and mirror our aspirations as a family. Taken in aggregate, they had a number of clear additional messages, discernible to us as members of the family. But I also noticed that our most idiosyncratic family conviction—that the arts are supremely important and certainly more important than money—was there even in that very first story, when my great-grandmother chose as her true love that talented but poor postman.

13   What struck me about my own family stories was first, how much under my skin they were; second, once my childhood was over, how little deliberate attention I ever paid to them; and third, how thoroughly invisible they were to anyone else. Going about my daily life, I certainly never told them aloud and

never even alluded to them. Based on all visible signs, those who talk of weakening family ties could have concluded that family was not one of my major concerns and that wherever it was I had come from, I had left it far behind. But they would have been wrong, as wrong about me as they may be about others. Those who say that America is a land of rootless nomads who travel light, uninstructed by memory and family ties, have missed part of the evidence.

14   The family storytelling that has always gone on in my family goes on in families everywhere. Like me, people grow up and walk around with their stories under their skin, sometimes as weightless pleasures but sometimes painfully tattooed with them, as Maxine Hong Kingston felt she was in *The Woman Warrior*. This is what I've learned after interviewing more than a hundred people from a variety of regions, races, ethnicities, ages, and classes. Loosely, their experiences have been the same as mine. Though family storytelling happens casually and unreflectively, the realms family stories invariably enter into are predictable. The family is our first culture, and, like all cultures, it wants to make known its norms and mores. It does so through daily life, but it also does so through family stories which underscore, in a way invariably clear to its members, the essentials, like the unspoken and unadmitted family policy on marriage or illness. Or suicide. Or who the family saints and sinners are, or how much anger can be expressed and by whom.

15   Like all cultures, one of the family's first jobs is to persuade its members they're special, more wonderful than the neighboring barbarians. The persuasion consists of stories showing family members demonstrating admirable traits, which it claims are family traits. Attention to the stories' actual truth is never the family's most compelling consideration. Encouraging belief is. The family's survival depends on the shared sensibility of its members.

16   The family's first concern is itself, but its second realm of concern is its relation to the world. Family stories about the world are usually teaching stories, telling members still at home the ways of the world according to the experiences its elders have had. Often the news is not good—money is too important in the world, in all sorts of ways, and the family, almost any family, seems to have too little of it. They don't measure up. Or the family's racial or ethnic group doesn't afford them a comfortable place on the social ladder. Family stories convey the bad news, but they also offer coping strategies as well as stories that make everyone feel better.

17   Family stories seem to persist in importance even when people think of themselves individually, without regard to their familial roles. The particular human chain we're part of is central to our individual identity. Even if we loathe our families, in order to know ourselves, we seem to need to know about them, just as prologue. Not to know is to live with some of the disorientation and anxiety of the amnesiac.

18   How else can one explain the persistent need of many adopted children to know more about where they "really" come from? Something intangible and

crucial is missing. To know themselves, they seem to need to know more of the collective family experience that predates their birth. They need their family stories.

19   All of us, long after we've left our original families, keep at least some of these stories with us, and they continue to matter, but sometimes in new ways. At moments of major life transitions, we may claim certain of our stories, take them over, shape them, reshape them, put our own stamp on them, make them part of us instead of making ourselves part of them. We are always in conversation with them, one way or another. The ancestral figures in them—especially grandparents or great-grandparents of the same sex as us—often become a major part of our imaginative life. They can, along with other powerful cultural archetypes, maybe from fiction or film, serve as our role models and guides.

☐ Discovering Meaning and Technique

1. In this selection, Stone argues the importance of storytelling to family life. Discuss her reasons for this viewpoint.

2. Cite some characteristics of Stone's family that are revealed by family stories.

3. What does Stone mean by the statement, "The family's survival depends on the shared sensibility of its members" (paragraph 15)?

4. Stone begins her essay with an anecdote about her great-grandmother. Why is this anecdote an effective beginning for her argument?

5. Where does Stone move from a discussion of her own family to a discussion of families in general?

6. Because Stone is supporting an argument, she refers to her family stories but does not tell them in the traditional oral style. Had she done so, would the essay have been more or less interesting?

☐ Writing Suggestions

1. Write an essay explaining how your family stories helped you define your personality.

2. Today's families are often made up of parents who have remarried and have thus brought different sets of ancestors and children together in the same household. Does this phenomenon destroy the possibility of family stories? Or does it allow an even richer heritage?

3. Rewrite the story of Annunziata in an oral style: "Let me tell you about your great-grandmother back in Sicily. . . ."

4. Tell your favorite family story or several of your favorites.

WHERE THE WORLD BEGAN

☐ **MARGARET LAURENCE**

[1] A strange place it was, that place where the world began. A place of incredible happenings, splendours and revelations, despairs like multitudinous pits of isolated hells. A place of shadow-spookiness, inhabited by the unknowable dead. A place of jubilation and of mourning, horrible and beautiful.

[2]   It was, in fact, a small prairie town.

[3]   Because that settlement and that land were my first and for many years my only real knowledge of this planet, in some profound way they remain my world, my way of viewing. My eyes were formed there. Towns like ours, set in a sea of land, have been described thousands of times as dull, bleak, flat, uninteresting. I have had it said to me that the railway trip across Canada is spectacular, except for the prairies, when it would be desirable to go to sleep for several days, until the ordeal is over. I am always unable to argue this point effectively. All I can say is—well, you really have to live there to know that country. The town of my childhood could be called bizarre, agonizingly repressive or cruel at times, and the land in which it grew could be called harsh in the violence of its seasonal changes. But never merely flat or uninteresting. Never dull.

[4]   In winter, we used to hitch rides on the back of the milk sleigh, our moccasins squeaking and slithering on the hard rutted snow of the roads, our hands in ice-bubbled mitts hanging onto the box edge of the sleigh for dear life, while Bert grinned at us through his great frosted moustache and shouted the horse into speed, daring us to stay put. Those mornings, rising, there would be the perpetual fascination of the frost feathers on windows, the ferns and flowers and eerie faces traced there during the night by unseen artists of the wind. Evenings, coming back from skating, the sky would be black but not dark, for you could see a cold glitter of stars from one side of the earth's rim to the other. And then the sometime astonishment when you saw the Northern Lights flaring across the sky, like the scrawled signature of God. After a blizzard, when the snowploughs hadn't yet got through, school would be closed for the day, the assumption being that the town's young could not possibly flounder through five feet of snow in the pursuit of education. We would then gaily don snowshoes and flounder for miles out into the white dazzling deserts, in pursuit

of a different kind of knowing. If you came back too close to night, through the woods at the foot of the town hill, the thin black branches of poplar and chokecherry now meringued with frost, sometimes you heard coyotes. Or maybe the banshee wolf-voices were really only inside your head.

5   Summers were scorching, and when no rain came and the wheat became bleached and dried before it headed, the faces of farmers and townsfolk would not smile much, and you took for granted, because it never seemed to have been any different, the frequent knocking at the back door and the young men standing there, mumbling or thrusting defiantly their requests for a drink of water and a sandwich if you could spare it. They were riding the freights, and you never knew where they had come from, or where they might end up, if anywhere. The Drought and Depression were like like evil deities which had been there always. You understood and did not understand.

6   Yet the outside world had its continuing marvels. The poplar bluffs and the small river were filled and surrounded with a zillion different grasses, stones, and weed flowers. The meadowlarks sang undaunted from the twanging telephone wires along the gravel highway. Once we found an old flat-bottomed scow, and launched her, poling along the shallow brown waters, mending her with wodges of hastily chewed Spearmint, grounding her among the tangles of yellow marsh marigolds that grew succulently along the banks of the shrunken river, while the sun made our skins smell dusty-warm.

7   My best friend lived in an apartment above some stores on Main Street (its real name was Mountain Avenue, goodness knows why), an elegant apartment with royal-blue velvet curtains. The back roof, scarcely sloping at all, was corrugated tin, of a furnace-like warmth on a July afternoon, and we would sit there drinking lemonade and looking across the back lane at the Fire Hall. Sometimes our vigil would be rewarded. Oh joy! Somebody's house burning down! We had an almost-perfect callousness in some ways. Then the wooden tower's bronze bell would clonk and toll like a thousand speeded funerals in a time of plague, and in a few minutes the team of giant black horses would cannon forth, pulling the fire wagon like some scarlet chariot of the Goths, while the firemen clung with one hand, adjusting their helmets as they went.

8   The oddities of the place were endless. An elderly lady used to serve, as her afternoon tea offering to other ladies, soda biscuits spread with peanut butter and topped with a whole marshmallow. Some considered this slightly eccentric, when compared with chopped egg sandwiches, and admittedly talked about her behind her back, but no one ever refused these delicacies or indicated to her that they thought she had slipped a cog. Another lady dyed her hair a bright and cheery orange, by strangers often mistaken at twenty paces for a feather hat. My own beloved stepmother wore a silver fox neckpiece, a whole pelt, *with the embalmed (?) head still on.* My Ontario Irish grandfather said, "sparrow grass," a more interesting term than asparagus. The town dump was known as "the nuisance grounds," a phrase fraught with weird connotations, as

though the effluvia of our lives was beneath contempt but at the same time was subtly threatening to the determined and sometimes hysterical propriety of our ways.

9   Some oddities were, as idiom had it, "funny ha ha;" others were "funny peculiar." Some were not so very funny at all. An old man lived, deranged, in a shack in the valley. Perhaps he wasn't even all that old, but to us he seemed a wild Methuselah figure, shambling among the underbrush and tall couchgrass, muttering indecipherable curses or blessings, a prophet who had forgotten his prophesies. Everyone in town knew him, but no one knew him. He lived among us as though only occasionally and momentarily visible. The kids called him Andy Gump, and feared him. Some sought to prove their bravery by tormenting him. They were the mediaeval bear baiters, and he the lumbering bewildered bear, half blind, only rarely turning to snarl. Everything is to be found in a town like mine. Belsen, writ small but with the same ink.

10   All of us cast stones in one shape or another. In grade school, among the vulnerable and violet girls we were, the feared and despised were those few older girls from what was charmingly termed "the wrong side of the tracks." Tough in talk and tougher in muscle, they were said to be whores already. And may have been, that being about the only profession readily available to them.

11   The dead lived in that place, too. Not only the grandparents who had, in local parlance, "passed on" and who gloomed, bearded or bonneted, from the sepia photographs in old albums, but also the uncles, forever eighteen or nineteen, whose names were carved on the granite family stones in the cemetery, but whose bones lay in France. My own young mother lay in that graveyard, beside other dead of our kin, and when I was ten, my father, too, only forty, left the living town for the dead dwelling on the hill.

12   When I was eighteen, I couldn't wait to get out of that town, away from the prairies. I did not know then that I would carry the land and town all my life within my skull, that they would form the mainspring and source of the writing I was to do, wherever and however far away I might live.

13   This was my territory in the time of my youth, and in a sense my life since then has been an attempt to look at it, to come to terms with it. Stultifying to the mind it certainly could be, and sometimes was, but not to the imagination. It was many things, but it was never dull.

14   The same, I now see, could be said for Canada in general. Why on earth did generations of Canadians pretend to believe this country dull? We knew perfectly well it wasn't. Yet for so long we did not proclaim what we knew. If our upsurge of so-called nationalism seems odd or irrelevant to outsiders, and even to some of our own people (*what's all the fuss about?*), they might try to understand that for many years we valued ourselves insufficiently, living as we did under the huge shadows of those two dominating figures, Uncle Sam and Britannia. We have only just begun to value ourselves, our land, our abilities.

We have only just begun to recognize our legends and to give shape to our myths.

15   There are, God knows, enough aspects to deplore about this country. When I see the killing of our lakes and rivers with industrial wastes, I feel rage and despair. When I see our industries and natural resources increasingly taken over by America, I feel an overwhelming discouragement, especially as I cannot simply say "damn Yankees." It should never be forgotten that it is we ourselves who have sold such a large amount of our birthwight for a mess of plastic Progress. When I saw the War Measures Act being invoked in 1970, I lost forever the vestigial remains of the naive wish-belief that repression could not happen here, or would not. And yet, of course, I had known all along in the deepest and often hidden caves of the heart that anything can happen anywhere, for the seeds of both man's freedom and his captivity are found everywhere, even in the microcosm of a prairie town. But in raging against our injustices, our stupidities, I do so *as family,* as I did, and still do in writing, about those aspects of my town which I hated and which are always in some ways aspects of myself.

16   The land still draws me more than other lands. I have lived in Africa and in England, but splendid as both can be they do not have the power to move me in the same way as, for example, that part of southern Ontario where I spent four months last summer in a cedar cabin beside a river. "Scratch a Canadian, and you find a phony pioneer," I used to say to myself in warning. But all the same it is true, I think, that we are not yet totally alienated from physical earth, and let us only pray we do not become so. I once thought that my lifelong fear and mistrust of cities made me a kind of old-fashioned freak; now I see it differently.

17   The cabin has a long window across its front western wall, and sitting at the oak table there in the mornings, I used to look out at the river and at the tall trees beyond, green-gold in the early light. The river was bronze; the sun caught it strangely, reflecting upon its surface the near-shore sand ripples underneath. Suddenly, the crescenting of a fish, gone before the eye could clearly give image to it. The old man next door said these leaping fish were carp. Himself, he preferred muskie, for he was a real fisherman and the muskie gave him a fight. The wind most often blew from the south, and the river flowed toward the south, so when the water was wind-riffled, and the current was strong, the river seemed to be flowing both ways. I liked this, and interpreted it as an omen, a natural symbol.

18   A few years ago, when I was back in Winnipeg, I gave a talk at my old college. It was open to the public, and afterward a very old man came up to me and asked me if my maiden name had been Wemyss. I said yes, thinking he might have known my father or my grandfather. But no. "When I was a young lad," he said, "I once worked for your great-grandfather, Robert Wemyss, when he had the sheep ranch at Raeburn." I think that was a moment when I realized all over again something of great importance to me. My long-ago families came

from Scotland and Ireland, but in a sense that no longer mattered so much. My true roots were here.

19   I am not very patriotic, in the usual meaning of that word. I cannot say "My country right or wrong" in any political, social or literary context. But one thing is inalterable, for better or worse, for life.

20   This is where my world began. A world which includes the ancestors—both my own and other people's ancestors who become mine. A world which formed me, and continues to do so, even while I fought it in some of its aspects, and continue to do so. A world which gave me my own lifework to do, because it was here that I learned the sight of my own particular eyes.

☐ Discovering Meaning and Technique

1. What does Laurence mean when she calls her home in Canada "where the world began"?

2. Laurence calls her home "a place of jubilation and of mourning, horrible and beautiful" (paragraph 1). Point out some details that support each of these opposing qualities.

3. Twice in the essay, Laurence states that her hometown was "never dull." How does she support this claim?

4. This selection is primarily description, although Laurence does generalize about her feelings toward Canada. Point out where she moves from descriptive details to generalizations.

5. What is the purpose of the anecdote (paragraph 18) about the man who worked for her grandfather?

6. Is Laurence's frequent use of sentence fragments an effective descriptive device?

☐ Writing Suggestions

1. Laurence organizes part of her essay around the seasons of winter and summer. Describe the place where you grew up, organizing your composition around the four seasons.

2. Describe one or several eccentric people you remember from childhood.

3. Explain how your childhood environment helped shape your current values.

400 MULVANEY STREET

☐ NIKKI GIOVANNI

1 I was going to Knoxville, Tennessee, to speak. I was going other places first but mostly to me I was going home. And I, running late as usual, hurried to the airport just in time.

2 The runway is like an airport carrier—sticking out in the bay—and you always get the feeling of drunken fly-boys in green airplane hats chomping wads and wads of gum going "Whooooopie!" as they bring the 747 in from Hackensack to La Guardia. It had been snowing for two days in New York and the runway was frozen. They never say to you that the runway is frozen and therefore dangerous to take off from, and in fact you'd never notice it because all the New York airports have tremendous backups—even on clear days. So sitting there waiting was not unusual but I did notice this tendency to slide to the side with every strong wind, and I peeked out my window and noticed we were in the tracks of the previous jet and I thought: death has to eat too. And I went to sleep.

3 The whole thing about going to Knoxville appealed to my vanity. I had gotten a call from Harvey Glover about coming down and had said yes and had thought no more of it. Mostly, as you probably notice, artists very rarely have the chance to go back home and say, "I think I've done you proud." People are so insecure and in some cases jealous and in some cases think so little of themselves in general that they seldom think you'd be really honored to speak in your home town or at your old high school. And other people are sometimes so contemptuous of home that they in fact don't want to come back. This has set up a negative equation between the artist and home.

4 I was excited about going to Knoxville but I didn't want to get my hopes up. What if it fell through? What if they didn't like me? Oh, my God! What if nobody came to hear me? Maybe we'd better forget about it. And I did. I flew on out to Cleveland to make enough money to be able to go to Knoxville. And Cleveland was beautiful. A girl named Pat and her policeman friend couldn't have been any nicer. And he was an intelligent cop. I got the feeling I was going to have a good weekend. Then my mother met me at the Cincinnati airport, where I had to change over, and had coffee with me and had liked my last television appearance. Then they called my flight, and on to Knoxville.

5 When we were growing up Knoxville didn't have television, let alone an airport. It finally got TV but the airport is in Alcoa. And is now called Tyson Field. Right? Small towns are funny. Knoxville even has a zip code and seven-digit phone numbers. All of which seems strange to me since I mostly remember Mrs. Flora Ford's white cake with white icing and Miss Delaney's blue furs and

Armentine Picket's being the sharpest woman in town—she attended our church—and Miss Brooks wearing tight sweaters and Carter-Roberts Drug Store sending out Modern Jazz Quartet sounds of "Fontessa" and my introduction to Nina Simone by David Cherry, dropping a nickel in the jukebox and "Porgy" coming out. I mostly remember Vine Street, which I was not allowed to walk to get to school, though Grandmother didn't want me to take Paine Street either because Jay Manning lived on it and he was home from the army and very beautiful with his Black face and two dimples. Not that I was going to do anything, because I didn't do anything enough even to think in terms of not doing anything, but according to small-town logic "It looks bad."

6   The Gem Theatre was on the corner of Vine and a street that runs parallel to the creek, and for 10 cents you could sit all day and see a double feature, five cartoons and two serials plus previews for the next two weeks. And I remember Frankie Lennon would come in with her gang and sit behind me and I wanted to say, "Hi. Can I sit with you?" but thought they were too snooty, and they, I found out later, thought I was too Northern and stuck-up. All of that is gone now. Something called progress killed my grandmother.

7   Mulvaney Street looked like a camel's back with both humps bulging—up and down—and we lived in the down part. At the top of the left hill a lady made ice balls and would mix the flavors for you for just a nickel. Across the street from her was the Negro center, where the guys played indoor basketball and the little kids went for stories and nap time. Down in the valley part were the tennis courts, the creek, the bulk of the park and the beginning of the right hill. To enter or leave the street you went either up or down. I used to think of it as a fort, especially when it snowed, and the enemy would always try to sneak through the underbrush nurtured by the creek and through the park trees, but we always spotted strangers and dealt. As you came down the left hill the houses were up on its side; then people got regular flat front yards; then the right hill started and ran all the way into Vine and Mulvaney was gone and the big apartment building didn't have a yard at all.

8   Grandmother and Grandpapa had lived at 400 since they'd left Georgia. And Mommy had been a baby there and Anto and Aunt Agnes were born there. And dated there and sat on the swing on the front porch and fussed there, and our good and our bad were recorded there. That little frame house duplicated twice more which overlooked the soft-voiced people passing by with "Evening, 'Fessor Watson, Miz Watson," and the grass wouldn't grow between our house and Edith and Clarence White's house. It was said that he had something to do with numbers. When the man tried to get between the two houses and the cinder crunched a warning to us, both houses lit up and the man was caught between Mr. White's shotgun and Grandfather's revolver, trying to explain he was lost. Grandpapa would never pull a gun unless he intended to shoot and would only shoot to kill. I think when he reached Knoxville he was just tired of running. I brought his gun to New York with me after he died but the forces

that be don't want anyone to keep her history, even if it's just a clogged twenty-two that no one in her right mind would even load.

9   Mr. and Mrs. Ector's rounded the trio of houses off. He always wore a stocking cap till he got tied back and would emerge very dapper. He was in love with the various automobiles he owned and had been seen by Grandmother and me on more than one occasion sweeping the snow from in front of his garage before he would back the car into the street. All summer he parked his car at the bottom of the hill and polished it twice a day and delighted in it. Grandmother would call across the porches to him, "Ector, you a fool 'bout that car, ain't cha?" And he would smile back. "Yes, ma'am." We were always polite with the Ectors because they had neither children nor grandchildren so there were no grounds for familiarity. I never knew Nellie Ector very well at all. It was rumored that she was a divorcée who had latched on to him, and to me she became all the tragic heroines I had read about, like *Forever Amber* or the *All This and Heaven Too* chick, and I was awed but kept my distance. He was laughs, though. I don't know when it happened to the Ectors but Mr. White was the first to die. I considered myself a hot-shot canasta player and I would play three-hand with Grandmother and Mrs. White and beat them. But I would drag the game on and on because it seemed so lonely next door when I could look through my bedroom window and see Mrs. White dressing for bed and not having to pull the shade anymore.

10   You always think the ones you love will always be there to love you. I went on to my grandfather's alma mater and got kicked out and would have disgraced the family but I had enough style for it not to be considered disgraceful. I could not/did not adjust to the Fisk social life and it could not/did not adjust to my intellect, so Thanksgiving I rushed home to Grandmother's without the bitchy dean of women's permission and that dean put me on social probation. Which would have worked but I was very much in love and not about to consider her punishment as anything real I should deal with. And the funny thing about that Thanksgiving was that I knew everything would go down just as it did. But I still wouldn't have changed it because Grandmother and Grandpapa would have had dinner alone and I would have had dinner alone and the next Thanksgiving we wouldn't even have him and Grandmother and I would both be alone by ourselves, and the only change would have been that Fisk considered me an ideal student, which means little on a life scale. My grandparents were surprised to see me in my brown slacks and beige sweater nervously chain-smoking and being so glad to touch base again. And she, who knew everything, never once asked me about school. And he was old so I lied to him. And I went to Mount Zion Baptist with them that Sunday and saw he was going to die. He just had to. And I didn't want that. Because I didn't know what to do about Louvenia, who had never been alone in her life.

11   I left Sunday night and saw the dean Monday morning. She asked where I had been. I said home. She asked if I had permission. I said I didn't need her

permission to go home. She said, "Miss Giovanni," in a way I've been hearing all my life, in a way I've heard so long I know I'm on the right track when I hear it, and shook her head. I was "released from the school" February 1 because my "attitudes did not fit those of a Fisk woman." Grandpapa died in April and I was glad it was warm because he hated the cold so badly. Mommy and I drove to Knoxville to the funeral with Chris—Gary's, my sister's, son—and I was brave and didn't cry and made decisions. And finally the time came and Anto left and Aunt Agnes left. And Mommy and Chris and I stayed on till finally Mommy had to go back to work. And Grandmother never once asked me about Fisk. We got up early Saturday morning and Grandmother made fried chicken for us. Nobody said we were leaving but we were. And we all walked down the hill to the car. And kissed. And I looked at her standing there so bravely trying not to think what I was trying not to feel. And I got in on the driver's side and looked at her standing there with her plaid apron and her hair in a bun, her feet hanging loosely out of her mules, sixty-three years old, waving good-bye to us, and for the first time having to go into 400 Mulvaney without John Brown Watson. I felt like an impotent dog. If I couldn't protect this magnificent woman, my grandmother, from loneliness, what could I ever do? I have always hated death. It is unacceptable to kill the young and distasteful to watch the old expire. And those in between our link commit the little murders all the time. There must be a better way. So Knoxville decided to become a model city and a new mall was built to replace the old marketplace and they were talking about convention centers and expressways. And Mulvaney Street was a part of it all. This progress.

12   And I looked out from a drugged sleep and saw the Smoky Mountains looming ahead. The Smokies are so called because the clouds hang low. We used to camp in them. And the bears would come into camp but if you didn't feed them they would go away. It's still a fact. And we prepared for the landing and I closed my eyes as I always do because landings and takeoffs are the most vulnerable times for a plane, and if I'm going to die I don't have to watch it coming. It is very hard to give up your body completely. But the older I get the more dependent I am on other people for my safety, so I closed my eyes and placed myself in harmony with the plane.

13   Tyson Field turned out to be Alcoa. Progress again. And the Alcoa Highway had been widened because the new governor was a football fan and had gotten stuck on the old highway while trying to make a University of Tennessee football game and had missed the kickoff. The next day they began widening the road. We were going to the University of Tennessee for the first speaking of the day. I would have preferred Knoxville College, which had graduated three Watsons ant two Watson progeny. It was too funny being at U.T. speaking of Blackness because I remember when Joe Mack and I integrated the theater here to see *L'il Abner.* And here an Afro Liberation Society was set up. Suddenly my body

remembered we hadn't eaten in a couple of days and Harvey got me a quart of milk and the speaking went on. Then we left U.T. and headed for Black Knoxville.

14 Gay Street is to Knoxville what Fifth Avenue is to New York. Something special, yes? And it looked the same. But Vine Street, where I would sneak to the drugstore to buy *Screen Stories* and watch the men drink wine and play pool—all gone. A wide, clean military-looking highway has taken its place. Austin Homes is cordoned off. It looked like a big prison. The Gem Theatre is now some sort of nightclub and Mulvaney Street is gone. Completely wiped out. Assassinated along with the old people who made it live. I looked over and saw that the lady who used to cry "HOT FISH! GOOD HOT FISH!" no longer had a Cal Johnson park to come to and set up her stove in. Grandmother would not say, "Edith White! I think I'll send Gary for a sandwich. You want one?" Mrs. Abrum and her reverend husband from rural Tennessee wouldn't bring us any more goose eggs from across the street. And Leroy wouldn't chase his mother's boyfriend on Saturday night down the back alley anymore. All gone, not even to a major highway but to a cutoff of a cutoff. All the old people who died from lack of adjustment died for a cutoff of a cutoff.

15   And I remember our finding Grandmother the house on Linden Avenue and constantly reminding her it was every bit as good as if not better than the little ole house. A bigger back yard and no steps to climb. But I knew what Grandmother knew, what we all knew. There was no familiar smell in that house. No coal ashes from the fireplaces. Nowhere that you could touch and say, "Yolande threw her doll against this wall," or "Agnes fell down these steps." No smell or taste of biscuits Grandpapa had eaten with the Alaga syrup he loved so much. No Sunday chicken. No sound of "Lord, you children don't care a thing 'bout me after all I done for you," because Grandmother always had the need to feel mistreated. No spot in the back hall weighted down with lodge books and no corner where the old record player sat playing Billy Eckstine crooning, "What's My Name!" till Grandmother said, "Lord! Any fool know his name!" No breeze on dreamy nights when Mommy would listen over and over again to "I Don't See Me in Your Eyes Anymore." No pain in my knuckles where Grandmother had rapped them because she was determined I would play the piano, and when that absolutely failed, no effort on Linden for us to learn the flowers. No echo of me being the only person in the history of the family to curse Grandmother out and no Grandpapa saying, "Oh, my," which was serious from him, "we can't have this." Linden Avenue was pretty but it had no life.

16   And I took Grandmother one summer to Lookout Mountain in Chattanooga and she would say I was the only grandchild who would take her riding. And that was the summer I noticed her left leg was shriveling. And she said I didn't have to hold her hand and I said I liked to. And I made ice cream the way Grandpapa used to do almost every Sunday. And I churned butter in the hand churner. And I knew and she knew that there was nothing I could do. "I just

want to see you graduate," she said, and I didn't know she meant it. I graduated February 4. She died March 8.

17   And I went to Knoxville looking for Frankie and the Gem and Carter-Roberts or something and they were all gone. And 400 Mulvaney Street, like a majestic king dethroned, put naked in the streets to beg, stood there just a mere skeleton of itself. The cellar that had been so mysterious was now exposed. The fireplaces stood. And I saw the kitchen light hanging and the peach butter put up on the back porch and I wondered why they were still there. She was dead. And I heard the daily soap operas from the radio we had given her one birthday and saw the string beans cooking in the deep well and thought how odd, since there was no stove, and I wanted to ask how Babbi was doing since I hadn't heard or seen "Brighter Day" in so long but no one would show himself. The roses in the front yard were blooming and it seemed a disgrace. Probably the tomatoes came up that year. She always had fantastic luck with tomatoes. But I was just too tired to walk up the front steps to see. Edith White had died. Mr. Ector had died, I heard. Grandmother had died. The park was not yet gone but the trees looked naked and scared. The wind sang to them but they wouldn't smile. The playground where I had swung. The courts where I played my first game of tennis. The creek where our balls were lost. "HOT FISH! GOOD HOT FISH!" The hill where the car speeding down almost hit me. Walking barefoot up the hill to the center to hear stories and my feet burning. All gone. Because progress is so necessary. General Electric says, "Our most important product." And I thought Ronald Reagan was cute.

18   I was sick throughout the funeral. I left Cincinnati driving Mommy, Gary and Chris to Knoxville. From the moment my father had called my apartment I had been sick because I knew before they told me that she was dead. And she had promised to visit me on the tenth. Chris and I were going to drive down to get her since she didn't feel she could fly. And here it was the eighth. I had a letter from her at my house when I got back reaffirming our plans for her visit. I had a cold. And I ran the heat the entire trip despite the sun coming directly down on us. I couldn't get warm. And we stopped in Kentucky for country ham and I remembered how she used to hoard it from us and I couldn't eat. And I drove on. Gary was supposed to relieve me but she was crying too much. And the car was too hot and it was all so unnecessary. She died because she didn't know where she was and didn't like it. And there was no one there to give a touch or smell or feel and I think I should have been there. And at her funeral they said, "It is well," and I knew she knew it was. And it was so peaceful in Mount Zion Baptist Church that afternoon. And I hope when I die that it can be said of me all is well with my soul.

19 So they took me up what would have been Vine Street past what would have been Mulvaney and I thought there may be a reason we lack a collective historical memory. And I was taken out to the beautiful homes on Brooks Road where

we considered the folks "so swell, don't cha know." And I was exhausted but feeling quite high from being once again in a place where no matter what I belong. And Knoxville belongs to me. I was born there in Old Knoxville General and I am buried there with Louvenia. And as the time neared for me to speak I had no idea where I would start. I was nervous and afraid because I just wanted to quote Gwen Brooks and say, "This is the urgency—Live!" And they gave me a standing ovation and I wanted to say, "Thank you," but that was hardly sufficient. Mommy's old bridge club, Les pas Si Bêtes, gave me beads, and that's the kind of thing that happens in small towns where people aren't afraid to be warm. And I looked out and saw Miss Delaney in her blue furs. And was reminded life continues. And I saw the young brothers and sisters who never even knew me or my family and I saw my grandmother's friends who shouldn't even have been out that late at night. And they had come to say *Welcome Home.* And I thought Tommy, my son, must know about this. He must know we come from somewhere. That we belong.

☐ Discovering Meaning and Technique

1. Early in the essay, Giovanni says, "Something called progress killed my grandmother" (paragraph 6). Does this seem to be the central point of the selection?

2. Point out some of the details that Giovanni uses to make the town of her childhood seem real and immediate.

3. What leads Giovanni to her conclusion: "And I thought Tommy, my son, must know about this. He must know we come from somewhere. That we belong" (paragraph 19)?

4. Giovanni weaves the progress of a plane trip to Knoxville with past memories of Knoxville. Which parts of the essay describe memories? Which parts describe the plane trip?

5. Giovanni makes use of very long as well as very short sentences. For example, in paragraph 10, she writes, "But I still wouldn't have changed it because Grandmother and Grandpapa would have had dinner alone and I would have had dinner alone and the next Thanksgiving we wouldn't even have him and Grandmother and I would both be alone by ourselves, and the only change would have been that Fisk considered me an ideal student, which means little on a life scale." Several sentences later, she writes, "He just had to." Discuss how this device makes her prose sound much like someone talking.

☐ **Writing Suggestions**

1. Relate an experience of returning home to the memories you have of that home.

2. If you have experienced the death of a close relative, explain how that death made you feel.

3. Giovanni makes her grandparents come alive for the reader by describing their simple habits—how they talked, what they cooked, what they wore. Describe a close relative using some of Giovanni's techniques.

UNCLE HAROLD

☐ RUSSELL BAKER

1 Uncle Harold was famous for lying.

2   He had once been shot right between the eyes. He told me so himself. It was during World War I. An underaged boy, he had run away from home, enlisted in the Marine Corps, and been shipped to France, where one of the Kaiser's soldiers had shot him. Right between the eyes.

3   It was a miracle it hadn't killed him, and I said so the evening he told me about it. He explained that Marines were so tough they didn't need miracles. I was now approaching the age of skepticism, and though it was risky business challenging adults, I was tempted to say, "Swear on the Bible?" I did not dare go this far, but I did get a hint of doubt into my voice by repeating his words as a question.

4   "Right between the eyes?"

5   "Right between the eyes," he said. "See this scar?"

6   He placed a finger on his forehead just above the bridge of his nose. "That's all the mark it left," he said.

7   "I don't see any scar," I said.

8   "It's probably faded by now," he said. "It's been a long time ago."

9   I said it must have hurt a good bit.

10   "Hurt! You bet it hurt."

11   "What did you do?"

12   "It made me so mad I didn't do a thing but pull out my pistol and kill that German right there on the spot."

13   At this point Aunt Sister came in from the kitchen with cups of cocoa. "For God's sake, Harold," she said, "quit telling the boy those lies."

14   People were always telling Uncle Harold for God's sake quit telling those

lies. His full name was Harold Sharp, and in the family, people said, "That Harold Sharp is the biggest liar God ever sent down the pike."

15   Aunt Sister, Ida Rebecca's only daughter, had married him shortly after my mother took Doris and me from Morrisonville. He'd spent sixteen years in the Marines by then, but at Aunt Sister's insistence he gave up the Marine Corps and the two of them moved to Baltimore. There they had a small apartment on Hollins Street overlooking Union Square. Our place was a second-floor apartment on West Lombard Street just across the square. It was easy for my mother to stroll over to Aunt Sister's with Doris and me to play Parcheesi or Caroms or Pick-Up-Sticks with the two of them, but the real pleasure of these visits for me came from listening to Uncle Harold.

16   It didn't matter that my mother called him "the biggest liar God ever sent down the pike." In spite of his reputation for varnishing a fact, or maybe because of the outrageousness with which he did the varnishing, I found him irresistible. It was his intuitive refusal to spoil a good story by slavish adherence to fact that enchanted me. Though poorly educated, Uncle Harold somehow knew that the possibility of creating art lies not in reporting but in fiction.

17   He worked at cutting grass and digging graves for a cemetery in West Baltimore. This increased the romantic aura through which I saw him, for I had become fascinated with the Gothic aspects of death since arriving in Baltimore. In Baltimore, disposing of the dead seemed to to be a major cultural activity. There were three funeral parlors within a one-block radius of our house, and a steady stream of hearses purred through the neighborhood. I had two other distant relatives from Morrisonville who had migrated to Baltimore, and both of them were also working in cemeteries. In addition, there was a fairly steady flow of corpses through our house on Lombard Street.

18   Our landlord there, a genial Lithuanian tailor who occupied the first floor, lent out his parlor to a young relative who was an undertaker and sometimes had an overflow at his own establishment. As a result there was often an embalmed body coffined lavishly in the first-floor parlor. Since our apartment could be reached only by passing the landlord's parlor, and since its double doors were always wide open, it seemed to me that instead of finding a home of our own, we had come to rest in a funeral home. Passing in and out of the house, I tried to avert my eyes from the garishly rouged bodies and hold my breath against inhaling the cloying odors of candle wax, tuberoses, and embalming fluid which suffused the hallway.

19   When Uncle Harold came over for an evening of card playing and found a corpse in the parlor, his imagination came alive. On one such evening I went down to let Aunt Sister and him in the front door. Noting the coffin in our landlord's parlor, Uncle Harold paused, strode into the room, nodded at the mourners, and examined the deceased stranger with professional scrutiny. Upstairs afterwards, playing cards at the dining-room table, Uncle Harold announced that the old gentleman in the coffin downstairs did not look dead to him.

20 "I could swear I saw one of his eyelids flicker," he said.

21 Nobody paid him any attention.

22 "You can't always be sure they're dead," he said.

23 Nobody was interested except me.

24 "A man I knew was almost buried alive once," he said.

25 "Are you going to play the jack or hold it all night?" my mother asked.

26 "It was during the war," Uncle Harold said. "In France. They were closing the coffin on him when I saw him blink one eye."

27 The cards passed silently and were shuffled.

28 "I came close to being buried alive myself one time," he said.

29 "For God's sake, Harold, quit telling those lies," Aunt Sister said.

30 "It's the truth, just as sure as I'm sitting here, so help me God," said Uncle Harold. "It happens every day. We dig them up out at the cemetery—to do autopsies, you know—and you can see they fought like the devil to get out after the coffin was closed on them, but it's too late by that time."

31 Uncle Harold was not a tall man, but the Marines had taught him to carry himself with a swaggering erect indolence and to measure people with the grave, cool arrogance of authority. Though he now shoveled dirt for a living, he was always immaculately manicured by the time he sat down to supper. In this polished man of the world—suits pressed to razor sharpness, every hair in place, eyes of icy gray self-confidence—I began to detect a hidden boy, in spirit not too different from myself, though with a love for mischief which had been subdued in me by too much melancholy striving to satisfy my mother's notions of manhood.

32 Admiring him so extravagantly, I was disappointed to find that he detested my hero, Franklin Roosevelt. In Uncle Harold's view, Roosevelt was a deep-dyed villain of the vilest sort. He had data about Roosevelt's shenanigans which newspapers were afraid to publish and occasionally entertained with hair-raising accounts of Rooseveltian deeds that had disgraced the Presidency.

33 "You know, I suppose, that Roosevelt only took the job for the money," he told me one evening.

34 "Does it pay a lot?"

35 "Not all that much," he said, "but there are plenty of ways of getting rich once you get in the White House, and Roosevelt's using all of them."

36 "How?"

37 "He collects money from everybody who wants to get in to see him."

38 "People have to give him money before he'll talk to them?"

39 "They don't give him the money face to face. He's too smart for that," Uncle Harold said.

40 "Then how does he get it?"

41 "There's a coat rack right outside his door, and he keeps an overcoat hanging on that rack. Before anybody can get in to see him, they've got to put money in the overcoat pocket."

42   I was shocked, which pleased Uncle Harold. "That's the kind of President you've got," he said.

43   "Do you know that for sure?"

44   "Everybody knows it."

45   "How do *you* know it?"

46   "A fellow who works at the White House told me how it's done."

47   This was such powerful stuff that as soon as I got home I passed it on to my mother. "Who told you that stuff?" she asked.

48   "Uncle Harold."

49   She laughed at my gullibility. "Harold Sharp is the biggest liar God ever sent down the pike," she said. "He doesn't know any more about Roosevelt than a hog knows about holiday."

50   Through Uncle Harold I first heard of H. L. Mencken. Mencken's house lay just two doors from Uncle Harold's place on Hollins Street. Uncle Harold pointed it out to me one day when we were walking around to the Arundel Ice Cream store for a treat. "You know who lives in that house, don't you?"

51   Of course I didn't.

52   "H. L. Mencken."

53   Who's H. L. Mencken?

54   "You mean to tell me you never heard of H. L. Mencken? He writes those pieces in the newspaper that make everybody mad," Uncle Harold said.

55   I understood from Uncle Harold's respectful tone that Mencken must be a great man, though Mencken's house did not look like the house of a great man. It looked very much like every other house in Baltimore. Red brick, white marble steps. "I saw Mencken coming out of his house just the other day," Uncle Harold said.

56   It's doubtful Uncle Harold had ever read anything by Mencken. Uncle Harold's tastes ran to *Doc Savage* and *The Shadow.* Still, I could see he was proud of living so close to such a great man. It was a measure of how well he had done in life at a time when millions of other men had been broken by the Depression.

57   He had left home in 1917 for the Marines, an uneducated fifteen-year-old country boy from Taylorstown, a village not far from Morrisonville, just enough schooling to read and do arithmetic, not much to look forward to but a career of farm labor. Maybe in the Marines he even became a hero. He did fight in France and afterwards stayed on in the Marines, shipping around the Caribbean under General Smedley Butler to keep Central America subdued while Yankee corporations pumped out its wealth. For a man with negligible expectations, he had not done badly by 1937 standards. Full-time cemetery labor; a one-bedroom apartment so close to a famous writer.

58   My first awe of him had softened as I gradually realized his information was not really intended to be information. Gradually I came to see that Uncle Harold was not a liar but a teller of stories and a romantic, and it was Uncle

Harold the teller of tales who fascinated me. Though he remained a stern figure, and I never considered sassing him, I saw now that he knew I no longer received his stories with total credulity, but that I was now listening for the pleasure of watching his imagination at play. This change in our relationship seemed to please him.

59   Over the Parcheesi board one evening he told a story about watching the dead in Haiti get up out of their shrouds and dance the Charleston. Aunt Sister and my mother had the usual response: "For God's sake, Harold, quit telling those lies."

60   His face was impassive as always when he issued the usual protest—"It's the truth, so help me God"—but I could see with absolute clarity that underneath the impassive mask he was smiling. He saw me studying him, scowled forbiddingly at me for one moment, then winked. That night we came to a silent understanding: We were two romancers whose desire for something more fanciful than the humdrum of southwest Baltimore was beyond the grasp of unimaginative people like Aunt Sister and my mother.

61   Still, it took me a while to understand what he was up to. He wanted life to be more interesting than it was, but his only gift for making it so lay in a small talent for homespun fictions, and he could not resist trying to make the most of it. Well, there was nothing tragic about his case. Our world in Baltimore hadn't much respect for the poetic impulse. In our world a man spinning a romance was doomed to be dismissed as nothing more than a prodigious liar.

☐ Discovering Meaning and Technique

1. How plausible are Uncle Harold's lies? Does he really expect them to be believed?

2. How does young Baker's attitude toward Harold differ from that of other family members?

3. Find the place in the essay where Baker and Harold become conspirators.

4. What two expressions do family members use to dismiss or explain Harold's behavior?

5. Baker manipulates language to make his experiences with the funeral business less grim than they might ordinarily be. Point out some of the humorous phrases, such as "disposing of the dead seemed to be a major cultural activity" (paragraph 17).

6. Point out other sources of the humor in the selection.

☐ **Writing Suggestions**

1. Baker claims that his uncle knew "that the possibility of creating art lies not in reporting but in fiction" (paragraph 16). Explain the quotation.

2. Discuss the progress of the boy's attitude toward his uncle as it changes from awe to understanding.

3. Describe an incident in your childhood when an adult told you a tall tale. Did you believe it? How did you find out the truth?

4. Describe a favorite relative from your childhood and explain why he or she interested you.

HOW PLAYING COUNTRY MUSIC TAUGHT ME TO LOVE MY DAD

☐ JAMES D. HOUSTON

*Deep within my heart
lies a melody,
a song of Old San Antone . . .*
—*BOB WILLS*—

1 I grew up listening to my father play the steel guitar. It was his pastime and his passion. Once or twice a month our front room would fill with fiddlers and guitar pickers who had come west from Texas and Oklahoma and Arkansas and other places farther south to make money in the fields and in the shipyards of World War Two. Dad was more or less the leader, since he had the most equipment—a little speaker, two mikes, an old Westinghouse recording machine. From upstairs, with my head and my radio under pillows and covers, where I was trying to concentrate on *The Shadow,* I could hear them ripping into *San Antonio Rose* or *Detour—There's a Muddy Road Ahead.* Clutching the radio I would groan and burrow deeper and, to fend off the guitars, imagine the look of The Shadow himself, my sinister and worldly night-time companion.

2 I thought I was groaning about the music. But it was dad who made me cringe. Coming of age in San Francisco, I was a smartass city kid, cool and sullen, and ashamed of all his downhome tastes and habits. During those years I lost a tremendous amount, resisting the things he cared about and denying

who he was. At the time I had no way of knowing how much was working against us. No two points of origin could have been farther apart.

3   His hometown was not a town at all. It was an east Texas village called Pecan Gap, where kids grew up chopping cotton. To escape he dropped out of highschool in the tenth grade and joined the Navy, on a hitch that sent him to Honolulu in the mid-1920s, for two years of submarine duty at Pearl Harbor. That was where he learned half the music he knew. In Texas he had learned enough rhythm guitar to accompany singing. Some Hawaiian taught him the flat-lap style, the right hand flashing with silver picks, the left moving its little steel bar across the strings, sliding, whining, yearning, dreaming. Until the day he died, the two tunes he played most, and loved most, were *The Steel Guitar Rag* and *The Hilo March.*

4   He also learned the ukulele over there. When I was fourteen I found one hanging in his closet. My first hour of aimless plinking jangled his nerves. I knew this, and I kept it up until he grabbed the uke and told me to sit still while he taught me three chords and a basic strum, which he described as "trying to shake somethin off the end of your fanger."

5   I started practicing that strum and those chords about two hours a day. After a week he hid the ukulele. One afternoon I came home from school and it was gone. First I accused my sister. Then I confronted my mother. When I told dad that his ukulele had disappeared he pursed his lips judiciously and said, "Gone, you say. Imagine that."

6   Who knows why he hid it? Maybe the sound I had been making, akin to the squawk of a rusty clothesline wheel, was too big a price to pay to have another musician in the family. Maybe he was getting even with me for refusing to listen to his band. I'm still not sure. We were both inexperienced at this game. He was my first and only father. I was his first and only son.

7   For two days I searched, and finally found the uke between the ceiling and the roof beams, shoved back under some insulation. When I came strumming into the front room, he turned red. His jaws bunched in the classic, teeth-grinding, Dust Bowler's way of holding it all inside. Then he tried to grin. With eyes lowered, he jerked his face sideways in that other classic gesture that can signify all moods from outrage to wonder. He said, "Looks like you scared it up."

8   Maybe this had been a little test, to measure my commitment. Before long he showed me the rest of his chords, another strum, a simple way to pick the melody to *Lovely Hula Hands.* About the time I had practiced all this to death, I graduated to the four-string banjo. I was in a neighborhood music store eyeing the long neck and stretched head and gleaming strings of a brand-new instrument, when the owner's seductive voice, from somewhere behind me, said I was welcome to do more than look. From there it was a short step to Dixieland Jazz which, in those days, around 1950, was the hottest sound in northern California. My songs were *The Muskrat Ramble* and *The Rampart Street Parade.* My new-

found heroes were Louis Armstrong, Jack Teagarden, Turk Murphy, Red Nichols and His Five Pennies.

9   Sometimes, say late on a Saturday afternoon, I would be practicing, and I would hear dad in the front room tuning up, as if by chance. Begrudgingly I would find myself in there with him, running through the changes for one of his big production numbers, *The Steel Guitar Rag,* the *Cow Cow Boogie.* But I was arrogant about these little rehearsals. His arrangements, his slides and flourishes, his idea of an impressive finale—this was ancient history. It was beneath me. It was worse than hicksville. It was Okie music. And I was anything but an Okie.

10   From Dixieland I soon moved toward modern jazz, and now my instrument was the upright bass. *How High The Moon. Darn That Dream. Willow, Weep For Me.* These were the songs you had to know, and how could dad and I even talk about such music? The tunes we listened to placed us on opposite sides of an uncrossable chasm, a Grand Canyon of taste—the augmented seventh chord as far from his vocabulary as a queen's pawn, or existentialism.

> Goin down to Cripple Creek,
> Goin on the run,
> Goin down to Cripple Creek
> To have a little fun . . .

11 Though music has never been my main line of work, I have always kept some gig or another going on the side, found some combo to sit in with. I inherited this from him, of course, a connection so obvious it eluded me for half my life. I have played in dance bands and in piano bars, at New Year's Eve parties and for weddings in June. I have played in total release sessions where anyone can get into the act, with any horn or rhythm-maker handy, to do whatever comes to mind.

12   For several years I spent half my mornings on classical and flamenco guitar. By that time he had pretty much quit playing. After the family moved down to Santa Clara Valley, his old picking buddies were too far away to meet with. Most of them had packed up their instruments anyhow, when their fingers gave out. And by that time I was married, living here in Santa Cruz, starting my own family, taking on a few guitar students for the extra cash, and trying to go the distance with the classical repertoire—Villa-Lobos, Tarrega, Fernando Sor. Those days now stand for what pushed me farthest from him. Call it my own yearning for sophistication. I was never much good at sophistication. It runs right against the grain. But I confess that I have hungered for it. In the preludes and the nocturnes, I could taste it, and in the numerous baroque guitar suites I tried to master, in the Elizabethan galliards, in the Fantasía written by some 16th century lutenist whose three surviving works had recently been transcribed from nearly indecipherable tablatures.

13   I still love the galliards. I always will. But it took me twenty years of part-time music life to discover, or rather to quit being ashamed of the fact and come right out and admit that I love *San Antonio Rose* more. If I am sitting in a honky tonk when the pedal steel begins to whine the opening bars of that song, I have no choice but to surrender. I hear a calling in the blood. It launches me. It fills me with unabashed glee.

14   I can now trace this change in outlook to a bluegrass band I happened to join, during the very year dad passed away. At the time I told myself I was "between gigs," looking for new musical allies and looking for something I had not tried. But I am convinced that more than coincidence brought this group together. It was another version of the ancient maxim: when the musician is ready, the band will appear.

15   Everyone else had played a lot of country music. The mandolin picker was a graduate student from North Carolina. The banjo player came from Knox-ville, Tennessee, by way of Viet Nam, discovering California like my dad did, passing through. I was the novice, and the first night we got together I was stupefied with boredom. One of the pleasures of playing string bass is working through a good set of chord changes, the challenging progression, the little surprise moves that have to be memorized. In bluegrass there are many tricky melodies to be executed by fiddle and banjo and mandolin, but no changes to speak of, three or four in most tunes, two in a lot of them, in some tunes no changes at all.

16   "Just hang on to that A minor, Jim baby!" the mandolin picker told me, as we began to play a modal breakdown featuring his shiny Gibson. "And for God sake, let me hear that A!"

17   It took some getting used to. It took a little while to hear what was really going on with five stringed instruments, all acoustic, all made of wood. They wove a tapestry of sound, a tight braid of mountain counterpoint, and I found that I could squeeze inside the braid, pushing notes up from underneath for the fiddle and banjo to loop around. The best way to feel it is to stand in a circle, get moving on a song like *Blackberry Blossom* or *Cripple Creek*. Then all the strings and resonating chambers pulse at one another in intricate, skin-whiffling ways.

18   I told myself that bluegrass is rural chamber music, which, in a certain sense, is true. But those were mainly academic words I needed, to talk myself into it.

19   I soon discovered, or remembered, that my head was full of songs I had grown up hearing on "The Grand Ol Opry" out of Nashville. Dad used to listen to that show every Saturday night. I started taking vocals on some of Roy Acuff's great hits, *Wreck on The Highway, The Wabash Cannonball.* The other guys were bringing in truck driving songs, gospel numbers, old Jimmie Rodgers yodels, anything that tickled us, as long as we could call it "country," as long as we

could do it acoustically and without piano and drums. We could afford to be purists because we all made our money other ways. We dressed up in boots and sting ties and colored shirts and drank whiskey in the parking lot. I would often think of dad while we were playing, wishing he could have seen and heard all this, sometimes wondering why he had to pass away before I could embrace what I had resisted for so long.

20   I guess this band had been together for a couple of years when he finally turned up, very briefly, at a country fair outside of town.

21   There's a long low valley winding inland from the ocean and the coast road called Highway One. About five miles back, in a big open meadow, wooden booths had been nailed up out of rough-hewn planks and hung with flags and banners. The meadow was recently mowed. Hay was raked into mounds for picnickers to loll against. Steep stands of madrone and bay and redwood sloped away on both sides and seemed to gather all the sunlight into this grassy basin. It wasn't hot. Little breezes eddied through there all day long. But from noon on, the sun was so bright, the haystacks shimmered so, you could hardly look at them with the naked eye.

22   There were clay pots for sale, and embroidered shirts, and buffaloes of welded iron, and roasting corn, and ice cream, and free draft beer for the band, to chase down the Jim Beam we had stashed behind our sound system. By the end of the second set we were so loose we played *Foggy Mountain Breakdown* faster than we ever thought we could. Not one of us missed a note. We all agreed it was the best we had sounded. The scene had lifted us to its own excellence. And it was just then, as I stepped back into the shade, looking for a drink, high from the music, yet already wistful, afraid we might never be that good again, that I spotted him leaning against one of the hay bales, in between our bandstand and the curving line of booths.

23   He looked mighty comfortable, like this was how he had hoped to spend the day. His legs were stretched in front of him, ankles crossed, hands behind his head. He wore white shoes, white duck pants, a white shirt open at the collar, and a white, broad-brim plantation owner's hat, watching me carefully and almost smiling. He never had smiled much. Somehow it was difficult for him. He gave me as wide a smile as he'd ever been able to deliver, followed by his ultimate statement, that all-purpose sideways twist of the head, which in this case signified approval, and perhaps a hint of true delight. Then a strolling couple passed between us, and he was gone.

24   I stared at the hay mound until my eyes blurred, trying to conjure him up again and wishing to hell I had been born ten years before World War One, so we could have toured east Texas together, around 1928, when he first got back from Honolulu, out of the Navy and looking for some action. He and his pals had about twenty-five tunes between them and an old bathtub Model T. They hit all the towns between Fort Worth and Corpus Christi, actually played

for a couple of months on a radio station out of Texarkana, two guitars and a country fiddle. He wore that white plantation owner's hat everywhere he went in those days, twenty-four years old at the time and a singing fool.

☐ Discovering Meaning and Technique

1. The central theme of the selection is Houston's conflict with his father: "I was a smartass city kid . . . and ashamed of all his downhome tastes and habits" (paragraph 2). How accurate is the title as the resolution of the conflict?

2. The narrative is organized around the stages of Houston's musical development, which parallel the stages of his growing up and the progress of the conflict. Point out where each stage begins and ends.

3. During the year the father died, the son joined a bluegrass band. Houston claims that this event illustrates the "ancient maxim: when the musician is ready, the band will appear" (paragraph 14). Have you ever heard this maxim? Do you think that it is true?

4. When the father "turned up, very briefly, at a country fair" (paragraph 20), Houston describes him as dressed all in white. Is the reader supposed to think the father is a ghost? Is the reader supposed to think that Houston is drunk?

5. Twice in the selection, the father makes the same gesture with his head: "he jerked his face sideways in that other classic gesture that can signify all moods from outrage to wonder" (paragraph 7) and "he gave me . . . that all-purpose sideways twist of the head" (paragraph 23). Discuss the fact that each instance marks a turning point in Houston's life.

6. Point out where Houston uses quotations to characterize his father's "down-home" style.

7. Why does Houston include the song lyrics?

8. Discuss the description of the country fair. Point out where Houston piles up details to paint the backdrop.

☐ Writing Suggestions

1. Choose a conflict you had with your parents; narrate its beginning, middle, and end.

2. Describe how your taste in music changed as you grew up.

3. Discuss how a person's taste in music indicates something about his or her personality.

4. Describe a period in your life when you were ashamed of a parent.

BOUND UPON A WHEEL OF FIRE

☐ SALLIE TISDALE

1 Every winter night of my childhood, my father built a fire. Every element of the evening's fire was treated with care—with the caress of the careful man. The wood, the wood box, the grate, the coal-black poker and shovel: He touched these more often than he touched me. I would hold back, watching, and when the fire was lit plant myself before it and fall into a gentle dream. No idea was too strange or remote before the fire, no fantasy of shadow and light too bizarre.

2   But for all the long hours I spent before his fires, for all the honey-colored vapors that rose like smoke from that hearth, these aren't the fires of memory. They aren't my father's fires. When I remember fire, I remember houses burning, scorched and flooded with flame, and mills burning, towers of fire leaping through the night to the lumber nearby like so much kindling, and cars burning, stinking and black and waiting to blow. I loved those fires with a hot horror, always daring myself to step closer, feel their heat, touch.

3   My father is a fireman. My submission to fire is lamentably obvious. But there is more than love here, more than jealousy—more than Electra's unwilling need. It is a fundamental lure, a seduction of my roots and not my limbs. I am propelled toward fire, and the dual draw of fascination and fear, the urge to walk into and at the same time conquer fire, is like the twin poles of the hermaphrodite. I wanted to be a fireman before, and after, I wanted to be anything else.

4   Firemen are big, brawny, young, and smiling creatures. They sit in the fire hall with its high ceilings and cold concrete floors and dim corners, waiting, ready. Firemen have a perfume of readiness. They wash their shiny trucks and hang the long white hoses from rods to dangle and dry. And when the alarm rings, firemen turn into hurrying bodies that know where to step and what to do, each with a place and duty, without excess motion. Firemen wear heavy coats and big black boots and hard helmets. They can part crowds. They are calescent and virile like the fire, proud, reticent, and most content when moving; firemen have their own rules, and they break glass, make messes, climb heights, and drive big loud trucks very fast.

5   Forgive me; I am trying to show the breadth of this fable. I wanted to be a fireman so much that it didn't occur to me for a long time that they might

not let me. Fires marked me; I got too close. The hearth fire was my first and best therapist, the fire-dreams were happy dreams of destruction and ruin. The andiron was the ground, the logs our house, and each black space between the logs a window filled with helpless people, my father and mother and siblings. The fire was the world and I was outside and above, listening to their calls for rescue from the darting blaze, and sometimes I would allow them to escape and sometimes not, never stirring from my meditative pose. If I felt uncharitable, I could watch the cinders crumble from the oak and cedar like bodies falling to the ground below and the fire turn to ashes while I, the fire fighter, sat back safe and clear and cool.

6   At odd times—during dinner, late at night—the alarm would sound, and my father would leap up, knocking dogs and small children aside as he ran from the house. I grew up used to surprise. He was a bulky man, and his pounding steps were heavy and important in flight; I slipped aside when he passed by.

7   The fire department was volunteer, and every fireman something else as well. My father was a teacher. We had a private radio set in the house, and we heard alarms before the town at large did. It was part of the privilege of fire. Before the siren blew on the station two blocks away, the radio in the hallway sang its high-pitched plea. He was up and gone in seconds, a sentence chopped off in mid-word, a bite of food dropped to the plate. Squeal, halt, go: I was used to the series; it was a part of our routine.

8   Then my mother would stop what she was doing and turn down the squeal and listen to the dispatcher on the radio. His voice, without face or name, was one of the most familiar voices in my home, crowned with static and interruptions. My mother knew my father's truck code and could follow his progress in a jumble of terse male voices, one-word questions, first names, numbers, and sometimes hasty questions and querulous shouts. She stood in the hallway with one hand on the volume and her head cocked to listen; she shushed us with a stern tension. She would not betray herself, though I knew and didn't care; in the harsh wilderness of childhood, my father's death in a fire would have been a great and terrible thing. It would have been an honor.

9   The town siren was a broad foghorn call that rose and fell in a long ululation, like the call of a bird. We could hear it anywhere in town, everyone could, and if I was away from our house I would run to the station. (I had to race the cars and pickups of other volunteer firemen, other teachers, and the butcher, the undertaker, an editor from the local newspaper, grinding out of parking lots and driveways all over town in a hail of pebbles.) If I was quick enough and lucky enough, I could stand to one side and watch the flat doors fly up, the trucks pull out one after the other covered with clinging men, and see my father driving by. He drove a short, stout pumper, and I waved and called to him high above my head. He never noticed I was there, not once; it was as though he ceased to be my father when he became a fireman. The whistle of the siren was the whistle of another life, and he would disappear around a corner, face pursed with concentration, and be gone.

10   Oh, for a fire at night in the winter, the cold nocturnal sky, the pairing of flame and ice. It stripped life bare. I shared a room with my sister, a corner room on the second floor with two windows looking in their turn on the intersection a house away. The fire station was around that corner and two blocks east, a tall white block barely visible through the barren trees. Only the distant squeal of the alarm downstairs woke us, that and the thud of his feet and the slam of the back door; before we could open the curtains and windows for a gulp of frigid air, we'd hear the whine of his pickup and the crunch of its tires on the crust of snow. The night was clear and brittle and raw, and the tocsin called my father to come out. Come out, come out to play, it sang, before my mother turned the sound off. He rushed to join the hot and hurried race to flames. We knelt at the windows under the proximate, twinkling stars, in light pajamas, shivering, and following the spin of lights on each truck—red, blue, red, blue, red—flashing across houses, cars, faces. We could follow the colored spin and figure out where the fire must be and how bad and wonder out loud if he'd come back.

11   There were times when he didn't return till morning. I would come downstairs and find him still missing, my mother sleepy-eyed and making toast, and then he would trudge in. Ashen and weary, my father, beat, his old flannel pajamas dusted with the soot that crept through the big buckles of his turnout coat, and smelling of damp, sour smoke.

12 I should be a fire setter. I should be that peculiar kind of addict, hooked on stolen matches and the sudden conflagration in mother's underwear and father's shoes. There are plenty of them, many children, thieving flame and setting its anarchic soul free in unexpected places. But I lack that incendiary urge; my Electra is more subtle, the knotty recesses of my own desires cunning even to me.

13   "What we first learn about fire is that we must not touch it," Gaston Bachelard writes in his book *The Psychoanalysis of Fire,* in the course of explaining the "Prometheus Complex" that the prohibition against fire creates. I talk about my father infrequently, always with hunger and anger; I build fires almost every winter night. But I've never built a wrong fire, and I worry over flammables like a mother hen. I'm scared of being burned and of all of fire's searing lesions. I class it with the other primitive, deadly joys: the sea deeps and flying—the runaway edge of control.

14   I fear one particular fire. My father was also an electrician, a tinker of small appliances. I am wary of outlets and wires of all kinds, which seem tiny and potent and unpredictable; the occult and silent river of electrical fire racing behind the walls can keep me awake nights. Electricity is just another flame, but flame refined. (In this way it is like alcohol: literally distilled.) Not long ago I put a pot of water to boil on my stove, and a little sloshed over; suddenly a roaring arc of electricity shot from beneath the pot and curved back upon itself. The kitchen air filled with the acrid smoke of burning insulation and the

crackling, sputtering sound of short circuits, and I didn't have the slightest idea what to do. I wanted my father to put it out, and he was 300 miles away. It seemed the most untenable betrayal, my stove lunging out at me in such a capricious way. It seemed *mean;* that arc of blue-white current burned down my adulthood.

15   Prometheus stole more than fire; he stole the *knowledge* of fire, the hard data of combustion. I wanted all my father's subtle art. I wanted the mystery of firewood and the burning, animated chain saw, the tree's long fall, the puzzle of splitting hardwood with a wedge and maul placed just so in the log's curving grain. I wanted to know the differences of quality in smoke, where to lay the ax on the steaming roof, how the kindling held up the heavy logs. What makes creosote ignite? How to know the best moment to flood a fire? What were the differences between oak and cedar, between asphalt and shake? And most of all I wanted to know how to go in to the fire, what virtue was used when he set his face and pulled the rim of his helmet down and ran inside the burning house. It was arcane, obscure, and unaccountably male, this fire business. He built his fires piece by piece, lit each with a single match, and once the match was lit I was privileged to watch, hands holding chin and elbows propped on knees, in the posture Bachelard calls essential to the "physics of reverie" delivered by fire.

16   I build fires now. I like the satisfying scritch-scratch of the little broom clearing ash. I find it curious that I don't build very good fires; I'm hasty and I don't want to be taught. But at last, with poorly seasoned wood and too much paper, I make the fire go, and then the force it exerts is exactly the same. That's something about fire: All fire is the same, every ribbon of flame the same thing, whatever that thing may be. There is that fundamental quality, fire as an irreducible element at large; fire is fire is fire no matter what or when or where. The burning house is just the hearth freed. And the fire-trance stays the same, too. I still sit cross-legged and dreaming, watching the hovering flies of light that float before me in a cloud, as fireflies do.

17   How I wanted to be a fireman when I grew up. I wanted this for a long time. To become a volunteer fireman was expected of a certain type of man— the town's steady, able-bodied men, men we could depend on. As I write this I feel such a tender pity for that little, wide-eyed girl, a free-roaming tomboy wandering a little country town and friend to all the firemen. I really did expect them to save me a place.

18   Every spring we had a spring parade. I had friends lucky enough to ride horses, others only lucky enough to ride bikes. But I rode the pumper and my father drove slowly, running the lights and siren at every intersection and splitting our ears with the noise. We the firemen's children perched on the hoses neatly laid in pleated rows, bathed in sunlight, tossing candy to the spectators as though, at parade's end, we wouldn't have to get down and leave the truck alone again.

19   He would take me to the station. I saw forbidden things, firemen's lives.

20   On the first floor was the garage with its row of trucks. Everything shivered with attention, ripe for work: the grunt of a pumper, the old truck, antique and polished new. And the Snorkel. When I was very small, a building burned because it was too high for the trucks to reach a fire on its roof; within a year the town bought the Snorkel, a basher of a truck, long, white, sleek, with a folded hydraulic ladder. The ladder opened and lifted like a praying mantis rising from a twig, higher and higher.

21   Above the garage was the real station, a single room with a golden floor and a wall of windows spilling light. The dispatcher lived there, the unmarried volunteers could bunk there if they liked; along one wall was a row of beds. No excess there, no redundancy, only a cooler of soda, a refrigerator full of beer, a shiny bar, a card table, a television. I guess I held my father's hand while he chatted with one of the men. In the corner I saw a hole, a hole in the floor, and in the center of the hole the pole plunging down; I peeked over the edge and followed the light along the length of the shining silver pole diving to the floor below.

22   I remember one singular Fourth of July. It was pitch dark on the fairgrounds, in a dirt field far from the exhibition buildings and the midway. Far from anything. It was the middle of nothing and nowhere out there on a moonless night, strands of dry grass tickling my legs, bare below my shorts. There was no light at all but a flashlight in one man's hand, no sound but the murmurs of the men talking to one another in the dark, moving heavy boxes with mumbles and grunts, laughing very quietly with easy laughs. My father was a silhouette among many, tall and black against a near-black sky. Then I saw a sparkle and heard the fuse whisper up its length and strained to see the shape of it, the distance. And I heard the whump of the shell exploding and the high whistle of its flight; and when it blew, its empyreal flower filled the sky. They flung one rocket after another, two and four at once, boom! flash! One shell blew too low and showered us with sparks, no one scared but smiling at the glowworms wiggling through the night as though the night were earth and we the sky and they were rising with the rain.

23 Only recently have I seen how much more occurred, hidden beneath the surface of his life. I presumed too much, the way all children do. It wasn't only lack of sleep that peeled my father's face bald in a fire's dousing. He hates fires. Hates burning mills; they last all night and the next day like balefires signaling a battle. He hated every falling beam that shot arrows of flame and the sheets of fire that curtain rooms. And bodies: I heard only snatches of stories, words drifting up the stairs in the middle of the night after a fire as he talked to my mother in the living room in the dark. Pieces of bodies stuck to bedsprings like steaks to a grill, and, once, the ruin of dynamite. When my mother died I asked about cremation, and he flung it away with a meaty hand and chose a solid, airtight coffin. He sees the stake in fire. He suffered the fear of going in.

24   I was visiting my father last year, at Christmastime. There are always fires at Christmastime, mostly trees turning to torches and chimneys flaring like Roman candles. And sure enough, the alarm sounded early in the evening, the same bright squeal from the same radio, for a flue fire. There have been a thousand flue fires in his life. (Each one is different, he tells me.)

25   As it happened, this time it was our neighbor's flue, across the street, on Christmas Eve, and I put shoes on the kids and we dashed across to watch the circus, so fortunately near. The trucks maneuvered their length in the narrow street, bouncing over curbs and closing in, and before the trucks stopped the men were off and running, each with a job, snicking open panels, slipping levers, turning valves. We crept inside the lines and knelt beside the big wheels of the pumper, unnoticed. The world was a bustle of men and terse voices, the red and blue lights spinning round, the snaking hose erect with pressure. The men were hepped up, snappy with the brisk demands. And the house—the neighbor's house I'd seen so many times before had gone strange, a bud blooming fire, a ribbon of light behind a dark window. Men went in, faces down.

26   My father doesn't go in anymore. He's gotten too old, and the rules have changed; young men arrive, old men watch and wait. He still drives the truck. He lives for it, for the history and the books, his models, the stories, meetings, card games. But he's like a rooster plucked; I have a girlish song for Daddy, but I sing it too far away for him to hear.

27   I wanted to feel the hot dry cheeks of fever and roast with the rest of them. I wanted to go in, and I kept on wanting to long after my father and the others told me I couldn't be a fireman because I wasn't a man. I wanted to be the defender, to have the chance to do something inarguably good, pit myself against the blaze. I wanted it long after I grew up and became something else altogether, and I want it still.

28   "That which has been licked by fire has a different taste in the mouths of men," writes Bachelard. He means food, but when I read that I thought of men, firemen, and how men licked by fire have a different taste to me.

29   I live in a city now, and the fire fighters aren't volunteers. They're college graduates in Fire Science, and a few are women, smaller than the men but just as tough, women who took the steps I wouldn't—or couldn't—take. Still, I imagine big, brawny men sitting at too-small desks in little rooms lit with fluorescent lights, earnestly taking notes. They hear lectures on the chemistry of burning insulation, exponential curves of heat expansion, the codes of blueprint. They make good notes in small handwriting on lined, white paper, the pens little in their solid hands.

30   Too much muscle and nerve in these men and women both, these fire-men; they need alarms, demands, heavy loads to carry up steep stairs. They need fires; the school desks are trembling, puny things, where they listen to men like my father, weary with the work of it, describing the secrets of go-ing in.

☐ Discovering Meaning and Technique

1. Explain the allusion to "Electra's unwilling need" in paragraph 3.

2. Explain the effect of the sound patterns in paragraph 2: the sequence of words ending with *ing* and the repetition of vowel and consonant sounds.

3. Do you think Tisdale has romanticized the profession of firefighters?

4. What do you think Tisdale's "fire-dreams" before the hearth signify?

5. What contradictions in Tisdale's feeling are revealed in the memoir?

6. Tisdale successfully varies sentence length. Illustrate the variety with a few examples.

7. Find examples of words used to convey sounds ("thud").

8. What is the "Prometheus Complex" (paragraph 13)? Why has it been given this name?

9. What is the significance of the father's refusing cremation at his wife's death?

☐ Writing Suggestions

1. Discuss the "fascination and fear" of fire.

2. Describe some familiar occupation from the perspective of a child.

3. Are some occupations still "unaccountably male" even though women often have been included?

4. Write about your childhood role models.

5. Write about women's ability to perform jobs previously denied them: police work, fire fighting, construction, combat, mail delivery.

6. What qualities are required of people holding dangerous jobs?

7. Describe the disappointment of realizing you would never be qualified for a desired profession.

WHY I LIVE AT THE P.O.

☐ **EUDORA WELTY**

1 I was getting along fine with Mama, Papa-Daddy and Uncle Rondo until my sister Stella-Rondo just separated from her husband and came back home again. Mr. Whitaker! Of course I went with Mr. Whitaker first, when he first appeared here in China Grove, taking "Pose Yourself" photos, and Stella-Rondo broke us up. Told him I was one-sided. Bigger on one side than the other, which is a deliberate, calculated falsehood: I'm the same. Stella-Rondo is exactly twelve months to the day younger than I am and for that reason she's spoiled.

2 She's always had anything in the world she wanted and then she'd throw it away. Papa-Daddy gave her this gorgeous Add-a-Pearl necklace when she was eight years old and she threw it away playing baseball when she was nine, with only two pearls.

3 So as soon as she got married and moved away from home the first thing she did was separate! From Mr. Whitaker! This photographer with the popeyes she said she trusted. Came home from one of those towns up in Illinois and to our complete surprise brought this child of two.

4 Mama said she like to made her drop dead for a second. "Here you had this marvelous blonde child and never so much as wrote your mother a word about it," says Mama. "I'm thoroughly ashamed of you." But of course she wasn't.

5 Stella-Rondo just calmly takes off this *hat,* I wish you could see it. She says, "Why, Mama, Shirley-T.'s adopted, I can prove it."

6 "How?" says Mama, but all I says was "H'm!" There I was over the hot stove, trying to stretch two chickens over five people and a completely unexpected child into the bargain, without one moment's notice.

7 "What do you mean—'H'm!'?" says Stella-Rondo, and Mama says, "I heard that, Sister."

8 I said that oh, I didn't mean a thing, only that whoever Shirley-T. was, she was the spit-image of Papa-Daddy if he'd cut off his beard, which of course he'd never do in the world. Papa-Daddy's Mama's papa and sulks.

9 Stella-Rondo got furious! She said, "Sister, I don't need to tell you you got a lot of nerve and always did have and I'll thank you to make no future reference to my adopted child whatsoever."

10 "Very well," I said. "Very well, very well. Of course I noticed at once she looks like Mr. Whitaker's side, too. That frown. She looks like a cross between Mr. Whitaker and Papa-Daddy."

11 "Well, all I can say is she isn't."

12 "She looks exactly like Shirley Temple to me," says Mama, but Shirley-T. just ran away from her.

13 So the first thing Stella-Rondo did at the table was turn Papa-Daddy against me.

14   "Papa-Daddy," she says. He was trying to cut up his meat. " Papa-Daddy!" I was taken completely by surprise. Papa-Daddy is about a million years old and's got this long-long beard. " Papa-Daddy, Sister says she fails to understand why you don't cut off your beard."

15   So Papa-Daddy l-a-y-s down his knife and fork! He's real rich. Mama says he is, he says he isn't. So he says, "Have I heard correctly? You don't understand why I don't cut off my beard?"

16   "Why," I says, " Papa-Daddy, of course I understand, I did not say any such of a thing, the idea!"

17   He says, "Hussy!"

18   I says, " Papa-Daddy, you know I wouldn't any more want you to cut off your beard than the man in the moon. It was the farthest thing from my mind! Stella-Rondo sat there and made that up while she was eating breast of chicken."

19   But he says, "So the postmistress fails to understand why I don't cut off my beard. Which job I got you through my influence with the government. 'Bird's nest'—is that what you call it?"

20   Not that it isn't the next to smallest P.O. in the entire state of Mississippi.

21   I says, "Oh, Papa-Daddy," I says, "I didn't say any such of a thing, I never dreamed it was a bird's nest, I have always been grateful though this is the next to smallest P.O. in the state of Mississippi, and I do not enjoy being referred to as a hussy by my own grandfather."

22   But Stella-Rondo says, "Yes, you did say it too. Anybody in the world could of heard you, that had ears."

23   "Stop right there," says Mama, looking at *me.*

24   So I pulled my napkin straight back through the napkin ring and left the table.

25   As soon as I was out of the room Mama says, "Call her back, or she'll starve to death," but Papa-Daddy says, "This is the beard I started growing on the Coast when I was fifteen years old." He would of gone on till nightfall if Shirley-T. hadn't lost the Milky Way she ate in Cairo.

26   So Papa-Daddy says, "I am going out and lie in the hammock, and you can all sit here and remember my words: I'll never cut off my beard as long as I live, even one inch, and I don't appreciate it in you at all." Passed right by me in the hall and went straight out and got in the hammock.

27   It would be a holiday. It wasn't five minutes before Uncle Rondo suddenly appeared in the hall in one of Stella-Rondo's flesh-colored kimonos, all cut on the bias, like something Mr. Whitaker probably thought was gorgeous.

28   "Uncle Rondo!" I says. "I didn't know who that was! Where are you going?"

29   "Sister," he says, "get out of my way, I'm poisoned."

30   "If you're poisoned stay away from Papa-Daddy," I says. "Keep out of the hammock. Papa-Daddy will certainly beat you on the head if you come within forty miles of him. He thinks I deliberately said he ought to cut off his beard after he got me the P.O., and I've told him and told him and told him, and he acts like he just don't hear me. Papa-Daddy must of gone stone deaf."

31   "He picked a fine day to do it then," says Uncle Rondo, and before you could say "Jack Robinson" flew out in the yard.

32   What he'd really done, he'd drunk another bottle of that prescription. He does it every single Fourth of July as sure as shooting, and it's horribly expensive. Then he falls over in the hammock and snores. So he insisted on zigzagging right on out to the hammock, looking like a half-wit.

33   Papa-Daddy woke up with this horrible yell and right there without moving an inch he tried to turn Uncle Rondo against me. I heard every word he said. Oh, he told Uncle Rondo I didn't learn to read till I was eight years old and he didn't see how in the world I ever got the mail put up at the P.O., much less read it all, and he said if Uncle Rondo could only fathom the lengths he had gone to to get me that job! And he said on the other hand he thought Stella-Rondo had a brilliant mind and deserved credit for getting out of town. All the time he was just lying there swinging as pretty as you please and looping out his beard, and poor Uncle Rondo was *pleading* with him to slow down the hammock, it was making him as dizzy as a witch to watch it. But that's what Papa-Daddy likes about a hammock. So Uncle Rondo was too dizzy to get turned against me for the time being. He's Mama's only brother and is a good case of a one-track mind. Ask anybody. A certified pharmacist.

34   Just then I heard Stella-Rondo raising the upstairs window. While she was married she got this peculiar idea that it's cooler with the windows shut and locked. So she has to raise the window before she can make a soul hear her outdoors.

35   So she raises the window and says, *"Oh!"* You would have thought she was mortally wounded.

36   Uncle Rondo and Papa-Daddy didn't even look up, but kept right on with what they were doing. I had to laugh.

37   I flew up the stairs and threw the door open! I says, "What in the wide world's the matter, Stella-Rondo? You mortally wounded?"

38   "No," she says, "I am not mortally wounded but I wish you would do me the favor of looking out that window there and telling me what you see."

39   So I shade my eyes and look out the window.

40   "I see the front yard," I says.

41   "Don't you see any human beings?" she says.

42   "I see Uncle Rondo trying to run Papa-Daddy out of the hammock," I says. "Nothing more. Naturally, it's so suffocating-hot in the house, with all the windows shut and locked, everybody who cares to stay in their right mind will have to go out and get in the hammock before the Fourth of July is over."

43   "Don't you notice anything different about Uncle Rondo?" asks Stella-Rondo.

44   "Why, no, except he's got on some terrible-looking flesh-colored contraption I wouldn't be found dead in, is all I can see," I says.

45   "Never mind, you won't be found dead in it, because it happens to be

part of my trousseau, and Mr. Whitaker took several dozen photographs of
me in it," says Stella-Rondo. "What on earth could Uncle Rondo *mean* by
wearing part of my trousseau out in the broad open daylight without saying so
much as 'Kiss my foot,' *knowing* I only got home this morning after my separation and hung my negligee up on the bathroom door, just as nervous as I
could be?"

46   "I'm sure I don't know, and what do you expect me to do about it?" I
says. "Jump out the window?"

47   "No, I expect nothing of the kind. I simply declare that Uncle Rondo looks
like a fool in it, that's all," she says. "It makes me sick to my stomach."

48   "Well, he looks as good as he can," I says. "As good as anybody in reason
could." I stood up for Uncle Rondo, please remember. And I said to Stella-Rondo,
"I think I would do well not to criticize so freely if I were you and came
home with a two-year-old child I had never said a word about, and no explanation
whatever about my separation."

49   "I asked you the instant I entered this house not to refer one more time
to my adopted child, and you gave me your word of honor you would not,"
was all Stella-Rondo would say, and started pulling out every one of her eyebrows
with some cheap Kress tweezers.

50   So I merely slammed the door behind me and went down and made some
green-tomato pickle. Somebody had to do it. Of course Mama had turned both
the niggers loose; she always said no earthly power could hold one anyway on
the Fourth of July, so she wouldn't even try. It turned out that Jaypan fell in
the lake and came within a very narrow limit of drowning.

51   So Mama trots in. Lifts up the lid and says, "H'm! Not very good for your
Uncle Rondo in his precarious condition, I must say. Or poor little adopted
Shirley-T. Shame on you!"

52   That made me tired. I says, "Well, Stella-Rondo had better thank her lucky
stars it was her instead of me came trotting in with that very peculiar-looking
child. Now if it had been me that trotted in from Illinois and brought a peculiar-
looking child of two, I shudder to think of the reception I'd of got, much less
controlled the diet of an entire family."

53   "But you must remember, Sister, that you were never married to Mr. Whitaker in the first place and didn't go up to Illinois to live," says Mama, shaking
a spoon in my face. "If you had I would of been just as overjoyed to see you
and your little adopted girl as I was to see Stella-Rondo, when you wound up
with your separation and came on back home."

54   "You would not," I says.

55   "Don't contradict me, I would," says Mama.

56   But I said she couldn't convince me though she talked till she was blue
in the face. Then I said, "Besides, you know as well as I do that that child is
not adopted."

57   "She most certainly is adopted," says Mama, stiff as a poker.

58   I says, "Why, Mama, Stella-Rondo had her just as sure as anything in this world, and just too stuck up to admit it."

59   "Why, Sister," said Mama. "Here I thought we were going to have a pleasant Fourth of July, and you start right out not believing a word your own baby sister tells you!"

60   "Just like Cousin Annie Flo. Went to her grave denying the facts of life," I remind Mama.

61   "I told you if you ever mentioned Annie Flo's name I'd slap your face," says Mama, and slaps my face.

62   "All right, you wait and see," I says.

63   "I," says Mama, *"I* prefer to take my children's word for anything when it's humanly possible." You ought to see Mama, she weighs two hundred pounds and has real tiny feet.

64   Just then something perfectly horrible occurred to me.

65   "Mama," I says, "can that child talk?" I simply had to whisper! "Mama, I wonder if that child can be—you know—in any way? Do you realize," I says, "that she hasn't spoken one single, solitary word to a human being up to this minute? This is the way she looks," I says, and I looked like this.

66   Well, Mama and I just stood there and stared at each other. It was horrible!

67   "I remember well that Joe Whitaker frequently drank like a fish," says Mama. "I believed to my soul he drank *chemicals.*" And without another word she marches to the foot of the stairs and calls Stella-Rondo.

68   " Stella-Rondo? O-o-o-o-o! Stella-Rondo!"

69   "What?" says Stella-Rondo from upstairs. Not even the grace to get up off the bed.

70   "Can that child of yours talk?" asks Mama.

71   Stella-Rondo says, "Can she what?"

72   "Talk! Talk!" says Mama. "Burdyburdyburdyburdy!"

73   So Stella-Rondo yells back, "Who says she can't talk?"

74   "Sister says so," says Mama.

75   "You didn't have to tell me, I know whose word of honor don't mean a thing in this house," says Stella-Rondo.

76   And in a minute the loudest Yankee voice I ever heard in my life yells out, "OE'm Pop-OE the Sailor-r-r-r Ma-a-an!" and then somebody jumps up and down in the upstairs hall. In another second the house would of fallen down.

77   "Not only talks, she can tap-dance!" calls Stella-Rondo. "Which is more than some people I won't name can do."

78   "Why, the little precious darling thing!" Mama says, so surprised. "Just as smart as she can be!" Starts talking baby talk right there. Then she turns on me. "Sister, you ought to be thoroughly ashamed! Run upstairs this instant and apologize to Stella-Rondo and Shirley-T."

79   "Apologize for what?" I says. "I merely wondered if the child was normal, that's all. Now that she's proved she is, why, I have nothing further to say."

80   But Mama just turned on her heel and flew out, furious. She ran right

upstairs and hugged the baby. She believed it was adopted. Stella-Rondo hadn't done a thing but turn her against me from upstairs while I stood there helpless over the hot stove. So that made Mama, Papa-Daddy and the baby all on Stella-Rondo's side.

81   Next, Uncle Rondo.

82   I must say that Uncle Rondo has been marvelous to me at various times in the past and I was completely unprepared to be made to jump out of my skin, the way it turned out. Once Stella-Rondo did something perfectly horrible to him—broke a chain letter from Flanders Field—and he took the radio back he had given her and gave it to me. Stella-Rondo was furious! For six months we all had to call her Stella instead of Stella-Rondo, or she wouldn't answer. I always thought Uncle Rondo had all the brains of the entire family. Another time he sent me to Mammoth Cave, with all expenses paid.

83   But this would be the day he was drinking that prescription, the Fourth of July.

84   So at supper Stella-Rondo speaks up and says she thinks Uncle Rondo ought to try to eat a little something. So finally Uncle Rondo said he would try a little cold biscuits and ketchup, but that was all. So *she* brought it to him.

85   "Do you think it wise to disport with ketchup in Stella-Rondo's flesh-colored kimono?" I says. Trying to be considerate! If Stella-Rondo couldn't watch out for her trousseau, somebody had to.

86   "Any objections?" asks Uncle Rondo, just about to pour out all the ketchup.

87   "Don't mind what she says, Uncle Rondo," says Stella-Rondo. "Sister has been devoting this solid afternoon to sneering out my bedroom window at the way you look."

88   "What's that?" says Uncle Rondo. Uncle Rondo has got the most terrible temper in the world. Anything is liable to make him tear the house down if it comes at the wrong time.

89   So Stella-Rondo says, "Sister says, 'Uncle Rondo certainly does look like a fool in that pink kimono!' "

90   Do you remember who it was really said that?

91   Uncle Rondo spills out all the ketchup and jumps out of his chair and tears off the kimono and throws it down on the dirty floor and puts his foot on it. It had to be sent all the way to Jackson to the cleaners and re-pleated.

92   "So that's your opinion of your Uncle Rondo, is it?" he says. "I look like a fool, do I? Well, that's the last straw. A whole day in this house with nothing to do, and then to hear you come out with a remark like that behind my back!"

93   "I didn't say any such of a thing, Uncle Rondo," I says, "and I'm not saying who did, either. Why, I think you look all right. Just try to take care of yourself and not talk and eat at the same time," I says. "I think you better go lie down."

94   "Lie down my foot," says Uncle Rondo. I ought to of known by that he was fixing to do something perfectly horrible.

95   So he didn't do anything that night in the precarious state he was in—

just played Casino with Mama and Stella-Rondo and Shirley-T. and gave Shirley-T. a nickel with a head on both sides. It tickled her nearly to death, and she called him "Papa." But at 6:30 A.M. the next morning, he threw a whole five-cent package of some unsold one-inch firecrackers from the store as hard as he could into my bedroom and they every one went off. Not one bad one in the string. Anybody else, there'd be one that wouldn't go off.

96   Well, I'm just terribly susceptible to noise of any kind, the doctor has always told me I was the most sensitive person he had ever seen in his whole life, and I was simply prostrated. I couldn't eat! People tell me they heard it as far as the cemetery, and old Aunt Jep Patterson, that had been holding her own so good, thought it was Judgment Day and she was going to meet her whole family. It's usually so quiet here.

97   And I'll tell you it didn't take me any longer than a minute to make up my mind what to do. There I was with the whole entire house on Stella-Rondo's side and turned against me. If I have anything at all I have pride.

98   So I just decided I'd go straight down to the P.O. There's plenty of room there in the back, I says to myself.

99   Well! I made no bones about letting the family catch on to what I was up to. I didn't try to conceal it.

100   The first thing they knew, I marched in where they were all playing Old Maid and pulled the electric oscillating fan out by the plug, and everything got real hot. Next I snatched the pillow I'd done the needlepoint on right off the davenport from behind Papa-Daddy. He went "Ugh!" I beat Stella-Rondo up the stairs and finally found my charm bracelet in her bureau drawer under a picture of Nelson Eddy.

101   "So that's the way the land lies," says Uncle Rondo. There he was, piecing on the ham. "Well, Sister, I'll be glad to donate my army cot if you got any place to set it up, providing you'll leave right this minute and let me get some peace." Uncle Rondo was in France.

102   "Thank you kindly for the cot and 'peace' is hardly the word I would select if I had to resort to firecrackers at 6:30 A.M. in a young girl's bedroom," I says back to him. "And as to where I intend to go, you seem to forget my position as postmistress of China Grove, Mississippi," I says. "I've always got the P.O."

103   Well, that made them all sit up and take notice.

104   I went out front and started digging up some four-o-clocks to plant around the P.O.

105   "Ah-ah-ah!" says Mama, raising the window. "Those happen to be my four-o'clocks. Everything planted in that star is mine. I've never known you to make anything grow in your life."

106   "Very well," I says. "But I take the fern. Even you, Mama, can't stand there and deny that I'm the one watered that fern. And I happen to know where I can send in a box top and get a packet of one thousand mixed seeds, no two the same kind, free."

107   "Oh, where?" Mama wants to know.

108   But I says, "Too late. You 'tend to your house, and I'll 'tend to mine. You hear things like that all the time if you know how to listen to the radio. Perfectly marvelous offers. Get anything you want free."

109   So I hope to tell you I marched in and got that radio, and they could of all bit a nail in two, especially Stella-Rondo, that it used to belong to, and she well knew she couldn't get it back, I'd sue for it like a shot. And I very politely took the sewing-machine motor I helped pay the most on to give Mama for Christmas back in 1929, and a good big calendar, with the first-aid remedies on it. The thermometer and the Hawaiian ukulele certainly were rightfully mine, and I stood on the step-ladder and got all my watermelon-rind preserves and every fruit and vegetable I'd put up, every jar. Then I began to pull the tacks out of the bluebird wall vases on the archway to the dining room.

110   "Who told you you could have those, Miss Priss?" says Mama, fanning as hard as she could.

111   "I bought 'em and I'll keep track of 'em," I says. "I'll tack 'em up one on each side the post-office window, and you can see 'em when you come to ask me for your mail, if you're so dead to see 'em."

112   "Not I! I'll never darken the door to that post office again if I live to be a hundred," Mama says. "Ungrateful child! After all the money we spent on you at the Normal."

113   "Me either," says Stella-Rondo. "You can just let my mail lie there and *rot,* for all I care. I'll never come and relieve you of a single, solitary piece."

114   "I should worry," I says. "And who you think's going to sit down and write you all those big fat letters and postcards, by the way? Mr. Whitaker? Just because he was the only man ever dropped down in China Grove and you got him—unfairly—is he going to sit down and write you a lengthy correspondence after you come home giving no rhyme nor reason whatsoever for your separation and no explanation for the presence of that child? I may not have your brilliant mind, but I fail to see it."

115   So Mama says, "Sister, I've told you a thousand times that Stella-Rondo simply got homesick, and this child is far too big to be hers," and she says, "Now, why don't you all just sit down and play Casino?"

116   Then Shirley-T. sticks out her tongue at me in this perfectly horrible way. She has no more manners than the man in the moon. I told her she was going to cross her eyes like that some day and they'd stick.

117   "It's too late to stop me now," I says. "You should have tried that yesterday. I'm going to the P.O. and the only way you can possibly see me is to visit me there."

118   So Papa-Daddy says, "You'll never catch me setting foot in that post office, even if I should take a notion into my head to write a letter some place." He says, "I won't have you reachin' out of that little old window with a pair of shears and cuttin' off any beard of mine. I'm too smart for you!"

119   "We all are," says Stella-Rondo.

120   But I said, "If you're so smart, where's Mr. Whitaker?"

121   So then Uncle Rondo says, "I'll thank you from now on to stop reading all the orders I get on postcards and telling everybody in China Grove what you think is the matter with them," but I says, "I draw my own conclusions and will continue in the future to draw them." I says, "If people want to write their inmost secrets on penny postcards, there's nothing in the wide world you can do about it, Uncle Rondo."

122   "And if you think we'll ever *write* another postcard you're sadly mistaken," says Mama.

123   "Cutting off your nose to spite your face then," I says. "But if you're all determined to have no more to do with the U.S. mail, think of this: What will Stella-Rondo do now, if she wants to tell Mr. Whitaker to come after her?"

124   "Wah!" says Stella-Rondo. I knew she'd cry. She had a conniption fit right there in the kitchen.

125   "It will be interesting to see how long she holds out," I says. "And now— I am leaving."

126   "Good-bye," says Uncle Rondo.

127   "Oh, I declare," says Mama, "to think that a family of mine should quarrel on the Fourth of July, or the day after, over Stella-Rondo leaving old Mr. Whitaker and having the sweetest little adopted child! It looks like we'd all be glad!"

128   "Wah!" says Stella-Rondo, and has a fresh conniption fit.

129   *"He* left *her*—you mark my words," I says. "That's Mr. Whitaker. I know Mr. Whitaker. After all, I knew him first. I said from the beginning he'd up and leave her. I foretold every single thing that's happened."

130   "Where did he go?" asks Mama.

131   "Probably to the North Pole, if he knows what's good for him," I says.

132   But Stella-Rondo just bawled and wouldn't say another word. She flew to her room and slammed the door.

133   "Now look what you've gone and done, Sister," says Mama. "You go apologize."

134   "I haven't got time, I'm leaving," I says.

135   "Well, what are you waiting around for?" asks Uncle Rondo.

136   So I just picked up the kitchen clock and marched off, without saying "Kiss my foot" or anything, and never did tell Stella-Rondo good-bye.

137   There was a nigger girl going along on a little wagon right in front.

138   "Nigger girl," I says, "come help me haul these things down the hill, I'm going to live in the post office."

139   Took her nine trips in her express wagon. Uncle Rondo came out on the porch and threw her a nickel.

140   And that's the last I've laid eyes on any of my family or my family laid eyes on me for five solid days and nights. Stella-Rondo may be telling the most horrible tales in the world about Mr. Whitaker, but I haven't heard them. As I tell everybody, I draw my own conclusions.

141   But oh, I like it here. It's ideal, as I've been saying. You see, I've got everything cater-cornered, the way I like it. Hear the radio? All the war news. Radio, sewing machine, book ends, ironing board and that great big piano lamp—peace, that's what I like. Butter-bean vines planted all along the front where the strings are.

142   Of course, there's not much mail. My family are naturally the main people in China Grove, and if they prefer to vanish from the face of the earth, for all the mail they get or the mail they write, why, I'm not going to open my mouth. Some of the folks here in town are taking up for me and some turned against me. I know which is which. There are always people who will quit buying stamps just to get on the right side of Papa-Daddy.

143   But here I am, and here I'll stay. I want the world to know I'm happy.

144   And if Stella-Rondo should come to me this minute, on bended knees, and *attempt* to explain the incidents of her life with Mr. Whitaker, I'd simply put my fingers in both my ears and refuse to listen.

☐ Discovering Meaning and Technique

1. How does the first paragraph establish the jealousy between the narrator and her sister?

2. Why is the child called Shirley-T.?

3. What first tells you that Uncle Rondo is a bit strange?

4. What details in the story indicate that it takes place at some time in the past?

5. The characters use a great many clichés, for instance, "as long as I live" and "as sure as shooting." Find other examples of clichés in the story.

6. What devices does Welty use to create the realistic dialogue?

7. The story is written from the first-person point of view; in other words, everything is told in the words of one of the characters. Do you think the story would be as effective if the author told the story from her point of view?

8. At what point in the story does the narrator decide to move and why?

☐ Writing Suggestions

1. Using the conflict between the two sisters as background, write about conflicts you have witnessed between children in the same family.

2. Many times families have problems getting along. Discuss possible solutions to these problems.

3. In the past it was common to have grandparents living in the home. Contrast this tradition to the current trend of placing old people in nursing homes.

School and Friends

■ ■ ■

THREE BOYS

☐ **JOHN UPDIKE**

1   *A, B,* and *C,* I'll say, in case they care. *A* lived next door; he *loomed* next door, rather. He seemed immense—a great wallowing fatso stuffed with possessions; he was the son of a full-fashioned knitter. He seemed to have a beer-belly— solid, portentous, proud. After several generations beer-bellies may become con- genital. Also his face had no features; it was just a blank ball on his shoulders. He used to call me "Ostrich," after Disney's Ollie Ostrich. My neck was not very long; the name seemed horribly unfair; it was its injustice that made me cry. But nothing I could say, or scream, would make him stop. And I still, now and then sometimes—in reading, say, a book review by one of the apple-cheeked savants of the quarterlies or one of the pious gremlins who manufacture puns for *Time*—get the old sensations: my ears close up, my eyes go warm, my chest feels thin as an eggshell, my voice churns silently in my stomach. From *A* I received my first impression of the smug, chinkless, irresistible *power* of stupidity; it is the most powerful force on earth. It says "Ostrich" often enough, and the universe crumbles.

2   *A* was more than a boy, he was a force-field that could manifest itself in many forms, that could take the wiry, disconsolate shape of wide-mouthed, tiny- eared boys who would now and then beat me up on the way back from school. I did not greatly mind being beaten up, though I resisted it. For one thing, it firmly involved me, at least during the beating, with the circumambient humanity that so often seemed evasive. Also, the boys who applied the beating were misfits, periodic flunkers, who wore knickers whose knees had lost the corduroy ribbing and men's shirts with the top button buttoned—this last an infallible sign of deep poverty. So that I felt there was some justice, some condonable revenge, being applied with their fists to this little teacher's son. And then there was the delicious alarm of my mother and grandmother when I returned home bloody, bruised, and torn. My father took the attitude that it was making a boy of me, an attitude I dimly shared. He and I both were afraid of me becoming a sissy—he perhaps more afraid than I.

3   When I was eleven or so I met *B.* It was summer and I was down at the

playground. He was pushing a little tank with moving rubber treads up and down the hills in the sandbox. I was a beautiful little toy, mottled with camouflage green; patriotic manufactuers produced throughout the war millions of such authentic miniatures which we maneuvered with authentic, if miniature, hate. Drawn by the toy, I spoke to him; though taller and a little older than I, he had my dull straight brown hair and a look of being also alone. We became fast friends. He lived just up the street—toward the poorhouse, the east part of the street, from which the little winds of tragedy blew. He had just moved from the Midwest, and his mother was a widow. Besides wage war, we did many things together. We played marbles for days at a time, until one of us had won the other's entire coffee-canful. With jigsaws we cut out of plywood animals copied from comic books. We made movies by tearing the pages out of Big Little Books and coloring the drawings and pasting them in a strip, and winding them on toilet-paper spools, and making a cardboard carton a theater. We rigged up telephones, and racing wagons, and miniature cities, using orange crates and cigar boxes and peanut-butter jars and such potent debris. We loved Smokey Stover and were always saying "Foo." We had an intense spell of Monopoly. He called me "Uppy"—the only person who ever did so. I remember once, knowing he was coming down that afternoon to my house to play Monopoly, in order to show my joy I set up the board elaborately, with the Chance and Community Chest cards fanned painstakingly, like spiral staircases. He came into the room, groaned, "Uppy, what are you doing?" and impatiently scrabbled the cards together in a sensible pile. The older we got, the more the year between us told, and the more my friendship embarrassed him. We fought. Once, to my horror, I heard myself taunting him with the fact that he had no father. The unmentionable, the unforgivable. I suppose we patched things up, children do, but nothing was quite right after that. He had a long, pale, serious face, with buck teeth, and is probably an electronics engineer somewhere now, doing secret government work.

4   So through *B* I first experienced the pattern of friendship. There are three stages. First, acquaintance: we are new to each other, make each other laugh in surprise, and demand nothing beyond politeness. The death of the one would startle the other, no more. It is a pleasant stage, a stable stage; on austere rations of exposure it can live a lifetime, and the two parties to it always feel a slight gratification upon meeting, will feel vaguely confirmed in their human state. Then comes intimacy: now we laugh before two words of the joke are out of the other's mouth, because we know what he will say. Our whole two beings seem marvelously joined, from our toes to our heads, along tingling points of agreement; everything we venture is right, everything we put forth lodges in a corresponding socket in the frame of the other. The death of the one would grieve the other. To be together is to enjoy a mounting excitement, a constant echo and amplification. It is an ecstatic and unstable stage, bound of its own agitation to tip into the third: revulsion. One or the other makes a misjudgment;

presumes; puts forth that which does not meet agreement. Sometimes there is an explosion; more often the moment is swallowed in silence, and months pass before its nature dawns. Instead of dissolving, it grows. The mind, the throat, are clogged; forgiveness, forgetfulness, that have arrived so often, fail. Now everything jars and is distasteful; the betrayal, perhaps a tiny fraction in itself, has inverted the tingling column of agreement, made all pluses minuses. Everything about the other is hateful, despicable; yet he cannot be dismissed. We have confided in him too many minutes, too many words; he has those minutes and words as hostages, and his confidences are embedded in us where they cannot be scraped away, and even rivers of time cannot erode them completely, for there are indelible stains. Now—though the friends may continue to meet, and smile, as if they had never trespassed beyond acquaintance—the death of the one would please the other.

5   An unhappy pattern to which *C* is an exception. He was my friend before kindergarten, he is my friend still. I go to his home now, and he and his wife serve me and my wife with alcoholic drinks and slices of excellent cheese on crisp crackers, just as twenty years ago he served me with treats from his mother's refrigerator. He was a born host, and I a born guest. Also, he was intelligent. If my childhood's brain, when I look back at it, seems a primitive mammal, a lemur or shrew, his brain was an angel whose visitation was widely hailed as wonderful. When in school he stood to recite, his cool rectangular forehead glowed. He tucked his right hand into his left armpit and with his left hand mechanically tapped a pencil against his thigh. His answers were always correct. He beat me at spelling bees and, in another sort of competition, when we both collected Big Little Books, he outbid me for my supreme find (in the attic of a third boy), the first Mickey Mouse. I can still see that book, I wanted it so badly, its paper tan with age and its drawings done in Disney's primitive style, when Mickey's black chest is naked like a child's and his eyes are two nicked oblongs. Losing it was perhaps a lucky blow; it began to wean me away from any hope of ever having possessions.

6   *C* was fearless. He deliberately set fields on fire; he engaged in rock-throwing duels with tough boys. One afternoon he persisted in playing quoits with me although—as the hospital discovered that night—his appendix was nearly bursting. He was enterprising. He peddled magazine subscriptions door-to-door; he mowed neighbors' lawns; he struck financial bargains with his father. He collected stamps so well his collection blossomed into a stamp company that filled his room with steel cabinets and mimeograph machinery. He collected money—every time I went over to his house he would get out a little tin box and count the money in it for me: $27.50 one week, $29.95 the next, $30.90 the next—all changed into new bills nicely folded together. It was a strange ritual, whose meaning for me was: since he was doing it, I didn't have to. His money made me richer. We read Ellery Queen and played chess and invented board games and discussed infinity together. In later adolescence, he collected records. He

liked the Goodman quintets but loved Fats Waller. Sitting there in that room so familiar to me, where the machinery of the Shilco Stamp Company still crowded the walls and for that matter the tin box of money might still be hiding, while my pale friend grunted softly along with that dead dark angel on "You're Not the Only Oyster in the Stew," I felt, in the best sense, patronized. The perfect guest of the perfect host. What made it perfect was that we had both spent our entire lives in Shillington.

☐ Discovering Meaning and Technique

1. According to Updike, what are the three stages of friendship? Explain how each stage is partly defined by one's attitude toward the death of a friend.

2. Many games and activities that Updike and his friends engaged in are still not out of date; others are. Discuss which are still current and which are dated.

3. Explain what Updike means in paragraph 6 by "his money made me richer."

4. Updike probably does not include all his memories of *A, B,* and *C.* Why do you think he selected the memories he includes?

5. In what order does Updike describe his three childhood friends?

6. Where in the selection does Updike place his digression on the stages of friendship? Why is it positioned there?

7. Updike's focus does not constantly remain in the past. Cite examples of when his focus is on the present.

8. Is the description of one friend presented in more colorful language than the others? If so, give examples to illustrate.

9. Explain the meaning of "the smug, chinkless, irresistible *power* of stupidity" (paragraph 1) and "circumambient humanity" (paragraph 2).

☐ Writing Suggestions

1. Updike enumerates three stages of friendship. Can you illustrate these stages with your past friendships? Or have your friendships progressed through different stages?

2. Some friendships come and go; others last. Write about the fickleness of some relationships and the permanence of others.

3. Describe one or several friendships from your past. Include some of the same kinds of information presented by Updike: appearance, behavior, toys, events.

THE CHASE

☐ ANNIE DILLARD

1 Some boys taught me to play football. This was fine sport. You thought up a new strategy for every play and whispered it to the others. You went out for a pass, fooling everyone. Best, you got to throw yourself mightily at someone's running legs. Either you brought him down or you hit the ground flat out on your chin, with your arms empty before you. It was all or nothing. If you hesitated in fear, you would miss and get hurt: you would take a hard fall while the kid got away, or you would get kicked in the face while the kid got away. But if you flung yourself wholeheartedly at the back of his knees—if you gathered and joined body and soul and pointed them diving fearlessly—then you likely wouldn't get hurt, and you'd stop the ball. Your fate, and your team's score, depended on your concentration and courage. Nothing girls did could compare with it.

2   Boys welcomed me at baseball, too, for I had, through enthusiastic practice, what was weirdly known as a boy's arm. In winter, in the snow, there was neither baseball nor football, so the boys and I threw snowballs at passing cars. I got in trouble throwing snowballs, and have seldom been happier since.

3   On one weekday morning after Christmas, six inches of new snow had just fallen. We were standing up to our boot tops in snow on a front yard on trafficked Reynolds Street, waiting for cars. The cars traveled Reyonlds Street slowly and evenly; they were targets all but wrapped in red ribbons, cream puffs. We couldn't miss.

4   I was seven; the boys were eight, nine, and ten. The oldest two Fahey boys were there—Mikey and Peter—polite blond boys who lived near me on Lloyd Street, and who already had four brothers and sisters. My parents approved of Mikey and Peter Fahey. Chickie McBride was there, a tough kid, and Billy Paul and Mackie Kean too, from across Reynolds, where the boys grew up dark and furious, grew up skinny, knowing, and skilled. We had all drifted from our houses that morning looking for action, and had found it here on Reynolds Street.

5   It was cloudy but cold. The cars' tires laid behind them on the snowy street a complex trail of beige chunks like crenellated castle walls. I had stepped on some earlier; they squeaked. We could have wished for more traffic. When a car came, we all popped it one. In the intervals between cars we reverted to the natural solitude of children.

6   I started making an iceball—a perfect iceball, from perfectly white snow, perfectly spherical, and squeezed perfectly translucent so no snow remained all the way through. (The Fahey boys and I considered it unfair actually to throw an iceball at somebody, but it had been known to happen.)

7   I had just embarked on the iceball project when we heard tire chains come clanking from afar. A black Buick was moving toward us down the street. We all spread out, banged together some regular snowballs, took aim, and, when the Buick drew nigh, fired.

8   A soft snowball hit the driver's windshield right before the driver's face. It made a smashed star with a hump in the middle.

9   Often, of course, we hit our target, but this time, the only time in all of life, the car pulled over and stopped. Its wide black door opened; a man got out of it, running. He didn't even close the car door.

10   He ran after us, and we ran away from him, up the snowy Reynolds sidewalk. At the corner, I looked back; incredibly, he was still after us. He was in city clothes: a suit and tie, street shoes. Any normal adult would have quit, having sprung us into flight and made his point. This man was gaining on us. He was a thin man, all action. All of a sudden, we were running for our lives.

11   Wordless, we split up. We were on our turf; we could lose ourselves in the neighborhood backyards, everyone for himself. I paused and considered. Everyone had vanished except Mikey Fahey, who was just rounding the corner of a yellow brick house. Poor Mikey, I trailed him. The driver of the Buick sensibly picked the two of us to follow. The man apparently had all day.

12   He chased Mikey and me around the yellow house and up a backyard path we knew by heart: under a low tree, up a bank, through a hedge, down some snowy steps, and across the grocery store's delivery driveway. We smashed through a gap in another hedge, entered a scruffy backyard and ran around its back porch and tight between houses to Edgerton Avenue; we ran across Edgerton to an alley and up our own sliding woodpile to the Halls' front yard; he kept coming. We ran up Lloyd Street and wound through mazy backyards toward the steep hilltop at Willard and Lang.

13   He chased us silently, block after block. He chased us silently over picket fences, through thorny hedges, between houses, around garbage cans, and across streets. Every time I glanced back, choking for breath, I expected he would have quit. He must have been as breathless as we were. His jacket strained over his body. It was an immense discovery, pounding into my hot head with every sliding, joyous step, that this ordinary adult evidently knew what I thought only children who trained at football knew: that you have to fling yourself at what you're doing, you have to point yourself, forget yourself, aim, dive.

14   Mikey and I had nowhere to go, in our own neighborhood or out of it, but away from this man who was chasing us. He impelled us forward; we compelled him to follow our route. The air was cold; every breath tore my throat. We

kept running, block after block; we kept improvising, backyard after backyard, running a frantic course and choosing it simultaneously, failing always to find small places or hard places to slow him down, and discovering always, exhilarated, dismayed, that only bare speed could save us—for he would never give up, this man—and we were losing speed.

15   He chased us throug the backyard labyrinths of ten blocks before he caught us by our jackets. He caught us and we all stopped.

16   We three stood staggering, half blinded, coughing, in an obscure hilltop backyard: a man in his twenties, a boy, a girl. He had released our jackets, our pursuer, our captor, our hero: he knew we weren't going anywhere. We all played by the rules. Mikey and I unzipped our jackets. I pulled off my sopping mittens. Our tracks multiplied in the backyard's new snow. We had been breaking new snow all morning. We didn't look at each other. I was cherishing my excitement. The man's lower pants legs were wet; his cuffs were full of snow, and there was a prow of snow beneath them on his shoes and socks. Some trees bordered the little flat backyard, some messy winter trees. There was no one around: a clearing in a grove, and we the only players.

17   It was a long time before he could speak. I had some difficulty at first recalling why we were there. My lips felt swollen; I couldn't see out of the sides of my eyes; I kept coughing.

18   "You stupid kids," be began perfunctorily.

19   We listened perfunctorily indeed, if we listened at all, for the chewing out was redundant, a mere formality, and beside the point. The point was that he had chased us passionately without giving up, and so he had caught us. Now he came down to earth. I wanted the glory to last forever.

20   But how could the glory have lasted forever? We could have run through every backyard in North America until we got to Panama. But when he trapped us at the lip of the Panama Canal, what precisely could he have done to prolong the drama of the chase and cap its glory? I brooded about this for the next few years. He could only have fried Mikey Fahey and me in boiling oil, say, or dismembered us piecemeal, or staked us to anthills. None of which I really wanted, and none of which any adult was likely to do, even in the spirit of fun. He could only chew us out there in the Panamanian jungle, after months or years of exalting pursuit. He could only begin, "You stupid kids," and continue in his ordinary Pittsburgh accent with his normal righteous anger and the usual common sense.

21   If in that snowy backyard the driver of the black Buick had cut off our heads, Mikey's and mine, I would have died happy, for nothing has required so much of me since as being chased all over Pittsburgh in the middle of winter—running terrified, exhausted—by this sainted, skinny, furious red-headed man who wished to have a word with us. I don't know how he found his way back to his car.

☐ Discovering Meaning and Technique

1. Dillard builds suspense with the reference to the iceball. Explain the ironic twist that results.

2. Why during the frightening chase does Dillard refer to every "joyous step," to "our hero," and to "cherishing" the "excitement"?

3. Although the primary event of the selection is the chase, Dillard begins by discussing football. What is the purpose of the introduction? Where is football referred to again?

4. Short clauses and sentences tend to slow down the prose; long structures can speed it up. Analyze the length of the structures in paragraph 1 and in paragraph 14.

5. Much of Dillard's description is vivid. Readers can "see" the "beige chunks" of snow "like crenellated castle walls." Find other vivid descriptions.

☐ Writing Suggestions

1. Write about games from your childhood.

2. Relate a personal experience when you got into trouble while playing.

3. Frequently, children find excitement in mischievous play like throwing snowballs at cars. Discuss when play becomes unwise and dangerous. How are children to learn the difference between excitement and danger?.

4. Discuss the different attitudes of adults toward children's games and playing.

MY EARLY YEARS AT SCHOOL

☐ PHILLIP LOPATE

1 In the first grade I was in a bit of a fog. All I remember is running outside at three o'clock with the others to fill the safety zone in front of the school building, where we whirled around with our bookbags, hitting as many proximate bodies as possible. The whirling dervishes of Kabul could not have been more ecstatic than we with our thwacking book satchels.

2   But as for the rest of school, I was paying so little attention that, once, when I stayed home sick, and my mother had to write a letter of excuse to the teacher, she asked me what her name was and I said I did not know. "You must know what your teacher's name is." I took a stab at it. "Mrs. . . . Latka?" I said, *latka* being the Jewish word for potato pancakes (this was around the time of Hanukkah celebrations). My mother laughed incredulously, and compromised with the salutation "Dear Teacher." As I learned soon after, my teacher's name was actually Mrs. Bobka, equally improbable. She wore her red hair rolled under a hairnet and had a glass eye, which I once saw her taking out in a luncheonette and showing to her neighbor, while I watched from a nearby table with my chocolate milk. Now, can it be possible that she really had a glass eye? Probably not; but why is it that every time I think of Mrs. Bobka my mind strays to that association? She had a hairnet and a very large nose, of that we can be sure, and seemed to have attained middle age. This teacher paid no attention to me whatsoever, which was the kindest thing she could have done to me. She had her favorite, Rookie, who collected papers and handed out pencils—Rookie, that little monster with the middy blouse and dangling curls, real name Rochelle. "Teacher's Pet!" we would yell at her.

3   Yet secretly I was attracted to Rookie, and admired the way she passed out supplies, as well as the attention she got.

4   Otherwise, I was so much in a daze, that once I got sent on an errand to a classroom on the third floor, and by the time I hit the stairwell I had already forgotten which room it was. Afterward, Mrs. Bobka never used me as her monitor.

5   The school itself was a wreck from Walt Whitman's day, with rotting floorboards, due to be condemned in a year or two; already the new annex that was to replace it was rising on the adjoining lot. But in a funny way, we loved the old school better. The boys' bathroom had zinc urinals with a common trough; the fixtures were green with rust, the toilet stalls doorless. In the Hadean basement where we went for our hot lunches, an overweight black woman would dish out tomato soup. Every day tomato soup, with a skim. Sometimes, when the basement flooded, we walked across a plank single file to get to the food counter. And that ends my memories from first grade.

6   In the second grade I had another teacher, Mrs. Seligman, whose only pleasure was to gossip with her teacher pals during lineups in the hall and fire drills (when *we* were supposed to be silent). Such joy came over her when another teacher entered our classroom—she was so bored with the exclusive company of children, poor woman, and lived for these visits.

7   By second grade, I had been anonymous long enough. One day we were doing show-and-tell, wherein each child bragged how he or she had been to the beach or had on a new pair of tap shoes. My parents had just taken me to see the movie *Les Misérables,* and Robert Newton as the tenacious gum-baring Inspector had made a great impression on me. Besides, I knew the story backwards

and forwards, because I had also read the Classics Illustrated comic book version. As I stood up in front of the class, something possessed me to elaborate a little and bend the truth.

8   "Mrs. Seligman, I read a book called *Les Misérables* . . ."

9   She seemed ready to laugh in my face. "Oh? Who is it by?"

10   "Victor Hugo." I stood my ground. There must have been something in my plausible, shy, four-eyed manner that shook her. Her timing was momentarily upset; she asked me to sit down. Later, when there was a lull in the activity, she called me over to her desk.

11   "Now tell me, did you honestly read *Les Misérbles?* Don't be afraid to tell the truth."

12   "Yes! it's about this man named Jean Valjean who . . ." and I proceeded to tell half the plot—no doubt getting the order confused, but still close enough to the original to give this old war-horse pause. She knew deep down in her professional soul that a child my age did not have the vocabularly or the comprehension to get through a book of that order of complexity. But she wanted to believe, I felt. If I stumbled she would dismiss me in a second, and I would probably burst into tears. Yet even then I knew (children know it better than adults) that in telling a lie, fidelity is everything. They can never be absolutely sure if you keep denying and insisting.

13   Just then one of her teacher pals came in, the awesome Mrs. McGonigle, who squeezed bad boys into wastebaskets.

14   "Do you know what? Phillip here says that he read Victor Hugo's *Les Misérables.*"

15   "Really!" cried her friend archly. "And you believe him?"

16   "I don't know."

17   "What's it about? *I've* never read it. He must be very smart if he read it and I haven't."

18   "Tell Mrs. McGonigle the story."

19   "It's about this man named Jean Valjean who stole a loaf of bread," I began, my heart beating as I recounted his crime, aware that I myself was committing a parallel one. By this time I had gotten more than the attention I wanted and would have done anything to return to my seat. Mrs. McGonigle was scrutinizing me sarcastically with her bifocals, and I was much more afraid of her seeing through my deception than Mrs. Seligman. But it came to me in a dim haze of surprise that Mrs. Seligman seemed to be taking my side; she was nodding, and shushing the other woman's objections. Perhaps nothing so exciting had happened to her as a teacher for months, even years! Here was her chance to flaunt a child prodigy in her own classroom before the other teachers. I told the story as passionately as I could, seeing the movie unroll scene by scene in my mind's eye, a foot away from the desk.

20   "There's only one way to find out," interrupted Mrs. McGonigle. "We will take him down to the library and see if he can read the book."

21   My teacher could not wait to try this out. She rose and took my arm. "Now, class, I'm leaving you alone for a few minutes. You are to remain quiet and in your seats!" So they marched me over to the school library. I was praying that the school had no such volume on its shelves. But the librarian produced Victor Hugo's masterpiece with dispatch—as luck would have it, a sort of abridged version for young adults. I knew enough how to sound out words so that I was able to stumble through the first page; fortunately, Mrs. Seligman snatched the book away from me: "See? I told you he was telling the truth." Her mocker was silenced. And Seligman was so proud of me that she began petting my head—I, who had never received more than distracted frowns from her all year long.

22   But it wasn't enough; she wanted more. She and I would triumph together. I was to be testimony to her special reading program. Now she conceived a new plan: she would take me around from class to class, and tell everyone about my accomplishment, and have me read passages from the book.

23   I begged her not to do this. Not that I had any argument to offer against it, but I gave her to understand, by turning dangerously pale, that I had had enough excitement for the day. Everyone knows that those who are capable of great mental feats are also susceptible to faints and dizzy spells. Insensitive as she was, she got the point, and returned me regretfully to the classroom.

24   Everyday afterward I lived in fear of being exhibited before each class and made to recount the deed that I had not done. I dreaded the truth coming out. Though my teacher did not ask me to "perform" *Les Misérables* anymore, nevertheless she pointed me out to any adult who visited the classroom, including the parents of other children. I heard them whispering about me. I bowed my head in shame, pretending that modesty or absorption in schoolwork made me turn red at the notoriety gathering around me.

25   So my career as genius and child prodigy began.

26   "Victor Hugo, *hélas!*" Gide said, when asked to name the greatest poet in the French language. I say "Victor Hugo, *hélas!*" for another reason. My guilt is such that every time I hear that worthy giant's name I cringe. Afterward, I was never able to read *Les Misérables*. In fact, irrationally or not, I have shunned his entire oeuvre.

☐ Discovering Meaning and Technique

1. The description of Mrs. Bobka's glass eye reveals the problem of memory. In a reminiscence can everything be true?

2. In a story, which is more interesting—successful or unsuccessful school experiences? A modern, clean school building or a "wreck" of a building?

3. If this narrative were fiction, do you think it would end in the same way?

4. This selection is divided very simply into two parts. How is the division indicated? Is the indication necessary?

5. Lopate alternates prose and dialogue. Is the alternation more interesting than writing exclusively with dialogue or without?

6. Words ending with *ing* tend to speed up prose. Why do you think several *ing* words appear in paragraph 1?

7. Explain "Hadean basement."

☐ Writing Suggestions

1. Write a narrative of your early years in school.

2. Contrast your favorite grammar-school teacher with your least favorite.

3. Discuss several techniques that students use to write book reports without reading the books.

LINCOLN SCHOOL

☐ ERNESTO GALARZA

¹ The two of us—my mother and I—walked south on Fifth Street one morning to the corner of Q Street and turned right. Half of the block was occupied by the Lincoln School. It was a three-story wooden building, with two wings that gave it the shape of a double-T connected by a certain hall. It was a new building, painted yellow, with a shingled roof that was not like the red tile of the school in Mazatlán. I noticed other differences, none of them very reassuring.

² We walked up the wide staircase hand in hand and through the door, which closed by itself. A mechanical contraption screwed to the top shut it behind us quietly.

³ Up to this point the adventure of enrolling me in the school had been carefully rehearsed. Mrs. Dodson had told us how to find it and we had circled it several times on our walks. Friends in the *barrio* explained that the director was called a principal, and that it was a lady and not a man. They assured us that there was always a person at the school who could speak Spanish.

4   Exactly as we had been told, there was a sign on the door in both Spanish and English: "Principal." We crossed the hall and entered the office of Miss Nettie Hopley.

5   Miss Hopley was at a roll-top desk to one side, sitting in a swivel chair that moved on wheels. There was a sofa against the opposite wall, flanked by two windows and a door that opened on a small balcony. Chairs were set around a table and framed pictures hung on the walls of a man with long white hair and another with a sad face and a black beard.

6   The principal half turned in the swivel chair to look at us over the pinch glasses crossed on the ridge of her nose. To do this she had to duck her head slightly as if she were about to step through a low doorway.

7   What Miss Hopley said to us we did not know but we saw in her eyes a warm welcome and when she took off her glasses and straightened up she smiled wholeheartedly, like Mrs. Dodson. We were, of course, saying nothing, only catching the friendliness of her voice and the sparkle in her eyes while she said words we did not understand. She signaled us to the table. Almost tiptoeing across the office, I maneuvered myself to keep my mother between me and the gringo lady. In a matter of seconds I had to decide whether she was a possible friend or a menace. We sat down.

8   Then Miss Hopley did a formidable thing. She stood up. Had she been standing when we entered she would have seemed tall. But rising from her chair she soared. And what she carried up and up with her was a buxom superstructure, firm shoulders, a straight sharp nose, full cheeks slightly molded by a curved line along the nostrils, thin lips that moved like steel springs, and a high forehead topped by hair gathered in a bun. Miss Hopley was not a giant in body but when she mobilized it to a standing position she seemed a match for giants. I decided I liked her.

9   She strode to a door in the far corner of the office, opened it and called a name. A boy of about ten years appeared in the doorway. He sat down at one end of the table. He was brown like us, a plump kid with shiny black hair combed straight back, neat, cool, and faintly obnoxious.

10   Miss Hopley joined us with a large book and some papers in her hand. She, too, sat down and the questions and answers began by way of our interpreter. My name was Ernesto. My mother's name was Henriqueta. My birth certificate was in San Blas. Here was my last report card from the Escuela Municipal Numero 3 para Varones of Mazatlán, and so forth. Miss Hopley put things down in the book and my mother signed a card.

11   As long as the questions continued, Doña Henriqueta could stay and I was secure. Now that they were over, Miss Hopley saw her to the door, dismissed our interpreter and without further ado took me by the hand and strode down the hall to Miss Ryan's first grade.

12   Miss Ryan took me to a seat at the front of the room, into which I shrank— the better to survey her. She was, to skinny, somewhat runty me, of a withering

height when she patrolled the class. And when I least expected it, there she was, crouching by my desk, her blond radiant face level with mine, her voice patiently maneuvering me over the awful idiocies of the English language.

13   During the next few weeks Miss Ryan overcame my fears of tall, energetic teachers as she bent over my desk to help me with a word in the pre-primer. Step by step, she loosened me and my classmates from the safe anchorage of the desks for recitations at the blackboard and consultations at her desk. Frequently she burst into happy announcements to the whole class, "Ito can read a sentence," and small Japanese Ito, squint-eyed and shy, slowly read aloud while the class listened in wonder: "Come, Skipper, come. Come and run." The Korean, Portuguese, Italian, and Polish first graders had similar moments of glory, no less shining than mine the day I conquered "butterfly," which I had been persistently pronouncing in standard Spanish as boo-ter-flee. "Children," Miss Ryan called for attention. "Ernesto has learned how to pronounce *butterfly!*" And I proved it with a perfect imitation of Miss Ryan. From that celebrated success, I was soon able to match Ito's progress as a sentence reader with "Come, butterfly, come fly with me."

14   Like Ito and several other first grades who did not know English, I received private lessons from Miss Ryan in the closet, a narrow hall off the classroom with a door at each end. Next to one of these doors Miss Ryan placed a large chair for herself and a small one for me. Keeping an eye on the class through the open door she read with me about sheep in the meadow and a frightened chicken going to see the king, coaching me out of my phonetic ruts in words like *pasture, bow-wow-wow, hay,* and *pretty,* which to my Mexican ear and eye had so many unnecessary sounds and letters. She made me watch her lips and then close my eyes as she repeated words I found hard to read. When we came to know each other better, I tried interrupting to tell Miss Ryan how we said it in Spanish. It didn't work She only said "oh" and went on with *pasture, bow-wow-wow,* and *pretty.* It was as if in that closet we were both discovering together the secrets of the English language and grieving together over the tragedies of Bo-Peep. The main reason I was graduated with honors from the first grade was that I had fallen in love with Miss Ryan. Her radiant, no-nonsense character made us either afraid not to love her or love her so we would not be afraid, I am not sure which. It was not only that we sensed she was with it, but also that she was with us.

15   Like the first grade, the rest of the Lincoln School was a sampling of the lower part of town where many races made their home. My pals in the second grade were Kazushi, whose parents spoke only Japanese; Matti, a skinny Italian boy; and Manuel, a fat Portuguese who would never get into a fight but wrestled you to the ground and just sat on you. Our assortment of nationalities included Koreans, Yugoslavs, Poles, Irish, and home-grown Americans.

16   Miss Hopley and her teachers never let us forget why we were at Lincoln: for those who were alien, to become good Americans; for those who were so

born, to accept the rest of us. Off the school grounds we traded the same insults we heard from our elders. On the playground we were sure to be marched up to the principal's office for calling someone a wop, a chink, a dago, or a greaser. The school was not so much a melting pot as a griddle where Miss Hopley and her helpers warmed knowledge into us and roasted racial hatreds out of us.

17   At Lincoln, making us into Americans did not mean scrubbing away what made us originally foreign. The teachers called us as our parents did, or as close as they could pronounce our names in Spanish or Japanese. No one was ever scolded or punished for speaking in his native tongue on the playground. Matti told the class about his mother's down quilt, which she had made in Italy with the fine feathers of a thousand geese. Encarnación acted out how boys learned to fish in the Phillippines. I astounded the third grade with the story of my travels on a stagecoach, which nobody else in the class had seen except in the museum at Sutter's Fort. After a visit to the Crocker Art Gallery and its collection of heroic paintings of the golden age of California, someone showed a silk scroll with a Chinese painting. Miss Hopley herself had a way of expressing wonder over these matters before a class, her eyes wide open until they popped slightly. It was easy for me to feel that becoming a proud American, as she said we should, did not mean feeling ashamed of being a Mexican.

18   The Americanization of Mexican me was no smooth matter. I had to fight one lout who made fun of my travels on the *diligencia,* and my barbaric translation of the word into "diligence." He doubled up with laughter over the word until I straightened him out with a kick. In class I made points explaining that in Mexico roosters said "qui-qui-ri-qui" and not "cock-a-doodle-doo," but after school I had to put up with the taunts of a big Yugoslav who said Mexican roosters were crazy.

19   But it was Homer who gave me the most lasting lesson for a future American.

20   Homer was a chunky Irishman who dressed as if every day was Sunday. He slicked his hair between a crew cut and a pompadour. And Homer was smart, as he clearly showed when he and I ran for president of the third grade.

21   Everyone understood that this was to be a demonstration of how the American people vote for president. In an election, the teacher explained, the candidates could be generous and vote for each other. We cast our ballots in a shoe box and Homer won by two votes. I polled my supporters and came to the conclusion that I had voted for Homer and so had he. After class he didn't deny it, reminding me of what the teacher had said—we could vote for each other but didn't have to.

22   The lower part of town was a collage of nationalities in the middle of which Miss Nettie Hopley kept school with discipline and compassion. She called assemblies in the upper hall to introduce celebrities like the police sergeant or the fire chief, to lay down the law of the school, to present awards to our athletic champions, and to make important announcements. One of these was that I had been proposed by my school and accepted as a member of the newly

formed Sacramento Boys Band. "Now, isn't that a wonderful thing?" Miss Hopley asked the assembled school, all eyes on me. And everyone answered in a chorus, including myself, "Yes, Miss Hopley."

23   It was not only the parents who were summoned to her office and boys and girls who served sentences there who knew that Nettie Hopley meant business. The entire school witnessed her sizzling Americanism in its awful majesty one morning at flag salute.

24   All the grades, as usual, were lined up in the courtyard between the wings of the building, ready to march to classes after the opening bell. Miss Shand was on the balcony of the second floor off Miss Hopley's office, conducting us in our lusty singing of "My Country tiz-a-thee." Our principal, as always, stood there like us, at attention, her right hand over her heart, joining in the song.

25   Halfway through the second stanza she stepped forward, held up her arm in a sign of command, and called loud and clear: "Stop the singing." Miss Shand looked flabbergasted. We were frozen with shock.

26   Miss Hopley was now standing at the rail of the balcony, her eyes sparking, her voice low and resonant, the words coming down to us distinctly and loaded with indignation.

27   "There are two gentlemen walking on the school grounds with their hats on while we are singing," she said, sweeping our ranks with her eyes. "We will remain silent until the gentlemen come to attention and remove their hats." A minute of awful silence ended when Miss Hopley, her gaze fixed on something behind us, signaled Miss Shand and we began once more the familiar hymn. That afternoon, when school was out, the word spread. The two gentlemen were the Superintendent of Schools and an important guest on an inspection.

28   I came back to the Lincoln School after every summer, moving up through the grades with Miss Campbell, Miss Beakey, Mrs. Wood, Miss Applegate, and Miss Delahunty. I sat in the classroom adjoining the principal's office and had my turn answering her telephone when she was about the building repeating the message to the teacher, who made a note of it. Miss Campbell read to us during the last period of the week about King Arthur, Columbus, Buffalo Bill, and Daniel Boone, who came to life in the reverie of the class through the magic of her voice. And it was Miss Campbell who introduced me to the public library on Eye Street, where I became a regular customer.

29   All of Lincoln School mourned together when Eddie, the blond boy every-body liked, was killed by a freight train as he crawled across the tracks going home one day. We assembled to say good-bye to Miss Applegate, who was off to Alaska to be married. Now it was my turn to be excused from class to interpret for a parent enrolling a new student fresh from Mexico. Graduates from Lincoln came back now and then to tell us about high school. A naturalist entertained us in assembly, imitating the calls of the meadow lark, the water ouzel, the oriole, and the killdeer. I decided to become a bird man after I left Lincoln.

30   In the years we lived in the lower part of town, La Leen-Con, as my family called it, became a benchmark in our lives, like the purple light of the Lyric Theater and the golden dome of the Palacio de Gobierno gleaming above Capitol Park.

☐ Discovering Meaning and Technique

1. Galarza's first experiences at Lincoln School were positive. In what ways was he lucky?

2. Galarza does not recognize the framed picture of a man "with a sad face and a black beard" (paragraph 5). Whose picture do you think it is?

3. Explain these statements:

> "Her radiant, no-nonsense character made us either afraid not to love her or love her so we would not be afraid" (paragraph 14).
> "The school was not so much a melting pot as a griddle" (paragraph 16).

4. Galarza has written a narrative about all his years at Lincoln School. Obviously, he cannot cover every occurrence. Which year does he cover in greatest detail? Why?

5. Discuss the effectiveness of the following comparisons:

> "thin lips that moved like steel springs" (paragraph 8)
> "She loosened me and my classmates from the safe anchorage of the desks" (paragraph 13).

6. Galarza's prose is straightforward and easy to read. Pick two paragraphs and calculate the average number of words in one of his sentences.

☐ Writing Suggestions

1. Describe the greatest fears and problems of going to a school where everyone speaks a foreign language.

2. Describe a teacher or principal who made you feel safe and protected.

3. Describe a teacher or principal who made you fearful or uneasy.

PRIMER CLASS

☐ **ELIZABETH BISHOP**

1 Every time I see long columns of numbers, handwritten in a certain way, a strange sensation or shudder, partly aesthetic, partly painful, goes through my diaphragm. It is like seeing the dorsal fin of a large fish suddenly cut through the surface of the water—not a frightening fish like a shark, more like a sailfish. The numbers have to be only up to but under a hundred, rather large and clumsily written, and the columns squeezed together, with long vertical lines between them, drawn by hand, long and crooked. They are usually in pencil, these numbers that affect me so, but I've seen them in blue crayon or blurred ink, and they produce the same effect. One morning our newspaper delivery man, an old Italian named Tony, whom I'd seen over and over again, threw back the pages of his limp, black, oilcloth-covered account book to my page, and there, up and down, at right angles to the pages' blue lines, he had kept track of my newspapers in pencil, in columns of ones and ones, twos and threes. My diaphragm contracted and froze. Or Faustina, the old black lottery-ticket seller, and *her* limp school notebook with a penciled-off half-inch column waveringly drawn for each customer. Or my glimpse of a barkeeper's apparently home-made, home-stitched pad, as he consulted long thin numbers referring to heaven knows what (how many drinks each of his customers had had?), and then put the pad away again, under the bar.

2 The real name of this sensation is memory. It is a memory I do not even have to try to remember, or reconstruct; it is always right there, clear and complete. The mysterious numbers, the columns, that impressed me so much—a mystery I never solved when I went to Primer Class in Nova Scotia!

3 Primer Class was a sort of Canadian equivalent of kindergarten; it was the year you went to school before you went to "First Grade." But we didn't sit about sociably and build things, or crayon, or play, or quarrel. We sat one behind the other in a line of small, bolted-down desks and chairs, in the same room with grades one, two, three, and four. We were at the left, facing the teacher, and I think there were seven or eight of us. We were taught reading and writing and arithmetic, or enough of them to prepare us for the "First Grade"; also, how to behave in school. This meant to sit up straight, not to scrape your feet on the floor, never to whisper, to raise your hand when you had to go out, and to stand up when you were asked a question. We used slates; only the real grades could buy scribblers, beautiful, fat writing pads, with colored pictures of horses and kittens on the covers, and pale tan paper with blue lines. They could also go up front to sharpen their pencils into the wastebasket.

4 I was five. My grandmother had already taught me to write on a slate my name and my family's names and the names of the dog and the two cats. Earlier

she had taught me my letters, and at first I could not get past the letter *g,* which for some time I felt was far enough to go. *My* alphabet made a satisfying short song, and I didn't want to spoil it. Then a visitor called on my grandmother and asked me if I knew my letters. I said I did and, accenting the rhythm, gave him my version. He teased me so about stopping at *g* that I was finally convinced one must go on with the other nineteen letters. Once past *g,* it was plain sailing. By the time school started, I could read almost all my primer, printed in both handwriting and type, and I loved every word. First, as a frontispiece, it had the flag in full color, with "One Flag, One King, One Crown" under it. I colored in the black-and-white illustrations that looked old-fashioned, even to me, using mostly red and green crayons. On the end pages I had tried to copy the round cancellation marks from old envelopes: "Brooklyn, N.Y. Sept. 1914," "Halifax, Aug. 1916," and so on, but they had not turned out well, a set of lopsided crumbling wheels.

5   The summer before school began was the summer of numbers, chiefly number eight. I learned their shapes from the kitchen calendar and the clock in the sitting room, though I couldn't yet tell time. Four and five were hard enough, but I think I was in love with eight. One began writing it just to the right of the top, and drew an S downwards. This wasn't too difficult, but the hardest part was to hit the bottom line (ruled on the slate by my grandmother) and come up again, against the grain, that is, against the desire of one's painfully cramped fingers, and at the same time not make it a straight line, but a sort of upside down and backwards S, and all this in *curves.* Eights also made the worst noise on the slate. My grandmother would send me outside to practice, sitting on the back steps. The skreeking was slow and awful.

6   The slate pencils came two for a penny, with thin white paper, diagonally striped in pale blue or red, glued around them except for an inch left bare at one end. I loved the slate and the pencils almost as much as the primer. What I liked best about the slate was washing it off at the kitchen sink, or in the watering trough, and then watching it dry. It dried like clouds, and then the very last wet streak would grow tinier and tinier, and thinner and thinner; then suddenly it was gone and the slate was pale gray again and dry, dry, dry.

7   I had an aunt, Mary, eleven or twelve years older than me, who was in the last, or next-to-last, year of the same school. She was very pretty. She wore white middy blouses with red or blue silk ties, and her brown hair in a braid down her back. In the mornings I always got up earlier than Aunt Mary and ate my porridge at the kitchen table, wishing that she would hurry and get up too. We ate porridge from bowls, with a cup of cream at the side. You took a spoonful of porridge, dipped it into the cream, then ate it; this was to keep the porridge hot. We also had cups of tea, with cream and sugar; mine was called "cambric tea." All during breakfast I listened for the school bell, and wished my aunt would hurry up; she rarely appeared before the bell started ringing, over on the other side of the river that divided the village in two. Then she

would arrive in the kitchen braiding her hair, and say, "That's just the *first* bell!" while I was dying to be out the door and off. But first I had to pat Betsy, our little dog, and then kiss Grandmother goodbye. (My grandfather would have been up and out for hours already.)

8   My grandmother had a glass eye, blue, almost like her other one, and this made her especially vulnerable and precious to me. My father was dead and my mother was away in a sanatorium. Until I was teased out of it, I used to ask Grandmother, when I said goodbye, to promise me not to die before I came home. A year earlier I had privately asked other relatives if they thought my grandmother could go to heaven with a glass eye. (Years later I found out that one of my aunts had asked the same question when she'd been my age.) Betsy was also included in this deep but intermittent concern with the hereafter; I was told that of course she'd go to heaven, she was such a good little dog, and not to worry. Wasn't our minister awfully fond of her, and hadn't she even surprised us by trotting right into church one summer Sunday, when the doors were open?

9   Although I don't remember having been told it was a serious offense, I was very afraid of being late, so most mornings I left Mary at her breakfast and ran out the back door, around the house, past the blacksmith's shop, and was well across the iron bridge before she caught up with me. Sometimes I had almost reached the school when the second bell, the one that meant to come in immediately from the schoolyard, would be clanging away in the cupola. The school was high, bare and white-clapboarded, dark-red-roofed, and the four-sided cupola had white louvers. Two white outhouses were set farther back, but visible, on either side. I carried my slate, a rag to wash it with, and a small medicine bottle filled with water. Everyone was supposed to bring a bottle of water and a clean rag; spitting on the slates and wiping them off with the hand was a crime. Only the bad boys did it, and if she caught them the teacher hit them on the top of the head with her pointer. I don't imagine that wet slate, by itself, had a smell; perhaps slate pencils do; sour, wet rags do, of course, and perhaps that is what I remember. Miss Morash would pick one up at arm's length and order the owner to take it outside at once, saying *Phaaagh,* or something like that.

10   That was our teacher's name, Georgie Morash. To me she seemed very tall and stout, straight up and down, with a white starched shirtwaist, a dark straight skirt, and a tight, wide belt that she often pushed down, in front, with both hands. Everything, back and front, looked smooth and hard; maybe it was corsets. But close to, what I mostly remember about Miss Morash, and mostly looked at, were her very white shoes, Oxford shoes, surprisingly white, white like flour, and large, with neatly tied white laces. On my first day at school my Aunt Mary had taken me into the room for the lower grades and presented me to Miss Morash. She bent way over, spoke to me kindly, even patted my head and, although told to look up, I could not take my eyes from those silent, independent-looking, powdery-white shoes.

11   Miss Morash almost always carried her pointer. As she walked up and down the aisles, looking over shoulders at the scribblers or slates, rapping heads, or occasionally boxing an ear, she talked steadily, in a loud, clear voice. This voice had a certain fame in the village. At dinner my grandfather would quote what he said he had heard Miss Morash saying to us (or even to me) as he drove by that morning, even though the schoolhouse was set well back from the road. Sometimes when my grandmother would tell me to stop shouting, or to speak more softly, she would add, "That Georgie!" I don't remember anything Miss Morash ever said. Once when the Primer Class was gathered in a semicircle before one of the blackboards, while she showed us (sweepingly) how to write the capital *C,* and I was considering, rather, the blue sky beyond the windows, I too received a painful rap on the head with the pointer.

12   There was another little girl in the Primer Class, besides me, and one awful day she wet her pants, right in the front seat, and was sent home. There were two little Micmac Indian boys, Jimmy and Johnny Crow, who had dark little faces and shiny black hair and eyes, just alike. They both wore shirts of blue cotton, some days patterned with little white sprigs, on others with little white anchors. I couldn't take my eyes off these shirts or the boys' dark bare feet. Almost everyone went barefoot to school, but I had to wear brown sandals with buckles, against my will. When I went home the first day and was asked who was in Primer Class with me, I replied, "Manure MacLaughlin," as his name had sounded to me. I was familiar with manure—there was a great pile of it beside the barn—but of course his real name was Muir, and everyone laughed. Muir wore a navy-blue cap, with a red-and-yellow maple leaf embroidered above the visor.

13   There was a poor boy, named Roustain, the dirtiest and raggediest of us all, who was really too big for Primer Class and had to walk a long way to school, when he came at all. I heard thrilling stories about him and his brother, how their father whipped them all the time, *horsewhipped* them. We were still horse-and-buggy-minded (though there were a few automobiles in the village), and one of the darkest, most sinister symbols in our imaginations was the horsewhip. It *looked* sinister: long, black, flexible at a point after the handle, sometimes even with lead in it, tasseled. It made a swish *whissh*ing sound and sometimes figured in nightmares. There was even a song about the Roustains:

> I'm a Roustain from the mountain,
> I'm a Roustain, don't you see,
> I'm a Roustain from the mountain,
> You can smell the fir on me.

Not only did their father whip them, but their mother didn't take care of them at all. There were no real beds in their house and no food, except for a big barrel of molasses, which often swarmed with flies. They's dip pieces of bread in the molasses, when they had bread, and that was all they had for dinner.

14   The schoolroom windows, those autumn days, seemed very high and bright.

On one window ledge, on the Primer Class side, there were beans sprouting up in jars of water. Their presence in school puzzled me, since at home I'd already grown "horse bean" to an amazing height and size in my own garden (eighteen inches square), as well as some radishes and small, crooked carrots. Beyond, above the sprouting beans, the big autumn clouds went grandly by, silver and dazzling in the deep blue. I would keep turning my head to follow them, until Miss Morash came along and gave it a small push back in the right direction. I loved to hear the other grades read aloud, unless they hesitated too much on words or phrases you could guess ahead. Their stories were better, and longer, than those in my primer. I already knew by heart "The Gingerbread Boy" and "Henny Penny," in my primer, and had turned against them. I was much more interested when the third grade read about Bruce watching the spider spin his web. Every morning school began with the Lord's Prayer, sitting down, then we stood up and sang "O maple leaf, our emblem dear." Then sometimes—and not very well, because it was so much harder—we sang "God save our gracious king," but usually stopped with the first verse.

15   Only the third and fourth grades studied geography. On their side of the room, over the blackboard, were two rolled-up maps, one of Canada and one of the whole world. When they had a geography lesson, Miss Morash pulled down one or both of these maps, like window shades. They were on cloth, very limp, with a shiny surface, and in pale colors—tan, pink, yellow, and green—surrounded by the blue that was the ocean. The light coming in from their windows, falling on the glazed, crackly surface, made it hard for me to see them properly from where I sat. On the world map, all of Canada was pink; on the Canadian, the provinces were different colors. I was so taken with the pull-down maps that I wanted to snap them up, and pull them down again, and touch all the countries and provinces with my own hands. Only dimly did I hear the pupils' recitations of capital cities and islands and bays. But I got the general impression that Canada was the same size as the world, which somehow or other fitted into it, or the other way around, and that in the world and Canada the sun was always shining and everything was dry and glittering. At the same time, I knew perfectly well that this was not true.

16   One morning Aunt Mary was even later than usual at breakfast, and for some reason I decided to wait for her to finish her porridge. Before we got to the bridge the second bell—the bell that really meant it—started ringing. I was terrified because up to this time I had never actually been late, so I began to run as fast as I possibly could. I could hear my aunt behind, laughing at me. Because her legs were longer than mine, she caught up to me, rushed into the schoolyard and up the steps ahead of me. I ran into the classroom and threw myself, howling, against Miss Morash's upright form. The class had their hands folded on the desks, heads bowed, and had reached "Thy kingdom come." I clutched the teacher's long, stiff skirt and sobbed. Behind me, my awful aunt was still *laughing.* Miss Morash stopped everyone in mid-prayer, and propelled

us all three out into the cloak-room, holding me tightly by the shoulder. There, surrounded by all the japanned hooks, which held only two or three caps, we were private, though loud giggles and whispering reached us from the schoolroom. First Miss Morash in stern tones told Mary she was *very* late for the class she attended overhead, and ordered her to go upstairs at once. Then she tried to calm me. She said in a very kindly way, not at all in her usual penetrating voice, that being only a few minutes late wasn't really worth tears, that everything was quite all right, and I must go into the classroom now and join in the usual morning songs. She wiped off my face with a folded white handkerchief she kept tucked in her belt, patted my head, and even kissed me two or three times. I was overcome by all this, almost to the point of crying all over again, but keeping my eyes fixed firmly on her two large, impersonal, flour-white shoes, I managed not to give way. I had to face my snickering classmates, and I found I could. And that was that, although I was cross with Aunt Mary for a long time because it was all her fault.

17   For me this was the most dramatic incident of Primer Class, and I was never late again. My initial experiences of formal education were on the whole pleasurable. Reading and writing caused me no suffering. I found the first easier, but the second was enjoyable—I mean *artistically* enjoyable—and I came to admire my own handwriting in pencil, when I got to that stage, perhaps as a youthful Chinese student might admire his own brushstrokes. It was wonderful to see that the letters each had different expressions, and that the same letter had different expressions at different times. Sometimes the two capitals of my name looked miserable, slumped down and sulky, but at others they turned fat and cheerful, almost with roses in their cheeks. I also had the "First Grade" to look forward to, as well as geography, the maps, and longer and much better stories. The one subject that baffled me was arithmetic. I knew all the numbers of course, and liked to write them—I finally mastered the eight—but when I watched the older grades at arithmetic class, in front of the blackboard with their columns of figures, it was utterly incomprehensible. Those mysterious numbers!

☐ Discovering Meaning and Technique

1. What evokes Elizabeth Bishop's memories? What comparison does she make to show how they emerge?

2. Describe Bishop's experiences learning to read, write, and count.

3. Why did Bishop live with her grandparents?

4. What two ideas worried Bishop about the "hereafter"?

5. What kinds of details does Bishop remember about the other students in her class?

6. What did Bishop like best in school?

7. Contrast Bishop's attitude toward getting to school with Mary's.

8. Elizabeth Bishop became a poet. Find evidence in her prose of a poetic style—descriptions that contain shapes, colors, and sounds; comparisons; rhythmic sentences.

9. Do you think Bishop deliberately begins and ends the selection by referring to numbers?

☐ Writing Suggestions

1. How did Bishop's early learning experiences resemble or differ from yours?

2. What memories do you have of schoolbooks, pens, pencils, chalk, tablets, and the like?

3. Some children mature faster than others and can read before they start to school; others cannot read. How can schools handle dissimilar skills?

4. Do you have memories of learning to read and write? If so, describe them.

5. Compare the punishments in school inflicted by Miss Morash with the teachers in your early education.

GRADUATION AT LAFAYETTE COUNTY TRAINING SCHOOL

☐ MAYA ANGELOU

[1] The children in Stamps trembled visibly with anticipation. Some adults were excited, too, but to be certain the whole young population had come down with graduation epidemic. Large classes were graduating from both the grammar school and the high school. Even those who were years removed from their own day of glorious release were anxious to help with preparations as a kind of dry run. The junior students who were moving into the vacating classes' chairs were tradition-bound to show their talents for leadership and management.

They strutted through the school and around the campus exerting pressure on the lower grades. Their authority was so new that occasionally if they pressed a little too hard it had to be overlooked. After all, next term was coming, and it never hurt a sixth grader to have a play sister in the eighth grade, or a tenth-year student to be able to call a twelfth grader Bubba. So all was endured in a spirit of shared understanding. But the graduating classes themselves were the nobility. Like travelers with exotic destinations on their minds, the graduates were remarkably forgetful. They came to school without their books, or tablets or even pencils. Volunteers fell over themselves to secure replacements for the missing equipment. When accepted, the willing workers might or might not be thanked, and it was of no importance to the pregraduation rites. Even teachers were respectful of the now quiet and aging seniors, and tended to speak to them, if not as equals, as beings only slightly lower than themselves. After tests were returned and grades given, the student body, which acted like an extended family, knew who did well, who excelled, and what piteous ones had failed.

2   Unlike the white high school, Lafayette County Training School distinguished itself by having neither lawn, nor hedges, nor tennis court, nor climbing ivy. Its two buildings (main classrooms, the grade school and home economics) were set on a dirt hill with no fence to limit either its boundaries or those of bordering farms. There was a large expanse to the left of the school which was used alternately as a baseball diamond or a basketball court. Rusty hoops on the swaying poles represented the permanent recreational equipment, although bats and balls could be borrowed from the P.E. teacher if the borrower was qualified and if the diamond wasn't occupied.

3   Over this rocky area relieved by a few shady tall persimmon trees the graduating class walked. The girls often held hands and no longer bothered to speak to the lower students. There was a sadness about them, as if this old world was not their home and they were bound for higher ground. The boys, on the other hand, had become more friendly, more outgoing. A decided change from the closed attitude they projected while studying for finals. Now they seemed not ready to give up the old school, the familiar paths and classrooms. Only a small percentage would be continuing on to college—one of the South's A&M (agricultural and mechanical) schools, which trained Negro youths to be carpenters, farmers, handymen, masons, maids, cooks and baby nurses. Their future rode heavily on their shoulders, and blinded them to the collective joy that had pervaded the lives of the boys and girls in the grammar school graduating class.

4   Parents who could afford it had ordered new shoes and ready-made clothes for themselves from Sears and Roebuck or Montgomery Ward. They also engaged the best seamstresses to make the floating graduating dresses and to cut down secondhand pants which would be pressed to a military slickness for the important event.

5   Oh, it was important, all right. Whitefolks would attend the ceremony,

and two or three would speak of God and home, and the Southern way of life, and Mrs. Parsons, the principal's wife, would play the graduation march while the lower-grade graduates paraded down the aisles and took their seats below the platform. The high school seniors would wait in empty classrooms to make their dramatic entrance.

6 In the Store I was the person of the moment. The birthday girl. The center. Bailey had graduated the year before, although to do so he had had to forfeit all pleasures to make up for his time lost in Baton Rouge.

7 My class was wearing butter-yellow piqué dresses, and Momma launched out on mine. She smocked the yoke into tiny crisscrossing puckers, then shirred the rest of the bodice. Her dark fingers ducked in and out of the lemony cloth as she embroidered raised daisies around the hem. Before she considered herself finished she had added a crocheted cuff on the puff sleeves, and a pointy crocheted collar.

8 I was going to be lovely. A walking model of all the various styles of fine hand sewing and it didn't worry me that I was only twelve years old and merely graduating from the eighth grade. Besides, many teachers in Arkansas Negro schools had only that diploma and were licensed to impart wisdom.

9 The days had become longer and more noticeable. The faded beige of former times had been replaced with strong and sure colors. I began to see my classmates' clothes, their skin tones, and the dust that waved off pussy willows. Clouds that lazed across the sky were objects of great concern to me. Their shiftier shapes might have held a message that in my new happiness and with a little bit of time I'd soon decipher. During that period I looked at the arch of heaven so religiously my neck kept a steady ache. I had taken to smiling more often, and my jaws hurt from the unaccustomed activity. Between the two physical sore spots, I suppose I could have been uncomfortable, but that was not the case. As a member of the winning team (the graduating class of 1940) I had outdistanced unpleasant sensations by miles. I was headed for the freedom of open fields.

10 Youth and social approval allied themselves with me and we trammeled memories of slights and insults. The wind of our swift passage remodeled my features. Lost tears were pounded to mud and then dust. Years of withdrawal were brushed aside and left behind, as hanging ropes of parasite moss.

11 My work alone had awarded me a top place and I was going to be one of the first called in the graduating ceremonies. On the classroom blackboard, as well as on the bulletin board in the auditorium, there were blue stars and white stars and red stars. No absences, no tardinesses, and my academic work was among the best of the year. I could say the preamble to the Constitution even faster than Bailey. We timed ourselves often: "WethepeopleoftheUnitedStates inordertoformamoreperfectunion . . ." I had memorized the Presidents of the United States from Washington to Roosevelt in chronological as well as alphabetical order.

12   My hair pleased me too. Gradually the black mass had lengthened and thickened, so that it kept at last to its braided pattern, and I didn't have to yank my scalp off when I tried to comb it.

13   Louise and I had rehearsed the exercises until we tired out ourselves. Henry Reed was class valedictorian. He was a small, very black boy with hooded eyes, a long, broad nose and an oddly shaped head. I had admired him for years because each term he and I vied for the best grades in our class. Most often he bested me, but instead of being disappointed I was pleased that we shared top places between us. Like many Southern Black children, he lived with his grandmother, who was as strict as Momma and as kind as she knew how to be. He was courteous, respectful and soft-spoken to elders, but on the playground he chose to play the roughest games. I admired him. Anyone, I reckoned, sufficiently afraid or sufficiently dull could be polite. But to be able to operate at a top level with both adults and children was admirable.

14   His valedictory speech was entitled "To Be or Not to Be." The rigid tenth-grade teacher had helped him write it. He'd been working on the dramatic stresses for months.

15   The weeks until graduation were filled with heady activities. A group of small children were to be presented in a play about buttercups and daisies and bunny rabbits. They could be heard throughout the building practicing their hops and their little songs that sounded like silver bells. The older girls (nongraduates, of course) were assigned the task of making refreshments for the night's festivities. A tangy scent of ginger, cinnamon, nutmeg and chocolate wafted around the home economics building as the budding cooks made samples for themselves and their teachers.

16   In every corner of the workshop, axes and saws split fresh timber as the woodshop boys made sets and stage scenery. Only the graduates were left out of the general bustle. We were free to sit in the library at the back of the building or look in quite detachedly, naturally, on the measures being taken for our event.

17   Even the minister preached on graduation the Sunday before. His subject was, "Let your light so shine that men will see your good works and praise your Father, Who is in Heaven." Although the sermon was purported to be addressed to us, he used the occasion to speak to backsliders, gamblers and general ne'er-do-wells. But since he had called our names at the beginning of the service we were mollified.

18   Among Negroes the tradition was to give presents to children going only from one grade to another. How much more important this was when the person was graduating at the top of the class. Uncle Willie and Momma had sent away for a Mickey Mouse watch like Bailey's. Louise gave me four embroidered handkerchiefs. (I gave her three crocheted doilies.) Mrs. Sneed, the minister's wife, made me an underskirt to wear for graduation, and nearly every customer gave me a nickel or maybe even a dime with the instruction "Keep on moving to higher ground," or some such encouragement.

19   Amazingly the great day finally dawned and I was out of bed before I knew it. I threw open the back door to see it more clearly, but Momma said, "Sister, come away from that door and put your robe on."

20   I hoped the memory of that morning would never leave me. Sunlight was itself still young, and the day had none of the insistence maturity would bring it in a few hours. In my robe and barefoot in the backyard, under cover of going to see about my new beans, I gave myself up to the gentle warmth and thanked God that no matter what evil I had done in my life He had allowed me to live to see this day. Somewhere in my fatalism I had expected to die, accidentally, and never have the chance to walk up the stairs in the auditorium and gracefully receive my hard-earned diploma. Out of God's merciful bosom I had won reprieve.

21   Bailey came out in his robe and gave me a box wrapped in Christmas paper. He said he had saved his money for months to pay for it. It felt like a box of chocolates, but I knew Bailey wouldn't save money to buy candy when we had all we could want under our noses.

22   He was as proud of the gift as I. It was a soft-leather-bound copy of a collection of poems by Edgar Allan Poe, or, as Bailey and I called him, "Eap." I turned to "Annabel Lee" and we walked up and down the garden rows, the cool dirt between our toes, reciting the beautifully sad lines.

23   Momma made a Sunday breakfast although it was only Friday. After we finished the blessing, I opened my eyes to find the watch on my plate. It was a dream of a day. Everything went smoothly and to my credit. I didn't have to be reminded or scolded for anything. Near evening I was too jittery to attend to chores, so Bailey volunteered to do all before his bath.

24   Days before, we had made a sign for the Store, and as we turned out the lights Momma hung the cardboard over the doorknob. It read clearly: CLOSED. GRADUATION.

25   My dress fitted perfectly and everyone said that I looked like a sunbeam in it. On the hill, going toward the school, Bailey walked behind with Uncle Willie, who muttered, "Go on, Ju." He wanted him to walk ahead with us because it embarrassed him to have to walk so slowly. Bailey said he'd let the ladies walk together, and the men would bring up the rear. We all laughed, nicely.

26   Little children dashed by out of the dark like fireflies. Their crepe-paper dresses and butterfly wings were not made for running and we heard more than one rip, dryly, and the regretful "uh uh" that followed.

27   The school blazed without gaiety. The windows seemed cold and unfriendly from the lower hill. A sense of ill-fated timing crept over me, and if Momma hadn't reached for my hand I would have drifted back to Bailey and Uncle Willie, and possibly beyond. She made a few slow jokes about my feet getting cold, and tugged me along to the now-strange building.

28   Around the front steps, assurance came back. There were my fellow "greats," the graduating class. Hair brushed back, legs oiled, new dresses and pressed

pleats, fresh pocket handkerchiefs and little handbags, all homesewn. Oh, we were up to snuff, all right. I joined my comrades and didn't even see my family go in to find seats in the crowded auditorium.

29   The school band struck up a march and all classes filed in as had been rehearsed. We stood in front of our seats, as assigned, and on a signal from the choir director, we sat. No sooner had this been accomplished than the band started to play the national anthem. We rose again and sang the song, after which we recited the pledge of allegiance. We remained standing for a brief minute before the choir director and the principal signaled to us, rather desperately, I thought, to take our seats. The command was so unusual that our carefully rehearsed and smooth-running machine was thrown off. For a full minute we fumbled for our chairs and bumped into each other awkwardly. Habits change or solidify under pressure, so in our state of nervous tension we had been ready to follow our usual assembly pattern: the American national anthem, then the pledge of allegiance, then the song every Black person I knew called the Negro National Anthem. All done in the same key, with the same passion and most often standing on the same foot.

30   Finding my seat at last, I was overcome with a presentiment of worse things to come. Something unrehearsed, unplanned, was going to happen, and we were going to be made to look bad. I distinctly remember being explicit in the choice of pronoun. It was "we," the graduating class, the unit, that concerned me then.

31   The principal welcomed "parents and friends" and asked the Baptist minister to lead us in prayer. His invocation was brief and punchy, and for a second I thought we were getting back on the high road to right action. When the principal came back to the dias, however, his voice had changed. Sounds always affected me profoundly and the principal's voice was one of my favorites. During assembly it melted and lowed weakly into the audience. It had not been in my plan to listen to him, but my curiosity was piqued and I straightened up to give him my attention.

32   He was talking about Booker T. Washington, our "late great leader," who said we can be as close as the fingers on the hand, etc. . . . Then he said a few vague things about friendship and the friendship of kindly people to those less fortunate than themselves. With that his voice nearly faded, thin, away. Like a river diminishing to a stream and then to a trickle. But he cleared his throat and said, "Our speaker tonight, who is also our friend, came from Texarkana to deliver the commencement address, but due to the irregularity of the train schedule, he's going to, as they say, 'speak and run.' " He said that we understood and wanted the man to know that we were most grateful for the time he was able to give us and then something about how we were willing always to adjust to another's program, and without more ado—"I give you Mr. Edward Donleavy."

33   Not one but two white men came through the door offstage. The shorter one walked to the speaker's platform, and the tall one moved over to the center

seat and sat down. But that was our principal's seat, and already occupied. The dislodged gentleman bounced around for a long breath or two before the Baptist minister gave him his chair, then with more dignity than the situation deserved, the minister walked off the stage.

34   Donleavy looked at the audience once (on reflection, I'm sure that he wanted only to reassure himself that we were really there), adjusted his glasses and began to read from a sheaf of papers.

35   He was glad "to be here and to see the work going on just as it was in the other schools."

36   At the first "Amen" from the audience I willed the offender to immediate death by choking on the word. But Amens and Yes, sir's began to fall around the room like rain through a ragged umbrella.

37   He told us of the wonderful changes we children in Stamps had in store. The Central School (naturally, the white school was Central) had already been granted improvements that would be in use in the fall. A well-known artist was coming from Little Rock to teach art to them. They were going to have the newest microscopes and chemistry equipment for their laboratory. Mr. Donleavy didn't leave us long in the dark over who made these improvements available to Central High. Nor were we to be ignored in the general betterment scheme he had in mind.

38   He said that he had pointed out to people at a very high level that one of the first-line football tacklers at Arkansas Agricultural and Mechanical College had graduated from good old Lafayette County Training School. Here fewer Amen's were heard. Those few that did break through lay dully in the air with the heaviness of habit.

39   He went on to praise us. He went on to say how he had bragged that "one of the best basketball players at Fisk sank his first ball right here at Lafayette County Training School."

40   The white kids were going to have a chance to become Galileos and Madame Curies and Edisons and Gauguins, and our boys (the girls weren't even in on it) would try to be Jesse Owenses and Joe Louises.

41   Owens and the Brown Bomber were great heroes in our world, but what school official in the white-goddom of Little Rock had the right to decide that those two men must be our only heroes? Who decided that for Henry Reed to become a scientist he had to work like George Washington Carver, as a bootblack, to buy a lousy microscope? Bailey was obviously always going to be too small to be an athlete, so which concrete angel glued to what country seat had decided that if my brother wanted to become a lawyer he had to first pay penance for his skin by picking cotton and hoeing corn and studying correspondence books at night for twenty years?

42   The man's dead words fell like bricks around the auditorium and too many settled in my belly. Constrained by hard-learned manners I couldn't look behind me, but to my left and right the proud graduating class of 1940 had dropped

their heads. Every girl in my row had found something new to do with her handkerchief. Some folded the tiny squares into love knots, some into triangles, but most were wadding them, then pressing them flat on their yellow laps.

43   On the dais, the ancient tragedy was being replayed. Professor Parsons sat, a sculptor's reject, rigid. His large, heavy body seemed devoid of will or willingness, and his eyes said he was no longer with us. The other teachers examined the flag (which was draped stage right) or their notes, or the windows which opened on our now-famous playing diamond.

44   Graduation, the hush-hush magic time of frills and gifts and congratulations and diplomas, was finished for me before my name was called. The accomplishment was nothing. The meticulous maps, drawn in three colors of ink, learning and spelling decasyllabic words, memorizing the whole of *The Rape of Lucrece*—it was for nothing. Donleavy had exposed us.

45   We were maids and farmers, handymen and washerwomen, and anything higher that we aspired to was farcical and presumptuous.

46   Then I wished that Gabriel Prosser and Nat Turner had killed all whitefolks in their beds and that Abraham Lincoln had been assassinated before the signing of the Emancipation Proclamation, and that Harriet Tubman had been killed by that blow on her head and Christopher Columbus had drowned in the *Santa María.*

47   It was awful to be Negro and have no control over my life. It was brutal to be young and already trained to sit quietly and listen to charges brought against my color with no chance of defense. We should all be dead. I thought I should like to see us all dead, one on top of the other. A pyramid of flesh with the whitefolks on the bottom, as the broad base, then the Indians with their silly tomahawks and teepees and wigwams and treaties, the Negroes with their mops and recipes and cotton sacks and spirituals sticking out of their mouths. The Dutch children should all stumble in their wooden shoes and break their necks. The French should choke to death on the Louisiana Purchase (1803) while silkworms ate all the Chinese with their stupid pigtails. As a species, we were an abomination. All of us.

48   Donleavy was running for election, and assured our parents that if he won we could count on having the only colored paved playing field in that part of Arkansas. Also—he never looked up to acknowledge the grunts of acceptance— also, we were bound to get some new equipment for the home economics building and the workshop.

49   He finished, and since there was no need to give any more than the most perfunctory thank-you's, he nodded to the men on the stage, and the tall white man who was never introduced joined him at the door. They left with the attitude that now they were off to something really important. (The graduation ceremonies at Lafayette County Training School had been a mere preliminary.)

50   The ugliness they left was palpable. An uninvited guest who wouldn't leave. The choir was summoned and sang a modern arrangement of "Onward, Christian

Soldiers," with new words pertaining to graduates seeking their place in the world. But it didn't work. Elouise, the daughter of the Baptist minister, recited "Invictus," and I could have cried at the impertinence of "I am the master of my fate, I am the captain of my soul."

51   My name had lost its ring of familiarity and I had to be nudged to go and receive my diploma. All my preparations had fled. I neither marched up to the stage like a conquering Amazon, nor did I look in the audience for Bailey's nod of approval. Marguerite Johnson, I heard the name again, my honors were read, there were noises in the audience of appreciation, and I took my place on the stage as rehearsed.

52   I thought about colors I hated: ecru, puce, lavender, beige and black.

53   There was shuffling and rustling around me, then Henry Reed was giving his valedictory address, "To Be or Not to Be." Hadn't he heard the whitefolks? We couldn't *be,* so the question was a waste of time. Henry's voice came out clear and strong. I feared to look at him. Hadn't he got the message? There was no "nobler in the mind" for Negroes because the world didn't think we had minds, and they let us know it. "Outrageous fortune"? Now, that was a joke. When the ceremony was over I had to tell Henry Reed some things. That is, if I still cared. Not "rub," Henry , "erase." "Ah, there's the erase." Us.

54   Henry had been a good student in elocution. His voice rose on tides of promise and fell on waves of warnings. The English teacher had helped him to create a sermon winging through Hamlet's soliloquy. To be a man, a doer, a builder, a leader, or to be a tool, an unfunny joke, a crusher of funky toadstools. I marveled that Henry could go through with the speech as if we had a choice.

55   I had been listening and silently rebutting each sentence with my eyes closed; then there was a hush, which in an audience warns that something unplanned is happening. I looked up and saw Henry Reed, the conservative, the proper, the A student, turn his back to the audience and turn to us (the proud graduating class of 1940) and sing, nearly speaking,

> "Lift ev'ry voice and sing
> Till earth and heaven ring
> Ring with the harmonies of Liberty . . ."

It was the poem written by James Weldon Johnson. It was the music composed by J. Rosamond Johnson. It was the Negro national anthem. Out of habit we were singing it.

56   Our mothers and fathers stood in the dark hall and joined the hymn of encouragement. A kindergarten teacher led the small children onto the stage and the buttercups and daisies and bunny rabbits marked time and tried to follow:

"Stony the road we trod
 Bitter the chastening rod
 Felt in the days when hope, unborn, had died.
 Yet with a steady beat
 Have not our weary feet
 Come to the place for which our fathers sighed?"

57 Every child I knew had learned that song with his ABC's and along with "Jesus Loves Me This I Know." But I personally had never heard it before. Never heard the words, despite the thousands of times I had sung them. Never thought they had anything to do with me.

58   On the other hand, the words of Patrick Henry had made such an impression on me that I had been able to stretch myself tall and trembling and say, "I know not what course others may take, but as for me, give me liberty or give me death."

59   And how I heard, really for the first time:

"We have come over a way that with tears
 has been watered,
 We have come, treading our path through
 the blood of the slaughtered."

60 While echoes of the song shivered in the air, Henry Reed bowed his head, said "Thank you," and returned to his place in the line. The tears that slipped down many faces were not wiped away in shame.

61   We were on top again. As always, again. We survived. The depths had been icy and dark, but now a bright sun spoke to our souls. I was no longer simply a member of the proud graduating class of 1940; I was a proud member of the wonderful, beautiful Negro race.

62   Oh, Black known and unknown poets, how often have your auctioned pains sustained us? Who will compute the lonely nights made less lonely by your songs, or the empty pots made less tragic by your tales?

63   If we were a people much given to revealing secrets, we might raise monuments and sacrifice to the memories of our poets, but slavery cured us of that weakness. It may be enough, however, to have it said that we survive in exact relationship to the dedication of our poets (include preachers, musicians and blues singers).

☐ Discovering Meaning and Technique

1. Discuss the conflict between the attitudes of the people and the world they live in and the futures they face.

2. Although the people in this selection are poor, they have a strong tradition of gift giving. Describe it.

3. What is the significance of the address by Mr. Donleavy?

4. Explain the significance of Angelou's praise of black poets: "Oh, Black known and unknown poets, how often have your auctioned pains sustained us? Who will compute the lonely nights made less lonely by your songs, or the empty pots made less tragic by your tales?" (paragraph 62).

5. Discuss how Angelou moves from a general overview to a specific focus.

6. The structure is primarily but not strictly chronological. What signposts make the chronology clear?

7. Angelou is a poet; she writes in this selection, "Sounds always affected me profoundly" (paragraph 31). Can you find phrases in this reminiscence that illustrate her interest in the sounds of language?

8. Discuss the effect of the following similes:

> "Years of withdrawal were brushed aside and left behind, as hanging ropes of parasitic moss" (paragraph 10).
> "Yes, sir's began to fall around the room like the rain through a ragged umbrella" (paragraph 36).

☐ Writing Suggestions

1. Compare or contrast the graduation in Stamps with one in your hometown.

2. Angelou's primary purpose is to picture the graduation. In addition, the reader learns much of black life in the South in the 1940s. Describe what you have learned. Supplement your description with information from magazines and newspapers published during the period.

3. What might have been the fate of a person like Henry Reed during this period of American history?

NOT ANOTHER WORD

☐ RICHARD THURMAN

[1] Because I was one of the bigger, healthier boys in the class—and also one of the biggest, smoothest liars, and thus apt to set an inspiring example for the others—Miss Devron would often begin the morning's inquisition with me. "Paul

Adam," she would say, beaming down upon me, "would you be kind enough to tell us what you had for breakfast this morning?"

2   Even in the third grade, we were perceptive enough to sense that Miss Devron's inquiries into our daily breakfast menus sprang from something deeper than a mere interest in keeping us healthy. One look at her size and you knew what supreme importance food had in her life, and since we were her children—those she would never have herself, because of age, temperament, and general appeareance—she apparently found it necessary to feel her way into our souls by following a glass of fruit juice and an egg and a slice of ham down our throats each morning. It wasn't just her zeal to know us personally through the food we ate that made us guard against her with a series of outrageous lies; she also wanted to know our families—their general way of life, their social and economic status in our small Utah town and whether or not they lived in accordance with the Mormon doctrines, which were as inseparable from our lives as the mountain air we breathed. And she had a nasty way of pointing out any deviation from her set of standards by interrupting the stream of breakfast reports. "Hominy grits!" I remember her saying on one of the first mornings we were in her class. "Did you hear, class? Ronald Adair had hominy grits for breakfast."

3   She smiled her closed smile of wisdom and commiseration at Ronald, and placed the index finger of her left hand like a hot dog between her second and third chins while waggling her free hand scoldingly in his direction. "It's a lucky thing for you, young man, that your parents somehow had the energy to come out West, where you can get a new start in life," she said. "It's food like hominy grits that has kept the South backward so long. Out *here* we eat bacon and ham-and-eggs and hot cereal and fresh fruit juices and good buttered toast with jam. You're very lucky, young man! My, yes."

4   With such tactics she soon taught us to lie, and regardless of what each of us had eaten at home, there in Miss Devron's class we began to share a breakfast as monotonous as it was sumptuous. It was only a variation in quantity that crept into our diets from the first student's report to the last, for if one egg and a modest piece of ham were enough to start Miss Devron's fingers strolling contentedly over the terraces of her chins, it took considerably more than this to keep them happy and moving by the time the class was half through its recital, and by the time the last student's turn came, Miss Devron's wolfish appetite responded to nothing less than a gorge. Lila Willig was the last student on our class list. She looked as if she were made from five laths, and in the hectic flush of her unhealthiness—perhaps caused by near-starvation at home—she would sometimes get a little hysterical and report that she had eaten twenty-five eggs and a whole ham. I'm sure now that this was not because of any native waggishness in Lila, but we thought it was then, and we always laughed until Miss Devron had to pound the desk with her ruler.

5   "Now, stop that foolishness, Lila," she would say briskly. "Tell the class right out how many eggs you had for breakfast."

6　　"Five," Lila would say, nervously scratching her frizzled yellow curls until they stood out like coiled wires. She could have said nothing else. The boy in front of her just reported a breakfast of five eggs; anything less from Lila would have been picked up by Miss Devron as an example of parental neglect.

7　　"That's better," the teacher would say, her fingers resuming their stroll. "And as I look over your faces this morning, class, I can already see the differences that good eating habits can make in one's life. How much brighter your eyes! How much stronger your backs!"

8　　We simpered back at her, only vaguely and uneasily aware that she was a tyrant who was flattening our individuality with the weight of her righteous self-assurance. In less than a month under her, we were reduced to a spineless group of syncophantic ham, egg, and cereal eaters, with only Lila's occasional lapses to show us what a dull mold we had been crushed into. And then our integrity was rescued in an unexpected way.

9　　The new boy who turned up in our class a month after the opening of school certainly looked like no hero. He was smaller than most of us, and while all of us boys were proudly wearing corduroy knickers, he still wore the short pants we scorned, and in the sharp air of that October morning his thin legs were mottled with a network of blue. We welcomed this pathetic figure with a fine generosity of spirit. "Where you from?" one of us asked him as we walked up to where he was standing, at the edge of the playground.

10　　"New York."

11　　"New York!" we said, and I now had an explanation of why he was such a puny-looking little rat. From the handful of Western movies and cowboy books I had already absorbed, I knew the kind of magic that enters into a man's blood when he is born west of the Mississippi River. His eye is clearer, his nerves are truer, his gait is more tireless, his aim is steadier, and in the very heart of his manliness there is a dimension that effete Easterners know nothing about. All this I knew as I looked down at the new boy's skinny blue legs.

12　　"New York, eh?" I said menacingly, moving up to him until I could have rested my chin on the top of his head.

13　　"That's right," he said, lounging against the top rail of the playground fence and casually lifting one foot to rest it over the lower rail.

14　　I eyed him with a steely coldness I had learned from a story about a man who had built the Union Pacific Railroad across the plains and who could drive a spike into a tie with two hammer blows. I put my fingers into my belt, just above where my six-shooters should have been. "Who's your old man voting for?" I asked. "Al Smith or Hoover?"

15　　"Al Smith."

16　　"Well, then, I guess I'll have to beat you up."

17　　Perhaps nowadays, what with the broadening horizons brought on by the Second World War, Korea, UNESCO, and the stress on social-adjustment patterns in modern education, a new student from, say, Siam or Afghanistan can take his place unobtrusively in an American schoolroom. I don't know. But I do know that in my part of America in 1928 a new student had to fight his way into school, particularly if he had come to us from more than five blocks away. It will be understood, then, that I had no unusual political precocity or passion at the age of eight, and that this difference in our fathers' political views was only a pretext for me to beat up the new boy, who had offended every one of us by coming all the way from New York, with his short pants and blue skin.

18   We sized each up for a second. Then he shrugged his thin shoulders and said "O.K.," and the quickness with which he squared away for battle gave me a little turn. We circled around each other, with everyone urging me to get in there and show him what was what. But just then the bell rang, and I felt a surge of relief that was just a bit disconcerting to anyone born as far west as I had been.

19   "I'll finish with you later," I said.

20   "O.K.," he said, with that same unnerving readiness.

21   Something more immediate than our fathers' political inclinations operated to bring us closer together that morning. Miss Devron put the new boy in the empty seat just in front of me, and I spent the first few minutes of class watching his blue neck turn pink in the warm room, while the pupils drearily went through their recital of breakfasts eaten that morning.

22   "And now the new boy, Robert Bloom," said Miss Devron, smiling down at him. "What did he have this morning?"

23   He had been listening carefully to what was going on, and once, when he turned his profile to me, I could see that he was enjoying himself. The rest of the pupils had answered from their seats, but he stood up in the aisle. He stood at attention like a soldier.

24   "I had a cup of coffee and a snail, Ma'am."

25   There was a stony quiet for a second, and then the dazzling irreverence of what he had said burst through us with shock waves of pure delight. Miss Devron pounded on the desk with her ruler, and her red chins trembled in front of her like molten lava. "Class!" she cried. "Class, we'll have order here! Come to order. Come to order this instant!"

26   But she was trying to calm down a madhouse.

27   "A cup of coffee and a snail, please!" somebody shouted.

28   "Give me a worm with mine!" somebody yelled back.

29   And on we went, up that enticing road of suggestibility, until we were eating snakes on muffins. The special delight, of course, was the coffee. *There* was the alluring evil and joy of what he had said, because most of us in that room, including Miss Devron, were Mormons, who felt, in a way beyond reason, that murder was no more than a high-spirited lark compared to drinking coffee or smoking. It wasn't until Miss Devron and her ruler and the powers of light finally triumphed over the dark joy in us that we began to realize the outrageousness of what he had said. We slunk back from debauchery to righteousness

under Miss Devron's glowering eye, and finally he was left standing there, all alone before the glare of our joint indignation.

30   "We should never laugh at those who don't know better, class," Miss Devron began, in a carefully controlled voice. "We must share our knowledge with those less fortunate, and help them to know the truth. Robert comes from a part of the country where they don't know what we know about health. Now then, Robert, that can't be all you had for breakfast, can it?" She looked at him with the pity, the heart-spoken prayer, and the tenderness of a missionary meeting with a cannibal for the first time.

31   "No, Ma'am," he said. "I had two cups of coffee."

32   The tight breath gathered in our throats again, but Miss Devron was in control now, and aside from a few blown cheeks and red faces there was no sign that we were not with her in spirit.

33   "Now, class," she continued, "I want to ask Robert's pardon for what I'm about to do, but I think we can all learn a great deal from what he has told us and from what we can see. Very soon now Robert will be as big and strong as any of you, because he will soon be eating the right foods. But look at him now. See how small he is? *This* is what comes from not eating the right foods and from drinking coffee."

34   We looked him over, almost seeming to pass him from desk to desk, as if he were a mounted disease-carrying bug we were studying. But what a happy, smiling bug! To judge from his face, he considered the attention we gave him an unexpectedly hearty welcome to his new school.

35   "I don't think it's the coffee, Ma'am," he suddenly added. "My dad says I steal too many of his cigarettes."

36   During the next couple of minutes, Miss Devron could have fired salvos of cannon shells over our heads without getting our attention. We were like an oppressed people hailing with insane joy the coming of a revolutionary leader. Even the girls in the room were caught up in the exultation of our victory. All the cigars, cigarettes, or drinking straws filled with grains of coffee that any of us had smoked in secret, all our uneasy past abandonments to appetite, curiosity, and lawlessness were suddenly recalled and made glorious by Robert's cheerful confession. We worshipped him instantly, and at the end of the day a lot of us walked home with him, proud to be seen with such a man. We were walking along with him, swearing, talking about smoking, and making faces at the girls on the other side of the street, when he stopped and tapped me on the arm.

37   "How about this place?" he said, pointing to a strip of grass between two houses.

38   "What do you mean?" I asked.

39   "Your old man's voting for Hoover, isn't he?"

40   "Sure, but . . ."

41   "Well, let's fight."

42   I wanted no part of the fight now, but Robert insisted. He proceeded to

support his political views with a ferocity I couldn't seem to match, and it wasn't until he hit me a hard one in the eye that I brought my personal enthusiasm to the fight. From then on, my size and strength started getting the better of him, but no one in the group around us was shouting for me. Those who had been beside me that morning were now yelling for Robert to kill me, and I must say that he did his best. But I finally knocked him down and sat on top of him, and kept his shoulders pinned to the grass until he admitted that Hoover would win the election. When he was up again, he expressed some strong reservations about this opinion, but the election a few days later proved I was right, and, with our political differences out of the way, we became the best of friends.

43   For the next two or three weeks, Miss Devron tried her best to change Robert's breakfast habits, or at least to get him to lie a little in the interests of classroom harmony. But his incorruptible honesty soon inspired the rest of us to tell what we had really had for breakfast. Variety returned to the menu, and Miss Devron's discovery that some of the larger, healthier children, like me, frequently ate what tasted good for breakfast, instead of simply what was good for them, seemed to undermine her spirit. She acknowledged defeat one morning when she opened class by reading aloud to us from a book of dog stories by Albert Payson Terhune. Subsequently, she read to us whenever there were spare minutes in the day, and the breakfast lists were forgotten. From that time on, she was one of our favorite teachers.

44   My first idea about Robert's father was that he was a sailor in the United States Navy. Robert showed me pictures of him in a sailor suit—pictures in which he was leaning against a palm tree; laughing, with his arms around two girls; pulling a rope; scrubbing the deck of a ship; or standing on his hands, with a distant and smoking volcano framed between his spread legs. Then I learned that he was no longer in the Navy but was selling something—"selling something out on the road," as Robert described it. With only that imagination-tickling description, I developed the permanent expectation of turning a corner in the city someday and seeing Robert's father selling something right in the middle of the road. What he would be selling I couldn't imagine, nor had I a clear idea of how he would be doing it. Salesmen were never allowed in my own neighborhood, and the only prototype of Mr. Bloom I could conjure up was a man I had seen at the circus the year before. He had been standing outside one of the tents—a man with a dark face and a croaking voice, who kept urging us to come in, trying to scoop us up over his shoulder and into the dark tent with a dipping swing of his straw hat. "Selling, selling, selling!" my mother had said to my father. "It's plain disgusting." And so the man with the straw hat became Mr. Bloom, and I always had the feeling that Robert's house, too, was somehow disgusting. But it was also the most exciting house I had ever been in.

45   The excitement would hit me as soon as I entered the front door—usually

in the form of Robert's dog, an overgrown mongrel lummox called Buddy. I think he was mostly a police dog, but any remnants of purebred respectability had worn thin through long association with the underworld of back alleys and garbage cans, and through personal vice, for the dog was a hopeless drunkard. At least once a week, Robert and I would take a bottle of beer from his refrigerator (and how thrilling it was to me to be in a house containing anything so illegal and wicked as a bottle of beer!) and pour some of it out into a saucer for the dog. He would go at it with a ravenous thirst, frothing the beer with slaps from his scooping tongue until the white suds were all over the floor and his muzzle. He looked as if he were mad, and soon he would act mad. He would lurch around the house, bumping into chairs and tables, and endangering ashtrays and bric-a-brac in his weaving course. I would hold him by the collar at one end of the living room while Robert called him from the other end, and negotiating those fifteen feet of open rug held for him all the peril and adventure of a walk on a slippery deck in a typhoon. Once he had made it to safety, he would sit down, brace himself against a chair, and look at us triumphantly. We would never get him drunk when Robert's mother was around, of course. That was the one thing I ever saw her really angry about. But she was a person of such unquenchable joy and good cheer that even the sight of Buddy drunk that one time didn't keep her angry for long.

46   She came home from town unexpectedly that day. Buddy's flank had just crashed into a floor lamp and Robert was juggling it back to equilibrium when his mother walked in the front door.

47   "Robert, have you got that dog drunk again?" she asked, after one look.

48   "Yes, Mom."

49   His truthfulness, both at school and at home, always amazed me. For me the truth was usually a fearful thing; my telling it often seemed to hurt my father or my mother, or someone else. But Robert was dauntless before it.

50   "I've *told* you not to, Robert," Mrs. Bloom said. "You know I have. Poor Buddy! Just look at him. That's no way to treat a dog."

51   We all looked at him, and I, at least, was conscience-stricken at what we had done. But none of us could remain remorseful for long. Deep in his cups, Buddy had misgauged the size and slipperiness of the low black leather hassock in front of the rocking chair, and though he had managed to plant one haunch on it, it kept sliding off. He would edge it back momentarily, his happy face conveying to all of us his certainty that he was seated there foursquare and in perfect dignity. I don't know what there was about him—perhaps a certain slack-jawed serenity—but we all started laughing helplessly at the same time. Robert's mother threw herself onto the couch, and Robert and I rolled on the floor in our laughter, while Buddy watched us out of one open eye.

52   She recovered enough after a time to continue her scolding, but she couldn't get more than a few words out without looking at Buddy, and then she would laugh again. Finally, she gave us some cookies and milk, and poured out a big

saucerful of thick cream for Buddy, which she said would sober him faster than anything else. While Robert was drinking his milk at the kitchen table, she came up behind him and slipped her arms under his and clasped her hands on his chest. She kissed him on his neck and on his cheek and up into his hair, and all this time he went on eating his cookies and drinking his milk. I hardly dared to look at them, but I *had* to see the way she kissed him. She was a young woman, with long, dark hair, and black eyes that opened very suddenly at times, then closed very slowly, the lids seeming to take great pleasure in their long trip back down. The nails of her fingers, clasped on Robert's chest, were buffed to a high polish, and her lips were full and red, and looked wonderfully soft against Robert's cheek. I was the fifth, and youngest, child in my family, and I had only been pecked at gingerly by thin lips pulled tight against clenched teeth, and now I could almost feel that cushioned touch of Robert's mother's kiss on my own cheek. I had no name for the feeling it gave me. I was simply fascinated.

53   She straightened up, put her hand to the back of her hair, and walked to the refrigerator again. "Boys, boys, boys!" she said. "Little devils, all of you. Little heartless devils, getting dogs drunk, pulling girls' hair, fighting, swearing. You're no good, any of you." As she said it, she dug two big scoops of applesauce out of a bowl and slapped them into two dishes.

54   "So why do I like you so much?" she said to me as she leaned over the table to put a dish in front of me. She was wearing the kind of low dress she usually wore, but I didn't dare look away from her face. I just looked at her smile, and that was everywhere. Then she leaned over and kissed my forehead.

55   By the time I left her home, Buddy was on his feet and feeling well enough to walk to the corner with Robert and me.

56   "I like your mother," I said.

57   "Ah, she's all right," he said, leveling his toe at a rock and kicking it out into the street.

58   "You bet she's all right. I'd like to marry her when I grow up."

59   "She's already married."

60   "I know she is. My gosh, don't I know that? I just said I'd like to, that's all."

61   We stood on the corner and kicked a few more rocks into the street. And then we were just standing there. Suddenly there was between us a strip of that infinite desolation that surrounds and crisscrosses life, which children must face without the comfort of philosophy or the retreat of memory.

62   Robert slapped the dog on the side as hard as he could. "Come on, you," he said to him, and I stood and watched them run down the street. I wondered why he never seemed to like the dog except when we got him drunk. I would have given anything for him, but it had been made clear to me at home long before that our yard was too beautiful to be ruined by a "dirty dog."

63 Besides Buddy, and Robert's mother, with whom I fell more and more in love as I sampled her cakes, home-canned fruit, dill pickles, candy, sandwiches, and lemonade, there were other charms at Robert's house that made my own seem intolerably dreary. Although it as nearly Christmas and I had known Robert for more than two months, I still hadn't met his father, and yet I had come to feel that I knew him as well as my own, or even better. My father's actual physical arrival at home, after a day spent seeing patients in his office or operating at the hospital or attending a church meeting, was the main thing that impressed his existence upon me. He was so neat, so disciplined in his habits, and so completely without vices, eccentricities, or hobbies that he carried himself completely with him wherever he went. But Robert's father lay scattered about the house in the form of pipes, fishing equipment, shotguns, whiskey bottles locked in a glass-front cabinet, a tennis racket, a set of rusty golf clubs, and a three-foot-long Chinese beheading sword, with a dragon engraved on the length of the blade and a dull, pewtery stain on the bright steel, which Robert said was blood. His father had brought the sword home from China when he was in the Navy, and it hung, with its handle wrapped in cords of scarlet silk, above the bed that he and Robert's mother slept in. I was so taken by the sword at that time that I thought anyone would die of pride to have it hanging above his bed, but I now see what a generous concession to his male taste it was for her to have it there. I remember the room as delicately feminine in décor, but it was his room, too, and he had chosen the exact thing to put his mark on it that I would have chosen if I had been married to Robert's mother.

64   Mr. Bloom did come home occasionally, but even then I didn't get to see him. He was sleeping, Robert would say, going on to explain how tired a salesman becomes after several weeks on the road. On two or three such afternoons, Robert's mother was also not to be seen, and he told me that she, too, was taking a nap and that we were to tiptoe carefully when we went past the closed door to their bedroom.

65 Christmas morning came and I was downstairs at 5 A.M., tearing into my carefully wrapped presents with impatient, greedy hands. The unexpected child of my parents' middle age, with all my brothers and sisters grown up and living away from home, I had spent the early hours of the past three Christmases all by myself, and I am certain that the pain of a child getting up on Christmas morning to find nothing under the tree cannot be much worse than the pain of one who finds everything there but has no one to show it to. It was not that my parents were really unfeeling. Indeed, they carefully kept my belief in Santa Claus alive beyond the customary age of disillusionment, perhaps because I *was* the last and much the youngest child—even telling me that all my Christmas presents, except for some clothing from my mother, had come from Santa Claus. But it never occurred to them to get up early on Christmas morning in order to share my excitement, and I can still remember the sick emptiness of the

hour and a half between my discovery of my presents and the first sound of someone else stirring in the house. That year, as usual, I finally heard the maid come upstairs from her basement room, and for the next ten minutes I held her captive while I gloated over each new addition to my wealth.

66   "Santa was certainly generous to you," she said, and it was so true that I didn't at all mind her saying it in the middle of a yawn.

67   "Look what Santa Claus left me!" I was able to say to my parents at last, when they came down for breakfast. I had been particularly struck that year by the great number of things he had given me compared to what my mother had given me, and I emphasized this difference by putting his gifts to me and hers in two piles, side by side. But a peck on the cheek and a cursory smile were all the tribute my parents paid to me, Christmas, and Santa Claus's generosity before they opened their own small presents from me, with an air of rather hasty embarrassment, and then turned to the newspaper and to breakfast.

68   Still, this year I knew someone who would take a second look at what I had received. It took some tight crowding, but I managed to tie all my presents onto my new sled with my new lariat, and I departed for Robert's house. I wasn't disappointed. Not only did Robert's eyes pop at some of the individual presents and at the sheer mass of what I had been given but his mother and, yes, his father, too, were as excited as Robert himself. Mr. Bloom, who got down on the floor to play with my new hook-and-ladder fire engine, turned out to be just the sort of man I had expected. He liked the fire engine so much that I wanted to give it to him, except that the idea of giving it up hurt too much. Out of this dilemma came a sudden inspiration to ask him if he would like to trade his sword for my fire engine. I was circling carefully about this idea, trying to approach it in the best way, when something happened to destroy the notion utterly.

69   It was not surprising that none of us had paid much attention to Robert's gifts during the first few minutes I was there. All three of the Blooms were too polite not to have gone all out to admire a sledful of gifts dumped into the middle of their living room by a guest as greedy for appreciation as I was. They would have done this even if my presents had come from the ten-cent store. But my gifts were both costly and impressive, and the Blooms, in their modest circumstances, had no need to be just polite; quite simply, they all gave in to the dream of having enough money to buy what I spread out before them, and wholly enjoyed themselves with my presents. I was too far lost in their appreciation to remember that Robert had also had a Christmas that day. But he soon reminded me of it.

70   "Look!" he said to me. He held in his cupped hands a bright, gold-colored wheel, suspended on a silver axle within a framework of two intersecting wire circles.

71   "What the heck *is* it?" I asked.

72   Robert's mother and father were both down on the floor with us, and

while Robert threaded a length of green string through a hole in the axle and then wound it carefully along the axle's length, I could feel their eyes looking from me to the wheel and back, excitedly waiting for my reaction. Then Robert gave the wound-up string a sudden vigorous pull, putting the muscles of his back and arm and the tension of his clenched teeth and closed eyes into it, and brought the top spinning to life. The golden wheel hummed softly within its unmoving world of wire circles. Robert placed the top carefully on the smooth surface of a box lid, and there it rested, poised on its projecting tip like a dancer on one leg.

73   "Watch," he said, and he picked up the wonderful toy and rested its cupped tip on the point of a pencil his father held up. Once the top was spinning there, Robert pushed it, a fraction of an inch at a time, until it was no longer a continuation of the pencil's length but was hanging horizontally out over space, held from falling only by the quiet humming and the touch of the pencil point on the cup.

74   "My *gosh!*" I said. "Where'd you get that?"

75   "Mom gave it to me."

76   "It's called a gyroscope," she said.

77   For the next five or ten minutes, we shared the excitement of watching the gyroscope ignore gravity in every position we could devise. I was ready to trade Robert all the solid excitement of my presents for the magic that I could feel spring to life when I pulled the green string. I held the gyroscope in my hand and laughed to feel that quiet, determined will fighting mine as I tipped the wheel away from the path it had chosen in the air. And then, suddenly, the magic would be gone and I would be left holding the toy dead in my hands.

78   "And what did your father give you?" I asked, staring down at the wheel.

79   "That Chinese beheading sword."

80   I gave him back the top, but I couldn't look at him. I could feel the cold, sharp edge of that sword in me.

81   "Where is it?" I asked at last.

82   "He hung it over my bed."

83   "Let's see it."

84   We stepped around the scattered toys and went into his bedroom. There is was, hanging over his bed, just as I had dreamed it might hang over mine.

85   "I'm not to touch it until I'm older, but she's all mine," Robert said.

86   I could easily have cried. My mother had given me ties, socks, gloves, shirts, pants, shoes, underwear—all the things a boy could easily do without. But Robert's mother had given him a gyroscope! And the sword had come from his father, while I didn't even think that my father had given me anything! I seemed to have only one real friend right then.

87   "What did Santa Claus bring you?" I asked.

88   "Santa Claus? *Santa Claus*?" he hooted. "There isn't any Santa Claus, you big dummy!"

89   I had heard there wasn't—but only speculatively, never with this final, crushing authority. I could think of only one way to defend myself against Robert's having everything and my not having even Santa Claus. I hit him twice, once on the chest and once in the face, and then I tied all my presents onto my sled with my lariat and started out of the living room, refusing to answer any of the questions his parents asked me. Robert followed me onto the porch, and when I was half a block away he called out to me, "What did you hit me for?"

90   "Shut up!" I yelled back, and I went home and put my presents under the tree for my relatives to see when they came around later.

91   Most of the rifts of childhood are as troubled, as tearing, and as quickly smoothed over as the wake of a small motorboat, and by the time Christmas vacation came to an end I had accepted the death of another illusion and Robert had forgotten my naïveté. We went on as before, with the abrasive honesty of his life wearing away at the hypocrisy of my own until I, too, occasionally knew some emotional truths. With that encouragement of truth which had been given him at home, he was quite free to say, for example, that he liked or disliked this or that person, this or that book, or a threatening gray or a clear blue sky. But I knew no such freedom. Caught within the attitude that this world was God's green acre and too sacred to be regarded critically by the likes of me, I wasn't free to decide whether I liked a dog better than a cat, or a mountain better than a rosebush. Any expression of vital choice on my part was seen as a blasphemous elevation and denigration of two aspects of the divine order, and, pressed down by the weight of my blasphemy, I lost the power to make any choice. But Robert restored this power during the next year of our friendship. He restored it with a series of shocks that showed me that what he had said about something and what I felt about it, way down, were often related. How exhilarating it was to have him come out with a truth that my bones knew but my tongue could not say!

92   "What do you think of Miss Brown?" I might ask him, speaking about the elementary-school art teacher.

93   "She's a nice lady," he answered, "but she doesn't know anything about art."

94   My heart pounded with the truth of what he had said. I half knew she didn't know anything about art, but she had been put in our classroom by authority as an art teacher, so it was certain that I must be wrong about her. "What do you mean, she doesn't know anything about art?" I asked—on his side, of course, but still fearful.

95   "All she draws is mountains," he said disgustedly. "Never people, or dogs, or flowers, or trees, or boats, or water, or houses, or clouds, or *anything* but mountains. And it's always the same mountain. You should have seen the teacher I had in New York. She could draw a face on the board in two seconds and everyone knew who it was. Boy, was she an artist!"

96   If I was impressed at the time by the fearlessness of what Robert knew and said, it is only now that I can appreciate the full miracle of his freshness surviving the hothouse atmosphere of souls under cultivation for adulthood that existed in our third- and fourth-grade classrooms. Having known Robert, I now seriously believe that the right sort of parents can emotionally equip a child to survive the "civilizing" process of education. But my real appreciation of Robert came mostly in retrospect, and most of whatever I now know about truth I had to learn the hard way, for in the late winter of our fourth-grade year—about a year and a half after our friendship started—I cut myself off from the hope that Robert would go on indefinitely helping me find the truth.

97   It was one of those false spring days that sometimes appear toward the end of winter—a sad, nostalgic day, when the air teased our bodies with the promise of games and picnics, and the earth was still locked up and unavailable for our use, beneath two feet of grimy snow. Robert and I were walking home together. "Mom just put up some more dill pickles last night," he said, and suddenly the day came alive.

98   "First one there gets the biggest," I said, and, with my longer legs, I was on the porch while Robert was still pounding up the sidewalk. We pushed the living-room door open, and when we weren't hit in the chest by a flying, dancing Buddy, we both understood the sign. Whenever Robert's father was out of town, his mother tried to keep Buddy in the house as a watchdog—I suppose on the theory that he might possibly trip up an intruder and break his neck as he frisked about him in indiscriminate welcome. But when Buddy was absent—off on some disreputable scavenging trip, no doubt—it usually meant that Mr. Bloom was home. Robert and I now peered out the back living-room window and saw the car in front of the garage, and he lifted his fingers to his lips. "Come on," he whispered. "Let's go into the kitchen."

99   We tiptoed past the closed door of his parents' bedroom and past the open door of his own bedroom. As usual, I looked in and saw the sword still hanging over his bed. The sharp pain of Robert's ownership of that sword had been replaced in me by a kind of dull wonder at his exasperating sense of honor. "No, I can't touch it until I'm twelve," he had insisted a dozen or more times that past year—times when nothing in the world but a three-foot-long Chinese beheading sword was appropriate to the game at hand. Now, in the kitchen, Robert whispered, "We better not have any pickles without asking Mom. Boy, was she ever mad the last time we ate them all! How about some apricot jam and bread?"

100   "Swell," I whispered back.

101   "Hey, would you rather have apricot or strawberry?" he whispered from the depths of the icebox.

102   "Let's have both," I said, regaining some of the excitement I had lost in my disappointment over the pickles.

103   He brought out the two jam jars, spooned large helpings of each kind

into a bowl, and began whipping them together with a fork. I stared, hypnotized, at the clean colors as they ran together and faded to a pinkish tan. "Boy, are you ever lucky!" I said. "Eating any old thing you want when you want! Do you think my mother, or that old maid of ours, would let me eat *anything* between meals? No, sir! Our maid says you're spoiled because you're an only child and your mother doesn't know any better."

104   "Well, maybe," he said, shaking fist-size globs of jam onto the bread. "But Mom told me they're going to try and get me a baby brother or a baby sister pretty soon."

105   "A baby brother or sister? Which kind would you rather have?"

106   "Oh, I don't care. They're both O.K., I guess." He returned the jars to the icebox, and came back to the table and picked up his bread and jam. "How about taking these out on the front porch to eat?"

107   "O.K."

108   We crept past the closed bedroom door again and went out on the porch, being careful not to let the door slam behind us. When we were comfortably settled on the front steps, with our mouths full of bread and jam, I suddenly decided to ask him a question that had occurred to me many times. "Robert, is there something wrong with your mother and father?"

109   "What do you mean, 'something wrong'?" he asked.

110   "Well, you know. The way they're always resting when we come here. Are they sick?"

111   It seemed to me that they must certainly be sick, or something more than sick. For me, bed was a concept that changed entirely with the time of day. Bed at night was a completely respectable thing, both for myself and for my parents—so respectable, in fact, that I usually put up a spirited fight against going to it. But after the sun rose over the high, gray mountains east of town, bed instantly became something slack and irresponsible, even on weekend mornings, when there was no immediate reason for getting out of it. "What?" my father would say, standing over me at seven o'clock on a rainy Saturday morning. "Not up yet?" He never said it harshly but always with a friendly smile, kept just thin enough to give me the message that bed simply wasn't the place to be at that hour. So grave was this obscure crime that even when I was sick enough to stay in bed all day, I dreaded the long morning and afternoon hours there, and never wholly relaxed until it was 8 P.M. again and really time for bed. If there was one aspect of the irregularity of Robert's house that I did not enjoy, it was this matter of bed in the afternoon. There *was* something sick about it.

112   "Heck, no, they're not sick," Robert said. "Dad gets tired out on the road. I *told* you that. And Mom likes to be with him. They're just taking a nap. Or maybe they're trying to find me that baby brother."

113   I stopped in the middle of a bite and stared at him. If he had spoken the last words in Latin he could not have lost me more completely.

114   "They're trying to find a baby? In *there*?"

115   "Well, of course," he said, stuffing the last of his bread and jam into his mouth. And then the full extent of my darkness must have shown on my face. He swallowed with a little choking cough. "Oh, my gosh!" he said. "You don't know about *that,* either, do you?"

116   "Of course I know about it," I said angrily. "I just didn't know what you meant."

117   But I couldn't cover up my ignorance or my need to know the truth, for he proceeded to tell me all about it. He told me in adequate detail and finished by saying that all babies were "found" in just this way.

118   *All* babies?"

119   "Yep—me, you, everybody. That's the way everybody's parents get their children."

120   I jumped up, and, seeing the expression on my face, Robert stood up, too, and then I hit him twice—once on the chest to knock him down and once on the nose as he was falling. In its most impersonal sense, the idea he had given me was just barely tolerable, but in relation to my parents it was an unthinkable blasphemy. After all they had done for me, hitting him seemed the very least I could do. I stood over him, breathing hard and with my fists clenched. He looked up at me from the top step, where he had fallen, and slowly rubbed his nose.

121   "You big damn dumb!" he said at last. "I'll never tell you another thing as long as I live!"

122   "You just better not," I said. "You just better never say another word to me if you know what's good for you!"

123   And he never did. From that day forward, I was on my own.

☐ Discovering Meaning and Technique

1. "Not Another Word" is a story told from the point of view of the narrator. Is the narrator a child or an adult?

2. Thurman develops the story through a series of conflicts. Name as many as you can.

3. Explain what Thurman means when he writes that "with such tactics" Miss Devron "soon taught us to lie" (paragraph 4).

4. Explain why Robert Bloom is viewed by the other students and especially by Paul Adam as a hero. Is he a likely hero?

5. Contrast the two boys' home life and Christmases.

6. How does Robert's truthfulness make Paul face reality (except for the one reality he could not face)?

7. The story falls into several episodes. What are they?

8. Is the phrase "the obsessive honesty of his life wearing away at the hypocrisy of my own" (paragraph 91) the thread that holds the story together? If so, why?

9. Thurman sometimes makes interesting comparisons. He writes, for example, that Miss Devron "placed the index finger of her left hand like a hot dog between her second and third chin" (paragraph 3). Can you find other examples of comparisons?

10. It is not always easy to recognize symbols. A bird, a cloud, a torn letter may be nothing more than a part of the scenery. At times, however, an object takes on additional importance and meaning. In this story, is the sword a symbol? If so, of what?

☐ Writing Suggestions

1. Relate a conflict you have had with another child.

2. Contrast your family with another that you envied.

3. According to Thurman, "The right sort of parents can emotionally equip a child to survive the 'civilizing' process of education" (paragraph 96). Does the statement by Thurman give you an idea for a composition?

4. Does dialogue make a story more realistic? To support your opinion, you could rewrite a passage from the story to eliminate the dialogue. Discuss which version is more effective—the rewrite or the original.

■ Combining Sources in a Composition

1. Stone maintains that family stories are important to an individual's sense of self. Explain how this idea relates to other selections in this section.

2. Family relationships, even close ones, can differ drastically from individual to individual. Contrast the relationship between Giovanni and her grandmother, Baker and his uncle, Houston and his father, Sister and Stella-Rondo, Tisdale and her father.

3. Using the selections by Angelou and Giovanni as source material, contrast life among rural and urban blacks in the South of the 1940s.

4. Several writers included in this section have enlivened their work with eccentric characters. What is it about eccentrics that make us smile? Consider, for example, Miss Devron in "Not Another Word"; the strange old ladies in "Where the World Began"; Mr. Ector in "400 Mulvaney Street;" and Uncle Rondo in "Why I Live at the P.O."

5. Many elementary school teachers use show-and-tell as a part of the educational process, as seen in Lopate, Galarza, and Thurman. Do you think this technique is effective?

6. Using the selections by Lopate, Galarza, Bishop, and Thurman as source material, discuss the effects that teachers can have on their students.

7. Several selections focus on typical youthful conflicts: Lopate, Angelou, Dillard, and Houston with adults; Updike and Thurman with other children. What do these conflicts contribute to growing up?

8. Gift-giving appears as a strong element in Angelou and Thurman. Discuss the tradition. What makes one gift more meaningful than another?

9. Robert in "Not Another Word" and Updike's friend C in "Three Boys" seem to be unlikely heroes—and yet they are. What qualities in a friend do you find heroic?

10. The school buildings described by Lopate, Bishop, and Angelou are not modern or physically appealing. What is the importance of the physical condition of a school building?

■ □ ■

■ ■ ■

■ ■ ■

C H A P T E R 2

TRADITIONS
Rituals and Celebrations

■ ■ ■

CHRISTMAS AND OTHER
FESTIVALS OF CONSUMPTION

□ DANIEL J. BOORSTIN

[1] In 1939, while the nation's business still suffered from the Depression, the month of November happened to have five Thursdays and Thanksgiving Day was scheduled to fall on November 30. But celebration of the holiday on the traditional last Thursday would have been unfortunate for the nation's merchants. With business lagging, they needed every fillip they could find, and by tradition the Christmas shopping season did not begin until the day after Thanksgiving. In New York City, Detroit, and elsewhere, the opening of the season was customarily marked by a Christmas-oriented Thanksgiving Day parade. It is not surprising, then, that under the circumstances an enterprising Ohio department-store owner, Fred Lazarus, Jr., proposed that the nation move the celebration of Thanksgiving to the earlier Thursday, November 23, which would add a whole week to the "Christmas shopping" season. The Ohio State Council of Retail Merchants and the Cincinnati *Enquirer* endorsed the idea. In Washington, President Franklin D. Roosevelt greeted the suggestion with enthusiasm, and proclaimed that in 1939 Thanksgiving should come on November 23.

2   President Roosevelt's "tampering with the calendar" (like the establishing of Standard Time a half-century before) was labeled by some as an interference with the divine order, but within a few years, all the states had fallen in line by enacting Thanksgiving as the fourth Thursday. Only a few continued to declare their independence from federal fiat by authorizing a Thanksgiving holiday on both the fourth and the last Thursday.

3   It was a little-known oddity of American life that the United States, unlike other nations, actually had no "national" holidays established by law. Under the federal system the legalizing of holidays had been left to the states. The President's only power over holidays was to issue proclamations focusing national attention and to give a day off to federal employees in the District of Columbia and elsewhere. Thanksgiving had grown up simply as a national custom. President Lincoln in 1863 was the first to issue a presidential Thanksgiving proclamation, and then the legal holiday was created by separate laws in each of the states. This trivial shift in the date of President Roosevelt's proclamation of a national Thanksgiving was significant mainly for what it revealed of the American Christmas; and for what it told of the transformation of this ancient festival into an American Festival of Consumption.

4   In the eyes of the early New England Puritans, Christmas was a menace to the pure Christian spirit. Fearing "popish" idolatry, the General Court of Massachusetts in 1659 passed an act punishing with a fine of five shillings for each offense "anybody who is found observing, by abstinence from labor, feasting, or any other way, any such days as Christmas day." By 1681 they felt secure enough against "popery" to repeal the law, but they still feared giving the day any ritualistic significance. In his diary for 1685, Judge Samuel Sewall, for example, expressed his satisfaction that on Christmas day he saw everybody conducting business as usual. During the next two centuries, while Christmas was somehow American- ized, it still remained a simple folk holiday marked by no grand religious obser- vance and with little commercial significance. The season is hardly recognizable, for example, in the pages of the New York *Tribune* for the month of December 1841, which are barren of flashy Christmas advertising and simply repeat the unchanging copy which merchants had run for months. In a few instances when gifts are mentioned, they are referred to as "Christmas and New Year's" presents; Santa Claus has not yet entered the Christmas scene.

5   By the era of the Civil War the old festival, characterized by folksy convivial- ity, was beginning to be transformed. There were signs that the holiday was on its way to becoming a spectacular nationwide Festival of Consumption. On Decem- ber 24, 1867, the first Christmas Eve when R. H. Macy's remained open until midnight, the store set a record with one-day receipts of $6,000. In 1874 Macy's offered its first promotional window displays to have an exclusively Christmas motif, featuring the Macy collection of dolls, and from then on the Christmas windows became an annual institution. During the next years, those Macy depart-

ments whose volume depended heavily on the Christmas trade increased their share of the store's total sales. Other department stores, too, began the practice of staying open late during the last two weeks before Christmas. December began to become the big month for retailers, and by 1870, December sales were already double those of May, the next best month.

6   Still, in 1880 Christmas was so undeveloped that a manufacturer of Christmas-tree ornaments had difficulty persuading F. W. Woolworth to take $25 worth of his product. Within a few years Woolworth's annual order of Christmas-tree ornaments from this supplier alone came to $800,000. In the next half-century, he drew on numerous suppliers and his orders totaled $25 million. "This is our harvest time," Woolworth instructed his store managers in December 1891. "Make it pay."

> Give your store a holiday appearance. Hang up Christmas ornaments. Perhaps have a tree in the window. Make the store look different. . . . This is also a good time to work off "stickers" or unsalable goods, for they will sell during the excitement when you could not give them away other times. Mend all broken toys and dolls every day.

By 1899 Woolworth's Christmas trade was reaching a half-million dollars. In order to avert a strike at that crucial time of year, Woolworth introduced a system of Christmas bonuses ($5 for each year of service, with a limit of $25).

7   The mail-order houses began to issue special Christmas catalogues. At the 1939 Christmas season Montgomery Ward and Company gave away 2.4 million copies of "Rudolph the Red-Nosed Reindeer," a versified story written by an employee in their advertising department. Gene Autry's singing version became a runaway best-selling record.

8   Display type was used for Christmas advertising even before it became common for other purposes. Newspaper advertising peaked in December, and then fell off sharply after Christmas. By 1910 more than one third of the nation's annual output of books was being delivered in the six weeks before Christmas. Before mid-century, one quarter of the whole year's jewelry purchases were being made in December.

9   The Christmas Club, which first appeared in 1910, was an arrangement by which a person deposited a specified amount every week during the year, to be accumulated in a special savings account for withdrawal at Christmas time. By 1950 there were more than 10 million members of such clubs in 6,200 banks, in all states of the Union; and their deposits for the year exceeded $950 million.

10   With the passing decades of the twentieth century, Christmas became overwhelmingly a season of shopping. Gifts which first had the force of good manners actually acquired the force of law. The Christmas bonus (soon "expected but not appreciated") became a part of the anticipated compensation of employees. In 1951, when a firm reduced its Christmas bonus and the union appealed to

the National Labor Relations Board, the board ruled the "Christmas" bonus to be not in fact a gift at all. The employer, they said, was not free to discontinue this practice. Christmas gifts to policemen, mailmen, janitors, and others tended to become a kind of insurance against poor service during the coming year. And the "executive gift" sometimes became a convenient device for evading the laws of bribery.

11 One of the most distinctive features of the American Christmas was Santa Claus, who was speedily transformed out of all recognition from his Old World character. There had been a real St. Nicholas, a fourth-century bishop of Myra in Asia Minor, who became the patron saint of Russia, and of mariners, thieves, virgins, and children. According to legend, St. Nicholas had saved three poor virgins from being forced to sell their virtue, by throwing a purse of gold through their windows on three successive nights.

12 In the United States, St. Nicholas early became a familiar figure of folklore and pseudo-folklore. His earliest conspicuous appearance in American literature was in Washington Irving's *Knickerbocker's History of New York* (1809), where St. Nicholas traveled through the skies in a wagon, and began to acquire some of his other features. The American Santa Claus's rotund figure, jolly mien, and white beard were conferred on him by Thomas Nast in his series of Christmas drawings for *Harper's Weekly* beginning in 1863. By the late nineteenth century, "belief" in Nast's Santa Claus had become a symbol of childhood innocence and adult warm-heartedness.

13 No sooner had Santa become the patron saint of a Saturnalia for children, "bringing treasures for the little rogues," than he was elevated to patron of a nationwide Saturnalia of consumption. The department store was the proper habitat of *Santa Claus Americanus.* And he above all others was responsible for moving the primary scene of the festival from the church to the department store. By 1914 a well-organized Santa Claus Association, with headquarters in New York City, had as its object "to preserve Children's faith in Santa Claus." The association aimed to secure from the post office the letters addressed to Santa Claus and then reply to them in the name of Santa with letters or gifts. When there was public objection, postal authorities intervened. "All I ask," the founder of the association urged, "is that these people don't sock it to us at this time of the year and spoil the faith of little children."

14 Widespread demand led to the founding of "schools" for "real" Santa Clauses. The curriculum of the first such school (in Albion, New York) included indoctrination in the history of Santa Claus, dressing for the role, wearing beards, handling children, and other special techniques. A firm called Santa's Helpers rented out trained Santas for special occasions. In 1948 the City Council of Boston, acting on the complaint of a council member that "there is a Santa on every corner and children are beginning to wonder," formally requested the mayor to "permit only one Santa in the city in 1949 and to station him on the historic Boston

Common." A bill in the California Senate in 1939 (required, a senator explained, by the sight of Santas "selling everything from bottled beer to automobiles") aimed legally to restrict the use of Santa's image.

15   "Belief" in Santa Claus was widely defended. A sentimental editorial, "Yes, Virginia, There Is a Santa Claus!," became the classic declaration of faith for agnostic Americans. When a savings bank in Muskegon, Michigan, displayed a sign in 1949 declaring "There Is No Santa Claus—Work—Earn—Save," local parents protested. And when the sign was removed, the bank president wryly commented, "The myth of Santa Claus is far-reaching and implies a nation of people who seem to accept a Santa Claus with headquarters at Washington." Judges issued facetious opinions from the bench *(ex parte Santa Claus)* to defend Santa, and held in contempt of court those who impugned him.

16   A few dared to put Santa Claus in the tradition of the great American hoaxes. But psychiatrists, the new authorities on national myths, could not take him so lightly. One solemnly declared that "any child who believes in Santa Claus has had his ability to think permanently injured." Others diagnosed the Santa myth as a symptom of parental insecurity, although some, including the influential Dr. Arnold Gesell, were not unduly alarmed.

17   The Christmas tree, too, acquired a special American character, and with its numerous accessories it became a significant seasonal industry. One story is that trimmed trees were first introduced to the United States during the Revolution by Hessian soldiers trying to recreate here the holiday of their homeland. In the nineteenth century the Christmas-tree custom was widespread in northern Europe. But the elaboration and electrification, and finally the syntheticizing of the Christmas tree, were reserved for the United States. By 1948 about 28 million Christmas trees were being distributed annually in the United States. The 100,000 acres devoted to Christmas trees were producing a crop valued at $50 million annually. At least after Woolworth began featuring Christmas-tree decorations in the 1880's, the business of decorations, ornaments and accessories flourished. The Christmas tree was officially recognized in 1923 when the President began the practice of lighting a tree on the White House lawn. Raising trees became more profitable with the development of the ingenious technique of "stump-culture" (by which the tree was severed above live-branch whorls, leaving a pruned number of these to grow, in turn, into trees for the next season). But the rising prices of trees, together with fire hazards and a growing interest in forest conservation, combined to create a new market for synthetic, plastic reusable Christmas trees.

18   Another thriving American industry—greeting cards—was a by-product of the American Christmas. Louis Prang, a sixteen-year-old refugee from the German revolutions, came to New York in 1850, acquired a reputation as a lithographer, and pioneered in making colored lithographs of famous works of art (he christened them "chromos" and the name stuck) which he sold for $6 apiece. In 1875 he

applied his techniques to producing colorful cards for Christmas, and these came to be esteemed as works of art. Prang's elegant eight-color chromos of the Nativity, of children, young women, flowers, birds, and butterflies (a few, too, of Santa Claus) gave a certain tone to the practice of sending greeting cards at Christmas and dominated the market until about 1890. When the Christmas card was democratized by the import of cheaper cards from Germany, Prang retired from the business, but even less expensive cards of American make recaptured the market within another twenty years. By the early twentieth century the practice of sending Christmas cards, and then other greeting cards, had become widespread. By mid-century, about 1.5 billion Christmas greeting cards were being sold each season.

19   As the custom became more widespread, cards tended to become less and less religious in motif. The message, even in Prang's first deluxe items, had never been predominantly religious. The friendly secularized texts became acceptable to Jews and others who did not subscribe to such theological message as still remained in the American Christmas.

20   Americans found other ingenious ways to elide religious issues in order to share in the national Festival of Consumption. While the Rabbinical Assembly of America in 1946 protested the school practice of singing Christmas carols as an infringement of freedom of religion, the Jews themselves helped "solve" the problem. They promoted Chanukah, historically only a minor Jewish festival, into a kind of Jewish Christmas, with *eight* gift-giving days. More than one Jewish child probably asked, "Mother, dear, are we having Chanukah for Christmas?"

21   In a nation of consumption communities, there was a tendency for all festivals somehow to become Festivals of Consumption. Mother's Day was an example.

22   Something like a Mother's Day—the fourth Sunday before Easter, a day to honor Mary, the mother of Jesus—had been observed in European countries. "Mothering Sunday" was when servants and apprentices were given a day off to "go a-mothering," to go visit their mothers. Sometimes the eldest son would bring his mother a "mothering cake," which was then shared by the family. There appears to be no evidence that Mother's Day was an American holiday before 1907. In that year an enterprising young lady from West Virginia, Anna Jarvis, much attached to her mother who had died two years before, consulted the Philadelphia merchant John Wanamaker about a suitable way to honor the nation's mothers. He advised her to campaign for a national observance. Helped by evangelists, newspaper editors, and politicians, the campaign for a nationwide Mother's Day quickly succeeded. The governor of West Virginia issued the first Mother's Day proclamation in 1912, and the Mother's Day International Association was founded. On May 9, 1914, pursuant to a Congressional Resolution, President Wilson issued the first presidential Mother's Day proclamation urging that the flag be flown on that day.

23   The simple old "mothering cake" was transmuted into a whole range of

Mother's Day gift merchandise. The practice of noting the day by going to church (wearing a red carnation for a living mother or a white carnation for one deceased) blossomed into a bonanza for telegraph and telephone companies, candy shops, florists, jewelers, and cosmetic manufacturers. Like other American festivals which had originated in church, Mother's Day too ended in the department store.

24   In 1934, when retailers needed every possible stimulus to business, Postmaster General James A. Farley ordered a Mother's Day stamp showing Whistler's "Mother." The stamp, said to have been personally designed by President Roosevelt, actually offered a cropped and barely recognizable version of Whistler's well-known painting, which had been improved for the purpose by a vase of carnations prominently added in the lower left-hand corner. While the American Artists' Professional League objected to this "mutilation" of Whistler's painting, Anna Jarvis, the mother of Mother's Day, went personally to the Postmaster General to protest the transformation of her holiday into an advertisement for the florists' trade. She finally secured an apology. On the occasion of Mother's Day 1961 (according to a retail association estimate), more than 55 million families bought Mother's Day gifts for a total of some $875 million.

25   It is not surprising, then, that there was also to be a Father's Day, and the authorship of this idea was claimed by many. In 1910 a lady in Spokane, Washington, supported by William Jennings Bryan, began to campaign for a Father's Day; in 1916 President Wilson pressed a button in Washington to open the Spokane celebration. In June 1921 the governor of Virginia was persuaded to proclaim a Father's Day by a young lady who in 1932 registered the name "National Father's Day Association" with the United States Patent Office. Then, in 1935, a National Father's Day Committee was established "dedicated to building a democratic world through wholesome child upbringing." The prime mover for this holiday, Mrs. John Bruce Dodd, unlike the founder of Mother's Day, was not troubled by the danger of commercialization or the practice of making the day a time for gifts. "After all," she observed, "why should the greatest giver of gifts not be on the receiving end at least once a year?" The gift idea, she explained, was "a sacred part of the holiday, as the giver is spiritually enriched in the tribute paid his father."

☐ Discovering Meaning and Technique

1. What was the motive for moving Thanksgiving to the fourth Thursday in November?

2. What were the first signs that the American Christmas was becoming a "Festival of Consumption"?

3. What industries were spawned by the commercialization of Christmas?

4. The material on Thanksgiving seems to serve as an introduction to the selection. What in particular produces that effect?

5. After the long section on Christmas, do the sections on Mother's Day and Father's Day seem unduly short (paragraphs 21–25)?

6. In general, what seems to be Boorstin's attitude toward his material? Is he objective and neutral? Sarcastic? Approving? Disapproving?

7. Does Boorstin's attitude seem to shift anywhere in the selection, or does it remain consistent?

☐ Writing Suggestions

1. It's fairly easy to attack the commercialization of Christmas. Try defending the American Christmas by focusing on its merits—for example, the jobs and industries created or the emphasis on home and family.

2. During Christmas, the emphasis on family tends to depress many people without families or "significant others." Describe ways that people alone can enjoy the Christmas season.

3. Suggest alternatives to the mania of buying expensive Christmas gifts for dozens of friends and relatives.

4. Controversy has long existed over the psychology of Santa Claus. For example, some psychologists applaud the "magic" of Santa Claus and the effect on children's imaginations. Others think that children are scarred when they find out that adults have tricked them. And, of course, parents fret about the appearance of Santa on every corner and in every department store. Defend or attack the Santa Claus myth.

5. Discuss another holiday as a "Festival of Consumption"—for example, Halloween or Valentine's Day.

MEGAWATT MIRACLES OF THE YULETIDE

☐ WILLIAM GEIST

1 White Plains Post Road in Scarsdale is aglow this holiday season with the festive brake lights of motorists happening upon the megawatt wonder that is the Prisco family's outdoor Christmas display.

2   "Santa won't have any trouble finding this house," Denise Dombrowsky, a passerby drawn out of her car by the sight, said to her five-year-old son, Alex. Not to mention intelligence satellites and nonstop flights from London to Chicago.

3   This is a time in the suburbs for hauling out the ladder and wrapping the bushes in lights—which seem rarely to work from one year to the next—or perhaps stringing them along the gutters. It is also a time for evening family outings to view the outdoor decorations that others have erected. As in all things, some residents carry the decorating tradition a little farther than others, to the great joy of many, the bemusement of others, and the absolute mortification of a few neighbors.

4   Anthony and Teresa Prisco have draped the bushes at the front of their yard with one thousand pulsating lights. Behind the bushes stands an eleven-piece polypropylene nativity scene, each translucent figure glowing with light bulbs within—all but the two baby lambs, which presumably will glow when they reach maturity.

5   Across the driveway, which is lined with three-foot-high candy canes, are three incandescent carolers and a wooden soldier. On the porch, which is decorated in garlands strung with lights, stand glowing plastic snowmen, three-foot-high candles, "Noel" lampposts, several Santas, and a drummer boy. Shrubs around the porch are decorated with blinking colored lights, and there is an enormous wreath strung with lights on the front of the house. On the roof is Santa Claus in a sleigh pulled by three reindeer.

6   While young Alex Dombrowsky found the Priscos' decorations "pretty," a neighbor suggested that they were "a little much," and another neighbor thought the place looked "like Las Vegas." Scarsdale is an affluent suburb where most people put up no outdoor Christmas decorations at all, and most who do keep their enthusiasm for the season firmly in check, displaying tasteful door wreaths of natural materials. The entire subject of outdoor Christmas decorations in such suburbs of studied reserve seems fraught with social peril.

7   It is difficult, perhaps impossible, to find a place in Scarsdale that sells plastic figures, one local resident suggesting that it might be illegal to sell such items over the counter in this village. In a visit over the line to the Flower Time shop in White Plains, Wayne Pritzker was considering the purchase of a four-foot plastic snowman and suggested that "Christmas is for the kids," that people who worry about the tastefulness of decorations "should lighten up a little."

8   Teresa Prisco loves her displays and said she did not particularly care if her decorations were causing a stir. She would prefer, however, that the other children stop teasing hers and "telling them that their mother is crazy."

9   Mrs. Prisco has been putting out her Christmas displays for twenty years, adding a few things each year. "Jesus, Mary, and Joseph are originals and do require maintenance," she explained.

10   "My husband thinks I'm crazy, too," she said. "Every year he says, 'I thought

we were going to cut down this year.' " Mrs. Prisco hides the December electric bill from Mr. Prisco.

11   "I think it's nice," Mr. Prisco observed. "The only problem is she goes a little too far." Many of the passing cars on this busy thoroughfare slow, some stop, and a few come right up the driveway. Some people get out of their cars at this roadside attraction to take photographs or to knock on the door and discuss the lavish display with the Priscos. Some mistake the Prisco home for some kind of store. They knock on the door and ask Mrs. Prisco, "Are you open?"

12   For all of this, most residents of this community can tell you that the Priscos' decorations are dim compared with those that Dr. John Salimbene used to put up at his house just down White Plains Post Road. One of the doctor's Wise Men moved his arm, by way of a barbecue grill motor, pointing to the star on the rooftop. Some people didn't even notice the moving arm, for all of the wooden elves sawing and hammering in the front yard, Santa and his sleigh on the lawn, the huge "Noel" sign, thousands of lights, the snowmen, the loud-speakers blaring carols, and at times Dr. Salimbene's nephews dressed as Mr. and Mrs. Claus.

13   "They had to put a policeman on the corner, for all the traffic," the physician said. "We had buses of people coming here."

14   He said that occasionally someone would make a derogatory comment and that he stopped erecting the bulk of his display about four years ago when a neighbor suggested Dr. Salimbene was less than patriotic—possibly an Arab sympathizer—for using all that electric power on a Christmas display.

15   Mrs. Prisco said that if Dr. Salimbene is not going to use them anymore, she is interested in buying his animated characters and "getting them out there."

☐ Discovering Meaning and Technique

1. What seem to be the most bizarre elements in the displays Geist describes?

2. From the dialogue that Geist supplies, try to imagine the relationship between Mr. and Mrs. Prisco.

3. Geist is clearly amused by and a bit sarcastic about his subject. Point out language that indicates his attitude.

4. Why does Geist use specific names and ample direct quotations in the selection?

5. Do you think that Geist is accurately quoting real people? Or has he fabricated the names and the quotations for an effect?

☐ **Writing Suggestions**

1. What prompts people to create elaborate Christmas displays?

2. Explain your attitude toward the "megawatt miracles." Do you find them interesting? Distasteful? Tacky? Amusing?

3. Considering the need to conserve energy, should "megawatt" displays be prohibited or limited by law?

4. Are you particularly fond of or appalled by other types of holiday decorations—such as those for Halloween, Easter, or Valentine's Day? Explain your reaction.

ODE TO THANKSGIVING

☐ MICHAEL J. ARLEN

1 It is time, at last, to speak the truth about Thanksgiving, and the truth is this. Thanksgiving is really not such a terrific holiday. Consider the traditional symbols of the event: Dried cornhusks hanging on the door! Terrible wine! Cranberry jelly in little bowls of extremely doubtful provenance which everyone is required to handle with the greatest of care! Consider the participants, the merrymakers: men and women (also children) who have survived passably well throughout the years, mainly as a result of living at considerable distances from their dear parents and beloved siblings, who on this feast of feasts must apparently forgather (as if beckoned by an aberrant Fairy Godmother), usually by circuitous routes, through heavy traffic, at a common meeting place, where the very moods, distempers, and obtrusive personal habits that have kept them all happily apart since adulthood are then and there encouraged to slowly ferment beneath the cornhusks, and gradually rise with the aid of the terrible wine, and finally burst forth out of control under the stimulus of the cranberry jelly! No, it is a mockery of a holiday. For instance: *Thank you, O Lord, for what we are about to receive.* This is surely not a gala concept. There are no presents, unless one counts Aunt Bertha's sweet rolls a present, which no one does. There is precious little in the way of costumery: miniature plastic turkeys and those witless Pilgrim hats. There is no sex. Indeed, Thanksgiving is the one day of the year (a fact known to everybody) when all thoughts of sex completely vanish, evaporating from apartments, houses, condominiums, and mobile homes like steam from a bathroom mirror.

3   Consider also the nowhereness of the time of year: the last week or so in November. It is obviously not yet winter: winter, with its death-dealing blizzards

and its girls in tiny skirts pirouetting on the ice. On the other hand, it is certainly not much use to anyone as fall: no golden leaves or Oktoberfests, and so forth. Instead, it is a no-man's-land between the seasons. In the cold and sobersides northern half of the country, it is a vaguely unsettling interregnum of long, mournful walks beneath leafless trees: the long, mournful walks following the midday repast with the dread inevitability of pie following turkey, and the leafless trees looming or standing about like eyesores, and the ground either as hard as iron or slightly mushy, and the light snow always beginning to fall when one is halfway to the old green gate—flecks of cold, watery stuff plopping between neck and collar, for the reason that, it being not yet winter, one has forgotten or not chosen to bring along a muffler. It is a corollary to the long, mournful Thanksgiving walk that the absence of this muffler is quickly noticed and that four weeks or so later, at Christmastime, instead of the Sony Betamax one had secretly hoped the children might have chipped in to purchase, one receives another muffler: by then the thirty-third. Thirty-three mufflers! Some walk! Of course, things are more fun in the warm and loony southern part of the country. No snow there of any kind. No need of mufflers. Also, no long, mournful walks, because in the warm and loony southern part of the country everybody drives. So everybody drives over to Uncle Jasper's house to watch the Cougars play the Gators, a not entirely unimportant conflict which will determine whether the Gators get a Bowl bid or must take another post-season exhibition tour of North Korea. But no sooner do the Cougars kick off (an astonishing end-over-end squiggly thing that floats lazily above the arena before plummeting down toward K. C. McCoy and catching him on the helmet) than Auntie Em starts hustling turkey. Soon Cousin May is slamming around the bowls and platters, and Cousin Bernice is oohing and ahing about "all the fixin's," and Uncle Bob is making low, insincere sounds of appreciation: "Yummy, yummy, Auntie Em, I'll have me some more of these delicious yams!" Delicious yams? Uncle Bob's eyes roll wildly in his head. Billy Joe Quaglino throws his long bomb in the middle of Grandpa Morris saying grace, Grandpa Morris speaking so low nobody can hear him, which is just as well, since he is reciting what he can remember of his last union contract. And then, just as J. B. (Speedy) Snood begins his ninety-two-yard punt return, Auntie Em starts dealing everyone second helpings of her famous stuffing, as if she were pushing a controlled substance, which it well might be, since there are no easily recognizable ingredients visible to the naked eye.

3   Consider for a moment the Thanksgiving meal itself. It has become a sort of refuge for endangered species of starch: cauliflower, turnips, pumpkin, mince (whatever "mince" is), those blessed yams. Bowls of luridly colored yams, with no taste at all, lying torpid under a lava flow of marshmallow! And then the sacred turkey. One might as well try to construct a holiday repast around a fish—say, a nice piece of boiled haddock. After all, turkey tastes very similar to haddock: same consistency, same quite remarkable absence of flavor. But then,

if the Thanksgiving *pièce de résistance* were a nice piece of boiled haddock instead of turkey, there wouldn't be all that fun for Dad when Mom hands him the sterling-silver, bone-handled carving set (a wedding present from her parents and not sharpened since) and then everyone sits around pretending not to watch while he saws and tears away at the bird as if he were trying to burrow his way into or out of some grotesque, fowl-like prison.

4   What of the good side to Thanksgiving, you ask. There is always a good side to everything. Not to Thanksgiving. There is only a bad side and then a worse side. For instance, Grandmother's best linen tablecloth is a bad side: the fact that it is produced each year, in the manner of a red flag being produced before a bull, and then is always spilled upon by whichever child is doing poorest at school that term and so is in need of greatest reassurance. Thus: "Oh, my God, *Veronica*, you just spilled grape juice [or plum wine or tar] on Grandmother's best linen tablecloth!" But now comes worse. For at this point Cousin Bill, the one who lost all Cousin Edwina's money on the car dealership three years ago and has apparently been drinking steadily since Halloween, bizarrely chooses to say: "Seems to me those old glasses are always falling over." To which Auntie Meg is heard to add: "Somehow I don't remember receivin' any of those old glasses." To which Uncle Fred replies: "That's because you and George decided to go on vacation to Hawaii the summer Grandpa Sam was dying." Now Grandmother is sobbing, though not so uncontrollably that she can refrain from murmuring: "I think that volcano painting I threw away by mistake got sent me from Hawaii, heaven knows why." But the gods are merciful, even the Pilgrim-hatted god of cornhusks and soggy stuffing, and there is an end to everything, even to Thanksgiving. Indeed, there is a grandeur to the feelings of finality and doom which usually settle on a house after the Thanksgiving celebration is over, for with the completion of Thanksgiving Day the year itself has been properly terminated: shot through the cranium with a high-velocity candied yam. At this calendrical nadir, all energy on the planet has gone, all fun has fled, all the terrible wine has been drunk.

5   But then, overnight, life once again begins to stir, emerging, even by the next morning, in the form of Japanese window displays and Taiwanese Christmas lighting, from the primeval ooze of the nation's department stores. Thus, a new year dawns, bringing with it immediate and cheering possibilities of extended consumer debt, office-party flirtations, good—or, at least mediocre—wine, and visions of Supersaver excursion fares to Montego Bay. It is worth noting, perhaps, that this true new year always starts with the same mute, powerful mythic ceremony: the surreptitious tossing out, in the early morning, of all those horrid aluminum-foil packages of yams and cauliflower and stuffing and red, gummy cranberry substance which have been squeezed into the refrigerator as if a reenactment of the siege of Paris were shortly expected. Soon afterward, the phoenix of Christmas can be observed as it slowly rises, beating its drumsticks, once again goggle-eyed with hope and unrealistic expectations.

☐ Discovering Meaning and Technique

1. Does Arlen's Thanksgiving Day sound familiar? If so, which details from the selection best describe your family's Thanksgiving dinners?

2. What ceremony does Arlen describe as beginning the Christmas season and the "true new year"?

3. Arlen attacks Thanksgiving on three fronts. The first is the symbols of Thanksgiving. What are the other two? Point out these three divisions of the essay.

4. What is the purpose of the exclamation points in the first paragraph?

5. Read aloud the sentence from paragraph 1 that begins "Consider the participants, the merrymakers. . ." What effect does Arlen achieve with this long and cumbersome structure? What is the effect of the exclamation point after such a structure?

6. Why does Arlen use specific names in the essay—Cousin May, Uncle Bob, Grandpa Sam?

7. The last paragraph points ahead to the coming of Christmas. What characteristics of Arlen's language and tone create the humor of this paragraph?

8. Find some of Arlen's humorous images, such as *a lava flow of marshmallow* and *primeval ooze of the nation's department stores.*

☐ Writing Suggestions

1. Write an essay explaining what is good about Thanksgiving as opposed, say, to Christmas. For example, Thanksgiving does not require weeks of shopping, decorating, spending, and dressing up. In your essay, give specific details as Arlen does.

2. Explain why Thanksgiving has not been commercialized.

3. Take another holiday, such as Valentine's Day or Halloween, and treat it humorously (as Arlen does Thanksgiving) by focusing on its sameness.

4. Propose another menu for Thanksgiving dinner—one equally as American but more inviting. Defend your choice of the items included.

THE AMERICAN WAY OF DEATH

☐ **JESSICA MITFORD**

> *How long, I would ask, are we to be subjected to*
> *the tyranny of custom and undertakers? Truly, it is*
> *all vanity and vexation of spirit—a mere mockery*
> *of woe, costly to all, far, far beyond its value; and*
> *ruinous to many; hateful, and an abomination to*
> *all; yet submitted to by all, because none have the*
> *moral courage to speak against it and act in definance*
> *of it.*
>   **—LORD ESSEX**

1 O death, where is thy sting? O grave, where is thy victory? Where, indeed. Many a badly stung survivor, faced with the aftermath of some relative's funeral, has ruefully concluded that the victory has been won hands down by a funeral establishment—in disastrously unequal battle.

2   Much has been written of late about the affluent society in which we live, and much fun poked at some of the irrational "status symbols" set out like golden snares to trap the unwary consumer at every turn. Until recently, little has been said about the most irrational and weirdest of the lot, lying in ambush for all of us at the end of the road—the modern American funeral.

3   If the Dismal Traders (as an eighteenth-century English writer calls them) have traditionally been cast in a comic role in literature, a universally recognized symbol of humor from Shakespeare to Dickens to Evelyn Waugh, they have successfully turned the tables in recent years to perpetrate a huge, macabre and expensive practical joke on the American public. It is not consciously conceived of as a joke, of course; on the contrary, it is hedged with admirably contrived rationalizations.

4   Gradually, almost imperceptibly, over the years the funeral men have constructed their own grotesque cloud-cuckoo-land where the trappings of Gracious Living are transformed, as in a nightmare, into the trappings of Gracious Dying. The same familiar Madison Avenue language, with its peculiar adjectival range designed to anesthetize sales resistance to all sorts of products, has seeped into the funeral industry in a new and bizarre guise. The emphasis is on the same desirable qualities that we have all been schooled to look for in our daily search for excellence: comfort, durability, beauty, craftsmanship. The attuned ear will recognize too the convincing quasi-scientific language, so reassuring even if unintelligible.

5   So that this too, too solid flesh might not melt, we are offered "solid copper—

a quality casket which offers superb value to the client seeking long-lasting protection," or "the Colonial Classic Beauty—18 guage lead coated steel, seamless top, lap-jointed welded body construction." Some are equipped with foam rubber, some with innerspring mattresses. Elgin offers "the revolutionary 'Perfect-Posture' bed." Not every casket need have a silver lining, for one may choose between "more than 60 color matched shades, magnificient and unique masterpieces" by the Cheney casket-lining people. Shrouds no longer exist. Instead, you may patronize a grave-wear couturière who promises "handmade original fashions— styles from the best in life for the last memory—dresses, men's suits, negligees, accessories." For the final, perfect grooming: "Nature-Glo—the ultimate in cosmetic embalming." And, where have we heard that phrase "peace of mind protection" before? No matter. In funeral advertising, it is applied to the Wilbert Burial Vault, with its ⅜-inch precast asphalt inner liner plus extra-thick, reinforced concrete—all this "guaranteed by Good Housekeeping." Here again the Cadillac, status symbol par excellence, appears in all its gleaming glory, this time transformed into a pastel-colored funeral hearse.

6   You, the potential customer for all this luxury, are unlikely to read the lyrical descriptions quoted above, for they are culled from *Mortuary Management* and *Casket and Sunnyside,* two of the industry's eleven trade magazines. For you there are ads in your daily newspaper, generally found on the obituary page, stressing dignity, refinement, high-caliber professional service and that intangible quality, *sincerity.* The trade advertisements are, however, instructive, because they furnish an important clue to the frame of mind into which the funeral industry has hypnotized itself.

7   A new mythology, essential to the twentieth-century American funeral rite, has grown up—or rather has been built up step by step—to justify the peculiar customs surrounding the disposal of our dead. And, just as the witch doctor must be convinced of his own infallibility in order to maintain a hold over his clientele, so the funeral industry has had to "sell itself" on its articles of faith in the course of passing them along to the public.

8   The first of these is the tenet that today's funeral procedures are founded in "American tradition." The story comes to mind of a sign on the freshly sown lawn of a brand-new Midwest college: "There is a tradition on this campus that students never walk on this strip of grass. This tradition goes into effect next Tuesday." The most cursory look at American funerals of past times will establish the parallel. Simplicity to the point of starkness, the plain pine box, the laying out of the dead by friends and family who also bore the coffin to the grave— these were the hallmarks of the traditional funeral until the end of the nineteenth century.

9   Secondly, there is the myth that the American public is only being given what it wants—an opportunity to keep up with the Joneses to the end. "In keeping with our high standard of living, there should be an equally high standard of dying," says the past president of the Funeral Directors of San Francisco.

"The cost of a funeral varies according to individual taste and the niceties of living the family has been accustomed to." Actually, choice doesn't enter the picture for the average individual, faced, generally for the first time, with the necessity of buying a product of which he is totally ignorant, at a moment when he is least in a position to quibble. In point of fact the cost of a funeral almost always varies, not "according to individual taste" but according to what the traffic will bear.

10   Thirdly, there is an assortment of myths based on half-digested psychiatric theories. The importance of the "memory picture" is stressed—meaning the last glimpse of the deceased in open casket, done up with the latest in embalming techniques and finished off with a dusting of makeup. A newer one, impressively authentic-sounding, is the need for "grief therapy," which is beginning to go over big in mortuary circles. A historian of American funeral directing hints at the grief-therapist idea when speaking of the new role of the undertaker—"the dramaturgic role, in which the undertaker becomes a stage manager to create an appropriate atmosphere and to move the funeral party through a drama in which social relationships are stressed and an emotional catharsis or release is provided through ceremony."

11   Lastly, a whole new terminology, as ornately shoddy as the satin rayon casket liner, has been invented by the funeral industry to replace the direct and serviceable vocabulary of former times. Undertaker has been supplanted by "funeral director" or "mortician." (Even the classified section of the telephone directory gives recognition of this; in its pages you will find "Undertakers—see Funeral Directors.") Coffins are "caskets"; hearses are "coaches," or "professional cars"; flowers are "floral tributes"; corpses generally are "loved ones," but mortuary etiquette dictates that a specific corpse be referred to by name only—as, "Mr. Jones"; cremated ashes are "cremains." Euphemisms such as "slumber room," "reposing room," and "calcination—the *kindlier* heat" abound in the funeral business.

12   If the undertaker is the stage manager of the fabulous production that is the modern American funeral, the stellar role is reserved for the occupant of the open casket. The decor, the stagehands, the supporting cast are all arranged for the most advantageous display of the deceased, without which the rest of the paraphernalia would lose its point—*Hamlet* without the Prince of Denmark. It is to this end that a fantastic array of costly merchandise and services is pyramided to dazzle the mourners and facilitate the plunder of the next of kin.

13   Grief therapy, anyone? But it's going to come high. According to the funeral industry's own figures, the *average* undertaker's bill in 1961 was $708 for casket and "services," to which must be added the cost of a burial vault, flowers, clothing, clergy and musician's honorarium, and cemetery charges. When these costs are added to the undertaker's bill, the total average cost for an adult's funeral is, as we shall see, closer to $1,450.

14   The question naturally arises, *is* this what most people want for themselves

and their families? For several reasons, this has been a hard one to answer until recently. It is a subject seldom discussed. Those who have never had to arrange for a funeral frequently shy away from its implications, preferring to take comfort in the thought that sufficient unto the day is the evil thereof. Those who have acquired personal and painful knowledge of the subject would often rather forget about it. Pioneering "Funeral Societies" or "Memorial Associations," dedicated to the principle of dignified funerals at reasonable cost, have existed in a number of communities throughout the country, but their membership has been limited for the most part to the more sophisticated element in the population—university people, liberal intellectuals—and those who, like doctors and lawyers, come up against problems in arranging funerals for their clients.

15   Some indication of the pent-up resentment felt by vast numbers of people against the funeral interests was furnished by the astonishing response to an article by Roul Tunley, titled "Can You Afford to Die?" in *The Saturday Evening Post* of June 17, 1961. As though a dike had burst, letters poured in from every part of the country to the *Post,* to the funeral societies, to local newspapers. They came from clergymen, professional people, old-age pensioners, trade unionists. Three months after the article appeared, an estimated six thousand had taken pen in hand to comment on some phase of the high cost of dying. Many recounted their own bitter experiences at the hands of funeral directors; hundreds asked for advice on how to establish a consumer organization in communities where none exists; others sought information about pre-need plans. The membership of the funeral societies skyrocketed. The funeral industry, finding itself in the glare of public spotlight, has begun to engage in serious debate about its own future course—as well it might.

16   Is the funeral inflation bubble ripe for bursting? A few years ago, the United States public suddenly rebelled against the trend in the auto industry towards ever more showy cars, with their ostentatious and nonfunctional fins, and a demand was created for compact cars patterned after European models. The all-powerful auto industry, accustomed to *telling* the customer what sort of car he wanted, was suddenly forced to *listen* for a change. Overnight, the little cars became for millions a new kind of status symbol. Could it be that the same cycle is working itself out in the attitude towards the final return of dust to dust, that the American public is becoming sickened by ever more ornate and costly funerals, and that a status symbol of the future may indeed be the simplest kind of "funeral without fins"?

☐ Discovering Meaning and Technique

1. Mitford wrote this selection in 1963. Does it seem outdated? Or does her description of the funeral industry apply today?

2. Why does Mitford think "the funeral industry has had to 'sell itself' on its articles of faith" (paragraph 7)?

3. What are those "articles of faith"?

4. What kinds of people does Mitford say belong to associations "dedicated to the principle of dignified funerals at reasonable cost" (paragraph 14)?

5. In general, what is Mitford's objection to the language of the funeral industry?

6. Find the section of the essay that lists the myths surrounding modern funerals. What makes the structure of this section easy to follow?

7. Mitford begins the selection with a quotation: "O Death, where is thy sting? O grave, where is thy victory?" What is the source of the quotation? If you don't know, look it up in a reference book such as *Bartlett's Familiar Quotations.*

8. Mitford uses a number of comparisons between two essentially dissimilar things. One, for example, occurs in paragraph 2 where she compares status symbols to "golden snares to trap the unwary consumer." Find other interesting comparisons in the selection.

9. What is the tone of the selection? That is, does Mitford seem amused, sarcastic, angry, neutral? How can you tell?

☐ Writing Assignments

1. Describe a traditional American funeral that you attended. Did the ritual provide, as the funeral industry contends, an emotional release for the bereaved? Or did the ritual provide, instead, a great deal of emotional stress?

2. Mitford suggests at the end of the selection that the American public might rebel against the funeral industry. But the selection was written in 1963, and still the public has not rebelled. Why?

3. Describe how you would like to have your own funeral conducted.

4. Try to find some information on current funeral practices and costs. Compare your findings with the information in the selection.

THE PARTY

☐ PAT ESSLINGER CARR

1 I steadied the present on my lap and took a deep breath that stopped at my tight damp skirt band. The streetcar wheels clicked, clicked against the rails. I

resisted the impulse to push back wet strands of hair at my temples and mash what little curl was left.

2   I didn't want to be on the hot trolley and I didn't want to go.

3   I pushed my glasses back up my greasy nose and wiped under the rims, carefully, not touching the glass with my knuckles. I had wanted so much more to stay in the porch swing with my book. John had just started telling his story; he was still with Beau and Digby, and we had all been together beneath sun spots of heat and sand, hearing the curses of the Legionnaires, smelling hot leather and camel fuzz. And then I had had to splash tepid water over my face, change from my shorts and wrap the hasty present my mother had bought at the dime store that morning. Matching fingernail polish and lipstick whose perfume made me slightly nauseated, but that Jan would probably like all right. I guessed she would, anyway, but I didn't much care. I begrudged the time I was having to lose. Over forty minutes each way on the trolley, and I would have to stay at least until 4:30 before I could break away politely. They usually played some kind of games until about 3:30 or so before they let you eat and escape.

4   I looked at the fat bland face of the watch hanging in its leather sheath beside the conductor: 2:20. I'd be a little late as it was and that would mean even more minutes lost at the end of the party; my mother said you should always stay at least two hours for politeness' sake. And I had the other two Beau books waiting in their faded blue covers when I finished this one. My whole Saturday afternoon wasted.

5   The click of the metal wheels chipped away at my world of sand and dry hot fortresses until the desert sun fell into pieces and then dissolved. I scooted the damp package higher up on my lap. I could feel drops of sweat collecting under my bare knees.

6   We were passing the cemetery. The gawky stone angels dotted the tombs and oozed green slime. They all had the same faces, the same stone cataracts for eyes. Guardian angels, stiffened and blind.

7   I settled back against the wooden seat, feeling the wet patch of blouse on my skin as we swayed along. It would be another ten minutes on the trolley and then an eight-block walk. My whole Saturday wasted.

8   When I climbed down from the awkward trolley steps, I realized the afternoon was even hotter than when I had started from home. The drops behind my knees gathered into rivulets that crawled with itching slowness down to the tops of my anklets. Hot branches hung like lank hair over the street, lifting and drooping with a faint hot breeze almost as if they were panting.

9   Half a block away I saw the house with its tight cluster of balloons tacked to the front door and its pink ribbon trailing from the brass knocker. Up close, I wasn't quite sure how to knock around the pink satin ribbon, so I finally used my knuckles and left damp imprints on the white door.

10   The door popped open immediately and a lady I guessed must be Jan's mother stood there beaming greedily at me.

11   "Here's your first guest," she half turned back and called happily without taking her eyes off me. "Do come in," she added to me and tried to open the door wider except that it was already open about as far as it could go. She reached out to take my arm, but when she saw me looking at her a little dumbfounded she didn't touch me and just motioned me in with her hand. I saw Jan behind her.

12   "Hi," I said, blinking a little with the shadow of the room as the door closed out the bright streak of balloons. I held out the little package with its moist wrapping paper.

13   "Hi," she said and took the package.

14   "Aren't you going to introduce your little friend to me, Jan?" her mother said brightly, birdlike, from beside me.

15   I winced and glanced at her as Jan mumbled my name and held the present in her hands, not seeming to know what to do with it. Although not as fat as Jan, her mother had the same tight curly hair and the same plump cheeks. She said something else bright and pecking while I was looking at her that I didn't hear and then she put a hand on each of our shoulders and pushed us slightly ahead of her into the next room.

16   "We decided to stack all the presents on the buffet, and yours can be the first." I could hear her beam behind us.

17   The room was a dining room, but it was so covered with pink crepe paper I couldn't tell at first. Pink twisted streamers bulged low from the overhead light and swung to the molding of every wall. The tablecloth was scalloped with pink crepe paper held on by Scotch tape, and the buffet where Jan's mother put my present was skirted with more taped pink paper. A massive pink frosted cake with a circle of twelve pink candles in flower holders sat in the center of the table, and the whole rest of the table top was jammed with pink paper plates holding a pink snapper each and a pink nut cup stuffed with cashew nuts. Enough for the whole class I guessed.

18   "We thought we'd just stand up for the cake and ice cream," her mother's voice smiled around me. I knew we would have pink ice cream with the cake. "We just don't have thirty-three chairs in the house," she almost giggled.

19   I didn't know what to say and Jan didn't say anything, so her voice added, "Why don't you show your little friend your new room, Jan? I'll be down here to catch the door as the rest of your guests arrive."

20   Jan made a kind of shrugging nod and led the way out the other side of the room, up some stairs that smelled of newly rubbed polish to a converted attic room.

21   Everything in the room was yellow. Bedspread, curtains, walls, lampshade on the desk. It was a bit like having been swallowed by a butterfly, but it wasn't as bad as the pink downstairs.

22   "It's new," Jan said offhandedly. "Daddy finished the walls and my mother made the bedspread and curtains." She glanced around casually, but I caught the glint of pride before she covered it up.

23   "It's nice," I said. "I like yellow."

24   "It's so sunny." I could almost hear her mother saying it.

25   I nodded and grappled for something else to talk about. "What's that?" I pointed to a cloth-covered scrap book. The cover was a tiny red and white check, and I somehow knew Jan had chosen that herself.

26   "Just some sketches." But she couldn't cover up the pride this time.

27   "Can I see them?" I said too heartily, but she didn't notice as she put the book tenderly on the bed.

28   I started turning the pages, commenting on each one. Some of them were bad, the heart-lipped beauties in profile we all tried once in a while in math class, a few tired magnolias, some lopsided buildings; but then I got to the animals. Round, furred kittens that you knew were going to grow into cats. Zoo monkeys, hanging on the bars, pretending to be people. Fat pigeons strutting among cigarette wrappers on their way to drop white splatters on Robert E. Lee.

29   I glanced up at her. She was watching me with the hungry expression I had seen on her mother at the door. "These are good." I couldn't keep the surprise out of my voice.

30   "Do you think so?" She waited to lap up my praise, her mouth parted and her plump cheeks blushing a little.

31   I nodded, turning to the animals again, telling her what I thought about each one. I don't know how long we were there when she said, "I guess we'd better go down." I hadn't heard anything, but she carefully closed the book and placed it on her desk.

32   Her mother was at the foot of the stairs waiting for us. There was a tight pulled look at the corners of her mouth. "What time is it, dear?" she said with that glittering, bird-sharp voice.

33   I saw the hall clock behind her in a brass star. The shiny brass hands had just slipped off each other and were pointing to 3:20.

34   "I can't imagine what has happened." Her voice slivered a little.

35   "You live pretty far out," I said, the excuse sounding pretty bad even to me.

36   She nodded abstractedly. "I suppose so." Then she added, "I'd better see about the ice cream."

37   She bustled off and Jan and I stood aimlessly at the foot of the stairs. I could see the pink crepe paper through the door of the dining room.

38   The silence lengthened uncomfortably and the hall clock pinged 3:30.

39   "You want to go in the back yard?" Jan said at last.

40   "Okay."

41   We trudged through the kitchen. Her mother was standing beside the refrigerator where I guessed she had just checked the cartons of ice cream. "You two go on outside. I'll be here to catch the door." Her voice was brittle, like overdone candy cracking on a plate.

42   I thought as we filed past that it would be better if she went up to take a nap and could have the excuse later of maybe having missed the knocker. It was getting awfully late.

43   We went out and took turns sitting on the swing in the oak tree they had out back and I told her about the book I was reading. I didn't much want to share it, but I had to talk about something. I told her she could have it after I finished even though I had intended to let my best friend Aileen read it next so we could make up joint Foreign Legion daydreams. We rocked back and forth a while, not really swinging, just sort of waiting and trying to limp along in a kind of conversation. I knew we were both listening, straining to hear a knock, a footstep on the sidewalk out front.

44   Her mother appeared at the back screen. "I thought you girls would like preview lemonade. It's so hot this afternoon."

45   "It really is," I agreed hastily. She somehow made me feel awful. I guess it was the word "preview" that did it. As if there were really going to be something to follow, the birthday party when the other thirty-one guests arrived. "Pink lemonade sounds great." I hadn't meant to say "pink," and as soon as I said it I could have stuffed my sweaty fist in my mouth.

46   She gave a little stilted laugh and I couldn't tell if she noticed. "It's all made."

47   We waited and took turns in the swing until she brought the two glasses out on a little tray. I saw her coming from the corner of my eye and said, "I bet you can't guess what I got you for your birthday."

48   Jan shook her head, looking at me and sort of grinning.

49   "It's something to wear," I said prolonging it. Then as her mother got there with the lemonade, I looked up, startled, as if I hadn't seen her. "That looks good," I said a little too loudly at the pink liquid. There wasn't any ice in it; the freezer part of their box was probably full of ice cream.

50   She strained out a smile. I thought I saw her lower lip quiver a little.

51   "I got so hot coming out here. I didn't know you lived so near the end of the trolley line." I tried to put over the idea of distance and maybe a confusion about their address. "This is great." I took a quick sip.

52   "Really great," Jan chorused.

53   But her mother was already on her way back to the kitchen, into the house where she'd be able to hear the door.

54   We stayed there in the hot shade, alternately leaning against the rough tree trunk and sitting in the swing until I guessed it must have been about 4:00 or so. We were still listening too hard to talk much.

55   "Want something to eat?"

56   I couldn't face that pink dining room with the crepe paper streamers and the thirty-three nut cups. I hesitated.

57   She must have understood. "We have some cupcakes, in case we ran out of. . ." Her voice trailed off.

58   "Fine. I love cupcakes," I said hurriedly.

59   As we came in her mother came from the front of the house.

60   "We thought we'd have a cupcake," Jan said.

61   "Oh, yes. That's a fine idea," she began. "And have a dip of the ice. . ." Then her face crumpled like a sheet of wadded paper. Her lips wavered over the word and a great sob hiccuped through her throat. She put her hand over her mouth as she turned and ran toward the hall, and I saw her back heaving as she disappeared beside the stairs.

62   We pretended we hadn't seen anything. Jan got the little pink cakes from a bin and dished out two great heaps of strawberry ice cream, and we stood beside the sink and ate them.

63   I had separate sensations of dry warmish crumbs and iced smoothness passing across my tongue, but I couldn't taste anything. But I ate the little cake and the bowl of ice cream and when she offered me another cupcake and more ice cream, I took them and ate them too.

64   I repeated some of my compliments about her sketches and added more as I thought of them and spooned up the chopped bits of strawberry in the bottom of the dish. We dragged out the ritual until shadows began to ease into the kitchen and I saw by the kitchen clock that it was after 5:30. I told her I had better leave to be able to get home before dark with such a long trolley ride back uptown. "Tell your mother," I began, but I couldn't think what she should tell her mother for me and I stopped.

65   As we went toward the front door I saw the pink paper of the dining room glowing in the afternoon sun.

66   "See you Monday. I'll bring the book," I said loudly at the front door.

67   She waved her hand and shut the door. The knot of balloons jogged, settled lightly against one another beneath the pink satin ribbon on the door knocker as I went down the sidewalk.

☐ Discovering Meaning and Technique

1. Identify the "Beau books" the narrator refers to in paragraphs 3, 4, and 43.

2. When does the reader first begin to suspect that the narrator will be the only guest?

3. When does the narrator realize that no one else is going to arrive?

4. What strategies does the narrator use to smooth over the embarrassing situation?

5. Which details in the story tell you that it is set in the South?

6. Explain what the narrator means in paragraph 64 when she says, "We dragged out the ritual. . . ."

7. Why does Carr emphasize the time of day in the third and fourth paragraphs?

8. What descriptive passages emphasize the birdlike character of Jan's mother?

9. How does the dialogue reveal the embarrassment of the characters?

☐ Writing Suggestions

1. Explain why the children in the story handle the situation better than the adult.

2. Recount a painfully embarrassing experience from your own childhood.

3. Describe an unusual or particularly interesting birthday party you attended.

4. Some parents see birthday parties as status symbols and consequently stage elaborate, expensive gatherings. Do you think children enjoy these lavish parties? Or do they prefer junk food and unstructured play?

Clothing

■ ■ ■

WE WERE WHAT WE WORE

☐ **INK MENDELSOHN**

1 A Chicago judge ruled in 1908 that a nightgown was a luxury, not a necessity, and thereupon issued a restraining order forbidding an eighteen-year-old girl from buying one against her father's wishes. "The only possible use of a night-gown," the judge explained, "is to keep off flies and mosquitoes, and the bedclothes will do just as well." The father testified: "She never wore a nightgown in her life, and neither did her parents. She's been associating with nifty people, that's the trouble with her." Clearly, as recently as this century, all Americans did not enjoy freedom of dress.

2 By the 1920s, however, production and distribution of ready-to-wear cloth-ing had reached a stage that enabled most men and women to dress stylishly at moderate cost. As a Midwestern businessman observed, "I used to be able to tell something about the background of a girl applying for a job as a stenographer by her clothes, but today I often have to wait till she speaks, shows a gold tooth or otherwise gives me a second clew."

3 This egalitarian confusion of class distinctions would seem to reflect the ideals of the early Republic, but in fact, it had evolved only gradually. For much of our history, according to Claudia Kidwell, the head curator of the Smithsonian Institution's Costume Division, "Clothing's most prevading function has been to declare status." From the beginning Americans have loved fine clothes. In 1676 Hannah Lyman and thirty-five other young women of Northampton, Massachusetts, were arrested for overdressing—specifically for wearing hoods. A defiant Hannah appeared in court in the offending garment and was censured and fined on the spot for "wearing silk in a fflonting manner, in an offensive way. . . ." Along with their style of dress, the colonists had brought from England laws like the 1621 Virginia resolution to "supress excess in cloaths" and to prevent anyone but high government officials from wearing "gold in their cloaths."

4 Declaring its "utter detestation and dislike" of men and women of "mean condition, education and calling" who would wear the "garb of gentlemen," the Massachusetts General Court in 1639 particularly prohibited Puritans of

low estate from wearing "immoderate great breeches, knots of riban, silk roses, double ruffles and capes." Women of low rank were forbidden silk hoods and scarves, as well as short sleeves "whereby the nakedness of the arms may be discovered"—the daring new fashion popular among the upper classes.

5   Such legislation hardly seems to have been necessary for the somber Puritans of popular imagery. Yet rich, elegant, and stylish clothing was as important to New England merchants as it was to Virginia cavaliers or to the good dames of New Amsterdam. Although the Puritan Church did in fact preach simplicity of dress, it was widely ignored by a flock that counted fine clothing as an outward sign of God's favor. Eventually the laws attempting to dictate dress in the American colonies proved unenforceable and were abandoned.

6   This meant that for New Englanders of means, plain and dull-colored dress was not among the hardships of the New World. Bills and inventories record "pinck hose," "green sleeves," "a Scarlet petticoat with Silver Lace." One Massachusetts governor was noted for the gold-fringed gloves he wore, and another ordered several dozen scarlet coats to be sent to him from England.

7   Shipping lists, portraits, advertisements, court records, and tailors' bills give evidence of the fashion ties that bound prosperous American colonists to their counterparts overseas. Norwich garters—decorative ornaments worn by Sir Walter Raleigh—came over on the *Mayflower,* and a Madame Padishal of Plymouth, Massachusetts, posed for her portrait in a low-necked black velvet gown with a lace whisk to cover her bare neck, the latest court fashion in France.

8 Class distinctions had not been left on Old World shores, and fashion was clear evidence of social standing. Affluent American settlers eagerly sought news of style changes in Europe.

9   Margaret Winthrop, the wife of the governor of Massachusetts, insisted on "the civilest fashion now in use" when she ordered gowns from John Smith, the family tailor in London. But at that distance even personal tailoring could not guarantee good fit, as Smith made clear in a letter accompanying a coat for the governor: "Good Mr. Winthrop, I have, by Mr. Downing's directions sent you a coat. . . . For the fittness I am a little vncerteyne, but if it be too bigg or too little it is esie to amend, vnder the arme to take in or let out the lyning; the outside may be let out in the gathering or taken in also without any prejudice."

10   Not all clothing in colonial America, however, was made by a tailor. Elegantly dressed ladies or gentlemen in silks and brocades from London were outnumbered by craftsmen in leather aprons, female servants in simple petticoats and jackets and the men in livery, seamen and farmers coming to market in homespun trousers, and, in the South, slaves in hand-me-downs. A person's clothing indelibly marked an eighteenth-century man or woman.

11   Housewives made most of the clothing worn by average people. Using

both imported and domestic fabrics, colonial women made their own clothes and their children's, and such simply constructed men's clothes as undergarments, shirts, and trousers. But a fashionably cut coat or smooth-fitting breeches were beyond their skills. By the second half of the eighteenth century, breeches were worn so skintight that—the story goes —in Alexandria, Virginia, they were hung on hooks and the wearer-to-be put them on by mounting three steps and letting himself into them from above. Small wonder, then, that the making of a jacket, waistcoat, and breeches was left to the art of the tailor.

12   Preindustrial American clothing was mostly made to order. The well-to-do kept measurements on file with a London tailor, ordering, perhaps, as one gentleman did, "A Suit of Lemmon Collour Brocaded or flowered Lustering the best that can be had for Ten Shillings pr yard made Fashionable and Genteel to the inclosed measures. . . ." And Americans—even after the Revolution—announced their stations in life sartorially. High-hatting went to a ridiculous extreme. Martha Washington may have worn a modest and democratic mobcap, but hats worn by her contemporaries abounded with flowers, vegetables, windmills (that turned), shepherds with their sheep, and, in one case, a naval battle featuring a spun-glass French ship of war. Feathers as much as a yard and a half high topped turbans and other hats. At a New Year's Assembly in 1814, according to a news account of the day, Dolley Madison's "towering feathers above the excessive throng distinctly pointed out her station wherever she moved."

13   "Do not conceive that fine clothes make fine men any more than fine feathers make fine birds," George Washington advised his nephew Bushrod. But Washington himself loved fine clothes and believed that the dignity of a new nation depended to a degree on the outward appearance of its leaders. Records show that John Hancock owned a scarlet velvet suit. And on July 4, 1776, the Declaration of Independence wasn't even mentioned in Thomas Jefferson's day-book. He made only one entry that day: "For Seven pair of Womens Gloves, 20 shillings."

14   Not all Americans followed the latest fashions. Benjamin Franklin, a plain dresser himself, urged his wife and daughter to eschew their feathers and silks for honest calico. And at Harvard College a dress code prohibited "Schollars" from wearing "strange, ruffian-like, or new-fangled fashions." But it is doubtful whether the "Schollars" abandoned their "lavish dress" any more than the Franklin women turned in their silks or the young Puritan Hannah Lyman gave up her hood.

15   By the end of the eighteenth century, class distinctions in dress were beginning to be threatened by new developments in technology. On December 20, 1791, Samuel Slater harnessed the waterwheel at Carpenter's Clothier Mill in Pawtucket, Rhode Island, to the falls of the Blackstone River and thereby brought the Industrial Revolution to this country. Slater, a young English immigrant, combined waterpower and a superior system of cotton yarn manufacture to

produce the first power-spun yarn in America. A few years later Eli Whitney's cotton gin pulled the fibers away from the cotton seeds—a technique that made the mass cultivation of cotton economically feasible. By 1814 the Boston business-man Francis Cabot Lowell had colaborated with the machinist Paul Moody to perfect a power loom superior to the English models. At Lowell's Boston Manufac-turing Company of Waltham, for the first time in history, every process of clothmak-ing was performed under one roof by power machinery.

16   An ample supply of fabric encouraged an emerging ready-to-wear industry. Early in the nineteenth century clothing manufacture also began to move to the factory, where, as the century progressed, steadily improved machinery was to make much shorter work of what hands alone could do.

17   One of the earliest clothing manufactories was the United States Army Clothing Establishment, begun in Philadelphia at the start of the War of 1812 to meet the need for enlisted men's uniforms. It organized production into several key operations. The uniform was cut from a standardized pattern; the pieces were packaged with buttons, padding, lining, facing cloth, and thread and then sent out for sewing to "widows and other meritorious females," who could by "close application . . . make twelve shirts pr week and the same number of pants." Civilian manufacturers followed the model of inside and outside labor division provided by this "immense Government Tailor's Shop."

18   Military organization may have been precise, but the fit of the uniforms was not. The real hero of the ready-to-wear revolution was the custom tailor. This specialist, who had once sewn only for those able to afford his individualized services, rescued ready-made clothing from the realm of "slops"—cheap, coarse, and ill-fitting garments that marked their wearers as second-class citizens. Early in the nineteenth century custom tailors began to modify their techniques in order to manufacture ready-made clothing that was cheaper than custom, yet fashionable and reasonably well fitting. The tailor had a new weapon: the tape measure. "Scientific principles" helped tailors establish standardized rules for measurement that meant they could make not only styles for individuals but apparel for everybody. By 1832 most tailors carried a large stock of ready-made clothing.

19   "Clothing is created out of motivation." says Claudia Kidwell. "The wealthy wanted to maintain distinctions. Everyone else wanted to close the gap. When the working man took off his apron, he wanted to be part of the gentry. He wore frockcoat, vest and trousers to work, then took off his coat and rolled up his sleeves."

20   By mid-century the editor Horace Greeley could write. "No distinction of clothing between gentlemen and otherwise can be seen in the United States." Men—but not women—could purchase in a range of prices a great variety of garments manufactured in Baltimore, Newark, Albany, Rochester, Philadelphia, and New York.

21   Representative of the Eastern manufactories was the New York retail clothing shop founded in 1818 by Henry Sands Brooks as a "gentlemen's store run by gentlemen" and by 1850 known as Brooks Bros. Before the widespread use of the sewing machine in clothing manufacture, cloth was inspected and cut, and trimmings for garments provided, by a small number of people in the shop. A pool of more than a thousand seamstresses on the outside sewed the pieces together by hand and added the finishing touches. Returned and found satisfactory, the garments then went to the sales department. In 1859 Brooks Bros. advertised a "large and complete assortment of Ready-Made Clothing and Furnishings Goods of superior style and make."

22   Thanks to ready-made clothes, a common style of dressing found favor across the land. Clothes made on the Eastern seaboard were available across the country. In Philadelphia the Clothing Palace offered "the most extensive assortment and the finest quality of READY-MADE GARMENTS for the lowest cash price in plain figures." Alfred Munroe of New Orleans challenged anyone to match his twenty-three hundred coats, nineteen hundred pantaloons, fifteen hundred vests, and eight thousand shirts. San Francisco's Keyes & Co. advertised "$100,000 stock in the very latest styles."

23   For promotional vigor, however, it was hard to top Boston's George Simmons, who described his store, Oak Hall, as a "Spacious Magnificent & Inviting TEMPLE, the Centre of Trade, the Wonder of an Admiring World." In pursuit of "large sales, small profits and quick returns." Simmons sent up balloons announcing bargains and threw free overcoats from his roof. Simmons boasted of the "largest and best assortment of Ready-Made Clothing and Furnishing Goods to be found in the United States." Here "the Man of Fashion, the Professional, Gentlemen Clerks with moderate salaries, Merchants, Mechanics and Farmers, Military and Naval Officers" could find "any article from a pair of Gloves to a superfine Dress or Frock coat." In short, Oak Hall and its counterparts had something for everybody—as long as everybody was male. Women would have to wait several decades to participate in the democracy of dress.

24 Ready-made clothing for women at midcentury consisted of the one-size-fits-all cloak, worn since the seventeenth century, and the corset. Blouses, skirts, and dresses that were complexly constructed, individually fitted, and subject to changes in style were still too formidable a challenge for clothing manufacturers before the Civil War. Women depended on their own sewing skills or on dressmakers, who were numerous and charged little, for the better part of their wardrobes.

25   "A Victorian lady stayed at home and stuck to her needlework," according to Pamela Puryear, the author of *Dressing Victorian* (1987). Puryear became interested in historical clothing when she moved into her great-grandparents' home in Navasota, Texas, and found her great-grandmother's 1873 wedding dress. A cousin then gave her twenty-two trunks of clothes belonging to his

grandparents and great-grandparents. Puryear discovered that in Texas Victorian women in a reasonably comfortable economic position dressed the same way as women in Boston or New York. "Clothing revealed a Victorian woman's station in life," Puryear writes. "Women wearing a tight corset, at least four petticoats, dresses with tight elbows and gloves *inside* the house, didn't do the cleaning and the washing. What you wore was you."

26   Hallie Gudger of Old Washington, Texas, wore for her portrait a dress with a satin bodice, double ruffled organdy at the neck, satin rosettes on the skirt and on the sleeves, a draped overskirt, an underskirt, and a bustle. Mary Frances Wickes of Houston was photographed in the late 1850s in a dress of "black silk with gathers in the bodice and triangular black gimp edging. The sleeves were sewn with a geometric interlace of a lighter-colored braid," probably done with the new sewing machine.

27   Between 1842 and 1895 the United States issued more than seven thousand patents for sewing machines and their accessories. Elias Howe and Isaac Singer fought for the right to be called the machine's inventor. But it was Allen B. Wilson who created the machine first adopted by the clothing manufacturers. A shirt that had taken fourteen hours and twenty-six minutes to sew by hand could be sewn on the "Wheeler and Wilson" in one hour and sixteen minutes. In the 1860s Brooks Bros. reported that a good overcoat, which had once required six days of sewing, could be done in half that time by machine.

28   Mechanization revolutionized the garment industry in the late nineteenth century. Powerful machines that were able to slice through a hundred layers of cloth at a time brought the speed of cutting clothes in line with the sewing operation. Completely automatic looms meant one weaver could produce four hundred yards of fabric an hour. Improved cylinder presses had the capability of printing from two to twelve colors simultaneously. As calico florals rolled off the cylinders, one of the most expensive fabrics of the eighteenth century became one of the cheapest of the nineteenth.

29   Almost all the processes of clothing manufacture had moved into the machine age. Only pressing was still done by hand. The heavy tailor's iron held its own until the early twentieth century, when Adon J. Hoffman of Syracuse dislocated his shoulder and invented a steam pressing machine operated by a foot pedal.

30   Foot power and hand power were needed in ever-greater quantity as production in the garment industry accelerated. New Americans, by and large, did the job. In the 1840s Irish tailors, cutters, and seamstresses came to America in unprecedented numbers. Later in the decade German tailors arrived and with their wives and children produced clothing at home. But it was the great migration from eastern and southern Europe—Poland, Russia, and Italy—beginning in 1880 that provided the garment industry with the cheap labor that permitted mass production in this country. Beryl Fried, a founder of the Cloakmaker's Union,

described working conditions as he knew them in 1885 and as they continued to be until immigrant clothing workers formed their own union in 1914: "Eighteen men and women were crowded into a small dark room: operators, pressers and finishers. During the season there was no time limit. We started working at dawn and stopped at ten or eleven at night. If a worker happened to be an hour late he was met by the others with ridicule. 'Here comes the doctor.' In their conception only a doctor could permit himself the luxury of sleeping so late."

31   In a crazy quilt of inside and outside shops, factory and home production, contracting and subcontracting, the men, women, and children of the garment industry worked long hours for low wages in overcrowded, unsanitary, and unsafe conditions. By their toil they gave a new word to the English language—*sweatshop*—and they gave to this country an immense variety of clothes that the majority of Americans could afford.

32   During the late 1890s the Sears, Roebuck catalog listed men's suits costing from ninety-eight cents to twenty dollars, and on a single day Sears sold nine thousand of them. The "trusty blue serge suit" was worn by store clerks, office workers, professionals, and businessmen, so that Giuseppe Giacosa, an Italian who visited in 1908, was struck by the fact that "no European would be able to pick out by eye who there represents the infinite variety of professions, trades, states, fortune, culture, education that may be encountered among the whole people . . . the shape and texture of the clothing in all shows the same care, the same cut, and almost the same easy circumstances." While visiting Chicago's slaughterhouses, he saw the workers at day's end change their bloody clothes and emerge "a lordly collection of gentlemen" in "handsome ties and plaid jackets."

33   Even the shirt, that once-reliable indicator of social status, dividing white collar from blue, no longer divided men—at least from a distance. Shirts with detachable collars and cuffs, as advertised by the Arrow Collar man, meant that every man could without excessive laundry costs wear what appeared to be a clean white shirt every day. Working men's blue shirts turned up as sportswear along with shirts in a kaleidoscopic array of colors and patterns. Some sense of proportion was retained, however, Boston's Jordan Marsh department store in 1883 announced selections that included "mostly neat designs, such as stripes, figures, spots etc. Large figures, stripes, pug dogs, armchairs etc. have been avoided."

34   Clothes even for occasions too formal for the trusty blue serge were available off the rack and were adapted to the American love of comfort. Thanks to Griswold Lorillard, who in 1886 appeared in a tailless evening coat at the Tuxedo Park Club's formal autumn ball, the tuxedo became part of America's sartorial style.

35   In the years before World War I, sports and leisure activites swept across America. One of the nation's largest manufacturers of clothing, Browning King,

proclaimed, "In these days of almost universal wheeling no man's or boy's wardrobe is complete without a bicycle suit." There were bathing suits, tennis suits, yachting suits, and golf clothes. But there were no blue jeans. Levi's waist pantaloons or overalls—in blue denim or brown duck—were still strictly work clothes.

36   Working clothes began to be important for women, too, after the Civil War. Many women came into the business world as "typewriters" to operate that clacking invention, and as retail establishments proliferated, there was a need for shopgirls. Thousands of immigrant women worked in factories. With no time to sew or suffer endless fittings at a dressmaker's, women needed ready-to-wear clothing. A women's garment industry emerged and grew, until by 1919 it exceeded the men's clothing industry in number of establishments and value of production.

37   Carson Pirie Scott & Co. of Chicago explained that its women's suits were "what the name was meant to imply—strictly man-tailored." But when the woman-on-the-go removed the jacket of her tailored suit, she stood revealed in shirtwaist and skirt, the American girl immortalized by the illustrator Charles Dana Gibson. For the first time in America, women had the equivalent of the trusty blue suit—a uniform that blurred social and economic distinctions. Once the basic investment in the suit had been made, the look could be changed for a mere dollar—the price of a blouse pleated at the shoulders "giving the pronounced Gibson effect."

38   Now there was a new pastime in America: shopping. "Consumer palaces" began to appear in America's cities in response to the large assortment of factory-made goods that were being produced. A typical department store early in the twentieth century was reported to have six miles of sales counters. In one window display, Jordan Marsh re-created the hall of Henri II's palace at Fontainebleau out of "ladies', misses', and children's silk, lisle, and cotton hose." Another store urged everybody to come in: "We want you to feel perfectly at home and free to inspect the goods and ask for information, regardless of whether you wish to buy or not."

39   "Before department stores," Kidwell points out, "if you wanted to see luxury goods, you had to be deemed a suitable client at a small specialty store." The department stores went out of their way to suit everyone. Wanamaker's held white sales; R. H. Macy & Co. gave away fans with its picture on them; and Jordan Marsh & Co. sent out free catalogs for mail-order service.

40   By 1872 small-town residents and farmers could also see all manner of goods simply by looking in a catalog. Aaron Montgomery Ward's first "catalog" was a one-page price list. But by 1875 it had grown to 152 pages listing 3,899 items including #1399—striped velvet vests for $2.50 each; #1406—Black Union Cassimere suit for $12.00; and #1456—2 pairs of Blue Denim Overalls for $1.25. Sears, Roebuck and Co., proudly calling itself the "Cheapest Supply House on Earth," had a 1,120-page catalog in 1898. Mail-order catalogs were the first outlets

for women's ready-to-wear clothing, and by the early twentieth century some ten million Americans shopped by mail.

41   By 1920 almost any American was able to acquire any article of apparel he or she was able to afford. The nation's garment industry had successfully achieved mass production of clothing at low-to-moderate prices. Now that the national closet could easily be filled, the question became, What would Americans choose to hang there?

42   Whatever they chose, it would soon go out of style. In the past, styles had changed slowly. Now, with almost unlimited capacity for production, there had to be a reason for buying new clothes, even if the closet was full. Fashions began to change with every season.

43   To report the rapidly changing styles, fashion communication itself became an industry. In the twenties Paris fashions were reported by newspapers all over the country. Papers ran fashion ads and featured fashion columns. There were fashion magazines for every audience. *Vogue* wanted to help the women of "more than average wealth and refinement with their clothes and social life." Magazines like *Woman's Home Companion* were content to offer advice to the millions of women with average wealth—the housewives of America. *Glamour of Hollywood,* later simply *Glamour,* was subtitled "For the Girl with a Job." And the males of America had *Esquire,* which, when begun in 1933, set as its goal "the establishment of elegance."

44   Before long the fashions these magazines were reporting came not from Paris but from Hollywood. When Clark Gable took off his shirt in *It Happened One Night* (1934) and revealed a bare chest, undershirt sales in America plummeted. And when Joan Crawford wore an Adrian-designed dress with multiruffled, puffed sleeves in *Letty Lynton* (1932), the story of a "girl who loved too often and too well," American women everywhere bought dresses with multiruffled, puffed sleeves. Who needed Paris when for $18.74 Macy's had a copy of the very gown Rita Hayworth wore to marry Aly Khan.

45   In the 1930s not only Hollywood but the rest of California, with its mild climate and casual way of life, began to influence what other Americans wore. California companies made an American contribution to international clothing history—sportswear. Even the French were impressed.

46   Levi Strauss, one of California's first clothing manufacturers, had gotten together with a tailor, Jacob Davis, in 1873 to give the world blue jeans. But not until the 1930s, when Western movies became popular and Easterners began visiting dude ranches in the West, did America decide that jeans were romantic. Soon young Americans made these guaranteed-to-shrink-and-fade blue denim pants the ultimate sartorial symbol of social equality.

47 Teen-agers all across the country began to wear blue jeans. In Los Angeles, in the 1940s, high schoolers walked around with one hand permanently protecting

the right buttock. The little red Levi's tab, the first external manufacturer's brand, was a lure to razor-wielding classmates who collected them. In the mid-fifties, James Dean, in the movie *Rebel without a Cause,* and Marlon Brando, in *The Wild Ones,* turned T-shirts and blue jeans into the emblems of youthful rebellion. In the sixties and seventies T-shirts and blue jeans became the universal uniform of social protest. "Blue jeans were adopted by the 'enemy'—adults," says the Smithsonian Institution's twentieth-century clothing specialist, Barbara Dickstein. Today Levi's—the all-American pants—are sold in at least seventy countries, including the U.S.S.R.

48   "Contemporary clothing blurs generational and social distinctions," Dickstein comments. The avant-garde designer Rudi Gernreich once explained it this way: "Clothes are just not that important. They're not status symbols any longer. They're for fun." Ultimately, the late designer decided that fashion for both sexes was "a kind of flaunting of one's personality."

49   Three hundred years earlier, in 1676, Hannah Lyman had "fflonted" her personality with a silk hood and become one of the first Americans to fight for equality in dress. By the mid-nineteenth century the democratization of clothing that we enjoy today was well under way. In Philadelphia the Great Central Clothing Depot was flourishing at Seventh and Market streets selling such "Fashionable Ready-made Clothing" as cloaks, dress and frock coats, and trousers.

50   Fittingly, in this very building, in 1776, one of America's earliest wearers of trousers, Thomas Jefferson, had created the pattern for a new nation's democracy—the Declaration of Independence.

☐ Discovering Meaning and Technique

1. Explain the meaning of the essay's title.

2. Point out some of the technological advances that made ready-to-wear clothing possible.

3. How did the history of ready-to-wear clothing for women differ from that for men?

4. What effect did the great waves of immigrants have on the clothing industry?

5. What prompted the rise of the "fashion communication" industry?

6. What did America—specifically California—contribute to international clothing history?

7. In paragraph 3 and paragraph 49, Mendelsohn mentions Hannah Lyman. Why is her experience a fitting example for the introduction and conclusion of this selection?

☐ Writing Suggestions

1. Mendelsohn describes the "ridiculous extreme" of hat decorations in Martha Washington's day, such as "windmills (that turned), shepherds with their sheep, and . . . a naval battle featuring a spun-glass French ship of war." Describe a fashion craze in your lifetime that reached a ridiculous extreme.

2. Differences still exist in the clothing services available to men and women. For example, most clothing stores do not charge to alter men's clothes, whereas women must pay for alterations. In addition, dry cleaning prices for women's clothes generally exceed those for men—regardless of the simplicity of the garment. Why do you think these differences exist? What could be done to correct the discrimination?

3. Mendelsohn quotes a businessman of the 1920s, who said, "I used to be able to tell something about the background of a girl . . . by her clothes, but today I often have to wait till she speaks, shows a gold tooth or otherwise gives me a second clew." Today, what clues might tell you about a person's background?

4. Mendelsohn says that "with almost unlimited capacity for production, there had to be a reason for buying new clothes, even if the closet was full. Fashions began to change every season." Defend or attack the control of the fashion industry over our buying habits.

5. How healthy is the concern of even small children with the "right" clothes and brand names?

THE LANGUAGE OF WHITE COSTUMES

☐ ALISON LURIE

1 In classical times, long before the "White" race was invented, white was the color of fair-weather clouds and the snow-topped mountains where the gods dwelt. It was sacred in Zeus, the king of gods: white horses drew his chariot, and white animals were sacrificed to him by white-robed priests. In the Christian church, white is the color of heavenly joy and purity, and is associated with Easter and the Resurrection. In Christian art, God the father, like Zeus, usually wears a long white robe.

2   In secular life white has always stood for purity and innocence. Logically, all-white outfits are most frequently worn by babies and very young children. They often become fashionable for unmarried young women, and sometimes (as in the early nineteenth century) for women of all ages. Innocent heroines in fiction customarily wear white on their first appearance, especially when—like Hardy's Tess or Henry James's Daisy Miller—they are destined for a tragic end. Because it is so easily soiled physically as well as symbolically, white has always been popular with those who wish to demonstrate wealth and status through the conspicuous consumption of laundry soap or conspicuous freedom from manual labor. It is traditionally worn by participants in the high-status sports of tennis and polo, especially in professional competition.

3   Perhaps because it soils easily, or perhaps because of its long association with infancy and early childhood, all-white clothing has often suggested delicacy, and even physical infirmity or weakness, especially when the material is fragile. Invalids in fiction and on stage—as well as in real life—often wear such clothes, and even today the woman who wishes to look especially innocent and dainty may wear an all-white costume. The man who imitates her, however, has usually been considered eccentric and dandified.

4   Today certain social roles and professions seem to us to require white garments. In some cases, this necessity is of recent date: the traditional white wedding dress, for instance, is only about fifty years old. Before the 1920s a bride usually wore a new evening gown in whatever color suited her: it might be white, but it might just as well be pink, yellow, blue or green. After the wedding it became her best party dress. Today most young women are married in a special all-white costume of antique cut and fabric which is generally assumed to be a symbol of innocence and purity, and which will be worn only once in a lifetime. White is considered unsuitable for second marriages, or for brides who are evidently pregnant, though in the latter case the rule is sometimes broken. A cynic might wonder why this expensive and archaic garment should have become fashionable just at the time when changes in social mores and the availability of birth control had made it much less likely than before that a bride was a pure virgin. Prudence Glynn, an erudite and witty commentator on British costume, has suggested that either the modern bride "wants one marvelous, escapist, romantic moment in an otherwise drab life." or perhaps, "by wearing archaic dress she is stating her unconscious belief that the ceremony itself is archaic." It is also possible that the function of the white wedding dress and veil is magical: that by putting it on the bride cancels out her previous experiences, so that she may enter marriage emotionally and symbolically if not physically intact.

5   Before the twentieth century, cleanliness and godliness were not necessarily associated with health, and medical men, wishing to appear serious and competent, dressed in dark, sober clothes. The discovery of germs and hygiene, and the transformation of medicine from an uncertain art into an uncertain science,

changed all that. The doctor was no longer a kind of skilled artisan who might relieve your aches and pains, but would never be asked to dinner in the best houses; he was now a godlike authority figure, an arbiter of life and death. This deified being gradually adopted a pristine white raiment, which today is the standard choice of members of the medical profession. Since any suggestion of their own weakness or illness is to be avoided, doctors and nurses wear garments of sturdy materials, starched as stiff as a board. Patients are also traditionally dressed in white; but their outfits are of a very different texture. When you enter a hospital, or go for a physical checkup, your own clothes are removed and replaced with a pale, shapeless, flimsy garment that fastens ineffectively up the back with strings or snaps like an infant's gown. You are thus simultaneously deprived of your chosen sartorial identity (in the language of clothes, struck dumb) and transformed into a half-naked, helpless, inarticulate creature that cannot even dress itself. (In some chic hospitals and examining rooms, the traditional infantine garment is very pale blue, suggesting trust and docility as well as helpless innocence, and perhaps therefore implying a slightly older baby.)

6   Stiffness and starch were also the mark of the traditional outfit of the Englishman in the tropics—though not that of the Englishwoman, which was usually made of flimsy, fragile muslin, satin and lace, as befitted her presumed delicacy and helplessness. What may be called British Colonial white, though seldom worn today, is familiar to all of us through films and cartoons. The white dress and hat of the female, the white shirt, trousers or shorts and topee of the male, were practical in a hot, sunny climate. But the British insistence upon the spotlessness and freedom from wrinkles of these garments also made them a portable sign of status, and symbolically transformed military occupation and commercial exploitation into justice and virtue, even into self-sacrifice. One of the most famous—and most ambiguous—cases of British Colonial white in fiction occurs in Conrad's *Lord Jim.* Jim (who is a lord only in the scornful designation of his peers) has deserted a sinking ship with a cargo of eight hundred native pilgrims. He always wears spotless white, which graphically expresses his incurable idealism and his identification with the romantic traditions of the British Empire. It is also a sign of false innocence shading into ignorance both of himself and of his world, and reminds us that one of the few negative associations of whiteness is with cowardice.

☐ Discovering Meaning and Technique

1. Why does Lurie say that white can "demonstrate wealth"?

2. To Lurie, the patient/doctor relationship is symbolized by clothes. Do you agreee with her description of that relationship?

3. Lurie and Prudence Glynn suggest reasons for the popularity of today's wedding gown. Do you think any of these reasons are particularly plausible or implausible?

4. The structure of the selection is enumeration—the listing of examples. What uses of white does Lurie enumerate?

5. In enumeration, examples usually support one or several generalizations. Find Lurie's generalizations throughout the essay. Does she have sufficient examples to support them?

6. Lurie discusses clothing over a long period of years—not always in chronological order. Which words and phrases help the reader to follow her discussion as she jumps back and forth in time?

☐ Writing Suggestions

1. Write an essay suggesting a different costume for brides than the one developed since the 1920s.

2. Present a negative view of white costumes—for example, ghost costumes and Ku Klux Klan robes.

3. Write an essay similar to this selection in which you enumerate the social and professional significance of black clothing.

THE JEANING OF AMERICA—AND THE WORLD

☐ CARIN C. QUINN

1 This is the story of a sturdy American symbol which has now spread throughout most of the world. The symbol is not the dollar. It is not even Coca-Cola. It is a simple pair of pants called blue jeans, and what the pants symbolize is what Alexis de Tocqueville called "a manly and legitimate passion for equality. . . ." Blue jeans are favored equally by bureaucrats and cowboys; bankers and deadbeats; fashion designers and beer drinkers. They draw no distinctions and recognize no classes; they are merely American. Yet they are sought after almost everywhere in the world—including Russia, where authorities recently broke up a teen-aged gang that was selling them on the black market for two hundred dollars a pair. They have been around for a long time, and it seems likely that they will outlive even the necktie.

2   This ubiquitous American symbol was the invention of a Bavarian-born Jew. His name was Levi Strauss.

3   He was born in Bad Ocheim, Germany, in 1829, and during the European

political turmoil of 1848 decided to take his chances in New York, to which his two brothers already had emigrated. Upon arrival, Levi soon found that his two brothers had exaggerated their tales of an easy life in the land of the main chance. They were landowners, they had told him; instead, he found them pushing needles, thread, pots, pans, ribbons, yarn, scissors, and buttons to housewives. For two years he was a lowly peddler, hauling some 180 pounds of sundries door-to-door to eke out a marginal living. When a married sister in San Francisco offered to pay his way West in 1850, he jumped at the opportunity, taking with him bolts of canvas he hoped to sell for tenting.

4   It was the wrong kind of canvas for that purpose, but while talking with a miner down from the mother lode, he learned that pants—sturdy pants that would stand up to the rigors of the diggings—were almost impossible to find. Opportunity beckoned. On the spot, Strauss measured the man's girth and inseam with a piece of string and, for six dollars in gold dust, had them tailored into a pair of stiff but rugged pants. The miner was delighted with the result, word got around about "those pants of Levi's," and Strauss was in business. The company has been in business ever since.

5 When Strauss ran out of canvas, he wrote his two brothers to send more. He received instead a tough, brown cotton cloth made in Nîmes, France—called *serge de Nîmes* and swiftly shortened to "denim" (the word "jeans" derives from *Gênes,* the French word for Genoa, where a similar cloth was produced). Almost from the first, Strauss had his cloth dyed the distinctive indigo that gave blue jeans their name, but it was not until the 1870's that he added the copper rivets which have long since become a company trademark. The rivets were the idea of a Virginia City, Nevada, tailor, Jacob W. Davis, who added them to pacify a mean-tempered miner called Alkali Ike. Alkali, the story goes, complained that the pockets of his jeans always tore when he stuffed them with ore samples and demanded that Davis do something about it. As a kind of joke, Davis took the pants to a blacksmith and had the pockets riveted; once again, the idea worked so well that word got around: in 1873 Strauss appropriated and patented the gimmick—and hired Davis as a regional manager.

6   By this time, Strauss had taken both his brothers and two brothers-in-law into the company and was ready for his third San Francisco store. Over the ensuing years the company prospered locally, and by the time of his death in 1902, Strauss had become a man of prominence in California. For three decades thereafter the business remained profitable though small, with sales largely confined to the working people of the West—cowboys, lumberjacks, railroad workers, and the like. Levi's jeans were first introduced to the East, apparently, during the dude-ranch craze of the 1930's, when vacationing Easterners returned and spread the word about the wonderful pants with rivets. Another boost came in World War II, when blue jeans were declared an essential commodity and were sold only to people engaged in defense work. From a company with fifteen salespeople, two plants, and almost no business east of the Mississippi in 1946,

the organization grew in thirty years to include a sales force of more than twenty-two thousand, with fifty plants and offices in thirty-five countries. Each year, more than 250,000,000 items of Levi's clothing are sold—including more than 83,000,000 pairs of riveted blue jeans. They have become, through marketing, word of mouth, and demonstrable reliability, the common pants of America. They can be purchased pre-washed, pre-faded, and pre-shrunk for the suitably proletarian look. They adapt themselves to any sort of idiosyncratic use; women slit them at the inseams and convert them into long skirts, men chop them off above the knees and turn them into something to be worn while challenging the surf. Decorations and ornamentations abound.

7   The pants have become a tradition, and along the way have acquired a history of their own—so much so that the company has opened a museum in San Francisco. There was, for example, the turn-of-the-century trainman who replaced a faulty coupling with a pair of jeans; the Wyoming man who used his jeans as a towrope to haul his car out of a ditch; the Californian who found several pairs in an abandoned mine, wore them, then discovered they were sixty-three years old and still as good as new and turned them over to the Smithsonian as a tribute to their toughness. And then there is the particularly terrifying story of the careless construction worker who dangled fifty-two stories above the street until rescued, his sole support the Levi's belt loop through which his rope was hooked.

8 Today "those pants of Levi's" have gone across the seas—although the company has learned that marketing abroad is an arcane art. The conservative-dress jeans favored in northern France do not move on the Côte d'Azur; Sta-Prest sells well in Switzerland but dies in Scandinavia; button fronts are popular in France, zippers in Britain.

9   Though Levi Strauss & Co. has since become Levi Strauss International, with all that the corporate name implies, it still retains a suitably fond regard for its beginnings. Through what it calls its "Western Image Program," employing Western magazine advertisements, local radio and television, and the promotion of rodeos, the company still pursues the working people of the West who first inspired Levi Strauss to make pants to fit the world.

☐ Discovering Meaning and Technique

1. What are the origins of the terms *jeans* and *denim?*

2. Why does Quinn say that blue jeans symbolize the American "passion for equality"?

3. Pick out the events in the selection that indicate something about the personality of Levi Strauss. What kind of a person does he seem to have been?

4. The selection is primarily a narrative—a recounting of specific events in chronological order. Point out where the narrative begins and ends.

5. Find examples of the selection's enumeration strategy—the listing of details or examples to make a point.

6. Explain the following words and terms from the selection: *deadbeats* (paragraph 1), *sundries* (paragraph 3), *eke out* (paragraph 3), *mother lode* (paragraph 4), *dude-ranch* (paragraph 6). Why do you think Quinn chose these words?

☐ Writing Suggestions

1. Quinn states that jeans can be "pre-washed, pre-faded, and pre-shrunk." It has even been fashionable to cut holes in the knees and tear off back pockets. Why do many consumers try to achieve what Quinn calls here the "suitably proletarian look"?

2. Many consumers claim to favor jeans because they are comfortable; yet these same people often wear them so tight that comfort is out of the question. Why do you suppose that people actually favor jeans?

3. Comment on the popularity of some contemporary costume, such as jeans, western belts, boots, and baseball caps.

4. Categorize people by the type and cut of their jeans.

5. What might explain the fondness for jeans in other countries, even in Russia?

ON HATS

☐ ROY BLOUNT, JR.

1 Clothes are not my strong suit, but I do know this: Public hanging ended in England because of the hat.

2   According to Richard D. Altick in *Victorian Studies in Scarlet,* a German named Müller murdered an elderly man on a North London Railway train in 1864 and was convicted because he accidentally exchanged hats with the victim after a struggle. His own hat was found in the compartment, and he was presently discovered wearing the victim's—only with the crown cut down so as to eliminate

the victim's name on the side. Forthwith there sprang up a stylish hat, like a topper only half as tall, called the Müller cut-down. The crowd that gathered during the night before Müller's hanging was unruly. Several well-dressed congregants were bonneted—that is, someone sneaked up from behind and pulled their hats down over their faces—garroted, and robbed. Parliament was at last provoked to forbid public executions.

3   The hat. Our most resonant garment. According to *Folk Beliefs of the Southern Negro,* by Newbell Niles Puckett, American slaves (who had to believe in something other than America) believed that if you put on another person's hat you'll get a headache unless you blow into the hat first; that it is bad luck to put your hat on inside out; that the bad luck promised by a rabbit's crossing the road ahead of you may be averted by putting your hat on backward; that if you desire eggs to hatch into roosters you should carry them to the nest in a man's hat; that a group of people was once crossing a field at noon when they suddenly saw a whole house coming after them, which passed so close that it knocked off their hats, and neither hats nor house was seen again; that if you eat with your hat on you will not get enough.

4   And yet it seems to me that people these days wear hats lightly. People have somehow gotten hold of the notion that a hat is a fun topping. Nothing in this world makes a person who is not a cowboy look less like a cowboy than wearing a cowboy hat, and yet we have recently passed through a period when every third nonpunk person in New York and Los Angeles was in for the full ten gallons.

5   Hey! You can't just walk around *wearing a cowboy hat.* I don't walk around wearing one, and I have herded cows. Somehow years ago I lost the tan felt cowboy hat I got (with the card inside that says "Like Hell It's Yours") at the White Front Store in Fort Worth. I wore it on working visits to a Texas cattle ranch to which I was then related by marriage. That hat and I were rained on twice, and the trained eye could discern traces of horse slobber on its brim and a touch of cow paddy (it can happen) on its crown. That hat fit me so well that—well, I'll tell you how well it fit me.

6   One evening a bunch of us were in the back of a pickup truck, hurtling through the night toward a mudhole to pull out a mired heifer. It was too dark for abandoned driving, but the driver, Herman Posey, got caught up in the holiday spirit pervading us visitors, and before we knew it he had us jouncing and plummeting, off the ground more than on it, over creek bed, armadillo, and cactus.

7   Bob Crittendon, the foreman, was with us in the back. He weighed a good deal more than two hundred pounds and didn't find any charm in being jounced. He was busy yelling, *"Herman, damn you, slow down!"*

8   And yet he took the time to mention, "Old Roy's the only one don't have to hold on to his hat."

9   And. Yet. I wouldn't wear that hat around town.

10   When I'm around town I don't want to be always *backing up* a hat. You might think it would back up that hat for me to tell that story about what Bob Crittendon said. But it wouldn't be the same as hearing Bob say it. To back up a cowboy hat you have to think of a remark of your own, like the one a man I know named Jimmy Crafton, in Nashville, thought of when a man picked his cowboy hat up off a bar and tried it on.

11   Crafton gave him a look.

12   The man thought better of what he had done, and apologized.

13   "That's all right," said Crafton. "That's why I wear a fifty-dollar hat. If it was a two-hundred-dollar hat," he explained, "I'da had to kill you."

14   I'll say another thing. Nobody ought to wear a Greek fisherman's cap who doesn't meet two qualifications:

1. He is Greek.
2. He is a fisherman.

15   What I am getting at is, a hat ought not to be on a head for a whim. Yeats once said that when a poem is finished it "comes right with a click like a closing box." That's what a hat ought to do for a person. Quite often today, though the person may think it does, it doesn't.

16 I like to wear a hat around home and driving, because it obviates hair combing and it helps keep the bugs off. (There is no hat that keeps you warm in serious winter. If they ever invented a hat that kept your ears and neck warm it would be a hood and it might as well be attached to your coat.) What I usually wear is some kind of billed, adjustable cap.

17   And these days those caps all, just about, have something written on them. I stay away from the ones that say "I'm a Real Dilly," or "Texas Turkey" (with a picture of an armadillo). For some time I wore one that said "Shakespeare" for Shakespeare brand fishing equipment, because those folks make good fishing equipment and I wasn't averse to paying indirect tribute to the author of *King Lear.* And I had been given that hat free. And it fit my head. You'd be surprised how many people walk around in hats that don't fit their heads, and also how many "One Size Fits All" adjustable hats don't fit all. But that one fit me. But I left it hanging in a Howard Johnson's on the interstate and couldn't go back for it.

18   Then for a while I had a cap that said "MF," for Massey-Ferguson farm and industrial equipment, and that cap brought home to me that a hat is language.

19   I was wearing that cap out on the road and one of my tires went flat and wouldn't hold air longer than twenty miles and nobody could seem to patch it, and I didn't have a spare. I had to go to a place that sold tires, and the man was just closing up, but he was kind enough to turn his lights back on and chain his dog back up and sell me a tire and put it on.

20   And he took my cap at face value. Assumed I was a Massey-Ferguson represen-

tative. Plunged into a series of questions about what kind of tractor would be best for working the little piece of land he had at home, and could I maybe get him some kind of deal on one.

21   And I had to tell him I didn't represent Massey-Ferguson. And he took it the wrong way. Here he was staying open late to help me out, and either I was fraudulent or else I didn't want to admit that I could get him a deal. He kept shooting looks over at my cap (so did his dog) while he worked, and I thought he was going to tell me to take it off. And I could see how he felt. But I didn't want to think that I was going to let somebody tell me to take my *hat* off, you know. I got out of there all right, except I think he charged me an extra ten dollars for my cap.

22   Then a couple of weeks later I had the same cap on and a friend from New York looked at it and said, "Oh, a football coach's cap."

23   "A what?" I said.

24   "A football coach's cap," she said. "That's what you call them. They're very big now in the gay community."

25   Now, a gay person has every bit as much right to wear a Massey-Ferguson cap as I have; more right if he's a Massey-Ferguson representative. Or owns a tractor that the cap came with. But I didn't like it that my cap all of a sudden had a term for it, among the fashion-conscious.

26   But that's the way a hat is, it's like a word: you have to keep up with all its shifting connotations if you're going to employ it. And you have to avoid assuming too quickly that you do know them. There is a telling hat scene in the movie *Deliverance.* The city guys stop at a gas station up in the hills. Bobby, the chubby character played by Ned Beatty, espies a toothless-looking, shuffling mountain man with an old felt hat pulled down over his ears. "Hey, we got a live one here," Bobby says. The man begins to fill their tank. "I love the way you wear that hat," Bobby tells him. The man takes off the hat, turns it around in his hands, looks at it, jams it back on his head.

27   "Mister," he says, "you don't know *nuthin'."*

28   If you saw the movie, you remember what happens to Bobby.

☐ Discovering Meaning and Technique

1. Why does Blount in the second and third paragraphs relate historical data and folklore about hats?

2. Why does Blount begin the fourth paragraph with the words, "And yet"?

3. Explain what Blount means by *"backing up* a hat" (paragraph 10).

4. What is the effect of the scene (paragraphs 19–21) in which Blount gets his tire changed? Is he able to "back up" his hat?

5. Blount begins a number of sentences with *and.* What is effect of this technique on his writing style?

6. Blount also uses sentence fragments. Does this technique have the same effect as beginning sentences with *and?*

☐ Writing Suggestions

1. Agree or disagree with Blount's idea that a person should be able to back up a hat. Use real or fictional experiences to support your position.

2. Write about another type of clothing that you should be able to back up—coats, boots, ties, or workout clothes, for example.

3. Classify people by the kinds of costumes they wear. Can you, for example, tell an art major from an accounting major?

4. An old joke involves a seasoned cowboy applying for a job as a ranch hand. When the ranch foreman asks the cowboy why he is wearing tennis shoes instead of boots, the cowboy replies, "I didn't want you to think I was a truck driver." Discuss one or more articles of clothing inappropriate to the wearer.

THE ORIGINS OF THE COWBOY BOOT

☐ ROLAND SODOWSKY

1 The first United States settlers in the Texas Occident were from New Hampshire. They were fruit-and-nut gatherers of English and Scottish descent who had for many centuries worn high, wide-topped boots in which to drop their food as they gathered it. This tradition was continued in the Occident, where a gatherer's specialty could usually be ascertained by the color of his boot tops, since over a period of years the seeping juices of the fruit and nuts stained the leather. Green mesquite beans, for example, produced a bright chartreuse color, which is still popular among cowboys today; dry mesquite beans produced a rich mahogany stain, darker than that of pecans; a rosy pink-red stain, also still popular, was produced by prickly pears and blood.

2   Many puzzled historians have noted that the Texas Occident boot resembles the contours of the human foot about as much as bandannas do bananas. Searching

for a reason why anyone would commit such violence on his own feet, some historians have mistakenly assumed that the Texas Occident boot was worn by devoutly religious cowboys as a form of penitence, like flagellation. Its severe discomfort, however, may be traced to a singular chain of events involving two men, Angus Macleoud and Arturo Shumacher II.

3   Macleoud was the first bootmaker in the Texas Occident. He settled in the once thriving community of Lindisfarne, set to work building a boot shop, and, like many of his comrades from New Hampshire, eventually sent for his family, as well as for his boot-making tools. He had traveled light on his trip westward in search of a new home. Unfortunately, the immigrant wagon train bringing Macleoud's family was attacked by Comanches on the Middle Concho River, southwest of San Angelo, and Macleoud's wife, his eight-year old daughter, Marie, and all his boot lasts were taken. His wife was never heard of again. One of the lasts—for a pair of women's boots—reappeared later in Galveston, as a result of the infamous Comanche sweep to the Gulf, in 1878; it had been sharpened and attached to a lance that wounded Augustus Kalplish, a Galveston land speculator. Macleoud had etched his name on the last, so it was traced to him in Lindisfarne. Kalplish sued him for damages under the Attenuated Responsibility Act in the well-known "Last Laughs" case, but was awarded only one dollar, and the last was returned to Macleoud, who immediately put it to use again.

4   Since many pioneers had lived in the Lindisfarne area for several decades without new footwear, demand for Macleoud's boots was intense. Using the sharpened last for women's boots, Macleoud produced boots for men and women alike as fast as he could make them, despite their uncomfortable, unstable, and impractical high heels. By the time other boot makers arrived in the Texas Occident, the tradition was established, and they were forced to throw away the lasts designed for more reasonable and wholesome low-heeled footwear and to follow the regional fashion.

5   "It was a love-hate relationship," Miguel Cervantes recalled many years later. Cervantes was the philosopher-foreman of the Kalplish Ranch and one of a handful of men who had been in the Texas Occident long before even the pioneers like Macleoud had arrived—had, in fact, "been here forever, I reckon."

6   Cervantes continued, "We all hated Macleoud's boots. The heel would wobble out from under you without warning, and at the worst times. Your toes always hurt. The boot always fit too tight, and your feet would sweat and then smell like—well, like they'd been in a cowboy boot all day."

7   Unreasonable though the first generation of Macleoud's boots were, the next generation were worse, thanks to the flamboyant young heir to the vast and ancient Shumacher Ranch, Arturo Shumacher II. By 1886 Arturo II was already one of the most popular figures in the Occident. Notwithstanding his strangely shaped feet, which, a contemporary wrote, "were as slender and sharp as yucca blades," he had won everyone's admiration with his gracious manners,

his quick wit, and his uncanny ability to find hackberries. It was this talent that, indirectly, led to his central role in one of the indelible legends of the Occident.

8   On August 23, 1886, Arturo II was picking hackberries near Horseshoe Springs when he espied Angus Macleoud's daughter, Marie, in a Comanche encampment. Emptying the hackberries from his boots into a hollow tree, he concealed himself in the thick willows along the creek and awaited his chance to rescue her. That opportunity came when, as most of the camp slept in the heat of the afternoon, Marie approached the creek near where Arturo II was hidden. She glanced around carefully and then removed her large and elaborate earmuffs, which she had been wearing since leaving New Hampshire many years before.

9   Arturo II was stunned.

10   "She was wildly beautiful," he wrote many years later, in Volume II of his autobiography. "For many minutes I could only gaze as she washed her thick, lustrous black hair. Then I remembered that the short time I had in which to save her was rapidly running out. I burst from my concealment, raced across the shallow creek, threw her over my shoulder, and began that long, desperate race across the desert toward Lindisfarne."

11   Actually, as Marie was to note in Volume III of *her* autobiography, which was written after Arturo II's death, the creek was not as shallow as her rescuer had thought, and he had to empty his boots of several gallons of water before he could even move, much less throw Marie over his shoulder. By the time he had poured the water out, she had recovered somewhat from her surprise at having a young, flamboyant stranger speaking a language she barely remembered burst from the willows wearing such outlandish footwear.

12   "He threw me over his shoulder and began running," Marie wrote, "but I recalled that I had left behind some ornaments for my earmuffs that I especially treasured. So I made him go by my tepee for them. Then he set out again, but I had another thought and made him go back to the tepee once more for a large, soggy, rather messy parcel that I also coveted."

13   By then, of course, the whole encampment had been alerted, and as Arturo II set out at a dead run in a southwest direction across the desert, with Marie thrown over his shoulder, all the Comanches in the camp came howling after them. After two or three miles they began to catch up, partly, Marie wrote, "because Arturo II was carrying me, but more because of his strange footwear, which made running nearly impossible."

14   Taking a bite from the soggy parcel they had returned for, Marie chewed for a moment and then said to Arturo II, "I'm very curious about something, and since the Comanches are about to catch us, and kill you, perhaps you should tell me now. Where are you taking me?"

15   "Why, to your father, Angus Macleoud, in Lindisfarne," Arturo II said.

16   "Oh." Marie jumped lightly down from her uncomfortable position over his shoulder. "Why didn't you tell me before? I can run much faster than you,

and we can easily outdistance our pursuers if you'll take off those ridiculous boots."

17   Arturo II glanced at his boots and pondered for a moment as arrows began to whiz all around them. Then he shook his head. "I couldn't do that. Tradition, you know."

18   "So," Marie concluded, "I grabbed him, threw him over *my* shoulder, and commenced running across those trackless wastes again. The Comanches soon lost heart then, for they knew I had the bear's strength and the hummingbird's speed, and they could never catch me."

19   Thus Marie was reunited with her father.

20   Now sixteen years old and, in addition to being wildly beautiful, addicted to raw buffalo liver, which was what the parcel they had returned for contained, Marie was married in October to Arturo II in the most elaborate wedding ever seen in the Occident. Macleoud, who was immeasurably grateful to Arturo, went into seclusion in his workshop a month before the wedding and crafted the young man a pair of boots especially designed for his dainty, spear-shaped feet.

21   At the wedding hundreds of impressionable young men—all of whom, if the truth be known, were secretly and hopelessly in love with Marie—watched Arturo II and Marie swirling gracefully in the center of the ballroom floor at the Shumacher Ranch. Long before the wedding week was over and Arturo II and his bride had departed to retrieve his cache of hackberries, Macleoud had more orders for the thin, impossibly pointed boots than he could ever hope to fill in his lifetime.

22   Many young men performed radical operations on their feet by their own hand, cutting off all or parts of several toes to achieve the desired foot configuration, and the practice has continued in some remote areas of the Texas Occident to this day, although most parents prefer to forestall such grim measures by binding their infant sons' feet.

23   It has never been determined why some people began to call the Macleoud boot a "cowboy" boot in the early 1920s; conservative Texas Occidentals still refer to it by its traditional name, the fruit boot.

☐ Discovering Meaning and Technique

1. What theory about the shape of the cowboy boot does the narrator set out to disprove?

2. Why was Macleoud's boot last so pointed? Why did his boots have high heels?

3. How does Arturo's strange footwear figure in the plot?

4. Why does Marie twice return to the Comanche camp?

5. How does the introductory paragraph set up the last line of the selection?

6. For the most part, the structure is a narrative. Where is it not?

7. Why does Sodowsky name his characters as he does?

8. Sodowsky mixes the ridiculous with a few realistic touches. List a few ridiculous and a few realistic details.

☐ Writing Suggestions

1. Describe in a fanciful or serious manner the origins of some other clothes—for example, a man's tie, penny loafers, a tuxedo, a football uniform.

2. Treat the subject of the origin of the cowboy boot seriously.

3. Illustrate that tradition in clothing is more important than practicality or comfort.

4. Visit stores that sell cowboy boots. Discuss the newest trends.

5. To what do you attribute the worldwide popularity of cowboy boots?

Eating

■ ■ ■

UNDERSTANDING SOCIETY AND CULTURE THROUGH EATING

☐ PETER FARB AND GEORGE ARMELAGOS

1 All animals feed but humans alone eat. A dog wolfs down every meal in the same way, but humans behave in a variety of ways while eating. In North American and European societies, for example, business negotiations are conducted over cocktails and lunch; seductions may begin with champagne and oysters; wedding and birthday parties center around an elaborately decorated cake; and gifts of food are part of the exchange at Christmastime. In simpler societies, eating is associated with initiation and burial rites, the roles of the sexes, economic transactions, hospitality, and dealings with the supernatural—virtually the entire spectrum of human activity.

2   Food faddists in recent decades have declared, "You are what you eat." Before them, so did Edmund Kean, the nineteenth-century Shakespearean actor, who ate mutton before going onstage in the part of a lover, beef when he was to play a murderer, and pork for the role of a tyrant. The classic formulation of this statement was set down a century and a half ago by Jean Anthelme Brillat–Savarin in his treatise on eating, *The Physiology of Taste:* "Tell me what thou eatest, and I will tell thee what thou art." But the attribution of character, behavior, and achievement to particular items in the diet did not originate with Brillat–Savarin. In *Julius Caesar,* Cassius says to Brutus: "Upon what meat doth this our Caesar feed/ That he is grown so great?" And the idea was around long before Shakespeare. It goes back thousands of years—to a statement in the *Bhagavad Gita,* the sacred Hindu text, that particular foods are appropriate for those of a particular temperament, and even to the ancient Greeks, who codified the idea into their medical teachings, eventually passing it on to much of the world by way of Arab learning. The linking of food with human behavior has even been applied to stereotypes about entire nations: The French subtlety of thought and manners is said to be related to the subtlety of their cuisine, the reserve of the British to their unimaginative diet, German stolidness to the quantities of heavy food they consume, and the unreliability of Italians to the large amounts of wine they drink.

3   An anthropologist who knows what the members of a society eat already knows a lot about them. Learning how the food is obtained and who prepares it adds considerably to the anthropologist's store of information about the way that society functions. And once the anthropologist finds out where, when, and with whom the food is eaten, just about everything else can be inferred about the relations among the society's members. This is possible because human behavior has evolved in great part as an interplay between eating behavior and cultural institutions—and because behavior, in turn, influences anatomy, physiology, and the evolution of the human organism itself. Eating, in short, is inseparable from the behavior and the biology of the human species and from the adaptation that humans have made to the conditions of their existence on the planet. Cultural traits, social institutions, national histories, and individual attitudes cannot be entirely understood without an understanding also of how these have meshed with our varied and peculiar modes of eating.

4   In all societies, both simple and complex, eating is the primary way of initiating and maintaining human relationships. In fact, the English word "companion" is derived from French and Latin words that mean "one who eats bread with another." The Bantu of southern Africa regard exchanging food as the formation of what amounts to a temporary covenant between individuals—"a clanship of porridge," as they call it. For most Chinese, social transactions are almost inseparable from eating transactions. The giving and sharing of food is the prototypic relationship in Chinese society, as if the word were literally made flesh. Only a Chinese living alone and in abject poverty would sit down to a solitary meal. It is usual to eat with one's family or kin; when these are unavailable, people eat in teashops or at work rather than by themselves. No important business transaction and no marriage arrangement is ever concluded without the sharing of food. The quality of the meal and its setting convey a more subtle social message than anything that is consciously verbalized; attitudes that would be impolite if stated directly are communicated through the food channel.

5   Food and drink have such intense emotional significance that they are often linked with events that have nothing to do with nutrition. The perpetrators of the Boston Tea Party were angry not over tea but over taxation; the breadline and apple-sellers of the Great Depression became symbols of what was wrong with the economy. Guests at a dinner party usually leave a little food on the plate to let their hosts know they have been fed to repletion. A child who misbehaves is sent to bed without dinner, while obedience is rewarded with candy or ice cream. The simple fact of sitting down to eat together may convey important statements about a society. The civil-rights movement in the southern United States during the 1950s began as a dispute about the right of blacks not simply to eat at lunch counters but to sit down there with whites; blacks insisted on that right because in North American society people customarily sit down to eat only as equals.

6   Eating is intimately connected with sex roles, since the responsibility for each phase of obtaining and preparing a particular kind of food is almost always allotted according to sex. Members of one sex, generally the males, may be served first, and particular foods may be regarded as appropriate to each sex. Husbands and wives in some parts of Melanesia and Polynesia are not supposed to see each other eat; in Arabia, Japan, and parts of eastern Europe, women do not eat until the men in the family have finished their meals. In some societies, on the other hand, eating with the family is so traditional that workers are given long midday breaks so that they can go home for lunch. After World War II, hungry Greeks preferred to carry home the hot soup given them by the Red Cross and eat it there with their families rather than in the warm Red Cross canteens. At marriage celebrations in northern Europe during the Middle Ages, it was considered an important moment when the couple ate together— which is apparently the origin of the custom that prevails today in North America and in parts of Europe of watching the new bride and groom share the first slice of wedding cake.

7   Each society's culture is transmitted to children through eating with the family, a setting in which individual personalities develop, kinship obligations emerge, and the customs of the group are reinforced. Children learn at mealtimes to express a formal reverence for food through the custom of saying grace, as in what Christians know as the Lord's Prayer ("Give us this day our daily bread"), and they become acquainted with the regulations governing what their society considers edible. For many African children, this amounts to learning that a meal is not a meal unless it includes porridge. Europeans are brought up to feel much the same way about bread, and many North Americans genuinely believe that dinner is not really dinner without meat.

8   Finally, what is eaten establishes one's social, religious, and ethnic member-ships. The coarse black bread that is the standard fare of a European peasant is a function of social rank, and so is the meal of roast dog that was served to the Aztec noble. Who can mistake the status of a German who drinks Trockenberenau-slese, a wine made from grapes so rare that finding enough to produce a single bottle is a day's work even for a skilled picker? The surest way of discovering a family's ethnic origins is to look into its kitchen. Long after dress, manners, and speech have become indistinguishable from those of the majority, the old food habits continue as the last vestiges of the previous culture. Taboos against certain foods mark one as an adherent of a particular religion: Moslems and Jews reject pork, Hindus beef, and some Protestant denominations alcohol. Food customs as a badge of rank are particularly evident in India, where rules for each caste define both whom a person is permitted to marry and also with whom that person is permitted to eat; the interweaving of these prohibitions tends to keep young people in the same caste as their parents.

9   With so much cultural importance attached to eating, it is no wonder that food to a large extent is what holds a society together. For example, the

rice that is fundamental to the existence of the Malays of Southeast Asia is believed to possess an essential life force; so the ceremonials that mark every stage of life—from birth through coming of age, marriage, and death—involve a symbolic meal of rice. For a Malay, rice is synonymous with food, and its presence is what distinguishes a meal. The Malays' first food of the day, at what North Americans and Europeans think of as the breakfast meal, usually consists of a sort of cake and coffee. Malays regard this as a snack rather than as a meal, simply because no rice is eaten. People in modern societies as well have notions about what is appropriate food for each meal. A typical North American breakfast consists of fruit, cereal, and a milk product—but strawberry shortcake, which includes all three, is considered inappropriate.

10   Maize interpenetrates the entire culture of the Pueblo Indians of the southwestern United States: the family, religion, hospitality, friendship, and the concept of sharing. It is inseparable from ritual; chants praise the eating of maize, the field amounts almost to an altar and cultivating the plant to an act of worship. Every Pueblo Indian who can walk takes part in the Corn Dance. The anthropologist Dorothy Lee has summarized the central place of maize in Pueblo culture: "When I take away corn from such people, I take away not only nutrition, not just a loved food. I take away an entire life and the meaning of life." Possibly the reason why numerous American Indian groups have surrounded maize with myths, legends, and religious ceremonies is that they have never found the plant growing wild. Seeming to exist by some miracle entirely for human benefit, and being of unknown origin, maize may have been deemed a gift of the supernatural.

11   For the Bemba of Zambia, daily life revolves around food and beer. The village echoes all day with shouts from hut to hut about what is to be eaten at the next meal, what was eaten at the previous meal, and what is in prospect for the future. The Bemba refer both to the various habitats within their environment and to the passing seasons in terms of eating, describing a certain place as "where only pumpkin leaves are eaten" or referring to a time of year as "the time when we eat mushrooms." The polite greeting to a returned traveler is not an inquiry about the things seen or the people met, but rather the question: "Have you eaten well?" Wealth among the Bemba is measured by the amount of food available to offer hospitality to others. A man has not been fully described without some mention of how much he has in his granary, how many relatives he feeds, and how much beer he contributed to the last feast.

12 The many associations between eating and human behavior can be seen most clearly in simple and isolated societies, such as that of the Trobriand Islands off the eastern tip of New Guinea. Trobrianders do not consider eating a biological necessity for sustaining life, nor do they consciously recognize certain foods as having a higher nutritive value than others. They eat not simply because they have an appetite but because eating is a social necessity. To give food is a

virtuous act, and the man who distributes large amounts of it is by definition a good man. The formal distribution of food is so important to all Trobriand festivals and ceremonies that some anthropologists describe it as a "cult of food." Distributions figure not only at feasts, at competitions between rival groups, and at an annual festival. They are particularly lavish at funerals, marriages, and certain rituals when food is offered not only to the human guests, but also to the spirits as an encouragement for them to participate.

13   Even when formal distributions are not involved, food is used as a medium for most economic exchanges. A Trobriander who wants to engage the services of a specialist, such as a canoe-maker, first sends a gift of food, which is followed up with a succession of others after the artisan has agreed to the project. Food is also a measure of a person's sense of worth and pride. Hunger, or even a lack of superabundance, is not considered an occasion for the exercise of charity but rather as an extreme cause of shame. To say to a man, *"Gala kam"* ("Thou hast no food"), is to insult him. People will endure real hunger rather than expose themselves to such derogatory comments by asking for food. Above all else, foodstuffs are a prime medium for the enhancement of prestige. Yams are accumulated because they are easily stored, but also because they can be displayed as valued possessions. The storehouse is built with openings between the beams wide enough so that everyone can admire the quantity and quality of the yams, which are so arranged that the best specimens are visible—much as grocers in European-derived societies display their produce in a store window. Before filling the storehouse, magic is performed to decrease the appetite of the owners and thus insure that the supplies will last as long as possible. The Trobrianders believe that this magic also prolongs supplies by encouraging the eating of breadfruit from the village groves and wild fruits from the bush. Such magic is nutritionally and ecologically advantageous; it forces the Trobrianders to exploit their environment more fully, to consume a wide range of foods, and thereby to obtain a greater variety of vitamins and minerals.

14   Given the social importance of food, it might seem strange to discover that the Trobrianders eat alone, retiring to their own hearths with their portions, turning their backs on one another and eating rapidly for fear of being observed. Whereas premarital sexual relations are an accepted feature of Trobriand social life, couples are prohibited from eating together before marriage. People in Western societies sometimes object when an unmarried couple share a bed; the Trobrianders object just as strongly when they share a meal. Food taboos further divide the Trobrianders along the lines of rank. Those of the highest rank obtain food from, and have it prepared by, people of similar rank because their diet is different from that of commoners. A man of the highest rank would never knowingly eat, for example, a bush pig or a stingray—and were he to learn that he had done so unwittingly, he would vomit up the meal.

15   The attitudes toward eating that prevail in the Trobriand Islands can be found in more complex societies as well. At one time in North America and

Europe, both tuberculosis and rickets, for example, were attributed to a lack of proper food, and thus were a source of shame for the afflicted and their families. Just as the Trobrianders pay an artisan with gifts of food, painters and sculptors during the Middle Ages and the Renaissance were often paid in food and wine. Trobrianders gain status through their display of yams, but we also achieve status through the consumption of certain rare or expensive foods: caviar, wild game, and the truffles that must be rooted out by trained dogs and hogs. And although we do not use food directly as a medium of exchange, we discharge obligations that cannot appropriately be repaid with money by inviting people to a lavish meal. Trobrianders use food to reward and punish, but Europeans and North Americans long punished prisoners by feeding them only bread and water. For all that we denigrate the magical beliefs connected with food in simpler societies, it should be remembered that some of us throw salt over a shoulder to ward off bad luck, or eat fish in the belief that it is a superior brain food, or order oysters with the hope of increasing sexual potency. All the major religions continue to attach symbolic meanings to food and drink (even though the Roman Catholic prohibition against eating meat on Friday has been lifted): the bread and wine of the Christian communion service, the taboo observed by Jews against mixing meat and dairy products at the same meal, and the reverence for the sacred cow in Hindu India. In the political sphere, injustice is dramatized by fasting, as practiced by Gandhi and Martin Luther King, Jr., among many others. And we continue, like the Trobrianders, to observe the rites of passage—birth, coming of age, marriage, and death—with food and drink.

☐ Discovering Meaning and Technique

1. What does Brillat–Savarin mean by "Tell me what thou eatest, and I will tell thee what thou art"?

2. From what does the tradition of a bride and groom sharing a wedding cake come?

3. Why are mealtimes important to the education of children?

4. What grains are associated with many societies' rituals?

5. Why do some anthropologists call the Trobriand society a "cult of food"?

6. A topic sentence sums up the idea of a whole paragraph. Which paragraphs in this selection contain topic sentences?

7. How do the authors move the reader's attention from their general discussion of eating to the specific discussion of the Trobrianders?

8. What characteristics make the writers' style seem formal and not conversational?

9. What kind of information appears in parentheses?

☐ **Writing Suggestions**

1. Describe some of the many human activities associated with eating.

2. Discuss whether preparing food is becoming less often the woman's responsibility.

3. Are food traditions becoming less and less important with the advent of fast food and frozen dinners?

4. From observing a family's kitchen and eating habits, analyze its social, religious, and ethnic associations.

5. How is the decline of "family dinners" affecting society?

6. Which cooking activities are traditionally associated with males?

THE ANTHROPOLOGY OF TABLE MANNERS FROM GEOPHAGY ONWARD

☐ GUY DAVENPORT

1 A businessman now risen to a vice-presidency tells me that in his apprentice days he used to cross deepest Arkansas as a mere traveling salesman, and that there were certain farms at which men from his company put up overnight, meals being included in the deal. Once, on a new route, he appeared at breakfast after a refreshing sleep in a feather bed to face a hardy array of buttery eggs, biscuits, apple pie, coffee, and fatback.

2 This latter item was unfamiliar to him and from the looks of it he was damned if he would eat it. He knew his manners, however, and in passing over the fatback chatted with the lady of the house about how eating habits tend to be local, individual, and a matter of how one has been raised. He hoped she wouldn't take it wrong that he, unused to consuming fatback, left it untouched on his plate.

3 The genial Arkansas matron nodded to this politely, agreeing that food is different all over the world.

4   She then excused herself, flapped her copious apron, and retired from the kitchen. She returned with a double-barreled shotgun which she trained on the traveling salesman, with the grim remark, "Eat hit."

5   And eat hit he did.

6   Our traveler's offense was to reject what he had been served, an insult in practically every code of table manners. Snug in an igloo, the Eskimo scrapes gunk from between his toes and politely offers it as garnish for your blubber. Among the Penan of the upper Baram in Sarawak you eat your friend's snot as a sign of your esteem. There are dinner parties in Africa where the butter for your stewed calabash will be milked from your hostess's hair. And you dare not refuse.

7   Eating is always at least two activities: consuming food and obeying a code of manners. And in the manners is concealed a program of taboos as rigid as Deuteronomy. We rational, advanced, and liberated Americans may not, as in the Amazon, serve the bride's mother as the wedding feast; we may not, as in Japan, burp our appreciation, or as in Arabia, eat with our fingers. Every child has suffered initiation into the mysteries of table manners: keep your elbows off the table, ask for things to be passed rather than reach, don't cut your bread with a knife, keep your mouth closed while chewing, don't talk with food in your mouth, and on and on, and all of it witchcraft and another notch upward in the rise of the middle class.

8   Our escapes from civilization are symptomatic: the first rule we break is that of table manners. Liberty wears her reddest cap; all is permitted. I remember a weekend away from paratrooper barracks when we dined on eggs scrambled in Jack Daniel's, potato chips and peanut brittle, while the Sergeant Major, a family man of bankerish decorum in ordinary times, sang falsetto "There Will be Peace in the Valley" stark naked except for cowboy boots and hat.

9   But to children, hardest pressed by gentility at the table, a little bending of the rules is Cockayne itself. One of my great culinary moments was being taken as a tot to my black nurse's house to eat clay. "What this child needs," she had muttered one day while we were out, "is a bait of clay." Everybody in South Carolina knew that blacks, for reasons unknown, fancied clay. Not until I came to read Toynbee's *A Study of History* years later did I learn that eating clay, or geophagy, is a prehistoric habit (it fills the stomach until you can bring down another aurochs) surviving only in West Africa and South Carolina. I even had the opportunity, when I met Toynbee at a scholarly do, to say that I had been in my day geophagous. He gave me a strange, British look.

10   The eating took place in a bedroom, for the galvanized bucket of clay was kept under the bed, for the cool. It was blue clay from a creek, the consistency of slightly gritty ice cream. It lay smooth and delicious-looking in its pail of clear water. You scooped it out and ate it from your hand. The taste was wholesome, mineral, and emphatic. I have since eaten many things in respectable restaurants with far more trepidation.

11   The technical names have yet to be invented for some of the submissions to courtly behavior laid upon me by table manners. At dinners cooked by brides in the early days of their apprenticeship I have forced down boiled potatoes as crunchy as water chestnuts, bleeding pork, gravy in which you could have pickled a kettle of herring, and a *purée* of raw chicken livers.

12   I have had reports of women with skimpy attention to labels who have made biscuits with plaster of Paris and chicken feed that had to be downed by timid husbands and polite guests; and my venturesome Aunt Mae once prepared a salad with witch hazel, and once, in a moment of abandoned creativity, served a banana pudding that had hard-boiled eggs hidden in it here and there.

13   Raphael Pumpelly tells in his memoirs of the West in the good old days about a two-gunned, bearded type who rolled into a Colorado hotel with a viand wrapped in a bandana. This he requested the cook to prepare, and seated at a table, napkined, wielding knife and fork with manners passably Eastern, consulting the salt and pepper shakers with a nicety, gave a fair imitation of a gentleman eating. And then, with a gleam in his eye and a great burp, he sang out at the end, "Thar, by God, I swore I'd eat that man's liver and I've done it!"

14   The meaning of this account for those of us who are great scientists is that this hero of the West chose to eat his enemy's liver in the dining room of a hotel, with manners. Eating as mere consumption went out thousands of years ago; we have forgotten what it is. Chaplin boning the nails from his stewed shoe in *The Gold Rush* is thus an incomparable moment of satire, epitomizing all that we have heard of British gentlemen dressing for dinner in the Congo (like Livingstone, who made Stanley wait before the famous encounter until he could dig his formal wear out of his kit).

15   Ruskin and Turner never dined together, though an invitation was once sent. Turner knew that his manners weren't up to those of the refined Ruskins, and said so, explaining graphically that, being toothless, he sucked his meat. Propriety being propriety, there was nothing to be done, and the great painter and his great explicator and defender were damned to dine apart.

16   Nor could Wittgenstein eat with his fellow dons at a Cambridge high table. One wishes that the reason were more straightforward than it is. Wittgenstein, for one thing, wore a leather jacket, with zipper, and dons at high table must wear academic gowns and a tie. For another, Wittgenstein thought it undemocratic to eat on a level fourteen inches higher than the students (at, does one say, low table?).

17   The code of Cambridge manners could not insist that the philosopher change his leather jacket for more formal gear, nor could it interfere with his conscience. At the same time it could in no wise permit him to dine at high table improperly dressed. The compromise was that the dons sat at high table, the students at their humbler tables, and Wittgenstein ate between, at a card table, separate but equal, and with English decorum unfractured.

18   Maxim's declined to serve a meal to Lyndon Baines Johnson, at the time President of the United States, on the grounds that its staff did not have a recipe for Texas barbecue, though what they meant was that they did not know how to serve it or how to criticize *Monsieur le Président's* manners in eating it.

19   The best display of manners on the part of a restaurant I have witnessed was at the Imperial Ramada Inn in Lexington, Kentucky, into the Middle Lawrence Welk Baroque dining room of which I once went with the photographer Ralph Eugene Meatyard (disguised as a businessman), the Trappist Thomas Merton (in mufti, dressed as a tobacco farmer with a tonsure), and an editor of *Fortune* who had wrecked his Hertz car coming from the airport and was covered in spattered blood from head to toe. Hollywood is used to such things (Linda Darnell having a milk shake with Frankenstein's monster between takes), and Rome and New York, but not Lexington, Kentucky. Our meal was served with no comment whatever from the waitresses, despite Merton's downing six martinis and the *Fortune* editor stanching his wounds with all the napkins.

20   Posterity is always grateful for notes on the table manners of the famous, if only because this information is wholly gratuitous and unenlightening. What does it tell us that Montaigne gulped his food? I have eaten with Allen Tate, whose sole gesture toward the meal was to stub out his cigarette in an otherwise untouched chef's salad, with Isak Dinesen when she toyed with but did not eat an oyster, with Louis Zukofsky who was dining on a half piece of toast, crumb by crumb.

21   Manners survive the test of adversity. Gertrude Ely, the Philadelphia hostess and patron of the arts, was once inspired on the spur of the moment to invite home Leopold Stokowski and his orchestra, together with a few friends. Hailing her butler, she said breezily that here were some people for pot luck.

22   "Madam," said the butler with considerable frost, "I was given to understand that you were dining alone this evening; please accept my resignation. Good night to you all."

23   "Quite," said Miss Ely, who then, with a graciousness unflummoxed and absolute, set every table in the house and distributed splinters of the one baked hen at her disposal, pinches of lettuce, and drops of mayonnaise, not quite with the success of the loaves and fishes of scripture, but at least a speck of something for everybody.

24   I, who live almost exclusively off fried baloney, Campbell's soup, and Snickers bars, would not find table manners of any particular interest if they had not, even in a life as reclusive and uneventful as mine, involved so many brushes with death. That great woman Katherine Gilbert, the philosopher and aesthetician, once insisted that I eat some Florentine butter that Benedetto Croce had given her. I had downed several portions of muffins smeared with this important butter before I gathered from her ongoing conversation that the butter had been given her months before, somewhere in the Tuscan hills in the month of August, and that it had crossed the Atlantic, by boat, packed with her books, Italian wild flowers, prosciutto, and other mementos of Italian culture.

25   Fever and double vision set in some hours later, together with a delirium in which I remembered Pico della Mirandola's last meal, served him by Lucrezia and Cesare Borgia. I have been *in extremis* in Crete (octopus and what tasted like shellacked rice, with P. Adams Sitney), in Yugoslavia (a most innocent-looking melon), Genoa (calf's brains), England (a blackish stew that seemed to have been cooked in kerosene), France (an *andouillette,* Maigret's favorite feed, the point being, as I now understand, that you have to be born in Auvergne to stomach it).

26   Are there no counter-manners to save one's life in these unfair martyrdoms to politeness? I have heard that Edward Dahlberg had the manliness to refuse dishes at table, but he lost his friends thereby and became a misanthrope. Lord Byron once refused every course of a meal served him by Breakfast Rogers. Manet, who found Spanish food revolting but was determined to study the paintings in the Prado, spent two weeks in Madrid without eating anything at all. Some *Privatdozent* with time on his hands should compile a eulogy to those culinary stoics who, like Marc Antony, drank from yellow pools men did die to look upon. Not the starving and destitute who in wars and sieges have eaten the glue in bookbindings and corn that had passed through horses, wallpaper, bark, and animals in the zoo; but prisoners of civilization who have swallowed gristle on the twentieth attempt while keeping up a brave chitchat with the author of a novel about three generations of a passionately alive family.

27   Who has manners anymore, anyhow? Nobody, to be sure; everybody, if you have the scientific eye. Even the most oafish teen-ager who mainly eats from the refrigerator at home and at the Burger King in society will eventually find himself at a table where he is under the eye of his father-in-law to be, or his coach, and will make the effort to wolf his roll in two bites rather than one, and even to leave some for the next person when he is passed a bowl of potatoes. He will, naturally, still charge his whole plate with six glops of catsup, knock over his water, and eat his cake from the palm of his hand; but a wife, the country club, and the Rotarians will get him, and before he's twenty-five he'll be eating fruit salad with extended pinky, tapping his lips with the napkin before sipping his sauterne Almaden, and talking woks and fondues with the boys at the office.

28   Archeologists have recently decided that we can designate the beginning of civilization in the concept of sharing the same kill, in which simple idea we can see the inception of the family, the community, the state. Of disintegrating marriages we note that Jack and Jill are no longer sleeping together when the real break is when they are no longer eating together. The table is the last unassailed rite. No culture has worn the *bonnet rouge* there, always excepting the Germans, who have never had any manners at all, of any sort.

29   The tyranny of manners may therefore be the pressure placed on us of surviving in hostile territories. Eating is the most intimate and at the same time the most public of biological functions. Going from dinner table to dinner table is the equivalent of going from one culture to another, even within the same

family. One of my grandmothers served butter and molasses with her biscuits, the other would have fainted to see molasses on any table. One gave you coffee with the meal, the other after. One cooked greens with fatback, the other with hamhock. One put ice cubes in your tea, the other ice from the ice house. My father used to complain that he hadn't had any cold iced tea since the invention of the refrigerator. He was right.

30   Could either of my grandmothers, the one with English country manners, the other with French, have eaten on an airplane? What would the Roi Soleil have done with that square foot of space? My family, always shy, did not venture into restaurants until well after the Second World War. Aunt Mae drank back the tiny juglet of milk which they used to give you for coffee, and commented to Uncle Buzzie that the portions of things in these cafés are certainly stingy.

31   I was raised to believe that eating other people's cooking was a major accomplishment, like learning a language or how to pilot a plane. I thought for the longest time that Greeks lived exclusively off garlic and dandelions, and that Jews were so picky about their food that they seldom ate at all. Uncles who had been to France with the AEF reported that the French existed on roast rat and snails. The Chinese, I learned from a book, begin their meals with dessert. Happy people!

32   Manners, like any set of signals, constitute a language. It is possible to learn to speak Italian; to eat Italian, never. In times of good breeding, the rebel against custom always has table manners to violate. Diogenes assumed the polish of Daniel Boone, while Plato ate with a correctness Emily Post could have studied with profit. Thoreau, Tolstoy, and Gandhi all ate with pointed reservation, sparely, and in elemental simplicity. Calvin dined but once a day, on plain fare, and doubtless imagined the pope gorging himself on pheasant, nightingale, and minced boar in macaroni.

33   Honest John Adams, eating in France for the first time, found the food delicious if unidentifiable, but blushed at the conversation (a lady asked him if his family had invented sex); and Emerson once had to rap the water glass at his table when two guests, Thoreau and Agassiz, introduced the mating of turtles into the talk. Much Greek philosophy, Dr. Johnson's best one-liners, and the inauguration of the Christian religion happened at supper tables. Hitler's table-talk was so boring that Eva Braun and a field marshal once fell asleep in his face. He was in a snit for a month. Generalissimo Franco fell asleep while Nixon was talking to him at dinner. It may be that conversation over a shared haunch of emu is indeed the beginning of civilization.

34   To eat in silence, like the Egyptians, seems peculiarly dreadful, and stiff. Sir Walter Scott ate with a bagpipe droning in his ear and all his animals around him, and yards of blabbling guests. Only the truly mad eat alone, like Howard Hughes and Stalin.

35   Eccentricity in table manners—one has heard of rich uncles who wear oilcloth aviator caps at table—lingers in the memory longer than other foibles.

My spine tingles anew whenever I remember going into a Toddle House to find all the tables and the counter set; not only set, but served. One seat only was occupied, and that by a very eccentric man, easily a millionaire. He was, the waitress explained some days later, giving a dinner party there, but no one came. He waited and waited. He had done it several times before; no one had ever come. It was the waitress's opinion that he always forgot to send the invitations; it was mine that his guests could not bring themselves to believe them.

36   And there was the professor at Oxford who liked to sit under his tea table, hidden by the tablecloth, and hand up cups of tea and slices of cake from beneath. He carried on a lively conversation all the while, and most of his friends were used to this. There was always the occasional student who came to tea unaware, sat goggling the whole time, and tended to break into cold sweats and fits of stammering.

37   I was telling about this professor one summer evening in South Carolina, to amuse my audience with English manners. A remote cousin, a girl in her teens, who hailed from the country and had rarely considered the ways of foreigners, listened to my anecdote in grave horror, went home and had a fit.

38   "It took us half the night to quiet down Effie Mae," we were told sometime later. "She screamed for hours that all she could see was that buggerman under that table, with just his arm risin' up with a cup and saucer. She says she never expects to get over it."

☐ Discovering Meaning and Technique

1. What does Davenport mean when he writes that a code of manners conceals "a program of taboos as rigid as Deuteronomy" (paragraph 7)?

2. Davenport makes two references to Liberty's red hat, or *bonnet rouge* (paragraphs 8 and 28). What is he referring to?

3. How does the effort to be polite lead to unfortunate eating experiences or, as Davenport calls it, "unfair martyrdoms to politeness" (paragraph 26)?

4. Whom does Davenport name as examples of people who refused to eat despite the pressures of politeness?

5. According to archeologists, what event marks the beginning of civilization?

6. How does Davenport illustrate that traditions may differ not only among cultures but also from one table to another?

7. What are some of the variations in table manners?

8. What two incidents illustrate extreme eccentricity associated with eating?

9. How many paragraphs would you say constitute the introduction to this selection?

10. Define the following—using either a dictionary or context: *Cockayne* (paragraph 9), *aurochs* (paragraph 9), *unflummoxed* (paragraph 23), *Privatdozent* (paragraph 26).

11. Davenport's style ranges from folksiness to pedantry. Cite passages that illustrate the two extremes.

☐ Writing Suggestions

1. Describe several examples of eating habits that are strange and unconventional.

2. Which foods are particularly hard to eat while one is trying to be polite?

3. Which pressures encourage youth to adopt manners at the table?

FUTURE EATING PATTERNS

☐ REAY TANNAHILL

¹ For thousands of years, the search for food has helped to shape the development of society. It has dictated population growth and urban expansion, profoundly influenced economic, social, and political theory. It has widened the horizons of commerce, inspired wars of dominion, played no small role in the creation of empires, precipitated the discovery of new worlds. Food has had a part in religion, helping to define the separateness of one creed from another by means of dietary taboos. In science, where the prehistoric cook's discoveries about the effect of heat applied to raw materials laid the foundations on which much of early chemistry was based. In technology, where the water wheel first used in milling grain was to achieve immense industrial importance. In medicine, which was based largely on dietary principles until well into the eighteenth century. In war, where battles were postponed until the harvest had been gathered in and where well-fed armies usually defeated hungry ones. And even in relations between peoples, where for twelve thousand years there has been a steady undercurrent of antagonism between those whose diet consists mainly of grain and those who depend on animal foods.

2   In the last analysis, of course, food is not only inseparable from the history of mankind but essential to it. Without food there would be no history, no mankind.

3   The truth of this—it might be thought, self-evident—proposition is frequently forgotten in a world preoccupied with currency crises, computers, and communications satellites, but if, in the decades to come, population growth and environmental pollution follow the catastrophic course forecast by a number of modern ecologists, acute food shortages could prove a harsh reminder of it.

4   The debate over whether or not there *will* be a major world food crisis within the next few decades takes the form of a war of opinion, in which the belligerents' weapons are forecasts, not facts. One side believes that scientific advances will ensure a food surplus, the other that there are too many destructive elements in the environment today, too many imponderables in the future, to allow of complacency.

5   Both sides agree that by the first decade of the twenty-first century the world's population will have doubled from the 3,706,000,000 of 1971 to over 7,000,000,000 in 2007. Although these figures attempt to take into account a possible reduction in the birth rate brought about by campaigns in favor of birth control, as well as a counterbalancing reduction in the number of deaths which may be expected to result from advances in medical knowledge, they cannot allow for the effects of age-slowing techniques which may emerge in the interim. *

6   On the present showing of improved wheat and rice plants, however, the optimists appear to be justified when they claim that the food future is satisfactory. If food grains can be trebled while the population does no more than double, and if scientists can produce a sufficiency of manufactured protein and other nutrients—then there would seem to be no problem (except for the gourmet, whose *tournedos Rossini* is probably doomed).

7   But the pessimist replies that nothing which has to do with food or society is as simple as that, that people are more than computer fodder. What kind, what quantity of food will the 7,000,000,000 people of the year A.D. 2007 want? African and Asian peasants who have had to make do in the past with one meal a day—the majority of the world's population—are now, in the present climate of optimism, beginning to ask for two. And who can blame them. Their demands being met, as they must be, there is another foreseeable consequence. In Japan in 1962 it was recorded that, as a result of the more balanced and ample diet which became common in the country after 1945, the average junior school student was as tall as the average adult had been in the years between 1868

---

* Large-scale human tests of anti-aging drugs have begun. Anti-aging foods are a possibility, too. Animal experiments have established that if calorie intake is reduced soon after birth to about sixty per cent of normal, the active life span can be prolonged by as much as forty per cent. The calorie-reduction technique would not, of course, begin to affect population figures before about 2050, but anti-aging drugs might have earlier effects.

and 1912. Two meals a day instead of one. Larger people needing larger meals than before. And, in all probability, two or three thousand million of them. All this could wreak havoc with the comfortable arithmetic of the optimists.

8   The pessimists are also concerned over the declining fertility of soil that has for centuries been overworked and over-irrigated. About the water supply, steadily being polluted by persistent inorganic chemicals. And about the crop-destroying insects which are proliferating because their natural predators are more effectively killed off by pesticides than the pests themselves.

9   The simple fact is that either the pessimists or the optimists *could* be right. But it is also a fact that if the pessimists have their way, and prove to have been wrong, comparatively little harm will have been done. If the optimists win, and prove to have been wrong, the results could be disastrous. A few years of famine could mean death for millions of people, and permanent brain damage for many of those who survive.

10   Most governments, by their very nature, favor the optimistic view as being less disruptive of the *status quo;* a policy of drift which requires no action other than an apparently forward-looking contribution to research finances, and perhaps a *douceur* to the opposition in the form of some mild legislation against pollution. More than this is needed, however, if only because whether the food supply situation develops well or badly, it is highly probable that it will develop differently from at present. It may in fact be necessary for governments to take a hand in changing the food habits of the people they govern.

11 What most peoples eat today is the product of thousands of years of dietary choice, the outcome, in effect, of an almost Darwinian process of natural selection. The foods which have survived in different regions of the world have been those best fitted not only to cultivation conditions but to the specific requirements of the inhabitants, requirements originally shaped as much by work and living conditions as by taste and preference. Men who lived in cold damp countries found that rich, fatty foods were not only comforting, but helped to build up a layer of flesh which acted as insulation against the weather. In less extreme climates, the field laborer used up considerable amounts of energy on digging, plowing, hoeing and other agricultural tasks; his need was for calorie-rich starches and sugars to replace that energy. In tropical lands, perspiration, evaporating from the skin, helps to cool the body; strong spices encouraged perspiration and also stimulated a thirst for the liquids which were necessary to replace it. Discoveries such as these—the product of observation and experience, not of scientific analysis—laid the foundations of many food traditions.

12   During the course of history, however, such logic as there may have been in the origins of food habits has become almost impenetrably complex. It has been distorted by shortages, by surpluses, by the introduction of new foods, and by any number of external developments. Even the commonplace human

desire to catch up with those next higher on the social scale has helped to alter adequate diets for the worse. * Only recently, too, has it been appreciated that food preferences are not necessarily the same as food prejudices, that taste and custom are sometimes related to forces † which cannot be readily adjusted by social manipulation.

13   But however confused, from the modern viewpoint, the logic of food customs may appear to be, history suggests that there has always been a conscious or subconscious attempt to direct food production toward what tradition shows to be the "best" kind of diet for local circumstances.

14   In any attempt to shape future eating habits, therefore, it would be important to remember just how deeply ingrained certain food traditions are—despite the fact that the late twentieth century is in the process of cutting away the ground on which many of those traditions once rested. Tastes cannot be changed, particularly in peasant societies, simply by taking away one foodstuff that is in short supply and replacing it with something else which, theoretically, ought to be a satisfactory substitute. Tradition is against it, and so too are levels of knowledge. In the Bengal famine of 1942–43, great numbers of rice-eating people died because they did not know what to do with the wheat they were given instead—and only the most blinkered optimist would deny the possibility of such a thing happening again, even if on a much reduced scale.

15 If Brillat–Savarin had been alive today, he might have thought twice before he said: "Tell me what you eat: I will tell you what you are." Certainly, he would have qualified it, for no sane analyst of gastronomic history could be expected to deduce a Liverpool pop singer from yogurt and unpolished rice, or a Manhattan millionaire from black-eyed peas and chitterlings; to connect Scotch whisky with a Frenchman, or French bread with a Japanese. But these apparently wild deviations from the logic of the table—although they have more to do with contemporary social pressures than with food—do reflect a new and more general attitude of flexibility in the prosperous countries of the world and among the richer classes in developing countries.

16   This flexibility stems partly from the psychological effect of increases in the availability of foreign and "exotic" foods, canned, frozen, or flown in fresh by air, during the present century; from the impact of foreign travel; from the furious activity, in all the communications media, of experts on cooking; even from the fact that the age balance of the population is currently tipped in the direction of the young, whose ethos includes the need to experiment.

---

* In Britain's industrial revolution, for example, the assumption that the food of the rich must be "better" persuaded large numbers of the population to live on white bread and tea, instead of the more nourishing brown bread and beer of earlier times.
    † Illustrated, for example, by the allergy of many Africans and Asians to milk, and the sensitivity of some Asians to barley beer and grape wine.

17   There are also, however, more fundamental influences at work. Men who live in cold damp countries no longer have to eat rich, fatty foods. Many of them work indoors, where the need for warmth and comfort is satisfied by central heating. The field laborer who once burned up calories on reaping and binding grain now drives a combine harvester, which takes rather less energy. In hot lands, perspiration is no longer the only way of cooling the body. Air conditioners make a better job of it.

18   Central heating, combine harvesters and air conditioning are still the prerogative of the rich, though office workers share in the benefits of the first and third. But food flexibility (as a matter of choice) is in any case usually a characteristic of affluent societies. The nearness of hunger breeds conservatism. Only the well-fed can afford to try something new, because only they can afford to leave it on the plate if they dislike it.

19   The combined effect of a more open-minded attitude to food and a radical change in living conditions has been to divorce the contemporary diet from contemporary needs. It is nonsensical for a chairbound executive who breakfasted at 8:30 A.M. to lunch in the latest French bistro on a *cassoulet de Castelnaudary* or a *chou farçi à la mode de Grasse*—dishes designed centuries ago to restore farmers who had been hard at work in the fields since dawn. But thousands do it every day, to the post-meridian ruin not only of their mental alertness but of their whole digestive system. Among the lower-income groups, whose food habits tend to be less mobile, the imbalance between diet and need is only slightly less pronounced. Although, in an expanding economy, carbohydrate foods usually lose ground to meat, one lamb chop rimmed with fat contains just as many calories as a slice of white bread and butter. The stomachs of rich and not-so-rich alike, therefore, frequently have more fuel pumped into them than they need or can contend with. Whereas scurvy and rickets were the characteristic diseases of the nineteenth century, over-eating is almost certainly that of the twentieth.

20 Any attempt to adjust future eating patterns must take account of three essential facts. Familiar food, preferably in a slightly "improved" form, is customarily regarded as "best." There is a willingness to try new foods, but as an extra and *not in place of* the old. And, however little people are aware of it, physiological needs have changed; carefully introduced correctives could help to improve the general level of health.

21   In effect, the redirection of food habits would present, in the late twentieth century, fewer problems than at any time for many hundreds of years. An intelligent grasp of the situation and serious attention to forward planning are the main prerequisites.

22   In what direction would people's food tastes have to be turned? The prospect of banqueting on a handful of nutrient pills belongs in the realm of nightmare. What is more probable is that much of the roast beef of the future will have

been woven out of protein made from fuel oil, the bacon from an extract of intensively grown algae.

23   Protein, carbohydrates, vitamins and fats can all be created in the laboratory out of a wide variety of materials. Protein, for example, can be drawn from soybeans, then treated in a coagulating bath, spun into threads and wound into hanks. These hanks are next bound with a mixture of flour, gums and other ingredients, passed through a flavoring solution, and then pressed or teased into a fair imitation of bacon rashers or forcemeat. Protein can also be extracted from fuel oil, and it is confidently predicted that natural gas will prove an equally valuable source. Potatoes, molasses, manioc, and many types of green leaves can also be used.

24   A factory-laboratory of the not too distant future, designed to serve perhaps fifty thousand people, might run on roughly the following lines. Dark-tinted water treated with chemical reagents would be exposed to artifically focused sunlight from which it would collect energy. The water would then be fed into tanks containing microscopic plants, which would grow at great speed (to the extent of about one ton per tank per day) by converting the active ingredients in the water as well as in the high-pressure atmosphere of the tanks. Some of this plant material would, with the addition of vitamins and minerals imported from specialized factories, be fed direct to live cattle, pigs and poultry, to provide real meat for gourmets and eggs for everyone. Some of it would be made into flour, oils, carbohydrates, and some processed through laboratory-grown milk-producing glands, to give milk for drinking or for conversion into butter and cheese. From some, protein would be extracted, to be spun and woven into "animal" muscle—long wrist-thick tubes of "fillet steak," for example, ready for automatic slicing into tournedos-sized portions. If the factory had a separate kitchen section, some of the finished substitutes could be cooked and packaged for distribution as soup, sausages, bread, TV dinners, and so on. Fruit and vegetables, not catered for in this system, would probably continue to come from private gardens and specialist growers.

25   The standardization which twentieth-century mass production has helped to bring about—aided and abetted by the Western housewife, who has preferred reliably mediocre food to food of erratic quality and price—undoubtedly makes the task of the scientist easier. A steak spun out of artifically produced protein may have considerably less flavor (and, at present, fewer supplementary nutrients) than an Aberdeen Angus entrecôte, but it need not differ much from the enzyme-injected "tenderized" steak which is already familiar. Bread made from carbohydrates which have been manufactured from, say, formaldehyde (a product of natural gas or coal) is unlikely to match the crusty perfection achieved by a good baker using good wheat flour, but neither does the latex foam which passes as bread today. A slice of spun-protein ham may not stand comparison with the genuine article from Bradenham or Virginia, but neither does the pink plastic sheeting of the contemporary supermarket.

26   Provided that the process of substitution is begun at an early stage and sensibly developed over a period of time, there would not be too much difficulty in persuading a majority of Western consumers to accept the newest offerings of science. Whether the same would prove true of currently underdeveloped countries is another matter. Unless the average income of their inhabitants climbs at an extremely steep rate, the problem here is likely to be as much economic as gastronomic.

27   Protein from soybeans is cheap, but as yet, insufficient attention seems to have been paid to the cost on a commercial basis of *wholly* manufactured foods. In the case of such a factory-laboratory as has been described above, there would be little differential in the production costs of different types of food, since the same basic materials, the same equipment, and the same complex and probably costly manufacturing control would be necessary for all. This means that a handful of "rice" would cost much the same as a "fillet steak" to manufacture. With factory-laboratories producing, either individually or in collaboration, a wide variety of foods salable over the full range of traditionally differentiated prices, expensive "steaks" would effectively subsidize cheap "grain." This system, however, would not work satisfactorily in places where the diet is limited, as in the rice-eating areas of Asia and the maize-dependent parts of Africa. "Grain" prices could not be subsidized by the sale of more expensive foods unless radical changes in the economy take place in the near future. Furthermore, manufactured foods are relevant only in a monetary (or paternalist) economy, and there remain comparatively large areas in underdeveloped countries today which still depend on subsistence agriculture.

28   It is not yet clear whether conventional mass-production economics—the larger the output, the lower the unit cost—would apply in the case of the factory-laboratory. Nor is it clear whether other types of establishment producing "grain" alone—on lines currently being researched—would be an economic or practical proposition.

29   The need for large quantities of substitute or wholly manufactured foods may never arise, and the world may never see a factory-laboratory of the type described—a type chosen because it is such a classic example of self-sufficiency. * But complete dependence on "natural" food will certainly be out of tune with the times by the end of the present century, and research cannot, in any case, stop short at merely discovering how to manufacture carbohydrates, protein, minerals, fats and vitamins, and how to weave them into eatable foods. It must go on to translate that knowledge into workable reality.

30 Despite the pundits, developments in the future are no easier to forecast than

* Most other methods of artificial food production currently being advocated make use either of traditional food materials cultivated by traditional methods (and therefore liable to run short in any major food crisis) or of fuel oils, which some—though by no means all—authorities believe will be in dangerously short supply in the future.

they have ever been. But it would be well within the historical tradition—a tradition only partially affected by the extraordinary pace at which the world has developed since 1945—if town dwellers in the years to come found themselves living largely on artificial food, while natural foods were consumed in the areas where they were grown.

31   This would run counter to the present agricultural trend toward specialized and ever larger farming units, because the specialized unit would have a place only in fruit and vegetable production. Diversification would in general be necessary on farms whose role was to provide local inhabitants with a balanced diet.

32   Such a pattern would have several advantages. It might make it possible for some countries to approach, once again, that position of being self-supporting in food which was destroyed in so much of Europe during the industrial revolution, and which could prove critical in any forthcoming world food crisis. Mixed farming, too, would employ proportionately far more farm workers than specialized units, and this could have the effect of reducing that drift to the towns which promises to be one of the more disruptive results of any large population increase. And the contrast between town and country food might even encourage a drift back to the land by those city dwellers whose tongue papillae each contain the statutory 245 taste buds in full working order.

33   It would be reassuring to believe that the world's governments had given more than cursory consideration to the food pattern of the future. But in recent years thousands of tons of fruit have had to be destroyed, thousands of tons of butter sold off as cattle fodder, furious price wars engaged in for the disposal of surplus grain, millions of hens slaughtered because there is a glut of eggs—and this general climate of world food surplus has encouraged administrators to remain complacent about food and agricultural policies, which are, in most countries, short-sighted, inconsistent, and archaic. It is a situation that must be remedied soon if the next few decades are to be faced with any degree of composure, for the role of food in the future will be no less decisive than it has been in the past.

☐ Discovering Meaning and Technique

1. Optimists and pessimists disagree on the possibility of a future famine. Which side does Tannahill favor?

2. Besides "taste and preference," which influences shape food traditions?

3. Why is flexibility in choosing food more common among the affluent?

4. Why does Tannahill believe that at the present time it might be possible to redirect people's food habits?

5. Describe briefly how food might be produced in a factory-laboratory.

6. Does paragraph 1 illustrate a classic paragraph form—a thesis statement plus supporting details?

7. Explain how the overall structure of this composition is the problem-solution pattern.

8. Common strategies for a concluding paragraph are summarizing, making a recommendation, giving a warning, and calling for further study. What strategy or strategies does Tannahill use in her concluding paragraph?

9. In paragraph 1, some of the details are presented as parallel fragments. Is this structure effective?

10. For transition, Tannahill often begins sentences with *and* and *but.* Find examples of this technique.

☐ Writing Suggestions

1. Do you think that people will ever accept artificial food?

2. How do you think people could avoid a critical food shortage?

3. Discuss how "deeply ingrained certain food traditions are."

4. Write a paper elaborating on Tannahill's statement: "Whereas scurvy and rickets were the characteristic diseases of the nineteenth century, over-eating is almost certainly that of the twentieth."

5. Describe the food one would likely eat in a typical day in the year 2500.

BLT, HOLD THE MAYO

☐ VERNON PIZER

1 In the world of snack foods, America is the undisputed superpower, totally unrivaled for that position by any other nation. (Only those who are mean in spirit and cynical in outlook might ask who would want to compete for such a dubious honor.) It is a position of superiority that sprouted from the humble potato.

2   The potato seemed destined to remain no more than a simple, staid, humdrum food, the kind that would always be picked out as a blue-collar intruder if it tried to move in white-collar circles. And then American innovation created a whole new dimension to the potato's personality, endowing it with a verve and sparkle it had never before enjoyed. It all took place in 1853 when a domineering industrial tycoon and a thin-skinned redskin crossed paths in Moon's Lake House, a resort in Saratoga Springs, the upstate New York spa favored by the wealthy.

3   The multimillionaire industrialist was Commodore Cornelius Vanderbilt; the Indian was George Crum, cook in the Lake House kitchen. The Lake House was not the posh sort of place Vanderbilt was accustomed to patronizing; nevertheless, he stopped in one day for lunch. When his food was served he was displeased with the fried potatoes placed before him. Complaining that they had been cut much too thick, he petulantly ordered the waiter to take them back to the kitchen and have them replaced by thinner slices.

4   Resentful of this criticism of his kitchen performance, Crum set out to teach Vanderbilt a lesson. Snatching up some potatoes, he sliced them to paper thinness, plunged them briefly in boiling oil, sprinkled them liberally with salt, and then sent them out to the table, confident that his critic would get the message. Vanderbilt looked at the unusual slivers of potato, tasted one, smiled, and praised its crispness and flavor. For the balance of the season he returned again and again to Moon's Lake House, bringing his friends along to introduce them to the pleasures of George Crum's "Saratoga chips." Though Crum was denied the satisfaction of getting even with Vanderbilt, at least he lived long enough to see the potato chip he had invented become the cornerstone of a burgeoning snack-food industry.

5   Today potato chips are established as an international favorite from Tokyo where they are flavored with seaweed, to New Delhi where they are flavored with curry, to Berlin where they are flavored with paprika. In the United States alone manufacturers send about $2 billion worth of potato chips to market each year. A feel for how many chips that amounts to can be gleaned from this awesome statistic: if all those chips were laid end to end they would encircle the globe more than 325 times. By anyone's standards, that's not small potatoes.

6   By a wide margin the potato chip is the most popular snack food to emerge from America, but it is not the first one to be launched on this side of the Atlantic. What is quite possibly the world's oldest snack, popcorn, is a New World native with a history dating back more than 5,000 years. Popping corn was one of the initial skills the American Colonists picked up from the Indians. It has been said by some, with little apparent basis in actual fact, that as the first Thanksgiving feast was drawing to a close Quadequina, brother of Chief Massasoit, brought out a batch of popped corn to finish off the meal.

7   Popcorn is overshadowed in importance by the peanut, the snack that

comes closest to rivaling potato chips in popularity. Like the others, the peanut is also a native of the Americas. It was cultivated in South America at least 3,800 years ago, was introduced to Africa by Portuguese explorers in the sixteenth century, and then was brought to North America aboard African slave ships.

8   A St. Louis doctor is credited with creating in 1890 what many consider to be the most exalted state of grace any ambitious nuts can aspire to: peanut butter. Promoting his peanut butter as a readily digestible, tasty, high-protein food, he gained a loyal circle of consumers in the St. Louis area. But it gained national exposure and national popularity when he introduced it at Chicago's Columbian Exposition of 1893. Soon grocers across the country were stocking it in bulk in large wooden tubs to satisfy customer demand. When the innovative agricultural scientist, George Washington Carver, developed an improved version of the butter, it attracted even more enthusiasts to the fold. Nowadays it takes about a third of all the peanuts grown in the United States just to satisfy the American appetite for peanut butter. How seriously Americans regard peanut butter becomes quite clear when one notes the presence in Chicago of The American Museum of Peanut Butter History.

9   Although it is unassailably true that it is in America that the snack enjoys its finest hour, fairness requires recognition that some other countries do make original contributions of their own. But it must be added, again in fairness, that from a distance some of these foreign offerings seem to suggest a form of self-abuse for consumers. A popular Spanish snack is *angulas,* miniature baby eels that look exactly like pale fishing worms and are swallowed whole in a pungent garlic oil. Japanese enjoy snacking on roasted and salted grasshoppers. The French are partial to the pulpy insides of raw sea urchins—spiny, golf ball-sized marine animals. The English are very enthusiastic about baked beans as a snack food. They consume enough baked beans to founder a less stalwart people—nearly 5 million pounds in a single day, much of it in the form of sandwiches.

10   Viewed against a backdrop of the *angulas,* grasshoppers, sea urchins, and baked bean sandwiches abroad, the American snack scene takes on added savor. Even unrelenting food snobs who profess to see nothing of merit in the American kitchen are forced to concede that when it comes to snacks Americans do seem to have an appealing, innovative touch. What happened to the sausage is proof of that.

11   There had for a long time been general agreement that the sausage represented one of mankind's happiest, most productive moments in the kitchen. So nearly perfect a food was the sausage that any further improvement was dismissed as unlikely, if not impossible. After all, some sausages were edible without any cooking by the consumer and those that did require cooking called for culinary skill of an irreducibly minimum level, so that even the laziest and most inept could not ruin a sausage. And it came in enough varied flavors, textures, sizes, and shapes so that monotony was not possible even if one ate only sausages, being able to choose among those made of such meats as pork, beef, veal, mutton,

goat, chicken, horse, venison, even armadillo, and flavored with such ingredients as beer, wine, milk, eggs, pig blood, tripe, liver, onions, potatoes, rice, oatmeal, herbs, and spices. If all this were not enough to commend it most strongly, the sausage was an overwhelmingly democratic food, comfortably at home with every social class and priced within reach of every economic level.

12   Considering what a paragon of virtues the sausage is, it would seem highly improbable that anyone could perceive in it something that is sinister and disreputable. Yet the improbable came to pass in 1981 when Moroccan police boarded one of their nation's vessels to arrest a French crewmember. The charge against the prisoner? Blaspheming King Hassan II of Morocco. And how had the prisoner committed blasphemy against the king? By removing Hassan's shipboard portrait and in its place hanging a sausage. Surely the delectable sausage deserves a better fate than to be used as a political weapon.

13   The world's first sausage must have been created fairly soon after Jacob cooked his famous red lentil pottage and traded it off to Esau for his birthright. By the time of the ancient Greeks and Romans, sausages were already widely known. Itinerant Roman hawkers used to sell sausages along the city's busiest streets. One of their best-selling sausages was made of finely diced fresh pork, bacon, nuts, and herbs. These pork sausages were known as *botuli.* In 1735 when European doctors looked for a suitable name with which to label a newly identified disease thought to come from spoiled sausages, they named it "botulism" for the *botuli* of old Rome.

14   Throughout the thousands of years that sausages have been one of man's favored foods they were adapted and altered and modified according to national tastes but they always managed to remain substantially what they had always been, their changes being changes of degree rather than changes of basic character. Then American culinary imagination came to the fore and fashioned an entirely new identity for the sausage. It emerged as a born-again food.

15   What American ingenuity did was to take a beef sausage—the frankfurter that originated in Germany—and place it within the gently cuddling embrace of a long, soft bun. Like most great ideas it sounds deceptively simple but it was a revolutionary development. It enhanced the frankfurter with an easy portability and mobility it never before had enjoyed, so that now it was entirely possible to eat one single-handedly while simultaneously attending to other matters. Beyond that, the sides of the bun created a sort of dam rising up along either flank of the recumbent frankfurter so that mustard and various gastronomic frivolities could be heaped on it with little danger of overflowing, except when maneuvered by the hopelessly sloppy.

16   Some historians credit a vendor at the 1904 St. Louis World's Fair with being the matchmaker who engineered the marriage between frankfurter and bun. Others assign that honor to a hawker in New York's Coney Island in 1867. This version seems to be the more credible since the frankfurter-in-a-bun was once widely known as a "Coney Island red hot." Whatever the name it once

had, there is no doubt of the year in which it gained the endearing, enduring, internationally recognized name it now bears. It was in 1906. T. A. Dorgan, a cartoonist known professionally as "Tad," was doodling with his pencil as he tried to brainstorm an idea for a cartoon. What his doodling developed into was a caricature frankfurter, looking like an elongated dachshund, stretched out in its bun. Tad labeled the houndlike frankfurter in his cartoon a "hot dog" and the name tickled the public's funny bone so insistently that it gained linguistic respectability and culinary immortality. Today hot dogs are consumed by Americans at the astonishing rate of some 16 billion each year.

[17]   Having elevated the hot dog to sausage stardom, American culinary innovators looked around for new heights to scale. They were not long in finding the opportunity they sought.

[18]   Back in the mid-1700s France had begun importing beef from Holland by way of the German port of Hamburg. When the beef reached the French restaurants much of it had been chopped and then cooked and served as "Hamburg steak" after the city from which it had arrived. What American kitchen visionaries now did was to take the Hamburg steak, standardize it into a round pattie, give it a hot dog's mobility and convenience by serving it in a bun, and replace its formality with a more easygoing image by streamlining its name to simply "hamburger" with a small "h."

[19]   The hamburger became hugely popular. Like the hot dog, it made eating a portable feast and it made eating fun. Once "hand food" had meant chicken, but now there was a growing menu to choose from. What had begun with snacks was now evolving into something else. The evolution gradually shaped that phenomenon of modern life: the franchised world of the fast foods.

[20]   Fast-food restaurants are clearly a made-in-America phenomenon. There are the hot dogs and hamburgers and fried chicken. There are the barbecues and the pizzas. (Although the pizza says "Italy" to those who can't see beyond a mere technicality, when it first saw the light of day a thousand years ago it was nothing more than a plain Italian bread; it was only after it became a naturalized American in the mid-1800s that it found its full gustatory potential.) There are the chili, the ribs, the clam rolls, and the sausage biscuits. And there are the colas, especially the colas. John Styth Pemberton may have misfired with his earlier concoctions of Triplex Liver Pills, Indian Queen Hair Dye, and Globe of Flowers Cough Syrup, but the Georgia pharmacist was on target when he compounded a syrup of coca leaves, cola nuts, and other ingredients in a backyard washtub in 1886. Once the claims for its ability to "whiten teeth, cleanse the mouth, harden the gums, and relieve mental and physical exhaustion" were abandoned in favor of promoting it simply as a soft drink, Coca-Cola was a smashing success that, together with the copycat colas, became a mighty river irrigating the fast-food industry.

[21]   And then there is the system that America created to make it all work: the streamlining of operation and administration, the mechanization, the central

controls, the merchandising, even the distinctive building designs and logos. The system is the real key because it was the element that made possible the creation of great networks of franchised restaurants that were efficiently functional clones of one another, all doing the same things in exactly the same ways just as the advertising jingles promised. There were no surprises and no disappointments because you knew what you were getting into before you ever opened the front door. Thus, every hamburger placed on a McDonald's grill weighed precisely 1.6 ounces and measured 3.875 inches in diameter and .221 inches in thickness, while every one of the Colonel's finger-lickin' good drumsticks was seasoned with the same quantity of the same mix of "secret" herbs and spices. The system bridged geography, language, culture, and politics so that there was a familiar sense of comfortable sameness whether the golden arches cast their neon glow in Melbourne or Montreal or Mexico City, whether the Colonel did his thing in Amsterdam or Altoona.

22   Although it was created by individual enterprise and initiative, the fast-food world flourishes because it carefully suppresses individualism. Undeviatingly committed to the old adage that too many cooks spoil the broth, the franchisers don't want innovators—or even real cooks—in the outposts of the culinary empires. What they want are obedient employees who will follow instructions from the home office exactly. All of the cooks, the technical staffs, and the planners are back in headquarters with top management studying their computer readouts and experimenting in their test kitchens. Their objective is to refine foolproof formulas for those out in the field and—to the greatest extent possible—to premix, prepackage, and precook the food before it is shipped out from the distribution points.

23   Critics of the fast-food chains condemn them as neon-lit assembly lines that are to gastronomy what painting-by-the-numbers is to art. They charge that the best things the chains turn out are the catchy jingles in their TV commercials, and they dismiss the food disdainfully as indifferent, dull, and monotonous, served in a plastic, sterile, depersonalized setting. Foreign critics are especially harsh in their appraisal. They get particular satisfaction in heaping abuse on the condiment most associated with fast foods—ketchup, or catsup if you prefer—condemning it as an American food barbarism slowly submerging the planet in a red sea too deep for a Moses to part. Here, at the very least, critics nail the wrong hide to the wall. It was the Chinese who invented the sauce, called *ke-tsiap* in its native land and originally composed mainly of the salted juices of mushrooms and other fungi. It was Dutch and English traders who brought the sauce out of China in the eighteenth century, added tomatoes and otherwise tampered with its formula, and then let it loose on the West. (That other popular fast-food condiment, mustard, is also a native of Asia; the Chinese were using it thousands of years ago.)

24   Supporters of the fast-food chains praise them as clean, bright, friendly places that invariably deliver a reasonably wholesome, reasonably priced, and

reasonably tasty product. What is more, they add, the chains do it speedily, efficiently, and without frittering away time and effort on costly frills that are superfluous, inflating a customer's check without improving his meal.

25   The truth lies somewhere between the two opposing points of view.

26   It is clear that if fast foods are not as praiseworthy as their supporters believe, neither are they as blameworthy as their faultfinders charge. Even in the very citadel of gastronomic snobbery and culinary chauvinism—France— fast-food restaurants have made marked inroads. In the Paris area alone there are more than a dozen McDonald's hamburger outlets and that number is targeted to balloon to 166 by the year 2000. So significant a role do fast-food restaurants now play in France that the government, mounting an unwinnable rearguard action to stem the advance of the American chains, has issued an edict banning any official use of the English-language term "fast-food restaurant." But even under its government-mandated label as a *restaurante rapide* serving food that is *prêt-à-manger* (ready to eat) there is no way to hide the fact that it is a wholly American-accented operation. It is also worth noting that the French— who take a perfectly good ham and cheese sandwich and heat it in a special gadget that seals the edges together to frustrate the consumer bent on adding mustard and pickle slices—stand to pick up some worthwhile pointers from America's fast-food expertise.

27   At the very least, even if one doesn't intend to eat there, a fast-food restaurant is worth a visit just for the show. If things move along as they are supposed to, the staffs put on a carefully choreographed performance that has the grace of a ballet and the economy of movement of a racetrack pit stop.

☐ Discovering Meaning and Technique

1. Which snack foods does Pizer enumerate to substantiate his assertion that America is the "superpower" in the "world of snack foods"?

2. What do people in other countries like for snacks?

3. How did Americans improve on the sausage?

4. According to Pizer, what are the origins of the terms *hot dog* and *hamburger?*

5. What did Americans contribute that is the "real key" to the success of fast-food restaurants?

6. What is Pizer's attitude about the quality of fast-food restaurants?

7. When Pizer moves from one topic to another, he usually writes a transitional sentence. Locate examples of Pizer's transitional sentences.

8. This selection has two major sections. What are they?

9. Why in paragraph 1 is the use of the word *sprouted* a good choice? Is the use of the term *small potatoes* in paragraph 5 also a good choice?

10. Does Pizer's use of specific details, such as names and figures, improve the reader's interest?

☐ Writing Suggestions

1. What is the appeal of your favorite fast-food restaurants?

2. Discuss the appeal of snack foods other than potato chips, popcorn, and peanuts—for example, nachos, pizza, candy, or cookies.

3. Write about the origin of one or more fast-food restaurants.

4. Describe the "choreographed performance" of employees in a busy diner or restaurant.

5. Many people concoct their own unusual snack foods—marshmallow sand-wiches or cheese and sweet-and-sour sauce on gingersnaps. Write a paper on unusual snacks you have eaten, seen, or heard about.

FAST FOOD

☐ JOSEPH MONNINGER

1   When I was ten, my brother was accepted into a college in Kansas. My parents decided to drive him out from New Jersey, using the opportunity to show both of us the countryside as we went. The year was 1963.

2   Because we were on a budget, we normally ate at Howard Johnson's restaurants. This was fine with me. I was allowed to order the same thing at every meal: a turkey club sandwich with a strawberry milk shake. My brother, more adventurous, ate clams whenever he found them on the menu, never giving a thought to the fact that we were squarely in the center of the country, a thousand miles in either direction from salt water.

3   But those meals are indistinct in memory. The meal I recall most vividly from that trip was a lunch we had somewhere in eastern Kansas. My father, tearing along the highway at the approved speed of eighty miles an hour, spotted a pair of golden arches rising above one of the few hills we encountered in an entire day of driving.

4   Now the next thing he said may seem remarkable, but keep in mind that it was 1963. Tapping his foot on the brake to release our Buick's Cruise-amatic, he veered off the highway and rocketed down the small ramp onto what would, I suppose, eventually become a strip of fast-food restaurants. Cutting off a slower-moving vehicle, he turned into a McDonald's parking lot and switched off the engine. "Let's try some regional food," he said.

5   The outcome was predictable. My brother and I loved the food, my father enjoyed the price, and my mother knitted. Apparently she and my father held a conference out of our hearing sometime later in the day, because try as we might, we could never get my father to stop at McDonald's again. We resumed eating at Howard Johnson's, where the food was a little more expensive, but the quality was, according to my mother, "guaranteed." Nevertheless, we believed for years afterward that we had discovered McDonald's before any of our neighbors and that we had the inside dope on the chain springing up from Kansas, where the beef was doubtless cheaper.

6   I don't mean to give the impression that we had never eaten a hamburger on the cheap before. For years we frequented a place called Hamburger Junction, where the menus and meals were sent around the counter on a Lionel train. The interior of Hamburger Junction was standard for its time: a Formica counter, orange stools, black metal napkin cartridges, and a jukebox selector, stationed between each pair of stools, with a small dial on top that turned the song lists. Although Hamburger Junction's addition of a toy train was novel, the architecture and interior furnishings were not distinguishable from countless diners along other highways. Neither was its menu. The items were cleverly named—B&O Burgers, Choo-Choo Colas—but they were essentially what you could order in any other diner. It was possible to get eggs and French toast. It was possible to get pot roast and mashed potatoes, complete with gravy and string beans.

7   The differences, however, between our meal at McDonald's and Hamburger Junction are more profound than one might think at first glance. Even the smallest details mark a change in the American conception of "fast food." For example, it is important to note that typical diner fare of that period was served on plates. Milk shakes were blended in steel cups by machines with spindles, then poured into fountain glasses. Knives and forks, ridiculously supple, accompanied each other. Place mats describing attractions in the local countryside were slipped under each table setting. The result was a meal that vaguely resembled dinner at a family table. The food might be poorly prepared or erratic in quality, but the goal of many restaurants, even down to their advertising, was to make the dinner seem "home cooked."

8   Fast food, as we have come to think of it, was anything but home-cooked. Fast food was, and is, designed for travel, for consumption out of the house, for people too busy to linger over a slower-paced restaurant meal. In many cases our cars became our restaurants. The homey touches, indeed even such amenities as indoor seating, were often conspicuously absent. What we now

perceive as a normal fast-food serving system—paper cups, styrofoam hamburger containers, even paper bags—were a unique experiment in the McDonald brothers' restaurant in 1948. Forty years later it is not even a matter of thought to eat french fries with our fingers, add ketchup from plastic capsules, pour milk shakes from quick-drawing machines.

9   But the phenomenon goes far beyond a change in eating habits. The food at Hamburger Junction was pretty good; but it might have been swill, and there would have been no way for the newcomer to know that until the plate was put down in front of him. For years, of course, the bromide had it that one should "eat where the truckers eat": at best, an erratic barometer of food quality. What the fast food chains offered—and it was an entirely new thing—was a predictable level of sanitation, service, and quality. The fortunes of the fast-food industry rose on this tide of assurance: you knew that whether you were entering a restaurant in Sante Fe or Bangor, you were going to get exactly the same meal. It is this standardization that most impresses foreign visitors when they are confronted with McDonald's or Burger King, and it is the reflection of a particularly American kind of industrial genius.

10   It may have started in 1921 at the Royce Hailey's Pig Stand in Dallas when drivers began pulling up for barbecued sandwiches. Doubtless it started with cars, a population pushing out of the cities into the suburbs, and a volume business based on large production at minimal costs: hamburger factories with retail outlets. Tracking down the earliest restaurants, however, is a formidable exercise in genealogy. Dunkin' Donuts begot Mister Donut, which then begot Tastee Donut. White Castle sired White Diamond, Royal Castle, and White Crest. Some of the names give themselves over to chants: Taco Bell and Taco Tico, Taco Villa, and Tico Taco. The burger dynasty has maintained a somewhat bovine sound, not unlike cow bells gently clanging on a summer night: Burger King, Burger Chef, Bun & Burger, Wendy's . . . Mooooooo. Compare the burger line to the clucking chicken family: Bojangles, Church's Fried Chicken, Kentucky Fried Chicken, Popeye's Famous Fried Chicken. In pizza there are the Italian uncles: Godfather's, Domino's, Pizza Hut. Presiding over dessert are the married monarchs Dairy King and Dairy Queen and their wicked stepson, Dairy Cheer.

11   The numbers associated with these restaurants are perhaps even more astonishing than the family tree. A statistical breakdown on McDonald's alone is an MBA's dream. John Love, author of *McDonald's: Behind the Arches,* gives the following summation:

12   Ninety-six percent of Americans have eaten at one of the McDonald's restaurants in the last year; slightly more than half of the U.S. population lives within three minutes of a McDonald's; McDonald's has served more than 55 billion hamburgers; McDonald's commands 17% of all restaurant visits in the U.S. and gets 7.3% of all dollars Americans spent eating out; McDonald's sells 32% of all hamburgers and 26% of french fries; McDonald's is the country's largest beef buyer; it purchases 7.5% of the U.S. potato crop; McDonald's has employed

about 8 million workers—which amounts to approximately 7% of the entire U.S. work force: and McDonald's has replaced the U.S. Army as America's largest job training organization.

13   So that you know what you missed, I should mention that a block of a hundred shares of McDonald's stock bought when the company went public two decades ago is now worth around $400,000. The original cost was $2,250.

14   But the numbers only hint at the impact fast-food restaurants have had on our country. If you want to know what the fast-food industry really means, ask the next ten-year-old you meet where he'd like to eat if given his choice. Walk past a construction site in New York City around noon and note what the workers are eating for lunch. Check a potato farmer's invoices and track down his biggest client. Ask the farmer how egg production received a boom with the introduction of McDonald's Egg McMuffins and Burger King's Bagel Sandwiches, or what it meant to the chicken industry when McDonald's began serving Chicken McNuggets. Visit a quick-serve restaurant early in the morning and stay for breakfast. Finally, close your eyes right now and confess, honestly, how many fast-food jingles you can hum. If you can't hum at least two or three, you've probably been unplugged for the past ten years.

15   For my money, the true fast-food boom—the light bulb switching on to mark a pioneering idea—began on a tennis court located on one side of the McDonald brothers' San Bernardino house. The brothers, Maurice and Richard, were transplants from New Hampshire to California. They had already founded a successful restaurant that catered to the booming region surrounding San Bernardino in the 1940s. Housed in a shiny octagonal building with glass sides, the McDonald brothers had established an extremely well-run car hop restaurant. The parking lot was crowded daily. Teen-agers flocked to McDonald's, as did the older lunch crews working on projects around the area. The McDonald brothers had become wealthy, not fabulously so, but rich enough to acquire a new Cadillac each year, a ninety-thousand-dollar mansion, and tickets to local boxing matches. Annual sales topped two hundred thousand dollars.

16   But the McDonalds began to sense the limitations of their restaurant. Car hop service was becoming increasingly burdensome. The turnover rate in their work force was accelerating. Not only were they being pressured by competitors copying their operation, but they were also forced to compete against other industries for employees. Moreover, because the typical car hop was young and naturally attracted an adolescent clientele, the theft of knives and forks was driving up their operational costs.

17   In the fall of 1948 the brothers made a bold move. Risking their entire operation, they closed the restaurant for three months in order to overhaul the business. They fired the car hops. The windows formerly used by car hops to fill orders were converted to self-serve windows where customers could place their own orders. The kitchen was streamlined; the standard three-foot grill gave way to two six-foot grills custom-built by a Los Angeles kitchen supply

company. Paper products replaced plates and flatware, thereby eliminating the need for a dishwasher. The menu was cut back from twenty-five items to nine: cheeseburgers, hamburgers, three soft-drink flavors, milk, coffee, potato chips, and a slice of pie. The reduced number of menu items limited customer choice and, in turn, made "precooking" possible. Because of the increased speed and volume of sales, the cost of a hamburger plunged from thirty cents to an incredible fifteen.

18   When the restaurant reopened, business was slow. Nevertheless, the McDonald brothers stuck to their new formula. Within six months their trade had begun to recover. They added milk shakes and french fries to the menu. The real boom, though, came from an unexpected, and up until that time largely untapped, market share: adults and families.

19   McDonald's, by getting rid of the car hops, was no longer a "hangout." Small children, fascinated by the newly honed kitchen techniques and the assembly-line method of making hamburgers, began to ask their parents to take them to McDonald's. Because of the cost, parents were happy to oblige. Entire lower- and middle-class families were at last able to go out to a restaurant. The price was right, the service was automated, Mom escaped the kitchen, and no one had to be left home to mind the children.

20   But what about the tennis court?

21   When it became evident that the new Speedy System, as the brothers were calling it, could revolutionize the industry, they sold their first franchise to Neil Fox, an independent gasoline retailer. Working with an architect named Stanley Meston, they designed a new store. Eventually they got everything to their liking, save for one crucial element. "When I came up with the idea of the so-called Golden Arches and designed them," Richard McDonald wrote recently, "I could not find an architect who would use them in the building plans. They simply did not like the arches. So finally, George Dexter of the Dexter Sign Co. told me to have an architect leave the arches out of the plans and he would cut a hole in each corner of the roof of the building and lower the arches down through the holes." The store opened for business arches and all, in Phoenix in 1953 (and last winter those original arches went on permanent exhibition at the Henry Ford Museum in Dearborn, Michigan).

22   It was in the design of the new kitchen, however, that the McDonald brothers revealed the depth of their ingenuity. Taking the night crew of their existing restaurant to their home tennis court, they persuaded them to go through the motions of making hamburgers. While the crew members pantomimed the routine of making burgers, shakes, and fries, the brothers followed them, marking in red chalk exactly where the kitchen equipment should be placed for maximum efficiency. They finished at 3:00 A.M. and knocked off for the night. The draftsman who had been hired to transcribe the plan to paper said he would get on it first thing the next morning. Unfortunately a rain came up and washed away the entire outline, leaving only a muddled red mess.

23   But I still think the true beginning of the fast-food industry is encapsulated in the image of the crew moving through the night, making imaginary hamburgers. It combines many of the crucial elements that were to spread throughout the fast-food industry: attention to detail, emphasis on speed and efficiency, a vision of the future, and a wonderful dose of pure whimsy.

24   As has happened in many industries, the McDonald brothers only refined ideas that were already in existence. As early as 1921 a Wichita, Kansas, man named E. W. Ingram served a five-cent hamburger and encouraged customers to buy them by the sack. The hamburgers were served with fried onions; the hamburger itself was steam-fried. He called the restaurant White Castle. The hamburgers caught on, and in a few years his restaurant chain had spread to eleven states. Capitalizing on Ingram's success and company name, competing owners opened up restaurants called White Tower or Royal Castle.

25   But the White Castle restaurants were not geared to truly fast service. They typically included counter seating with a two-person staff to perform all functions in the restaurant: cooking, cleaning, and ringing up bills. Their clientele tended to be male, a fact that reduced the customer pool significantly. White Castles did not—as McDonald's was to do so successfully later—find a way to make their restaurants family-oriented. White Castles were often referred to in those early days as "truck stops," even though many were located in urban centers.

26   A&W appeared in 1924. The name was derived from the initials of its founders, Allen and White. A&W was based on a single product: Allen and White's root beer syrup. It did not begin serving food until much later, a fact that eventually spelled the chain's decline.

27   Though A&W is not a thriving chain today, it is still noted for its earliest franchises—the ones in Washington, D.C., where J. Willard Marriott got his start in the restaurant business. By 1928 Marriott had changed the name of his A&W stands to Hot Shoppe, forming a restaurant chain specializing in barbecue sandwiches. The sandwiches proved popular. The profits Marriott realized on the Hot Shoppes served as the foundation for the Marriott Corporation, one of America's largest hotel chains.

28   The path followed by Marriott was one Howard Johnson had already traveled. In 1925 Johnson scraped together five hundred dollars and invested it in a money-losing drugstore located in Quincy, Massachusetts. The drugstore contained a soda fountain, but the previous owner had served only three flavors of ice cream, all purchased from a local supplier. Johnson decided the ice cream was not rich enough for his clientele, so he set about producing a blend that doubled the butterfat content common in ice cream at the time. Working in his basement with a hand ice-cream maker, he came up with a product that soon had customers lined up. Riding on his success, he quickly added hot dogs and hamburgers to the menu. What started out as a soda fountain gradually expanded into a restaurant.

29   Others had also turned failing restaurants around, but it was Johnson who brought something wholly new to the game. In 1929 he once again expanded his operation. He opened a second restaurant in Quincy, using the techniques he had refined in the first. With the success of the second restaurant assured, he naturally began thinking of opening more. He would supply them himself from his own food-processing system, above all maintaining the high quality of his ice cream.

30   The Depression, however, proved formidable. Tight money cut into Johnson's sales, and made it difficult to expand. Surveying the situation, Johnson decided on a plan that would be followed by every food chain for the next sixty years: he would franchise.

31   Johnson convinced a restaurant owner on Cape Cod to use the Howard Johnson name and began supplying the new restaurant from his food-processing plant. By supplying the food himself, Johnson was able to maintain quality control while increasing the visibility of his chain. The new restaurant was a success, and more franchisees came forward. Six years later there were twenty-five Howard Johnson restaurants along the East Coast. By 1940 the Howard Johnson chain had expanded to a hundred restaurants, lining the Eastern seaboard. They were linked by a consistency in food quality and by the orange roofs that effectively attracted passing travelers.

32   Even if Howard Johnson's did not rely on a true fast-service system for its success (though it would later introduce Ho Jo's in an unsuccessful attempt to compete with the newer chains), it established a needed precedent when it came to franchising. Investors saw that properly franchised fast-serve restaurants could be big business. Perhaps no one understood this better than Harry Axene, the dominant force behind Dairy Queen.

33   Axene was on a family visit when he stopped at a Dairy Queen in East Moline, Illinois, in the 1940s. The store was operated by Jim Elliott, but the ice-cream manufacturing process was owned by John McCullough from Davenport, Iowa. McCullough had purchased the rights to the manufacturing process from Harold Oltz, who had invented a five-foot-long cylinder that chilled a liquid dairy mix. By opening a spigot on a machine and gently rotating the cone beneath the flow, the countermen were able to produce a serving in seconds.

34   McCullough saw potential in soft ice cream, but he did not know how to market it. Axene did. They formed a partnership with the intended purpose of franchising Dairy Queen nationally. To do so, however, they needed backing. With the advice and help of a Chicago ice-cream-cone manufacturer, Axene rounded up twenty-six investors from the ice-cream trade to attend a meeting in a Moline hotel. Axene approached the meeting as a businessman, with extensive charts detailing the potential profits in a typical Dairy Queen franchise. The investors, it turned out, were just as interested in the ice cream. They devoured the samples Axene provided, and Axene realized the product sold itself.

35   To a man, the investors bit. Some bought territories that covered an entire

state. The up-front prices ranged from twenty-five to fifty thousand dollars. Axene also charged each new franchise forty-five cents on every gallon of dairy mix. As a result of the chain's success, Axene became one of the nation's first fast-food millionaires virtually overnight.

36   The tremendous growth of Dairy Queen was based on several factors besides a popular product. For one thing, the menu was naturally limited. Because no elaborate equipment was required to open a store, the cost of franchising was kept low—only thirty thousand dollars in most cases. The minimal cost, combined with the chance to run one's own business, held tremendous appeal for the returning GIs of World War II. GI loans were plentiful; the economy was in a growth spurt. By the time Axene moved from Dairy Queen in1948 to start the Tastee Freeze line with Leo Moranz—on the basis of a purportedly superior freezer and ice-cream process—there were twenty-five hundred Dairy Queen outlets in operation.

37   On the hamburger front it was Bob Wian and his Big Boy restaurants that began the franchising boom in the late 1930s around California. The key product was a result of serendipity. When a regular customer asked for something different late one night, Wian responded with a hamburger that gave customers "the works"—two hamburger patties; served on a triple-deck bun. Soon customers were lined up for a taste, and Wian began selling Big Boy franchises around the country.

38   In chicken there was only one name: Harlan Sanders. His story is remarkable. In 1952, while he was the owner of a successful service station and restaurant, Sanders met a Utah man named Pete Harmon who was looking for a specialty item to add to the menu at his hamburger stand. The Colonel taught him the secret recipe to his fried chicken, and when he later visited Harmon's restaurant he had to squeeze through a throng of customers waiting to taste the "Kentucky Fried Chicken" that now accounted for half of Harmon's business.

39   On the same day in 1955 that he received his first Social Security check of $105, Sanders auctioned off his property. The business for which he had earlier refused an offer of $164,000 had been ruined by a new interstate highway that diverted traffic seven miles to the west. With unusual tenacity and Harmon's encouragement, Harlan Sanders took to the road armed with a pressure cooker, eleven herbs and spices, and an idea. He stopped at random restaurants and offered to cook for them if they would consider placing his Southern fried chicken on their menu. Before long Colonel Sanders stopped traveling: the chicken that had been a regional legend in his Kentucky restaurant was attracting restaurant owners to him. Operating his business from an office he built behind his house in Shelbyville, Kentucky, the Colonel with the white suit and goatee had by 1960 sold two hundred franchises, and was selling almost as many again annually.

40   Where were all these fast-food franchises opening? Consider a parcel of land five miles outside the city limits. You've seen thousands of building lots like it: high grass, Queen Anne's lace, tansy, blue aster, highway litter stuck in

the mud, and tire tracks that border the street side of the land. If you were around in the early 1950s, the land might appear to hold little value compared with prime corners within the city's center. But to the early franchisers such parcels of land were the perfect cribs for their new industry.

41   The competition was fierce, but the American appetite appeared insatiable. During the 1950s and early 1960s, doughnuts, pizza, fish sticks, spicy chicken, barbecued sandwiches, and Mexican tacos acquired brand names that were almost synonymous with the products themselves. Although it is extraordinary to calculate the amount of food these chains produce and sell, it is perhaps even more extraordinary to think of their use of real estate.

42   Food franchises changed the face, and character, of American towns. In step with other franchises—True Value, Sears, Midas, Firestone, 7-Eleven, car dealerships of all makes and models. B. Dalton's, Toys "R" Us, Shell, K Mart, Channel Home Centers, Mobile, Sunoco, Dino's, Sinclair, Esso, A&P, Food Town, and various movie theaters—fast-food outlets abandoned the towns and claimed the nation's highways and major roads. The commercial centers of many towns shifted and often all but died. Malls eventually became the focus of Saturday shopping trips, but originally it was underdeveloped highway land, or "strips" as they are sometimes called, that altered the physical makeup of suburban and country life.

43   It is not surprising, therefore, to find that McDonald's is the world's largest owner of real estate. It passed Sears in real estate holdings in 1982 and is still growing. If we add to its holdings the real estate owned by the other major food franchises, it's possible to glimpse the sheer scope of land they control. American towns are dominated, architecturally and in terms of landscape, by fast-food outlets. It is not simply an imagined perception one has when driving down the nation's highways that the roads are lined with franchises of all descriptions. It is almost more accurate than we can allow ourselves to believe.

44   The late Ray Kroc, founder of McDonald's Corporation, the man who is credited with franchising McDonald's around the world, sometimes flew over prospective sites to look for church steeples and schools, taking them as signs that the community had a solid middle class. He liked isolated locations on cheap lots, well away from existing businesses. Because McDonald's parking lots were designed in a U shape to guarantee a steady flow of traffic around the restaurant, he was happy with parcels in the middle of a block. He did not have to compete with the gas stations that preferred corner locations, a fact that greatly reduced the cost of franchising.

45   By the time McDonald's hit its stride, somewhere in the mid-1960s, the company could not put in an outlet without alerting other franchises that the overlooked location was prime. Other fast-food chains moved in quickly, and the strip was born. Even today lesser chains keep an eye on the major chains and build in their shadows, hoping to catch some of the runoff business, secure that the "majors" have done research to determine the best location.

46   Zoning could not keep pace during the infancy of the fast-food boom. Perhaps no one saw that a redefinition of our highways was about to take place, or perhaps local businessmen and politicians were pleased to see depressed land values suddenly soar in price. In any case, the rush was on.

47   Even now the zoning regulations concerning fast-food franchises are confusing and inconsistent. If you look closely at a typical strip, you can see the quality of curbing changes from one zoning jurisdiction to another. In one place the restaurants are fronted by sidewalks; in other locations there are no sidewalks at all. Long-range planning, in most cases, was nonexistent. As a result, our highways are now crammed with franchise signs that, by most reasonable standards, must be considered eyesores.

48   Understandably, over the years the strips have ignited a good deal of political action and considerable ill will. In Oregon the state legislature introduced bills in 1979 and 1980 to outlaw throw-away containers. Both bills failed, but they have added fuel to the growing controversy around the country. Garden clubs are now asking that signs and roofs be constructed with neutral colors. Resort towns guard their scenic stature by stipulating that the restaurants agree to limit the sizes, and colors, of their signs. Careful landscaping is slowly becoming the rule. Most fast-food franchises realize that proper community relations are essential to good business, and they are quick to comply. In direct response to requests from conservation groups, franchises are building new outlets that attempt to blend with surrounding architecture. On college campuses, or in historic districts, it's possible to come across a McDonald's or Burger King with a brick facade marred only by a minuscule sign advertising its product.

49   The gaudy hamburger and ice-cream stands of the early 1940s and 1950s are being lost, and with them, a genuine period in American architecture. In fact, the most recent push by fast-food franchises is being made in our major cities. The urban population, once courted by White Castle and the corner soda fountain, is now patronizing McDonald's and Kentucky Fried Chicken and Pizza Hut and Burger King. Some of the chains are experimenting with what is called "vertical rub-off stores"—two or three restaurants located on evenly spaced floors in a high rise, with each one stimulating purchases up and down the honeycomb of offices. Kroc, not long before he died, looked seriously at Chicago's Sears Tower as a prospective site for three stores. "All three would have done well, with the trade from one rubbing off to the others and not encroaching at all," he said in his book *Grinding It Out.* "We didn't do that for various reasons, but we might try it somewhere in the future."

50   The food franchises have entered our cultural history; Ronald McDonald is as well known as Ronald Reagan. "Where's the beef?" became a throw-off line for politicians around the country. Colonel Sanders, before his death, was one of the most widely recognized individuals in the nation. A bearded gentlemen dressed up as the "Burger King" never quite caught on, but the phrase "Have it your way" and the name Whopper provide instant identification.

51   But the food franchises have also entered our cultural history as "experiences"—which is an entirely different matter. I remember, for example, a night in the middle of the summer sometime around 1970 when I went out to a Gino's and inadvertently entered into my first and only fistfight. I was a member of the Westfield High School football team and, together with friends, got into a shoving match with rival football players from Clark, New Jersey. We fought it out—two or three punches thrown, one landed—in the restaurant parking lot. On another night I took my girl friend to the same restaurant, and we necked for twenty minutes before going in to dinner. As trivial as these moments appear in retrospect, they were nevertheless rites of passage for me.

52   We support the fast-food franchises. We go in station wagons, on lunch hours, and for quick summer dinners. We go to celebrate a Little League victory or a junior high school graduation. In the South I have seen prayer meetings held in an empty bay of a McDonald's restaurant. We go when our schedules get too busy to cook dinner or when we simply need a break. Many restaurants now offer playgrounds for the kids or special promotional games to keep the children busy while the parents steal a few minutes to relax. People seem to be happy in fast-food restaurants for the most part. They know what to expect: they know what things cost.

53   We go for the taste—something we should not overlook. We go, too, because massive advertising campaigns push us to go. But in a strange way I believe we also go because the food franchises represent free enterprise. Individuals—friends and neighbors—run the franchises up and down our highways. The idea of opening a business, of making a success, is at the heart of American attitudes. We like to visit food franchises because the concept behind them is something we can grasp. One person can start cooking hamburgers in a different way, or begin churning ice cream with more butterfat, and become a millionaire. The message is clear to all of us: You could do this too. Look, isn't it easy?

☐ Discovering Meaning and Technique

1. What does Monninger consider the major difference between the modern fast-food restaurants and the diners of yesterday?

2. Explain what Monninger means when he says that "originally it was underdeveloped highway land, or 'strips' as they are sometimes called, that altered the physical makeup of suburban and country life" (paragraph 42).

3. What is a "vertical rub-off store" (paragraph 49)?

4. What influence did the automobile have upon the development of fast-food restaurants?

5. What prompted the McDonald brothers to change the style of their original restaurant?

6. The essay is primarily a series of narratives that relate the history of fast-food chains. How many different narratives does Monninger relate?

7. Where does the introduction seem to stop and the body of the essay begin? Explain your choice.

8. Where does the conclusion seem to begin? Explain your choice.

☐ Writing Suggestions

1. Monninger ends his essay by suggesting that Americans eat fast food because it tastes good, because advertising is massive, and because the franchises represent free enterprise. Which reason seems the most valid to you? The least valid? Can you suggest reasons that Monninger overlooks?

2. Compare fast food with the food in other restaurants or with home-cooked meals. Try to focus on a few points of comparison—for example, taste, nutritional value, social interaction.

3. Monninger remembers Hamburger Junction, where menus and food "were sent around the counter on a Lionel train." Describe an unusual or unusually good restaurant that you remember from childhood.

4. Discuss the effects that fast-food chains have had on the environment, for example architectural appearance, use of nondegradable containers, and litter.

THE DINNER PARTY

☐ A. R. GURNEY, JR.

1 *"The dinner party is the ultimate celebration of what it means to be civilized," my father used to say. "There is nothing better in this world than to settle down around a lovely table and eat good food and say interesting things with one's friends."*

2 When I was growing up, or thought I was, in Buffalo before World War II,

Saturday-night dinner parties were an essential element in my parents' lives. They spent a lot of time talking about them, going to them, and giving them. Time and again my sister and brother and I would come home from sledding in Delaware Park to find an extra maid clucking in the kitchen, polishing the silver, teetering on a stepladder to get at the good china, while the cook distractedly set out soup and sandwiches for us on the kitchen table before she returned to basting the great, sizzling roast of beef in the oven or shelling the fresh green peas.

3 *"Dinner parties require immense amounts of labor," my father would say. "While the servants are toiling in the kitchen, your mother and I are working just as hard elsewhere, making sure that our guests are comfortable and happy. All of us happen to feel it's worth the effort."*

4 We children couldn't go into the living room the night of a party, but we could see from the doorway that someone had already neatened up the copies of *Life* in the magazine rack, and tucked the sheet music back in the piano bench, and laid out the Chesterfields in the cut-glass cigarette boxes. There would be a screen in front of the dining-room door, but we could still catch a glimpse of the lace tablecloth and the curly candlesticks and the blue and silver salt dishes, with the little spoons, that spilled so easily and fresh flowers and the twelve crystal water goblets that came from Cooperstown. It all looked as sacred and mysterious as the altar at Trinity Church, where we'd go the next day if our parents weren't too tired.

5 *"Now I do expect you children to come downstairs and shake hands. Remember to look people in the eye and call them by name, and speak up clearly when they talk to you. Half of our friends don't listen, and the other half don't hear. You don't have to bow or curtsy, though I think people would be very pleased if you did. Then get out promptly, so we can continue with our cocktails and our conversation."*

6 For most of the evening the strange, exotic sounds of the dinner party would waft upstairs, punctuating our radio programs and finally even penetrating our dreams: the ring of the doorbell, the greetings in the front hall, the rhythmic rattle of the cocktail shaker, the buzzer in the kitchen indicating they were "almost" ready to eat, the oohs and aahs and muffled slidings of chairs when they did, the clink of glasses when there were toasts, the whoops of laughter when there were jokes, the continual activity in the kitchen underneath it all. Afterward there might be singing around the piano or even dancing, if the Victrola had been fixed and my mother had remembered to buy a new needle. Then, finally, the good-byes in the hall, more at the door before its last closing thud, and the strained sound of cars starting outside the storm windows in the cold winter air.

7   This was the dinner party, and this was what my parents went out to on all those nights when they weren't "entertaining" at home. Almost always they'd "dress"—a long evening gown for my mother, black tie for my father, though on some occasions he'd wear his tails.

8   *"The jacket must always come below the waistcoat. Otherwise you'll look like a waiter and might be mistaken for one. But for most dinners wear your dinner jacket. And remember to call it that, rather than a tuxedo or tux. And say trousers, rather than pants."*

9   I suppose that the dinner party was one way my parents had of cheering themselves up during the gray days of the Depression. They also were simply perpetuating a custom that they had inherited from their parents, now amplified and lubricated by lengthy cocktail hours. Certainly they didn't have huge amounts of money— or if they did, they didn't have huge amounts for me. It was simply what they like to do when they wanted to be with their friends. Cooks and maids were fairly inexpensive then, until the war came along and they discovered they could make more money pounding rivets than passing the vegetables. After the war the custom cropped up again, though on a lesser scale. Even today, when I go home to visit, my mother does what she can to "get a maid."

10   *"How can I enjoy my family if I'm slaving away in the kitchen? How can I relax if there's a stack of dirty dishes waiting in the sink? I believe in being civilized, thank you very much."*

11   The dinner party was hardly a phenomenon confined to twentieth-century Buffalo. Homer's heroes always seem to be giving good dinner parties, and the Olympian gods put on even better ones. The Romans were no slouches at it, and even the Last Supper could be called a dinner party, if a not totally sucessful one. In nineteenth-century Europe, with the rise of an affluent bourgeoisie and the domestication of women, the custom bloomed extravagantly. The recently rich enjoyed it as a way of displaying their possessions, servants, and recipes. In America, if the Puritans always had difficulty with it, the Southern gentry had none. In any case the dinner party somehow found its way up the Erie Canal to Buffalo, where it was embraced with some fervor by my grandparents, by my parents, and ultimately, like it or not, by me. Or at least, if I didn't embrace it, I absorbed it so thoroughly that even now my father's various admonitions on the subject pervade my thinking at any social gathering we give or go to. Indeed, I find myself almost compelled to pass on his advice, for whatever it's worth, to whoever will listen. Some nuggets follow herewith:

12   • When your guests arrive, don't try to greet them at the door. Let the maid do that. Then, after you've given the man time to adjust his tie and the woman

to comb her hair, try to come in upon them with great enthusiasm, as if you had just been doing something terribly important, but their arrival is much more so.

13 • When serving cocktails, remind yourself to use plenty of ice, even if people say they don't want it. Ice does two essential things: It keeps the party under control and saves on liquor.

14 • Conversation is at the heart of a good party. If a conversation is going well, it will draw others to it, like moths to a flame. People will lean over or sidle up. When they do, be sure to include them immediately. Say. "We were discussing this," or "We were talking of that." Ask their opinion on the subject even if you're not interested in it. In this way, if everyone is concentrating, the entire room can catch fire.

15 • If you're having difficulty conversing with a woman, try complimenting her. Even if she's homely, search for something attractive to mention: her hair, her feet, her shoulders. You'd be surprised how many women have lovely shoulders. Don't compliment her clothes. Other women will do that. Your job is to focus on something more essential. Try the shoulders.

16 • Men are harder to start, like old cars on cold days. You can normally jump-start them with a question on sports, but sports conversations normally lack development and tend to confuse the women. Movies are good to talk about with men. Most men like movies. And, of course, travel. Ask a man if he's traveled recently, and he'll tell you. Make sure, though, you have an out, since he'll go on too long.

17 • When you go in to dinner, always guide your companion by touching the back of her elbow. She usually knows where she's going better than you, but guide her anyway. Before you sit, push in her chair. If there's a thick rug, this can be tricky, but get her to help, by sort of humping her chair up and down. Don't scamper around the table, pushing in too many chairs, though. You'll look like a fool.

18 • Never make remarks about the food. If it's bad, and you say it is, you're being rude. If it's bad, and you say it's good, you're encouraging bad cooking. If it's good, and you say that, you're being redundant. Just assume it's good, and eat it with quiet relish. Try to finish at the same time as the people sitting around you. Otherwise you'll be watching them eat, or they'll be watching you. Either way it's unpleasant. Eating is not basically an attractive habit. Who wants to watch people putting things in their mouths? That's why we have table manners, to disguise the process.

19 • Apparently, in the Navy, officers are advised not to talk about three things in their wardroom: politics, sex, and religion. Supposedly these topics lead to trouble when the ship's at sea. Now obviously we don't want brawls at a dinner party, but these inhibitions seem unduly stringent. Politics is an awkward topic because it invites argument, and people tend to make their points simply by assertion. Particularly if they've been drinking. It's very difficult to rebut them since the statistics aren't readily available, and it's disconcerting if you leave the table to get them. So perhaps the Navy is right about politics. Sex, on the other hand, is fun to talk about, as long as you maintain some discretion. It's a subject everyone knows something about. If people don't, they should. It's also a subject in which no one has any special expertise. If people do, they shouldn't. Religion, finally, hardly ever comes up. Most people who go to dinner parties aren't terribly religious. If they are, they probably shouldn't be there.

20 • Don't talk to the servants, except to say thank you when they pass the asparagus. It's very difficult for them to hold those great silver platters on one arm while tipping them so you can get at the butter. It's good to acknowledge that quietly. Otherwise it's better to pretend that the servants aren't there. We live in a democracy, and the idea of being waited on by somebody else goes against the very grain of our heritage. It's embarrassing on both sides. After the dinner is over, however, it's always good to slip into the kitchen and compliment everyone in sight.

21 Now that I have put them down, some of these admonitions seem like rather poor advice for a dinner party these days. A man can get slugged for complimenting a woman's shoulders, for example. And at least in New York you should probably speak to the servers whenever you can. Most of them are actors or artists and have more intelligent things to say than many of the guests. Still, these old rules from my father continue to roll around in my head. Try as I might, it is no more possible for me to strike out into totally new modes of social behavior than it is for an Atlantic salmon to spawn in the Nile. Meanwhile, no matter how I behave, I suspect dinner parties will continue to go on all over the world— some of them, darn it all, without me.

☐ Discovering Meaning and Technique

1. Which signs in the Gurney household alerted the children to an impending dinner party?

2. Pick out details that indicate the elegance of the Gurney's dinner parties.

3. Pick out details that indicate the era of the dinner parties.

4. What is the purpose of the italicized print in the essay?

5. Which paragraphs in the essay serve as a set of instructions? How does Gurney mark these paragraphs?

6. Which parts of the essay are written in the imperative mood (verbs of command), and why?

☐ Writing Suggestions

1. Which of the father's rules for conduct seem inappropriate today, and why?

2. Does the father's attitude toward women seem sexist or merely gentlemanly?

3. Do you (or would you) enjoy attending or giving formal dinner parties with formal dress and maids serving several courses? Why or why not?

4. Provide rules for a different type of gathering—such as a barbecue, a Super Bowl party, a college dance, a cocktail party.

5. Why do you think the dinner party is less common today than in the past?

■ Combining Sources in a Composition

1. Using the selections by Mendelsohn, Lurie, Quinn, and Blount as source material, write an essay explaining how our clothes reflect the attitudes of our society.

2. Write an essay on customs that encourage either excess or irrational behavior, or both. You can find material in the selections by Boorstin, Mendelsohn, Geist, and Mitford.

3. What does the popularity of fast foods and snack foods suggest about the American character?

4. Boorstin discusses American "Festivals of Consumption," designed to benefit the merchants. Compare his ideas with Mitford's view of the American funeral, which is designed to benefit the morticians.

5. In two selections ("Understanding Society and Culture Through Eating" and "Future Eating Habits"), the authors refer to Brillat–Savarin's famous remark, "Tell me what you eat: I will tell you what you are." Compare the authors' purposes in using the quotation.

6. Using the selection by Pizer and the selection by Farb and Armelagos to suggest ideas, discuss food traditions of other countries that seem particularly bizarre. You might want to do further research in the library.

7. Discuss some American traditions that reflect our democratic spirit. You can find material in the selections by Mendelsohn and Quinn.

8. Discuss the traditions and customs associated with eating that could be destroyed by modern society. You can find material for the composition in the selections by Farb and Armelagos, Davenport, Tannahill, and Gurney.

CHAPTER 3

ENTERTAINMENT

Film and Television

■ ■ ■

JOHN WAYNE: A LOVE SONG

☐ **JOAN DIDION**

[1] In the summer of 1943 I was eight, and my father and mother and small brother and I were at Peterson Field in Colorado Springs. A hot wind blew through that summer, blew until it seemed that before August broke, all the dust in Kansas would be in Colorado, would have drifted over the tar-paper barracks and the temporary strip and stopped only when it hit Pikes Peak. There was not much to do, a summer like that: there was the day they brought in the first B-29, an event to remember but scarcely a vacation program. There was an Officers' Club, but no swimming pool; all the Officers' Club had of interest was artificial blue rain behind the bar. The rain interested me a good deal, but I could not spend the summer watching it, and so we went, my brother and I, to the movies.

[2]   We went three and four afternoons a week, sat on folding chairs in the darkened Quonset hut which served as a theater, and it was there, that summer of 1943 while the hot wind blew outside, that I first saw John Wayne. Saw the walk, heard the voice. Heard him tell the girl in a picture called *War of the Wildcats* that he would build her a house, "at the bend in the river where the

cottonwoods grow." As it happened I did not grow up to be the kind of woman who is the heroine in a Western, and although the men I have known have had many virtues and have taken me to live in many places I have come to love, they have never been John Wayne, and they have never taken me to that bend in the river where the cottonwoods grow. Deep in that part of my heart where the artificial rain forever falls, that is still the line I wait to hear.

3   I tell you this neither in a spirit of self-revelation nor as an exercise in total recall, but simply to demonstrate that when John Wayne rode through my childhood, and perhaps through yours, he determined forever the shape of certain of our dreams. It did not seem possible that such a man could fall ill, could carry within him that most inexplicable and ungovernable of diseases. The rumor struck some obscure anxiety, threw our very childhoods into question. In John Wayne's world, John Wayne was supposed to give the orders. "Let's ride," he said, and "Saddle up." "Forward *ho*," and "A man's gotta do what he's got to do." "Hello, there," he said when he first saw the girl, in a construction camp or on a train or just standing around on the front porch waiting for somebody to ride up through the tall grass. When John Wayne spoke, there was no mistaking his intentions; he had a sexual authority so strong that even a child could perceive it. And in a world we understood early to be characterized by venality and doubt and paralyzing ambiguities, he suggested another world, one which may or may not have existed ever but in any case existed no more: a place where a man could move free, could make his own code and live by it; a world in which, if a man did what he had to do, he could one day take the girl and go riding through the draw and find himself home free, not in a hospital with something going wrong inside, not in a high bed with the flowers and the drugs and the forced smiles, but there at the bend in the bright river, the cottonwoods shimmering in the early morning sun.

4   "Hello, there." Where did he come from, before the tall grass? Even his history seemed right, for it was no history at all, nothing to intrude upon the dream. Born Marion Morrison in Winterset, Iowa, the son of a druggist. Moved as a child to Lancaster, California, part of the migration to that promised land sometimes called "the west coast of Iowa." Not that Lancaster was the promise fulfilled; Lancaster was a town on the Mojave where the dust blew through. But Lancaster was still California, and it was only a year from there to Glendale, where desolation had a different flavor: antimacassars among the orange groves, a middle-class prelude to Forest Lawn. Imagine Marion Morrison in Glendale. A Boy Scout, then a student at Glendale High. A tackle for U.S.C., a Sigma Chi. Summer vacations, a job moving props on the old Fox lot. There, a meeting with John Ford, one of the several directors who were to sense that into this perfect mold might be poured the inarticulate longings of a nation wondering at just what pass the trail had been lost. "Dammit," said Raoul Walsh later, "the son of a bitch looked like a man." And so after a while the boy from Glendale became a star. He did not become an actor, as he has always been careful to

point out to interviewers ("How many times do I gotta tell you, I don't act at
all, I *re*-act"), but a star, and the star called John Wayne would spend most of
the rest of his life with one or another of those directors, out on some forsaken
location, in search of the dream.

> Out where the skies are a trifle bluer
> Out where friendship's a little truer
> That's where the West begins.

5   Nothing very bad could happen in the dream, nothing a man could not
face down. But something did. There it was, the rumor, and after a while the
headlines. "I licked the Big C," John Wayne announced, as John Wayne would,
reducing those outlaw cells to the level of any other outlaws, but even so we
all sensed that this would be the one unpredictable confrontation, the one shoot-
out Wayne could lose. I have as much trouble as the next person with illusion
and reality, and I did not much want to see John Wayne when he must be (or
so I thought) having some trouble with it himself, but I did, and it was down
in Mexico when he was making the picture his illness had so long delayed,
down in the very country of the dream.

6 It was John Wayne's 165th picture. It was Henry Hathaway's 84th. It was number
34 for Dean Martin, who was working off an old contract to Hal Wallis, for
whom it was independent production number 65. It was called *The Sons of
Katie Elder,* and it was a Western, and after the three-month delay they had
finally shot the exteriors up in Durango, and now they were in the waning
days of interior shooting at Estudio Churubusco outside Mexico City, and the
sun was hot and the air was clear and it was lunchtime. Out under the pepper
trees the boys from the Mexican crew sat around sucking caramels, and down
the road some of the technical men sat around a place which served a stuffed
lobster and a glass of tequila for one dollar American, but it was inside the
cavernous empty commissary where the talent sat around, the reasons for the
exercise, all sitting around the big table picking at *huevos con queso* and Carta
Blanca beer. Dean Martin, unshaven. Mack Gray, who goes where Martin goes.
Bob Goodfried, who was in charge of Paramount publicity and who had flown
down to arrange for a trailer and who had a delicate stomach. "Tea and toast,"
he warned repeatedly. "That's the ticket. You can't trust the lettuce." And Henry
Hathaway, the director, who did not seem to be listening to Goodfried. And
John Wayne, who did not seem to be listening to anyone.

7   "This week's gone slow," Dean Martin said, for the third time.
8   "How can you say that?" Mack Gray demanded.
9   "*This . . . week's . . . gone . . . slow,* that's how I can say it."
10   "You don't mean you want it to end."
11   "I'll say it right out, Mack, I want it to *end.* Tomorrow night I shave this
beard, I head for the airport, I say *adiós amigos!* Bye-bye *muchachos!*"

12   Henry Hathaway lit a cigar and patted Martin's arm fondly. "Not tomorrow, Dino."

13   "Henry, what are you planning to add? A World War?"

14   Hathaway patted Martin's arm again and gazed into the middle distance. At the end of the table someone mentioned a man who, some years before, had tried unsuccessfully to blow up an airplane.

15   "He's still in jail," Hathaway said suddenly.

16   "In jail?" Martin was momentarily distracted from the question whether to send his golf clubs back with Bob Goodfried or consign them to Mack Gray. "What's he in jail for if nobody got killed?"

17   "Attempted murder, Dino," Hathaway said gently. "A felony."

18   "You mean some guy just *tried* to kill me he'd end up in jail?"

19   Hathaway removed the cigar from his mouth and looked across the table. "Some guy just tried to kill *me* he wouldn't end up in jail. How about you, Duke?"

20   Very slowly, the object of Hathaway's query wiped his mouth, pushed back his chair, and stood up. It was the real thing, the authentic article, the move which had climaxed a thousand scenes on 165 flickering frontiers and phantasmagoric battlefields before, and it was about to climax this one, in the commissary at Estudio Churubusco outside Mexico City. "Right," John Wayne drawled. "I'd kill him."

21   Almost all the cast of *Katie Elder* had gone home, that last week; only the principals were left, Wayne, and Martin, and Earl Holliman, and Michael Anderson, Jr., and Martha Hyer. Martha Hyer was not around much, but every now and then someone referred to her, usually as "the girl." They had all been together nine weeks, six of them in Durango. Mexico City was not quite Durango; wives like to come along to places like Mexico City, like to shop for handbags, go to parties at Merle Oberon Pagliai's, like to look at her paintings. But Durango. The very name hallucinates. Man's country. Out where the West begins. There had been ahuehuete trees in Durango; a waterfall, rattlesnakes. There had been weather, nights so cold that they had postponed one or two exteriors until they could shoot inside at Churubusco. "It was the girl," they explained. "You couldn't keep the girl out in cold like that." Henry Hathaway had cooked in Durango, *gazpacho* and ribs and the steaks that Dean Martin had ordered flown down from the Sands; he had wanted to cook in Mexico City, but the management of the Hotel Bamer refused to let him set up a brick barbecue in his room. "You really missed something, *Durango,*" they would say, sometimes joking and sometimes not, until it became a refrain, Eden lost.

22   But if Mexico City was not Durango, neither was it Beverly Hills. No one else was using Churubusco that week, and there inside the big sound stage that said LOS HIJOS DE KATIE ELDER on the door, there with the pepper trees and the bright sun outside, they could still, for just so long as the picture lasted, maintain a world peculiar to men who like to make Westerns, a world of loyalties and fond raillery, of sentiment and shared cigars, of interminable desultory recol-

lections; campfire talk, its only point to keep a human voice raised against the night, the wind, the rustlings in the brush.

23   "Stuntman got hit accidentally on a picture of mine once," Hathaway would say between takes of an elaborately choreographed fight scene. "What was his name, married Estelle Taylor, met her down in Arizona."

24   The circle would close around him, the cigars would be fingered. The delicate art of the staged fight was to be contemplated.

25   "I only hit one guy in my life," Wayne would say. "Accidentally, I mean. That was Mike Mazurki."

26   "Some guy. Hey, Duke says he only hit one guy in his life, Mike Mazurki."

27   "Some choice." Murmurings, assent.

28   "It wasn't a choice, it was an accident."

29   "I can believe it."

30   "You bet."

31   "Oh boy. Mike Mazurki."

32   And so it would go. There was Web Overlander, Wayne's makeup man for twenty years, hunched in a blue Windbreaker, passing out sticks of Juicy Fruit. "*Insect* spray," he would say. "Don't tell us about insect spray. We saw insect spray in Africa, all right. Remember Africa?" Or, "*Steamer* clams. Don't tell us about steamer clams. We got our fill of steamer clams all right, on the *Hatari!* appearance tour. Remember Bookbinder's?" There was Ralph Volkie, Wayne's trainer for eleven years, wearing a red baseball cap and carrying around a clipping from Hedda Hopper, a tribute to Wayne. "This Hopper's some lady," he would say again and again. "Not like some of these guys, all they write is sick, sick, sick, how can you call that guy *sick,* when he's got pains, coughs, works all day, *never complains.* That guy's got the best hook since Dempsey, not *sick.*"

33   And there was Wayne himself, fighting through number 165. There was Wayne, in his thirty-three-year-old spurs, his dusty neckerchief, his blue shirt. "You don't have too many worries about what to wear in these things," he said. "You can wear a blue shirt, or, if you're down in Monument Valley, you can wear a yellow shirt." There was Wayne, in a relatively new hat, a hat which made him look curiously like William S. Hart. "I had this old cavalry hat I loved, but I lent it to Sammy Davis. I got it back, it was unwearable. I think they all pushed it down on his head and said *O.K., John Wayne*—you know, a joke."

34   There was Wayne, working too soon, finishing the picture with a bad cold and a racking cough, so tired by late afternoon that he kept an oxygen inhalator on the set. And still nothing mattered but the Code. "That guy," he muttered of a reporter who had incurred his displeasure. "I admit I'm balding. I admit I got a tire around my middle. What man fifty-seven doesn't? Big news. Anyway, that guy."

35   He paused, about to expose the heart of the matter, the root of the distaste, the fracture of the rules that bothered him more than the alleged misquotations,

more than the intimation that he was no longer the Ringo Kid. "He comes down, uninvited, but I ask him over anyway. So we're sitting around drinking mescal out of a water jug."

36   He paused again and looked meaningfully at Hathaway, readying him for the unthinkable denouement. "He had to be *assisted* to his room."

37   They argued about the virtues of various prizefighters, they argued about the price of J & B in pesos. They argued about dialogue.

38   "As rough a guy as he is, Henry, I still don't think he'd raffle off his mother's *Bible*."

39   "I like a shocker, Duke."

40   They exchanged endless training-table jokes. "You know why they call this memory sauce?" Martin asked, holding up a bowl of chili.

41   "Why?"

42   "Because you *remember it in the morning.*"

43   "Hear that, Duke? Hear why they call this memory sauce?"

44   They delighted one another by blocking out minute variations in the free-for-all fight which is a set piece in Wayne pictures; motivated or totally gratuitous, the fight sequence has to be in the picture, because they so enjoy making it. "Listen—this'll really be funny. Duke picks up the kid, see, and then it takes both Dino and Earl to throw him out the door—*how's that?*"

45   They communicated by sharing old jokes; they sealed their camaraderie by making gentle, old-fashioned fun of wives, those civilizers, those tamers. "So Señora Wayne takes it into her head to stay up and have one brandy. So for the rest of the night it's 'Yes, Pilar, you're right, dear. I'm a bully, Pilar, you're right, I'm impossible.' "

46   "You hear that? Duke says Pilar threw a table at him."

47   "Hey, Duke, here's something funny. That finger you hurt today, get the Doc to bandage it up, go home tonight, show it to Pilar, tell her she did it when she threw the table. You know, make her think she was really cutting up."

48   They treated the oldest among them respectfully; they treated the youngest fondly. "You see that kid?" they said of Michael Anderson, Jr. "What a kid."

49   "He don't act, it's right from the heart," said Hathaway, patting his heart.

50   "Hey, kid," Martin said. "You're gonna be in my next picture. We'll have the whole thing, no beards. The striped shirts, the girls, the hi-fi, the eye lights."

51   They ordered Michael Anderson his own chair, with "BIG MIKE" tooled on the back. When it arrived on the set, Hathaway hugged him. "You see that?" Anderson asked Wayne, suddenly too shy to look him in the eye. Wayne gave him the smile, the nod, the final accolade. "I saw it, kid."

52 On the morning of the day they were to finish *Katie Elder,* Web Overlander showed up not in his Windbreaker but in a blue blazer. "Home, Mama," he

said, passing out the last of his Juicy Fruit. "I got on my getaway clothes." But he was subdued. At noon, Henry Hathaway's wife dropped by the commissary to tell him that she might fly over to Acapulco. "Go ahead," he told her. "I get through here, all I'm gonna do is take Seconal to a point just this side of suicide." They were all subdued. After Mrs. Hathaway left, there were desultory attempts at reminiscing, but man's country was receding fast; they were already halfway home, and all they could call up was the 1961 Bel Air fire, during which Henry Hathaway had ordered the Los Angeles Fire Department off his property and saved the place himself by, among other measures, throwing everything flammable into the swimming pool. "Those fire guys might've just given it up," Wayne said. "Just let it burn." In fact this was a good story, and one incorporating several of their favorite themes, but a Bel Air story was still not a Durango story.

53   In the early afternoon they began the last scene, and although they spent as much time as possible setting it up, the moment finally came when there was nothing to do but shoot it. "Second team out, first team in, *doors closed,*" the assistant director shouted one last time. The stand-ins walked off the set, John Wayne and Martha Hyer walked on. "All right, boys, *silencio,* this is a picture." They took it twice. Twice the girl offered John Wayne the tattered Bible. Twice John Wayne told her that "there's a lot of places I go where that wouldn't fit in." Everyone was very still. And at 2:30 that Friday afternoon Henry Hathaway turned away from the camera, and in the hush that followed he ground out his cigar in a sand bucket. "O.K.," he said. "That's it."

54   Since that summer of 1943 I had thought of John Wayne in a number of ways. I had thought of him driving cattle up from Texas, and bringing airplanes in on a single engine, thought of him telling the girl at the Alamo that "Republic is a beautiful word." I had never thought of him having dinner with his family and with me and my husband in an expensive restaurant in Chapultepec Park, but time brings odd mutations, and there we were, one night that last week in Mexico. For a while it was only a nice evening, an evening anywhere. We had a lot of drinks and I lost the sense that the face across the table was in certain ways more familiar than my husband's.

55   And then something happened. Suddenly the room seemed suffused with the dream, and I could not think why. Three men appeared out of nowhere, playing guitars. Pilar Wayne leaned slightly forward, and John Wayne lifted his glass almost imperceptibly toward her. "We'll need some Pouilly-Fuissé for the rest of the table," he said, "and some red Bordeaux for the Duke." We all smiled, and drank the Pouilly-Fuissé for the rest of the table and the red Bordeaux for the Duke, and all the while the men with the guitars kept playing, until finally I realized what they were playing, what they had been playing all along: "The Red River Valley" and the theme from *The High and the Mighty.* They did not quite get the beat right, but even now I can hear them, in another country and a long time later, even as I tell you this.

☐ Discovering Meaning and Technique

1. You could consider that this selection falls into either three or four sections. How many are there, in your opinion? Defend your choice.

2. In Didion's view, what was John Wayne's appeal?

3. When recounting the making of *The Sons of Katie Elder,* Didion relies primarily on dialogue between the people involved. What is the effect of this technique?

4. In paragraph 3, Didion says that Wayne "determined forever the shape of certain of our dreams." Then, in paragraph 4, she says that Wayne spent most of his movie career "on some forsaken location, in search of the dream." Finally, in the last paragraph, she says that "the room seemed suffused with the dream." To what dreams does Didion refer? Are they all the same?

☐ Writing Suggestions

1. Discuss Didion's assessment of Wayne's appeal, and agree or disagree with that assessment.

2. Describe your own childhood movie hero or heroes, and explain their appeal.

3. In the first two paragraphs of the selection, Didion briefly describes the summer of her eighth year, when she and her brother had nothing to do but go to the movies. Describe a summer in your own childhood, giving specific details that you remember (like Didion's memory of the B-29, the artificial rain in the Officers' Club, the folding chairs of the Quonset hut).

RECONSIDERATION: *GONE WITH THE WIND,* THE MOVIE

☐ ROGER ROSENBLATT

1 Her name, O'Hara, is deliberately Irish. Her Irishness is to be associated with impetuosity, wild courage, low class and the ability to lie charmingly. All these Scarlett has and does, though not once in the movie does she refer to her Irish heritage. She pretends to no ancestry other than Tara. Her father, played by Thomas Mitchell, is the stock Irishman of the piece, speaking as no Irishman

has ever spoken and showering himself in as many Irishisms as the plot allows. He dies mad, on his horse. We learn from his tombstone that he was born in County Wicklow, made famous by J. M. Synge who incidentally wrote of the mad in Wicklow, and of other riders thrown from their horses.

2   O'Hara does provide one key to Scarlett, however. At the outset of the movie when Scarlett is frantic having learned that "her" Ashley Wilkes is about to announce his engagement to Melanie Hamilton, she disclaims interest in her homestead. Her father, dismayed, tells her that there is nothing as lasting as land, nothing as important to an Irishman. This, of course, is true as the themes of most Irish plays testify. He tells her this as the camera rises showing Scarlett and the lovely land before her, an effect that is repeated later when the land before Scarlett is covered with dead and dying Confederate soldiers.

3   When her father has died, Scarlett vows to protect the land. She cultivates crops with her bare hands and makes her reluctant sisters do likewise. They do not know what Scarlett knows, that the land means money. Earlier Scarlett returned to Tara to find her father crazed and her mother dead. Her Ashley, married to Melanie, is at war. Her beautiful clothing is gone, as are the gracious Southern parties. Good talk is gone. Even the skies are not golden anymore. But when she stumbles into the fields, she finds a potato growing. She gags on it, in the obvious discovery of her own roots. Standing in the middle of her land, she vows never to go hungry again. By this point Scarlett has done some changing. No longer content to capture the heart of every man in the county, she wants the county.

4   There is reason to suspect that she can get what she wants. Scarlett does not merely live by her imagination; she controls reality by her imagination. She literally does not see what she will not see—thus she first *sees* the soldier's amputation when she is to participate as nurse; then she turns away so that she does not see it, and leaves her duty. Nor does she listen to what she will not know. Her boyfriends talk of impending war, but Scarlett will not hear of it, and threatens to go inside the house if they persist. She will not hear of Melanie's friendship, which she wishes not to exist. She will not hear of Lee's surrender.

5   But Scarlett is seen and heard by all. Wherever she goes she is the center of attention and activity because she is stunningly beautiful (more beautiful in Vivien Leigh than in Margaret Mitchell's heroine), and because she wishes herself to be noticed, and by imagining her own centrality, creates it. When the sisters complain to mother, they complain about Scarlett. When Scarlett overhears the local girls whisper on the stairs of the Wilkes mansion, they are talking about Scarlett. All gossip is of Scarlett. When Scarlett walks through the streets, men mutter. When she rides through Shantytown, men claw at her. At a dance Rhett Butler "bids" for her, offering the highest amount for Scarlett O'Hara Hamilton, the elaborately outrageous merry widow.

6   Who, after all, could not help noticing the color scarlet, or Rhett (red?) Butler? Yet, although Rhett occasionally can overpower Scarlett, he can never

outdazzle her. He knows this. He loves her not because they are so much alike, but because she is better and brighter at their common game. They both seek power, but compared to Scarlett, Rhett is an amateur. For all his avowed practicality, he is as wistful as they come. For all her avowed romanticism, Scarlett is absolutely clearheaded.

7   She is most clearheaded about her own romanticism. Agreeing to marry Melanie's brother in order to retaliate for Ashley's wedding, she is aware of her falsehood. She does not wish to hurt Ashley by this hasty decision, but to prove something to him; that she has a will of iron, one capable of superintending impulses. Ashley is correct when he contrasts Scarlett's fortitude to his weakness. When Scarlett finally does give up on Ashley, she is painfully exasperated because he could not be made strong enough to be worthy of her.

8   Slowly we begin to become aware of the size and force of Scarlett's mind. She is able to think Ashley into becoming someone who deserves her. She is able to think her way into having husbands, property, wealth, gaiety, her own strength. Yet she is neither contemplative nor plotting. She gets what she wants by the massive exertion of mind over matter. She manufactures her world piece by piece. There is a physical outer world disintegrating about her; she simply will not stand for it.

9 Scarlett is not the fatal woman of the European romantics, not Carmen or incarnations of Cleopatra and Helen of Troy. Men would die for her, and do, not because they are spellbound by the softness of Scarlett's skin, but by her will. Her will provides the only erotic element in the movie. Possessing Scarlett's body is not difficult; possessing her spirit is the light that draws the lovers.

10   Meanwhile Rhett Butler swaggers in and out of her life, feigning to bear reality. The most important thing about Rhett is that he is played by Clark Gable. Anyone with less handsome a grin would have been seen through at once, but this Rhett manages to keep the truth from us for a long time: that he is a fool and near imbecile. Where there is a grandstand stunt to be pulled, there is Rhett bidding $150 in gold for his lady love. Where there is a banality to be expressed there too is Rhett, his massive pop culture conscience having caught up with him as he suddenly wishes to catch up with his Confederate comrades. "I don't like fighting for a lost cause until it's really lost," explains Rhett. And when Scarlett's other gallant gentlemen have all departed, who is still hanging around but Rhett who, mocking the others for their futile persistence, has outbid them all?

11   Rhett directs his own scenes. He pretends to play to Scarlett's passion for melodrama when he is about to join the war. Kiss a departing soldier, he tells her; not Rhett, but a movie hero going into battle. Scarlett kisses neither Rhett nor the melodrama. The scene is Rhett's. He is ever making comments such as "at this point" or "now" when he is alone with Scarlett, as if he is blocking out his own ardor. Rhett is incapable of not looking intensely amused or intensely

troubled. He must always prove to someone outside himself that he is feeling something.

12   But Scarlett is equally intensely uninterested. She is not attracted to Rhett; Rhett is an essential ingredient of her maturity, as in fact are all the men in Scarlett's life: the Hamilton boy whom she marries first who is innocence; Frank Kennedy whom she marries next, who is business and finance; and finally Rhett who is experience and vitality. Scarlett's monogram changes accordingly: from surprise (S.O.H.) to stability (S.O.K.) to savvy (S.O.B.). She marries none of her husbands out of love, only practical need. Her love, she says, she reserves for Ashley, who is to her as she is to Rhett. At one point she vainly uses Rhett's own language of seduction on Ashley, absurdly begging him to flee with her to Mexico.

13   Ashley is the constant in her life, her fixed star. Scarlett is always married twice simultaneously: to innocence and Ashley; to money and Ashley; to power and Ashley. Ashley is constant because he is a version of history and tradition, specifically nostalgia. As he too often acknowledges, he represents the old, dead world. There is nothing to indicate that Scarlett could be content in such a world—Rhett rightly tells her so—yet she clings to the idea of Ashley nevertheless, because she needs nostalgia. That too is essential. Like Margaret Mitchell herself she knows nothing of the past but that it is "gone." In her conventional mind that fact alone makes it valuable.

14   On all levels *Gone with the Wind* is the most conventional of pictures. The O'Haras' black Mammy is everybody's black mammy, a little of Faulkner's Dilsey, a little more of Hattie McDaniel's "Beulah" (the radio character whom McDaniel later became) full of folk wisdom, stamina, common sense and character pseudoanalysis. Butterfly McQueen as Prissy the cowardly scatterbrain is similarly stereotyped, a female Mantan Moreland. Melanie Hamilton Wilkes is dutiful, resourceful, saccharine and kind, and shows no sign of ever being otherwise. Scarlett's silly sisters are as silly as we would wish them to be; Rhett is as dashing; Ashley as melancholy; the ladies of the town as gossipy; the young men as reckless, and so forth. There is something suspicious in this. Why should these people be so extraordinarily true to form?

15   They are *not* merely true to form but are gross exaggerations of the forms they represent. Clark Gable does not simply flash his sardonic grin; he is his grin, and nothing more. Similarly Ashley is his sighing, Melanie her virtue. There is a telling point in that scene at the start of the movie when O'Hara displays his Tara before Scarlett. The camera rises and backs up to frame the scene with the side of a huge tree. This is accompanied by the theme music making an enormous crescendo. If you had walked in on that scene, you would think it was the end of the picture. Like the characters, the tableau is allegorical, an exaggeration, a "humor" of itself.

16   Because they are so exaggerated, the movie's conventions become unconventional. They are bigger and more consistent than we ever would expect

them to be. Among and through them walks Scarlett, who is bigger yet: she who is conventional in essence, and the more so for being tagged by the others as rebellious. Meanwhile none of the other figures is in the slightest way transformed by Scarlett's presence. Instead what she does is to bring out, heighten and clarify their characteristics, as no one in the movie is ever quite as much himself as he is with Scarlett.

17   She goes her own way to the end. Riches and a comfortable marriage to Rhett mean no more to her than her former poverty. She is no more or less Scarlett when she wants or when she has. At the end she has pursued Ashley once too often, and Melanie learns the truth. Yet when Melanie dies, and Ashley might be Scarlett's at last, despite his protests, Scarlett gives up under the pretext that she now believes that Ashley really did love Melanie after all. It clearly is a pretext. Scarlett never did want to marry Ashley; she sought what he could offer, which was not only the past, but the cognizance of death. His name is Ashley, a man like the dead.

18   When Scarlett Butler throws herself at Ashley for the last time, which is the moment when it becomes clear even to Rhett that Scarlett does not care for him, Scarlett is most brilliantly herself. At Rhett's goading she wears a dazzling scarlet gown to a tea at the Wilkes's. To Rhett such a dress is the standard emblem of adultery, but to Scarlett this is her confirmation gown, the cloth and color of her astounding pride in being the only nonhypocrite of the story. Rhett's cool and swagger disguise his vapidity, particularly from himself. Ashley's "traditions" did the same for him. But Scarlett is never disguised nor self-deceived. She knows what she wants, though what she wants is "tomorrow" and elusive.

19   With her self-assertion she reaches what are commonly called "mythic proportions." Yet she is not a god in the mythic sense; she makes no judgments about her creations, and is thoroughly unconcerned with her world. Rather her immense size and power derive from her concentrations inward. Scarlett never leaves Scarlett for a moment. She is solely preoccupied with herself—not with her individual ups or downs, her looks or feelings, but with her whole contained existence.

20   I believe there is only one brief scene in those three hours and 45 minutes in which Scarlett does not appear (the "quittin' time" scene in the fields). If *Gone with the Wind* were intended as an epic, that imbalance would be impossible. We would need to know what was going on in the legislatures, in the battlefields, in the hospitals, and so forth, apart from Scarlett. In terms of dramatic effectiveness such excursions would explain Scarlett more thoroughly. But Scarlett has no need for excursions or for exposition. She is the epic.

21   Because she is all action, Scarlett takes us back to a civilization gone with the wind: antebellum, ante-Darwin, ante-Freud. We take to her not because we feel that one can and should live only the surfaces, but because we realize that it is

in fact impossible. Watching Scarlett and only Scarlett hour upon hour is like watching magic: a set of interlocking rings that miraculously dissolve, a glass of water turned to confetti, a dove in a man's hand. In the instance of Scarlett, the trick is character.

22   At the start of the country, as at the start of *Gone with the Wind,* hopes were high, resources were infinite, and the end of good times was not in sight. When our various wars of mind and body arrived, as with *Gone with the Wind,* promise gave way to reality. In response we invented illusion, the means by which we learned to live with promise brought low by reality: minstrel shows, circuses, and movies most of all. Scarlett is an illusion brought to us by an illusion. When she consoles herself that tomorrow is another day, she means promise, but we only hear illusion. Of course, tomorrow is another day; that is exactly what it is.

23   What Scarlett could just as well have said is, "tomorrow, *be* another day." She could have stood at the door of her house and shouted an order. It is certain to have been carried out. Tomorrow would have complied and been at Scarlett's door bright and early, just as surely as if Scarlett had cupped her hands to her mouth and ordered a ham and cheese, easy on the mayo. For Scarlett is the muse of ham and cheese, the all-American fatal woman with the soul of a perky car-hop.

24   "I never liked Scarlett," Vivian Leigh said once. "I knew it was a marvelous part, but I never cared for her." That is probably why she played the part so well—precisely because Scarlett did not care for herself either. In many ways she is too much to care for: an amalgam of popular wishes poured into a cliché—a Southern belle, a Hollywood star—who is not likeable because she is too grand for such considerations. We took our car-hop, dressed her in a hoop skirt, and set up a trust fund. We gave her everything we had: the daughter of Rosie O'Grady, hard-hearted Hannah, the girl that I marry, the girl of my dreams.

☐ Discovering Meaning and Technique

1. Rosenblatt weaves a good deal of the movie's plot into his discussion. Does he recount enough of the plot for readers who have not seen the movie?

2. In spite of his criticism of Scarlett, Rosenblatt seems to admire her. Point out some of his criticisms. Then, point out passages that indicate his admiration for the character. What qualities about Scarlett does the author particularly seem to like?

3. Rosenblatt calls Rhett Butler "a fool and near imbecile" (paragraph 10). On what grounds does Rosenblatt base this charge? Do you agree with him?

4. Find the passage where Rosenblatt lists the stereotypical characters in the movie. If you have seen the movie, comment on whether these characters seem stereotyped to you.

5. Although the title of the selection suggests that the author will discuss the movie in general, he focuses primarily upon Scarlett. Explain how he structures the essay around her, using her character to discuss plot, meaning, and other characters.

6. The essay ends with two sentences that summarize Scarlett's character. Do you think that they also summarize the essay? Or do they seem to depart from the rest of the selection?

□ Writing Suggestions

1. At the end of the essay, Rosenblatt calls Scarlett "a Southern belle." Describe the stereotype of the Southern belle, and explain why Scarlett does or does not fit the image.

2. Characterize Scarlett as a typical "Steel Magnolia," a stereotype somewhat different from that of the Southern belle.

3. Clearly, Rosenblatt dislikes the character of Rhett Butler. Defend or attack Rosenblatt's opinion.

4. Write your own review of *Gone with the Wind.* Does it deserve its popular acclaim? Why? Or why not?

5. Many viewers see Melanie as the epitome of virtue. Others think she is an exasperating wimp. What is your opinion?

6. Using Rosenblatt's essay as a model, review the strengths and weaknesses of another film.

MY CREATURE FROM THE BLACK LAGOON

□ STEPHEN KING

1 The first movie I can remember seeing as a kid was *Creature from the Black Lagoon.* It was at the drive-in, and unless it was a second-run job I must have been about seven, because the film, which starred Richard Carlson and Richard Denning, was released in 1954. It was also originally released in 3-D, but I cannot remember wearing the glasses, so perhaps I did see a rerelease.

2   I remember only one scene clearly from the movie, but it left a lasting impression. The hero (Carlson) and the heroine (Julia Adams, who looked absolutely spectacular in a one-piece white bathing suit) are on an expedition somewhere in the Amazon basin. They make their way up a swampy, narrow waterway and into a wide pond that seems an idyllic South American version of the Garden of Eden.

3   But the creature is lurking—naturally. It's a scaly, batrachian monster that is remarkably like Lovecraft's half-breed, degenerate aberrations—the crazed and blasphemous results of liaisons between gods and human women (It's difficult to get away from Lovecraft). This monster is slowly and patiently barricading the mouth of the stream with sticks and branches, irrevocably sealing the party of anthropologists in.

4   I was barely old enough to read at that time, the discovery of my father's box of weird fiction still years away. I have a vague memory of boyfriends in my mom's life during that period—from 1952 until 1958 or so; enough of a memory to be sure she had a social life, not enough to even guess if she had a sex life. There was Norville, who smoked Luckies and kept three fans going in his two-room apartment during the summer; and there was Milt, who drove a Buick and wore gigantic blue shorts in the summertime; and another fellow, very small, who was, I believe, a cook in a French restaurant. So far as I know, my mother came close to marrying none of them. She'd gone that route once. Also, that was a time when a woman, once married, became a shadow figure in the process of decision-making and bread-winning. I think my mom, who could be stubborn, intractable, grimly persevering and nearly impossible to discourage, had gotten a taste for captaining her own life. And so she went out with guys, but none of them became permanent fixtures.

5   It was Milt we were out with that night, he of the Buick and the large blue shorts. He seemed to genuinely like my brother and me, and to genuinely not mind having us along in the back seat from time to time (it may be that when you have reached the calmer waters of your early forties, the idea of necking at the drive-in no longer appeals so strongly . . . even if you have a Buick as large as a cabin cruiser to do it in). By the time the Creature made his appearance, my brother had slithered down onto the floor of the back and had fallen asleep. My mother and Milt were talking, perhaps passing a Kool back and forth. They don't matter, at least not in this context; nothing matters except the big back-and-white images up on the screen, where the unspeakable Thing is walling the handsome hero and the sexy heroine into . . . into . . . *the Black Lagoon!*

6   I knew, watching, that the Creature had become *my* Creature; I had bought it. Even to a seven-year-old, it was not a terribly convincing Creature. I did not know then it was good old Ricou Browning, the famed underwater stuntman, in a molded latex suit, but I surely knew it was some guy in some kind of a monster suit . . . just as I knew that, later on that night, he would visit me in

the black lagoon of my dreams, looking much more realistic. He might be waiting in the closet when we got back; he might be standing slumped in the blackness of the bathroom at the end of the hall, stinking of algae and swamp rot, all ready for a post-midnight snack of small boy. Seven isn't old, but it is old enough to know that you get what you pay for. You own it, you bought it, it's yours. It is old enough to feel the dowser suddenly come alive, grow heavy, and roll over in your hands, pointing at hidden water.

7   My reaction to the Creature on that night was perhaps the perfect reaction, the one every writer of horror fiction or director who has worked in the field hopes for when he or she uncaps a pen or a lens: total emotional involvement, pretty much undiluted by any real thinking process—and you understand, don't you, that when it comes to horror movies, the only thought process really necessary to break the mood is for a friend to lean over and whisper, "See the zipper running down his back?"

8   I think that only people who have worked in the field for some time truly understand how fragile this stuff really is, and what an amazing commitment it imposes on the reader or viewer of intellect and maturity. When Coleridge spoke of "the suspension of disbelief" in his essay on imaginative poetry, I believe he knew that disbelief is not like a balloon, which may be suspended in air with a minimum of effort; it is like a lead weight, which has to be hoisted with a clean and a jerk and held up by main force. Disbelief isn't light; it's heavy. The difference in sales between Arthur Hailey and H. P. Lovecraft may exist because everyone believes in cars and banks, but it takes a sophisticated and muscular intellectual act to believe, even for a little while, in Nyarlathotep, the Blind Faceless One, the Howler in the Night. And whenever I run into someone who expresses a feeling along the lines of, "I don't read fantasy or go to any of those movies; none of it's real," I feel a kind of sympathy. They simply can't lift the weight of fantasy. The muscles of the imagination have grown too weak.

9   In this sense, kids are the perfect audience for horror. The paradox is this: children, who are physically quite weak, lift the weight of unbelief with ease. They are the jugglers of the invisible world—a perfectly understandable phenomenon when you consider the perspective they must view things from. Children deftly manipulate the logistics of Santa Claus's entry on Christmas Eve (he can get down small chimneys by making himself small, and if there's no chimney there's the letter slot, and if there's no letter slot there's always the crack under the door), the Easter Bunny, God (big guy, sorta old, white beard, throne), Jesus ("How do you think he turned the water into wine?" I asked my son Joe when he—Joe, not Jesus—was five; Joe's idea was that he had something "kinda like magic Kool-Aid, you get what I mean?"), the devil (big guy, red skin, horse feet, tail with an arrow on the end of it, Snidely Whiplash moustache), Ronald McDonald, the Burger King, the Keebler Elves, Dorothy and Toto, the Lone Ranger and Tonto, a thousand more.

10   Most parents think they understand this openness better than, in many

cases, they actually do, and try to keep their children away from anything that smacks too much of horror and terror—"Rated PG (or G in the case of *The Andromeda Strain*), but may be too intense for younger children," the ads for *Jaws* read—believing, I suppose, that to allow their kids to go to a real horror movie would be tantamount to rolling a live hand grenade into a nursery school.

11   But one of the odd Döppler effects that seems to occur during the selective forgetting that is so much a part of "growing up" is the fact that almost *everything* has a scare potential for the child under eight. Children are literally afraid of their own shadows at the right time and place. There is the story of the four-year-old who refused to go to bed at night without a light on in his closet. His parents at last discovered he was frightened of a creature he had heard his father speak of often; this creature, which had grown large and dreadful in the child's imagination, was the "twi-night double-header."

12   Seen in this light, even Disney movies are minefields of terror, and the animated cartoons, which will apparently be released and rereleased even unto the end of the world,* are usually the worst offenders. There are adults today, who, when questioned, will tell you that the most frightening thing they saw at the movies as children was Bambi's father shot by the hunter, or Bambi and his mother running before the forest fire. Other Disney memories which are right up there with the batrachian horror inhabiting the Black Lagoon include the marching brooms that have gone totally out of control in *Fantasia* (and for the small child, the real horror inherent in the situation is probably buried in the implied father-son relationship between Mickey Mouse and the old sorcerer; those brooms are making a terrible mess, and when the sorcerer/father gets home, there may be PUNISHMENT. . . . This sequence might well send the child of strict parents into an ecstasy of terror); the night on Bald Mountain from the same film; the witches in *Snow White* and *Sleeping Beauty,* one with her enticingly red poisoned apple (and what small child is not taught early to fear the idea of POISON?), the other with her deadly spinning wheel; this holds all the way up to the relatively innocuous *One Hundred and One Dalmatians,* which features the logical granddaughter of those Disney witches from the thirties and forties—the evil Cruella DeVille, with her scrawny, nasty face, her loud voice (grownups sometimes forget how terrified young children are of loud voices, which come from the giants of their world, the adults), and her plan to kill all the dalmatian puppies (read "children," if you're a little person) and turn them into dogskin coats.

---

*In one of my favorite Arthur C. Clarke stories, this actually happens. In this vignette, aliens from space land on earth after the Big One has finally gone down. As the story closes, the best brains of this alien culture are trying to figure out the meaning of a film they have found and learned how to play back. The film ends with the words *A Walt Disney Production.* I have moments when I really believe that there would be no better epitaph for the human race, or for a world where the only sentient being absolutely guaranteed of immortality is not Hitler, Charlemagne, Albert Schweitzer, or even Jesus Christ—but is, instead, Richard M. Nixon, whose name is engraved on a plaque placed on the airless surface of the moon.

13   Yet it is the parents, of course, who continue to underwrite the Disney procedure of release and rerelease, often discovering goosebumps on their own arms as they rediscover what terrified them as children . . . because what the good horror film (or horror sequence in what may be billed a "comedy" or an "animated cartoon") does above all else is to knock the adult props out from under us and tumble us back down the slide into childhood. And there our own shadow may once again become that of a mean dog, a gaping mouth, or a beckoning dark figure.

14   Perhaps the supreme realization of this return to childhood comes in David Cronenberg's marvelous horror film *The Brood,* where a disturbed woman is literally producing "children of rage" who go out and murder the members of her family, one by one. About halfway through the film, her father sits dispiritedly on the bed in an upstairs room, drinking and mourning his wife, who has been the first to feel the wrath of the brood. We cut to the bed itself . . . and clawed hands suddenly reach out from beneath it and dig into the carpeting near the doomed father's shoes. And so Cronenberg pushes us down the slide; we are four again, and all of our worst surmises about what might be lurking under the bed have turned out to be true.

15   The irony of all this is that children are better able to deal with fantasy and terror *on its own terms* than their elders are. You'll note I've italicized the phrase "on its own terms." An adult is able to deal with the cataclysmic terror of something like *The Texas Chainsaw Massacre* because he or she understands that it is all make-believe, and that when the take is done the dead people will simply get up and wash off the stage blood. The child is not so able to make this distinction, and *Chainsaw Massacre* is quite rightly rated R. Little kids do not need this scene, any more than they need the one at the end of *The Fury* where John Cassavetes quite literally blows apart. But the point is, if you put a little kid of six in the front row at a screening of *The Texas Chainsaw Massacre* along with an adult who was temporarily unable to distinguish between make-believe and "real things" (as Danny Torrance, the little boy in *The Shining* puts it)—if, for instance, you had given the adult a hit of Yellow Sunshine LSD about two hours before the movie started—my guess is that the kid would have maybe a week's worth of bad dreams. The adult might spend a year or so in a rubber room, writing home with Crayolas.

16   A certain amount of fantasy and horror in a child's life seems to me a perfectly okay, useful sort of thing. Because of the size of their imaginative capacity, children are able to handle it, and because of their unique position in life, they are able to put such feelings to work. They understand their position very well, too. Even in such a relatively ordered society as our own, they understand that their survival is a matter almost totally out of their hands. Children are "dependents" up until the age of eight or so in every sense of the word; dependent on mother and father (or some reasonable facsimile thereof) not only for food, clothing, and shelter, but dependent on them not to crash the

car into a bridge abutment, to meet the school bus on time, to walk them home from Cub Scouts or Brownies, to buy medicines with childproof caps, dependent on them to make sure they don't electrocute themselves while screwing around with the toaster or while trying to play with Barbie's Beauty Salon in the bathtub.

17   Running directly counter to this necessary dependence is the survival directive built into all of us. The child realizes his or her essential lack of control, and I suspect it is this very realization which makes the child uneasy. It is the same sort of free-floating anxiety that many air travelers feel. They are not afraid because they believe air travel to be unsafe; they are afraid because they have surrendered control, and if something goes wrong all they can do is sit there clutching air-sick bags or the in-flight magazine. To surrender control runs counter to the survival directive. Conversely, while a thinking, informed person may understand intellectually that travel by car is much more dangerous than flying, he or she is still apt to feel much more comfortable behind the wheel, because she/he has control . . . or at least an illusion of it.

18   This hidden hostility and anxiety toward the airline pilots of their lives may be one explanation why, like the Disney pictures which are released during school vacations in perpetuity, the old fairy tales also seem to go on forever. A parent who would raise his or her hands in horror at the thought of taking his/her child to see *Dracula* or *The Changeling* (with its pervasive imagery of the drowning child) would be unlikely to object to the baby sitter reading "Hansel and Gretel" to the child before bedtime. But consider: the tale of Hansel and Gretel begins with deliberate abandonment (oh yes, the stepmother masterminds that one, but she is the symbolic mother all the same, and the father is a spaghetti-brained nurd who goes along with everything she suggests even though he know it's wrong—thus we can see her as amoral, him as actively evil in the Biblical and Miltonian sense), it progresses to kidnapping (the witch in the candy house), enslavement, illegal detention, and finally justifiable homicide and cremation. Most mothers and fathers would never take their children to see *Survive,* that quickie Mexican exploitation flick about the rugby players who survived the aftermath of a plane crash in the Andes by eating their dead teammates, but these same parents find little to object to in "Hansel and Gretel," where the witch is fattening the children up so she can eat them. We give this stuff to the kids almost instinctively, understanding on a deeper level, perhaps, that such fairy stories are the perfect points of crystallization for those fears and hostilities.

19   Even anxiety-ridden air travelers have their own fairy tales—all those *Airport* movies, which, like "Hansel and Gretel" and all those Disney cartoons, show every sign of going on forever . . . but which should only be viewed on Thanksgivings, since all of them feature a large cast of turkeys.

20   My gut reaction to *Creature from the Black Lagoon* on that long-ago night was a kind of terrible, waking swoon. The nightmare was happening right in

front of me; every hideous possibility that human flesh is heir to was being played out on that drive-in screen.

21   Approximately twenty-two years later, I had a chance to see *Creature from the Black Lagoon* again—not on TV, with any kind of dramatic build and mood broken up by adverts for used cars, K-Tel disco anthologies, and Underalls panty-hose, thank God, but intact, uncut . . . and even in 3-D. Guys like me who wear glasses have a hell of a time with 3-D, you know; ask anyone who wears specs how they like those nifty little cardboard glasses they give you when you walk in the door. If 3-D ever comes back in a big way, I'm going to take myself down to the local Pearle Vision Center and invest seventy bucks in a special pair of prescription lenses: one red, one blue. Annoying glasses aside, I should add that I took my son Joe with me—he was then five, about the age I had been myself, that night at the drive-in (and imagine my surprise—my *rueful* surprise—to discover that the movie which had so terrified me on that long-ago night had been rated G by the MPAA . . . just like the Disney pictures).

22   As a result, I had a chance to experience that weird doubling back in time that I believe most parents only experience at the Disney films with their children, or when reading them the Pooh books or perhaps taking them to the Shrine or the Barnum & Bailey circus. A popular record is apt to create a particular "set" in a listener's mind, precisely because of its brief life of six weeks to three months, and "golden oldies" continue to be played because they are the emotional equivalent of freeze-dried coffee. When the Beach Boys come on the radio singing "Help Me, Rhonda," there is always that wonderful second or two when I can re-experience the wonderful, guilty joy of copping my first feel (and if you do the mental subtraction from my present age of thirty-three, you'll see that I was a little backward in that respect). Movies and books do the same thing, although I would argue that the mental set, its depth and texture, tends to be a little richer, a little more complex, when re-experiencing films and a lot more complex when dealing with books.

23   With Joe that day I experienced *Creature from the Black Lagoon* from the other end of the telescope, but this particular theory of set identification still applied; in fact, it prevailed. Time and age and experience have all left their marks on me, just as they have on you; time is not a river, as Einstein theorized—it's a big fucking buffalo herd that runs us down and eventually mashes us into the ground, dead and bleeding, with a hearing-aid plugged into one ear and a colostomy bag instead of a .44 clapped on one leg. Twenty-two years later I knew that the Creature was really good old Ricou Browning, the famed underwater stuntman, in a molded latex suit, and the suspension of disbelief, that mental clean-and-jerk, had become a lot harder to accomplish. But I did it, which may mean nothing, or which may mean (I hope!) that the buffalo haven't got me yet. But when that weight of disbelief was finally up there, the old feelings came flooding in, as they flooded in some five years ago when I took Joe and my daughter Naomi to their first movie, a reissue of *Snow White and*

the Seven Dwarfs. There is a scene in that film where, after Snow White has taken a bite from the poisoned apple, the dwarfs take her into the forest, weeping copiously. Half the audience of little kids was also in tears; the lower lips of the other half were trembling. The set identification in that case was strong enough so that I was also surprised into tears. I hated myself for being so blatantly manipulated, but manipulated I was, and there I sat, blubbering into my beard over a bunch of cartoon characters. But it wasn't Disney that manipulated me; I did it myself. It was the kid inside who wept, surprised out of dormancy and into schmaltzy tears . . . but at least awake for awhile.

24   During the final two reels of *Creature from the Black Lagoon,* the weight of disbelief is nicely balanced somewhere above my head, and once again director Jack Arnold places the symbols in front of me and produces the old equation of the fairy tales, each symbol as big and as easy to handle as a child's alphabet block. Watching, the child awakes again and knows that this is what dying is like. Dying is when the Creature from the Black Lagoon dams up the exit. Dying is when the monster gets you.

25   In the end, of course, the hero and heroine, very much alive, not only survive but triumph—as Hansel and Gretel do. As the drive-in floodlights over the screen came on and the projector flashed its GOOD NIGHT, DRIVE SAFELY slide on that big white space (along with the virtuous suggestion that you ATTEND THE CHURCH OF YOUR CHOICE), there was a brief feeling of relief, almost of resurrection. But the feeling that stuck longest was the swooning sensation that good old Richard Carlson and Julia Adams were surely going down for the third time, and the image that remains forever after is of the creature slowly and patiently walling its victims into the Black Lagoon; even now I can see it peering over that growing wall of mud and sticks.

26   Its eyes. Its ancient eyes.

☐ Discovering Meaning and Technique

1. King contends that "kids are the perfect audience for horror" (paragraph 9). How does he support this contention throughout the selection?

2. Do you agree with King's assessment of the horror in Disney movies and fairy tales?

3. How does King explain Coleridge's notion of the "suspension of disbelief"?

4. King weaves his discussion of horror and fantasy around a personal experience: seeing *Creature From the Black Lagoon* at a drive-in movie. Point out the places in the selection where he refers to this experience.

5. King's style is informal; he seems to be talking casually to the reader. Point out some of the techniques that help him achieve this effect.

6. What is the effect of the material about King's mother and her boyfriends. Why do you think King included those details?

7. At the end of the selection, King refers to the traditional "sign off" of the drive-in movie: GOOD NIGHT, DRIVE SAFELY. ATTEND THE CHURCH OF YOUR CHOICE. Why is this detail effective?

8. What influences on King's work are revealed in this selection?

☐ Writing Suggestions

1. Describe your own childhood reaction to the first movie or television program that really frightened you.

2. Expand on King's idea that children are *dependents* "in every sense of the word" and that this dependency causes anxiety.

3. What do you think might have accounted for the rise and fall of drive-in movies?

4. Suggest a better rating system for movies—one that more accurately describes content.

5. What sorts of horror movies, if any, should children be allowed to watch? Defend your position.

6. Describe an irrational childhood anxiety.

WHERE THE MEDIA CRITICS WENT WRONG

☐ WALTER KARP

1 Way back when I was a teenager, it was common knowledge that the mass media—newly reinforced by television—were generating mass conformity, mass passivity, and mass "loss of autonomy." They were even producing a new kind of dismal American, a truly ominous being, grimly referred to as "mass man." In other words, it was common knowledge that the one thing we could not expect from the forthcoming 1960s—still hidden then in the womb of time— was exactly what we got from that turbulent era: a vast revival of political activity, a vast throwing off of the chains of conformity, and an exhibition of

youthful autonomy so appalling to many a media critic that when last heard from they were blaming television for breeding unrest and political rebellion. Not since it was common knowledge that international trade made war obsolete (this was in 1914) had humankind's bottonless capacity for mischief proved so many reputable social thinkers so devastatingly wrong.

2   To find out why the early media critics had gone so far astray—for it is not easy to be completely wrong—I decided not long ago to return to the scene of the accident, by which I mean those anxious postwar years when "What Is Television Doing to Us?" (*The New York Times Magazine,* June 12, 1949) was a question to which every right-thinking American expected an unpleasant answer—and invariably got one. Whether it was the famed theologian Reinhold Niebuhr predicting in 1949 that "much of what is still wholesome in our lives will perish under the impact of this visual aid" or hack writers predicting the death of conversation and the onset of mass myopia ("Does Television Cause Eyestrain?," *House Beautiful,* August 1950), virtually the entire discussion of television's influence took place in an atmosphere of hand-wringing hysteria.

3   Curiously enough, this hysterical atmosphere had nothing directly to do with television itself. What inspired it was the unnerving national experience of wartime propaganda. Four years of "Rosie the Riveter," "Loose Lips Sink Ships," and "Uncle Joe" Stalin, combined with terrifying reports of Hitler's irresistible "big-lie technique," had persuaded a remarkable number of Americans that mass propaganda was a new power too great for "the masses" to withstand.

4   "Politically, a lever of frightening efficiency has been devised," warned Mahonri Sharp Young in the Spring 1948 issue of *The American Scholar.* "New techniques of mass persuasion are being designed to manipulate a supposedly spontaneous public opinion. The existence of radio's influence can hardly be doubted. Argument occurs only over its extent and its depth." Two issues later in the same learned journal, Joseph T. Klapper observed that it was now commonly believed that "never before" in human history "has public opinion lain so completely at the mercy of whoever may be in control" of the mass media. Now add the visual impact of television to this "frightening" power of radio, MGM, and *Life* magazine and the mass media truly looked like the new master and dictator of the world. They had become, warned the eminent critic Gilbert Seldes, "as powerful in shaping our lives as our schools, our politics, our system of government."

5   But was it? The power of the wartime propaganda rested on the fact that every means of persuasion had been concerted and coordinated to convey the same basic message: "V for Victory," "Beat the Axis," "E for Effort," win the war, and do your bit. If the mass media were really as powerful as the critics believed, then mass entertainment in peacetime America was not only a *potential* instrument of mass propaganda—which, of course, it is—but already the conveyer of concerted, coordinated mass propaganda. Beneath the surface of miscellaneous amusements, the mass media carried a propaganda message, and the early critics

thought they knew exactly what it was. "The message is invariably that of identification with the *status quo*," wrote T. W. Adorno, the social psychologist, in 1954. "These media have taken on the job of rendering mass publics conformative to the social and economic status quo," said Paul Lazarsfeld in his authoritative study *Radio and the Printed Page.* "The whole entertainment side of broadcasting which surrounds the communication of ideas," wrote Seldes, "tends to create a mood of consent and acceptance. It cannot afford to stir and agitate the mind." Agitation does not sell soap; agitation displeases the sponsors. Inevitably, wrote Lazarsfeld, "commercially-sponsored mass media indirectly but effectively restrain the cogent development of a genuinely critical attitude."

6   The very popularity of the mass media preserved the status quo. Popularity demanded the purveying of the "nationally common denominator of attitudes," and the early critics had few doubts about what Americans held in common: a view of life so shallow that, according to Adorno, "the 'message' of adjustment and unreflecting obedience seems to be dominant and all-pervasive today." Donald Duck was popular with the masses, observed Irving Howe, because he "has something of the SS man in him," and the American people, "having something of the SS man in us, naturally find [him] quite charming."

7   The mass media operated on the mass audience like a deadly opiate. They "expedited flight from unbearable reality," Leo Lowenthal pointed out in a 1950 issue of the *American Journal of Sociology.* "Wherever revolutionary tendencies show a timid head, they are mitigated and cut short by a false fulfilment of wish-dreams, like wealth, adventure, passionate love, power, and sensationalism in general."

8   A poisonous passivity was entering the national bloodstream. "Increasing dosages of mass communication may be inadvertently transforming the energies of men from active participation into passive knowledge," warned Lazarsfeld. "The occurrence of this narcotizing dysfunction can scarcely be doubted," and almost nobody did doubt it. Like an electronic vampire, the mass media sucked the life-force out of the people, robbing them of their inner strength. "The repetitiveness, the self-sameness, and the ubiquity of modern mass culture tend to make for automatized reactions," said Dr. Adorno, "and to weaken the forces of individual resistance." Gunther Anders, a radical, called this inner weakening "depersonalization." Ernest Van Der Haag, a conservative, called it "de-individualization." Whatever it was called, it was reducing Americans to a state of zombielike inner docility, especially the children, whose "strength and imagination" were being steadily sapped by television, according to Marya Mannes, the TV critic of the *Reporter* magazine.

9   Television shows were full of gunplay, fisticuffs, and crime stories. The inevitable result, said the critics, was that Americans were growing "callous" toward human suffering. News programs and variety shows mixed so many different things together, according to the critics, that the audience could make little sense of anything. Seeing Edward R. Murrow interview Krishna Menon, India's

ambassador to the United States, in the first segment of "Person to Person" and Eva Gabor immediately following could only lead viewers to conclude, warned Murray Hausknecht, that the two were of "equal value." Early television was full of petty impostures. The hostess of a celebrity talk show, circa 1950, would hear the doorbell ring in her studio "living room" and exclaim, "Now who can that be?" as if the celebrities dropped in by surprise. This constant exposure to deception, warned Mannes, meant the "dulling of perception between true and false." The "senses" of the American people were becoming so "blunted" by television deceptions, warned Seldes, "they cannot tell truth from falsehood."

10   In short, whatever seemed likely to keep Americans in a state of vassalage the media effectively supplied—or so the students of "mass culture" insisted until a great democratic revival erupted in America for the first time in fifty years. Before the upheaval subsided, the alleged victims of the mass propaganda of "unreflecting obedience" had cast two Presidents—Johnson and Nixon—out of the White House.

11   Why had the great engine of passivity failed so badly, and why had the mass propaganda of conformity had so little effect? The answer is that commercial mass entertainment in America is a wonderfully inefficient tool of mass persuasion. The reason the early critics of the media failed to see this was that they assumed its efficiency in advance, made that "frightening efficiency" their starting point, and were blind to all evidence to the contrary.

12   The comedian Milton Berle is a good case in point. While the critics wrote of the media's "selfsameness" and their "stereotypes," the comic persona of the most dominating figure on television in those years was an outrageous egomaniac, so extravagantly shameless that nobody could have invented him except himself. So far from affirming "sanctioned attitudes," as the media were supposed to do, Berle trampled on every rule of decorum. Nor did he generate the required "mood of consent," since he was not only the most popular entertainer on television but also, as polls showed, the most widely detested one. I knew people who would drive nerve-racking miles on near-empty gas tanks just to avoid buying Texaco gasoline, the sponsor of the Berle show. To well-bred, right-thinking people, Berle's "message" was all too anarchic.

13   When Jackie Gleason supplanted Berle in public favor, the media critics did not modify by an iota their belief that the media "expedited flight from unbearable reality." Yet Gleason's Ralph Kramden in "The Honeymooners" was almost unbearably real. Envy and vanity made him a fool, and folly made him cruel and dishonest. The portrait was pitiless, as Seldes himself admitted, and the moral a harsh one, harsh yet profoundly humane: It takes strength and integrity just to be decent. Such was the weekly theme of an immensely popular television program while the critics were accusing the media of reproducing the smugness and intellectual passivity that seem to fit in with totalitarianism.

14   Blind to any virtues in popular things, the media critics took it for granted, noted Lowenthal in a survey of mass-culture studies, that the "media are estranged

from values and offer nothing but entertainment and distractions." If something amused a vast number of Americans, it has to be degrading, or how else could it serve as mass propaganda?

15   In that bigoted spirit the critics could see nothing valuable, for example, in the American Western except infantile violence. According to Mannes, the entire genre could be summed up as "good men and bad men who rode horses over magnificent country and decided issues by shooting each other." Yet it was the grand and terrible theme of the old-time Western that some issues could not be peaceably resolved: The dusty wooden cowboy town is in thrall to a tyrant, the local cattle baron, or the gambling casino owner; the sheriff is the tyrant's drunken tool; the churchgoing good folk are helplessly dithering. Nothing but armed insurrection can overthrow the tyranny and "clean up the town." Where is the message of subservience in that? Many Westerns could have been denounced as "subversive" had they not been so thoroughly American.

16   When a Senate judiciary subcommittee began investigating the influence of television on the juvenile crime rate in 1954, the senators saw precious little "narcotic dysfunction" generated by television. What worried them was television's all-too-stimulating incitement to mischief. Nor were they impressed by the media's power to "engineer consent." In its final report the subcommittee complained bitterly that television's judges, lawyers, and policemen were too often dishonest, incompetent, and stupid. Two decades later conservatives complained that big businessmen on television were too often portrayed as downright criminals. To the political leadership of America, the mass media have been, if anything, a little too *irreverent* for comfort.

17   Interestingly enough, the one truly prescient observation made in the 1950s about the impact of television was made by professional politicians. After seeing what the plot-ridden Republican National Convention looked like on television in 1952, politicians freely predicted that "TV would be the making of the direct Presidential primary," as Walter Goodman reported in *The New Republic.* And so it was, although it took a rebellion against an unpopular war to complete the job television had begun.

18   The reason the politicians were right goes a long way toward explaining why the media critics were wrong. America's politicians understood television's menace to the old nominating system because they never lost sight of the central truth about American life: that the American people believe devoutly in democracy, that we hate to see it openly violated, that we love to see its values affirmed and triumphant, even in our "entertainment and distractions." That is why the mass media performed so poorly as an engine of social control and passive obedience. In America you cannot promote deference and successfully sell soap. You cannot promote servility and amuse a vast audience. The popular understanding of democracy may not be precise or exacting; but our love of democracy runs deep, and that love has done more to shape the media than the media have done to shape us. That was what the early critics overlooked so completely.

Appalled by the power of mass propaganda, they concluded that the masses everywhere were empty and pliant and that Americans cherished nothing strongly enough to resist the designs of lawless ambition. That they were so largely in error is a truth well worth remembering in our darker hours.

☐ Discovering Meaning and Technique

1. In what specific ways did Milton Berle, Jackie Gleason, and the American Western contradict the media critics?

2. According to Karp, who in the 1950s made the only accurate prediction about the impact of television? What was that prediction?

3. What, in Karp's view, did the media critics overlook when making their predictions about television and society?

4. What does Karp say inspired the "hysterical atmosphere" about television in the postwar years?

5. Karp uses quite a few direct quotations from the critics. What is the purpose of this technique? Is it effective?

☐ Writing Suggestions

1. Expand on Karp's synopsis of the American Western. Using one or more films or television programs as support, describe the typical plot, principal characters, conflict, and conclusion.

2. Choose another film or television genre (such as the police detective story, the space odyssey, the family situation comedy). Describe the obligatory and the optional components.

3. What is the effect of waging political campaigns on television? Is the public better informed on issues? Or does the victory go to the candidate who has the best advertising agency?

4. Were the media critics right in any sense? Is television an "instrument for mass propaganda"? If so, how has television affected the behavior and values of Americans?

HOW PARENTS SURVIVED BEFORE TELEVISION

☐ **MARIE WINN**

1 Before television, in the thirties and forties, at the very height of the transformation of child rearing from a parent-centered to a child-centered business, the metaphysics of the new child-rearing philosophy was of necessity tempered by the empirical reality of everyday life with children. In order to survive, parents needed some time for themselves away from the incessant demands of their small children. Thus they were required to develop certain strategies, which, being parent-centered rather than child-centered, went somewhat against the modern grain. Although originating in the parents' needs, these proved to be of value to the child himself because they counterbalanced certain of the excesses of a child-centered upbringing.

2   Parents abandoned many of these disciplines when television presented itself as an easier alternative. In trying to assess the meaning of the television experience in children's lives today, it is important to consider what parents of the thirties and forties actually *did* when they simply had to get away from their children for a bit. By examining these courses of action we may discover what they offered the child, even as they offered the parent some relief.

Observing with an Eagle Eye

3 Before television the mother of a small child had a great need to develop her child's ability to play by himself for periods of time. But this was never a simple matter. The mothers had to find ways to ensure that the child would become truly involved in play for a time, leaving the mother to her own pursuits.

4   Thus the mother of the past was wont to observe her small children with an eagle eye to obtain a subtle picture of their changing development, not out of intellectual curiosity necessarily, but because this accumulation of information was useful to her in finding ways to get her children to entertain themselves successfully and reliably. A mother might take pains to discover, for instance, if her three-year-old was capable of learning to cut with a pair of blunted scissors. If this activity amused the child, it would be worth the mother's while to *work* on it a bit, to help the child learn how to cut properly, to provide a supply of colored papers or old magazines, a jar of paste perhaps, because her reward would be a self-entertaining child once the skill was acquired. For similar reasons the mother might provide buttons or beans for sorting, or dough for molding, or blocks for building, spurred not entirely by devotion to her child's happiness, but also by a certain amount of healthy self-interest.

5   Capturing her child's nascent interests and utilizing them to serve her own needs was once an important element for success as a mother. But as it

happens the intimate knowledge of her child gained through sharp observation of his development necessarily led the mother to a more satisfying relationship with her child, with greater opportunities for shared pleasures as well as a reduced likelihood of misunderstandings and inadvertently inflicted suffering.

6   From the child's point of view the period of solitary play augmented by the mother's efforts to make sure that it actually "worked" led to the development of important skills and to actual, tangible accomplishments—constructions, drawings, sculptures, collages, animal parades, whatever. These skills and accomplishments, in turn, gave the child a sense of competence, and thereby helped to counteract those feelings of helplessness and utter dependence that dominate early childhood.

7   Indeed the heightened attentiveness to children's needs and interests that parents once displayed affected the entire family in a beneficial way. Parents became experts on their children, and the information inevitably enabled them to raise their children more humanely, more effectively.

8   Without doubt the availability of television as a child-rearing tool has reduced parents' immediate *need* to know their children well. Though still inspired by affection or a sense of duty to observe their children and communicate with them in a variety of ways, parents make diminished efforts to understand their children because their own needs are no longer a motivating force.

The Father as a Survival Aid

9   Before television another source of relief for a child-ridden mother appeared on her doorstep at five-thirty with a lunch pail or a briefcase. The father was once a traditional survival aid. Arriving home from his job, he was often greeted with a baby to feed or a child to play with. Though he often accepted this job with a certain reluctance, he found it a different kind of work than his daily labors, and more often than not he enjoyed it.

10   The mother dumped the kids on the father and went for a walk or took a bath or did some work or read a book. This was a course of action necessary for her survival and she was refreshed and replenished by it. The father was left to amuse the children. In order to preserve the peace and his sanity during his spells of child care, he had to discover his children's likes and dislikes, their weaknesses and strengths. In order to succeed as a caretaker, he was obliged to figure out how his children thought and why they behaved as they did. It is not hard to see that this knowledge gained by necessity would stand him in good stead in his future relationship with them, allowing him to form deeper bonds based on real experiences rather than on idealized images.

11   Children in such a situation are stimulated by learning to get along with a person who is not their principal caretaker, though an important part of the family. Their interest is stirred by his new ways of behaving when he is actually in charge of them. They devise new strategies that do not work on their mother

in order to get their way. They evolve new games and rituals to perform with their father that differ in important ways from those they play with their mother, routines that require time to develop.

12   Of course, taking care of small children is often a trying occupation for a father weary from a long work day. Though he has much to gain from playing with his children for regular periods each day, it is only natural that he would forgo these advantages were there an alternative child-minder available to allow him to settle down after work with a drink and a newspaper.

13   A mother reports:

14   "Whenever my husband spells me off with the kids he has them watching TV. That's his way of taking care of them, turning the TV on. He lets the networks do it for him."

15   Television offers an irresistible alternative to the weary father impressed into child care. But children suffer a serious deprivation as a result of this new strategy: fewer opportunities to establish and consolidate a relationship with their father.

The Nap

16 The most dependable survival aid for mothers, however, was the nap. There was a time in the not too distant past when children took naps regularly during their entire early childhood, often until they began school. It wasn't necessarily that the child *needed* a nap, nor that he *wanted* a nap: he *had* to nap, quite simply. The nap was as inevitable and accepted a part of life as going to bed at night or getting dressed or brushing teeth or doing any of those many things that children don't particularly want to do but simply have to do in the course of their childhood.

17   The nap was inevitable because mothers needed that regular hiatus from child care. They saved up their telephone calls, their letter writing, reading, or sustained thinking for that interval of the day when an eye or an ear didn't have to be cocked in the direction of a small child.

18   Babies still spend the greatest part of their day sleeping, and children during their first two years continue to sleep for certain intervals during the day. But a great many of today's children give up napping during their third year, when they cease to require that daytime interval of sleep physiologically. This was the point when mothers of the past had to make a great effort to retain the nap. Since the child no longer fell asleep automatically at nap time, he naturally did his best to gain access to his mother's time and attention. This he did by "fussing," as mothers called it. But as a result of firmness based on a certain desperation and an almost physical need for time away from the child, mothers of the past persevered in their efforts to retain the nap, and the sleep nap gradually turned into a play nap, during which time the child was required to remain in his room, playing or dreaming or puttering about quietly. Mothers generally

managed to retain the nap as a regular part of their daily routine until school brought the opportunity of a new daily break.

[19]   Today parents do not "work" to keep the nap. Instead, with relief in sight second only to the relief they feel when their child is asleep at night, parents work on their young children to encourage them to watch television for reliable periods of time, a far easier job than working on a child to stay in his room during a nap. Perhaps some of the child's deep affection for the television experience in his later years is rooted in his earliest experiences with the medium when his mother, seeing television as a survival aid, made special and seductive efforts to "plug him in."

[20]   Here a young, well-educated mother in need of relief from the hardships of life with a small child describes her efforts to establish her child on a television-watching routine:

[21]   "Last spring, when Jeremy was one and a half, he gave up his morning nap. It was a difficult time, for him and for us. At that point I first started to try 'Sesame Street.' I made an effort to interest him in the program. I'd turn the set on and say, 'Look! There's a car!' or whatever. But he showed absolutely no interest. It really didn't seem worth working at then.

[22]   "Then, in the fall, when he was two, he gave up his nap entirely. The day loomed so long that I began to make another effort to interest him in 'Sesame Street.' He was more verbal then, and I thought there was a better chance that he'd understand it. I'd turn it on, and he'd show an initial interest in the first moments. It was an event. He'd look at it briefly, and then go on to other things. I'd leave it on and he'd pass by and look at it on his way to somewhere else. I might sit in front of it myself for a while, to try to make it more inviting, to try to coax him to watch. If he asked for a bottle, I'd certainly let him have it there, in front of the television set. Sometimes I'd even suggest a bottle.

[23]   "Anytime we were home and 'Sesame Street' was on, around four o'clock, I'd turn it on and try to interest him by commenting about things on the screen. 'Oh, look at the snow!' and things like that. Then I bought a book on 'Sesame Street' and we looked at it together. I think that helped get him interested. It took from about October to Christmas. Finally it 'took.' It was quite gradual. But now he watches every day, with a bottle, always, in the morning and in the afternoon. And 'Mr. Rogers,' too, most of the time, and it's really a great breathing spell for me.

[24]   "I know television probably isn't great for kids, but a few hours a day can't really be so bad. I suppose if I hadn't had a TV set I would have tried to establish some quiet-time routine in his room, a play-nap sort of thing. But it would have been hard. He's a very determined little boy. He probably wouldn't have stayed there."

[25]   In choosing television over the nap today's mother is following a simple imperative of human nature: always choose the easier of two possible courses of action, other things being equal. Pre-television mothers who persevered in

enforcing a regular nap were operating on the same principle—in their case the harder alternative was to have a child underfoot all day. But is there an essential difference between these two "easier" courses, the nap and television watching? Probably, for when the child who took a regular daily nap throughout his early years outgrew the need for actually sleeping, the nap period began to serve a new function: it provided him with his first regular opportunity to experience free time. An understanding of the importance of free time in a child's life reveals how great a deprivation its loss may be.

☐ Discovering Meaning and Technique

1. What does Winn mean by "parent-centered" and "child-centered" upbringing?

2. According to Winn, how did mothers in the thirties and forties help develop their children's ability to play alone?

3. Why, in Winn's view, did mothers help develop this ability?

4. Why does Winn refer to the pre-television father as a "survival aid"?

5. What role did the nap play in pre-television children?

6. Winn frequently uses *he, him,* and *his* to refer to both the male and female child. Do you find this practice annoying?

7. Are the headings useful? Would the selection be as clear without them?

☐ Writing Suggestions

1. In the pre-television family Winn describes, the father worked outside the home, while the mother stayed at home with the children. Might the changes in modern parenting be attributed not only to television but also to the fact that most mothers now work outside the home?

2. Can nursery schools help develop skills that mothers once did?

3. Today, a great deal of marital strife occurs because many husbands expect working wives to do all the shopping, cooking, cleaning, and child-tending. This problem is particularly acute if the male grew up in a home where his father made the living while his mother attended to the house and children. Suggest a solution or solutions to this common problem.

4. If families watched less television, would children learn more social and creative skills—such as table manners, conversational skills, cooperation, respect for elders, art, music, writing, invention?

5. Describe the day-to-day activity of your early childhood. How does it compare and contrast to the pre-television era that Winn describes?

6. Discuss your own theories of parenting. Try to be realistic about family income, parent employment, and housing.

ANOTHER WORLD

☐ GWEN KINKEAD

1   What do Erika Slezak, Jacklyn Zeman and Susan Lucci have in common? Long, grueling hours as soap queens, the workhorses of broadcasting. They slave twelve-hour days to produce, respectively, such shows as *One Life to Live, General Hospital* and *All My Children,* which earn the highest profit margins in television. Thanks to the vixens—the storm centers of every soap—and the matriarchs, nurses, newlyweds, lawyers, Mary Magdalenes and Liliths, prime-time TV in lean years is kept on the air.

2   An astonishing 20 million people tune in daily to the soaps for their emotional fix—14 million women, 4 million men and more than a million teens. Fewer women watch than once did, because more are working, but men and teens have taken their places. Many career women, however, tape the shows to watch on their VCRs in the evening. Top-rated *The Young and the Restless* alone has an average daily audience of 9 million. Soapland is a great big wonderfully wicked world.

3   And one whose appeal cuts across societal lines. Feminists can say nothing good about the shows—they stereotype, they're not political, women in them win by deceit, not merit. But many people who consider themselves intelligent find the shows relaxing. Betty Ford watches them. So do Carol Burnett, Joyce Brothers and Supreme Court Justice Thurgood Marshall. Even *New Yorker* writer Renata Adler admits to having once watched them. College students set class schedules around them—two recent studies found that 70 percent of the students at two large midwestern colleges follow at least one show a week. So do some of their professors. These days, being a soap fan has lost its stigma.

4   The appeal of soaps is that they become surrogate friends and psychologists. "Especially today as we move around so much, separated from our families, we can turn on the set and have an instant family every day, someone and something to depend on," says Lee Bell, who, with her husband Bill, created the top-ranked *The Young and the Restless.* "People need that help." Meredith Berlin, editor of the trade bible *Soap Opera Digest,* agrees that the intimacy of the shows makes them popular. "The characters talk among themselves about things you

might not even discuss with your best friend—like possibly having an abortion. It's comforting."

5   "Soaps are the closest form of entertainment to real life," echoes Agnes Nixon, the doyenne of the business who has worked on nearly every show and created three. "Every day is a new episode and there are no reruns. And we make 'em laugh, we make 'em cry and we make 'em wait."

6 Nowhere else in show business is there anything like the attachment between soap actors and viewers. Soap fans often watch just one of the eleven shows. When a character changes or is killed off, mail floods the studios. New characters have to wait about six months to a year before viewers accept them. Actresses being divorced on set get consolation gifts and religious instruction in the mail. Pregnant actresses are sent sets and sets of baby clothes, some hand-stitched. When Jacklyn Zeman's character was a villainess on *General Hospital,* she needed bodyguards to protect her on the streets. Leon Russom, a former bad guy on *Another World,* was not so lucky. Walking down Fifth Avenue, he was attacked by a handbag-wielding fan, irate that he was treating his screen beloved shabbily.

7   Soaps have always been a medium about women by women. Originally radio dramas, created by the dictatorial Irna Phillips, early soap operas centered on the life and loves of one small town girl. In the '50s, they made the jump to TV, and expanded to fifteen minutes. Phillips decreed that the plots be about families, love triangles, incurable diseases and tragic accidents *only,* and *only* in middle-class white communities. Even when soaps moved out of the kitchen by the '70s to embrace entire towns, the conventions were kept because the big suds manufacturer Procter & Gamble owned many of the shows and enforced the strictures.

8   New soaps like *All My Children,* created in 1970 by Nixon, and *The Young and the Restless,* created in 1973, made soaps both sexy and relevant. Then *General Hospital* added action and adventure to the formulas about romance and infidelity, transforming the genre in the process. Now soaps pay as much attention to makeup, wardrobe, jewelry, hairstyles and sets as they do to emotional dilemmas.

9   Characters are younger too, to appeal to preteens. Nearly all women on soaps work, and—horrors—not all always have a man. The last of Irna Phillips' taboos, interracial romance and homosexuality, have been broken. *General Hospital* married its first black-white couple last year, and an interracial love triangle is simmering on *All My Children. As the World Turns* has successfully introduced a homosexual leading man, long thought to be a sure turn-off to the typical female viewer. Men sometimes are the focus of the plots, though editor Berlin estimates that most plots, called story lines, still revolve around women.

10   The soaps may have a new look, but their larger-than-life melodramas have not changed. Daytime drama produces 260 episodes a year. By comparison, nighttime soaps like *Dynasty* film only 26 new episodes. The demand for material

is never-ending, and, consequently, so are the love stories. Unrequited love, intrigue, illicit love, star-crossed—any kind of love. No leading lady has a work life as interesting or complicated as her love life. Though shows like *One Life to Live, The Young and the Restless* and *As the World Turns* feature professionals juggling career and home life, in many cases work is an excuse to get ladies out of the house and into more romantic liaisons. "Loving is the most important thing we do," says Nixon. "Ambition! People have ambitions because they want love—they want applause. And depression! That's the absence of love."

11   Love can be blissful—but not for long. "If you put on a soap and everyone was happy, your ratings would go into the toilet," says *General Hospital*'s executive producer, Wes Kenney. "Look what happened to J. R. on *Dallas.* People who watch don't want sitcoms—they're looking for the intensity brought on by emotioal problems, cliffhangers and suspense."

12   To stir up the pot, every soap has a meddlesome bitch—"Usually an older one like Lucinda Walsh, whom Elizabeth Hubbard plays on our show," says Douglas Marland, head writer of *As the World Turns.* "And an incipient one who is learning her tricks. They're the movers and the shakers. They make things happen." Colleen Zenk, who plays Barbara Ryan on *As the World Turns,* speculates that manipulative women dominate soaps because "women out there in the real world feel so helpless in their work or home or marriage. They feel saddled by their children and they wish they could change their lives but they don't have the power to, so they live vicariously through the beautiful, powerful bitches."

13   Every soap also has a rich family, frequently contrasted with a family of modest means, such as the Brooks family and the Fosters on *The Young and the Restless.* NBC's new soap, *Generations,* features a poor white family and a rich black one, one of whose members used to be a housekeeper for the white family. Plot devices such as comas, diseases, kidnappings or car crashes are called in whenever characters need a change of heart or a rethinking by the writers. Pasts are deep and dark, and everyone has one. Usually they contain at least one child. Children with scrambled parentage are constantly turning up on the soaps. Says Marland, "Audiences like that device, that's why it's done so many times. They love the surprise—oh no! Oh my God, she's so-and-so's daughter!" Relatives also appear. Monica Quartermaine on *General Hospital* bedded a young tennis pro who turns out to be her nephew—a secret she's trying to hide from her husband, who has homicidal tendencies when he suspects infidelity.

14   Soap tradition decrees that people always pay for their sins. Good characters pay even more than vixens. Viki Buchanan on *One Life to Live* is one of the few women on soaps who has been married to her occasionally philandering hubbie for more than a few years, but perhaps that's because she's been so busy with a split personality and a brain tumor, which took her to heaven during an out-of-body experience. Now that she's back on earth, she's been occupied with a kidnapping and the discovery that she has a daughter.

¹⁵ But for the millions hooked on daytime, the more ludicrous the soaps are, in the end, the better. Last year one of *All My Children*'s principals, Skye Cudahy, stormed to the love nest of her husband Tom to kill Barbara, his lover. The scene went like this: Skye, aiming her gun, tells Barbara, "You made yourself available to my husband! There's no other way to look at it—you are a *whore.*"

¹⁶   "Oh, go ahead, call me that," says Barbara. "I'm sure the world would agree with you."

¹⁷   Skye cocks the trigger. "Do you have any clue, any inkling of what I've been through, of what it feels like to be betrayed? It feels like having your *guts* ripped out." Skye then commands Barbara to lie down on the bed.

¹⁸   "It's rather poetic justice, don't you think, to die on the field of dishonor?" Skye continues. "I think a bullet through the heart would be best. Maybe I should have brought *silver* bullets."

¹⁹   Cut to Tom watching through the window.

²⁰   Back to Skye: "This is no time to be vain, you want to look your best for Tom." She tells Barbara to take off her clothes. Tom sneaks in. Barbara starts to unbutton her blouse. She tells Skye to look behind her. Skye refuses: "Ever since I've met you, you've been trying to pull the wool over my eyes." Tom shouts at his wife. Skye points the gun at him, then back at Barbara, shouting for him to stand back, "unless you want me to send this slut to Kingdom Come right now!"

²¹   Cut to the commercials for mint-flavored dog biscuits and Pampers.

☐ Discovering Meaning and Technique

1. What changes have taken place in the soaps since the 1950s?

2. According to the head writer of *As the World Turns,* who are the prime movers and shakers of soap-opera plots?

3. Why do fewer women watch soaps now than in the past?

4. What plot lines are standard features of soaps?

5. The selection consists of assorted facts about soap operas. Outline the selection, indicating the general topics Kinkead uses to organize these facts.

6. Reread the last seven paragraphs of the selection. Is this an effective technique for ending an essay on soap operas?

☐ **Writing Suggestions**

1. Compare the daytime soap operas with prime-time soaps. Organize your details under general categories.

2. What do you think is the best or the worst daytime soap and why?

3. Why do you think soap operas are so popular?

4. Have the soaps gotten too sexually explicit for daytime, network television?

5. Are soap operas true to life? For example, do the characters dress, work, and raise children like ordinary people in the same income brackets?

Travel

■   ■   ■

DISCOVERING THE LAND OF LIGHT

☐ **N. SCOTT MOMADAY**

1 It is indeed the land of light. But as I think of it now, the country is less than easy, less than wholly hospitable. There is an ancient resistance in it, something of itself withheld. From the plain, at a distance, you look at the mountains, and they are grand and sharply defined on the blue sky; they are beautiful as in a photograph. On postcards they are glossy and imminent. But in the round they are formidable, even forbidding. You approach them and they recede; their far summits ride across the pure, cold light, and even the deer do not attain them. This landscape has always been remote, in some sense inaccessible, and it is an anachronism. Northern New Mexico lags a bit behind the times; it persists in the spirit of the frontier, and in its high fastnesses it is still a wilderness.

2 One autumn morning in 1946 I awoke at Jemez Pueblo. I had arrived there in the middle of the night and gone to sleep. I had no idea of where in the world I was. Now, in the very bright New Mexican morning, I began to look around and settle in.

3 When my parents and I moved to Jemez I was twelve years old. I could not have imagined a more beautiful or exotic place. The village and the valley, the canyons and the mountains had been there from the beginning of time, waiting for me, so it seemed; they were my discovery. Marco Polo in the court of Kublai Khan had nothing on me. I was embarked upon the greatest adventure of all; I had come to the place of my growing up.

4 The landscape was full of mystery and of life. The autumn was in full bloom. The sun cast a golden light upon the adobe walls and the cornfields; it set fire to the leaves of willows and cottonwoods along the river; and a fresh, cold wind ran down from the canyons and carried the good scents of pine and cedar smoke, of bread baking in the beehive ovens and of rain in the mountains. There were horses in the plain and angles of geese in the sky.

5 Gradually and without effort I entered into the motion of life there. In the winter dusk I heard coyotes barking by the river, the sound of drums in the kiva and the voice of the village crier, ringing at the rooftops. And on summer

nights of the full moon I saw old men in their ceremonial dress, running after witches.

6   I had a horse named Pecos, a fleet-footed roan gelding, which was my great glory for a time. I did a lot of riding in those days, and I got to be very good at it; my Kiowa ancestors, who were centaurs, would have been proud of me. I came to know the land by going out upon it in all seasons, getting into it until it became the very element in which I lived my daily life.

7   This was discovery, crucial, once and for all. And it was, I see now, a matter of some moment and intricacy. For not only did I discover an incomparable landscape in all of its colors and moods, but I discovered myself within it. From that time I have known that the sense of place is a dominant factor in my blood. It happens that I have traveled far and wide, and I have made my home elsewhere. But some elemental part of me remains in the hold of northern New Mexico. And when I sojourn there I am ever mindful of a line in Isak Dinesen, "In the highlands you woke up in the morning and thought: Here I am, where I ought to be."

8   Above Jemez Pueblo, San Diego Canyon ascends from the plain to the mountains. On Saturdays and Sundays, when the good people of Albuquerque and Corrales and Bernalillo drive up to take the mountain air, the women of Jemez Pueblo sell fresh bread at the side of the road at Canyon. The bread is baked in outdoor ovens, or *hornos,* and it is heavy and sweet and delicious, especially good for dipping into the very hot chili that is served in the pueblo on feast days. The rock formations at Canyon are of a red that cannot easily be imagined.

9   The village of Jemez Springs is huddled in this canyon at an elevation of 6,200 feet. The upper end of the village is dominated by the magnificent ruin of the church of San José de Jemez, built in the early seventeenth century and destroyed in the Indian rebellions that followed. In places the walls are eight feet thick. The little rooms of the old Indian town of Guisewa lie adjacent to the church, and they are like a maze. Prehistoric cave dwellings are numerous in this region, and there are ancient rock paintings about.

10   When I was a boy I climbed into the great octagonal bell tower of the church—the view commands the whole of the village of Jemez Springs and indeed the whole of the canyon to its mouth. It is a breathtaking sight. The walls of the canyon rise hundreds of feet directly above the village, and the hours of daylight are relatively few, but the consequent early morning and later afternoon light is extraordinary. It exists for a time as a diaphanous aura on the high skyline, then it touches fire to the western vertical face of the cliff; and in the afternoon the shadow of the west wall rises slowly on the east wall until the great rock face, above timber, half red and half white, blazes above the dark canyon floor. Snow comes down from the north with the big logging trucks, hauling their tons of pine. In summer the canyon is lime green with aspens and willows and cottonwoods, and yellow with paintbrush and chamisa.

11   Jemez Springs is named for the hot waters that rise out of the earth in this vicinity and which are said to be as rich in their mineral content as any springs in the country. In the center of the village is a bathhouse where an attendant will wrap you up after your bath and you can melt yourself down through your pores—and Los Ojos Bar, where you can build yourself up again.

12   A few miles north and east toward the summit of the range, there is one of the most beautiful valleys in the world. Valle Grande is a huge caldera, formed a million years ago when there was great volcanic activity here. The magma chambers under the volcanoes collapsed and whole mountains were engulfed and formed the valley below. Cattle graze far below eye level; they appear to be dark pinpoints of color on the immense field of bright grass. This is an enchanted place, kept by eagles. Once I drove along this road in winter. The snow reached almost to the tops of the fenceposts, and on the other side and close by were working cowboys. I thrilled to see them in their sheepskins and chaps, their horses steaming and lunging in the deep snow. And on another occasion, years later, I counted seventeen elk, as they emerged one by one from the woods on the valley's rim.

13   Across the summit the Rio Grande Valley lies out in the blur of distance, the Sangre de Cristos, southern horn of the Rockies, looming beyond. The ancient city of Santa Fe glints in the south, but the way of this journey is north, against the current of the great river. Espanola, once the capital of the territory, touches upon a circle that describes the heart of northern New Mexico.

14   The village of Abiquiu is situated on a hill overlooking the long, undulant depression of the Rio Chama. It is a various landscape—grassy banks, rolling plains, bluffs of red and rose and purple and blue. Abiquiu is an old Penitente village (the Penitentes were a religious society composed of men who scourged themselves to blood and carried heavy wooden crosses on the Fridays of Lent and especially during Holy Week), and the birthplace of one of New Mexico's great and enigmatic men of history, Padre Martinez, of whom more later. It is also the home of the artist Georgia O'Keeffe. One day in the early '70s I called upon this venerable lady—she was already in her eighties—for the first time. She met me at the door in a black suit and a white shirt. Her hair was swept severely back, and she seemed quite handsome and impressive in her formality. We sat in the front room among objects rare and beautiful—paintings, skulls and skeletons, boxes filled with smooth, colored stones.

15   We talked for a time, and she told me of how she had made the fireplace before which we sat, quite a lovely earthen sculpture, with her own hands. I saw that her hands were large and expressive, and I could easily imagine them shaping the delicate arch of the firebox. Then it occurred to Miss O'Keeffe that she had neglected to offer me refreshment, and she became slightly flustered. "Oh, I am sorry," she said. "Wouldn't you like a drink?" I replied that I was

quite comfortable, but she pressed the point and I said that I would have a scotch, please.

16   She excused herself and went out of the room. Long minutes passed, and she did not return. I grew uneasy, then concerned. There was a din, a rattling of metal objects, which I took to come from the kitchen. I got up, sat down again, wrung my hands; I wondered whether or not I should investigate. Then, to my great relief, she reappeared. But she was empty-handed, and there was a consternation in her face. "It's my maid's day off, and I do not know what she did with the key to the liquor pantry," she explained. "Oh, please, don't give it a thought," I blurted. "Really, I'm fine."

17   But Georgia O'Keeffe had got it into her head that I was going to have my drink, and to my deep distress she excused herself again. Another long time elapsed, again the banging of pots and pans, more wringing of my hands. And then, with pronounced dignity and not a hair out of place, she entered the room with my drink on a small silver tray. Later she confided to me with a twinkle in her eye, did this octogenarian, that she had taken the pantry door off at the hinges with a screwdriver.

18
> And then, in those days, too,
> I made you the gift of a small, brown stone,
> And you described it with the tips of your fingers
> And knew at once that it was beautiful—
> At once, accordingly you knew,
> As you knew the forms of the earth at Abiquiu:
> That time involves them and they bear away,
> Beautiful, various, remote,
> In failing light, and the coming of cold.

19   So ends a poem I dedicated to her.

20   On another occasion, over wine and goat cheese, she said to me, "This is simply the place that I like best in the world."

21   Farther north the village of Tierra Amarilla lies in the plain of the Rio Arriba. It is indeed a yellow land, shining with pale winter grass or gleaming with fawn lilies and mariposa tulips. To the north is Chama and the narrow-gauge railroad that runs over Cumbres Pass into Colorado, and to the west the wilds of the Jicarilla Apache reservation. There I used to drive out upon the dirt roads to corrals far away in the mountains where slim Apache boys and girls, their boots taped about the insteps, broke their sleek horses. And in the early sunlit mornings herds of elk ventured out upon the snowfields. But the circle turns to the east. The road runs just south of the Rio Brazos for a time, then across the west branch of the Carson National Forest to Tres Piedras, then southeastward across the Rio Grande Gorge to Taos.

22   Taos is definitive. There is something quintessential in its character. Of all places, Taos seems to me to represent best the soul of the Southwest in general and that of northern New Mexico in particular. It is Sante Fe, Gallup, Scottsdale and Tombstone concentrated into a single point of remarkable density and energy. Certainly it is not everyone's cup of tea. The cold can be bitter, the locals exclusive, the streets muddy and the conveniences of the modern world elsewhere. And Taoseños complain of Taos in the very way that New Yorkers complain of New York. But in the March dusk, say, sitting before a piñon fire and looking through the swirls of snow to the last light on the mountain peaks, *la sangre de Cristo,* you know that you inhabit the real world and that here, just here, the real world is ineffably beautiful.

23   There are many ghosts in Taos; in a very little while you are aware of their presence. Charles Bent and Kit Carson lived here, and their homes are museums. The stark and simple beauty of the Hacienda Martinez is like that of the church of San Francisco de Asis at Ranchos de Taos. It remains in the mind's eye for its own sake. The hacienda was the home of Severino Martinez, then of his famous son, Don Antonio José Martinez (1793–1867), the "dark priest" of whom Willa Cather wrote in *Death Comes for the Archbishop.* From obscure beginnings in his birthplace of Abiquiu he rose up to become a revolutionary force at Taos and in the territory. So controversial was he that at last Bishop Lamy was moved to pronounce upon him the most grave sentence of excommunication.

24   But Padre Martinez served his people well. Concerned that they be literate, he introduced the first printing press into New Mexico, and he published the first newspaper. He made of his home a kind of monastery to which the best young men of his time and place came to study and to formulate ideas. He made of Taos a center of learning in the nineteenth century.

25   One cannot be long in Taos without coming upon the ghost of D. H. Lawrence. His books, and books about him, are plentiful in the bookshops. Some of his paintings are on display at La Fonda, on the Taos plaza. Half a century after his death, his name is dropped about, especially by nonresidents. Lawrence lived here less than two years, all told, between 1922 and 1925, but he seems to have done a remarkable lot of work in that time, including the writing of *St. Mawr* and *The Woman Who Rode Away,* in which he evokes the landscape of northern New Mexico. Actually, he lived on a ranch some twenty miles north of Taos, near the village of San Cristobal. The Lawrence Ranch, at an elevation of 8,600 feet, is a magnificent 160-acre expanse of timbered mountainside overlooking the vast plain of the Rio Grande. The log cabin in which he lived remains intact, and there is a small chapel in which Lawrence's ashes are interred.

26   D. H. Lawrence, too, made a profound discovery of this landscape. "In the magnificent fierce morning of New Mexico," he wrote, "one sprang awake, a new part of the soul woke up suddenly, and the old world gave way to the new." And again, "What splendor! Only the tawny eagle could really sail out into the splendor of it all."

27   The sojourner in this land, this *tierra de la luz y el encanto,* would do well to close the circle by going the old mountain way through the Penitente villages of Penasco, Las Trampas and Truchas to Chimayo and Espanola. On the east is the jagged spine of the Sangre de Cristos, on the west the sandstone cliffs, the long, low peneplain that descends to the great river. Horses and cattle graze in the mountain meadows. Bright strings of chilies gleam. There is everywhere the smell of pine and cedar. Here are the weavers and woodcarvers whose antecedents came from Spain, then Mexico, bearing the old santos and reredos, the trappings of that aged, hard-bitten Christianity to an even more ancient world.

28   And in this place of discovery, that at last is what is discovered: the New World, ancient, as the poet has it, as light.

☐ Discovering Meaning and Technique

1. What is Momaday's purpose in referring to the land as "it," not letting the reader know where "it" is until the last sentence of the first paragraph?

2. What is the contrast in the introductory paragraph?

3. Momaday shifts between the present and past. Is it clear when he switches from one to the other?

4. What does Momaday mean by "the sense of place" (paragraph 7)?

5. Some of Momaday's prose sounds like poetry; it is rhythmic and alliterative (similar sounds reverberate)—for example, "the voice of the village crier, ringing at the rooftops" (paragraph 5). Find other examples of poetic phrasing.

6. What details emphasize Momaday's cultural closeness to the area?

7. Explain the many geological references: canyons, caldera, magma, bluffs, plains, peneplain.

8. Who is Georgia O'Keeffe? What does the story of Momaday's meeting with her reveal about her character?

9. What is the connection between the British writer D. H. Lawrence and New Mexico?

10. How does the conclusion point back to the introduction?

☐ Writing Suggestions

1. Have there been moments in your life when you awoke and thought "Here I am, where I ought to be"?

2. Momaday discusses a few of the ghosts that inhabit Taos. Try to capture the essence of a place by describing a few of its ghosts. They need not be famous people.

3. Describe a journey to a region of your state.

WALT'S WONDERFUL WORLD TURNS OUT TO BE FLAT

☐ **MANUELA HOELTERHOFF**

¹ Another happy, sunny day. I am having breakfast on Main Street, USA, the long, shoplined street that leads to Cinderella's Castle—the heart of Walt Disney World's Magic Kingdom. Music fills the air. Friendly birds pick crumbs off the restaurant's balustrade. And here's a gaily decked out pony pulling smiling visitors in a festooned wagon.

² By day's end, about 35,000 adults and children (adults outnumber kids four to one) will have strolled up Main Street. By year's end, the admirers of Donald, Dumbo, Mickey and Pluto are expected to reach 13.2 million, making Disney World even more popular than the older Disneyland in Anaheim, California. Since Disney World opened ten-and-a-half years ago, it has clocked over 131 million visitors. In fact, my travel guide says this is the most popular vacation spot on this planet. As the large 36-year-old child who accompanied me said: "Opera isn't everything, kid. You got to learn about America and talk to the people."

³ Over there at an adjacent table is a middle-aged couple forking in pancakes. His shortsleeved shirt reveals a tattoo; her print slack ensemble is as happily colored as a flower bed. We chat about their trip and she tells me that he is a construction worker and she a bookkeeper. They are celebrating their 25th anniversary here in Disney. Good choice? I ask. "Oh, God, yes," she says. "We're so amazed. It's better, its more than we imagined. Everything is so clean." They were hoping to spend their next vacation here.

⁴ Their satisfaction was echoed in varying decible levels by virtually everyone I spoke to during my four-day stay. "We wouldn't change anything," said a retired couple from Mississippi. "I've been here 11 times; it's an uplifting place," said a young lawyer from Ohio. And a Vermont-based doctor and his wife sang a duet of praise of which one stanza focused on the place's cheerfulness and another on its efficiency.

⁵ This joyous ensemble of voices is offered for reasons of balance. I did not have a great time. I ate food no self-respecting mouse would eat, stayed in a hotel that could have been designed by the Moscow corps of engineers and

suffered through entertainment by smiling, uniformed young people who looked like they had their hair arranged at a lobotomy clinic. Somehow the plastic heart of Disney didn't beat for me.

6   Still, I have to give Walt credit for standing in the swamplands surrounding Orlando and envisioning a drained, jillion-dollar amusement/vacation spot presided over by a castle and courtly mouse. Walt's world is simply immense. You need to be Peter Pan to cover its 27,400 acres. As our guide kept telling us: Disney World is much, much more than just the Magic Kingdom with its rides, attractions and restaurants. It's hotels, golf courses, a heap of shops and such other components of the perfect vacation as horseback riding, boating and swimming. The entire fiefdom is laced together by a battalion of buses and a monorail that zooms above your head and right through the Contemporary Resort Hotel (my happy home).

7   Anyway, you're thinking, this all sounds neat enough, nobody promised you Paris, poisonous food is at every streetcorner, so what if people smile a lot and what really is your problem, you Fair Isle-sweater-wearing snob? Well, let me offer some highlights of Disney and its parameters, and if it seems really good and you act quickly, you can probably still book a room in the Contemporary sometime next year. The waiting list here is longer than at the George V in Paris.

8   The Magic Kingdom is divided into various areas bearing such names as Tomorrowland, Adventureland and Frontierland. In Adventureland we stop at an attraction called the Enchanted Tiki Birds, which has a long line of mostly adults waiting to get into "the sunshine pavilion." While we wait, two robot (or, in Disney jargon, AudioAnimatronic) parrots entertain us with a story that starts "many birdbaths ago." One of the many sunny young folks who keep things running smoothly in the kingdom pops out dressed in a disgusting orange outfit. "Aloha!" he shouts. The people stare at him. "I said, 'Aloha,'" he yells smiling madly. "Aloha!" the audience shouts back, making up in volume what it had lacked in spontaneity. "Everyone raise his arm and wave goodbye!" he commands. And everyone raises his arm and waves goodbye.

9   Any minute, we figured, he's going to have them saluting and clicking their sandals.

10   We decided to break ranks and headed for Tomorrowland, where we bobbed about in the air sitting in something called sky jets and had some lunch at the Space Port shop. So many choices. We picked Splashdown Peach Punch over a Cosmic Cooler and settled for a Satellite sandwich. In Disney, language lovers will quickly note, Mickey Mouse and Donald Duck worked wonders with alliteration and little rhymes, though it must be said that Walt was no Whitman.

11   Fortified, we took in a short movie introducing EPCOT (the acronym for Experimental Prototype Community of Tomorrow), a new 600-acre attraction scheduled to open this fall. "Relax and enjoy," says the smooth-voiced narrator as a tenorino begins to croon: "Dreams of the future, lalala, the world belongs

to the dreamer, the dreamer inside you." The future apparently includes homes that look like aquariums and people cavorting with dolphins dressed up in pretty outfits. The level of the narration is such that it could be understood by an AudioAnimatronic audience.

12   In contrast, there is nothing futuristic or fantastical about the next stop, our hotel, except for that monorail speeding through its innards. That was a terrific design idea. And when the hotel opened, the decor had other 21st century touches. But visitors apparently felt uncomfortable with the unfamiliar and the rooms were redecorated. As I dial to a religious program on the TV, I sit on a purple-green bedspread surrounded by swimming-pool-blue plastic furniture, enormous lamps with tumor-like bases and textured green and beige walls. I look out over a parking lot and carefully planted vegetation that is pure Middle America—boring trees and dinky little flowers. I may be in tropical Florida, but there isn't a palm tree in sight. The beach behind the parking lot is as dully laid out as the golf course.

13   Once outside the fun and games of the Magic Kingdom, the rest of Disney World looks like a condo village. Which is a large part, I would argue, of its attraction. Many Americans spend most of their life preparing for a retirement community and Disney provides a good prelude with its own security force and hassle-free, clean living. Unlike in Europe, you don't have to deal with funny languages, funny-colored money or funny food. And there's no garbage. Never. The smallest scrap of litter is instantly sucked underground, and rushed via pipes to the most fabulous compactor in the universe. The place is obsessively antiseptic. When the Disney characters dance and ride up Main Street in the parade scheduled for every afternoon, a special squad equipped with scoopers follows the ponies.

14   There's nothing left to chance here, nothing at all. The instant you arrive, you are watched over and taken care of. This place has crowd control down to a science. Mazes set up in front of the popular attractions like "20,000 Leagues Under the Sea," which features plastic-looking, half-submerged submarines paddling past plastic monsters, keep the people-flow smooth and constant. Even though it took us 30 minutes to meet the mermaid, we had the impression our sub was just around the corner. The only time I saw the system break down was in front of the Haunted Mansion. "Disney World is your land" as the song frequently heard hereabouts goes. But not if you're fat. One unhappy girl got stuck in the turnstyle and had to be pushed back out. Like Cinderella's stepsisters, no matter how hard she tried, she just wouldn't fit.

15   Evenings, too, were crammed with events. One night we dined at the Papeete Bay Verandah restaurant in the Polynesian Village hotel, *the* place if you aren't at the Contemporary. An overamplified and oversimplified combo entertained us as we sipped a Chi-Chi, particularly popular, the menu points out, in Pago Pago, and stared at prawns blown up with breading to look like chicken legs.

16   But the unquestioned highlight was the Hoop-Dee-Doo Revue at Pioneer Hall in the camping area. "Enthusiastic performers sing, dance and joke up a storm until your mouth is as sore from laughing as your stomach is from ingesting all the food," promises my guide book. I couldn't have said it better. As we sat down, the hearty sextet appeared singing "Hoop-de-doo, hoop-dee-doo." Then they beat pans and washboards and established friendly rapport with the eating audience. With Robert, for instance, of Virile Beach (could have been Floral Beach, those washboards get noisy). And Chris. Let's hear it for Chris from Daytona Beach! He's 29 today! Let's hear it for Chris! People waved their napkins in Chris's direction. "Hoop-dee-doo" sang the ensemble, jumping up and down.

17   Our meal—greasy ribs and chicken—arrived in little buckets. When we were done staring again, the hearty sextet reappeared and rubbed their bellies as they sang: "Mom's in the kitchen fixing up a special dessert just for *you.*" Out came globs of possibly strawberry shortcake and then more jokes like "You got a wooden head; that's better than a cedar chest. Think about that for a while." Everybody did and whooped and hollered.

18   Was nothing nice in Disney? Oh, all right. We had a scary time on the roller coaster ride through darkness on Space Mountain; I always enjoy carousels and Disney has one with handsome horses. And I had a fine meal at the Empress Room aboard a riverboat anchored by the shopping complex, probably the only restaurant on the premises that doesn't microwave toast.

19   The next day, we left Disney World for Cypress Gardens, one of the many attractions beckoning in the Orlando area and bearing names like Sea World, Wet 'n Wild, Gatorland, Circus World, Monkey Jungle. And so on. The landscape is flat and straggled-out. The big thing seems to be gas stations with restaurants attached, chicken salad bars and shacks selling hot boiled peanuts. "Yahoo," says my pal. "Wouldn't mind trying a bag of them hot boiled peanuts." We buy a bag. They are soggy and awful. Our proximity to Cypress Gardens is periodically announced by signs for 12 million flowers and the chief attraction, dramatic ducks. (You're in Luck: A Banjo-Playing Duck.)

20   The gardens are much, much more than just a botanical garden. A water ski show is going on in the stadium. "He hit a wet spot!" exclaims the announcer as a performer disappears into the water. The audience jeers. A child in a carriage leans over and dribbles on my foot. "I wish you'd stop calling America a land of morons," says my friend. "It's not fitting for a foreigner." We pass 12 million flowers and don't miss a one, thanks to helpful signs like: "Look up! Don't miss the orchid." Look has little eyes painted into the o's. "Don't miss the scenic waterfall coming up on your right," warns another sign. "Have you forgotten to load your camera?" wonders a third. "Is America turning into a land of morons?" wonders my companion.

21   We are too early for the gator show (watch them make pocketbooks right in front of your eyes?). But Bill the Wackie Quackie man is setting up the duck follies and we sit down just in time to see a duck waddle out onto a tiny stage,

and peck at a tiny piano with its beak. "Waddaya call a rich duck?" asks Bill the Wackie-Quackie man of the audience. "A Ritzy Quacker!" he shouts. "Argh, argh" laughs the man in front of us, tugging at his visor cap. Liberace Duck leaves, followed by Kentucky Ducky playing "The Ballad of the Mallard." The Valeducktorian is introduced to a pleased audience as we fly to our car.

22   We press on to Circus World, which seems to have suffered an unexplained evacuation prior to our arrival. It doesn't seem to affect the place, which looks designed and run by a computer. A sound system keeps churning out electronic organ grinder music, the rides dip and turn even though there is no one waiting to get on. Holding pre-wrapped cotton candy we stand for a few horrible minutes on the deserted Avenue of Spins and Grins before peering into the concrete Big Top. An announcer is introducing what he calls "our ponderous pachyderms." The beasts do headstands in a ring without sawdust in front of a listless little crowd. The memories of my childhood circuses are stronger than any scent in the wind.

23   What's it all add up to? The only message I can offer after a few days down here in Central Florida is that America is getting cutified at a far more rapid rate than many of us may be aware of. In gritty New York this mania for babble, alliteration, dumb rhymes—and understandably, sanitation—had largely escaped me. Very few of the places I visited in Disney or its environs seemed to be expecting any functioning adults or intelligent children. They were expecting cartoon characters. And the visitors behaved accordingly. At Cypress Gardens, a number of able oldsters very happily tucked themselves into wheel-barrow-shaped wheelchairs. At Sea World, a theme park offering large fish in large tanks, adults obligingly stuffed kids into dolphin-shaped carriages.

24   In fact, it was at Sea World that I had a brief encounter with insanity. There I was holding a snack bought at Snacks 'n Suds, wandering past Fountain Fantasy on my way to Hawaiian Punch Village. Shamu, I thought. Got to find Shamu, the much-praised killer whale. So I fluttered about, finally coming to this big pool with a dark half-submerged hulk at one end. It was very still, not showing an inch of killer tail. Then it moved and I thought, this can't be real, it's a plastic submarine. Shamu? Submarine? I just couldn't tell anymore. It was time to go.

25   And quicker than you could say Mickey Mouse, we were in the friendly skies having another indescribable meal. Hoop-de-doo, we sang. Hoop-de-doo.

☐ Discovering Meaning and Technique

1. In the first paragraph, how does Hoelterhoff hint at her attitude about Disney World?

2. What is the purpose of the second paragraph?

3. Hoelterhoff could have picked many types of visitors. Why does she pick the particular people she describes and quotes?

4. In what paragraph does Hoelterhoff explicitly state her attitude?

5. Hoelterhoff avoids writing in generalities like "Disney World is enormous." Instead, she chooses specifics. What details and terms does she include to convey the immensity of Disney World?

6. What is the meaning of the statement following the description of the robot parrot: "Any minute, we figured, he's going to have them saluting and clicking their sandals" (paragraph 9)?

7. Explain "Walt was no Whitman" (paragraph 10).

8. What are some of the expressions of time ("by day's end") that Hoelterhoff uses to orient the reader?

9. Does Hoelterhoff find anything nice about Disney World?

10. Hoelterhoff's visit is not exclusively to Disney World but also to other sites in the Orlando area. Do you think the variety ruins the unity of the selection?

☐ Writing Suggestions

1. Argue that Hoelterhoff's attitude toward Disney World is prejudiced, written by an opera-loving "snob."

2. Describe entertainments that make America seem a "land of morons."

3. Critique some other tourist attraction.

4. Discuss how people on vacation seem to prefer fantasy to reality.

WHY I DON'T GET AROUND MUCH ANYMORE

☐ JEAN STAFFORD

1 The old Cunard Line slogan, "Getting There Is Half the Fun," is as obsolete as the Cunard Line is obsolescent. Getting there is about as much fun as riding a condemned roller coaster and *there,* if revisited, is unrecognizably altered for the worse or, if seen for the first time, is having an unseasonable heat wave or a general strike.

2   For close on forty years, I have traveled considerably and for most of those years, I have, on reflection, been sure that the sights I have seen have exhilarated and ennobled me, that the dilemmas have really been larks (arriving alone in a strange city at 3:34 A.M. without a hotel reservation and without a word of the language spoken there), and that the spiritual and cultural profits accruing to these peregrinations have far outweighed the fear and trembling (on a derelict launch crossing Pillsbury Sound, locally known as The Graveyard, between the islands of St. Thomas and St. John, the skipper told me, the only passenger, that he had been as drunk as a billy goat for four days and had been having a whale of a time scaring the living daylights out of his voyagers. His condition was conspicuously unchanged. When we cast off at eight A.M., he sent a boy below for a bottle of rum and two beat-up tin cups and I drank faster than he did while he told me that this tide rip where the Caribbean joined the Atlantic was likely the most perilous stretch of water in all the Seven Seas), the acute discomfort (sitting bolt upright in third-class carriages jam-packed with people eating garlic sandwiches, or standing bolt upright in third-class corridors jam-packed with Hitler's or Mussolini's bootleg troops going to or coming from the Spanish Civil War and drinking bootleg moonshine imported from the Kentucky hills), and acute distress of mind (I am so cowardly that guilt is written in neon all over my face, attracting border police).

3   Indeed, I am very glad that I have ridden on the Orient Express, have seen Old Faithful go off on schedule, have sat in a splintery wooden saddle on a horse the size of a coyote on the island of Samothrace, and that I studied *Julius Kaiser* under a Brownshirt at Heidelberg in 1937—the bard who wrote this play, Wilhelm Schäkespier, had been born in Frankfurt-am-Main and had invented National Socialism. Thank God my consultation with the oracle at Delphi is behind me: On both the ascent and descent of Mt. Parnassus, with a Barney Oldfield manqué at the wheel, we were attacked by hail and thunderbolts from the arsenal of Zeus whose ichor was boiling.

4   Five years ago, I made a journey to France during which not one mishap, not one delay, not one moment of inclement weather, not one cross word marred my passage thereby to derange my mind and harden my heart. The night plane I took to Geneva was almost empty and there was not a single moist and vocal baby aboard. I stretched out at length on three seats, tucked in with a soft blanket by an angelic maiden with flaxen locks and azure eyes; she woke me in the radiant morning to give me croissants and coffee, baked and brewed in a god's kitchen. Other gods were in the drivers' seats and they lowered my cradle to earth as gently as doves. A little car materialized on the tarmac, its neat backside imprinted with the hospitable enjoinder, FOLLOW ME. We did as we were bade by this wee red shepherd and we alit noiselessly and thudlessly. I was met and taken by car over the Juras, verdant and abloom. I arrived at teatime on a Thurday, and the following Thursday at teatime, after a perfect week in a perfect house with perfect friends, I was driven to Lyons

where I took a plane to London to spend the night. The following morning at eleven, I boarded a plane for New York: I had two seats to myself and there was, once again, an absence of mewling and puking infants and, at least in my neighborhood, anyone with a bad head cold. We were two hours early at Kennedy, the visibility was one hundred percent, there was no stacking; the customs and the immigration fellows waved us through—I think they were planning a jollification and wanted to shut up shop ahead of time to make the civil-service sockdolager punch—and I found a porter at once who led me to a telephone booth in which the instrument worked. I called (no busy signal, no wrong number) the air service to my town and, minutes later, a Port Authority car came to fetch me to Butler field. I was the only passenger on the eight-seater, but paid only the scheduled flight fare and the copilot came back to tell me a perfectly marvelous dog-food joke. Our flying time was twenty-one minutes. By five-thirty in the afternoon, I was unpacked, bathed, dressed and ready to go across the road for a drink and a light collation. Jet lag set in at ten that evening and was closed at ten the next morning.

5   I doubt that I will ever go abroad again, unwilling to challenge that record and come a mighty cropper.

6 Every now and again, I am invited by a college or a university to take part in a forum which will examine the reasons why the novel is dead, or to give a lecture proving that the novel is as fit as a fiddle. Compulsively I accept because, I tell myself, I will see a part of the country hitherto unknown to me; the fee is attractive; the date is so far in the future that it will never come.

7   It comes. I see no rain forests or striking geological phenomena or aboriginal Kansans in native tattoo. I see only lecture halls, seminar rooms and faculty clubs where dangerous cocktail parties and soirees are held: Next to summer vacationers in East Hampton, academicians are the hardest-drinking crew I have ever met up with. I also see airports and motels. The honorarium does not begin to cover medical expenses when I come home, and the things I have lost are irreplaceable.

8   Depending on my destination and the length of time I shall be gone, it takes me from two full days or two full weeks to prepare for my departure. On my return, I need a week to a month to shake off the virus acquired in alien corn, to get my bearings and settle back into my cozy rut.

9   To begin with, there is the matter of my luggage, which looks like a mule skinner's traps. It dates from the days of trains and steamships when porters teemed in terminals. Empty, it is heavy; packed, it has the heft of sea chests made of lignum vitae filled with spare parts for heavy-duty farm equipment. It is scuffed, scarred and stained, wanting in essential hardware (hasps, hinges, catches), and while I am mortally ashamed to be seen in public with it, I don't replace it because each time I venture beyond my township, I vow I will never do so again.

10   About two weeks before I leave, I go up to the attic to fetch these frightful old bags; I realize that before I do anything else, I must clean and tidy the attic, which is enormous and disproportionate to my small house. In it are dozens of grosses of empty cartons, pieces of furniture bought at auction that didn't work out, extra leaves for dining-room tables long since taken to the dump, sealed boxes labeled "Odds and Ends" which may contain keys to forgotten houses and apartments and offices, together with pieces of chalk, lengths of grosgrain ribbon and passementerie braid, finials to lamps no longer in my possession. The windowsills are charnel houses of unnumbered hornets and flies.

11   Now I am in for an exhausting season: The whole house, from attic to cellar, and the tool shed must be thoroughly cleaned lest I die in my absence. I wash the woodwork, the windows, the mirrors and the pictures under glass; I polish the silver and brass and the copper pots and skillets; I defrost; I oil and rub the furniture, put new paper in every drawer, sort the nails and arrange them according to length and head size; using a Q-tip moistened and dipped in Bab-o, I scour the interstices on kitchen appliances.

12   Two days before the taxi comes to pick me up, I am ready, wearing my hat and gloves. I do not want to dirty the stove, so I subsist on saltines, which I eat standing up.

13   In order to get a train or a plane to take me north or south or west, I must go to New York City on the Long Island Rail Road, which does not run: It hops like a cricket with a sprained foreleg, and between hops it rests a long time. As soon as the sun goes down, the pale lights are turned off. Sometimes there is drinking water but there are no cups, at other times there are cups but no water, a situation reminiscent of the rule on the other side of The Looking-Glass spelled out to Alice by the White Queen, ". . . jam to-morrow and jam yesterday—but never jam *to-day.*" The outer windows have been shattered by rocks and bullets and the inner ones are the color of a chimney sweep's work clothes; the lavatories would make the Augean stables look like the ladies' room at the Yale Club. The roadbed is so lumpy, so sagging, so pocked with lacunae that even if there were any light, it would be impossible for a passenger to read: The book won't hold still—it jumps up, giving the nose a smart wallop and knocking off the eyeglasses. In the summer, the air conditioning works in fits and starts; in the winter, there is no heat at all or there is so much that you get the feeling of being face to face with a Bessemer steel-processing furnace.

14   The only thing I dread more than a ride out of my town on those rails is changing planes in a big airport. Kennedy is awful, Kansas City is awful, Washington is awful, but the one that beats them all hollow is O'Hare in Chicago. I have never boarded a plane in any airport at Gate 2 or Gate 10: I go out at 19 or 27 and come in at gates similarly distant from my luggage and the taxi rank. At O'Hare, I arrive at Gate 72, located, I think, in the purlieus of Gary, Indiana,

and I hike cross-country to Gate 119 just east of Boise, Idaho. There is standing room only in the waiting rooms in Chicago. Most of the bars and most of the eating concessions have no chairs or stools; those that have are closed for repair. It is not possible to change planes in O'Hare in less than four hours.

15   Once I went to a university in Texas to be subjected to students. The room in the motel where I was lodged faced a swimming pool which was in use round the clock by hydrophiles addicted to rock music coming to them over transistor radios. I could not open the curtains lest I be on view. I could not regulate the air conditioning and the temperature was that of my Deep-freeze back home—back home! Oh, how far away I was from my own dear bed! On the bed here, there was one blanket, a cotton one, and there was a hole in the dead center with a diameter of about two feet. There was no room service and there was no restaurant. I had declined dinner on the plane (I do not fancy eating grey meat and waterlogged vegetables at four o'clock in the afternoon) and I had counted on a steak sandwich sent to my room which I would eat as I watched television. I returned to the lobby, splashed en route by the sportive swimmers in the floodlit pool, where I found a machine that dispensed peanuts and candy bars. The enormous color-TV set had an enormous voice, but its pictures were only those of dancing polka dots and what appeared to be paramecia, amoebae and other pseudopodal protozoans slinking through slime mold.

16   A few months later, in the dead of winter, I went to serve a two-week stretch at a university in the Allegheny Mountains. I could not fly because the airfield there had no provisions for instrument landing and visibility ended with the first blizzard that annually struck during the second week of September and did not begin again until the line storm shortly before Memorial Day. So at five in the afternoon, I boarded *The Spirit of St. Louis,* a train I remembered with respect and affection as being fast and grand and having good food well served. The trip was to take only four hours, but I engaged a room because I like dining in privacy on trains. When the porter showed me to my cold, crepuscular cell, he told me, in a tone of defiant glee, that meals were served only in the dining car. I had a drink in the bar car and watched the jaundiced New Jersey meadows inch past as *The Spirit of St. Louis* lumbered leisurely along. And then I went into the dining car, which was in total darkness except for a few candles. The waiter told me that the cookstove was on the fritz and I could have only what was ready: shrimp salad. I am allergic to shellfish. The following colloquy ensued:

17   I: Is there nothing else?

18   He: Not to eat, there isn't.

19   I: Could I have some crackers and cheese?

20   He: Only if you order the whole dinner.

21   I: But there is no dinner.

22   He: Sorry, lady, that's the policy of the line.

23   The headwaiter, hearing our bootless talk, ambled over and said he thought there was an auxiliary cooking apparatus somewhere around and I could have a cheeseburger.

24   I: That would be very nice, but could I have a plain hamburger?

25   Waiter (accusingly): She said she wanted crackers and cheese.

26   Headwaiter: You can have a plain hamburger but that will be two dollars and twenty-five cents. The cheeseburger is a dollar seventy-five.

27   I (baffled as a rat in a maze): I'll have the cheeseburger.

28   Time passed. The waiter returned to say that the Bunsen burner was out of fuel and there would be "nothing more in the food line" except shrimp salad. I went back to my room and ate a box of cough drops.

29   My stay was not comfortable. The television worked reasonably well, but, quite inexplicably, it was placed at an angle high above the bed and I could view it only by sitting on a chair designed to punish the flesh, craning my neck. The room was so cold that in order to watch *NYPD,* I had to swaddle myself in all the bedding. For two days, a Canadian opera company was in residence and a tenor, dedicated to his performing art, practiced scales and sang arias from *The Ring* at all times when he was not onstage. While he was my neighbor, I spent most of my time in the ladies' room reading *Complete Short Stories of Robert Louis Stevenson,* and Mr. Hyde began to insinuate himself into my character.

30   I traveled by ship for the last time in 1959. My husband and I took an American Export vessel from Piraeus in early November, attracted by a brochure that promised us visits to "glamorous Mediterranean ports, then ten carefree days along the Sun Lane." Except for us, the passengers were low-echelon State Department employees whose shoptalk was memorably uninteresting. By the time we reached Naples, the first port of call, we were sick and tired of that tub, but we were broke and couldn't switch to a plane. After Gibraltar, we had seas the like of which had not been recorded since *The Wreck of the Hesperus:* The hairdressing machinery broke down in Barcelona; the cap of one of my upper front teeth disintegrated in the Azores; my hair looked and felt like matted wire coat hangers, and my husband pretended he didn't know me.

31   Far from broadening, travel in this unenlightened age has narrowed my mind to a hairsbreadth. Chatty seatmates on planes, trains and buses have made me misanthropic; motels and hotels with no or with lackadaisical service have made me undemocratic. If I ever go farther than six miles from home, it will be by ambulance and I will be under a general anesthetic.

32   This is, of course, a whopping lie. Just now my house is as neat as a pin and it smells of ammonia and lemon oil. My satchels and valises and portmanteaus are packed. Day after tomorrow, I will go to New York City on the punitive (and grossly culpable) L.I.R.R. and proceed from Penn Station to Kennedy where I will emplane for Chicago and horrendous O'Hare, there to change to a craft, something a little larger than a crop duster, for Cedar Rapids. When I have

fastened my seat belt and have obediently fixed my eye upon the NO SMOKING sign, I will recite to myself a prayer taught me by a friend who composed it in a moment of panic and common sense. It is perhaps less a prayer than a business proposition: "Unto Thee, O Lord, I commend my spirit and with all my worldly goods I Thee endow."

☐ Discovering Meaning and Technique

1. What is Stafford's attitude toward travel? When do you first discover her attitude?

2. Who or what are the following people and places?

> Barney Oldfield (paragraph 3)
> Brownshirts (paragraph 3)
> Mt. Parnassus (paragraph 3)
> charnel houses (paragraph 10)
> Augean stables (paragraph 13)

3. Stafford mixes sophisticated and folksy language such as "peregrinations" and "drunk as a billy goat." Find other examples of both levels of language.

4. Discuss why you think Stafford chose the phrase in the first column over the phrase with a similar meaning in the second column.

wee red shepherd	small red shepherd
alit noiselessly and thudlessly	landed silently and smoothly
jaundiced meadows	yellow-green meadows
teemed in terminals	crowded in terminals

5. What comparison does Stafford use to describe the Long Island Rail Road?

6. Had Stafford omitted the last paragraph, what would be your impression? What does the last paragraph add?

☐ Writing Suggestions

1. Write about the ordeal of travel today by air, train, bus, or ship.

2. Are Stafford's motel accommodations and experiences typical? If not, what are typical in your experience?

3. Discuss the kinds of food available to travelers.

4. Examine travel ads and brochures. Do you think the trips will live up to the expectations they arouse?

UNFOLDING THE NATION

☐ **BEN YAGOTA**

[1] On Thanksgiving Day in 1895 the Chicago *Times-Herald* sponsored a fifty-four-mile road race from Jackson Park to Waukegan and on to Lincoln Park. The prize was five thousand dollars. The eventual winner, a man by the name of Frank Duryea, had at least two advantages over his competitors. First, unlike some of them, he was driving a car propelled by gasoline. Second, Duryea had noticed that the paper had published a rough plotting of the course, and he'd had the good sense to rip it out and use it. He thus made not only money but history. By virtue of his action the *Times-Herald* illustration transcended newspaper graphics to become the first American automobile road map.

[2]   The distinction is significant only in retrospect; at the time its effects were nil. After all, what need was there for road maps when, even in 1900, there were a mere eight thousand registered automobiles in the entire country? But as the century shifted into gear, things changed. By 1910 almost a million cars had been registered; by 1915 more than two million. With this new popularity came innovations in the superstructure of motoring, innovations that, considering their improvised character, proved to be surprisingly durable. In 1908 came the first concrete road, a mile-long stretch of Detroit's Woodward Avenue. Almost immediately motorists from hundreds of miles around made pilgrimages to drive on it. This was a year after the first pedestrian safety island, in San Francisco, and three years before the first painted dividing line, in Michigan. In 1914 Cleveland introduced the first electric traffic signal, and Buffalo put up the first no-left-turn sign in 1916.

[3]   Previously motoring had been a form of on-the-edge recreation, something like hang gliding today. Now it was transportation, and motorists needed guidance on how to get where they wanted to go. The roads in a good many urban areas were already mapped, thanks to the bicycle craze of the 1880s and 1890s. But bicycle maps were next to useless to motorists. Cyclists could negotiate mountain trails, pedal their way through alleys or, in an emergency, carry their vehicles across streams; motorists could not. Something new was needed.

[4]   As it happened, that something did not—at least at first—turn out to be the road map. Starting not long after the turn of the century, various concerns—tire companies, automobile associations, newspapers, car manufacturers, and resorts—began issuing road guides, in bound, folded, or pamphlet form, each spelling out one or more specific routes. For every turn along the way there was a

precise mileage reading, which the motorist was to find on his odometer. In a book put out in 1898 by the White Company, for example, Route 56 is a 110-mile journey from South Bend to Chicago; the driver is told to get ready at mile 80.3, and "at the next corner turn left passing 'Mike's Place' on the right." Publishing the guide was hardly a civic-minded gesture on the part of White, a manufacturer of steam cars. Not only is the book filled with advertisements, but almost every route in it ends at a branch of the firm.

5   These early road guides generally included a map or two, but they were not to be relied on. As the Hartford Rubber Works, a tire concern, admitted in its *Automobile Good Roads and Tours,* published in 1905, "A very thorough preliminary search showed that there were no maps which could be used as a basis for this work. . . . Much has been willingly left to geographical sense, and the tourist's own constructive faculty."

6   There was considerable variation in the books. In one or another you could find promotional claims ("That the White raises less dust than any other car was proven beyond question in the 'Dust competition' held last year by the Royal Automobile Club of England on the Brooklands race-track"); useful advice ("Look out for auto-trap [speed trap], especially in the thinly settled part of town"); and even navigational tips that suggest the precarious nature of motoring early in the century. One book gives detailed instructions, complete with a sketch of the Big Dipper, on how to find "true north."

7   A major innovation in the guidebooks was the use of photographs of key points along the route; some included a picture of every turn. (Early examples show a car making the maneuver in question, while later ones, their authors' having learned an important lesson, showed the turn from the perspective of the driver.) An obvious problem for the compilers of photo guides was that if the enterprise wasn't to take an intolerable amount of time, at least two researchers were needed: one to drive, and one to take odometer readings, pictures, and notes. Andrew McNally II, son of the founding partner of Rand McNally & Company, solved this problem by enlisting his bride; the *Rand McNally Chicago to Milwaukee Photo-Auto Guide* of 1909 is a record of their honeymoon trip.

8   Another difficulty with the guidebooks was that landmarks on the order of Mike's Place were not permanent. So, in the 1910s, a number of guidebook makers took the sensible step of making their *own* landmarks, in the middle of the decade, the Goodrich tire company began putting up guideposts, described as follows in one of their books: "Erected for the express purpose of guiding motor travel. This sign is made of porcelain enamel in three colors, erected on 4-inch oak posts, ten feet long. Each post is thoroughly creosoted and planted three feet into the ground." The company's guidebooks then supplied directions keyed to the markers.

9   The guides were useful, but they could not hold sway for very long. As new roads were built, the books, which had gotten more unwieldy every year, simply could not cover all the possible routes. It was time for the road map.

10   Maps designed exclusively for autos had been produced at least as early

as 1900, the date of a series of pocket maps put out by George Walker of Boston, which can be found in the map collection of the New York Public Library. His maps are in perfect condition, printed in delicate colors and handsome typography, beautifully bound and backed with stiff gauze covers, and—miraculously, considering the legendary difficulties later generations of drivers have had with the task—effortless to fold.

11   There was no shortage of other maps produced in the following years, many of them published by the American Automobile Association, founded in 1902. (In the early teens the AAA began putting out what later became known as Trip-Tiks, elongated, horizontal strip maps customized to guide members on their travels. It provides the same service today.) But there was one drawback in using maps for directional guidance at this time: roads had no names or at best had local, unofficial ones (Lincoln Highway, Dixie Highway, Post Road), that changed as you went from one town to another. How were these roads to be identified on maps?

12   A solution to this problem was hit on by John Brink, a draftsman on the staff of Rand McNally. In 1916 the company ran a contest, offering a hundred dollars to the employee who suggested the best new map product. Brink suggested road maps specifically designed for motorists. To deal with the route-naming difficulty, he proposed that Rand McNally take the Goodrich trial markers one step better and put up posts that *numbered* major routes, which would then be correlated with the maps. Brink, named head of Rand McNally's new Blazed Trails Department, put his scheme into practice in 1917, when his Illinois *Auto Trails* map was published. The next year Brink used his summer vacation to blaze the route from Kalamazoo, Michigan, to Cincinnati.

13   In his diary he recorded his method: "I started out for the field with my car loaded with 400 cardboard signs (coated to resist the weather), ten pounds of broadhead tacks, and a magnetic hammer, not to mention a pair of overalls. Commencing at Kalamazoo, I worked south, and in nine working days, reached Richmond, Ind. I had blazed 180 miles of road, tacking up 355 signs that consumed 22 pounds of tack."

14   Brink's idea might have been too good. It so clearly made sense that now dozens of civic organizations, auto clubs, state road departments, and map companies began blazing trails, with the confusing result that some roads were marked by as many as a dozen contradictory signposts. Clearly, government intervention was called for. It started to arrive in 1920, when Wisconsin became the first state to number its roads; by 1924 twenty-one other states had followed its lead. By the end of the decade, 75,884 miles of "U.S. Routes" were in place, the precursor to the Interstate Highway System of the 1950s.

15   A map innovator perhaps the equal of John Brink was an advertising man named William B. Akin. In 1913 the Gulf Refining Company erected, on a Pittsburgh street corner, the nation's very first drive-in gasoline service station. In the fall of 1913, Akin suggested that Gulf print up some maps of the county's roads and give them away to customers as promotional tools.

16   The idea caught on. By 1920 Gulf was giving away sixteen million Eastern states maps a year, and before long, with every other gasoline company following its lead, free road maps were the way virtually very American motorist figured out how to get from one place to another. From the thirties on, these folded maps of cities, states, and regions changed very little in form, except for occasional experiments like a 1955 map Esso put out of the route from New York to Florida. It is a cartographic fact of life that some people find it hard to use a map to proceed south, when a line veering off the the right represents a left turn. In an attempt to rectify the situation, Esso put Florida on the top. The break with convention proved to be too great, and after ten years the experiment was abandoned.

17   By this time free road maps had come to seem an American institution, something of an inalienable right. In the fifties, a publication of the General Drafting Company, one of the companies that, along with Rand McNally, designed and sold the road maps to the oil companies, mused: "It seems to us that there is a close parallel between maps and television. Both are free to the public, both have mass appeal. Both depend on high quality to produce low-cost results for advertisers. Both call for human interest, novelty, attractiveness and good taste in their commercials. "There is one big plus for maps. They have retention value. Their commercials live on for months, even years."

18   Such pride would not go unpunished. In 1972, two hundred and fifty million free maps were produced for the oil companies, more than ever before. The very next autumn the Arab oil embargo struck, an event that proved to be the death knell for the free road map. Shortages and gas lines did away with the intense competition that had spawned promotional giveaways. By 1978 the free road map had gone the way of the Packard, Ebbets Field, and the fifteen-cent cup of coffee. Today maps are available at gas stations and bookstores, but they can cost up to three dollars.

19   Still, free road maps left their mark. For one thing, they taught several generations of Americans a skill that had once been the esoteric province of yachtsmen, surveyors, and generals. Indeed, officers who served in both world wars found that in the Second their men could read reconnaissance maps more proficiently than they could in the First. The reason was road maps.

20   By definition realistic, road maps have also touched a lyrical vein in the American sensibility, offering an image of the country that is almost poetic. Unfolding a state map and following a crooked line to a town called, say, Clarion, is a potent imagination experience: it makes you ponder.

21   To Jack Kerouac the open road was "one long red line called Route 6 that led from Cape Cod clear to Ely, Nevada, and then dipped down to Los Angeles." A more recent writer, William Least Heat Moon, also sees the road map as a metaphor of sorts. In the preface to his book *Blue Highways,* he writes: "On the old highway maps of America, the main routes were red and the back roads blue. Now even the colors are changing. But in those brevities just before dawn and a little after dusk—times neither day nor night—the old

roads return to the sky some of its color. Then, in truth, they carry a mysterious cast of blue, and it's that time when the pull of the blue highway is strongest, when the open road is a beckoning, a strangeness, a place where a man can lose himself."

☐ Discovering Meaning and Technique

1. Which differences distinguish early road maps from current ones?

2. How did commercialism affect map making?

3. What were some of the difficulties in early map making?

4. Why did Esso print an upside-down map?

5. Which strategies does Yagota use to introduce and conclude the selection?

☐ Writing Suggestions

1. Describe the difficulties of using modern road maps.

2. Describe an imaginary road journey in the early 1900s before modern maps were available. Include details about maps, cars, conditions, and sights along the roads.

3. What improvements could be made to maps and road signs?

4. Using a road map, write about interesting or unusual place names.

5. If you can get both an old and a recent map of the same state, compare the two.

6. Compare travel on interstate highways and on back roads.

ON WATERINESS

☐ JAN MORRIS

1 Among the midnight disturbances that beset the traveller—the reverberation of gear-changes, the clanking of shunted railway-wagons, the dawn garbage trucks, the Last Waltz, the muffled announcement of Flight 538 to Georgetown—among

them all, one generic noise offers only solace. It is the sound of water outside one's bedroom window.

2   Sometimes, in old and elaborate city centres, it speaks of Bernini or Lescot, ancient conduits spouting through sculptured allegory into sentimental pools. Sometimes, on Atlantic shores, it suggests the secret convoys of the sea-trout, upstream through the darkness to hereditary mountain lakes. It may be only the splash of an ornamental runnel in a garden. It may be the terrific cycle of the ocean surf, the succession of thunder, suck and warning silence that gives an unforgettable rhythm to a tropical insomnia.

3   Whatever its origin, for some of us that intimation of water is a necessary dimension of travel. We may be bored to distraction by scorched posh beaches, we may prefer five crowded hours on a jumbo jet to an age without a name on a cruise ship, but our instinct leads always, wherever we are; like lemmings to the water's edge. It offers a reassurance, perhaps, of nature's dignity. It reminds us that the seas, lakes and rivers have no parking meters still, that the fish are masters of their own migrations, and that somewhere beyond our credit-card conformities, somewhere out there at the end of the pier, grand, green or fragrant things are always happening.

4   The waters of the world are sovereign Powers. We may pollute them, dam them or divert them, but they remain beyond our degradation. They are better and older than us. John Burns the radical was right, when he called the Thames 'liquid 'istory'. Many a politician, withdrawing to the Commons terrace or the Kennedy Center balcony from the heady puerilities of debate, must have been sobered into wiser judgement by the dark calm flow of the river below, and there are places in the world where this partnership of the water, at once aesthetic and functional, sets the whole tone of a society, and gives it the particular steady assurance that goes with an organic purpose.

5   Take, for example, the Mississippi. Abraham Lincoln thought it the most powerful force on earth, and certainly its progress through the American South is masterful more than slavish. Its yellowish muddy motion there, and the endless traffic of the river-craft through its shoals and cut-offs, still dictates the character of the country along its banks; and nothing in travel is more satisfying than to leave your car in a cotton-field of Arkansas or Tennessee, scramble to the ridge of the dusty levee, and discover the great river there at your feet, with the long line of a tow thudding its way to Vicksburg or New Orleans—the radar twirling on its wheelhouse, the sun glinting on its paintwork, and the off-duty crew stripped to the virile waist with mugs of coffee around the galley door.

6   Or think of a city like Singapore. It is not the most beautiful of towns, but because of the water that is its *raison d'être,* it is one of the most formidable. It was built to a purpose, designed for a trade, and it lives by the sea. Its prospect is the Strait, looking across to Sumatra and the archipelago, and littered with tangled melancholy islands. Its promenade is the waterfront, intermittently dressed up with esplanades and monuments, but in essence a working quay.

Everywhere the sea seeps through Singapore, in canals and backwaters and crowded wharfs, and always in the roadsteads lie the ships that are its familiars—opulent tankers from the west—shambled coasters from the island trade—junks, dhows, Malay schooners, warships—and all those myriad bum-boats, ferry-boats, rafts, punts, lighters and antique company launches which seem, in all such Oriental water-cities, never actually to have been constructed, but simply to have been washed up and encrusted on the land's edge, like oysters.

7 The rush of water is a traveller's elixir! Nothing can beat one of the great waterfalls, when it comes to the exhilaration of foreign travel. At Tisisat, on the Blue Nile below Lake Tana, you may sit meditatively beneath a gourd beside the water's turmoil, lolloped about by occasional baboons, interrogated sometimes by courteous tribesmen, and feeling like one of those distant poised figures in the background of explorers' engravings. At Tequendama in Colombia, on the other hand, you may feel yourself physically shaken by the force of the water—more an eruption than a fall, as though some hidden giant has been blocking the Rio Bogota with his thumb, like a boy with a bath tap. And undiminished remains the marvel of those tremendous cousins of the spectacular, Niagara and Victoria, the touch of whose spray upon one's cheek can still give the most blasé wanderer a sense of complacency.

8   At another level of excitement there is the joy of a fast river rushing immediately beside your sleeping quarters—a delight which Frank Lloyd Wright tried to reproduce in architecture, and which can give an extra fizz to every awakening. There is an inn on the French side of the Pyrenees, in the Basque village of St. Étienne-de-Baigorry, which perfectly expresses this stimulation for me. The river Nive rushes furiously past this inn, separated from its bedrooms only by a little terrace for eating *truite au bleu* upon, and filling the whole hostelry with its enthusiasm.

9   I stayed there once, and all day long, up to their thighs in the shaly mountain water beside the inn, an exquisite middle-aged French couple silently fly-fished: he unshakeably urbane with his pipe in his mouth, she miraculously unruffled, as vivid and intense as the river itself, as it pursued its headlong way towards the Bay of Biscay. They never caught a thing, but their failure was wonderfully stylish.

10 Often just the presence of water is enough—motionless, inaudible, perhaps even out of sight but for the special washed texture of sea air. For me even Delphi would lose half its mystery without that glorious blue remembrance of the sea far below at Itea, with its cruise-ship riding at anchor in the bay, and its vision of heroes and sea-nymphs.

11   Wherever mountains touch the sea, or are tipped with high silent lakes, they acquire an altogether different kind of magic: in Norway where the fjords

creep into the hills for shelter, in Iceland where the volcano Hekla smokes villainously above an icy ocean, among the memsahib's houseboats in Kashmir or best of all in Wales, where the allegorical hills of Snowdonia stand lapped in legend above Cardigan Bay—'There is no corner of Europe that I know', Belloc once wrote, 'which so moves me with the awe and majesty of great things as does this mass of the northern Welsh mountains seen from this corner of their silent sea.'

12   Nowhere is water's presence more ennobling than it is in New York, a sea-city that has forgotten its origins. There are days when almost everyone seems to be miserable in New York, if only in awful fits and starts: but when the shopkeepers are at their rudest, the traffic jams at their cruellest, the head waiters at their most preposterous, the tycoons at their least sincere, when the whole of Manhattan seems distorted with violence, dirt and disillusion—even then you have only to ride an elevator to the top of any skyscraper, and there on the edge of the city you will see the waters of New York Bay, that grandest lagoon of the New World, spanned by the slender blue steel of the Verrazano Bridge and traversed with majestic sagacity by the ships of the world.

13 And there are some places where the water is more than just a consolation, an antidote or a mechanism, but supplies something like an ideology. These are the water-civilizations, and there to the delights of ear and eye are added extra insubstantial satisfactions, sensual but profound, which can sometimes make a journey a fulfilment.

14   Among the water-reflections of Venice I have often felt this grace, as my small boat has taken me warily from one side of the city to the other, down back-canals evocative with age and rot and dampness, past hidden water-basins and busy shopping arcades above—beneath a hundred high-arched bridges, through the shadows of portentous palaces—sidelong between the dustbin barges and the *vaporetti,* boldly across the Grand Canal—until at last we chug beneath the Bridge of Sighs and I find myself in the Basin of St. Mark's, still to my mind the supreme spectacle of travel, where the lagoon seems to dance before my prow, the tankers tread grandly past Giudecca, and the whole panorama is radiant with the life and light of the sea.

15   But I have felt it even more suggestively, this limpid, liquid quality of a civilization, in the island of Japan. Everything that is most beautiful about that tantalizing country seems to me of a watery beauty. I think of fragile cedar pavilions balconied beside pools, and shrines rising strangely out of sea-shallows. I remember wooded islands in mountain lakes, and neat little coloured ducks in stone-slabbed castle moats. And at night sometimes, between the clatter of the cutlery and the unidentifiable recurrent hum from somewhere behind the wardrobe, I hear in my imagination the soft hollow plonk of the deer-scarers— through whose wooden channels a trickle of water flows perpetually backwards and forwards, throwing the little instrument from one balance to the through

the darkness, to create that gentle water-percussion of Kyoto, and keep the timid herds out of the moss-garden.

☐ Discovering Meaning and Technique

1. In the introduction (paragraph 3), Morris sums up the attraction of water. Why are people inclined to travel to some kind of body of water?

2. In the second section of the composition, what examples does Morris give of water being "aesthetic and functional"?

3. Which similes does Morris use to describe the force of the waterfall at Tequendama in Colombia (paragraph 7)? (Remember that a simile is a comparison containing the word *like* or *as*.)

4. Which kinds of bodies of water does Morris include in the composition?

5. Which cities serve to illustrate water-civilizations?

☐ Writing Suggestions

1. Explain the appeal to a traveler of water, mountains, sand, snow, country roads, interstate highways, trains, or museums.

2. Think of a river you have visited, or visit one in your vicinity. What is the charm? Is it endangered? How has it shaped the area and the people around it?

3. Discuss the advantages of having a wide variety of travel experiences.

4. Compare a city on a body of water with one that is landlocked.

THE OCEAN

☐ BOBBIE ANN MASON

¹ The interstate highway was like the ocean. It seemed to go on forever and was a similar color. Mirages of heat were shining in the distance like whitecaps, and now and then Bill lost himself in his memories of the sea. He hummed happily. Driving the fancy camper made Bill feel like a big shot.

2   Finding the interstate had been a problem for Bill and Imogene Crittendon. Not trusting the toll roads, they had blazed a trail to Nashville. They figured it was a three-hour drive to Nashville, but it took five, including the time they spent getting lost in the city. After driving past the tall buildings downtown and through the poor areas on the outskirts, Bill finally pulled over to the curb and Imogene said, "Hey!" to a man in a straw hat who was walking along thoughtfully.

3   "Which way's 65!" she yelled.

4   The entrance to it turned out to be around the corner. The man's eyes roved over the big camper cruiser as if in disbelief.

5   "We're going to Florida," Bill said, more to himself than to the man.

6   The man told them I-65 wasn't the best way to go. It wasn't the most direct.

7   "He's not in any hurry," Imogene said.

8   "Yes, I am," said Bill. "Going through Alaska to get there wasn't my idea."

9   Imogene hit him with the map.

10   "I didn't recognize a thing in Nashville," Bill said a little later, as they sailed down the vast highway.

11   "It's been thirty-five years," said Imogene. "Hey, watch where you're going."

12   "You can't talk about all the wrecks there's been out here. You don't know the history."

13   Imogene had a habit of telling the history of the wrecks on any given stretch of road. There was one long hill east of town, and whenever they drove down it she would tell about the group of women who hit a bump there and scattered all over the highway. They were all killed except one woman, who insisted on going to work anyway, but she was in such a state later that they had to take her home.

14   "That happened twenty years ago," Bill would say when Imogene told the story. "I remember her. She was the one that prayed. How do you know the others didn't pray too?"

18   "Well, that's what they always said. Of course, she's dead now too," Imogene had said.

16   Bill was getting the hang of interstate driving. He hummed awhile, then burst loudly into an old song he remembered.

> Don't go walking down lovers' lane
> With anyone else but me
> Till I come marching home.

The song made him feel young and hopeful. He pictured himself with his hands in his pockets, whistling and walking along. He couldn't wait to be walking along the beach.

17   "He'll never do it," Imogene had always told all the kinfolks. "He won't set foot off this place for the rest of his born days. He's growed to it."

18   But he had. He had shown everybody. He had fifteen hundred dollars in his billfold right this minute and more in the bank. All the big money made him delirious. He spent hours adding figures, paying this, paying that. He had always carried a wad of bills with him, but not to spend. He just had them handy. Now he was spending right and left. The figures danced in his head.

19   Bill stopped at a roadside rest area, and they ate potato salad and fried chicken Imogene had made that morning.

20   "This place ain't big enough to cuss a cat in," she said when they bumped into each other.

21   She opened a new jar of her squash pickles.

22   "Don't expect this grub to last," she said. "I can't can on the road."

23   "You won't have to," said Bill.

24   "You'll be wanting some field peas and country ham," said Imogene.

25   After eating, they lay down to rest, with the fan going and the traffic whizzing by. Bill studied the interior of the mobile home. He was not really familiar with it yet. He had bought the luxury model to please Imogene. He could live in a truckbed himself. He stretched out and shaded his eyes with his Worm-and-Germ cap from the feed mill.

26   A large family arrived at the rest area and noisily hauled out a picnic. They were laughing and talking and Bill couldn't get comfortably into his snooze. He got up and watched a boy and his dog play Frisbee. The boy was about eighteen, Bill guessed, and wore cut-off jeans. Bill was afraid the dog was going to run out in the road. It made him nervous to watch. Once the Frisbee sailed near the road and Bill had to fight to keep himself from racing after the dog. The dog did wild leaps trying to catch the Frisbee. Bill had seen dogs play Frisbee on television. Bill had never played Frisbee. He missed having a dog.

27   They drove on. The scenery changed back and forth from hills to flatlands, from fields to woods. Bill couldn't get over the fact that he was really going to see the ocean again. He just wanted to sit and look at it and memorize it. He drove along, singing. He liked the way they could sit up high in the camper, looking down on the other cars. He loved the way the camper handled, and the steady little noise of gasoline flowing through the carburetor.

28   Imogene sat with her hands in fists. When cars passed she grabbed the handle in front of her. Bill pointed out that with these wide highways she didn't have to worry about meeting traffic head-on, but Imogene said the cars sneaking around you were worse.

29   "I always heard when you retired you could start all over again at the beginning," said Imogene. "But my nerves is in too bad a shape."

30   She had said that over and over. She had cried at the sale and cried when she gave away her belongings to Judy and Bob and Sissy. She said it was her nerves.

31   "You're a lot of fun," said Bill in an exasperated tone. "I oughtn't to have brought you along."

32   "I've got this hurtin' in my side," she said.

33   Bill passed Volkswagens and Pintos and even trucks. He felt exhilarated when he passed another camper. He had a queer feeling inside, as though his whole body might jolt apart.

34   "You're going over fifty-five," Imogene said after a while.

35   Bill was an expert driver. He knew every road and cow path and Indian trail in the Jackson Purchase. If he was late coming home, Imogene always thought he had had a wreck. But he had never even been in a ditch, except on the tractor.

36   Imogene said, "Gladys had a hurtin' like this and come to find out she had kidney disease. She had to go to the bathroom every five minutes. At her husband's funeral she had to set by the door."

37   "Are you going to bellyache the whole way?"

38   Imogene laughed. "Listen to us! We'll kill each other before we get there. I'll be to bury. Or you'll have to put me in a asylum, one."

39   Bill laughed. A truck slowed him down, and he shifted gears. "You couldn't do this in China!" he exclaimed suddenly.

40   "Do what?"

41   "Go taking off like this. In China you can't go from one county to the next without a permit. And if you could, you'd have to go by bicycle."

42   "I think we might be in China before long, at the rate we're going. You're over fifty-five again."

43   "We'll be just like the Chinese if our goofy President has his way!" said Bill, ignoring Imogene's remark about the speed.

44   "What's this business about China again?" Imogene never read the papers, but Bill read the *Sun-Democrat* every night and watched NBC.

45   Bill tried to explain. "Well, see, after the war, the Chinese government was forced over to Taiwan, which was Formosa. And the rebels set up another country on the mainland, but China was on the island of Formosa. That was the true China. The ones that stayed back were Communists. The United States supported the true China." Bill looked at Imogene. "Are you listening?"

46   "Unh-huh. Go on." Imogene was clutching the sides of her seat. A Greyhound bus was passing them.

47   "And so the United States has a treaty with Taiwan, to protect them from the Communists."

48   "And so we broke the treaty," Imogene finished for him.

49   "That's right! And now our peanut President decides to be buddies with the Communists and he's going to have us in a war before you know it!"

50   Bill got upset when he thought of the President, with his phony grin. Bill couldn't stand him. He could see through every move he made. Bill had known too many like him.

51   "He gave Taiwan away, just like he did the Panama Canal," Bill said.

52   "I still want to see Plains," said Imogene.

53   "So you can see Billy Carter?" Bill laughed.

54   "I'd just like to say I went to the President's hometown."

55   "Well, O.K. We can probably get there tomorrow."

56   "Billy's always showing up somewhere—on a special or a talk show," said Imogene. "I bet he don't spend half his time in Plains anymore."

57   They looked for a campground. Imogene studied the guidebook and tried to watch the road at the same time. She located one that seemed reasonable, but Bill missed the turn.

58   "I think it was right back there," Imogene said. "Quick, turn around."

59   Bill made a U-turn, crossing the grassy strip. A car honked at him.

60   "Maybe you weren't supposed to do that," said Imogene, looking behind her.

61   The campground was pleasant. Music was playing and there were large shade trees and lots of dogs. Bill walked around the park while Imogene made supper. Being in a far-off place, wandering among strangers with license plates from everywhere, made Bill feel like a kid, off on his own. He nodded to a young man who hurried past him. The man, wearing rubber thong sandals and carrying a plastic shopping bag, had murmured a faint hello. For a moment Bill felt a desire to stop and have a conversation, a desire he felt only rarely.

62   Imogene made pork chops, butter beans, corn, slaw, and corn bread for supper, and they ate during the news. Bill made a face when the President came on.

63   "The days is getting longer," he said later, looking out the window.

64   "We're further south," said Imogene. She finished the dishes and sat down. "I don't hardly know what to do with myself. Without Mama to feed and watch over. Her complaining every ten minutes. I was thinking about her suppertime. I would go in there with her tray, her cornflakes and a little applesauce. And then get her ready for bed and bring her milk of magnesia and make sure she was covered up."

65   "Do you wish we had her along?" Bill asked, teasing. He knew Imogene would keep on if he let her. "We could have started out five years ago. I could have slept here, and you and she could have that bed."

66   "Oh, quit it! It hasn't been a month since we put her in the ground."

67   "I just thought you probably missed her snoring."

68   She shook her fist at him. "I tell you one thing. None of my younguns is going to have to put up with what I put up with." Imogene belched. "I've eat too much," she said.

69   Bill had a hard time sleeping. First the dogs barked half the night. Then a man kept hollering in the distance. And at one point during the night a motorcycle came roaring into camp, setting off the dogs again. Bill lay half awake, thinking of the ocean and remembering the rocking, cracking old ship that he had feared would sink. The U.S.S. *Shaw* was a destroyer that had been sunk at Pearl Harbor

and then raised and reoutfitted in an amazingly short time. He still heard the sounds of the guns. They woke him sometimes at night. And he would occasionally catch himself somewhere, standing as though in a trance, still passing ammunition to the gunners, rhythmically passing shell after shell. He had sailed the Pacific, but the Atlantic was connected—or it had been until Carter gave the canal away, Bill thought in disgust as he rolled over on the narrow bed.

70   "We might get there today!" Bill said when they got up at four. No one else in the camp was up.

71   "You thought it was milking time," Imogene said. "I couldn't sleep either. I was too wound up."

72   After a large breakfast of bacon, eggs, toast, and cereal, they drove awhile, then stopped for a nap.

73   "We'll never get there," said Bill.

74   They drove south to Birmingham, then across several smaller routes toward Plains. There was a lot of traffic on the small roads. Georgia drivers were worse than Kentucky drivers, Bill thought, as he tailed a woman who was straddling the line in a battered old Buick with its rear end dragging.

75   "Look, there's a old mansion!" Imogene cried. "One of those with the white columns!"

76   The mansion was so close to the road there was no yard, and they could look through the front door and out the back. Weeds had grown up around the place.

77   "See them old shacks out back," said Bill. "That's where the slaves used to live."

78   "Looks like they're still living there," said Imogene, pointing to some ragged black children. "Law, I thought we had poor people at home."

79   In Plains, Imogene bought postcards and sent them to the kids, who were scattered all over. Imogene wrote the same message on each card: "Your daddy and me's headed out to see the world. Will let you know how it comes out. If I live that long. (Oh!)" Bill and Imogene walked down the tiny main street, which was crowded with buses and campers. People from everywhere were there. Imogene wanted to take the tourist bus, but Bill said they had a new twenty-thousand-dollar vehicle of their own and knew how to drive it, so they drove around awhile, doubling back on themselves. Then, at Imogene's insistence, Bill stopped at Billy Carter's filling station.

80   "I think that's him," Imogene said, peering toward the back of the station, where there was a crowd of people standing around. "No, that's not him. Looked like him, though."

81   A sweaty man in an undershirt with skinny straps filled up the tank.

82   "Reckon Billy ain't around," said Imogene, leaning over toward Bill's window.

83   "No, he's off. He's off over to Americus." The man pointed.

84   "We went through there," said Imogene.

85   "No, we didn't," said Bill.

86   "All these tourists just driving you folks crazy, I expect," said Imogene, ignoring Bill.

87   "Oh, you get used to it," the man said, leaning against the gas pump. "You never know what you're liable to see or who you'll meet. We get some characters in here, I tell you."

88   "I 'magine."

89   "Are you ready?" Bill asked Imogene.

90   "I guess."

91   "Y'all come back now, hear?" the man said.

92   "We will," said Imogene, waving.

93   "Seen enough?" Bill asked.

94   "I can say I've been here anyway."

95   Bill was getting tired, and he drove listlessly for a while. He could not make the connection between Plains and the White House. Plains looked like the old slave shacks outside the mansion they had passed. The mansion was the White House. Bill thought of Honest Abe splitting rails, but that was a long time ago. Things were more complicated now. Bill hated complications. If he were running the show, it would be pretty simple. He never had trusted those foot-washing, born again Baptists anyway. And now the President had let a whole country in the Middle East be taken over by a religious maniac. It made him sick. What if Billy Graham decided to take over the United States? It would be the same thing.

96   Bill and Imogene, no longer talking, meandered throughout Georgia, through tiny towns that looked to Bill as though they hadn't changed since 1940. The grocery stores had front porches. Georgia still had Burma-Shave signs. Bill almost ran onto the shoulder trying to read one.

> YOUR HUSBAND
> MISBEHAVE
> GRUNT AND GRUMBLE
> RANT AND RAVE
> SHOOT THE BRUTE SOME
> BURMA-SHAVE

There was a word missing. The signs were faded and rotting.

97   Between Plains and the Florida border, Bill counted five dead animals—a possum, a groundhog, a cat, a dog, and one unidentifiable mass of hide and gristle. He tried to slow down.

98   They stopped at a camp on the border, and Bill filled up the water tank. The camper was dusty but still looked brand-new. Imogene checked to see if anything was broken.

99   "I don't see why this gas stove don't explode," she said. "All this shaking in this heat. They say not to take a gas can in your car."

100   "A camper is different," Bill said.

101   They walked around the campground. A lot of vehicles had motorcycles strapped onto them, and some people had already cranked up their motorcycles. The noise bothered Bill, but he liked to see the bikes take off, disappearing behind a swirl of dust.

102   Bill stopped to pet a friendly collie.

103   "That's Ishmael," said the girl who held the collie by a leash. "He's so friendly I never have any trouble meeting people. I meet lots of guys that way! People do that with dogs, you know?"

104   "You're a good boy," said Bill, patting the dog. "Nice boy."

105   Ishmael licked Bill's hand and then tried to sniff up Imogene's dress.

106   "Ishmael, don't be so obnoxious. He's always this friendly," the girl said apologetically. She had on a halter top and shorts. Her legs were smooth and brown, with golden hairs on her thighs.

107   "He loves dogs," said Imogene. "He can't stand to be without a dog. Or a cow or something! We sold all our cows and everything and here we are. Our whole farm's tied up in this." She waved at the camper.

108   "Wow, that's nice. That must have cost a fortune," the girl said, shading her eyes as she looked at the camper.

109   "Where are you headed?" Bill asked, with unusual politeness, which embarrassed him slightly.

110   "Oh, I was on the Coast, but it got to be a drag, so now I'm on my way to Atlanta, where I think I know this guy. I met him out in L.A. and he said if I was ever in Atlanta, to look him up. I hope he remembers me."

111   The girl said her name was Stephanie. Bill thought she might be college age. He wasn't sure. She looked very young to be traveling around alone. He thought of Sissy, his youngest daughter. Sissy had come home from San Francisco finally and had lived to tell the tale, though there was not much she would say about it.

112   "See, Ishmael is number one," Stephanie was saying. "If a guy can't take my dog, then I'm going to leave, right?" She looked up at Bill, as if for approval. Bill patted Ishmael, and the dog licked Bill's hand again.

113   "I got a ride with this guy who customizes rec-v's," Stephanie went on. She pointed to a beige van with designs of blue and red fish painted on the side. "See, people buy them stripped and he outfits them. He's supposed to be back any minute. He's checking out a deal." She looked around the campground. "See his license plate," she said. "KOOL-II. Isn't that cute? Here, look inside."

114   Bill and Imogene peered inside the van. It was lined with shag rug. In the back, crosswise, was a king-sized bed with a leopard-skin cover. The ceiling was shag carpeting too, white, with a red heart positioned above the bed.

115   "There's not a kitchen in it," said Imogene.

116   "Just a refrigerator, and a bar," said Stephanie. "Isn't it something? This interior just blows me away."

117   She let Ishmael inside the van and took his leash off. Ishmael hopped onto the bed and stretched his paws out. The bed seemed to ripple with the dog's movements.

118   "It's a water bed," Stephanie said with a laugh.

119   "We've been tied down on a farm all this time," said Imogene.

120   "We're going to travel around till we get it out of our system," said Bill, again feeling embarrassed to be telling the girl things about himself.

121   "That's really sweet," said Stephanie, pulling at her halter. "Wow, that's really sweet. Here I travel around and don't think anything about it, but I bet you've been waiting all these years!"

122   "You come and eat some supper with us," Imogene said. "You don't have a kitchen."

123   "Oh, no, thanks. I better wait for this guy. We were going to check out the McDonald's up on the highway. I'm sort of waiting around for him, see? Hey, thanks anyway."

124   Stephanie waved good-bye and wished them luck.

125   "We'll need it," said Imogene.

126   After supper Imogene and Bill sat in their folding chairs outside and watched the lights come on in the campers. It was still hot and they swatted at giant mosquitoes.

127   "I gave my antique preserve stand to Sissy," said Imogene. "She won't appreciate it."

128   Bill was quiet. He was listening to the sounds, the TV sets and radios all blending together. He watched a blond-headed boy enter the KOOL-II van.

129   "Can you just imagine the trouble that girl has been in?" said Imogene thoughtfully. "I believe she was one of those runaways they talk about."

130   "How do you know?"

131   "You never know, with people you meet, out."

132   Bill watched as the blond-headed boy emerged from the van and headed toward the shower building. Bill liked the way the boy walked, with his towel slung over his shoulder. He had hair like a girl's, and a short beard. The boy walked along so freely, as though he had nothing on his mind except that van with the red heart on the ceiling. Bill thought uncomfortably of how he had once promised Imogene that they would see the world, but they never had. He always knew it was a failure of courage. After the war he had rushed back home. He hated himself for the way he had stayed at home all that time.

133   Later, Imogene started crying. Bill was trying to watch *Charlie's Angels,* and he tried to pretend he didn't notice. In a few minutes she stopped. Then after a commercial she started again.

134   "Years ago," Imogene said, wiping her face, "when I took your mama to the doctor—when she had just moved in with us and I took her for a checkup?— I went in to talk to the doctor and he said to me, 'How are *you?*' and I said, 'I didn't come to see the doctor, I brought *her,*' and he said, 'I know, but how

are *you?'* He said to me, 'She'll kill you! I've seen it before, and she'll kill you. You think they won't be much trouble and it's best, but mark my words, you may not see it now, but she'll take it out of you. She could destroy you. You could end up being a wreck.' He said, 'Now I'm not a psychiatrist'—or whatever they call them—'but I've seen it too many times. I'm just warning you.' I read about this woman that lived with her son and daughter-in-law and lived to be a hundred and three! Nobody ought to live that long!"

135   "Are you finished?" Imogene had interrupted a particularly exciting scene in *Charlie's Angels.* Bill didn't say anything and the program finished. Imogene made him nervous, bringing up the past. If she was going to do that, they might as well have stayed at home. Bill didn't know what to say. Imogene got a washrag and wiped her face. Her face was puffed up and red.

136   "I've been working up to say all that, what I just said," she went on later. "I get these headaches and I've got this hurtin'. And I can't taste."

137   "It's all in your mind," said Bill, teasing her gently. "You've been listening to too many old women talk."

138   "I get all sulled up," Imogene said. "Just some little something will bring it on. It wouldn't matter if we were here or in China or Kalamazoo."

139   "You just have to have something to bellyache about," Bill said. He would have to try to humor her.

140   "She was *your* mama," Imogene continued. "And I'm the one that took care of her all that time, keeping her house, putting up her canning, putting out her wash, and then waiting on her when she got down. And you never lifted a finger. You couldn't be around old people, you said; it give you the heebie-jeebies. Well, listen, buster, your time's a-coming and who's going to wait on you? You can stick me in a rest home, for all I care. And another thing, you don't see Miz Lillian living at the White House."

141   Bill felt sick. "You would go to a rest home and leave me by myself?" he asked, with a little whine.

142   "I've a good mind to," she said. She measured an inch off her index finger. "I like about this much from it," she said.

143   "You wouldn't do me that way, would you? Who would cook?"

144   "You can eat junk."

145   "I bought you this pretty playhouse. You don't want to leave me in it all by myself, do you?" He tousled her hair. "You're not any fun anymore. Always got to tune up and cry over some little something."

146   "I can't help it." She put her head in a pillow. "Don't tease me."

147   Awkwardly, Bill put his arms around her.

148   "You don't make over me anymore," she said.

149   "You just wait till we get to the ocean," Bill said, petting her. He felt like a fool. The muscles in his arms were so rigid he thought they were going to pop. His mouth was dry.

150   That night Bill slept fitfully. He could not get used to a foam rubber mattress.

He had a nightmare in which his mother and Imogene sat in rocking chairs on either side of him, having a contest to see who could rock the longest. Bill's job was to keep score, but they kept on rocking. His kids gathered around, mocking him, wanting to know the score. The steady, swinging, endless rocking was making him feel seasick. He woke up almost crying out, but awake he could not understand why the rocking chairs frightened him so. He told himself he was an idiot and eventually he calmed himself down by thinking pleasant thoughts about Stephanie and the blond-headed boy. He imagined what they were doing in the van with the red heart on the ceiling. Later, he dreamed that he had a job driving a van across the country. He wore a uniform, with a cowboy hat that said KOOL-II on the front. He drove the van at top speed and when he got to the ocean he boarded a ferry, which turned out to be a destroyer. The destroyer zoomed across the ocean. Imogene did not show up in the dream at all.

151   When he woke up he looked at her sleeping, with her mouth open and a soft little snore coming out. He recalled the time in the Andrew Jackson Hotel in Nashville when he watched her sleep for a full hour, wanting to remember her face while he was overseas. Then she had awakened, saying, "I knew somebody was watching me. I dreamed it. You liked to stared a hole through me." They had not been married long, and they had stayed awake most of the night, holding each other.

152   Now Imogene's face was fat and lined, but he could still see her young face clearly. Her hair was gray and cut in short, curly layers. Each curl was distinctly separate, like the coils of a new pad of steel wool.

153   Bill bent down close to her and bellowed, "Rise and shine!" Then he sang, "You're an angel, lighting up the morning." Imogene woke up and glared at him.

154   "I can't wait to show you the ocean," said Bill. He pulled on his clothes and slapped his cap on his head. He looked out the window to see if KOOL-II had left. He had.

155   "KOOL-II's done gone," Bill said.

156   "She was a nice girl," said Imogene, getting up. "But taking up with that boy like that, I just don't know. There's so much meanness going on."

157   She put water and bacon strips on the stove and started dressing. Bill turned on the portable television. The *Today* show was in Minnesota. Jane Pauley was having breakfast with a farmer, who said that in fact it *was* possible to make a living as a dairy farmer these days.

158   "You have to like cows first," he said. He said he didn't name his cows anymore. He gave them numbers, "like social security numbers," the man said, laughing.

159   "How could you keep a cow without a name?" asked Bill. "How would you talk to it?"

160   "He's a big-dude farmer," said Imogene. "He couldn't remember all their names, he's got so many."

161   The farmer's wife claimed she was not a working wife, but Jane Pauley pointed out that the woman worked all the time making butter and cheese, dressing chickens, raising children, and so forth.

162   "That's fun work," she replied.

163   "If it don't kill you," said Imogene.

164   One of the farmer's seven children said he would be going to college. This day and age you had to be a businessman to be in agriculture. There was a lot his father couldn't teach him about the farm.

165   "Can you see us on TV, having breakfast and talking?" asked Imogene.

166   "Shoot," said Bill. "I'd be embarrassed to death. I'd go crawl in a hole."

167   The show switched to the original *Little House on the Prarie,* also in Minnesota. Tom Brokaw was interviewing Mike Landon. Mike Landon was telling how back then everybody lived mainly in one small room and they were forced to live together, to cooperate, to work together. You couldn't hide. Nowadays a kid could be off in his room and have a drug problem for six months and nobody would know. That couldn't have happened in the nineteenth century, Mike Landon said.

168   "Bet he lives in a mansion," said Bill, who was pacing the floor. "How does he explain that?"

169   Mike Landon said it didn't depend on the number of rooms, as long as you can communicate. His kids don't watch TV during the week, he said, except for *Little House on the Prairie.* "Or I give them a beating!" He laughed.

170   Bill grew more and more restless as they drove down into Florida. He kept an eye on the left side of the horizon so that he could catch that first glimpse of the ocean. He was afraid it might appear any second and he might miss it. He hardly noticed the changing terrain and the tourist signs.

171   "I thought I saw orange trees," Imogene said.

172   Imogene had stopped flinching every time a car passed, and she seemed to be in a better mood, Bill thought.

173   "I can't wait to show you the ocean," he said for the tenth time.

174   "Some folks is happy just to stay home," she said. "But that farmer on television—he had money. He could retire to Florida and still have something to show for all his years."

175   After bypassing Jacksonville, Bill headed for a campground. He still could not see the ocean.

176   "Whoa!" cried Imogene suddenly. "What's the matter with you? You scared the wadding out of me. You nearly run into that truck."

177   "That truck was half a mile down the road! Keep your britches on. We're almost there."

178   As they drove into the campground, which had a swimming pool but no trees, Imogene said, "You can tell this is Florida. Old folks everywhere."

179   Bill liked it better at the other places, with the dogs and the younger people. He didn't see any dogs here. They passed a man struggling along on a metal walker.

180   "I hope we don't get like that," said Imogene.

181   After selecting and paying for their parking place, they drove to the ocean, a couple of miles away. Bill's first sight of it was like something seen through a keyhole. Then it grew larger and larger.

182   "Is this what you brought me here to see?" said Imogene, as they examined the Atlantic from their high perches in the camper. "It all looks the same."

183   Bill was silent as they got out and locked the van. He dropped his keys in the sand, he was so nervous. They walked down a narrow pathway to the beach, and Bill kept wanting to break into a run, but Imogene was too slow. They walked down the beach together, now and then stopping while Bill faced the ocean. He kept his arm around Imogene's waist, in case she stumbled in the sand. She had on her straw wedgies.

184   Bill stopped her then and they stood still for a long while. Bill's eyes roved over the rolling sea. It was the same water, carried around by time, that he had sailed, but it was bluer than he remembered. He remembered the feeling of looking out over that expanse, fearing the sound of the Japanese planes, taking comfort at the sight of the big battleship and its family of destroyers. He had seen a kamikaze dive into a destroyer. The explosion was like a silent movie that played in his head endlessly, like reruns of *McHale's Navy.*

185   "How long will you be?" asked Imogene. "I need to find me some shade."

186   "I'll be along directly," said Bill, gazing out at battleships and destroyers riding on the horizon. He could not tell if they were coming or going, or whose they were.

☐ Discovering Meaning and Technique

1. Imogene's character is developed through her habits: enumerating wrecks, cooking, fearing diseases and accidents, not reading. What kind of person is she?

2. How did Bill get the money to buy the luxury-model camper-cruiser?

3. What are some of the things Bill and Imogene have lost by going on the road?

4. When does this story take place? How do you know?

5. What is the significance of the episode at the campground with Ishmael, Stephanie, and the "guy who customizes rec-v's" (paragraphs 102–32)? Of the episode with Jane Pauley's and Tom Brokaw's interviews (paragraphs 157–169)?

6. After Bill thinks of his failed promise to "see the world," we are told, "He always knew it was a failure of courage" (paragraph 132). Explain this statement.

7. Explain how the language Bill and Imogene use reveals their background.

8. What could be the meaning of Bill's dreams about the rocking-chair contest and his job driving a van (paragraph 150)?

9. Explain the possible meaning of the ending,

☐ Writing Suggestions

1. Move from the quotation "Driving the fancy camper made Bill feel like a big shot" to a discussion of how the cost of a vehicle affects a driver's self-image.

2. What is the appeal and/or drawback of travel in a recreational vehicle?

3. Describe life at a campground.

4. There was not much to enjoy in Plains, Georgia. Imogene says at the end of the visit, "I can say I've been here anyway." How much traveling is done so that people can say they have been to some famous place?

5. Write a story about a journey from home to some idealized place by train, bus, motorbike, bicycle, on horseback or foot.

6. Write about the conflict between home and strange places, between security and adventure.

Sports

■ ■ ■

GREG PRATT IS DEAD

☐ **RHETA GRIMSLEY JOHNSON**

1 It is all around, the Sunday morning rubble from the Saturday afternoon carnage. Pop tops and potato chip bags. Enough cans to see a roadside aluminum prospector through retirement.

2 Once again it has seduced me, this game of college football. It has thrown me across my own couch and had its way. Again, I have been suckered into believing the ol' alma mater, Auburn University, plays for me and me alone. Those knights carry my colors, my prestige and honor across a field mined with muscle.

3 That Greg Pratt fell dead as Auburn's football fortunes were rising and its season coming alive has bothered but not deterred me. My mind has been experiencing temporary technical difficulties; stay tuned and the interference will fade.

4 Here, beneath the empty cellophane sacks and mutilated snacks, is a reprieve. A copy of the coroner's report. The same thing could have happened to Pratt if he'd been cutting grass. That's what it says.

5 The official line, the final word to expunge the record of both a state institution and a national preoccupation. It's what Lee County Coroner Jon Williams discovered about the heatstroke that killed the fullback from Albany, Georgia. "That it happened during a football physical (workout) is purely coincidental," Williams wrote.

6 The August heat, the series of 440 sprints and Pratt's history of heat-related problems brushed neatly aside, perhaps it could have happened anytime, anywhere.

7 Moment of silence. Play ball.

8 Pratt's funeral delayed practice one day, but any fool believing his death might stop for one moment the actual game is as green as new Astroturf. After all, injuries are a part of the game. They are tallied and assessed and moaned about on the Sunday-after. And a player who "stays hurt" is about as popular as one who fumbles.

9 There is money in college football, and fun and prestige are mere afterthoughts. Coaches coach to make it. Players play for tuition or their own profes-

sional prospects. The Auburn Alumni Association recently purchased Pat Dye's $412,000 house from a Montgomery bank and will grant Dye the title if he stays at Auburn 14 more years. All he has to do is stay and win.

10   If college athletes and coaches were in it just for the fine fellowship, they'd all join the astronomy club.

11   A couple of lonely voices were raised in protest lately, politely suggesting that not enough questions had been asked about young Pratt's death. Two Auburn alumni, John E. Martin and John A. Fairbank, penned a letter to the college newspaper and dared to prick conscience.

12   "Why, we ask on the first day of practice, during one of the hottest, most humid days of the summer, was a talented young man with a clear history of exercise-related heat problems pushed beyond his physical capacity to endure? He apparently was having such difficulty completing the grueling series of sprints that two coaches had to run alongside him, according to the reports we read."

13   The two men also begged members of Auburn's coaching staff to say they didn't say they hoped the Pratt tragedy wouldn't affect their team's performance. "Please tell us that we are not that callous and self-serving, that this was a misquote."

14   Coaches who coddle are not in demand. Their contracts, not their mortgages, are bought up in short order and alumni help pack the bags. Cowering in the face of adversity is not part of The Code. You don't scratch a practice because of, for heaven's sakes, humidity. In the best circles, and in the most awesome conferences, it simply is not done.

15   Memphis Showboats Coach Pepper Rodgers stayed in trouble with Georgia Tech alumni, because he made the mistake of treating college football as a game. His boys roomed where they liked, not in a single athletic dormitory, and went to the playing field to have a good time. And they had a good time but didn't win enough games. So Tech got a new coach.

16   There will be no good answers to the questions Martin and Fairbank raised. We don't want them. Besides, the "official" investigation is complete. Greg Pratt is dead. College football is not.

17   All because of fans like me.

☐ Discovering Meaning and Technique

1. What is Johnson's attitude toward football and the death of Gregg Pratt?

2. What is the attitude of the coaches toward football?

3. Why does Johnson bring up the subject of Coach Pepper Rodgers?

4. How effective are the introduction and conclusion?

5. Locate examples of Johnson's frequent use of sentence fragments. Are these effective?

6. All of Johnson's paragraphs are short—some only a single sentence. What is the effect?

☐ Writing Suggestions

1. Is football as safe as it could be?

2. Johnson writes, "There is money in college football, and fun and prestige are mere afterthoughts." Support or refute this statement.

3. Find a letter to a newspaper or magazine and use it as the basis for a composition.

4. Discuss the tendency of fans to overlook the violence of sports.

BASEBALL'S HITS AND MISSES

☐ LEONARD KOPPETT

1 Baseball fans have witnessed many developments in their game of choice during the 40 years since the end of World War II, some favorable, some not so. In my opinion, the three worst have been:

1. Artificial turf.
2. Expansion.
3. The evisceration of the minor league system.

The three best developments have been:

1. The television camera.
2. The playoffs.
3. The return of the stolen base.

2   It is also my opinion that, unfortunately for fans, the worst far outweigh the best.

3   Before zeroing in on these developments, I should begin by making the following four assumptions:

4   First, fans dislike change. One of baseball's greatest assets is continuity. If a time machine whisked you back, say, to the 1912 World Series between the New York Giants and the Boston Red Sox, you would have no trouble following the game. All the basic rules and techniques would be the same as they are now. But a 1912 football or basketball or hockey game would mystify anyone who knew only today's rules and styles.

5   Second, fans like action they can see, which means scoring. A steady diet of 9–7 games with 20 or more hits and the lead changing hands a few times is more enjoyable than a steady diet of 2–1 games, as tense and artistic as these may seem to the professionals involved.

6   Next, fans like identifiable heroes and exceptional performances. The sports industry pays lip service to "parity" these days, which means spreading victory around to as many markets as possible, but the price of parity is the absence of champions who fire the imagination the way the old New York Yankees, Green Bay Packers, Joe Louis, Muhammad Ali and Arnold Palmer did.

7   And finally, every fan has a personal Golden Age, coinciding roughly with the first decade of that person's interest in baseball, whether it starts at the age of 6 or 26. That era, for that individual, sets the norm to which everything afterward is related.

8   For me, that was the decade of the 1930's. But after some 35 years of being paid to watch and report baseball for daily newspapers, mostly in New York, and interacting with those who make their living playing or promoting the game, I've gotten too close to things ordinary fans have no access to. So I no longer qualify as an unadulterated fan and it would be presumptuous to speak as one. On the other hand, all my training, inclination, job requirements and accumulated data have centered on the question, "What does the fan want to know about what happened?" So I don't share the myopia of those who live entirely within the baseball community. I can identify fan concerns with no ax to grind.

9   All that said, here are my reasons:

10   ARTIFICIAL TURF: This hard, smooth homogeneous surface distorts the basic principles of the game: hitting, pitching and fielding. A fundamental esthetic is altered as well: Because of the way artificial turf makes a baseball bounce, the game often looks as if it's being played with a tennis ball.

11   We think of pitchers as trying to get "outs" and hitters as trying to get "hits." Of course. But outs and hits are consequences of more basic conscious intentions.

12   A pitcher actually tries to accomplish two things. He wants to upset the batter's timing, so that he can't hit the ball squarely. And, according to the game situation, he wants to induce the batter to hit either a fly ball or a grounder.

13   A hitter can do nothing more than try to hit the ball hard. He can control its direction to some degree, but he must still hit the ball sharply enough to get it by a fielder.

14   Traditionally, hitters have wanted line drives and long drives that enable them and base runners to advance more than one base, and pitchers want grounders most of the time. On natural grass, each bounce takes some steam out of a batted ball. Under ordinary conditions, the four infielders and three outfielders can cover the gaps and field balls that aren't hit too sharply, while the offense benefits from balls hit very sharply and very far.

15   But artificial turf spoils all the formulas and ruins the rhythm of the game, especially in the outfield. A soft fly—in a sense, a victory for the pitcher—that falls in front of an in-rushing outfielder may well bounce over his head. And a modest line drive (or even a grounder) into an outfield gap cannot be cut off before it skids to the fence. To compensate, outfielders must play deeper and come in more cautiously, making the gaps between them even wider. At the same time, though infielders can play deeper—since a bouncing ball reaches them a little sooner, leaving them a bit more time to throw to first—grounders still scoot by them more quickly than they do on natural grass.

16   The result is more "undeserved" hits, particularly extra-base hits—and a much less attractive game to the spectator's eye. Artificial turf decreases the possibility of the most elegant plays, when fielders move laterally to intercept the ball and throw to a base for a close play.

17   The surface is enough like a running track to enhance running speed, so fleet outfielders can reach just about any long drive that doesn't hit or clear a fence. But the difficult shoestring catch has become a bad gamble. So we see countless two-base hits on grounders past the second baseman, or pop-fly triples that bounce away, and fewer "authentic" doubles and triples hit over outfielders' heads or out of their reach in the alleys.

18   If all baseball were played on artificial turf, we would simply adapt to the new parameters. But only 10 of the 26 major league parks have it—enough to make everyone deal with it, not enough to create a new norm. And, of course, in all the habit-forming years from Little League through the minors, players hone their reflexes on natural fields.

19   EXPANSION: The usual argument against expansion is that it "dilutes" playing talent. This is true but misleading. It is not true that there aren't enough "good" players to go around. Players with enough natural ability to reach the majors improve with the chance to play regularly. The player who would have been on the bench or in the minors behind someone slightly better in the old days now may surpass his original rival after developing on another team.

20   What *is* true is that, by definition, the best 400 players, when there were 16 teams, formed a higher density of excellence than the best 650 players on today's 26 teams.

21   More teams mean basic changes in statistics and schedule. Statistics are a key feature of baseball enjoyment, more so than statistics in other sports, and they became embedded in well-known regularities that existed, roughly, from 1903 to 1960. The 154-game schedule, in each league, had every team playing

every other team 22 times. Such milestones as 20 victories for a pitcher or 100 runs batted in for a hitter acquired their significance in that context; but, more important, the frequency and uniformity of matchups among the teams in a league enhanced the "breaks-even-up-over-time" concept that adds to the validity of statistics.

22   In 1961, the year the American League expanded to 10 teams, the schedule had to be increased to 162 games (with each team meeting each opponent 18 times). And a celebrated flap arose right away, when Roger Maris and Mickey Mantle launched an assault on Babe Ruth's record of 60 homers, set in 1927. Commissioner Ford Frick, once a close friend of Ruth's, declared that a new record "wouldn't count" unless it was accomplished in 154 games—an emotion-driven, illogical, unjustifiable restriction that would poison Maris's achievement of hitting 61, and would make "asterisks" into confusing addenda to all of baseball's record-keeping. The issue had real emotional force, and after leagues were broken into divisions, and more teams produced more players who did not face opponents an equal number of times, many statistics lost their power to excite.

23   Also weakened has been the fan's capability for attention. In the 16-team days, true fans knew the regular players on all teams, their records and characteristics of their play. Not only were there far fewer players, but each team came to town more often. Now, with 26 teams in action and other sports having gained in both media attention and viewer interest, and with an Oakland coming to New York for only two series three months apart, no fan can keep up with all the players. This increases home-team-only rooting, intensifying partisanship, but attenuating fan involvement in baseball as a whole.

24   Expansion, of course, benefits fans in cities with new teams. But it does so at the expense of the potential enjoyment of the game by those who had local teams in the old setup, and by the millions who don't live in any major league city but follow the game passionately with free choice of favorites.

25   In an eight-team league, 10 superstars (in fan perception, aside from statistics) may well be scattered among six teams; in a 14-team league, more than half the teams are likely to be without a superstar.

26   And too, more sparsely sprinkled talent means that offense suffers. With fewer teams, more good hitters are concentrated in any one batting order, and they "protect" each other. But when a batting order has only one or two outstanding hitters in it, the opposition pitches around them and gives them less opportunity to do damage. It wasn't a coincidence that when Maris hit 61 homers, Mantle (with 54) was hitting behind him, or that Lou Gehrig was on deck when Ruth came to bat.

27   THE MINORS: It used to take several years of minor league seasoning to produce a major leaguer, and the proportion of top-level minor to major league teams was about 2 to 1. Now the proportion is 1 to 1, and every minor league system is strictly a developmental device for the majors, arousing little local interest.

28   Why does this concern the major league fan? Because the present system tends to depress offense and retard the development of hitting stars. Pitchers can, by and large, perfect their craft by practicing their deliveries; hitters can become good hitters only by honing their reflexes against good pitchers. A young hitter with natural talent can be ruined if he is overmatched too early, i.e., by bringing him to the majors; but he will stagnate at a certain level if the minor leaguers he faces aren't good enough to keep testing him.

29   In the old days, the high minors had many experienced pitchers who had been in the majors or would have been there if there had been 26 pitching staffs instead of 16. Young hitters faced them for a couple of years, and either improved or dropped out. Today, minor league rosters consist only of promising youngsters and temporary major league convalescents, with only a few marginals—who are marginal in the context of 26, not 16, teams. Today, potentially talented hitters get minimum minor league experience and rapid promotion to the majors. The best do well enough, but not as many develop to their highest potential as did in the days of the strong minor leagues.

30   O.K., those are the worst developments. Now what about the best?

31   THE TELEVISION CAMERA: Thanks to television, fans like my son, who was born in 1967, see more major league baseball and hear more sophisticated discussion of it before the age of 12 than I was exposed to by the time I was 30.

32   Television's greatest gift to baseball is the camera angle that lets fans see the pitcher-hitter battle as it really takes place.

33   This, after all, is the whole ball game. It takes exceptionally sharp and well-trained vision to judge the speed and path of a thrown baseball. Managers learn to do it from the dugout, and professional scouts operate behind home plate or in a press box. But how many people sitting in the stands can really pick out the fine, individual qualities of a pitched ball, aside from noting that it is too high, in the dirt, or wild? Fans react to the umpire's signal, the batter's and catcher's movements, and the flight of the batted ball, but they don't really "see" pitching.

34   On television they do, and with slow-motion replays no less. Fans see it from the catcher-umpire angle sometimes, from the pitcher's angle sometimes, but with center-of-the-screen clarity always.

35   That alone is blessing enough. But when you add to it close-ups of facial expressions, split screens of base runners taking leads, replays of long hits and funny bounces and spectacular catches—well, television has opened up the richness of baseball details to all fans in a way that only a few professionals actually on the field used to know.

36   THE PLAYOFFS: Purists scoff at playoffs, but if you think you'd be fascinated watching teams battle for 11th place in late August, or just playing out the string in September, think again. Breaking up leagues into divisions has its drawbacks, as we've seen, but it is the only sensible solution to too many teams. The same forces that created a World Series between two league champions operate to create and hold interest in preliminary rounds. Four "pennant races,"

whatever their quality, are better than two of the same quality. And the kind of excitement a one-survivor playoff series generates is not obtainable any other way.

37   THE STOLEN BASE: When Babe Ruth proved what home runs could do, a whole baseball generation converted itself to long-ball thinking. In the process, the attempt to steal a base, a basic scoring weapon before the 1920's, was put aside as a poor risk. The homer or double will score a man from first; a man thrown out stealing won't score when the next man hits a homer, and that out will decrease the number of times the home-run hitters get to bat.

38   The stand-around-and-wait-for-a-homer style, which prevailed through the 1940's and 1950's, promoted unwanted byproducts: strikeouts and walks. Hitters, swinging from the heels, didn't mind striking out if they connected a few other times. Pitchers, fearing the homer, stayed out of the strike zone.

39   But fans want to see the batted ball in play. Walks and strikeouts are stop-action plays. By the late 1960's, as factors such as the increasingly effective use of relief pitchers made homers harder to hit, stop-action reached a peak. In 1968, when scoring slumped to a low of 6.8 runs a game (by both teams), about 25 percent of all the players coming to bat walked or struck out—no action one-fourth of the time.

40   Beginning around 1960, Maury Wills of the Los Angeles Dodgers and Luis Aparicio of the Chicago White Sox initiated a base-stealing revolution. In the last 25 years, after standing pat for more than four decades, the record for stolen bases in a season has been broken three times, by Wills, by Lou Brock, and finally by Rickey Henderson, who stole 130 for the Oakland A's in 1982. And as a result, many managers have plugged stealing back into their strategies. The threat of a steal worries the pitcher and affects what he throws. It makes infielders move around and affects defensive strategy. Willingness to steal means that the walk ceases to be a stop-action play; it is now perceived as the prelude to a steal attempt.

41   If you went to 10 games in 1958, you saw, on the average, 86 runs scored, 18 home runs and 6 stolen bases. In 1985, you saw 87 runs scored, 17 home runs and 15 stolen bases. In other words, we haven't lost any of the pleasures of power or production, but we're seeing more action.

42 Needless to say, there have been other developments that have affected the fan, many of them well-publicized. There is the recent outrage, for example, over drug use by players, and other factors that have served to alienate the fan from the game: ever-escalating ticket prices; exorbitant player salaries; two players strikes and one umpire strike during the 1980's; the uncertain economics of many franchises; and rowdyism in the stands. But drug abuse, price inflation, labor strife, bad behavior and selfishness are not peculiar to baseball, and as well they're concerns that are tangential to the actual playing of the game, operating outside the baselines.

43   So what about the ones I've cited? Has the game itself improved for the

fan? Is the effect of the bad balanced by the good? I would say no. Artificial turf and expansion have caused far more damage to the game than television and playoff excitement can compensate for. Fortunately, it hasn't been enough to spoil the special pleasures baseball affords, as constantly rising attendance and impassioned literary expressions continue to prove. But is baseball somewhat less fun than it used to be? Alas, yes.

44   And this raises another question, for each reader to answer alone: what isn't?

☐ Discovering Meaning and Technique

1. Do you agree with Koppett's four assumptions?

2. Koppett argues to prove the three worst developments and the three best. Is each of the six arguments effective? Why or why not?

3. Why does Koppett devote more space to the worst developments in baseball than to the best?

4. The structure of this selection is carefully delineated. What devices does Koppett use to make the structure completely clear?

5. How many paragraphs do you think constitute the conclusion?

6. Koppett tells us that he has been a newspaperman for about thirty-five years. Are there any stylistic characteristics in this selection that derive from journalism?

7. Does Koppett use baseball jargon, or does he use nonexpert language that anyone can understand?

☐ Writing Suggestions

1. Discuss change in sports. According to Koppett, baseball has changed little over time, but football, basketball, and hockey have changed a lot. Do you agree?

2. Write a similar composition on the "hits and misses" in some sport other than baseball.

3. Are all sports equally effective when seen on television? Or do some sports lend themselves to the television screen better than others?

4. Discuss artificial turf and football.

5. As Koppett writes at the conclusion, "There have been other developments that have affected the fan, many of them well-publicized." Discuss one or several of these developments.

BASKETBALL: THE PUREST SPORT OF BODIES

☐ **DONALD HALL**

1 Professional basketball combines opposites—elegant gymnastics, ferocious ballet, gargantuan delicacy, colossal precision. . . . It is a continuous violent dream of levitating hulks. It is twist and turn, leap and fly, turn and counterturn, flick and respond, confront and evade. It is monstrous, or would be monstrous if it were not witty.

2   These athletes show wit in their bodies. Watching their abrupt speed, their instant reversals of direction, I think of minnows in the pond—how the small schools slide swiftly in one direction, then reverse-flip and flash the opposite way. NBA players are quick as minnows, and with an adjustment for size great whales drive down the road. As a ball careens from a rim, huge bodies leap with legs outspread; then two high hands grasp the ball, propel it *instantly* downcourt to a sprinting guard, and *instantly* seven to ten enormous bodies spin and sprint on the wooden floor, pass, dribble, pass, pass, shoot—block or whoosh. . . .

3   Then the same bodies flip-flash back to the place they just departed from, fast as an LED display from a punched button—an intricate thrashing, a mercury-sudden pack of leviathans. . . .

4 In all sport, nothing requires more of a body than NBA basketball; nothing so much uses—and celebrates—bodily improvisation, invention, and imagination.

5   In football they measure forty-yard sprints. Nobody runs forty yards in basketball. Maybe you run the ninety-four feet of the court but more likely you sprint ten feet; then you stop, not on a dime, but on Miss Liberty's torch. In football you run over somebody's face.

6 When I was growing up, the winter sport was hockey. At high school, hundreds of us would stand outside at 0 degrees Fahrenheit beside a white rink puffing out white air, stamping our painful feet, our toes like frozen fishsticks. On the ice, unhelmeted shoulder-padded thick-socked blocky young men swept up and down, wedded to the moves of a black hard-rubber disk and crushing each other into boards, fighting, crashing, shooting, fighting again. Then we tromped

home to unfreeze by the hot-water radiators, red-cheeked and exhausted with cold, exhilarated with pain and crowd-fight.

7   But basketball was a sweaty half-empty gym on a Friday afternoon, pale white legs clomping down court below billowing gym shorts; it was the two-handed set shot: pause, arch, aim, *grunt.* In the superheated dim gymnasium, twenty-seven friends and relatives watched the desultory to-and-fro of short, slow, awkward players who were eternally pulling up twelve feet from the basket to clatter a heavy brown beachball harmlessly off a white backboard. Always we lost thirty-eight to nineteen.

8   It was a hockey town, and New England was hockey country.

9   Meantime, elsewhere—in city parks, in crepuscular gymnasiums after school with the heat turned off, or in Indiana farmyards with a basket nailed to the side of a barn—other children practiced other motions . . . and the best of these motions found their showcase, over the decades and for decades ahead, in New England's metropolis, in the leaky old ship of Boston Garden.

10 When I was at college, I took the subway to Boston to watch college double-headers. My Harvard team was better than the high school I went to . . . but I do not recollect that we were invited to the NIT. I watched Harvard, Boston College, Boston University—and Holy Cross. Of course I remember the astonishment of one young man's innovations: the infant Robert Cousy, who played for Holy Cross, dribbled behind his back and passed with perfect swift accuracy in a direction opposite the place toward which he gazed. Or he faked a pass, put the ball to the floor, and cut past bewildered defenders for an easy and graceful layup. As far as I am concerned, it was Robert Cousy, and not Colonel Naismith, who invented basketball.

11 One of the extraordinary qualities of basketball is its suddenness of change, in pace and in momentum.

12   Years ago, when I lived in Michigan, I frequented Cobo Hall when the Detroit Pistons played there. I watched good players on bad teams: great Bob Lanier, Big-Foot with bad knees, enormous and delicate and always hurt; Dave Bing and Chris Ford, who ended their careers with the Celtics. Once I took my young son to see the Detroit Pistons play the Boston Celtics in a play-off game. It was 1968, the first time the poor Pistons made the play-offs. It was Bill Russell's next-to-last year as player-coach of the Celtics; they went on to beat the Lakers for the championship.

13   I sat with my boy and his friend David, who was a Celtics fan because he had lived in Boston until he was eight months old, and watched three periods of desultory play. There were good moments from Bing and Lanier, good moments from Havlicek and White—my man Cousy retired in 1963—but Bill Russell looked half asleep even as he blocked shots. In the fourth quarter the Pistons, astonishingly, led—and I entertained notions of an upset. . . .

14   Then my small charges developed a desire for hot dogs; I dashed out for a few minutes, and as I returned laden, I heard a swelling of wistful applause from the knowledgeable Cobo crowd. I looked toward the floor to see Bill Russell floating through the air to sink a basket. In the space of two hot dogs, Boston had gone up by ten points—or rather, not Boston but the usually inoffensive Russell. He had waked up—and when Russell opened his eyes it was over for Detroit. . . .

15   "Momentum" is a cliché of the football field, but it is a habit of the wooden floor. Basketball is a game not so much of important baskets or of special plays as of violent pendulum swings. One team or another is always on a run, like a madcap gambler throwing a dozen sevens. When the Celtics are down by a dozen points in the second quarter, looking listless, hapless, helpless, we know that suddenly they can become energized—rag dolls wired with springy, reactive power. We know that twelve points down can be six points up with a crazy suddenness.

16   Sometimes one player does it all by himself. On a night when Cedric Maxwell has twelve thumbs and Kevin McHale three knees, when every pass hits vacant air, when the four-shooter clanks it off the rim, suddenly Larry Bird (usually it is Larry Bird) grows five inches taller and five seconds faster. With legs outspread he leaps above the rim to take a rebound, pivots, and throws a fastball the length of the court to Gerald Henderson who lays it up. Then as the Knicks (or the Bulls, or the Bullets . . .) go into their half-court offense, he appears to fall asleep. His slack jaw sags and he does his Idiot Thing . . . only to swoop around a guard and steal the ball cleanly, like plucking a sheep-tick off a big dog, then sprint down court and float a layup. Then he steals the inbound pass and, as the power-forward fouls him, falls heavily to the floor; only while he falls, he loops the ball up with his left hand over a high head into the basket— an *impossible* three-point play. The he fast-breaks with Maxwell and Parish, zapping the ball back and forth, and leaps as if to shoot over an immense center. But, looking straight at the basket, he passes the ball blind to Robert Parish on his left, who stuffs it behind the center's head. . . .

17   We have just run off nine points.

18   This is a game you can study on television because it is small enough to fit in the box; and through television's slow-motion replay, we study at our leisure the learned body's performances—as when Dr. J. or George Gervin soars from the base line, ball in the right hand, appears to shoot, pauses in midair, and, when a shot-blocker hovers beside him, transfers the ball to the left hand, twists the body, and stuffs the ball through the hoop.

19   It is only two points. If this were gymnastics or diving from the high board at the Olympics, it would be *ten* points.

20 The Celtics play team ball, passing, seeking the open man when defenders double-team Bird or Parish. The ball moves so rapidly, it is like a pinball machine in which the steel ball gathers speed as it bounces off springs, rioting up and out, down and across. Zany ball, with its own wild life, always like the rabbit seeking its hole.

Or.

The Game.

Slows.

Down.

21   Despite the twenty-four-second clock, there are passages of sheer stasis. The point guard bounces the ball: once, twice, three times. The guard in front of him is all alert nerves, arms spread and quivering. Will he drive right? Left?

Bounce.

Bounce . . .

Bounce. . . . . .

22   He goes right NO-he-only-seemed-to-go-right-he-is-left-around-his-man, he rises into the *air* and . . . blocked-by-a-giant-under-hands-to-his-own-giant . . . who backward-stuffs it. BANG.

23 Oh, my. Basketball is the purest sport of bodies.

☐ Discovering Meaning and Technique

1. Explain what Hall means by "then you stop, not on a dime, but on Miss Liberty's torch" (paragraph 5).

2. Identify the flashbacks and explain why you think Hall inserted them.

3. Summarize why Hall insists, "Basketball is the purest sport of bodies."

4. Would the thesis (the last sentence) be more effective as the first sentence?

5. In the introduction, how does Hall develop his statement that "professional basketball combines opposites"?

6. Hall makes several comparisons—for example, of NBA players and minnows. Find other comparisons and discuss their effectiveness.

7. Why do you think Hall frequently uses ellipses (a series of periods) in this selection?

8. Hall often lists a series of words to enhance the vividness of a description. Locate the series and identify them as adjectives, verbs, or some other construction.

9. Find passages that seem to capture the different paces in a basketball game.

☐ Writing Suggestions

1. Contrast a professional game with one played by amateurs.

2. Compare two sports. Include such aspects as the pace, the physical requirements, and the amount of equipment needed.

3. Describe several brilliant athletic performances that would rate ten points on a scale from one to ten.

ON BOXING AND PAIN

☐ JOYCE CAROL OATES

1 Years ago in the early 1950s when my father first took me to a Golden Gloves boxing tournament in Buffalo, New York, I asked him why the boys wanted to fight one another, why they were willing to get hurt. As if it were an explanation my father said, "Boxers don't feel pain quite the way we do."

2   Pain, in the proper context, is something other than pain.

3   Consider: Gene Tunney's single defeat in a thirteen-year career of great distinction was to a notorious fighter named Harry Greb who seems to have been, judging from boxing lore, the dirtiest fighter in history. Greb was infamous for his fouls—low blows, butting, "holding and hitting," rubbing his laces against an opponent's eyes, routine thumbing—as well as for a frenzied boxing style in which blows were thrown from all directions. (Hence, "The Human Windmill.") Greb, who died young, was a world middleweight champion for three years but a flamboyant presence in boxing circles for a long time. After the first of his several fights with Greb the twenty-two-year-old Tunney was so badly hurt he had to spend a week in bed; he'd lost an astonishing two quarts of blood during the fifteen-round fight. Yet, as Tunney said some years later:

> Greb gave me a terrible whipping. He broke my nose, maybe with a butt. He cut my eyes and ears, perhaps with his laces . . . My jaw was swollen from the right temple down the cheek, along under the chin and partway up the other side. The referee, the ring itself, was full of blood . . . But it was in that first fight, in which I lost my American light-heavyweight title, that I knew I had found a way to beat

Harry eventually. I was fortunate, really. If boxing in those days had been afflicted with the Commission doctors we have today—who are always poking their noses into the ring and examining superficial wounds—the first fight with Greb would have been stopped before I learned how to beat him. It's possible, even probable, that if this had happened I would never have been heard of again.

Tunney's career, in other words, was built upon pain. Without it he would never have moved up into Dempsey's class.

4   Tommy Loughran, light-heavyweight champion in the years 1927–29, was a master boxer greatly admired by other boxers. He approached boxing literally as a science—as Tunney did—studying his opponents' styles and mapping out ring strategy for each fight, as boxers and their trainers commonly do today. Loughran rigged up mirrors in his basement so that he could watch himself as he worked out, for, as he said, no boxer ever sees himself quite as he appears to his opponent. He sees the opponent but not himself as an opponent. The secret of Loughran's career was that his right hand broke easily so that he was forced to use it only once each fight: for the knockout punch or nothing. "I'd get one shot then the agony of the thing would hurt me if the guy got up," Loughran said. "Anybody I ever hit with a left hook I knocked flat on his face, but I would never take a chance for fear if my [left hand] goes, I'm done for."

5   Both Tunney and Loughran, it is instructive to note, retired from boxing well before they were forced to retire. Tunney became a highly successful businessman, and Loughran a highly successful sugar broker on the Wall Street commodities market. (Just to suggest that boxers are not invariably stupid, illiterate, or punch-drunk.)

6   Then there was Carmen Basilio!—much loved for his audacious ring style, his hit-and-be-hit approach. Basilio was world middle- and welterweight champion 1953–57, stoic, determined, a slugger willing to get hit in order to deal powerful counter-punches of his own. Onlookers marveled at the punishment Basilio seemed to absorb though Basilio insisted that he didn't get hit the way people believed. And when he was hit, and hit hard—

> People don't realize how you're affected by a knockout punch when you're hit on the chin. It's nerves is all it is. There's no real concussion as far as the brain is concerned. I got hit on the point of the chin [in a match with Tony DeMarco in 1955]. It was a left hook that hit the right point of my chin. What happens is it pulls your jawbone out of your socket from the right side and jams it into the left side and the nerve there paralyzed the whole left side of my body, especially my legs. My left knee buckled and I almost went down, but when I got back to my corner the bottom of my foot felt like it had needles about six inches high and I just kept stamping my foot on the floor, trying to bring it back. And by the time the bell rang it was all right.

Basilio belongs to the rough-and-tumble era of LaMotta, Graziano, Zale, Pep, Saddler; Gene Fullmer, Dick Tiger, Kid Gavilan. An era when, if two boxers wanted to fight dirty, the referee was likely to give them license, or at least not to interfere.

7 Of Muhammad Ali in his prime Norman Mailer observed, "He worked apparently on the premise that there was something obscene about being hit." But in fights in his later career, as with George Foreman in Zaire, even Muhammad Ali was willing to be hit, and to be hurt, in order to wear down an opponent. Brawling fighters—those with "heart" like Jake LaMotta, Rocky Graziano, Ray Mancini— have little choice but to absorb terrible punishment in exchange for some advantage (which does not in any case always come). And surely it is true that some boxers (see Jake LaMotta's autobiographical *Raging Bull*) invite injury as a means of assuaging guilt, in a Dostoyevskian exchange of physical well-being for peace of mind. Boxing is about being hit rather more than it is about hitting, just as it is about feeling pain, if not devastating psychological paralysis, more than it is about winning. One sees clearly from the "tragic" careers of any number of boxers that the boxer prefers physical pain in the ring to the absence of pain that is ideally the condition of ordinary life. If one cannot hit, one can yet be hit, and know that one is still alive.

8 It might be said that boxing is primarily about maintaining a body capable of entering combat against other well-conditioned bodies. Not the public spectacle, the fight itself, but the rigorous training period leading up to it demands the most discipline, and is believed to be the chief cause of the boxer's physical and mental infirmities. (As a boxer ages his sparring partners get younger, the game itself gets more desperate.)

9 The artist senses some kinship, however oblique and one-sided, with the professional boxer in this matter of training. This fanatic subordination of the self in terms of a wished-for destiny. One might compare the time-bound public spectacle of the boxing match (which could be as brief as an ignominious forty-five seconds—the record for a title fight!) with the publication of a writer's book. That which is "public" is but the final stage in a protracted, arduous, grueling, and frequently despairing period of preparation. Indeed, one of the reasons for the habitual attraction of serious writers to boxing (from Swift, Pope, Johnson to Hazlitt, Lord Byron, Hemingway, and our own Norman Mailer, George Plimpton, Ted Hoagland, Wilfrid Sheed, Daniel Halpern, et al.) is the sport's systematic cultivation of pain in the interests of a project, a life-goal: the willed transposing of the sensation we know as pain (physical, psychological, emotional) into its polar opposite. If this is masochism—and I doubt that it is, or that it is simply— it is also intelligence, cunning, strategy. It is an act of consummate self-determination—the constant reestablishment of the parameters of one's being. To not only accept but to actively invite what most sane creatures avoid—pain, humiliation, loss, chaos—is to experience the present moment as already, in a sense, past. *Here* and *now* are but part of the design of *there* and *then:* pain now but control, and therefore triumph, later. And pain itself is miraculously transposed by dint of its context. Indeed, it might be said that "context" is all.

10 The novelist George Garrett, an amateur boxer of some decades ago, reminisces about his training period:

I learned something . . . about the brotherhood of boxers. People went into this brutal and often self-destructive activity for a rich variety of motivations, most of them bitterly antisocial and verging on the psychotic. Most of the fighters I knew of were wounded people who felt a deep, powerful urge to wound others at real risk to themselves. In the beginning. What happened was that in almost every case, there was so much self-discipline required and craft involved, so much else besides one's original motivations to concentrate on, that these motivations became at least cloudy and vague and were often forgotten, lost completely. Many good and experienced fighters (as has often been noted) become gentle and kind people . . . They have the habit of leaving all their fight in the ring. And even there, in the ring, it is dangerous to invoke too much anger. It can be a stimulant, but is very expensive of energy. It is impractical to get mad most of the time.

Of all boxers it seems to have been Rocky Marciano (still our only undefeated heavyweight champion) who trained with the most monastic devotion; his training methods have become legendary. In contrast to reckless fighters like Harry "The Human Windmill" Greb, who kept in condition by boxing all the time, Marciano was willing to seclude himself from the world, including his wife and family, for as long as three months before a fight. Apart from the grueling physical ordeal of this period and the obsessive preoccupation with diet and weight and muscle tone, Marciano concentrated on one thing: the upcoming fight. Every minute of his life was defined in terms of the opening second of the fight. In his training camp the opponent's name was never mentioned in Marciano's hearing, nor was boxing as a subject discussed. In the final month Marciano would not write a letter since a letter related to the outside world. During the last ten days before a fight he would see no mail, take no telephone calls, meet no new acquaintances. During the week before the fight he would not shake hands. Or go for a ride in a car, however brief. No new foods! No dreaming of the morning after the fight! For all that was not *the fight* had to be excluded from consciousness. When Marciano worked out with a punching bag he saw his opponent before him, when he jogged he saw his opponent close beside him, no doubt when he slept he "saw" his opponent constantly—as the cloistered monk or nun chooses by an act of fanatical will to "see" only God.

11   Madness?—or merely discipline?—this absolute subordination of the self. In any case, for Marciano, it worked.

☐ Discovering Meaning and Technique

1. Oates writes, "Pain, in the proper context, is something other than pain" (paragraph 2). How does she develop this idea?

2. Whose stories illustrate that all boxers are not "stupid, illiterate, or punch-drunk"?

3. What does Oates mean by "a Dostoyevskian exchange of physical well-being for peace of mind" (paragraph 7)?

4. What does Oates suggest that boxing is "primarily about"?

5. Oates frequently places information in parentheses. Which kind of information does she choose to enclose?

6. What are the similarities between professional writers and boxers?

7. How did Marciano's training methods reflect "monastic devotion"?

☐ Writing Suggestions

1. Explain what Oates means by "Pain, in the proper context, is something other than pain"?

2. Why do you think people take up boxing knowing they will probably get hurt?

3. In the library, gather information to write a profile of one of the boxers Oates mentions.

4. Compare boxing's rigorous training to the kinds of training required by other sports.

5. Argue for or against the abolition of boxing.

TOWARD BETTER HUMAN UNDERSTANDING

☐ NIKKI GIOVANNI

1 OK, ladies, I'm going to help you out. I know I'm a poet and that poets are not supposed to be interested in these things, but let's file it under "Toward Better Human Understanding." That allows our subject to be considered either political or sociological. Men and women are different, and no matter what kind of data we uncover we will still see the differences . . . and sports proves it.

2   I'm not talking simply anatomy. Women, since the days of slavery, have been strong and physically capable, and we're not just discussing Black American slavery here. The Great Pyramids were as much built by female Jewish slaves

as by male. The great Roman roads were laid by women and men. The stuff
you see in movies and on television defies logic. The women were not simply
lovingly dressed and taken into concubinage while the men gathered the straw.
Both did bedroom duty; both did fieldwork. Black American slavery does at
least openly admit women were worked like men, though I think the term is
"worked like a . . ." (It's not, by the way, that I'm against using certain pejorative
terms, but when every comedian and left-wing politician thinks he can show
he's hip and prejudice-free by using the term it's time for those of us who had
a more familial connection to desert the field.) Anybody who thinks the women
who went West in covered and uncovered wagons to open the frontier just
stayed around the home fire fretting about the town gossip and baking biscuits
is nuts, too. We shot Indians, marauding Mexicans and crazy white men who
bothered us. We tilled fields, harvested the crops, fought weather, loneliness
and sometimes our mates—the same as we do today. The myth of the delicate
woman is very recent and very inaccurate. You had your historical crazies like
the Chinese peasants who bound the feet of their wives and daughters because
the Chinese rich did it. Of course, the rich did it to show that they were rich.
The poor did it in pitiful imitation of the rich. Foot-binding is as sick as the cry
for virgin women. It's simply a sign of men talking to men. "Hey man, I'm so
rich my ol' lady want to go someplace I have Chester, here, to carry her!"
"Babe, you too much. Do she walk to bed or do he carry her there, too?"
(With a lot of eye-rolling and back-slapping.) Like soft hands. Some pitiful woman
married to a normal factory guy or schoolteacher or policeman for that matter
is expected to have hands that look and feel like she never washed a pair of
socks or cleaned a greasy skillet or scrubbed the ring from around the tub. I
mean, if you work with your hands, your hands will show it. And I say Hurrah.
What a false sense of ego some men must have. How foolish of the women not
to protest. All those overlong, splitting nails, patchy red-polished dishpan hands
trying to make, hoping to believe, that Jergens or Palmolive or some miracle
would make their hands to be less red, less cracked, less dry. Scarlett should
have said to Rhett, "There's a war going on, dummy. What the hell do you
mean, what's wrong with my hands?" I'm simply trying to establish that women
have used, and always will use, our bodies for real work. What we have been
reluctant to use ourselves for is real play. Women don't like to sweat.

3   I do. I love sweat dripping from my chin or running down the back of
my neck. I wear an Afro so I don't have to worry about my hairstyle. I can
shower after a tennis match and wash my hair and go on about my business. In
all fairness to the younger women, I'm also forty-three and figure what I haven't
had I won't get. Athletics are fun. I've been totally cheered by the female body-
builders. People thought they were nuts ("I don't see what they gonna do with
all them muscles. No man ain't gonna want them"). Though those of us who
have followed the history of men know men want any and every thing. My
favorite sport is tennis, though as a two-pack-a-day smoker, I either have to

win early or accept defeat graciously. I am, of course, very gracious. I bowl in the high 100's, of which I am very proud, and can run a quarter mile in fifteen minutes. I've even joined a spa lately, where I have been known on rare occasions to do ten sit-ups, though they are not my favorite. Aerobics. I like the music, the side-to-side motion, the look of my AMF red-velvet heavy hands flinging into space calorie after calorie, which are burned, incinerated, banished to that place where lost weight goes on hiatus until it finds another woman to descend upon. I've learned something else. Why men like to look at sports.

4   I need to take a minute to, if not explain something, then at least admit it. Since turning forty I have found that I drift off the subject. Many's the year I had to hear that I was too direct, without humor, did not see the shadings. It never used to bother me until I turned forty. I never used to cry at commercials either. I never used to get choked up at poignant endings. Just a few scant years ago I would have torn apart a movie like *The Trip to Bountiful.* I would have found the son too weak, the daughter-in-law too stark, the mother too much a caricature. But I watched that movie and threw popcorn at the screen screaming, "Let her sing a hymn!" I just couldn't take it. I should have known it was coming because I used to get tears in my eyes watching that kid take the shirt from the football player in that Coke commercial. I mean, the kid looked so happy to have that sweaty shirt and it was so sweet of the player to give it to him. All right, I'll admit it. A tear or two fell when Pete Rose broke Ty Cobb's record. It was so touching. I had to be helped from the room when that Swiss female marathoner, Gabriele Anderson, limped crazily into the arena at the Los Angeles Olympics. "Don't touch her! Don't touch her!" I yelled until my mother, realizing I had once again been gotten to, put a steady hand on my elbow and took me into the kitchen muttering, "She'll be all right. She'll finish."

5   Unfortunately for me, my mother just loves *Little House.* Now, I can take the girls being blind and seeing again and all the fires and operations because I don't emotionally identify. But the show where the aging wrestler needs the money for his dying wife . . . well, I refused to look at it for the third time. It's just too much. I can't watch the *Highway to Heaven* where the actor ascends in front of the curtain to heaven after asking God to give him a sign that He understood the actor had tried to live a good life. It seemed that he asked for so little and it's only right that it be granted. And let's not even discuss *Star Trek.* The idea that Spock might die just broke me up. I had taken my son and two of his friends to see it and they all were horribly embarrassed by me. I got them back with *E.T.* Everybody heaved through that one. So I admit emotion has come into my life and, in many ways, I cannot control it. Honestly, I cried like a baby after amassing 346 points at Scrabble only to go down in defeat. But that's understandable. Most men like to watch sports because they refuse to admit they cry at commercials. They like to watch sports because they like to think that a group of men playing a game together are friends and really care about each other. They like to use terms like "Teamwork" and "I'll quarter-

back this" and "Let's run this up the middle" to get their subordinates to work harder. They sit around on Friday nights (fights), Saturday (college ball), Sunday (pro), and Monday (pro) wanting to believe that man does not struggle alone. That his fellows are there with him. That the team concept is alive and well. They cheer loudly and argue insistently about plays because it's also the only time they can show great and intense emotion without someone trying to analyze it. They can scream and holler and curse and thank the various deities without having to worry that someone will attach any deeper meaning. They watch sports, ladies, for the same reason you watch *General Hospital, The Young and the Restless, Dynasty* and *Dallas.* They need a fantasy. One other thing I should mention. They like sports because they are the undisputed master of the ERA, at-bats, percentages against left-handers vs. percentages against right-handers. This from a man who cannot remember his anniversary and occasionally forgets his wife's name (*"Honey,* will you bring me a beer?") Something primordial and personal happens when a man watches sports. He doesn't have to talk to women.

6   Most women don't like to watch sports because we are jealous of the men enjoying themselves without our help. We hear the same animal grunts and groans, the same urgings to come on, to finish it off, as we hear in private moments, and women don't want to compete with the New York Jets for private moments. I'm surprised some mate has not reported his significant other as running into the room near tears during the Super Bowl saying, "But, Timothy, I thought that was our grunt." And in our genetic jealousy we seek, not understanding of our negative emotions, but excuses. "I don't like boxing," (with lips pursed) "because it's too violent." Have you ever been to a department store the day after Christmas? Have you ever been in any grocery store when 96-ounce Coke was announced as on sale for the next twenty minutes for 76 cents? Did you never seek a Cabbage Patch doll for your child or grandchild? How can women really discuss violence?

7   Boxing is a marvelous sport. Except for the heavyweights you have two wonderfully muscled men in the ring in shorts outpointing each other. Yes, I will admit that you sometimes find real hackers who are simply trying to hurt the other man, but real boxing—and we do have to look at the heavyweights now—is an art. You take Muhammed Ali who at the peak of his career raised boxing to liquid sculpture. No one would compare Ali to Sonny Liston, Joe Frazier or Larry Holmes, because they, as Ali liked to say, were just big bears. Sugars Ray, both Robinson and Leonard, were a joy to watch. And Michael Spinks has shown it's not size but skill. Will boxing learn Michael's lesson? Probably not. But when you see a Lonnie Smith, who unfortunately lost his title, you see a man moving with a purpose. But mostly, whether you or I or the American Medical Association like it or not, boxing is here to stay. Men will always test themselves against each other. Someone is bound to say, "But we don't have to support it . . . it's barbaric." So is the stock exchange; so are interest rates; so

are farm foreclosures; so is life. Most women don't want to think that someone could really enjoy hitting or getting hit by someone else. It's probably quite fair to say no one enjoys getting hit. Hitting . . . well, that's another matter.

8   Football is fun, too. My sister once asked me, "Why do they get up close to each other and scrunch down?" I realized right away why she doesn't enjoy the sport. She doesn't know what's going on. My answer was, of course, a very patient, "I don't know." Because I don't. I'm not only not a sport historian, I don't intend to become one. They line up because that's the way the game is played. A better question, and one that can be quite a conversation opener is, "Why don't they throw on first down?" Your significant other will try to explain the importance of establishing a running game, which can take up quite a bit of time. If you occasionally ask something like, "Well, why don't they go for it on fourth down and inches? That front line isn't all that tough," you can talk all afternoon. Do not, I repeat, do not ask that if his team is playing against the Chicago Bears. You will look like the imposter you are. With any other team it'll do just fine. One minor thing you need to know: The object of football is first downs—not touchdowns, first downs. Your mate will be perfectly happy to have his favorite team lose if they get more first downs. Now that may not make sense but I'm not trying to make sense, I'm trying to save your relationship.

9   Shortly before the actual close of football—well, truthfully before the World Series is played—the NBA will raise its head. If your spouse is not a football nut you can count on losing him during basketball season. The trick to understanding basketball is calling the foul. You jump up and down saying, "FOUL! HE FOULED HIM! OH, WOW! DID YOU SEE THAT!" It won't matter whether or not a foul is called because someone is always fouling in basketball. You can always throw in a bunch of I-don't-believe-it-how-could-they-overlook-its and win the respect of every man in the room. Basketball, by the way, is the only sport where points are important. In the other majors it's the process.

10   Now baseball is called the American game and not for naught. It would take American ingenuity to come up with a sport that you do not have to be in good shape for, that takes all day, that you can get both mental and physical work done without interfering with your enjoyment of the contest. You simply must watch tennis and basketball to know what's going on. You need to see football replays so that you can talk about the tight end or nose tackle. It would help if you knew how the bowler was throwing in the first frame as compared to the ninth. A horse race isn't a race unless you are there when they say ". . . And they're off." But baseball . . . you can cook, clean, do your lawn work, read a book, play Scrabble, or pinochle. You can sleep, run errands, make love and still know what's going on. It's the perfect pastime because it demands nothing. The men who play it climb into their pajamas, wad up their mouths with tobacco or gum and stand around spitting all afternoon. Everybody can play baseball. If it wasn't such an institution I'm sure women would have tackled it way before they tried to break into the NBA or football or boxing. It makes

far more sense for an all-female team to play against men in baseball than any other sport. Billie Jean and Martina played and defeated men in tennis, and though Bobby Riggs is old, tennis is not necessarily a game that yields to age. Bobby was not in that bad shape. But baseball? My home team has two of the oldest players in professional ball and the Cincinnati Reds are still making a run for it. Have you seen the bellies on those guys? If baseball doesn't work out for them they can always go to Japan and try sumo wrestling. Ladies, what I am suggesting is that you've been intimidated by sports and for no good reason. You've been cowered into being weekend widows because you think sweat is sacred. Open that sports page, learn what a batting average is, pick a team, grab a beer and cheer. Just one PS here. Always take the underdog and points. Take the underdog even if you can't get points. I took the Dolphins over Chicago last year, and do you know that made me look like a genius? I was hot stuff. Always take the underdog, though, for another, more primordial reason. We're women. Somebody has to love the losers, too.

☐ Discovering Meaning and Technique

1. What does Giovanni believe was the woman's role in history? Does this role conflict with the idea that women should have "soft hands"?

2. Why have women been "reluctant" to engage in "real play"?

3. Why do men like to watch sports? Why do women not like to watch sports?

4. Where does Giovanni insert a digression? Where does it begin and end? What is its point?

5. Giovanni enumerates the appeal of several sports. What are those sports? Do you think there is any logic to the order in which they are presented?

6. How does Giovanni create a conversational style?

7. By looking at the language, determine the readers that Giovanni had in mind when she wrote this selection.

8. Conservatives in grammar think an infinitive (for example, *to look, to write*) should not be split—that is, the *to* should not be separated from the following verb. Most people today, however, agree with Strunk and White, who wrote in *The Elements of Style* that "some infinitives seem to improve on being split." What do you think about Giovanni's sentence: "I need to take a minute to, if not explain something, then at least admit it"?

☐ **Writing Suggestions**

1. Why do you think women are traditionally less involved in sports than are men?

2. Give advice on how to enjoy watching a particular sport.

3. Argue against one of Giovanni's views—for example, that women don't like to sweat, that women get jealous of men enjoying themselves without women, that a player does not have to be in shape to play baseball.

■ Combining Sources in a Composition

1. Marie Winn's "How Parents Survived before Television" was published in 1977. Have her fears proved as groundless as those of the social critics in Walter Karp's essay?

2. Both Joan Didion and Stephen King explore children's reactions to movies. Explore the subject further, using your own experiences as additional source material.

3. Compare Roger Rosenblatt's interpretation of Scarlett O'Hara to the manipulative soap-opera heroines described by Gwen Kinkead.

4. Using the selections by Rosenblatt and Didion for suggestions, write an essay on the typical Hollywood "he-man."

5. Some people view travel as exciting, educational, romantic; others view it as exasperating, depressing, difficult. Using material from the selections, contrast the various reactions to travel.

6. Through travel, some people look for meaning and fulfillment, searching for a place where they can say, in Isak Dinesen's words, "Here I am, where I ought to be." Apply this quotation to the selections by N. Scott Momaday, Jan Morris, and Bobbie Ann Mason.

7. In the selections by Morris and Mason, water is the attraction. Discuss why we are drawn "like lemmings to the water's edge."

8. Using the selections by Rheta Grimsley Johnson and Joyce Carol Oates as part of your material, discuss the violence of many sports.

9. Different sports have different attractions. Discuss the various attractions of sports, including Oates's fascination with boxing and Donald Hall's with basketball.

10. Do men and women have different tastes in sports? In addition to your own views, you can include Oates's attraction to the masculine world of boxing and Nikki Giovanni's comparison of men's and women's involvement in sports.

C H A P T E R 4

NATURE

Plants and Animals

■ ■ ■

THE POTATO

☐ **JOHN STEWART COLLIS**

1 I am anxious to say a word about the potato. . . . We sing the flower, we sing the leaf: we seldom sing the seed, the root, the tuber. Indeed the potato enters literature with no very marked success. True, William Cobbett abused it, and Lord Byron made it interesting by rhyming it with Plato; but for the most part it enters politics more easily and has done more to divide England from Ireland than Cromwell himself.

2 Yet if we praise the potato we praise ourselves, for it is an extreme example of artificiality. "The earth, in order that she might urge us to labour, the supreme law of life," says Fabre, "has been but a harsh stepmother. For the nestling bird she provides abundant food; to us she offers only the fruit of the Bramble and the Blackthorn." Not everyone realizes this, he said. Some people even imagine that the grape is today just like that from which Noah obtained the juice that made him drunk; that the cauliflower, merely with the idea of being pleasant, has of its own accord evolved its creamy-white head; that turnips and carrots, being keenly interested in human affairs, have always of their own motion done their best for man; and that the potato, since the world was young, wishing to

please us, has gone through its curious performance. The truth is far otherwise. They were all uneatable at first: it is we who have forced them to become what they now are. "In its native countries," says Fabre, "on the mountains of Chili and Peru, the Potato, in its wild state, is a meagre tubercle, about the size of a Hazel-nut. Man extends the hospitality of his garden to this sorry weed; he plants it in nourishing soil, tends it, waters it, and makes it fruitful with the sweat of his brow. And there, from year to year, the Potato thrives and prospers; it gains in size and nourishing properties, finally becoming a farinaceous tuber the size of our two fists."

3   During my first year in the agricultural world I decided to have a good look at the potato and carefully watch its operations. I had never done this before. In fact I had little idea how potatoes actually arrive. With me it is always a question of either knowing a thing or not knowing it, of knowing it from A to Z or not at all; the man who knows a little about everything, from A to B, is incomprehensible to me. Thus I could approach the potato with the clear head of ignorance.

4   I took one in my hand and offered it my attention. It looked like a smooth stone; a shapeless shape; so dull in appearance that I found it hard to look at it without thinking of something else. I took a knife and cut it in two. It had white flesh extremely like an apple. But it had nothing in the middle, no seed-box, no seeds. How then can it produce more of itself? Well, the season had now come to put it down into the earth. So we planted them into the prepared field, at a distance of one foot from each other—plenty of space in which laboratory they could carry out any work they desired.

5   In about a fortnight's time I decided to dig up one and see if anything had happened. The first I came to had not changed in appearance at all. From the second, however, two white objects, about the length of a worm, were protruding. On a human face, I reflected, such protuberances would have seemed like some dreadful disease. One of them looked like a little white mouse trying to get out. I covered up these phenomena again and left them to it, wondering what they would do next.

6   After a few weeks I again visited this earthly laboratory to see how things were getting on. I found that the protuberances had become much longer and had curled round at their ends—now white snakes coming out of the humble solid. They had curly heads like purplish knots, and some of these knots had half opened into a series of green ears. And now there was another addition: at the place where these stems, as we many now call them, came out of the potato, a network had been set up, of string, as it were, connecting the outfit with the soil. These, the roots, went downwards seeking the darkness of the earth, while every stem rose up to seek the light. But as yet there was no indication where or how new potatoes could appear.

7   During these early weeks the surface of the field showed no sign that anything was going on underneath. Later the whole brown surface began to

change into rows of green—the light-seeking stalks had risen into the air and unfurled their leaves. As the weeks passed, and the months, these little green bushes grew in size and complexity until in late July they were all flowering— and a very pretty field it then looked. As all flowers have fruit, so had these— potato fruits, of course. But not the ones we eat.

8   Even after the green rows had appeared above-board and I made a further examination below I still did not see where the crop of potatoes was going to come from. Eventually the problem cleared itself up. I found them forming at the end of the network of roots. A few of the roots began to swell at their extremity—first about the size of a bird's egg, then a baby's shoe, getting larger and larger until some of them were four times the size of the original potato planted in the ground. And here we come to the curious thing about potatoes. The substance which grows at the end of the root is not itself a root. It is a *branch.* It is not a root, the botanists say, because roots do not bear buds and do not bear leaves, while this, the potato, does have buds and does have leaves (in the shape of scales). It is a subterranean branch, swollen and misshapen, storing up food for its buds; and botanists, no longer having the courage to call it a branch, call it a tuber. So when we plant a potato we are not planting a seed, we are not planting a root; we are planting a branch from whose gateways, called "eyes," roots reach down and stalks reach up.

9   To complete the circle, what happens to the original potato? It conforms to the rule of eternal return by virtue of which the invisible becomes visible, and the visible takes on invisibility. It darkens, it softens, it becomes a squashy brown mash, and finally is seen no more. I used to enjoy taking it up in my hand when I saw it lying on the ground looking like an old leather purse. It had performed a remarkable act. Now its work was done. All the virtue had gone out of it. It had given its life to the green stalks above and the tubers below. Here I seemed to see a familiar sight in nature; many things coming from one thing, much from little, even something out of nothing. This is what we seem to see. Yet it is not so. True, the original potato started the business going, sending down those roots and sending up those stalks; but they in their turn built the building. The earth is not a solid; it is chiefly gas. The air is not thin; it is massed with food. Those roots sucked gases from the earth, those leaves sucked gases from the sky, and the result was the visible, hard, concrete potato. When we eat a potato we eat the earth, and we eat the sky. It is the law of nature that all things are all things. That which does not appear to exist today is tomorrow hewn down and cast into the oven. Nature carries on by taking in her own washing. That is Nature's economy, contrary to political econ- omy; so that he who cries "Wolf! Wolf!" is numbered amongst the infidels. "A mouse," said Walt Whitman, "is enough to stagger sextillions of infidels." Or a potato. What is an infidel? One who lacks faith. What creates faith? A miracle. How then can there be a faithless man found in the world? Because many men have cut off the nervous communication between the eye and the brain. In the

madness of blindness they are at the mercy of intellectual nay-sayers, theorists, theologians, and other enemies of God. But it doesn't matter; in spite of them, faith is reborn whenever anyone chooses to take a good look at anything—even a potato.

☐ Discovering Meaning and Technique

1. What does Collis mean when he says in the first paragraph that the potato "has done more to divide England from Ireland than Cromwell himself"?

2. At the beginning of paragraph 2, Collis remarks that "if we praise the potato we praise ourselves, for it is an extreme example of artificiality." What does Collis mean by this statement? Why should we praise artificiality?

3. Summarize briefly the growing stages of the potato. Then examine how Collis manages to embellish these stages with description and commentary.

4. What is the difference between a root and a branch?

5. Point out some phrases and sentences that sound almost like Ecclesiastes, such as "That which does not appear to exist today is tomorrow hewn down and cast into the oven" (paragraph 9).

6. Comment on Collis's style. Does it seem consistent throughout the selection? Or does it seem to change in some paragraphs?

☐ Writing Suggestions

1. Explain what Collis means when he says (in the last sentence) that "faith is reborn whenever anyone chooses to take a good look at anything—even a potato." Do you agree with him?

2. Collis call the potato "a miracle." Is he speaking only of the potato? Or does he intend some larger meaning?

3. Describe the growth process of some other plant.

4. If you have ever planted a garden, describe your experience. Was it rewarding? Frustrating? Educational?

5. Discuss how we often overlook fascinating things merely because they are ordinary or hidden from sight.

HOW FLOWERS CHANGED THE WORLD

☐ **LOREN EISELEY**

1   If it had been possible to observe the Earth from the far side of the solar system over the long course of geological epochs, the watchers might have been able to discern a subtle change in the light emanating from our planet. That world of long ago would, like the red deserts of Mars, have reflected light from vast drifts of stone and gravel, the sands of wandering wastes, the blackness of naked basalt, the yellow dust of endlessly moving storms. Only the ceaseless marching of the clouds and the intermittent flashes from the restless surface of the sea would have told a different story, but still essentially a barren one. Then, as the millennia rolled away and age followed age, a new and greener light would, by degrees, have come to twinkle across those endless miles.

2   This is the only difference those far watchers, by the use of subtle instruments, might have perceived in the whole history of the planet Earth. Yet that slowly growing green twinkle would have contained the epic march of life from the tidal oozes upward across the raw and unclothed continents. Out of the vast chemical bath of the sea—not from the deeps, but from the element-rich, light-exposed platforms of the continental shelves—wandering fingers of green had crept upward along the meanderings of river systems and fringed the gravels of forgotten lakes.

3   In those first ages plants clung of necessity to swamps and watercourses. Their reproductive processes demanded direct access to water. Beyond the primitive ferns and mosses that enclosed the borders of swamps and streams the rocks still lay vast and bare, the winds still swirled the dust of a naked planet. The grass cover that holds our world secure in place was still millions of years in the future. The green marchers had gained a soggy foothold upon the land, but that was all. They did not reproduce by seeds but by microscopic swimming sperm that had to wriggle their way through water to fertilize the female cell. Such plants in their higher forms had clever adaptations for the use of rain water in their sexual phases, and survived with increasing success in a wet land environment. They now seem part of man's normal environment. The truth is, however, that there is nothing very "normal" about nature. Once upon a time there were no flowers at all.

4   A little while ago—about one hundred millions years, as the geologist estimates time in the history of our four-billion-year-old planet—flowers were not to be found anywhere on the five continents. Wherever one might have looked, from the poles to the equator, one would have seen only the cold dark monotonous green of a world whose plant life possessed no other color.

5   Somewhere, just a short time before the close of the Age of Reptiles, there occurred a soundless, violent explosion. It lasted millions of years, but it was

an explosion, nevertheless. It marked the emergence of the angiosperms—the flowering plants. Even the great evolutionist, Charles Darwin, called them "an abominable mystery," because they appeared so suddenly and spread so fast.

6   Flowers changed the face of the planet. Without them, the world we know— even man himself—would never have existed. Francis Thompson, the English poet, once wrote that one could not pluck a flower without troubling a star, Intuitively he had sensed like a naturalist the enormous interlinked complexity of life. Today we know that the appearance of the flowers contained also the equally mystifying emergence of man.

7   If we were to go back into the Age of Reptiles, its drowned swamps and birdless forests would reveal to us a warmer but, on the whole, a sleepier world than that of today. Here and there, it is true, the serpent heads of bottom-feeding dinosaurs might be upreared in suspicion of their huge flesh-eating compatriots. Tyrannosaurs, enormous bipedal caricatures of men, would stalk mindlessly across the sites of future cities and go their slow way down into the dark of geologic time.

8   In all that world of living things nothing saw save with the intense concentra- tion of the hunt, nothing moved except with the grave sleepwalking intentness of the instinct-driven brain. Judged by modern standards, it was a world in slow motion, a cold-blooded world whose occupants were most active at noonday but torpid on chill nights, their brains damped by a slower metabolism than any known to even the most primitive of warm-blooded animals today.

9   A high metabolic rate and the maintenance of a constant body temperature are supreme achievements in the evolution of life. They enable an animal to escape, within broad limits, from the overheating or the chilling of its immediate surroundings, and at the same time to maintain a peak mental efficiency. Creatures without a high metabolic rate are slaves to weather. Insects in the first frosts of autumn all run down like little clocks. Yet if you pick one up and breathe warmly upon it, it will begin to move about once more.

10   In a sheltered spot such creatures may sleep away the winter, but they are hopelessly immobilized. Though a few warm-blooded mammals, such as the woodchuck of our day, have evolved a way of reducing their metabolic rate in order to undergo winter hibernation, it is a survival mechanism with drawbacks, for it leaves the animal helplessly exposed if enemies discover him during his period of suspended animation. Thus bear or woodchuck, big animal or small, must seek, in this time of descending sleep, a safe refuge in some hidden den or burrow. Hibernation is, therefore, primarily a winter refuge of small, easily concealed animals rather than of large ones.

11   A high metabolic rate, however, means a heavy intake of energy in order to sustain body warmth and efficiency. It is for this reason that even some of these later warm-blooded mammals existing in our day have learned to descend into a slower, unconscious rate of living during the winter months when food may be difficult to obtain. On a slightly higher plane they are following the

procedure of the cold-blooded frog sleeping in the mud at the bottom of a frozen pond.

12   The agile brain of the warm-blooded birds and mammals demands a high oxygen consumption and food in concentrated forms, or the creatures cannot long sustain themselves. It was the rise of the flowering plants that provided that energy and changed the nature of the living world. Their appearance parallels in a quite surprising manner the rise of the birds and mammals.

13   Slowly, toward the dawn of the Age of Reptiles, something over two hundred and fifty million years ago, the little naked sperm cells wriggling their way through dew and raindrops had given way to a kind of pollen carried by the wind. Our present-day pine forests represent plants of a pollen-disseminating variety. Once fertilization was no longer dependent on exterior water, the march over drier regions could be extended. Instead of spores simple primitive seeds carrying some nourishment for the young plant had developed, but true flowers were still scores of millions of years away. After a long period of hesitant evolutionary groping, they exploded upon the world with truly revolutionary violence.

14   The event occurred in Cretaceous times in the close of the Age of Reptiles. Before the coming of the flowering plants our own ancestral stock, the warm-blooded mammals, consisted of a few mousy little creatures hidden in trees and underbrush. A few lizard-like birds with carnivorous teeth flapped awkwardly on ill-aimed flights among archaic shrubbery. None of these insignificant creatures gave evidence of any remarkable talents. The mammals in particular had been around for some millions of years, but had remained well lost in the shadow of the mighty reptiles. Truth to tell, man was still, like the genie in the bottle, encased in the body of a creature about the size of a rat.

15   As for the birds, their reptilian cousins the Pterodactyls, flew farther and better. There was just one thing about the birds that paralleled the physiology of the mammals. They, too, had evolved warm blood and its accompanying temperature control. Nevertheless, if one had been seen stripped of his feathers, he would still have seemed a slightly uncanny and unsightly lizard.

16   Neither the birds nor the mammals, however, were quite what they seemed. They were waiting for the Age of Flowers. They were waiting for what flowers, and with them the true encased seed, would bring. Fish-eating, gigantic leather-winged reptiles, twenty-eight feet from wing tip to wing tip, hovered over the coasts that one day would be swarming with gulls.

17   Inland the monotonous green of the pine and spruce forests with their primitive wooden cone flowers stretched everywhere. No grass hindered the fall of the naked seeds to earth. Great sequoias towered to the skies. The world of that time has a certain appeal but it is a giant's world, a world moving slowly like the reptiles who stalked magnificently among the boles of its trees.

18   The trees themselves are ancient, slow-growing and immense, like the red-wood groves that have survived to our day on the California coast. All is stiff, formal, upright and green, monotonously green. There is no grass as yet; there

are no wide plains rolling in the sun, no tiny daisies dotting the meadows underfoot. There is little versatility about this scene; it is, in truth, a giant's world.

19   A few nights ago it was brought home vividly to me that the world has
changed since that far epoch. I was awakened out of sleep by an unknown
sound in my living room. Not a small sound—not a creaking timber or a mouse's
scurry—but a sharp, rending explosion as though an unwary foot had been put
down upon a wine glass. I had come instantly out of sleep and lay tense, unbreath-
ing. I listened for another step. There was none.

20   Unable to stand the suspense any longer, I turned on the light and passed
from room to room glancing uneasily behind chairs and into closets. Nothing
seemed disturbed, and I stood puzzled in the center of the living room floor.
Then a small button-shaped object upon the rug caught my eye. It was hard
and polished and glistening. Scattered over the length of the room were several
more shining up at me like wary little eyes. A pine cone that had been lying in
a dish had been blown the length of the coffee table. The dish itself could
hardly have been the source of the explosion. Beside it, I found two ribbonlike strips of a velvety-green. I tried to place the two strips together to make a
pod. They twisted resolutely away from each other and would no longer fit.

21   I relaxed in a chair, then, for I had reached a solution of the midnight
disturbance. The twisted strips were wistaria pods that I had brought in a day
or two previously and placed in the dish. They had chosen midnight to explode
and distribute the multiplying fund of life down the length of the room. A plant,
a fixed, rooted thing, immobilized in a single spot, had devised a way of propelling
its offspring across open space. Immediately there passed before my eyes the
million airy troopers of the milkweed pod and the clutching hooks of the sandburs.
Seeds on the coyote's tail, seeds on the hunter's coat, thistledown mounting on
the winds—all were somehow triumphing over life's limitations. Yet the ability
to do this had not been with them at the beginning. It was the product of
endless effort and experiment.

22   The seeds on my carpet were not going to lie stiffly where they had dropped
like their antiquated cousins, the naked seeds on the pine-cone scales. They
were travelers. Struck by the thought, I went out next day and collected several
other varieties. I line them up now in a row on my desk—so many little capsules
of life, winged, hooked or spiked. Every one is an angiosperm, a product of the
true flowing plants. Contained in these little boxes is the secret of that far-off
Cretaceous explosion of a hundred million years ago that changed the face of
the planet. And somewhere in here, I think, as I poke seriously at one particularly
resistant seedcase of a wild grass, was once man himself.

23 When the first simple flower bloomed on some raw upland late in the Dinosaur
Age, it was wind pollinated, just like its early pine-cone relatives. It was a very
inconspicuous flower because it had not yet evolved the idea of using the surer
attraction of birds and insects to achieve the transportation of pollen. It sowed

its own pollen and received the pollen of other flowers by the simple vagaries of the wind. Many plants in regions where insect life is scant still follow this principle today. Nevertheless, the true flower—and the seed that it produced— was a profound innovation in the world of life.

24   In a way, this event parallels, in the plant world, what happened among animals. Consider the relative chance for survival of the exteriorly deposited egg of a fish in contrast with the fertilized egg of a mammal, carefully retained for months in the mother's body until the young animal (or human being) is developed to a point where it may survive. The biological wastage is less—and so it is with the flowering plants. The primitive spore, a single cell fertilized in the beginning by a swimming sperm, did not promote rapid distribution, and the young plant, moreover, had to struggle up from nothing. No one had left it any food except what it could get by its own unaided efforts.

25   By contrast, the true flowering plants (angiosperm itself means "encased seed") grew a seed in the heart of a flower, a seed whose development was initiated by a fertilizing pollen grain independent of outside moisture. But the seed, unlike the developing spore, is already a fully equipped *embryonic plant* packed in a little enclosed box stuffed full of nutritious food. Moreover, by featherdown attachments, as in dandelion or milkweed seed, it can be wafted upward on gusts and ride the wind for miles; or with hooks it can cling to a bear's or a rabbit's hide; or like some of the berries, it can be covered with a juicy, attractive fruit to lure birds, pass undigested through their intestinal tracts and be voided miles away.

26   The ramifications of this biological invention were endless. Plants traveled as they had never traveled before. They got into strange environments heretofore never entered by the old spore plants or stiff pine-cone-seed plants. The well-fed, carefully cherished little embryos raised their heads everywhere. Many of the older plants with more primitive reproductive mechanisms began to fade away under this unequal contest. They contracted their range into secluded environments. Some, like the giant redwoods, lingered on as relics; many vanished entirely.

27   The world of the giants was a dying world. These fantastic little seeds skipping and hopping and flying about the woods and valleys brought with them an amazing adaptability. If our whole lives had not been spent in the midst of it, it would astound us. The old, stiff, sky-reaching wooden world had changed into something that glowed here and there with strange colors, put out queer, unheard-of fruits and little intricately carved seed cases, and, most important of all, produced concentrated foods in a way that the land had never seen before, or dreamed of back in the fish-eating, leaf-crunching days of the dinosaurs.

28   That food came from three sources, all produced by the reproductive system of the flowering plants. There were the tantalizing nectars and pollens intended to draw insects for pollenizing purposes, and which are responsible also for that wonderful jeweled creation, the hummingbird. There were the juicy and

enticing fruits to attract larger animals, and in which tough-coated seeds were concealed, as in the tomato, for example. Then, as if this were not enough, there was the food in the actual seed itself, the food intended to nourish the embryo. All over the world, like hot corn in a popper, these incredible elaborations of the flowering plants kept exploding. In a movement that was almost instantaneous, geologically speaking, the angiosperms had taken over the world. Grass was beginning to cover the bare earth until, today, there are over six thousand species. All kinds of vines and bushes squirmed and writhed under new trees with flying seeds.

29   The explosion was having its effect on animal life also. Specialized groups of insects were arising to feed on the new sources of food and, incidentally and unknowingly, to pollinate the plant. The flowers bloomed and bloomed in ever larger and more spectacular varieties. Some were pale unearthly night flowers intended to lure moths in the evening twilight, some among the orchids even took the shape of female spiders in order to attract wandering males, some flamed redly in the light of noon or twinkled modestly in the meadow grasses. Intricate mechanisms splashed pollen on the breasts of hummingbirds, or stamped it on the bellies of black, grumbling bees droning assiduously from blossom to blossom. Honey ran, insects multiplied, and even the descendants of that toothed and ancient lizard-bird had become strangely altered. Equipped with prodding beaks instead of biting teeth they pecked the seeds and gobbled the insects that were really converted nectar.

30   Across the planet grasslands were now spreading. A slow continental upthrust which had been a part of the early Age of Flowers had cooled the world's climates. The stalking reptiles and the leather-winged black imps of the seashore cliffs had vanished. Only birds roamed the air now, hot-blooded and high-speed metabolic machines.

31   The mammals, too, had survived and were venturing into new domains, staring about perhaps a bit bewildered at their sudden eminence now that the thunder lizards were gone. Many of them, beginning as small browsers upon leaves in the forest, began to venture out upon this new sunlit world of the grass. Grass has a high silica content and demands a new type of very tough and resistant tooth enamel, but the seeds taken incidentally in the cropping of the grass are highly nutritious. A new world had opened out for the warm-blooded mammals. Great herbivores like the mammoths, horses and bisons appeared. Skulking about them had arisen savage flesh-feeding carnivores like the new extinct dire wolves and the saber-toothed tiger.

32   Flesh eaters though these creatures were, they were being sustained on nutritious grasses one step removed. Their fierce energy was being maintained on a high, effective level, through hot days and frosty nights, by the concentrated energy of the angiosperms. That energy, 30 percent or more of the weight of the entire plant among some of the cereal grasses, was being accumulated and concentrated in the rich proteins and fats of the enormous game herds of the grasslands.

33   On the edge of the forest, a strange, old-fashioned animal still hesitated. His body was the body of a tree dweller, and though tough and knotty by human standards, he was, in terms of that world into which he gazed, a weakling. His teeth, though strong for chewing on the tough fruits of the forest, or for crunching an occasional unwary bird caught with his prehensile hands, were not the tearing sabers of the great cats. He had a passion for lifting himself up to see about, in his restless, roving curiosity. He would run a little stiffly and uncertainly, perhaps, on his hind legs, but only in those rare moments when he ventured out upon the ground. All this was the legacy of his climbing days; he had a hand with flexible fingers and no fine specialized hoofs upon which to gallop like the wind.

34   If he had any idea of competing in that new world, he had better forget it; teeth or hooves, he was much too late for either. He was a ne'er-do-well, an in-betweener. Nature had not done well by him. It was as if she had hesitated and never quite made up her mind. Perhaps as a consequence he had a malicious gleam in his eye, the gleam of an outcast who has been left nothing and knows he is going to have to take what he gets. One day a little band of these odd apes—for apes they were—shambled out upon the grass; the human story had begun.

35   Apes were to become men, in the inscrutable wisdom of nature, because flowers had produced seeds and fruits in such tremendous quantities that a new and totally different store of energy had become available in concentrated form. Impressive as the slow-moving, dim-brained dinosaurs had been, it is doubtful if their age had supported anything like the diversity of life that now rioted across the planet or flashed in and out among the trees. Down on the grass by a streamside, one of those apes with inquisitive fingers turned over a stone and hefted it vaguely. The group clucked together in a throaty tongue and moved off through the tall grass foraging for seeds and insects. The one still held, sniffed, and hefted the stone he had found. He liked the feel of it in his fingers. The attack on the animal world was about to begin.

36   If one could run the story of that first human group like a speeded-up motion picture through a million years of time, one might see the stone in the hand change to the flint ax and the torch. All that swarming grassland world with its giant bison and trumpeting mammoths would go down in ruin to feed the insatiable and growing numbers of a carnivore who, like the great cats before him, was taking his energy indirectly from the grass. Later he found fire and it altered the tough meats and drained their energy even faster into a stomach ill adapted for the ferocious turn man's habits had taken.

37   His limbs grew longer, he strode more purposefully over the grass. The stolen energy that would take man across the continents would fail him at last. The great Ice Age herds were destined to vanish. When they did so, another hand like the hand that grasped the stone by the river long ago would pluck a handful of grass seed and hold it contemplatively.

38   In that moment, the golden towers of man, his swarming millions, his

turning wheels, the vast learning of his packed libraries, would glimmer dimly there in the ancestor of wheat, a few seeds held in a muddy hand. Without the gift of flowers and the infinite diversity of their fruits, man and bird, if they had continued to exist at all, would be today unrecognizable. Archaeopteryx, the lizard-bird, might still be snapping at beetles on a sequoia limb; man might still be a nocturnal insectivore gnawing a roach in the dark. The weight of a petal has changed the face of the world and made it ours.

☐ Discovering Meaning and Technique

1. Where does the selection divide into two separate sections?

2. If Eiseley's overall purpose is to show how flowers changed the world, what is the purpose of first section?

3. What was the "soundless, violent explosion" just before the end of the Age of Reptiles?

4. Eiseley uses interesting, unusual phrases and sentences to describe plants and animals—for example, "A few lizard-like birds with carnivorous teeth flapped awkwardly on ill-aimed flights among archaic shrubbery" (paragraph 14) or "All kinds of vines and bushes squirmed and writhed under new trees with flying seeds" (paragraph 28). Find other examples of vivid phrasing.

5. Why does Eiseley reason that "a high metabolic rate and the maintenance of a constant body temperature are the supreme achievements in the evolution of life" (paragraph 9)?

6. Compare the spore with the seed plant.

7. What are the three sources of concentrated foods "Produced by the reproductive system of the flowering plants" (paragraph 28)?

8. Who is the "strange, old-fashioned animal" in paragraph 33?

☐ Writing Suggestions

1. Why does Eiseley conclude that without flowers, "the world we know—even man himself—would never have existed"? Reconstruct his argument in a shorter, simpler form.

2. Shorten and simplify Eiseley's comparison of the world before flowering plants with the world after their appearance.

3. How did flowering plants lead to human domination of the earth?

4. How has human behavior been shaped by the fact that "nature had not done well" when creating humans?

5. In the last three paragraphs, Eiseley touches briefly on human history from the time of the Ice Age herds to the time of wheat cultivation. Research that period in the library and summarize the developments in human society during that period.

THE CUTTHROAT TROUT

☐ **SALLY CARRIGHAR**

1 Only a sharpened, seeing look in the Trout's eyes proved that he had wakened. No shift of the eyes had flashed their crystalline shine. The wrongness of some sound had roused him. He peered from his nook along the west shore of the pond; was there a glisten of wet fur in the polished darkness? Or did he see the pale clouds hung in the water, moonlight, which had turned to luminous froth the bubbles clinging to the underwater plants?

2 His shelter was a groove among the sticks of the beaver house. He was holding himself as still as the sticks, so quiet in their tangle that a slippery ooze had grown upon them. His breathing lightened until the water drained through his gills with no perceptible beat, no pulse to send its circular waves out through the pond, revealing that he lay at the center of them.

3 From the edge of the Beaver's sunken pile of aspen boughs a string of small globes, faintly silver, smoked to the top. Some animal must have touched a branch and rubbed out air that was held within its fur. The water swayed; the creature had begun to swim. Its stroke was not familiar to the Trout, not one of the rhythms that he knew as harmless or a threat. It had more pulse than the Beaver's paddling or the striding of a moose. It was rougher than the swimming of a fish and heavier than a muskrat's sculling. At first the Trout must ready himself with his fins to keep from being slapped against the sticks. But the underwater waves diminished. The last of them struck the shores and clattered back, a liquid echo. The only motion in the pond then was its regular mottling flow, a current from the brook to the beaver dam.

4 The surging had torn the film of sleep from a thousand little minds. After it ceased, constrained breaths made the pond seem lifeless. But hunger was a danger too. It rose above the fear of the animals, one by one—of the smallest first. Soon the twinkling prowls of the mayfly nymphs, the quick strokes of the water-boatmen, and the foraging of even tinier creatures mingled in a hum like

that of insects in the air, but louder. The lightest sounds were wave-beats in the pond. To the Trout's ears came the twanging of minute activity.

5   Night was nearly over. The Trout knew by the brightening of the water, by his hunger, and the stiffness in his muscles. He saw the webs of the pelican start to push the bird's breast over the top of the pond. Its wing-tips dipped in the water, the webs were shoveling back with greater vigor, the breast was shrinking upward. Only the kick of the feet now broke the surface. When the bird was gone, the fin on the Trout's back stood a little higher, and a ripple scalloped from its front edge to the rear.

6   The Beaver swam to the entrance of the house and climbed in onto the floor. His angry voice came through the wall. He was driving from his bed the muskrat he allowed to share his home. The feet of a mother moose and her calf had waded off the bank. They dragged their splashes down the shore to a patch of horsetail. The big soft muffles plunged beneath the surface, closed around the plants and pulled them dripping from the water. Even yet the Trout would not risk showing himself. He was the wariest of all the animals in the pond.

7   Beside the stranger's threat, a more familiar danger kept him hiding. Three times a day the Osprey dived in the pond for fish. The Trout's good time-sense held him under cover when its strike was due: at dawn, as soon as the hawk could see its prey; at noon; and at sunset, with the first receding wave of light. Most mornings the Trout went out for an early swim, returning to his nook before he would be visible from the air; but not on this day.

8   His wait was an exquisite balancing of instincts. Hunger was sufficient reason to start forth, and the pond's flow was a stimulation. The current, passing through the walls of the beaver house, divided around the Trout. All night its touch had slid along his skin, from nose to tail, as though he ceaselessly swam forward. Now he was awake to feel the fine strokes down his sides—the touch of moving water; only the sight of moving prey could be more quickening to a trout. But he submitted to the quieting urge. He stayed in his groove, with ears and lateral lines both listening for the hawk.

9   The fluffs of moonlight disappeared in a tremulous green shine. No wind rocked the surface now, but the Trout could see the current draining toward the dam. It was a checkered wavering, unhurried and unaltering. Daylight reached the bottom, where the water's ripples had been fixed in sandy silt.

10   Directly over him the Trout could look into the air. His view was circular, and small; his own length would have spanned it. Beyond that opening the surface was an opaque silver cover, stretching to the shores. Reflected in it were the floor of the pond, the swimming animals, and the underwater plants. The Trout could see the lustrous belly of a leopard frog spring past. He also saw, in the mirror spread above, the frog's bronze, spotted back. The pond was a shallow layer of the world, with a ceiling on which its life was repeated upside-down.

11   Upon the surface crashed a huge light-feathered breast. Claws reached

and speared a bullhead. A brown throat, then a beak and eyes came through the top of the pond, and wings and tail. A shower of bubbles scattered downward as the long wings lowered in a sweep. The wings began to lift the Osprey. A final thrashing took him out of the surface, leaving the reverberations of his dive.

12   The wariness of the Trout released its check. He floated from his groove, still seeming motionless, as if the current had dislodged him. Slowly his fins commenced a ribbonlike stroke. His tail pressed gently on the water, left and right.

13   Freeing his entire strength in a tail-thrust then, he was across the pond. A spinning turn, and, energy closely held, he slanted toward the bottom silt—the touch, and a spasm of upward speed had flung him into the dangerous dazzling air.

14   A slicing dive back deep in the pond, a glimpse of another trout, and he whipped in its pursuit. But just before his teeth would have nicked its tail, he whirled, and the trout ahead whirled too, in perfect unison.

15   He cut forward in the channel of the current, throwing his tail from side to side as he tried to find in his own speed some full outlet for his strength. The water of the pond would give him nowhere more than a mild and yielding pressure. He was a native cutthroat of the Snake, a turbulent swift river, but the placid pond and little brook that fed it were the only home that he had known. In early summer of the year the beavers built the pond, his parents had come up the brook to spawn. The new dam trapped them and their offspring. The river poured along the east side of the marsh, so near that the Trout could feel its deep vibration. He had not seen it, but his spirit cried for its stronger flow, its more combative force.

16   Yet idle swimming could be pleasant. He glided to the backwash past the brook, toward food not scented, seen, or heard, but certain to appear. Sculled by his tail, he wove through bare elastic water-lily stalks, beneath a cover of translucent leaves. He was at rest in motion, fins outspread to ride the smooth support, his slippery skin quick-sliding through the wetness. But he stiffened, shot ahead, bent nose to tail, kicked back the tail in a sharp return, perhaps to savor the grace of a body incapable of awkwardness in an element incapable of angles: beautiful play.

17   He saw a streaming like fine grasses drawn by the current—dace! With a forward spring he snatched a minnow at the side of the school. Alarm flashed through them all, and the leaders swung to flee into the brook. The milling of the others would have made each one available to the Trout, but he swerved away.

18   He'd seen a pair of reedy, jointed legs, seeming to be rooted in the silt, but still, not quivering as reeds would in the flow of the pond. The dace swam toward them. The dace had left the safety of the shallows because a harmless moose was splashing there. The Trout had captured one, and now the great

blue heron certainly would catch another. But would not catch the Trout! Already he was far beyond the stab of the bird's beak.

19   Near the shore the water swished with the feet of ducks. A quick look: no mergansers' feet, with paddle-toes for diving, there among the webs of mallards, pintails, and of baldpates. The Trout swam under them. He need not dread an enemy's unexpected dive here while the feet were moving the ducks about in search of food, while they were easy, pushing webfuls of water back and folding in and drawing forward; not while one foot hung, a pivot, and the other swung an oval breast; or both of a duck's webs splashed at the surface, holding him bill-down. As long as no fear tensed the feet, the Trout felt safe.

20   The long stripe on a pintail's neck shone white as it lowered the bird's head, swanlike, to the bottom. But swiftly it was pulled above the surface. Now all the feet were quiet, spread from the feathered bellies, ready for a leap. The Trout, alert, poised in midwater.

21   He did not know what animal had frightened the ducks. While they continued their wary wait, the white keel of the pelican dipped through the surface, slid ahead, and, checked by its wide webs, glided to a stop. The Trout streamed off, away from the watchful ducks, and gradually forgot their warning.

22   When he was a young fish, nearly every animal he saw seemed hungry for him. One by one then he outgrew the threat of frogs, kingfishers, snakes, and larger trout. He learned the tricks of human fishermen. Minks and mergansers chased him still but could not capture him. No other creature in the pond was quite so swift. And he almost was too heavy to be carried by an osprey. Soon the Trout might reach security that few wild creatures know, unless the alien of the early morning proved a danger.

23   Every instinct whispers some command; for him the loudest command was always, *live.* He listened for it, always deferred his other urges to it. Survival was so strong an impulse in him that the most involuntary workings of his body helped him hide. The pale sheen on his belly matched the cover of the pond, to an eye below. One watching from across the surface might confuse the iridescence of his scales with scales of sunlight on the ripples. The black spots spattered on his skin disguised his shape when seen from any angle. To a mate or rival he might show two crimson gashes on his throat, but usually he folded them beneath his jaws.

24   When his alarm had quieted, he started to the beaver house. First he passed a bank of sedges. In summer when their shade was green, the Trout had turned to emerald here. This autumn day the grass was tawny, and its color, focused in his eyes, had caused the grains of yellow in his skin to scatter out and tint him olive. If the inborn guardian in his tissues could arrange it, he would live. Yet other animals also had ingenious aids, some useful in attack.

25   He circled the island on the dam, now moving through a tunnel of grasses, bent with the tips of the blades awash. The sun was laying gold bars over him. He moved with a little flourish, for it seemed that he was really safe. Beyond

the far side of the island a floating log pressed down the top of the pond. He started under—and was circled with a crash.

26   Escape! Escape to a nook in the dam! He split the water and was there. Wheeling, he shot in the hole and flung out his fins to check him. The water bulged in after him, as the one who chased him surged to a stop outside.

27   He had not seen what creature dived from the log. But his dash to the shelter, finished between heartbeats, was long enough to tell him that the other gained. Gained! Did panic echo, now, from days when the rush of most pursuers swept upon him like a wave?

28   His refuge was a space in the roots of a cottonwood, the dead tree anchoring the dam. Through interwoven fibres he could see his enemy, an animal he did not know, the Otter. The creature darted around the root-maze, trying to peer in. His eyes would show in one place, reaching for the Trout. A drive with a quick foot, and the brown-furred face would push into another hole. Eagerly it was weaving forward, cocked ears sharp as claws.

29   The Otter found a looser tangle, which his paws began to tear. The water was tainted with the scent of his excitement, acrid in the nostrils of the Trout. Close beside the Trout's face now a lean webbed paw had grasped a root. The claws were scratching as the toes kept tightening in convulsive grips. The Otter tried to burrow through, but the tangle held. Should the Trout attempt to reach the sturdier beaver house? No longer was there safety in a flight. He tensed his tail for a great thrust; yet he hesitated.

30   As suddenly then as if the Otter had seen a more accessible fish, he drew back out of the roots. He swam away with a vertical sculling, so that each roll took him to the top. The pulses in the water matched the surging that had stirred the pond at dawn.

31   The water beat for some time with his strokes and other creatures' startled movements. When the Trout could feel the light quick overlap of wavelets nearly spent, he knew that the Otter had gone to the far end of the pond. Then he could have fled to the beaver house, but he was waiting for the Osprey's midday dive. His new fear had not blurred his sense of the older menace.

32   The Osprey's perch was in the tree whose roots now hid him. He could not see the hawk, but when the spread wings glided from the upper boughs, they came into his air-view. He watched, as he never had from the beaver house, the way the Osprey hovered high above his victim, and how he plunged, so slanting his dive that he dropped from behind an unsuspecting fish. The Trout could recognize the jolting of the pond, the splashing as the Osprey struggled from the water, the sudden quiet, and widening of the echoes. The hawk returned in his air-view, carrying a mountain sucker to his branch. After he ate the fish, he flew back down to clean his claws. The Trout could see them cross the pond, thin hooks that cut the surface, trailing silvered sacs of air.

33   At last the water near the cottonwood roots sucked up, a motion meaning that some heavy animal was climbing out. A gust of drops fell onto the surface,

as the creature shuddered the moisture from its fur. Feet ran over the top of the dam. As they passed the base of the tree, a sift of dirt fell through the roots and briefly struck to the mucous coating on the skin of the Trout.

34   The pond was all in motion, for the wind had risen. The wind had stirred the marsh for several days, with short lulls. The Trout sensed that it brought a change of season. He could even taste the proof of summer's end, as dust, seeds, crumbling leaves and bark washed through the pond.

35   Bright-edged shadows of the waves were racing over the bottom silt. They swept across the underwater plants and seemed to shake them. The surface layer of the pond was blowing to the upper end of the backwash. There the water turned below, to sweep back down along the bottom. Against the dam this flowing sheet rolled up. It pressed beneath the Trout's fins as a breeze will lift the wings of a bird.

36   Whenever the wind would strain the top of the rigid dead tree, he could feel a pulling in the roots. Abruptly they began to writhe, to tear. The Trout was out of the maze and back in the beaver house as if the water had parted for him.

37   The Osprey's tree, upturned by the wind, fell into the pond. Billows met rebounding billows, whirls and eddies struggled, surges rocked the Trout. Gradually the violence quieted. Through a cloud of mud he dimly saw that the trunk of the tree was under the surface, propped up from the bottom on its boughs.

38   He settled himself to feel the current's long touch on his sides. But what disturbing change was this: the water's stroking soon was regular, yet took a new course—not from his nose to tail but downward now. The water's pressure was becoming lighter and its color rosier. The top of the pond was falling.

39   Inherited memories warned him that the change was ominous. But he did not leave his shelter, for it seemed that a greater danger threatened him outside: the Otter had returned. Sometimes the Trout could hear him in the water, sometimes out along the narrowing shores. The Trout would not be caught through panic. He lay in his nook and watched the surface drop.

40   Only when it reached the nook itself did he nose outside. Feeling the Otter's surging near, he turned down to a refuge lower in the wall. The top of the pond descended on him there. The water, draining off the bank beside the house, was roily, so that he could not see where he would go. But he entered it and let its motion guide him.

41   The currents were not flowing in familiar paths. They all converged in a powerful new suction. Since the roots of the cottonwood tree had been interwoven with the dam, its fall had torn apart the beaver's masonry of mud and sticks. The whole marsh seemed to be swirling toward the gap and plunging through it.

42   The Trout turned back. He would escape to the brook. He sensed that he must leave the doomed pond and would seek the water's source, as many of the other fish had done. He could not reach it. While he, the one most wary,

stayed in the house to escape the Otter, the pond had shrunk below the mouth of the brook. The only water now connecting them was a thin sheet crinkling over a pebble bar.

43   Gone, lost above the surface, were the undercut banks of roots, the grassy tunnels, brush, and other shoreline hideaways. The Trout returned to the lower end of the pond. He glided with his fins streamlined in the depressions in his sides, and with so slight a sculling that he might be trying to make smoothness hide him. As he approached the dam, he saw the Otter. Dodging up the bottom toward the island, he slipped beneath the log, which drifted now with one end resting on the silt.

44   The Otter was walking on the pond floor, moving with a swing from his shoulders to his high arched rump. He somersaulted to the surface for a breath; then looped and tumbled through the water. He straightened toward the hole in the dam. The fluent column of his body merged with the strands of the current and he vanished.

45   The surface soon was shattered by a splash. The Otter was back. He had climbed up over the dam, beside the gap. He dived in, disappeared through the break, and again returned. A plunge, a joining with the water's sweep, and a swift ride: he had found a game.

46   The Trout was holding down his top fin, tense with fear. He spread it, and it struck the under side of the log. And yet his belly touched the silt. The log was the pond's last refuge, but the water soon would leave it.

47   Nothing in the Trout's experience could help him. He only could give himself to the urge that so intensely pressed to have him live. He waited until the Otter had dived and once more swung out through the hole. Leaving the log with a jet of speed, the Trout had reached the gap. A gushing force took hold of him. It hurled him through the break. Too quick for thought he dodged the wreckage of the dam. He leapt to pass the brink of the fall and dropped in the foam beneath. The cascade lightened, slowed, and he found himself in a shallow creek-bed, moving over cobblestones.

48   His high emotion quickened his choice of route: to the left, through streamers of emerald algae; right, along a slit between the stones; here a turn to miss a piece of driftwood, there to pass a boulder. The air was seldom far above his topmost fin. Sometimes he drew a breath of it, and it seared his gills with dryness. Avoiding one by one the unfamiliar hazards, he progressed.

49   His lateral lines were jarred by a new sound, a tremendous heavy pouring. He swam around a bend in the creek and slid across a bar. And there a torrent plunged upon him, water more swift than any he had known. He was in the river, the violent tumult of the Snake.

50   It nearly overwhelmed him, but he found a milder flow along the bank. A curve there held a pool as in a shell. The pool was covered by a sweeper, a willow with its caught debris. The Trout discovered the refuge, entered it, and spiraled down into the cool green quiet.

51   Through the afternoon he stayed there, gaining back his poise and fitting his spirit to the strange new shape of his life. Most of the time he hung in the water, motionless, but now and then a ripple ran through his fins, and he chopped his breaths as with excitement. When the first gray wave of dusk washed over the pool, he rose to the top.

52   He swam along the bank, where ripples pattered into crevices among the roots. The motion of the water here was light and peaceful, like the pond's. Turning out, he met a crisper current, stimulating as the pond had never been. An even greater challenge growled from the center of the river, from grinding rocks that yielded to the push of water irrresistibly strong. The Trout began to slant his strokes into the torrent. With a leap he sprang to the very heart of its taut pressure. Enormous weight bore down upon him, but he gripped it, driving his way against it with exultant power.

53   To fight! To fight the turbulent flow! To sharpen his nerves on its chill; to cut quick arcs through the weaving water; to throw so much force into his muscles' swing that they could drive him upstream, past the rocks beneath, with the whole flood pounding toward him; to fling himself out into the air and see the river under him, a river wider than the pond, wide for his play— all this, the heritage of a trout, he knew now for the first time.

54   He faced the flood and, sculling exactly at the current's pace, remained above the same stone. Swirling past were many insects, blown in the river. He stayed to take a cricket only, for exhilaration sang in his nerves. He leapt—

55   But stopped, caught. Talons had stabbed into his flesh, were now locked through it. They were holding him in the center of a splash. A feathered throat was lowering before his eyes. Wings were sweeping down at the sides, enclosing him. The Osprey, forgotten in his conquest of the river, had made its sunset dive.

56   His torn nerves stung the Trout to action. The claws were powerful that bound him, but his thrashing bent their grip. They almost rigidly resisted, but they did bend. They were a pressure, like the river's force—to fight!

57   His instinct focused on one urge, to get himself in deeper water. Arching his body downward, he furiously tried to scull from side to side. The hawk's wings beat, attempting to lift his own weight and the Trout's. The wings and the driving paddle of the Trout's tail pulled against each other. So far the Trout had not been able to drag the bird down, but he held himself under the surface of the water.

58   The river was aiding the fish. For the Osprey was growing desperate for a breath. At first the spines on the pads of his feet had pierced the skin of the Trout. They passed their hold no longer. And the Trout could feel the talons in his flesh release their clutch. The hawk was trying to withdraw them, but their curving points were caught securely.

59   The bird and fish were swirling downstream. They jolted to a stop, snagged by the willow sweeper. The water's force was beating at them. It poured through

the Osprey's feathers. The push of the wings was weakening. They suddenly relaxed, awash in the flow. And the claws were limp.

60   The Trout had fought another pressure, his exhaustion. When the straining of the talons ceased, he too relaxed. For long enough to gather a little strength, he waited. Then he began an intermittent thrashing. With bursts of effort he tried to jerk himself away. One by one the claws worked out, some slipping loose but more of them tearing through his sides. Finally a twist of his body sent him forward, free.

61   He turned down under the willow, lower and lower in the dark pool. With his flesh so cut, his lateral lines no longer clearly caught the echo of his motions, thus to guide him. He was careful therefore not to swim against the bottom. His chin touched, and he sank upon a stone. The stone was smooth, and soft with slime-coat algae. Soon he had drifted over on his side. His eyes were dull and his fins closed. His consciousness sank lower.

62   The Trout had been so stimulated by the river that he had ignored his innate caution. But now he was listening again to instinct, not to the water's roar. As he lay and waited for his strength to seep back into him, no creature could have been more passive, none more acquiescent.

63   The water's cold had numbed the anguish in his severed nerves. It would draw his wounds together. Already it had put in winter sluggishness the parasites that possibly would enter his exposed flesh. And gradually, as he rested, the cold became a tonic to his temper. Cold was as sharpening to him as the warm sun is to insects. By midnight he was swimming experimentally around the bottom. He circled higher. The Osprey was gone from the willow sweeper. The Trout moved out of the pool.

64   He found a backwash near the bank and held himself on the edge, where a smooth flow passed. Moonlight, falling on the surface, showed that a drift of small debris was swirling by. Drowned insects should be in it. His eyes discovered a bright bit up ahead. He swayed forward. His mouth opened, touched it, and it broke with a singing snap. More came floating toward him—little round stars. Some winked out. He let the others pass.

65   But here was what he liked, a mayfly. Earlier in the day the year's last swarm had left the river for their brief erotic life. Now their delicate spent bodies would be nourishment for the Trout. Many others came his way. After his hunger had been satisfied, he took one more, and shot it out of his mouth for the chance of catching it again, of biting it in two and tossing out and snapping up the pieces.

66   Now he was not shaped like a smooth wedge, for the cover of one gill was hanging loose, and his sides were ragged. And so his balance in the turns of the water was not perfect. His fins were spread, all needed to aid his sculling tail. Yet the fins were rippling with an easy motion, easy as a creature can be only when it feels that more of living is ahead.

67   The winter, when a trout is quiet, would be long enough for his wounds

to heal, and for his nerves to sharpen. Soon the last migrating Osprey would be gone—but would come back. And otters might be hunting here. The Trout must learn the dangers of this flood, and learn to be wary even while he was exhilarated by it. He would. The wisdom of instinct, as of intelligence, can be disregarded, and it also can be drawn upon.

68   By the time he would be ready to try his strength once more against the river, the Snake would be a slapping, dodging, driving, wild spring torrent.

☐ Discovering Meaning and Technique

1. The setting of this selection is Teton March, at Jackson Hole, Wyoming. Are you familiar with the animals in the drama—the cuttthroat trout, osprey, bullhead, dace, pintail, otter, merganser? If not, look them up in an encyclopedia.

2. How did the trout come to live in the pond rather than in the Snake River, his native home?

3. What threats does the trout experience in the pond?

4. What violent, natural act abruptly changes the trout's life?

5. How does this act affect the trout's natural caution?

6. Carrighar presents the events of the trout's day as a story—with characters, plot, conflict, and resolution. Further, the story is told from the trout's point of view: We know what motivates him and how he responds to events. Nevertheless, the selection never sounds like children's literature, in which animals take on human characteristics. How does Carrighar achieve this effect?

7. Although the selection sounds like a story, it includes a remarkable amount of information about the trout: its physiology, environment, habits, and so on. Is this an efficient technique for relating scientific information?

☐ Writing Suggestions

1. Relate an event that could occur in the life of an animal with which you are very familiar—for example, a squirrel, cat, dog, horse, green snake, chameleon, wild duck, rabbit, gopher, parakeet, or hamster. Try to relate the event in such a way that you give information about the animal's habits.

2. Using the library, research an animal and write about its habits and environment.

3. By simplifying and shortening the selection, rewrite it as a children's story.

4. Discuss how nature is a system of the eaters and the eaten. How do humans fit in the system?

5. Explore the subject of what various animals are capable of perceiving. Carrighar mentions that the trout "knows," "expects," and "dreads." Do these sensations seem realistic?

THE COURAGE OF TURTLES

☐ **EDWARD HOAGLAND**

1 Turtles are a kind of bird with the governor turned low. With the same attitude of removal, they cock a glance at what is going on, as if they need only to fly away. Until recently they were also a case of virtue rewarded, at least in the town where I grew up, because, being humble creatures, there were plenty of them. Even when we still had a few bobcats in the woods the local snapping turtles, growing up to forty pounds, were the largest carnivores. You would see them through the amber water, as big as greeny wash basins at the bottom of the pond, until they faded into the inscrutable mud as if they hadn't existed at all.

2   When I was ten I went to Dr. Green's Pond, a two-acre pond across the road. When I was twelve I walked a mile or so to Taggart's Pond, which was lusher, had big water snakes and a waterfall; and shortly after that I was bicycling way up to the adventuresome vastness of Mud Pond, a lake-sized body of water in the reservoir system of a Connecticut city, possessed of cat-backed little islands and empty shacks and a forest of pines and hardwoods along the shore. Otters, foxes and mink left their prints on the bank; there were pike and perch. As I got older, the estates and forgotten back lots in town were parceled out and sold for nice prices, yet, though the woods had shrunk, it seemed that fewer people walked in the woods. The new residents didn't know how to find them. Eventually, exploring, they did find them, and it required some ingenuity and doubling around on my part to go for eight miles without meeting someone. I was grown by now, I lived in New York, and that's what I wanted on the occasional weekends when I came out.

3   Since Mud Pond contained drinking water I had felt confident nothing untoward would happen there. For a long while the developers stayed away, until the drought of the mid-1960s. This event, squeezing the edges in, convinced the local water company that the pond really wasn't a necessity as a catch basin, however; so they bulldozed a hole in the earthen dam, bulldozed the

banks to fill in the bottom, and landscaped the flow of water that remained to wind like an English brook and provide a domestic view for the houses which were planned. Most of the painted turtles of Mud Pond, who had been inaccessible as they sunned on their rocks, wound up in boxes in boys' closets within a matter of days. Their footsteps in the dry leaves gave them away as they wandered forlornly. The snappers and the little musk turtles, neither of whom leave the water except once a year to lay their eggs, dug into the drying mud for another siege of hot weather, which they were accustomed to doing whenever the pond got low. But this time it was low for good; the mud baked over them and slowly entombed them. As for the ducks, I couldn't stroll in the woods and not feel guilty, because they were crouched beside every stagnant pothole, or were slinking between the bushes with their heads tucked into their shoulders so that I wouldn't see them. If they decided I had, they beat their way up through the screen of trees, striking their wings dangerously, and wheeled about with that headlong, magnificent velocity to locate another poor puddle.

4   I used to catch possums and black snakes as well as turtles, and I kept dogs and goats. Some summers I worked in a menagerie with the big personalities of the animal kingdom, like elephants and rhinoceroses. I was twenty before these enthusiasms began to wane, and it was then that I picked turtles as the particular animal I wanted to keep in touch with. I was allergic to fur, for one thing, and turtles need minimal care and not much in the way of quarters. They're personable beasts. They see the same colors we do and they seem to see just as well, as one discovers in trying to sneak up on them. In the laboratory they unravel the twists of a maze with the hot-blooded rapidity of a mammal. Though they can't run as fast as a rat, they improve on their errors just as quickly, pausing at each crossroads to look left and right. And they rock rhythmically in place, as we often do, although they are hatched from eggs, not the womb. (A common explanation psychologists give for our pleasure in rocking quietly is that it recapitulates our mother's heartbeat *in utero.*)

5   Snakes, by contrast, are dryly silent and priapic. They are smooth movers, legalistic, unblinking, and they afford the humor which the humorless do. But they make challenging captives; sometimes they don't eat for months on a point of order—if the light isn't right, for instance. Alligators are sticklers too. They're like war-horses, or German shepherds, and with their bar-shaped, vertical pupils adding emphasis, they have the *idée fixe* of eating, eating, even when they choose to refuse all food and stubbornly die. They delight in tossing a salamander up towards the sky and grabbing him in their long mouths as he comes down. They're so eager that they get the jitters, and they're too much of a proposition for a casual aquarium like mine. Frogs are depressingly defenseless: that moist, extensive back, with the bones almost sticking through. Hold a frog and you're holding its skeleton. Frogs' tasty legs are the staff of life to many animals— herons, raccoons, ribbon snakes—though they themselves are hard to feed. It's not an enviable role to be the staff of life, and after frogs you descend down the evolutionary ladder a big step to fish.

6 Turtles cough, burp, whistle, grunt and hiss, and produce social judgments. They put their heads together amicably enough, but then one drives the other back with the suddenness of two dogs who have been conversing in tones too low for an onlooker to hear. They pee in fear when they're first caught, but exercise both pluck and optimism in trying to escape, walking for hundreds of yards within the confines of their pen, carrying the weight of that cumbersome box on legs which are cruelly positioned for walking. They don't feel that the contest is unfair; they keep plugging, rolling like sailorly souls—a bobbing, infirm gait, a brave, sea-legged momentum—stopping occasionally to study the lay of the land. For me, anyway, they manage to contain the rest of the animal world. They can stretch out their necks like a giraffe, or loom underwater like an apocryphal hippo. They browse on lettuce thrown on the water like a cow moose which is partly submerged. They have a penguin's alertness, combined with a build like a Brontosaurus when they rise up on tiptoe. Then they hunch and ponderously lunge like a grizzly going forward.

7   Baby turtles in a turtle bowl are a puzzle in geometrics. They're as decorative as pansy petals, but they are also self-directed building blocks, propping themselves on one another in different arrangements, before upending the tower. The timid individuals turn fearless, or vice versa. If one gets a bit arrogant he will push the others off the rock and afterwards climb down into the water and cling to the back of one of those he has bullied, tickling him with his hind feet until he bucks like a bronco. On the other hand, when this same milder-mannered fellow isn't exerting himself, he will stare right into the face of the sun for hours. What could be more lionlike? And he's at home in or out of the water and does lots of metaphysical tilting. He sinks and rises, with an infinity of levels to choose from; or, elongating himself, he climbs out on the land again to perambulate, sits boxed in his box, and finally slides back in the water, submerging into dreams.

8   I have five of these babies in a kidney-shaped bowl. The hatchling, who is a painted turtle, is not as large as the top joint of my thumb. He eats chicken gladly. Other foods he will attempt to eat but not with sufficient perseverance to succeed because he's so little. The yellow-bellied terrapin is probably a yearling, and he eats salad voraciously, but no meat, fish or fowl. The Cumberland terrapin won't touch salad or chicken but eats fish and all of the meats except for bacon. The little snapper, with a black crenelated shell, feasts on any kind of meat, but rejects greens and fish. The fifth of the turtles is African. I acquired him only recently and don't know him well. A mottled brown, he unnerves the green turtles, dragging their food off to his lairs. He doesn't seem to want to be green—he bites the algae off his shell, hanging meanwhile at daring, steep, head-first angles.

9   The snapper was a Ferdinand until I provided him with deeper water. Now he snaps at my pencil with his downturned and fearsome mouth, his swollen face like a napalm victim's. The Cumberland has an elliptical red mark on the side of his green-and-yellow head. He is benign by nature and ought to be as

elegant as his scientific name *(Pseudemys scripta elegans),* except he has contracted a disease of the air bladder which has permanently inflated it; he floats
high in the water at an undignified slant and can't go under. There may have
been internal bleeding, too, because his carapace is stained along its ridge. Unfortunately, like flowers, baby turtles often die. Their mouths fill up with a white
fungus and their lungs with pneumonia. Their organs clog up from the rust in
the water, or diet troubles, and, like a dying man's, their eyes and heads become
too prominent. Toward the end, the edge of the shell becomes flabby as felt
and folds around them like a shroud.

10   While they live they're like puppies. Although they're vivacious, they would
be a bore to be with all the time, so I also have an adult wood turtle about six
inches long. Her shell is the equal of any seashell for sculpturing, even a Cellini
shell; it's like an old, dusty, richly engraved medallion dug out of a hillside.
Her legs are salmon-orange bordered with black and protected by canted, heroic
scales. Her plastron—the bottom shell—is splotched like a margay cat's coat,
with black ocelli on a yellow background. It is convex to make room for the
female organs inside, whereas a male's would be concave to help him fit tightly
on top of her. Altogether, she exhibits every camouflage color on her limbs
and shells. She has a turtleneck neck, a tail like an elephant's, wise old pachyder-
mous hind legs and the face of a turkey—except that when I carry her she
gazes at the passing ground with a hawk's eyes and mouth. Her feet fit to the
fingers of my hand, one to each one, and she rides looking down. She can walk
on the floor in perfect silence, but usually she lets her shell knock portentously,
like a footstep, so that she resembles some grand, concise, slow-moving id. But
if an earthworm is presented, she jerks swiftly ahead, poises above it and strikes
like a mongoose, consuming it with wild vigor. Yet she will climb on my lap
to eat bread or boiled eggs.

11   If put into a creek, she swims like a cutter, nosing forward to intercept a
strange turtle and smell him. She drifts with the current to go downstream,
maneuvering behind a rock when she wants to take stock, or sinking to the
nether levels, while bubbles float up. Getting out, choosing her path, she will
proceed a distance and dig into a pile of humus, thrusting herself to the coolest
layer at the bottom. The hole closes over her until it's as small as a mouse's
hole. She's not as aquatic as a muck turtle, not quite as terrestrial as the box
turtles in the same woods, but because of her versatility she's marvelous, she's
everywhere. And though she breathes the way we breathe, with scarcely perceptible movements of her chest, sometimes instead she pumps her throat ruminatively,
like a pipe smoker sucking and puffing. She waits and blinks, pumping her throat,
turning her head, then sets off like a loping tiger in slow motion, hurdling the
jungly lumber, the pea vine and twigs. She estimates angels so well that when
she rides over the rocks, sliding down a drop-off with her rugged front legs
extended, she has the grace of a rodeo mare.

12   But she's well off to be with me rather than at Mud Pond. The other

turtles have fled—those that aren't baked into the bottom. Creeping up the brooks to sad, constricted marshes, burdened as they are with that box on their backs, they're walking into a setup where all their enemies move thirty times faster than they. It's like the nightmare most of us have whimpered through, where we are weighted down disastrously while trying to flee; fleeing our home ground, we try to run.

13   I've seen turtles in still worse straits. On Broadway, in New York, there is a penny arcade which used to sell baby terrapins that were scrawled with bon mots in enamel paint, such as KISS ME BABY. The manager turned out to be a wholesaler as well, and once I asked him whether he had any larger turtles to sell. He took me upstairs to a loft room devoted to the turtle business. There were desks for the paper work and a series of racks that held shallow tin bins atop one another, each with several hundred babies crawling around in it. He was a smudgy-complexioned, serious fellow and he did have a few adult terrapins, but I was going to school and wasn't actually planning to buy; I'd only wanted to see them. They were aquatic turtles, but here they went without water, presumably for weeks, lurching about in those dry bins like handicapped citizens, living on gumption. An easel where the artist worked stood in the middle of the floor. She had a palette and a clip attachment for fastening the babies in place. She wore a smock and a beret, and was homely, short and eccentric-looking, with funny black hair, like some of the ladies who show their paintings in Washington Square in May. She had a cold, she was smoking, and her hand wasn't very steady, although she worked quickly enough. The smile that she produced for me would have looked giddy if she had been happier, or drunk. Of course the turtles' doom was sealed when she painted them, because their bodies inside would continue to grow but their shells would not. Gradually, invisibly, they would be crushed. Around us their bellies—two thousand belly shells—rubbed on the bins with a mournful, momentous hiss.

14   Somehow there were so many of them I didn't rescue one. Years later, however, I was walking on First Avenue when I noticed a basket of living turtles in front of a fish store. They were as dry as a heap of old bones in the sun; nevertheless, they were creeping over one another gimpily, doing their best to escape. I looked and was touched to discover that they appeared to be wood turtles, my favorites, so I bought one. In my apartment I looked closer and realized that in fact this was a diamond-back terrapin, which was bad news. Diamondbacks are tidewater turtles from brackish estuaries, and I had no sea water to keep him in. He spent his days thumping interminably against the baseboards, pushing for an opening through the wall. He drank thirstily but would not eat and had none of the hearty, accepting qualities of wood turtles. He was morose, paler in color, sleeker and more Oriental in the carved ridges and rings that formed his shell. Though I felt sorry for him, finally I found his unrelenting presence exasperating. I carried him, struggling in a paper bag, across town to the Morton Street Pier on the Hudson. It was August but gray and

windy. He was very surprised when I tossed him in; for the first time in our association, I think, he was afraid. He looked afraid as he bobbed about on top of the water, looking up at me from ten feet below. Though we were both accustomed to his resistance and rigidity, seeing him still pitiful, I recognized that I must have done the wrong thing. At least the river was salty, but it was also bottomless; the waves were too rough for him, and the tide was coming in, bumping him against the pilings underneath the pier. Too late, I realized that he wouldn't be able to swim to a peaceful inlet in New Jersey, even if he could figure out which way to swim. But since, short of diving in after him, there was nothing I could do, I walked away.

☐ Discovering Meaning and Technique

1. Point out a few of the comparisons that Hoagland makes between turtles and people.

2. What is Hoagland's attitude toward the fate of the wildlife when Mud Pond is spoiled by developers?

3. For what reasons did Hoagland choose the turtle as "the particular animal I wanted to keep in touch with" (paragraph 4)?

4. What is the overall effect of the scene in which the woman is painting the turtles' shells?

5. In the last paragraph, Hoagland relates a rather sad experience with a turtle. Why did Hoagland find "his unrelenting presence exasperating"?

6. Why is the selection named "The Courage of Turtles"?

☐ Writing Suggestions

1. Hoagland relates some of his experiences as a boy and as a young man with the outdoors. Write a paper on your own experiences in the outdoors. What activities and animals interested you and why?

2. Hoagland describes a surprising variety of turtles—their appearance, behavior, and eating habits. Write a paper on the behavior of different members of another animal group—such as snakes, frogs, deer, fish, dogs, cats, or horses.

3. Describe an experience in which you observed wilderness and wildlife destroyed by land developers.

4. Hoagland tells us that painting their shells is fatal to turtles. Should there be laws against cruelty to animals for the amusement of people? Describe other such practices harmful to animals.

5. Should we establish wildlife preserves that people are not allowed to visit?

HAS SUCCESS SPOILED THE CROW?

☐ **DAVID QUAMMIN**

[1] Any person with no steady job and no children naturally finds time for a sizable amount of utterly idle speculation. For instance, me—I've developed a theory about crows. It goes like this:

[2]   Crows are bored. They suffer from being too intelligent for their station in life. Respectable evolutionary success is simply not, for these brainy and complex birds, enough. They are dissatisfied with the narrow goals and horizons of that tired old Darwinian struggle. On the lookout for a new challenge. See them there, lined up conspiratorially along a fence rail or a high wire, shoulder to shoulder, alert, self-contained, missing nothing. Feeling discreetly thwarted. Waiting, like an ambitious understudy, for their break. Dolphins and whales and chimpanzees get all the fawning publicity, great fuss made over their near-human intelligence. But don't be fooled. Crows are not stupid. Far from it. They are merely underachievers. They are bored.

[3]   Most likely it runs in their genes, along with the black plumage and the talent for vocal mimicry. Crows belong to a remarkable family of birds known as the Corvidae, also including ravens, magpies, jackdaws and jays, and the case file on this entire clan is so full of prodigious and quirky behavior that it cries out for interpretation not by an ornithologist but a psychiatrist. Or, failing that, some ignoramus with a supple theory. Computerized ecologists can give us those fancy equations depicting the whole course of a creature's life history in terms of energy allotment to every physical need, with variables for fertility and senility and hunger and motherly love; but they haven't yet programmed in a variable for boredom. No wonder the Corvidae dossier is still packed with unanswered questions.

[4]   At first glance, though, all is normal: Crows and their corvid relatives seem to lead an exemplary birdlike existence. The home life is stable and protective. Monogamy is the rule, and most mated pairs stay together until death. Courtship is elaborate, even rather tender, with the male doing a good bit of bowing and dancing and jiving, not to mention supplying his intended with food; eventually he offers the first scrap of nesting material as a sly hint that they get on with it.

While she incubates a clutch of four to six eggs, he continues to furnish the groceries, and stands watch nearby at night. Then for a month after hatching, both parents dote on the young. Despite strenuous care, mortality among fledglings is routinely high, sometimes as high as 70 percent, but all this crib death is counterbalanced by the longevity of the adults. Twenty-year-old crows are not unusual, and one raven in captivity survived to age twenty-nine. Anyway, corvids show no inclination toward breeding themselves up to huge numbers, filling the countryside with their kind (like the late passenger pigeon, or an infesting variety of insect) until conditions shift for the worse, and a vast population collapses. Instead, crows and their relatives reproduce at roughly the same stringent rate through periods of bounty or austerity, maintaining levels of population that are modest but consistent, and which can be supported throughout any foreseeable hard times. In this sense they are astute pessimists. One consequence of such modesty of demographic ambition is to leave them with excess time, and energy, not desperately required for survival.

5   The other thing they possess in excess is brain-power. They have the largest cerebral hemispheres, relative to body size, of any avian family. On various intelligence tests—to measure learning facility, clock-reading skills, the ability to count—they have made other birds look doltish. One British authority, Sylvia Bruce Wilmore, pronounces them "quicker on the uptake" than certain well-thought-of mammals like the cat and the monkey, and admits that her own tamed crow so effectively dominated the other animals in her household that this bird "would even pick up the spaniel's leash and lead him around the garden!" Wilmore also adds cryptically: "Scientists at the University of Mississippi have been successful in getting the cooperation of Crows." But she fails to make clear whether that was as test subjects, or on a consultative basis.

6   From other crow experts come the same sort of anecdote. Crows hiding food in all manner of unlikely spots and relying on their uncanny memories, like adepts at the game of Concentration, to find the caches again later. Crows using twenty-three distinct forms of call to communicate various sorts of information to each other. Crows in flight dropping clams and walnuts on highway pavement, to break open the shells so the meats can be eaten. Then there's the one about the hooded crow, a species whose range includes Finland: "In this land Hoodies show great initiative during winter when men fish through holes in the ice. Fishermen leave baited lines in the water to catch fish and on their return they have found a Hoodie pulling in the line with its bill, and walking away from the hole, then putting down the line and walking back on it to stop it sliding, and pulling it again until [the crow] catches the fish on the end of the line." These birds are bright.

7   And probably—according to my theory—they are too bright for their own good. You know the pattern. Time on their hands. Under-employed and over-qualified. Large amounts of potential just lying fallow. Peck up a little corn, knock back a few grasshoppers, carry a beak-full of dead rabbit home for the

kids, then fly over to sit on a fence rail with eight or ten cronies and watch some poor farmer sweat like a sow at the wheel of his tractor. An easy enough life, but is this *it?* Is this *all?*

8   If you don't believe me just take my word for it: Crows are bored.

9 And so there arise, as recorded in the case file, these certain . . . no, *symptoms* is too strong. Call them, rathern, *patterns of gratuitous behavior.*

10   For example, they play a lot.

11   Animal play is a reasonably common phenomenon, at least among certain mammals, especially in the young of those species. Play activities—by definition— are any that serve no immediate biological function, and which therefore do not directly improve the animal's prospects for survival and reproduction. The corvids, according to expert testimony, are irrepressibly playful. In fact, they show the most complex play known in birds. Ravens play toss with themselves in the air, dropping and catching again a small twig. They lie on their backs and juggle objects (in one recorded case, a rubber ball) between beak and feet. They jostle each other sociably in a version of "king of the mountain" with no real territorial stakes. Crows are equally frivolous. They play a brand of rugby, wherein one crow picks up a white pebble or a bit of shell and flies from tree to tree, taking a friendly bashing from its buddies until it drops the token. And they have a comedy-acrobatic routine: allowing themselves to tip backward dizzily from a wire perch, holding a loose grip so as to hang upside down, spreading out both wings, then daringly letting go with one foot; finally, switching feet to let go with the other. Such shameless hot-dogging is usually performed for a small audience of other crows.

12   There is also an element of the practical jokester. Of the Indian house crow, Wilmore says: ". . . this Crow has a sense of humor, and revels in the discomfort caused by its playful tweaking at the tails of other birds, and at the ears of sleeping cows and dogs; it also pecks the toes of flying foxes as they hang sleeping in their roosts." This crow is a laff riot. Another of Wilmore's favorite species amuses itself, she says, by "dropping down on sleeping rabbits and rapping them over the skull or settling on drowsy cattle and startling them." What we have here is actually a distinct subcategory of playfulness known, where I come from at least, as Cruisin' For A Bruisin'. It has been clinically linked to boredom.

13   Further evidence: Crows are known to indulge in sunbathing. "When sunning at fairly high intensity," says another British corvidist, "the bird usually positions itself sideways on to the sun and erects its feathers, especially those on head, belly, flanks and rump." So the truth is out: Under those sleek ebony feathers, they are tan. And of course sunbathing (like ice-fishing, come to think of it) constitutes prima facie proof of a state of paralytic ennui.

14   But the final and most conclusive bit of data comes from a monograph by K. E. L. Simmons published in the *Journal of Zoology,* out of London. (Perhaps

it's for deep reasons of national character that the British lead the world in the study of crows; in England, boredom has great cachet.) Simmons's paper is curiously entitled "Anting and the Problem of Self-Stimulation." *Anting* as used here is simply the verb (or to be more precise, participial) form of the insect. In ornithological parlance, it means that a bird—for reasons that remain mysterious—has taken to rubbing itself with mouthfuls of squashed ants. Simmons writes: "True anting consists of highly stereotyped movements whereby the birds apply ants to their feathers or expose their plumage to the ants." Besides direct application, done with the beak, there is also a variant called *passive anting:* The bird intentionally squats on a disturbed ant-hill, allowing (inviting) hundreds of ants to swarm over its body.

15   Altogether strange behavior, and especially notorious for it are the corvids. Crows avidly rub their bodies with squashed ants. They wallow amid busy ant colonies and let themselves become acrawl. They revel in formication.

16   Why? One theory is that the formic acid produced (as a defense chemical) by some ants is useful for conditioning feathers and ridding the birds of external parasites. But Simmons cites several other researchers who have independently reached a different conclusion. One of these scientists declared that the purpose of anting "is the stimulation and soothing of the body," and that the general effect "is similar to that gained by humanity from the use of external stimulants, soothing ointments, counter-irritants (including formic acid) and perhaps also smoking." Another compared anting to "the human habits of smoking and drug-taking" and maintained that "it has no biological purpose but is indulged in for its own sake, for the feeling of well-being and ecstasy it induces. . . ."

17   You know the pattern. High intelligence, large promise. Early success without great effort. Then a certain loss of purposefulness. Manifestations of detachment and cruel humor. Boredom. Finally the dangerous spiral into drug abuse.

18   But maybe it's not too late for the corvids. Keep that in mind next time you run into a raven, or a magpie, or a crow. Look the bird in the eye. Consider its frustrations. Try to say something stimulating.

☐ Discovering Meaning and Technique

1. Quammin gives a good deal of scientific information about crows, but his tone remains light and amusing. How does the first paragraph establish the tone?

2. To maintain this tone throughout the selection, Quammin uses such techniques as sentence fragments, amusing word choice, and varying sentence lengths. Find specific examples of these techniques in the selection.

3. Throughout the selection, what problem does Quammin maintain accounts for the unusual behavior of crows?

4. Which kinds of behavior demonstrate the crow's intelligence?

☐ Writing Suggestions

1. Research the characteristics of the bluejay (another member of bird family Corvidae), and compare the jay with the crow. You can use the library's card catalog or an encyclopedia of ornithology to find information.

2. Compare Quammin's description of the crow with the general attitude toward crows as pests.

3. A good bit of folklore surrounds crows; people have long used their appearance as omens—for example, one crow signals woe; two signal mirth; four signal a birth; and so on. Write an essay on crows and other birds in folklore and soothsaying. You might find information by interviewing elderly people or by researching folklore in the library.

4. Write an essay on the behavior of another bird or animal common to your region. You can rely solely upon your own observations, or you can do library research on the subject.

PLANTS AND ANIMALS IN WINTER

☐ PHYLLIS S. BUSCH

1 Step outside on a bitter winter day and you are immediately struck by the immense quiet—a hushed enveloping stillness. If the landscape is under a cover of snow the whiteness emphasizes the silence. Recall the recent assertive notes of the katydid and colorful songbirds, the gentle tinkle of the peepers—all gone. It is as if thousands of actors, each having appeared on stage, gave a rehearsed performance, finished on cue, then slowly made their exit, leaving behind a cold stillness.

2 The silence may be broken by the sudden creak of a bare limb or the gentle swoosh of a swaying evergreen branch. The sounds call attention to their living presence. The trees remain in place like permanent stage props. Both deciduous and evergreen trees are very much alive, carrying on their vital functions throughout the year, with or without leaves. Plants, other than trees, are also thriving in a variety of interesting forms. The stage is not empty. It is the settings that are different in winter.

3   Some of the animals did leave to go to warmer climates. Those remaining have just changed their costumes. The winter cast of characters may look slightly or vastly different from the original group, but each one has been endowed with its inherent genetic material which will protect its identity and help it to survive the winter.

4   The ways in which some animals survive the winter are most dramatic. In others, life-preserving is carried on in subtle and inconspicuous ways. The change might be one of dress as in the white-tailed deer. Its reddish slender-haired summer coat has been replaced by a grayish brown winter coat with stout crinkled hollow hairs to provide excellent insulation. The brown northern weasel's fur is replaced with white in winter. Even the common gray squirrel changes its thin and brown-tinged summer fur to a thicker clear gray in winter.

5   Remaining active animals often cluster together in the cold weather. Birds that choose not to migrate may be seen traveling in flocks. Small bands of robins and bluebirds are a fairly common winter sight. The flash of a blue jay or cardinal, its feathers renewed, often makes a Christmas card appearance, adding color to the scene. Some of these leftovers mingle with the juncoes and evening grosbeaks that have come down from the north, and as a special treat there is always the chance of sighting a snowy owl.

6   Birds depend greatly on their feathers for warmth because they provide perfect insulation from the cold. Some birds add more down in winter, trapping even more air that can be heated. Birds are further aided by being able to regulate their body temperature. Fluffing up their feathers when it is cold traps the air next to the body furnishing a warm blanket of heated air. As the temperature rises, the bird compresses its feathers to get rid of the trapped warm air.

7   Insects, too, may huddle. Ladybirds often band together in the cold. A mass of these adult beetles, possibly thousands, may form a cluster among the dead leaves at the base of a tree. Farther up the trunk some loose bark may provide shelter for another gathering of these insects.

8   Fallen branches and loose bark coverings often reveal attractive designs. During their winter sojurn bark beetles, also called engraver beetles, leave markings on the wood and the inside of the bark covering the wood. The resulting patterns are a clue to a part of the designer's life. Not only does the beetle engrave a characteristic design, it also selects a specific tree. Elm beetles choose elm trees. The female European elm beetle digs a vertical gallery in which to deposit her eggs, and the hatched larvae dig their feeding galleries at right angles to it. The female American elm beetle digs a horizontal groove for her eggs, and the hatchlings dig at right angles to this structure. Each completed engraving on the wood and its image mirrored by the bark covering it, resembles a many-legged centipede-like animal climbing up the tree or around it, depending on the species.

9   Winter is the strange breeding time for some kinds of insects. During a February or March thaw one may commonly find insects massed on the snow.

Long-legged crane flies, harmless common insects that superficially resemble mosquitoes, come out of the soil through the snow looking for mates. Once mating is accomplished, they return to the soil to lay their eggs.

10   Snowfleas, primitive wingless insects, are most abundantly visible in winter as thousands emerge to march over the snow in search of food. They are also called springtails because of their little tail-like structures which propel the insects in a spring-like thrust. They can actually jump several centimeters.

11   The bees, crowded in their hives, are very much alive and active all winter long. They keep the hive clean and warm and take special care of the queen for she will lay many, many eggs the following spring. During the cold weather, as in warm weather, the bees have to keep on eating. They make short trips outdoors to dispose of their wastes. Bees sometimes wander too far from the hive and are overtaken with the cold before they return. They become numb, fall on the snow, and can be mistakenly taken for dead. It is best not to pick them up because a quick revival in the hand can result in a sting. If one knows how to handle bees, the fallen ones can be warmed and then freed to return to their hive.

12   A large number of insects spend winter as a collection of eggs. In this form the adults pass on their genetic material before frost kills them. The eggs will hatch in the spring and give rise to the next generation. Egg hunting in winter is a rewarding sport.

13   One kind of egg mass that is soon recognized is, unfortunately, that of the gypsy moth. Batches may be found all over—on trees, stones, buildings, ground litter. Although frequently clustered on the lower parts of tree trunks, these eggs are also found high up in the tree. The approximately five hundred eggs are laid in a fairly large straw-colored mass. During egg-laying the female mixes hair from her body with the eggs, making the eggs rough to the touch.

14   Tiny black creatures may be found crawling among the gypsy moth eggs. These are parasitic wasps originally imported from Japan. They are laying their eggs inside the moth eggs. Black specks can be seen inside parasitized eggs. In areas where these wasps have been introduced, both the number and size of the egg masses have decreased.

15   Tent caterpillars also lay overwintering eggs, about two hundred to a clump. Waterproofed shiny bands of eggs are arranged around twigs of a variety of trees and shrubs. Wild black cherry, apple and related trees are most frequently affected by the tent caterpillar.

16   The most attractive case of eggs is the one laid by the praying mantis. The female deposits her several hundred to a thousand eggs on a twig, a board, or even the side of a building. She then covers them with a frothy blanket which hardens to form a protective cover against rain, cold and predators.

17   A most interesting egg case is the one made by the bagworm. Bags, about an inch and a half long, are decorated with bits of leaves and twigs similar to the material that the larvae had used for food. The bags hang from twigs suspended

by silken threads. Those which had been occupied by males are now empty. As with the gypsy moth, only males fly. The female's bag will contain several hundred yellow eggs.

18   A large number of insects do not overwinter as adults or as eggs but as larvae, and in a most obscure way, for they are not easily visible. They are snugly encased in plant homes where they are warm and well fed. Here they remain all winter long, eating and growing until it is time for the transformed adult to emerge in the spring. Hunting for these insects can begin in a stand of goldenrod. One conspicuous home in the shape of a small brown ball about an inch in diameter, can be easily spotted along the stem. There may be one or more on a single plant. It can be pried open to reveal a small white grub. It is the larval stage of the peacock fly, so called because the adult is attractive and struts as it walks. The previous spring the female had deposited a fertilized egg in the growing stem of the Canada goldenrod. The egg hatched and the tiny larva, looking somewhat like a small white segmented worm, began to eat its way down the stalk. Chemicals in the larva's saliva helped to dissolve the tissue as it made its way down the path of the stem. Other salivary chemicals stimulated the plant to form a round swelling called a gall. By July the winter home was completed. The larva lives here all winter, finally changing to a pupa if not disturbed. Before changing into a pupa, at which times its mouthparts prevent it from biting and feeding, the larva excavates an exit tunnel from which it will emerge some time in March.

19   It is quite simple to locate galls of at least three different species of insects in a single stand of goldenrods. The one mentioned, the goldenrod ball gall, caused by a fly, is the most common one. A bunch of dried leaves on top of a stalk indicates the presence of the goldenrod bunch gall. It is caused by a midge, a mosquito-like insect. The elliptical goldenrod gall, usually found low on the stem, owes its presence to a moth. All three are apt to be found on a single stem, a veritable apartment house occupied by three different kinds of tenants.

20   The larvae, though presumably secure, are not always safe. Woodpeckers, mice and squirrels may prey upon them. Or they may be consumed by parasites. Sometimes the gall is empty, its contents destroyed by a virus. Jonathan Swift expresses these hazards well;

> So, naturalists, observe a flea
> Hath smaller fleas that on him prey;
> And these hath smaller fleas to bit em,
> And so proceed ad infinitum.

21   Some larvae inhabit plants, which, unlike those inhabiting goldenrod, produce very slight changes in the host. Burdock, a common wayside plant is a good example. Its persistent winter fruits have hooked spines which account for the common name, "stickers," and for good reason. They catch onto clothing, hair and fur, resulting in their wide dispersal. It is said that a Mr. Velcro was so impressed by these tenacious hooks that he was inspired to develop the now

famous velcro fastener. A fruit head of burdock can be easily pried open with one's fingers. Opening a portion that is bunched together to form a hard clump is where a fat little white grub with a golden head might be found. It was preparing itself to issue forth as a moth the following spring. It has been calculated that one burdock plant may bear 400,000 seeds and harbor about thirty thousand larvae.

22   Large numbers of animals may not be an obvious presence in winter but they are around. They are to be found in the meadow and woodland, on the surface of land or snow or below, as well as in the numerous microhabitats these areas provide—trees, rocks, walls, caves, underground. Bear, fox, chipmunk, mouse or shrew—each is programmed for its particular winter location, duration and extent of activity.

23   The cold season's life is not restricted to the land. Many survivors exist in ponds and streams. Ice-cold standing or moving water, whether clear or covered with snow, presents a vast new world for inspection. Because pond water is many degrees warmer than the air above, there is considerable activity below the surface. Patience and warm clothing is a must for the observer. The discovery of a beaver lodge would suggest looking for underwater stores of food and active beavers. Slow-moving fish such as perch, can be seen moving about. One might find some salamanders, perhaps, or a foraging muskrat.

24   The activities of the larger animals initiates movement by smaller creatures. There are some very tiny animals, barely discernible with the naked eye that appear to be constantly swimming. Water fleas, also known as daphnia, are a good example. They are transparent little animals often found together with the slightly larger fairy shrimp.

25   Spring-fed streams, another interesting winter habitat, harbor a variety of aquatic insects. Large numbers of stone flies, which have left the water, often cluster along its banks searching for food and mates. Fertilized eggs are deposited in the water where they will hatch and develop until, like their parents, they are ready to emerge next winter.

26   Here, too, are to be found May flies, the curious waterpenny beetles attached to the undersides of rocks, and many, many others. They thrive in what, to us as land animals, appears as a cold hostile environment. The clue is adaptation, and these many and varied organisms are most elegantly suited for their world.

27   Less obvious, perhaps, than animals, but equally dramatic, are the ways of overwintering plants. Deciduous trees do not drop their leaves before a large percentage of their manufactured food enters the trees' circulatory systems. The food is stored in the trunks or roots as a continued source of nourishment. There are many kinds of trees, and each has a unique way of protecting and providing its seeds to assure a next generation of trees.

28   Birch, and its many species, are among our common and frequently planted trees. The fruits of birch are little chunky catkins. A stiff wind or other source of pressure, such as from one's finger, causes a catkin to release hundreds of

delicate, small, rarely noticed seeds. Rain or snow somehow conveys them down onto the soil and below where, if they find suitable growing conditions, they germinate, each one with the potential of growing into a birch tree. Many things apparently interfere to prevent this from happening since the world is not a vast birch forest. Such is the prodigality of nature.

29   More interesting than the birch seeds is the packing material in the birch fruit that protects the seeds. These are scales, tightly arranged between the seeds. Larger than the seeds and shaped like miniature birds or airplanes, they are called "mimic birds." The scales in each kind of birch catkin have a unique color, shape and size. They can be used to identify the kind of birch even though the trees are nowhere in sight. "Mimic birds" can be found peppering the snow many miles from their original source.

30   Another common deciduous tree is the sycamore. This sturdy forest tree has been hybridized for city environments and then becomes known as the plane tree. Its beauty and tolerance for polluted air make it an ideal urban choice. The sycamore has seed-carrying balls which can be seen hanging from the branches all winter long. When wind and storm cause these tree fruits to fall, they dash to the ground, break apart and release the seeds. These are drawn earthward where many of the trees' fallen leaves can still be found, as well as rolls of its shredded bark. Both leaves and seed balls produce a natural herbicide, a toxic chemical which leaches into the soil and is detrimental to the growth of other plants. The areas under these trees are likely to be quite bare as a result.

31   Evergreen trees carry on active photosynthesis all winter long when the sun shines. Excessive cold from snow is avoided since snow does not linger long on the slender needles. A slight breeze or even a landing bird stirs the branches of pine, spruce and hemlock preventing an accumulation of snow. Robert Frost, observing a crow on a hemlock in winter, gave us this short bit of eloquence:

> The way a crow
> Shook down on me
> The dust of snow
> From a hemlock tree
>
> Has given my heart
> A change of mood
> And saved some part
> Of a day I had rued.

32   Rhododendrons, wild or cultivated, are attractive broad-leaved evergreen shrubs, exceptionally well adapted to survive the cold. A waxy covering over the leaves and a sensitivity to temperature changes prevent excessive water loss and freezing. As the temperature decreases the leaves conserve water and heat by rolling up ever more tightly. A rising temperature stimulates the leaves

to relax and uncurl. Besides rolling up in very cold weather, the rhododendron leaves droop, exposing less leaf surface to the air, conserving heat and reducing evaporation. There is a definite correlation between the degree of coldness and the angle of droop. Rhododendron thermometer scales have been developed based upon the plant's drooping reaction to the changes in temperature.

33   There are thousands of plants other than trees that provide overwintering seeds for the next spring's growth. The winter landscape is dotted with withered stalks, their shredded seed heads still attached: aster, goldenrod, ragweed, wild carrot, others. Many of their seeds have been scattered about. A handful of speckled snow will reveal a great variety of seeds, all waiting for warmer days. Seeds have a number of protective devices for surviving the cold and wetness of this raw season such as extra thick seed coats, layers of waxy coverings or mantles of thick hair. Meanwhile many of the seeds on the ground, on the snow or remaining in the fruits of leftover standing plants, help wild animals to survive on the rich stored nutrients within.

34   Some of the non-woody plants form winter rosettes at the bottoms of their stems before dying. Rosettes are beautiful and symmetrical circles of green leaves that hug the ground all winter. They are usually quite different from the upper leaves. It is from their midst that the plants of the following spring will grow. The air below the circle is considerably warmer than the above. Among some common plants that produce overwintering rosettes are dandelions, ox-eyed daisies, plantain, thistles, asters, goldenrods, mullein, evening primrose, mustards.

35   Many plants disappear altogether from sight, then reappear the following spring. These plants did not die in the fall without leaving a structure, characteristic of their species, underground. Such well-protected devices are tubers, corms, bulbs, rhizomes. These are flesh organs complete with buds, flowers and leaves in miniature, ready to develop fully when the plants' body clocks stimulate them to grow.

36   The strategies used by plants and animals of all kinds to withstand the northern winters are many. Even the shortest outdoor foray will provide a glimpse into this fascinating world to an observing eye. Any venture is bound to be not only productive, but satisfying to the mind and comforting to the spirit. One could be happily alone but never lonely while knowingly surrounded by such an abundance of vitality—plants and animals thriving and surviving above, below, within—everywhere.

☐ Discovering Meaning and Technique

1. In the first paragraph, Busch makes a comparison between a deserted stage and nature in winter. Do you think the comparison is a good one?

2. Where does Bush use the comparison a second time?

3. List, by type, some of the changes that animals undergo in winter.

4. Make a similar list for plants.

5. What was the inspiration for Velcro's invention of the hook-and-loop fastener?

6. What do the literary quotations from Swift and Frost contribute to the selection?

☐ Writing Suggestions

1. Using the lists you made in questions 3 and 4 above, summarize the natural changes that occur in winter.

2. Describe a winter scene as it looks to an observer unaware of the hidden changes.

3. Research the habits of a plant, animal, or insect over the course of four seasons, and report your findings.

4. This selection shows the author to be a keen observer of nature. If our schools educated us to be better observers of nature, would we be less likely to destroy it?

AM I BLUE?

☐ ALICE WALKER

"Ain't these tears in these eyes tellin' you?" *

1 For about three years my companion and I rented a small house in the country that stood on the edge of a large meadow that appeared to run from the end of our deck straight into the mountains. The mountains, however, were quite far away, and between us and them there was, in fact, a town. It was one of the many pleasant aspects of the house that you never really were aware of this.

2 It was a house of many windows, low, wide, nearly floor to ceiling in the

* ©1929 Warner Bros., Inc. (renewed). By Grant Clarke and Harry Akst. All rights reserved. Used by permission.

living room, which faced the meadow, and it was from one of these that I first saw our closest neighbor, a large white horse, cropping grass, flipping its mane, and ambling about—not over the entire meadow, which stretched well out of sight of the house, but over the five or so fenced-in acres that were next to the twenty-odd that we had rented. I soon learned that the horse, whose name was Blue, belonged to a man who lived in another town, but was boarded by our neighbors next door. Occasionally, one of the children, usually a stock teen-ager, but sometimes a much younger girl or boy, could be seen riding Blue. They would appear in the meadow, climb up on his back, ride furiously for ten or fifteen minutes, then get off, slap Blue on the flanks, and not be seen again for a month or more.

3   There were many apple trees in our yard, and one by the fence that Blue could almost reach. We were soon in the habit of feeding him apples, which he relished, especially because by the middle of summer the meadow grasses—so green and succulent since January—had dried out from lack of rain, and Blue stumbled about munching the dried stalks half-heartedly. Sometimes he would stand very still just by the apple tree, and when one of us came out he would whinny, snort loudly, or stamp the ground. This meant, of course: I want an apple.

4   It was quite wonderful to pick a few apples, or collect those that had fallen to the ground overnight, and patiently hold them, one by one, up to his large, toothy mouth. I remained as thrilled as a child by his flexible dark lips, huge, cubelike teeth that crunched the apples, core and all, with such finality, and his high, broad-breasted *enormity;* beside which, I felt small indeed. When I was a child, I used to ride horses, and was especially friendly with one named Nan until the day I was riding and my brother deliberately spooked her and I was thrown, head first, against the trunk of a tree. When I came to, I was in bed and my mother was bending worriedly over me; we silently agreed that perhaps horseback riding was not the safest sport for me. Since then I have walked, and prefer walking to horseback riding—but I had forgotten the depth of feeling one could see in horses' eyes.

5   I was therefore unprepared for the expression in Blue's. Blue was lonely. Blue was horribly lonely and bored. I was not shocked that this should be the case; five acres to tramp by yourself, endlessly, even in the most beautiful of meadows—and his was—cannot provide many interesting events, and once rainy season turned to dry that was about it. No, I was shocked that I had forgotten that human animals and nonhuman animals can communicate quite well; if we are brought up around animals as children we take this for granted. By the time we are adults we no longer remember. However, the animals have not changed. They are in fact *completed* creations (at least they seem to be, so much more than we) who are not likely *to* change; it is their nature to express themselves. What else are they going to express? And they do. And, generally speaking, they are ignored.

6   After giving Blue the apples, I would wander back to the house, aware that he was observing me. Were more apples not forthcoming then? Was that to be his sole entertainment for the day? My partner's small son had decided he wanted to learn how to piece a quilt; we worked in silence on our respective squares as I thought . . .

7   Well, about slavery: about white children, who were raised by black people, who knew their first all-accepting love from black women, and then, when they were twelve or so, were told they must "forget" the deep levels of communication between themselves and "mammy" that they knew. Later they would be able to relate quite calmly, "My old mammy was sold to another good family." "My old mammy was ____ ____." Fill in the blank. Many more years later a white woman would say: "I can't understand these Negroes, these blacks. What do they want? They're so different from us."

8   And about the Indians, considered to be "like animals" by the "settlers" (a very benign euphemism for what they actually were), who did not understand their description as a compliment.

9   And about the thousands of American men who marry Japanese, Korean, Filipina, and other non-English-speaking women and of how happy they report they are, *"blissfully,"* until their brides learn to speak English, at which point the marriages tend to fall apart. What then did the men see, when they looked into the eyes of the women they married, before they could speak English? Apparently only their own reflections.

10   I thought of society's impatience with the young. "Why are they playing the music so loud?" Perhaps the children have listened to much of the music of oppressed people their parents danced to before they were born, with its passionate but soft cries for acceptance and love, and they have wondered why their parents failed to hear.

11   I do not know how long Blue had inhabited his five beautiful, boring acres before we moved into our house; a year after we had arrived—and had also traveled to other valleys, other cities, other worlds—he was still there.

12   But then, in our second year at the house, something happened in Blue's life. One morning, looking out the window at the fog that lay like a ribbon over the meadow, I saw another horse, a brown one, at the other end of Blue's field. Blue appeared to be afraid of it, and for several days made no attempt to go near. We went away for a week. When we returned, Blue had decided to make friends and the two horses ambled or galloped along together, and Blue did not come nearly as often to the fence underneath the apple tree.

13   When he did, bringing his new friend with him, there was a different look in his eyes. A look of independence, of self-possession, of inalienable *horse*-ness. His friend eventually became pregnant. For months and months there was, it seemed to me, a mutual feeling between me and the horses of justice, of peace. I fed apples to them both. The look in Blue's eyes was one of unabashed "this is *it*ness."

14   It did not, however, last forever. One day, after a visit to the city, I went out to give Blue some apples. He stood waiting, or so I thought, though not beneath the tree. When I shook the tree and jumped back from the shower of apples, he made no move. I carried some over to him. He managed to half-crunch one. The rest he let fall to the ground. I dreaded looking into his eyes—because I had of course noticed that Brown, his partner, had gone—but I did look. If I had been born into slavery, and my partner had been sold or killed, my eyes would have looked like that. The children next door explained that Blue's partner had been "put with him" (the same expression that old people used, I had noticed, when speaking of an ancestor during slavery who had been impregnated by her owner) so that they could mate and she conceive. Since that was accomplished, she had been taken back by her owner, who lived somewhere else.

15   Will she be back? I asked.

16   They didn't know.

17   Blue was like a crazed person. Blue *was*, to me, a crazed person. He galloped furiously, as if he were being ridden, around and around his five beautiful acres. He whinnied until he couldn't. He tore at the ground with his hooves. He butted himself against his single shade tree. He looked always and always toward the road down which his partner had gone. And then, occasionally, when he came up for apples, or I took apples to him, he looked at me. It was a look so piercing, so full of grief, a look so *human*, I almost laughed (I felt too sad to cry) to think there are people who do not know that animals suffer. People like me who have forgotten, and daily forget, all that animals try to tell us. "Everything you do to us will happen to you; we are your teachers, as you are ours. We are one lesson" is essentially it, I think. There are those who never once have even considered animals' rights: those who have been taught that animals actually want to be used and abused by us, as small children "love" to be frightened, or women "love" to be mutilated and raped. . . . They are the great-grandchildren of those who honestly thought, because someone taught them this: "Women can't think," and "niggers can't faint." But most disturbing of all, in Blue's large brown eyes was a new look, more painful than the look of despair: the look of disgust with human beings, with life; the look of hatred. And it was odd what the look of hatred did. It gave him, for the first time, the look of a beast. And what that meant was that he had put up a barrier within to protect himself from further violence; all the apples in the world wouldn't change that fact.

18   And so Blue remained, a beautiful part of our landscape, very peaceful to look at from the window, white against the grass. Once a friend came to visit and said, looking out on the soothing view: "And it *would* have to be a *white* horse; the very image of freedom." And I thought, yes, the animals are forced to become for us merely "images" of what they once so beautifully expressed. And we are used to drinking milk from containers showing "contented" cows, whose real lives we want to hear nothing about, eating eggs and drumsticks

from "happy" hens, and munching hamburgers advertised by bulls of integrity who seem to command their fate.

19   As we talked of freedom and justice one day for all, we sat down to steaks. I am eating misery, I thought, as I took the first bite. And spit it out.

☐ Discovering Meaning and Technique

1. The first two paragraphs establish the spaciousness of the house, the expansive view from the windows, and the confinement of the horse to five fenced-in acres. How do these details forecast the rest of the selection?

2. How does Walker first discover that Blue is lonely?

3. Which subjects does the horse's loneliness and boredom prompt Walker to reflect upon? Why?

4. Explain what Walker means when she says that Blue's "new friend" gave him "a look . . . of inalienable *horse*ness" (paragraph 13).

5. Explain why Walker says first that "Blue was like a crazed person" and then that "Blue *was*, to me, a crazed person" (paragraph 17)?

6. Reviewing the entire selection, point out where Walker compares the treatment and feelings of animals with those of humans.

7. From the selection, pick out the myths used by society to abuse animals, children, women, and minorities.

8. What do you think is the point of the selection? Is it stated or implied?

☐ Writing Suggestions

1. In paragraph 17, Walker says that we forget what animals try to tell us: "Everything you do to us will happen to you; we are your teachers, as you are ours. We are one lesson." Explain what she means.

2. Explore one of the myths used by society to justify abuse. Use historical research, your own experiences, or a combination of both.

3. In the last paragraph, Walker is unable to eat her steak, because, "I am eating misery, I thought, as I took the first bite. And spit it out." Do you think it cruel or barbaric to eat flesh?

4. State your own views on animal rights. You might want to consider, for example, the use of laboratory animals in medical research, the raising of domestic animals specifically for slaughter, and hunting and fishing for sport.

5. In paragraph 17, Walker describes the new look in Blue's eyes as "the look of hatred." She says, "It gave him, for the first time, the look of a beast. And what that meant was that he had put up a barrier within to protect himself from further violence." Apply this idea to the reactions of abused humans.

Humans and the Environment

■   ■   ■

"BUT A WATCH IN THE NIGHT"
A SCIENTIFIC FABLE

☐ **JAMES C. RETTIE**

1   Out beyond our solar system there is a planet called Copernicus. It came into existence some four or five million years before the birth of our Earth. In due course of time it became inhabited by a race of intelligent men.

2   About 750 million years age the Copernicans had developed the motion picture machine to a point well in advance of the stage that we have reached. Most of the cameras that we now use in motion picture work are geared to take twenty-four pictures per second on a continuous strip of film. When such film is run through a projector, it throws a series of images on the screen and these change with a rapidity that gives the visual impression of normal movement. If a motion is too swift for the human eye to see it in detail, it can be captured and artificially slowed down by means of the slow-motion camera. This one is geared to take many more shots per second—ninety-six or even more than that. When the slow-motion film is projected at the normal speed of twenty-four pictures per second, we can see just how the jumping horse goes over a hurdle.

3   What about motion that is too slow to be seen by the human eye? That problem has been solved by the use of the time-lapse camera. In this one, the shutter is geared to take only one shot per second, or one per minute, or even one per hour—depending upon the kind of movement that is being photographed. When the time-lapse film is projected at the normal speed of twenty-four pictures per second, it is possible to see a bean sprout growing up out of the ground. Time-lapse films are useful in the study of many types of motion too slow to be observed by the unaided, human eye.

4   The Copernicans, it seems, had time-lapse cameras some 757 million years

ago and they also had superpowered telescopes that gave them a clear view of what was happening upon this Earth. They decided to make a film record of the life history of Earth and to make it on the scale of one picture per year. This photography has been in progress during the last 757 million years.

5   In the near future, a Copernican interstellar expedition will arrive upon our Earth and bring with it a copy of the time-lapse film. Arrangements will be made for showing the entire film in one continuous run. This will begin at midnight of New Year's eve and continue day and night without a single stop until midnight of December 31. The rate of projection will be twenty-four pictures per second. Time on the screen will thus seem to move at the rate of twenty-four years per second; 1440 years per minute; 86,400 years per hour; approximately two million years per day; and sixty-two million years per month. The normal life-span of individual man will occupy about three seconds. The full period of Earth history that will be unfolded on the screen (some 757 million years) will extend from what the geologists call Pre-Cambrian times up to the present. This will, by no means, cover the full time-span of the Earth's geological history but it will embrace the period since the advent of living organisms.

6   During the months of January, February, and March the picture will be desolate and dreary. The shape of the land masses and the oceans will bear little or no resemblance to those that we know. The violence of geological erosion will be much in evidence. Rains will pour down on the land and promptly go booming down to the seas. There will be no clear streams anywhere except where the rains fall upon hard rock. Everywhere on the steeper ground the stream channels will be filled with boulders hurled down by rushing waters. Raging torrents and dry stream beds will keep alternating in quick succession. High mountains will seem to melt like so much butter in the sun. The shifting of land into the seas, later to be thrust up as new mountains, will be going on at a grand scale.

7   Early in April there will be some indication of the presence of single-celled living organisms in some of the warmer and sheltered coastal waters. By the end of the month it will be noticed that some of these organisms have become multicellular. A few of them, including the Trilobites, will be encased in hard shells.

8   Toward the end of May, the first vertebrates will appear, but they will still be aquatic creatures. In June about 60 percent of the land area that we know as North America will be under water. One broad channel will occupy the space where the Rocky Mountains now stand. Great deposits of limestone will be forming under some of the shallower seas. Oil and gas deposits will be in process of formation—also under shallow seas. On land there will still be no sign of vegetation. Erosion will be rampant, tearing loose particles and chunks of rock and grinding them into sand and silt to be spewed out by the streams into bays and estuaries.

9   About the middle of July the first land plants will appear and take up the tremendous job of soil building. Slowly, very slowly, the mat of vegetation will spread, always battling for its life against the power of erosion. Almost foot by foot, the plant life will advance, lacing down with its root structures whatever pulverized rock material it can find. Leaves and stems will be giving added protection against the loss of the soil foothold. The increasing vegetation will pave the way for the land animals that will live upon it.

10   Early in August the seas will be teeming with fish. This will be what geologists call the Devonian period. Some of the races of these fish will be breathing by means of lung tissue instead of through gill tissues. Before the month is over, some of the lung fish will go ashore and take on a crude lizard-like appearance. Here are the first amphibians.

11   In early September the insects will put in their appearance. Some will look like huge dragon flies and will have a wingspread of 24 inches. Large portions of the land masses will now be covered with heavy vegetation that will include the primitive spore-propagating trees. Layer upon layer of this plant growth will build up, later to appear as the coal deposits. About the middle of this month, there will be evidence of the first seed-bearing plants and the first reptiles. Heretofore, the land animals will have been amphibians that could reproduce their kind only by depositing a soft egg mass in quiet waters. The reptiles will be shown to be freed from the aquatic bond because they can reproduce by means of a shelled egg in which the embryo and its nurturing liquids are sealed in and thus protected from destructive evaporation. Before September is over, the first dinosaurs will be seen—creatures destined to dominate the animal realm for about 140 million years and then to disappear.

12   In October there will be a series of mountain uplifts along what is now the eastern coast of the United States. A creature with feathered limbs—half bird and half reptile in appearance—will take itself into the air. Some small and rather unpretentious animals will be seen to bring forth their young in a form that is a miniature replica of the parents and to feed these young on milk secreted by mammary glands in the female parent. The emergence of this mammalian form of animal life will be recognized as one of the great events in geologic time. October will also witness the high water mark of the dinosaurs—creatures ranging in size from that of the modern goat to monsters like Brontosaurus that weighed some 40 tons. Most of them will be placid vegetarians, but a few will be hideous-looking carnivores, like Allosaurus and Tyrannosaurus. Some of the herbivorous dinosaurs will be clad in bony armor for protection against their flesh-eating comrades.

13   November will bring pictures of a sea extending from the Gulf of Mexico to the Arctic in space now occupied by the Rocky Mountains. A few of the reptiles will take to the air on bat-like wings. One of these, called Pteranodon, will have a wingspread of 15 feet. There will be a rapid development of the modern flowering plants, modern trees, and modern insects. The dinosaurs will

disappear. Toward the end of the month there will be a tremendous land disturbance in which the Rocky Mountains will rise out of the sea to assume a dominating
place in the North American landscape.

14   As the picture runs on into December it will show the mammals in command
of the animal life. Seed-bearing trees and grasses will have covered most of the
land with a heavy mantle of vegetation. Only the areas newly thrust up from
the sea will be barren. Most of the streams will be crystal clear. The turmoil of
geologic erosion will be confined to localized areas. About December 25 will
begin the cutting of the Grand Canyon of the Colorado River. Grinding down
through layer after layer of sedimentary strata, this stream will finally expose
deposits laid down in Pre-Cambrian times. Thus in the walls of that canyon
will appear geological formations dating from recent times to the period.when
the earth had no living organisms upon it.

15   The picture will run on through the latter days of December and even up
to its final day with still no sign of mankind. The spectators will become alarmed
in the fear that man has somehow been left out. But not so; sometime about
noon on December 31 (one million years ago) will appear a stooped, massive
creature of man-like proportions. This will be Pithecanthropus, the Java ape
man. For tools and weapons he will have nothing but crude stone and wooden
clubs. His children will live a precarious existence threatened on the one side
by hostile animals and on the other by tremendous climatic changes. Ice sheets—
in places 4000 feet deep—will form in the northern parts of North America
and Eurasia. Four times this glacial ice will push southward to cover half the
continents. With each advance the plant and animal life will be swept under or
pushed southward. With each recession of the ice, life will stuggle to reestablish
itself in the wake of the retreating glaciers. The wooly mammoth, the musk ox,
and the caribou all will fight to maintain themselves near the ice line. Sometimes
they will be caught and put into cold storage—skin, flesh, blood, bones and all.

16   The picture will run on through supper time with still very little evidence
of man's presence on the earth. It will be about 11 o'clock when Neanderthal
man appears. Another half hour will go by before the appearance of Cro-Magnon
man living in caves and painting crude animal pictures on the walls of his dwelling.
Fifteen minutes more will bring Neolithic man, knowing how to chip stone
and thus produce sharp cutting edges for spears and tools. In a few minutes
more it will appear that man has domesticated the dog, the sheep and, possibly,
other animals. He will then begin the use of milk. He will also learn the arts of
basket weaving and the making of pottery and dugout canoes.

17   The dawn of civilization will not come until about five or six minutes
before the end of the picture. The story of the Egyptians, the Babylonians, the
Greeks, and the Romans will unroll during the fourth, the third and the second
minute before the end. At 58 minutes and 43 seconds past 11:00 P.M. (just 1
minute and 17 seconds before the end) will come the beginning of the Christian
era. Columbus will discover the new world 20 seconds before the end. The

Declaration of Independence will be signed just 7 seconds before the final curtain comes down.

18   In those few moments of geologic time will be the story of all that has happened since we became a nation. And what a story it will be! A human swarm will sweep across the face of the continent and take it away from the primitive red men. They will change it far more radically than it has ever been changed before in a comparable time. The great virgin forests will be seen going down before ax and fire. The soil, covered for aeons by its protective mantle of trees and grasses, will be laid bare to the ravages of water and wind erosion. Streams that had been flowing clear will, once again, take up a load of silt and push it toward the seas. Humus and mineral salts, both vital elements of productive soil, will be seen to vanish at a terrifying rate. The railroads and highways and cities that will spring up may divert attention, but they cannot cover up the blight of man's recent activities. In great sections of Asia, it will be seen that man must utilize cow dung and every scrap of available straw or grass for fuel to cook his food. The forests that once provided wood for this purpose will be gone without a trace. The use of these agricultural wastes for fuel, in place of returning them to the land, will be leading to increasing soil impoverishment. Here and there will be seen a dust storm darkening the landscape over an area a thousand miles across. Man-creatures will be shown counting their wealth in terms of bits of printed paper representing other bits of a scarce but comparatively useless yellow metal that is kept buried in strong vaults. Meanwhile, the soil, the only real wealth that can keep mankind alive on the face of this earth is savagely being cut loose from its ancient moorings and washed into the seven seas.

19   We have just arrived upon this Earth. How long will we stay?

☐ Discovering Meaning and Technique

1. Suggest why Rettie might have chosen to call his mythical planet "Copernicus."

2. Make an outline of the Copernican film by listing each month and the major developments of that month.

3. To help the reader understand the newness of human beings, Rettie capsules 757 million years into one year. This technique, in which one thing is explained in terms of another, is called *extended analogy.* Do you think the technique is effective? Why or why not?

4. Consider the last two paragraphs of the essay. How much "film time" is occupied by each of the developments described?

5. What seems to be the major point of this selection? Where do you find it in the essay?

☐ **Writing Suggestions**

1. Use an extended analogy to explain a period of time. For example, describe your life in terms of twelve months; a typical relationship in terms of a week; high school in terms of one day.

2. What is your answer to the last sentence in the selection: "How long will we stay?"

3. "A watch in the night" comes from the Bible, Psalm 90. Look up the Psalm and explain why the phrase is an appropriate title for this selection.

4. Here is Rettie's description of money in paragraph 18: ". . . bits of printed paper representing other bits of a scarce but comparatively useless yellow metal." When considered objectively, money really is a rather curious concept. Explore the idea that scraps of paper represent power, status, and privilege.

5. How is the pursuit of money connected to our wanton destruction of the environment?

6. Expand on Rettie's statement that soil is "the only real wealth."

■   ■   ■

WHO OWNS CROSS CREEK?

☐ MARJORIE KINNAN RAWLINGS

¹ The question once arose. "Who owns Cross Creek?" It came to expression when Mr. Marsh Turner was turning his hogs and cattle loose on us and riding drunkenly across the Creek bridge to drive them home. Tom Morrison, who does not own a blade of corn at the Creek, but is yet part and parcel of it, became outraged by Mr. Marsh Turner's arrogance. Tom stood with uplifted walking stick at the bridge, a Creek Horatio, and turned Mr. Marsh Turner back.

² "Who do you think you are?" he demanded. "How come you figure you can turn your stock loose on us, and then ride up and down, whoopin' and hollerin'? You act like you own Cross Creek. You don't. Old Boss owns Cross Creek, and Young Miss owns it, and old Joe Mackay. Why, you don't own six feet of Cross Creek to be buried in."

3   Soon after this noble gesture was reported to me by Martha, I went across the Creek in April to gather early blackberries. I had not crossed the bridge for some weeks and I looked forward to seeing the magnolias in full bloom. The road is lined with magnolia trees and is like a road passing through a superb park. There were no magnolia blossoms. It seemed at first sight that there were no magnolia trees. There were only tall, gray, rose-lichened trunks from which the branches had been cut. The pickers of magnolia leaves had passed through. These paid thieves come and go mysteriously every second or third year. One week the trees stand with broad outstretched branches, glossy of leaf, the creamy buds ready for opening. The next, the boughs have been cut close to the trunks, and it will be three years before there are magnolia blossoms again. After long inquiry, I discovered the use for the stripped leaves. They are used for making funeral wreaths. The destruction seemed to me a symbol of private intrusion on the right of all mankind to enjoy a universal beauty. Surely the loveliness of the long miles of magnolia blooms was more important to the living than the selling of the bronze, waxy leaves for funerals of the dead.

4   I had a letter from a friend at this time, saying, "I am a firm believer in property rights."

5   The statement disturbed me. What is "property" and who are the legitimate owners? I looked out from my veranda, across the acres of grove from which I had only recently been able to remove the mortgage. The land was legally mine, and short of long tax delinquency, nothing and nobody could take it from me. Yet if I did not take care of the land lovingly, did not nourish and cultivate it, it would revert to jungle. Was it mine to abuse or to neglect? I did not think so.

6   I thought of the countless generations that had "owned" land. Of what did that ownership consist? I thought of the great earth, whirling in space. It was here ahead of men and could conceivably be here after them. How should one man say that he "owned" any piece or parcel of it? If he worked with it, labored to bring it to fruition, it seemed to me that at most he held it in fief. The individual man is transitory, but the pulse of life and of growth goes on after he is gone, buried under a wreath of magnolia leaves. No man should have proprietary rights over land who does not use that land wisely and lovingly. Steinbeck raised the same question in his *Grapes of Wrath*. Men who had cultivated their land for generations were dispossessed because banks and industrialists believed they could make a greater profit by turning over the soil to mass, mechanized production. But what will happen to that land when the industrialists themselves are gone? The earth will survive bankers and any system of government, capitalistic, fascist, or bolshevist. The earth will even survive anarchy.

7   I looked across my grove, hard fought for, hard maintained, and I thought of other residents there. There are other inhabitants who stir about with the same sense of possession as my own. A covey of quail has lived for as long as I have owned the place in a bramble thicket near the hammock. A pair of blue-

jays has raised its young, raucous-voiced and handsome, year after year in the hickory trees. The same pair of red-birds mates and nests in an orange tree behind my house and brings its progeny twice a year to the feed basket in the crepe myrtle in the front yard. The male sings with a *joie de vivre* no greater than my own, but in a voice lovelier than mine, and the female drops bits of corn into the mouths of her fledglings with as much assurance as though she paid the taxes. A black snake has lived under my bedroom as long as I have slept in it.

8   Who owns Cross Creek? The red-birds, I think, more than I, for they will have their nests even in the face of delinquent mortgages. And after I am dead, who am childless, the human ownership of grove and field and hammock is hypothetical. But a long line of red-birds and whippoorwills and blue-jays and ground doves will descend from the present owners of nests in the orange trees, and their claim will be less subject to dispute than that of any human heirs. Houses are individual and can be owned, like nests, and fought for. But what of the land? It seems to me that the earth may be borrowed but not bought. It may be used, but not owned. It gives itself in response to love and tending, offers its seasonal flowering and fruiting. But we are tenants and not possessors, lovers and not masters. Cross Creek belongs to the wind and the rain, to the sun and the seasons, to the cosmic secrecy of seed, and beyond all, to time.

☐ Discovering Meaning and Technique

1. Rawlings uses "man" and "he" to refer to humans in general. Do you find this practice offensive? Would it have been more offensive if the selection had been written by a man instead of by a woman? (Remember that the selection was published in 1961).

2. Near the end of paragraph 3, Rawlings refers to "the right of all mankind to enjoy a universal beauty." Do humans indeed have such a "right?" How could this right be granted?

3. In paragraph 3, Rawlings describes the practice of stripping magnolia trees to make funeral wreaths. According to Rawlings, what does the practice symbolize?

4. Who does Rawlings think might actually own Cross Creek?

5. Define the following words from paragraphs 5–8: *veranda, fief, covey, joie de vivre, hammock.*

☐ **Writing Suggestions**

1. Write an answer to the questions posed by Rawlings in paragraph 5: "What is 'property' and who are the legitimate owners?"

2. Write your own definition of "property rights."

3. Agree or disagree with Rawlings's statement that no one "should have proprietary rights over land who does not use that land wisely and lovingly" (paragraph 6). How can wise and loving use be determined?

4. Describe the plants and animals that inhabit your own yard, garden, or apartment.

PARTLY CLOUDY

☐ **ELEANOR PERÉNYI**

1 The drought is serious, the corn crop threatened, lawns are burning up and water restrictions forbid us to water them. Turn to the evening weather forecast and there is a grinning young man surrounded with weather maps and radarscopes to assure us we haven't a worry in the world: "The threat of shower activity has passed and it looks like a gorgeous weekend." Or it is winter and a snowfall in prospect. Panic: "It could be as much as four inches and travelers' warnings are out for the metropolitan area and eastern Long Island." Nightly, some variation on these themes is enacted in the grotesque ritual called a weather forecast but more accurately described as pandering to infantilism. It is a frightening revelation of how insulated we have become from the natural world.

2   I assume that in those parts of the country where sufficient rain is still a life-and-death matter the forecasters show a little more sensitivity, though I wouldn't bet on it; and surely the states whose economy depends on snow to activate the ski resorts don't allow an imminent storm to be forecast as though it were a plague of locusts. Elsewhere, the weather is treated as something between a threat and a joke. The "meterologist," having read out the figures we can see for ourselves on the screen and relayed predictions that come to him from computers at the National Weather Service as though they were his own, then engages in heavy banter with the fellow who broadcasts the news: "Don't give us any more of the white stuff, Bill." "I'll do my best, Jim." Thus is the power once attributed to Jove and his thunderbolts transferred to a man in a sports jacket—a quaint conceit indeed in a scientific age, and one with disturbing implications that the viewer is a child on perpetual holiday, his only interest in going out to play.

3   Unfortunately, that assumption seems to be correct. Americans resent the vagaries of weather to a degree unknown to other peoples. England's generally abominable climate is forecast in positively poetic terms—"Intervals of sun and cloud over East Anglia"—and in Italy a light chop on the Mediterranean sounds Vergilian. The majority of Americans crave a sunlit perfection, as if hell itself weren't a warm, well-lighted place, and have accordingly migrated by the millions to the Sun Belt, where the real prediction, not often uttered, is that they and their crops, planted in areas never intended by nature to support such exploitation, will die of thirst within twenty years unless a miracle occurs. Not only that: Bulldozed and overbuilt southern California is regularly burnt over by man-kindled fires and bids fair to be destroyed by mud-slides well before the long-predicted earthquake comes along. Californians are only continuing the well-worn practice of building where floods and washouts are regular events—all our alluvial plains are examples of the same recklessness. We aren't, of course, the only people who have chosen to live on the brink. Ancient history testifies to that. From the flood plains of Mesopotamia to volcanic regions around the world, always heavily populated, the record is of one catastrophe after another, beginning with the Flood. But we are surely, in modern times, the least realistic and least equipped to deal with quite ordinary and predictable happenings. Our cars are so constructed (they didn't used to be) that an inch or two of snow is enough to swamp the roads with accidents. I don't know how they do it, but in northern and Alpine Europe (and Japan's northernmost island, Hokkaido), trains race through blizzards and arrive on the minute. In the United States, a commuter railroad like the Long Island, with no mountain passes to cross, no elaborate connections to be made with other international trains, can and has collapsed for more than a week after a snowstorm. No wonder the prospect of a little bad weather makes us nervous. We aren't equipped to handle it physically or—what is more important in the long run—psychologically either.

4   Weather is a force we have lost touch with. We feel entitled to dominate it, like everything else in the environment, and when we can't are more panic-stricken than primitives who know that when nature is out of control they can only pray to the gods. We pray, too—to the electric company on whose vulnerable wires our lives depend. When we first moved here, the local company was called the Mystic Light & Power, a name that made me laugh whenever I made out a check. Now it is Northeast Utilities, which doesn't inspire the same confidence. Nor has Northeast moved to change the scary system of wires, strung overhead where they can be smitten by lightning and tree limbs, that was installed about the turn of the century. In Europe, these tangles are underground and not allowed to disfigure the streets and endanger the citizenry. Why are they here? Nobody can tell me. There they hang, one more reason to fear the winds that can't be stopped from blowing. Only last week, lightning struck the maple across the street, bringing down the wires interlaced in its branches and leaving us powerless for a night and half a day. Powerless is the word. It was almost comic that I couldn't even brew a cup of coffee.

5   It probably goes without saying that that particular storm didn't figure in the evening forecast—neither its violence nor where it would strike. "Possible late afternoon or late evening thundershowers" is a prediction we hear day after day all summer and have learned to ignore until we see the thunderheads. It is the forecasters' way of not getting caught, just as ever since the unannounced 1938 hurricane of terrible memory they have been careful to inform us of the least tropical depression developing in the Caribbean. But having lived through many later hurricanes, I have noticed that the nearer the storm, the less accurate the plotting of its probable strike. We are told the "eye" will pass over Montauk (which on the usual north by east course means, in short order, us), or no—it will pass over Bridgeport (which doesn't), or it has already gone out to sea. The same with snow, which will accumulate to two inches, four inches or, suddenly, amount to little or nothing. Not the least of the sins of the forecasters is their unreliability. Many years ago, my father believed there would be a revolution in forecasting as soon as Arctic weather stations and an efficient system of radio communication were established at various points across the globe. A Navy man, he had a particular interest in the subject, especially as it applied to military operations like the Normandy landings, which it will be recalled nearly foundered on account of an unforseen storm. He died before the invention of weather satellites and other advanced technology like computers, which would have given him even higher hopes. What would have been his feelings to learn, thirty years later, that our military weathermen in the Arabian Sea were unaware of a vast sandstorm hovering over the Iranian plateau at a critical moment—a locality where such storms are common at that time of year? Is it reasonable to expect the little chap on the TV screen, who gets his information from a less vitally concerned source, to do better? I would rather trust the farmer who holds his finger to the wind, anyone, indeed, who lives outside the technological cocoon. I remember that when my father was in charge of a naval station on a West Indian island in the 1920s, he had received no official word of an approaching hurricane. It was the inhabitants who gave him warning of the need to take precautions. Reading the motion of the sea, the clouds, feeling in the barometer of their bones a sudden drop a thousand miles away, they muttered for days, "Hurricane coming, hurricane coming." They were right. A couple of hours after the official warning arrived, the storm struck the island like a sandblasting machine and nearly blew us off the map.

6   Such skills have largely been lost. Hence, in part, the inordinate fear of weather and the dependence on the idiot box to feed the dream of eternal sunshine, or the nightmare of a couple of inches of snow. In our civilization, if that is what it is, only farmers and gardeners are free of these fantasies. We don't care if your weekend *is* ruined by the rain we need. We curse the wind the Sunday sailor wants for his outing (it dries up our peas, just coming to perfection), and bless the snow that blocks your roads but keeps our plants and the winter wheat safe. We must collaborate with nature whether we like it or not and perhaps need a special weather service of our own.

7   Something of the sort exists, and I don't mean the old black magic, not but what I don't rely on it on occasion, and in the short run. Rain really is imminent when the leaves turn their backs to the wind, smoke goes to ground and the earthworms rise to the surface. It may not be true that if St. Martin's Day is fair and cold the winter will be short, but I would give it a try. A Mexican-Indian gardener once told me at the beginning of the dry season in October that it would rain heavily for three days in February—I forgot which saint's fiesta was involved and anyway the saint was undoubtedly a thinly disguised Aztec god—and not thereafter for three months. The prediction was correct and amazed me at the time. It doesn't amaze me now. It never pays to underestimate folk wisdom. Neither does it pay to overestimate it. The "natives" don't know everything or they wouldn't be "natives." But neither do we, or we wouldn't be in the awful pickle we are. What I seek is a scientific approach that takes into account information gathered down the ages by observant human beings—and goes on from there.

8   Such a minor discipline is at hand in a development called phenology: the study of the growth stages of plants, which can be used to predict the approach of spring and all that implies about planting dates, the emergence of insects and other data vital to farmers and gardeners. The name is modern, the practice as old as the hills. The Chinese and the ancient Romans were using phenological calendars a couple of thousand years ago, and real farmers, as opposed to those engaged in mass agriculture, have always been aware of the principle—which simply consists in noting the dates when one or more plants known as 'indicators' burst into leaf or bloom. Given this information, it is then possible to predict other events like the warming of the soil, the likelihood of one area remaining persistently colder than another, and so on. It has long been understood that plants are sensitive weather instruments, registering temperature and humidity. Indicator plants are simply more reliable than others. The common lilac, for instance, won't open its buds until it is safe to do so (which is why the flowering can vary by as much as three weeks from one season to another), and the farmer or gardener who takes phenology for his guide will watch for this flowering rather than go by the books and perform certain tasks at a fixed date. In Montana, the blooming of the lilacs tells farmers they have ten days to cut the alfalfa and eliminate the first brood of alfalfa weevils. Truck farmers on Long Island count on the flowering forsythia to signal the arrival of the cabbage-root maggot. In New England we used to plant our corn when the elm leaves were the size of a squirrel's ear, knowing the ground would then be warm enough for the seed to germinate. The elms are nearly gone but oak or maple will do as well. Using the lilac, or the dogwood—another indicator plant—it should also be possible to locate the best place on a property to plant a tender fruit tree like an apricot. Where either of these flowered consistently earlier than others of their kind would be a warm spot that could save the fruit buds from late freezes.

9   A number of countries in Europe maintain networks to gather phenological

information as part of their national weather services. We don't. Such a network was established here in 1904 by the Weather Bureau but abandoned for lack of funds. Now, however, there seems to be a revival of interest. A few states are developing programs and the Department of Agriculture is collaborating with some of them. Phenological maps have been compiled. But it will be a long time before the nightly forecast includes the latest word on lilac time. Meanwhile, there is nothing to stop the amateur from making his own observations. I scored a minor success, though not with phenology, in long-range forecasting in the fall of 1979, when we had an exceptionally early snowfall, one that took place while the roses were still in bloom and the leaves green on the trees. That, I announced grandly, meant we would have no more snow until February and an exceptionally dry winter. This was based on nothing more than notes in my garden log which recorded two similarly premature snowfalls in the early 1970's, both followed by dry winters. It may well have been coincidence, but I turned out to be right. On the number of times I have been wrong, misled by the behavior of squirrels with nuts and the amount of moss on the north sides of trees, time-honored omens, I naturally don't enlarge. But then I notice that those who predict weather never do mention, or apologize for, their failures.

☐ Discovering Meaning and Technique

1. What, according to Perényi, seems to be the only interest Americans have in the weather?

2. Why does Perényi claim that "we are surely, in modern times, the least realistic and least equipped to deal with quite ordinary and predictable happenings" (paragraph 3)?

3. What are Perényi's specific complaints about weather forecasters and forecasting?

4. Point out some of the "folk wisdom" about weather predicting that appears in the selection.

5. What is phenology?

6. Which kinds of predictions can we make by using phenology? Be specific.

7. What does Perényi mean by "real farmers, as opposed to those engaged in mass agriculture" (paragraph 8)?

☐ **Writing Suggestions**

1. At the end of the first paragraph, Perényi says that the television weather forecast demonstrates "how insulated we have become from the natural world." Describe other modern phenomena that also demonstrate our insulation—such as air conditioning, enclosed shopping malls, indoor sports arenas.

2. Perényi says that we are dependent on the power company even for a cup of coffee. Imagine living for twenty-four hours without any form of power, and describe how "powerless" you would be. For example, how would you get to school or work? How would you work or study? Fix your hair? Prepare a meal? Clean house?

3. Relate any folklore you know about predicting weather. Which lore is reliable and which is not?

4. Watch several different weather forecasters on television. Do you agree that they treat the weather as "something between a threat and a joke"?

5. In what ways does bad weather change the routines of our lives?

6. Which would you trust to predict the weather more accurately, a computer model based on satellite information or a farmer experienced in growing crops?

ONE THAT GOT AWAY

☐ ROBERT FINCH

1 This is something in the nature of a confession, I suppose. But the trouble is that even now, long after the event, I am still not sure what it is I have to confess: a recklessness or a cowardice, a sin of commission or omission, a drama of ultimate limits or a trivial matter of twenty minutes and a leaky boot.

2 I have some idea of what might have brought it on. It may have had something to do with a dream I had the night before, or with a certain feeling of self-containment that had grown upon me as an oppression during the previous week. . . .

3 But since, even at this distance, I am still not sure *what* occurred, there is little point in analyzing motives or rationalizing behavior beforehand. Let me simply try to describe the incident as it happened and see what emerges. And you, reader, keep your distance a little from the narrative. Do not get too caught up in what I am trying to remember. Do not listen too closely to the shifts and withdrawals of emotion that underlie and punctuate its progress. Imagine yourself,

if you will, raised up above the action, a little like gods, perhaps, or in a stadium, or on one of those hills on which generals used to stand to watch the clash of their armies in the valleys below. Keep your eye on the movements, and let that tell you what happened, more than whatever cries or shouts of combat come up from below.

⁴ It happened in late February. There had been continuous rains, heavy at times, and strong easterly gale winds throughout the weekend. That morning the weather, though still wet and gusty, was mild and misty. It seemed like a good day to drive up to Eastham and watch the ocean overwash the barrier spit at Coast Guard Beach. Storm breakthroughs at this beach had become a regular, even a familiar and anticipated event since a great winter northeaster had first ripped its dune ridge to shreds the winter before. Conditions once more seemed ripe for a breakthrough. High course tides were due just before noon, in conjunction with a partial solar eclipse—part of the last total eclipse of the sun over North America for another thirty-eight years. Things seemed propitious.

⁵ I put on my rain gear and headed for Coast Guard Beach, arriving about 10:30 A.M. Already a crowd of cars had begun to gather in the storm overlook area behind the old Coast Guard station. At the bottom of the hill was the former site of the beach's parking lot. Slightly more than a year ago, record storm surges had ripped up its asphalt and demolished the bathhouse, yet now it looked as if there had never been anything there but beach.

⁶ It was nearly an hour and a half to high tide, but already the salt marsh behind the long barrier spit had turned into a broad dark-blue lake, beating against the mainland shore to the west. Wide, thick mats of muddy foam were strewn about on the marsh side of the beach, washed over on last night's tide. Several of the snow fences placed across the cut to trap sand had been flattened and carried away, but some had miraculously held. Beyond the cut, the long, ravaged spit of Coast Guard Beach stretched a mile and a half southward, but it was too misty to see any of the remaining beach cottages from the overlook, to tell if any of them had been hit again. And to the east there loomed the cause of it all, the great advancing storm-tossed ocean, erupting majestically upon the beach, while legions of sullen, determined clouds raced inland overhead. It was a day to be careful what you asked the flounder.

⁷ The occupants of the dozen or so cars in the parking area remained inside, so I decided to take the opportunity to have an unimpeded view of the storm at close range. Pulling on a pair of waders and buttoning up my slicker, I got out and walked down the hill toward the beach, shrouded in wind-driven mist and spray. As I stood at the bottom of the blocked-off road, watching great cascades of white foam piling up onto the beach, I could see that the next series of overwashes had already begun. The tops of the crashing swells were just beginning to urge themselves up over the hump of the upper beach, spilling down the long sloping backside toward the marsh. So far they were only shallow

sheens and braided little rivulets of water, but they gave notice that a wide salt river would soon course through here again at high tide.

8   On the far side of the destroyed lower parking lot, standing at the base of the foredunes just above the reach of the surf, was the silhouette of a very large gull, its head bent down, eating something on the beach. I walked closer to the cut-through to see better, and as I did it grew into the rounded, hull-shaped body of a white goose. I stood marveling: could it be a snow goose? Then, as I fumbled for my binoculars, the rain let up and the mist cleared momentarily; the white form loomed larger still, uncurled an incredibly long neck up into the air, and blossomed into the improbable but unmistakable shape of a swan.

9   What on earth was a *swan* doing here on the Outer Beach in the middle of a raging northeaster? What had brought it here, and what had it been eating? Its appearance seemed avatarlike and strangely compelling. It was, I realized, hidden from view to those in the cars up on the hill. I thought of waving them down to see it, but before I could, the bird turned its head toward me, unsheathed its huge white wings, and sailed low and quickly, like some enormous milkweed seed, down the length of the beach in front of the dune ridge and out of sight.

10   Rain and mist swirled again, but I looked through the binoculars to see if the swan might have landed farther down the beach. Where it had been, the beach seemed to have shaped itself to the storm, forming a perfectly smooth curving battlement up which the breakers ran halfway, doing little dances, and rolling back. But further down, the waves were already crashing into vertical sand walls four or five feet high, foaming for several seconds into an element neither land nor sea, but both, and carrying visible sections of dune away with each sucking withdrawal. The tops of the low dune walls cracked and slid, and the long, naked pale-yellow roots of beach grass trailed down into the foamy water like strands of rock kelp pulled seaward on granite shores. There was no sign of the swan.

11   I could also see now, through moving rips in the mist, two of the three surviving cottages on the far side. One was heavily damaged and precariously exposed at the north end of the dune ridge, but the second, a bit farther down and set back from the beach, still sat relatively secure and untouched in a hollow just behind one of the few undamaged dunes.

12   And as I watched, a thought, one that had been growing slowly and unawares in the back of my mind for the past several minutes, now suddenly surged forward an seized me in a rush: *I would cross over.*

13   It came, not as a decision, but as a fully formed conviction. I knew what I was going to do. And more: I knew exactly how I was going to do it, as though I had been unconsciously preparing for it all morning and was now simply giving a final review to my plans. I would cross the open plain of the cut to the far side before the washovers grew any deeper or more frequent. I already had everything I needed: my slicker and waders would keep me dry, and in

my pocket was a stale jelly doughnut. There, on the last remaining stretch of high dunes on Coast Guard Beach, I would spend the duration of the high tide, alone with the three cottages, the swan, and the storm. It was a good storm, but not big enough to pose any serious threat to my safety. The tide would subside by four o'clock, five at the latest, giving me plenty of time to get back across before dark. It was enough. I was ready.

14 It looked easy enough. The rain had let up, the mist had cleared. It was, at most, a minute's run, even in waders, across the wide, smooth plain of the overwash area to the storm-ravaged barrier spit.

15   I walked over to the edge of the former parking lot, where the sand was highest and some snow fencing still remained. To the east the storm waves were now beginning to crest over the top of the beach, spilling down the backslope and sinking into the sands before they reached the flooded marsh behind. In front of me the water ran by in rapid little channels, only a few inches deep and a few yards wide. Beyond them, a clear, flat plain of moist sand. And beyond that, the eroding dunes, the surviving cottages, the apparition of the white swan, and the solitude of the storm.

16   Piece of cake, as they say. Yet I knew I had better not hesitate; the tide was still coming in, and very soon the overwashes would begin in earnest. Also, the impulsive adventurer today always hears at his back the government official hovering near: though there were no signs around saying "Do Not Cross Over During Storms," a Seashore ranger might show up at any moment and order me ignominiously off the beach.

17   So, without further thought, I set off confidently across the first of the small channels—and instantly received a shock, more of surprise than cold, as my right foot filled with icy seawater. I looked down: there was a slit in the waders, a small tear less than a half-inch long just above the ankle. *Damn!* I thought, *Damn it anyway!* There goes comfort, there goes protection, there goes everything. For however appealing the romantic scenario I had been fashioning for myself, I had no intention of spending several hours out on a barrier beach with a cold, soaked foot.

18   I stood, thwarted, on the far side of the first channel I had just crossed, staring down with anger and frustration at the small but decisive chink in my armor. Looking back up at the cars parked behind the old Coast Guard station, I saw that they had grown in number and now lined the road that sloped down the hill toward the beach. If I did not want to be an uncomfortable adventurer, neither did I want to be just one of them, a mere observer, a spectator of spectacles.

19   The desire and promise of the storm rose before me again. I wanted to be part of it, to experience the obliteration of this long beach, not from some heightened perspective, but from inside; to be out there riding the bare dune ridge into the foamy teeth of destruction, to feel the sand shake beneath me

with each onslaught of the sea, to watch the muddy surges gouge and slice off clumps of beach grass from around my feet. Perhaps I might even get to see one of the three remaining cottages nudged off its foundations and sent sidling and waddling, like some ungainly hippopotamus, down into the flooded marsh.

20   I had to get across, but the soaked foot, as cold as reality, still held me back. Then I had an idea: I might be able to hop across these deeper but narrow channels on one leg, keeping my leaky foot in the air, and still manage to get across relatively dry. It would be a less than graceful crossing, but it seemed so silly, so *stupid,* to be turned back at this point by something as trivial as a leaky boot. At any rate, I had to try.

21   Stepping back and taking a short run, I did manage to skip successfully across the second channel on one foot, and from there strode determinedly out across the lower rounded plain of the cut-through. But as I did, a low, wide surge of water came up over the crest of the beach and began to roll toward me. At first it looked like a mere sheen of water upon the sand, but when it reached me it was about eight inches deep. Still, I managed to keep hopping in place while it passed, or rather, nearly in place, for with each jump I found myself nudged gently backward toward the marsh by the force of the shallow current.

22   After the surge had gone by, I trotted back to higher ground, where I stopped and stood again, facing the cut. Once more it was only a plain of wet sand, but this time I knew the truth. If I were to get across to the barrier island, I would not get there dry. The shallow surges, which had looked like mere skins of water from here, were deeper than they seemed. I cursed the cheap Japanese waders I wore and wished (with the trite hell of mundane truth seen too late) that I had brought along my good pair. But there was no time to go back for them now—and perhaps it was too late in any case. I asked myself if a little stupid cold water was going to stop me, and found myself answering, yes, I guessed it was.

23   So, resigned to discretion, I started up from the beach, and as I did I became aware of what a curious and conspicuous sight I must have presented to the cars above: a man, dressed in a red-orange slicker and waders, hopping on one foot back and forth across the beach. What did they think of me, all those watchers on the hill? What did they make of all my indecisive comings and goings? Did they think I was dancing, or did they divine what I was up to? And if they did, did they cheer me or chastise me in their minds?

24   I began to feel not so much like a dissatisfied or frustrated spectator, but like a performer in an arena, one who was not only testing himself but carrying with him the expectations and vicarious aspirations of the crowd. Strangely, people still remained in their cars, though the rain had virtually stopped. Were they, perhaps, mesmerized by my efforts? Did they think that by coming out now they might discourage me, break my resolve? Their staying inside began to seem a sort of vote of confidence, a silent encouragement, a sign that the

outcome still lay in the balance. The people watching on the hill, warm and dry inside their vehicles, became not a threat but an inspiration and a responsibility. I found myself thinking that, after all, the water inside my right boot was not that bad. Already my body heat had warmed it up, creating a wet-suit effect that would actually act as insulation against subsequent soakings.

25   I turned back. Across the cut the truncated hulk of eroding dune cradled its diminishing collection of moribund structures in the face of the storm. It gained a renewed and intense desirability, commensurate with its vulnerability and increasing inaccessibility. A situation like this might come again, but never this opportunity, never this moment. I longed for the sea change it offered, but first I had to cross over to it, on its terms, not mine. I was being kept off only by a barrier of my own making, a petty fear of cold, wet feet. But what was a little physical discomfort in exchange for such a rare chance?

26   I began racing out across the overwash plain, knowing this time I would not turn back, splashing heedlessly through the shallow channels, out over the rounded sea-washed plain. I no longer cared what would happen once I reached that island, only that I wanted to be there, to become for an afternoon's space part of that good destruction, a witness and human measure of its uncircumferenced power.

27   I ran on, my feet splashing and leaving little pools behind in the wet sand, my wader legs slapping against one another rhythmically, as the dunes and their little cottages grew closer, ever more possible, ever more real. And then, nearly halfway across, I saw, too late, that I had misjudged again. A major surge lifted itself up over the crest of the beach to my left and began to roll straight across the cut at right angles to my own progress. I knew I could not outrace it, that I had to stop short and brace myself broadside to the surge, or I would be knocked over and swamped. Even so, when it hit, I felt the force of the water moving me, sliding me back, back and down toward the marsh. The sand itself began to slide with me under my feet, and I thought of the VW that had been swept, driverless, off the parking lot and out into the marsh on the night of the great storm a year ago. The overwash was itself half water and half sand. The grains sparkled and glistened like stars as they tumbled and fell around me. The water began to pour into another tear in my waders, larger and higher up around my thighs, and I felt it clutch at my groin with a deep chill.

28   *Hang on, hang on,* was all I thought as the surge continued to rise and push against me. I could see only water flowing around me now, and had the strange sensation that I was not being pushed backward, but rather was rushing headlong toward the seething ocean beyond, an ocean which, as in a dream, did not get any closer as I rushed forward, but even seemed to be receding.

29   The surge had crested to my waist now, pushing with a steady but immeasurable force. Only my concentration on keeping my balance kept me from giving way to panic, though somewhere, far below, I was still convinced I was in no real danger. In summer, meeting such a swell head-on would have been great

fun; but this was no play; this was cold primal power, this was the end to all rules and all options, the ultimate naysayer and decision maker. And when I finally felt myself stop moving, when I sensed that the force, the pulse of the surge, had rolled past and the waters had begun to subside, I also knew which way I would go. . . .

30   But I went back laughing, partly from relief, but also with a strange sense of elation. I knew I would now have to be satisfied with a rather tame view of the flood from the secure battlements on the hill. I also knew I could likely have made it across before the next swell caught me; and, if not, it had only been the delay of my earlier hesitations that now made the crossing impossible.

31   Still, I had at least made a full effort, and in so doing had perhaps come closer to what I aimed at than I had really intended. And if in the end I was turned back, at least it had not been by considerations of human comfort, nor by official interference, nor even by what it would now have been much too easy to call common sense, but by the overwhelming and undeniable authority of that time and tide which, as ever, wait for no man.

32   As I climbed back up the hill, I passed the line of idling cars parked along the roadside. None of the occupants gave any sign they had been watching me, except for one man who, rolling down his window, remarked in a noncommittal tone, "I thought you were fishing out there."

33   I wanted to say that I was, and that the big one had gotten away. But the truth is, it just proved too big and I cut bait.

☐ Discovering Meaning and Technique

1. Reread the first three paragraphs of the selection. Do you think that instructing the reader is an effective way to begin?

2. Finch relates the experience in the first person *(I)*. Would the selection have been as effective if told in the third person *(he)?*

3. Why does the narrator initially decide to cross over the open plain?

4. Point out the places in the selection where the narrator makes decisions about whether to turn back or not. Why does he make the decisions he makes?

5. Do the people in the cars understand the narrator's motives, or does he merely imagine that they do? On what do you base your answer?

☐ **Writing Suggestions**

1. Describe an experience of your own during a storm, flash flood, hurricane, or tornado.

2. Why do humans pit themselves against nature—riding rapids, climbing mountains, sailing alone across the sea?

3. Describe something you have done that tested your courage and jeopardized your safety. Why did you do it? How did you feel afterward?

4. Why do children "take dares"? Describe something foolish that you once did on a dare—such as climbing a water tower, swimming in freezing water, jumping from a rooftop, taking a drug. Why does peer pressure often overcome common sense?

TO THE OPEN WATER

☐ JESSE HILL FORD

1 When the teal leaped from the grass it flew up so swiftly that it was already out of range by the time he fired. At the sound of the shotgun a few blackjacks put up. They rose reluctantly in the cold air and circled a moment before flying straight up channel towards the neck of the bottoms.

2   He quickly climbed the embankment to the road and ran to the bridge to watch the ducks. Slicing through the sky like arrows, they flew almost out of sight before they veered left, folded suddenly into a soft spiral, and went down beyond the trees.

3   The open water would be there, where they went down. He knew the place, a logjam island. It would be, perhaps, the only open water to be found on such a day when even the coves along the Tennessee River were frozen solid. Ice was skimming the main channel itself in places.

4   Even where the pale afternoon sun had shone on the windless side of the levee the air was pinching cold. Since early morning he had scouted the banks about the bottoms without venturing on the ice. Until he saw the teal he had seen only two snipe. He had killed one of them and missed the other.

5   He left the bridge and walked about seventy yards up the levee, then down the embankment through dead briers and dormant honeysuckle vines. The johnboat lay where he had left it, bottom upward on the bank. He stepped out on the ice.

6   He stamped his foot. The ice held, solid as concrete, hard as glass it seemed,

too thick to break a way through it for the boat. Besides, the boat was small and of light-gauge aluminum, not meant to take the punishment of jagged, broken ice. It was made to be sculled through the bottoms on warmer days, to be ghosted along like a feather by the merest dip and twitch of the paddle, to go more quietly than man could walk or duck could fly.

7   He looked up. By hauling the little boat up the levee to the road he could carry it on his shoulders to the channel and put in at the bridge. He was a stout man of two hundred pounds, well used to work. Had it been morning he wouldn't have hesitated. Time, however, was against him now. Walk fast though he might, carrying the boat, and once in the channel with it, paddle swiftly though he would, there was small chance he could reach the logjam island before sundown. By that time it would be too late to shoot, and he would have labored for nothing.

8   His only chance was to slide the little johnboat over the ice straight out towards the logjam island, to sled along swiftly directly to his destination, pushing the little craft ahead of him and, for safety, leaning forward over the stern as he went. In that way, should he run upon rotten ice, he would fall in the boat as it cracked through.

9   He had gone over the ice this way many times before, but never this late in the afternoon, never with the bottoms so silent. The freeze kept other hunters close at home or sitting beside stoves in crossroads country stores. None but the most determined, not even professional guides, would try to find open water in weather such as this, even though once it was found and reached, the shooting was beyond compare. With no other place to land, the ducks would leave when jumped, only to return again and again.

10   The desire to be where they were this very instant made his throat ache. Once before as he slid over the ice he had cracked through in a bad place several hundred yards out and had been forced to stay where he was until after midnight, when the bottoms froze sufficiently solid for him to walk out and drag the little boat after him. Every other time, though, he had made it to the open water. There was a line of trees marking the grave of an old road buried by the winter flood. By leaping into the boat just there, it was possible to coast off the edge of the ice into the water. He had done it with never an accident, a dozen times perhaps, all before he married. Since his marriage six years ago, he had never attempted the trick.

11   From the time he was ten until the day of his marriage, he had hunted every day of every duck season, every day after school, even Sundays after church, though Sunday hunting was frowned upon. He had hunted them because he loved them then with the same passionate ache in his throat that he felt now for those creatures settled there on the open water by the thousands, their wild hearts calling his own, it seemed.

12   Marriage had pinched him down. His wife had ambitions for the farm. It wasn't enough to spend spring, summer, and fall riding a tractor, driving a cotton

picker, loading and unloading his truck, working at times until long after nightfall, waiting five hours to get his cotton trailer under the suck at the gin. A wife had to have chickens and geese and cattle. Coonhounds and mules weren't creatures enough to care for, not in a wife's estimation. There must be winter duties too—even, finally, a dairy barn. God help him if he once failed to be home in time to milk.

13   He hadn't gone over the ice in six long years because there had been too many creatures dependent on him, nearly all of them female. First a wife, then infant daughters, and finally the wife's gentle-eyed Jerseys with their slender hips and heavy udders.

14   A mallard susie quacked in the distance. He turned the johnboat right side up and laid his heavy parka in it next to his gun. Besides two extra boxes of shells in the pockets of the parka, he carried twenty-three magnum loads in a shooting vest which he wore buttoned snugly about his chest for warmth. He opened his half-pint and took a drink of white moonshine whiskey. Over the bottoms the air was still.

15   With a practiced heave he pushed the boat out ahead of him on the ice, keeping his weight forward, ready to leap in the boat if the ice failed. As he gathered speed, his legs moving in a regular rhythm, running easily, the boat set up a screeching, thundering racket, scraping past trees and cracking through thickets. Mallards rose from the red oak thickets and flew towards the channel. Now in an open space he paused and watched them a moment. Then he pushed on, going even faster now as the open spaces between thickets got wider and wider. He began sweating a little and slowed down.

16   Farther out, he stopped to rest. He sat on the stern of the little boat, boots on the ice, elbows on knees, looking down at the hard, slick, olive-drab surface. He looked up at the levee, about six hundred yards away now, a long, straight elevated outline. The road was desolate in both directions. Only hunters, trappers, fishermen, or an occasional logger used it. Far down to the left, he saw the black outline of his pickup truck. He had parked it that morning before starting along the north edge of the bottoms where he had killed the snipe.

17   He leaned back and got the bird from the game pocket of his parka. The little body was frozen. Strangest of all were the eyes; black with life's memory, they seemed, in the instant after death, before the cold seeped into them and did its work. Frozen now, the eyes were white.

18   He stood up and tossed the snipe into the front of the boat, turning at the same time and leaning forward. The ice cracked. The crack ran under him and on ahead of the boat through the dark-green ice. Though a crack it most surely was, it didn't seem to be a very serious one. He held the sides of the boat, leaning forward to distribute his weight, braced like an athlete preparing to do push-ups. He waited. The ice held.

19   Fifty yards to the right stood a duck blind. The decoys in front of it were frozen solid into the ice and glazed with white frost. Red oak saplings shaded

the ice in their direction. There the ice looked pale, almost white. It would be thicker. He could turn back now in that direction and reach the levee.

20   Far away to his left over the long open stretches he saw the line of trees marking the lost road. Beyond the flat glare he saw the logjam island, and around it the still blue gulf of the open water, reflecting the sky. In ten minutes he could reach the trees for the final, sliding rush.

21   He skidded the boat left and made straight for the trees, getting up speed first and then making only so much effort with his legs as would keep the boat sliding. Now and again the ice cracked, but the boat outran the cracks, one after the other as he pushed on, keeping his weight carefully distributed forward, over the boat.

22   Suddenly, with no warning the ice gave under him, and he fell into the boat just in time, just before it cracked through, and not an instant too soon, for the icy water had bitten him almost to mid-thigh, wetting him well above his insulated rubber knee boots. It had happened this way before. It was like being burned, like the sting of flames licking about his legs. He lay face down and still, waiting for his trousers to freeze. It needed only a little patience. When he sat up at last, remembering to wiggle his toes and flex his calf muscles to keep the circulation going, even the splashes had frozen. They looked like drops of candle wax.

23   Flared by the commotion of his fall, the ducks had flown up. Now they flocked and circled low around the edge of the open water. He slipped a magnum shell into the magazine of the automatic to replace the one fired at the teal. Then he put the parka over his head and shoulders and sat very still. He quacked with his mouth. A susie answered. He quacked again. He patted his lips, making the intimate, stuttering feed call. He tried the raucous call of the wise old susie. It all proved a false hope. The entire drove splashed in beside the island with a brisk rush of sound that set his heart beating faster.

24   When he put the gun down and took off the parka, his toes were numb. He moved them and rubbed his legs and finally admitted it to himself. He had cracked through; maybe the ice *was* rotten. Very well, but he had broken through only one time in several hundred yards of running, after all. He *had* managed to fall very neatly into the johnboat, hadn't he?

25   Though it was a ticklish sort of job, there was still a chance that he could get the boat back up on the ice. He moved back cautiously and sat on the stern, balancing his weight until the bow rose high out of the water and less than four inches of freeboard remained beneath him. Then he dipped the paddle and drove the boat hard against the edge, and moving at once, fast, before it could slide off again, he went quickly forward on all fours. The ice cracked, the long, brittle sound of a marble rolling over a glass tabletop. Crouched in the bow, he waited, holding his breath, a dull pain beating in his throat just under the Adam's apple. The ice held. Cautiously, slowly, he leaned far out over the prow and caught a willow limb in his gloved hand and pulled. The

boat eased forward with him. He caught another limb and then another, getting farther and farther up on firm ice, hauling the boat painfully hand over hand until at last his arms gave out and he turned carefully and lay on his back breathing the cold, clean air through his mouth, cupping his hands and breathing into them. Lying thus, looking straight up, the depth of the clear sky was blue and magnificent. When he held his breath there was not a stir of sound anywhere to be heard. He might have been the last creature left alive on earth. A feeling of independence entered him like the slow onset of sleep.

26   When it was time to move again he found he was tired. He moved awkwardly, stiff in his joints, his shoulders aching in the sockets, his toes numb because he had neglected to keep moving them. He took the flat, half-pint bottle from his parka and drank it empty in three long swigs and flung the bottle away. It smashed. The clear little shards of glass slid on for several yards before they finally stopped, gleaming at rest in the waning sunlight like white jewels.

27   The levee had never before seemed so far away. The slanting sun perhaps added to the illusion. When he stood up he could not see the truck. Willow thickets blocked the way. In the other direction, just ahead, the island loomed from the open water, a tangled mass of roots and black tree trunks. Low in the water all around it the ducks rested, very still, as though waiting for him.

28   Although they were out of range, he was tempted to fire at them anyway, to put them up for the joy of seeing them fly, for the satisfaction, knowing that though they might circle the whole bottoms, they would come back. The cold air would drive them down again, here, in the last of the open water, perhaps the last open water to be found anywhere about, except in the mid-river channel.

29   The liquor's warmth caught hold. He hadn't eaten since before daylight. It didn't matter. He had taught himself not to want food. He had taught himself not to want anything but the beautiful joy of killing. He had always hunted this way.

30   Now he took the bow line, and without hesitating, stepped out on the ice and put it over his shoulder and towed the boat after him. Once started, it seemed to follow him willingly, coming after him across the patch of firm, white ice like a docile beast. When the ice shaded into olive green again, he stopped and fended his way around to the stern to rest a moment before making the final dash for trees at the edge of the open water.

31   Once the boat slid free he would be in range. The ducks would come up and circle, dipping their dark wings to his call, and he would lovingly kill them. He would scull coaxingly after the cripples one by one, coming so slowly on them that they would hardly know the boat was moving at all. While they flirted in that final, zigzag hesitation, he would suddenly raise the gun and shoot their heads off clean. Their blood would boil below them like a cloud into the dark, clear water.

32   A whistling flight of teal drove in, wings already set, and pitched in beyond the island. A susie quacked. He drew a deep breath and shoved. The boat groaned

against the willows and slid forward. Faster and faster, he pushed on. Exhilaration shook him like a sudden wind among dead leaves. With less than fifty yards to go, speed was in his favor. Instinctively, at the right instant, he would leap lightly forward.

33   As though struck suddenly blind, however, he was groping, wet to the armpits, his breath coming so fast that his chest seemed about to burst. He saw the johnboat beside him. It had cracked through. He caught its side. Water spilled in, so he pushed back, trying to swim, his hands already so numb he could hardly feel them.

34   *"Still, be still!"* he commanded aloud, using words he spoke to the restless cows at milking. The cold drove in from every direction like nails, driving and driving in, searching his vitals.

35   He must think! Of course, only keep a clear head! Make every move carefully! Sound judgment, no wasted time or motion. *Easy, careful,"* he said, speaking to the fiery grip of the cold, which now became more powerful than anything he had ever before imagined, for it was taking him over.

36   In the place of the strong, obedient body he had so long been accustomed to command, he felt a strange and foolish despair at this heaving, disquieted thing that would no longer obey.

37   In spite of every caution to the contrary, his body suddenly fought like a cat snared on a string. Thrashing and fighting like a dying fish, he fended himself clumsily around to the prow and threw himself hard upon it. Short of seeing it, he could never have believed such an utterly foolish panic to be possible. Already almost in the wink of an eye, he had destroyed his best hope. The incredible, the *impossible* thing happened. The boat filled almost as quickly as he had moved, and rolled down from under him.

38   Water covered his face. When he had fought to the surface and taken breath, he felt his hair and his eyebrows freezing.

39   Bottom up now and barely afloat, the boat was another creature entirely, as though it too, the docile beast of a moment before, had now lost all notion of what it was logically supposed to be, and do.

40   When he touched it, it rolled. When he caught at it, the weird creature shook him off; it threw him a second time, and he gentled cautiously against it, the cold biting clean through his shoulders now, like teeth. His body's least twitch made the boat heave and swing. Holding the boat, huddling on it and fighting its strange movements, he realized for the first time that the shooting vest with its cargo of magnum shells was his enemy now, the perfect weight to sink a man and kill him. Propping a hand and both knees against the boat, he tried the vest's buttons. Briefly his fingers stung back to life, but they were useless against buttons.

41   He tried to balance himself on the boat and rip the vest apart with both hands, no trick for a strong man in his early prime, yet each time he tried it the other creature, the rebellious animal self, seized him. His arms failed. They

disobeyed. His hands groped warily forward like burned stumps, to rest against the boat and balance him.

42   He remained thus awhile, motionless, not even shivering, such was the marvel of it, his head just above the surface of the freezing water. The thin winter sunlight and the desolate, utter silence of the bottoms, great spanning miles of it, dinned and drummed at him.

43   He knew he must shout soon. It would be no use, of course. No earthly man would hear. Yet soon he would begin screaming. The body would have that too; the body would have it, though he knew shouting must only exhaust him the sooner and hasten the end. Screams began gathering in his throat like a queer nausea.

44   If he had only thought to take off the vest before his fingers numbed, to get out of his boots, even kick off his trousers. Then he might have gotten back in the boat. He would have wrung out his clothes and put them back on and huddled under the parka until night froze the bottoms in, and then he would have walked out to the road and gotten in the truck. He would have driven it home and tottered into the house and asked his wife to draw him a hot bath. Once he was warm and rested he would have gotten a friend or two and come back after his boat and the gun.

45   If they ever found it, anytime within a week or two, the gun would be all right. He kept it oiled, and with the water so cold the oil would stick. The gun wouldn't rust quickly. Perhaps they would find it. He hoped they would.

46   Finding the gun shouldn't be hard with the boat frozen in the ice right over it. A sudden ruthless pain in his back, above the beltline, jerked his head forward. For the first time he began shuddering. He heard himself shouting, screaming for help, the cries already hoarse though hardly even well begun. The ducks came up and began wheeling and circling above him. Their curved wings were more beautiful than any he had seen before, cupping as gently as a kiss, skimming like a long caress, each pair shaped like the touch of a woman's hands in love.

47   He stopped yelling and slid peacefully down into the white darkness under the surface.

☐ Discovering Meaning and Technique

1. Why is the hunter so eager to reach the "open water"? Is it only his desire to shoot ducks?

2. What is the hunter's attitude toward marriage? What do you suppose his relationship is with his wife? Might this relationship have anything to do with his desire to reach the open water?

3. What details does Ford include to indicate the extreme cold?

4. Point out the paragraphs near the end of the selection where the hunter seems to be two people—one acting and one observing.

5. Explain the attitude described in these passages from the selection: "he hunted them because he loved them" (paragraph 11); "the beautiful joy of killing" (paragraph 29); "he would lovingly kill them" (paragraph 31). Explain also this passage from paragraph 46, as the hunter is about to drown: "Their curved wings were more beautiful than any he had seen before, . . . each pair shaped like the touch of a woman's hands in love."

6. Compare the last paragraph with the description of the dead snipe's eyes (paragraph 17).

☐ **Writing Suggestions**

1. Some readers might feel that the hunter's death is nature's revenge. Is that what Ford thinks? What seems to be Ford's attitude toward this particular hunter?

2. Explain the psychology of hunting. Is it purely an exercise in *machismo?* Or are there other explanations?

3. Explain the story as the hunter's attempt to reassert his independence and manhood.

4. Describe a personal hunting experience that was particularly memorable.

5. Describe any personal experience that involved nature and danger. How did it affect you?

6. Why do you suppose that whereas many people oppose hunting, relatively few oppose fishing?

THE OBLIGATION TO ENDURE

☐ RACHEL CARSON

1 The history of life on earth has been a history of interaction between living things and their surroundings. To a large extent, the physical form and the habits of the earth's vegetation and its animal life have been molded by the environment. Considering the whole span of earthly time, the opposite effect, in which life actually modifies its surroundings, has been relatively slight. Only within the moment of time represented by the present century has one species—man—acquired significant power to alter the nature of his world.

2   During the past quarter century this power has not only increased to one of disturbing magnitude but it has changed in character. The most alarming of all man's assaults upon the environment is the contamination of air, earth, rivers, and sea with dangerous and even lethal materials. This pollution is for the most part irrecoverable; the chain of evil it initiates not only in the world that must support life but in living tissues is for the most part irreversible. In this now universal contamination of the environment, chemicals are the sinister and little-recognized partners of radiation in changing the very nature of the world—the very nature of its life. Strontium 90, released through nuclear explosions into the air, comes to earth in rain or drifts down as fallout, lodges in soil, enters into the grass or corn or wheat grown there, and in time takes up its abode in the bones of a human being, there to remain until his death. Similarly, chemicals sprayed on croplands or forests or gardens lie long in soil, entering into living organisms, passing from one to another in a chain of poisoning and death. Or they pass mysteriously by underground streams until they emerge and, through the alchemy of air and sunlight, combine into new forms that kill vegetation, sicken cattle, and work unknown harm on those who drink from once pure wells. As Albert Schweitzer has said, "Man can hardly even recognize the devils of his own creation."

3   It took hundreds of millions of years to produce the life that now inhabits the earth—eons of time in which that developing and evolving and diversifying life reached a state of adjustment and balance with its surroundings. The environment, rigorously shaping and directing the life it supported, contained elements that were hostile as well as supporting. Certain rocks gave out dangerous radiation; even within the light of the sun, from which all life draws its energy, there were short-wave radiations with power to injure. Given time—time not in years but in millennia—life adjusts, and a balance has been reached. For time is the essential ingredient; but in the modern world there is no time.

4   The rapidity of change and the speed with which new situations are created follow the impetuous and heedless pace of man rather than the deliberate pace of nature. Radiation is no longer merely the background radiation of rocks, the bombardment of cosmic rays, the ultraviolet of the sun that have existed before there was any life on earth; radiation is now the unnatural creation of man's tampering with the atom. The chemicals to which life is asked to make its adjustment are no longer merely the calcium and silica and copper and all the rest of the minerals washed out of the rocks and carried in rivers to the sea; they are the synthetic creations of man's inventive mind, brewed in his laboratories, and having no counterparts in nature.

5   To adjust to these chemicals would require time on the scale that is nature's; it would require not merely the years of a man's life but the life of generations. And even this, were it by some miracle possible, would be futile, for the new chemicals come from our laboratories in an endless stream; almost five hundred annually find their way into actual use in the United States alone. The figure is

staggering and its implications are not easily grasped—five hundred new chemicals to which the bodies of men and animals are required somehow to adapt each year, chemicals totally outside the limits of biologic experience.

6   Among them are many that are used in man's war against nature. Since the mid-1940s over two hundred basic chemicals have been created for use in killing insects, weeds, rodents, and other organisms described in the modern vernacular as "pests"; and they are sold under several thousand different brand names.

7   These sprays, dusts, and aerosols are now applied almost universally to farms, gardens, forests, and homes—nonselective chemicals that have the power to kill every insect, the "good" and the "bad," to still the song of birds and the leaping of fish in the streams, to coat the leaves with a deadly film, and to linger on in soil—all this though the intended target may be only a few weeds or insects. Can anyone believe it is possible to lay down such a barrage of poisons on the surface of the earth without making it unfit for all life? They should not be called "insecticides," but "biocides."

8   The whole process of spraying seems caught up in an endless spiral. Since DDT was released for civilian use, a process of escalation has been going on in which ever more toxic materials must be found. This has happened because insects, in a triumphant vindication of Darwin's principle of the survival of the fittest, have evolved super races immune to the particular insecticide used, hence a deadlier one has always to be developed—and then a deadlier one than that. It has happened also because, for reasons to be described later, destructive insects often undergo a "flareback," or resurgence, after spraying, in numbers greater than before. Thus the chemical war is never won, and all life is caught in its violent crossfire.

9   Along with the possibility of the extinction of mankind by nuclear war, the central problem of our age has therefore become the contamination of man's total environment with such substances of incredible potential for harm—substances that accumulate in the tissues of plants and animals and even penetrate the germ cells to shatter or alter the very material of heredity upon which the shape of the future depends.

10   Some would-be architects of our future look toward a time when it will be possible to alter the human germ plasm by design. But we may easily be doing so now by inadvertence, for many chemicals, like radiation, bring about gene mutations. It is ironic to think that man might determine his own future by something so seemingly trivial as the choice of an insect spray.

11   All this has been risked—for what? Future historians may well be amazed by our distorted sense of proportion. How could intelligent beings seek to control a few unwanted species by a method that contaminated the entire environment and brought the threat of disease and death even to their own kind? Yet this is precisely what we have done. We have done it, moreover, for reasons that collapse the moment we examine them. We are told that the enormous and expanding use of pesticides is necessary to maintain farm production. Yet is

our real problem not one of *overproduction?* Our farms, despite measures to remove acreages from production and to pay farmers *not* to produce, have yielded such a staggering excess of crops that the American taxpayer in 1962 is paying out more than one billion dollars a year as the total carrying cost of the surplus-food storage program. And is the situation helped when one branch of the Agriculture Department tries to reduce production while another states, as it did in 1958, "It is believed generally that reduction of crop acreages under provisions of the Soil Bank will stimulate interest in use of chemicals to obtain maximum production on the land retained in crops."

12   All this is not to say there is no insect problem and no need of control. I am saying, rather, that control must be geared to realities, not to mythical situations, and that the methods employed must be such that they do not destroy us along with the insects.

13 The problem whose attempted solution has brought such a train of disaster in its wake is an accompaniment of our modern way of life. Long before the age of man, insects inhabited the earth—a group of extraordinarily varied and adaptable beings. Over the course of time since man's advent, a small percentage of the more than half a million species of insects have come into conflict with human welfare in two principal ways: as competitors for the food supply and as carriers of human disease.

14   Disease-carrying insects become important where human beings are crowded together, especially under conditions where sanitation is poor, as in time of natural disaster or war or in situations of extreme poverty and deprivation. Then control of some sort becomes necessary. It is a sobering fact, however, as we shall presently see, that the method of massive chemical control has had only limited success, and also threatens to worsen the very conditions it is intended to curb.

15   Under primitive agricultural conditions the farmer had few insect problems. These arose with the intensification of agriculture—the devotion of immense acreages to a single crop. Such a system set the stage for explosive increases in specific insect populations. Single-crop farming does not take advantage of the principles by which nature works; it is agriculture as an engineer might conceive it to be. Nature has introduced great variety into the landscape, but man has displayed a passion for simplifying it. Thus he undoes the built-in checks and balances by which nature holds the species within bounds. One important natural check is a limit on the amount of suitable habitat for each species. Obviously then, an insect that lives on wheat can build up its population to much higher levels on a farm devoted to wheat than on one in which wheat is intermingled with other crops to which the insect is not adapted.

16   The same thing happens in other situations. A generation or more ago, the towns of large areas of the United States lined their streets with the noble elm tree. Now the beauty they hopefully created is threatened with complete destruction as disease sweeps through the elms, carried by a beetle that would

have only limited chance to build up large populations and to spread from tree to tree if the elms were only occasional trees in a richly diversified planting.

17   Another factor in the modern insect problem is one that must be viewed against a background of geologic and human history: the spreading of thousands of different kinds of organisms from their native homes to invade new territories. This worldwide migration has been studied and graphically described by the British ecologist Charles Elton in his recent book *The Ecology of Invasions.* During the Cretaceous Period, some hundred million years ago, flooding seas cut many land bridges between continents and living things found themselves confined in what Elton calls "colossal separate nature reserves." There, isolated from others of their kind, they developed many new species. When some of the land masses were joined again, about 15 million years ago, these species began to move out into new territories—a movement that is not only still in progress but is now receiving considerable assistance from man.

18   The importation of plants is the primary agent in the modern spread of species, for animals have almost invariably gone along with the plants, quarantine being a comparatively recent and not completely effective innovation. The United States Office of Plant Introduction alone has introduced almost 200,000 species and varieties of plants from all over the world. Nearly half of the 180 or so major insect enemies of plants in the United States are accidental imports from abroad, and most of them have come as hitchhikers on plants.

19   In new territory, out of reach of the restraining hand of the natural enemies that kept down its numbers in its native land, an invading plant or animal is able to become enormously abundant. Thus it is no accident that our most troublesome insects are introduced species.

20   These invasions, both the naturally occurring and those dependent on human assistance, are likely to continue indefinitely. Quarantine and massive chemical campaigns are only extremely expensive ways of buying time. We are faced, according to Dr. Elton, "with a life-and-death need not just to find new technological means of suppressing this plant or that animal"; instead we need the basic knowledge of animal populations and their relations to their surroundings that will "promote an even balance and damp down the explosive power of outbreaks and new invasions."

21   Much of the necessary knowledge is now available but we do not use it. We train ecologists in our universities and even employ them in our governmental agencies but we seldom take their advice. We allow the chemical death rain to fall as though there were no alternative, whereas in fact there are many, and our ingenuity could soon discover many more if given opportunity.

22   Have we fallen into a mesmerized state that makes us accept as inevitable that which is inferior or detrimental, as though having lost the will or the vision to demand that which is good? Such thinking, in the words of the ecologist Paul Shepard, "idealizes life with only its head out of water, inches above the limits of toleration of the corruption of its own environment . . . Why should we tolerate a diet of weak poisons, a home in insipid surroundings, a circle of

acquaintances who are not quite our enemies, the noise of motors with just enough relief to prevent insanity? Who would want to live in a world which is just not quite fatal?"

23   Yet such a world is pressed upon us. The crusade to create a chemically sterile, insect-free world seems to have engendered a fanatic zeal on the part of many specialists and most of the so-called control agencies. On every hand there is evidence that those engaged in spraying operations exercise a ruthless power. "The regulatory entomologists . . . function as prosecutor, judge and jury, tax assessor and collector and sheriff to enforce their own orders," said Connecticut entomologist Neely Turner. The most flagrant abuses go unchecked in both state and federal agencies.

24   It is not my contention that chemical insecticides must never be used. I do contend that we have put poisonous and biologically potent chemicals indiscriminately into the hands of persons largely or wholly ignorant of their potentials for harm. We have subjected enormous numbers of people to contact with these poisons, without their consent and often without their knowledge. If the Bill of Rights contains no guarantee that a citizen shall be secure against lethal poisons distributed either by private individuals or by public officials, it is surely only because our forefathers, despite their considerable wisdom and foresight, could conceive of no such problem.

25   I contend, furthermore, that we have allowed these chemicals to be used with little or no advance investigation of their effect on soil, water, wildlife, and man himself. Future generations are unlikely to condone our lack of prudent concern for the integrity of the natural world that supports all life.

26   There is still very limited awareness of the nature of the threat. This is an era of specialists, each of whom sees his own problem and is unaware of or intolerant of the larger frame into which it fits. It is also an era dominated by industry, in which the right to make a dollar at whatever cost is seldom challenged. When the public protests, confronted with some obvious evidence of damaging results of pesticide applications, it is fed little tranquilizing pills of half truth. We urgently need an end to these false assurances, to the sugar coating of unpalatable facts. It is the public that is being asked to assume the risks that the insect controllers calculate. The public must decide whether it wishes to continue on the present road, and it can do so only when in full possession of the facts. In the words of Jean Rostand, "The obligation to endure gives us the right to know."

☐ Discovering Meaning and Technique

1. At the end of paragraph 3, Carson says that "in the modern world there is no time." Explain what she means.

2. What are some of the reasons for what Carson calls "man's war against nature"?

3. Give several reasons for the spread of destructive insects in modern times and explain each.

4. Why does Carson contend that "the chemical war is never won"?

5. What does Carson see as the trouble with specialists?

☐ Writing Suggestions

1. Describe the power of humans to "alter the nature" of the earth—both for good and harm.

2. What can a single individual do to reduce pollution?

3. Read the caution information on various insecticides and herbicides. Do you think that the dangers of the products are made sufficiently clear? How could the information be made more noticeable?

4. Since the word *biocide* means "capable of killing life," do you agree with Carson that insecticides should be renamed "biocides"?

5. Assume that you are a historian in the twenty-fourth century—a time in which humans have evolved into a civilized and wise society. Looking back to the twentieth century, describe how people treated the environment.

6. Are humans or insects more likely to survive the future?

7. Some studies have shown that farmers lose the same harvest to insects as they lost before using insecticides. Research this subject in current periodicals, and write a short paper on it.

8. Research and discuss the battle against the Mediterranean fruit fly in California.

9. Should we be concerned about passing on today's problems to future generations?

10. To the pollution problem, apply Walt Kelly's statement, "We have met the enemy and he is us."

■ Combining Sources in a Composition

1. Compare the ways in which some of the writers in this section view animals. Which view seems the most realistic to you? Which seems the most interesting?

2. Write an essay on the altering of nature, using for source material the selections by Carson, Rettie, Rawlings—or any other selection that seems appropriate.

3. Discuss some inventive ways in which plants feed, protect, and reproduce themselves. You can find source material in the selections by Eiseley, Busch, and Collis.

4. Carson says that we need a better approach to controlling insects. Could naturalists (like Busch) be more helpful than chemists?

5. Compare the conflict between humans and the environment in the selections by Robert Finch and Jesse Hill Ford.

6. After reading the selections by Perényi and Busch, do you think that plants and animals are better weather indicators than computers?

7. Write a composition on the ways in which humans are out of touch with nature. For source material, use selections such as those by Perényi, Collis, Carrighar, and Walker.

8. Using the selections by Rettie, Carson, Hoagland, and Rawlings for source material, discuss how greed contributes to human destruction of nature.

C H A P T E R 5

SCIENCE AND TECHNOLOGY
The Computer

THE POET AND THE COMPUTER

NORMAN COUSINS

1 A poet, said Aristotle, has the advantage of expressing the universal; the technician or specialist expresses only the particular. The poet, moreover, can remind us that man's greatest energy comes not from his dynamos but from his dreams. The notion of where a man ought to be instead of where he is; the liberation from cramped prospects; the intimations of immortality through art—all these proceed naturally out of dreams. But the quality of man's dreams can only be a reflection of his subconscious. What he puts into his subconscious, therefore, is quite literally the most important nourishment in the world.

2 Nothing really happens to a man except as it is registered in the subconscious. This is where event and feeling become memory and where the proof of life is stored. The poet—and I use the term to include all those who have respect for

and speak to the human spirit—can help to supply the subconscious with material to enhance its sensitivity, thus safeguarding it. The poet, too, can help to keep man from making himself over in the image of his electronic marvels. The danger is not so much that man will be controlled by the computer as that he may imitate it.

3   There once was a time, in the history of this society, when the ability of people to convey meaning was enriched by their knowledge of and access to the work of creative minds from across the centuries. No more. Conversation and letters today, like education, have become enfeebled by emphasis on the functional and the purely contemporary. The result is a mechanization not just of the way we live but of the way we think, and of the human spirit itself.

4   The delegates to the United States Constitutional Convention were able to undergird their arguments with allusions to historical situations and to the ideas of philosophers, essayists, and dramatists. Names such as Thucydides, Aristotle, Herodotus, Plutarch, or Seneca were commonly cited to support their positions. They alluded to fictional characters from Aristophanes, Marlowe, or Shakespeare to lend color to the exploration of ideas. The analytical essays by Hamilton, Madison, and Jay that appeared in *The Federalist Papers* were an excursion into the remote corners of history.

5   Men such as Jefferson, Adams, Franklin, and Rush could summon pertinent quotations from Suetonius or Machiavelli or Montaigne to illustrate a principle. If they referred to Bacon's opinion of Aristotle, they didn't have to cite particulars; they assumed such details were common knowledge. Their allusions were not the product of intellectual ostentation or ornamentation but the natural condiments of discourse, bringing out the full flavor of the cultivated intelligence.

6   The same was true of correspondence. People regarded letters as an art form and a highly satisfying way of engaging in civilized exchange. The correspondence of Jefferson and Adams and Priestley was not so much a display of personal matters as a review of the human condition. It was not unusual for the writers to range across the entire arena of human thought as a way of sharing perceptions. Allusion was common currency. Today, we rarely turn to letters as a way of embarking on voyages of intellectual discovery.

7   The essential problem of humankind in a computerized age remains the same as it has always been. That problem is not solely how to be more productive, more comfortable, more content, but how to be more sensitive, more sensible, more proportionate, more alive. The computer makes possible a phenomenal leap in human proficiency; it demolishes the fences around the practical and even the theoretical intelligence. But the question persists and indeed grows whether the computer makes it easier or harder for human beings to know who they really are, to identify their real problems, to respond more fully to

beauty, to place adequate value on life, and to make their world safer than it now is.

8   Electronic brains can reduce the profusion of dead ends involved in vital research. But they can't eliminate the foolishness and decay that comes from the unexamined life. Nor do they connect a man to the things he has to be connected to—the reality of pain in others; the possibilities of creative growth in himself; the memory of the race; and the rights of the next generation.

9   The reason these matters are important in a computerized age is that there may be a tendency to mistake data for wisdom, just as there has always been a tendency to confuse logic with values, and intelligence with insight. Unobstructed access to facts can produce unlimited good only if it is matched by the desire and ability to find out what they mean and where they would lead.

10   Facts are terrible things if left sprawling and unattended. They are too easily regarded as evaluated certainties rather than as the rawest of raw materials crying to be processed into the texture of logic. It requires a very unusual mind, Whitehead said, to undertake the analysis of a fact. The computer can provide a correct number, but it may be an irrelevant number until judgment is pronounced.

11   To the extent, then, that people fail to make the distinction between the intermediate operations of electronic intelligence and the ultimate responsibilities of human decision and conscience, the computer could obscure awareness of the need to come to terms with himself. It may foster the illusion that he is asking fundamental questions when actually he is asking only functional ones. It may be regarded as a substitute for intelligence instead of an extension of it. It may promote undue confidence in concrete answers. "If we begin with certainties," Bacon said, "we shall end in doubts; but if we begin with doubts, and we are patient with them, we shall end in certainties."

12   The computer knows how to vanquish error, but before we lose ourselves in celebration of victory, we might reflect on the great advances in the human situation that have come about because men were challenged by error and would not stop thinking and probing until they found better approaches for dealing with it. "Give me a good fruitful error, full of seeds, bursting with its own corrections," Ferris Greenslet wrote. "You can keep your sterile truths to yourself."

13   Without taking anything away from the technicians, it might be fruitful to effect some sort of junction between the computer technologists and the poet. A genuine purpose may be served by turning loose the wonders of the creative imagination on the kinds of problems being put to electronic tubes and transistors. The company of poets may enable the men who tend the machines to see a larger panorama of possibilities than technology alone may inspire.

14   Poets remind men of their uniqueness. It is not necessary to possess the ultimate definition of this uniqueness. Even to speculate on it is a gain.

☐ Discovering Meaning and Technique

1. How does Cousins define a poet?

2. What is Cousins's criticism of modern society?

3. How does Cousins support his contention that society once had "access to the work of creative minds across the centuries" (paragraph 3)?

4. Name the qualities that Cousins thinks human beings should develop.

5. Name the characteristics that the computers can contribute to human beings.

6. What is the computer incapable of ever doing, according to Cousins?

7. What is the difference between asking fundamental questions and functional questions?

☐ Writing Suggestions

1. Do you agree that technicians are less creative than poets?

2. Argue that it is not the computer but something else that has made modern life more mechanized.

3. Do you think it is more important to have computers today than it was in the past?

4. Compare writing on a computer, on a typewriter, and by hand.

COMMAND PERFORMANCE

☐ TOM BODETT

1 Up until a few days ago I was one of those people who didn't know a megabyte from an overbite, but that's all history now. I've joined the technocrats, that global group of future-minded individuals who embrace advanced technology and use it to their utmost advantage. I bought a personal computer.

2 Now, a personal computer is unlike all those other kinds in that, like a checking account or deodorant stick, you have it all to yourself. Other people can't just bop in and use it even if the spirit did move them to. This one is all mine, so keep your hands off while I run you through the details.

3   Like most new technology, computers can be a little scary to the uninitiated. The cavemen who first discovered fire no doubt circled around it cautiously, poking at it with sticks while daring each other to touch it. New computer owners do much the same with their machines. Once our cavemen finally did break down and touch the fire, they quickly got an idea of its basic properties. Technological advancement can be a very real and moving experience. Fortunately, most of the name-brand computers won't singe the hair off your knuckles. In fact, we don't even have hair on our knuckles anymore. You can see we've come a long way since fire was discovered.

4   Unlike fire, computers are what they call "user-friendly." Now, what I think that means is that those little boxes of microchips *like* you and want to hang around with you. Like dogs do. Just like our dogs, they are happiest when they're doing things for us. They want us to give them commands. So let's try a command here.

>SIT<

5   Let's see what it does with that.

<BAD COMMAND—TRY AGAIN>

6   You know, it's right. "Sit" is a bad command. It has domineering overtones and doesn't really suggest the friendship we're trying to develop here. Let's try this, then:

>PLEASE TAKE A SEAT<

7   That's better.

<BAD COMMAND—TRY AGAIN>

8   Oops. There it goes again. Obviously it either doesn't feel like sitting, knows it already is sitting, or considers it too elementary a command to deal with. Maybe it's looking for something a little more complex. Probably wants to impress me and win my undying friendship. Let me find a more advanced function. Here's a key that says SEARCH on it. Let's see what that does.

>SEARCH<
<SEARCH FOR WHAT!>

9   Now we're getting somewhere.

>NORTHWEST PASSAGE<

10   That should keep it busy. Oh good, it's making little noises. Must be working on it.

<NOT FOUND>

11   Not found? It sure couldn't have looked very hard. That's all right. I know where it is anyway, and it's a stupid route to take. Let's have it look around for something a little more practical and closer to home. I'll have it search for my lug-nut wrench. I haven't been able to find it all summer. Here goes nothing:

>LUG WRENCH<
<NOT FOUND>

12   There it is again. What good is this thing? How about this:

>SEARCH FOR YOUR PLASTIC BUTT WITH
BOTH HANDS<
<NOT FOUND>

13   I knew it. Either I've got a real lemon of a computer here, or an exceptionally lazy one. How about this MOVE key:

<MOVE WHAT?>
>MOVE YOU!<

14   That oughta burn its brain box.

<MOVE WHERE?>

15   Oh, how easily it fell into my trap. Let it flop this around its disk drive for a while:

>SEATTLE! HOUSTON! BACK TO SILICON
VALLEY! I DON'T CARE JUST GO!<
<BAD COMMAND—TRY AGAIN>

16   A mutiny, is it? I might not be able to move this overrated high-tech stick-in-the-mud to do a darn thing for me, but I'll tell you one function I know how to use. It's this big red switch on the side of it that says OFF.

< >

17   There, that worked.

18   So, as you can tell, these computers are nothing to be afraid of. Now you know as much about them as I do. If you have any questions, just give me a call. I'd be happy to walk you through this last procedure.

☐ Discovering Meaning and Technique

1. To what does Bodett compare a new computer owner's behavior?

2. Trace Bodett's increasing irritation with his computer.

3. What is Bodett's ultimate weapon against the computer?

☐ Writing Suggestions

1. Bodett reacts to his computer as if it were human. Explain why this reaction is common.

2. Describe what you think a truly "user-friendly" computer would be like.

3. Describe your feelings when you first used a computer or some other piece of equipment such as a VCR.

4. Write a story in which a computer mutinies.

CHILDHOOD LOST

☐ CRAIG BROD

1 A headline in *USA Today,* the national tabloid coming to us "via satellite," read "USA's Whiz Kids Rule the Computer World," and the full-color cover story was subtitled, "They show their elders new ways to think." The story described startling accomplishments by youngsters: an eleven-year-old in Texas writes a syndicated newspaper column about computers; numerous children across the country make substantial sums of money (up to $60,000 a year) inventing computer games; a sixteen-year-old in California has founded a company that offers uncopiable systems to protect against computer piracy. His company is a leader in the field. One seventeen-year-old in New Jersey helped his school system

buy seventy-six computers and trained teachers to operate them, and was then hired by a New York firm to rewrite the software. He is about to graduate from high school and, in the words of his principal, has "been recruited as if he were a seven-foot basketball player." The youngster spoke at his old elementary school, and, says one of those attending, "it was like Rocky. The kids were standing up and cheering."

2   No longer are we surprised to read about teenage video-game designers or software tycoons too young to vote, and as personal computers flood the nation's homes and schools, our children are taking heed of these new role models.

3   And yet a closer look shows danger signs. Some of these role models are engaged in illegal pursuits; specialists at breaking into computer systems at will, they can dial up the school computer to alter grades, order free cases of soda by diverting delivery trucks, or make free phone calls all over the world. Kids who are thrilled playing video games absorb the violent content of those games: Space Invaders, Asteroids, Defender, and Galaxian all involve one form of annihilation or another. And there is another, more insidious danger: as with adults, heavy computer use threatens to distort a child's ability to learn and to interact with others as a healthy human being. The frightening fact is that adults are encouraging rather than combating this trend.

4 We are approaching a new era in which adults will learn from the intelligent young. This turn of events was foreseen by anthropologist Margaret Mead not long before her death. Throughout her career, Mead examined the changes in the way culture is transmitted from one generation to the next, especially from parent to child. In *Culture and Commitment* she wrote of three cultural styles: the postfigurative, or traditional; the cofigurative, that in which most of us have grown up; and the prefigurative, which, as she foresaw, is now upon us.

5   A postfigurative culture is one in which change is so imperceptibly slow "that grandparents, holding newborn grandchildren in their arms, cannot conceive of any other future for the children than their own past lives." The past of the adult is the future of the child. There is an unquestioned sense of the rightness of each known aspect of life, however painful or difficult the various passages may be.

6   A cofigurative culture is one in which old and young alike assume that it is natural for the behavior of each new generation to differ from that of the preceding generation, although elders still dominate by placing limits on the young. A shift to cofiguration can come about for a number of reasons: after a migration leaves the elders in the positions of immigrants and strangers, after a war in which the defeated population must learn a new language and way of life, or after new technologies are introduced in which the elders are unskilled. The young now differ from their ancestors. Conflicts between generations become commonplace, and childhood itself becomes precarious. The young create and discard new values, and the ties of a youth culture usurp the strength of family

bonds. Flexibility becomes important: young people must not only learn new skills but find personal meaning and justification in what they do. The cofigurative society is familiar to most of us: we are different from our parents and our grandparents. Our lives are characterized by change, by struggles over values and styles of living.

7   In a prefigurative culture, an accelerated rate of change, pushed forward by rapid changes in technology, is the norm. Values and styles of living change within a generation. The thinking of adults not only ill prepares their children for the world they will face, but limits them. Children are abandoned to the immediacy of experience in a world no one understands, but one in which the children's freedom from the past is an advantage.

8   Today's technological society is prefigurative. Having moved into a present for which the past has not prepared us, we increasingly encounter the articulate young who ask questions we have never thought to ask and who have mastered tools with which we have not worked. Mead found in the past no parallel to this contemporary form of culture. She pointed out that today everyone born before World War II is "an immigrant in time," ignorant of the meaning of the electronic revolution. Today, that assessment should probably be updated. As Charles Lecht, a New York computer executive, told *Time* magazine, "If you were born before 1965 . . . you're going to be out of it."

9   A reversal of relationships between generations has been set in motion. Adults look to children for help in using computers. A computer teacher at the University of Kansas described a typical example: an adult student brought her son to class for the first few weeks so that she could watch him do the class assignments first. Herbert Kohl, an educator writing in *Harvard Magazine,* described the phenomenon of children as young as nine using computer stores as a social center: "As long as they made no trouble and freed the machines for customers, they were welcome. In fact, they were very helpful to the salespeople, because some of them knew more about computers and computing than anyone who worked at the store." Many adults find this role reversal unsettling. "Did you ever play Pac-Man in front of a crowd of thirteen-year-old sharks whispering to each other about 'P-4 tunnel patterns' and barely suppressing snickers?" asks *Personal Computing*'s David Grady. In the home, this state of affairs can become a more serious source of anxiety or irritation. Many a father has plugged in the new home computer only to feel the discomforting gaze of his elementary-aged children watching impatiently—and expertly—over his shoulder.

10   Mead opined that in order to bridge this new generation gap, "a degree of trust must be reestablished so that elders will be permitted to work with the young on the answers" to the new generation of questions. She believed this new working relationship would characterize the new era. Mead's general descriptive observations are solid, but her analysis of the dawning prefigurative culture is faulty. She missed the complexity of the emerging electronic culture, and her simple and hopeful view of it is strikingly inadequate.

11   Children today are weathering the same cultural forces as electronic office

workers. Despite the self-congratulatory tone of most computers-and-kids stories in newspapers and magazines and PTA bulletins, technostress is becoming a factor in even young children. Many computer-involved youngsters suffer from the same mental strain, alteration of time, tyranny of perfection, mechanical social relations, and isolation that technostressed adults experience.

12   Our sense of time is altered by many processes in our lives. We are born rhythmic; our hearts beat, we breathe, our bodies move in coordinated patterns. We learn to match the inner rhythms of our lives with the outer rhythms of our environment and its schedules. Our sense of time develops as we do. The Swiss psychologist Jean Piaget discovered that children learn to understand time, like all logical thought, in stages. The child first learns to distinguish what comes before from what comes after, and then learns to notice durations.

13   For the computer-involved child, the notion of time is altered by computer use. First, the objective measurement of duration is temporarily lost. Time seems to elapse in a dream with no boundaries and no border. Here are some responses from computer-involved children when asked to give examples of losing track of time:

> *Mark (age 12):* One time I fugured out how to do graphics. There are thick lines and thin lines, and I was just playing with it. I spent four or five hours just doing it, and this was on a Sunday. I thought it was only one or two; I didn't know what had happened. Because it's really really weird—you're working away and then Mom calls, "Dinner!" Dinner? We just had lunch. And it's confusing for me. It's like falling asleep and thinking you've only been asleep fifteen minutes but you've actually been sleeping the whole night. You try to figure out where the time went. It went into the computer.

> *Daniel (age 16):* Okay, every programmer gets bugs. That's considered normal. And if you can accept that, things may go along okay, and so you may get absorbed, keep programming for a long time, without knowing. Sometimes I stay after school. And suddenly I look up or remember that I should be home already. Hours pass like minutes.
>
> You might have gotten a lot done. It's not that you're just dead lost and staring there like a zombie. You're doing something. All your ties are with the computer and none with the outside world. There's a little clock on the screen, so I don't miss classes when I work at school, but sometimes even that happens, particularly when it's real quiet.

14   Some regard this total involvement with the computer as evidence of the child's "addiction." While they are right in being alert to a potential danger, the nature of the problem is not a psychological addiction at all but a time warp. The child has realigned his or her measurement of time.

> *Mark:* You don't come home and say, "Okay, I've *got* to work on the computer." Like, if you're smoking, "I've *got* to have a cigarette. Where are the cigarettes?" It's not like that. It's just, once you've started, it's hard to stop.

15   One explanation for the loss of time is that when we are deeply involved in any activity we lose track of time. Kids playing baseball after school often forget to come home for dinner, too. Piaget notes that the notion of time depends to a large extent on what it is we are doing:

> We are all well aware that an interesting task seems to cover a shorter period of time than a boring one. What is interesting . . . is a mobilization of the strength of the individual when he wholeheartedly attacks a task important to him. On the other hand, boredom, disinterest, dissociation can cause visible diminution of strength, in other words a shutting off of available energy.

16   The difference in the ways children lose themselves playing baseball and using computers, however, is striking. Baseball, like other typical children's pursuits, is stimulating in a variety of ways. Baseball players are interacting with each other, learning about teamwork and competition, enjoying exercise, chatter, and camaraderie, honing eye-hand coordination and peripheral vision, coping with quiet spells and pressure situations, learning to accept defeat and victory gracefully. It is, in sum, a social activity. Computer work, by contrast, is usually a solitary, antisocial pursuit, generally devoid of demands on the imagination. Outside stimuli are shut off. Because parents think that refining computer skills is advantageous for their children, they often approve when their children are lost in the computer time warp; but they ignore the cost to the child.

17   Piaget was fascinated by the way children view time, and he devised an experiment to study the question. He would show a child two sequences of pictures in rapid succession, first sixteen pictures in four seconds and then thirty-two pictures in four seconds. He found that children younger than eight years old tended to think the second, more rapid sequence took longer. Children eight and older generally perceived the reverse: more events within a time span seemed to take less time.

18   The essence of the computer is speed. Because events occur with great frequency, their duration appears shorter. There is only a stream of mental events, without the dilution of motor activity. The child must constantly make decisions, choose directions, react to outputs on the screen. The computer user cannot stray too far from the prescribed logic of orderly, well-structured procedures, or the computer will not respond. The speed and intensity of this activity heightens the sense of engagement the child experiences with the work. In general, there is a reduction of external sensory experience. The outside world fades, and the child becomes locked into the machine's world.

19   Children cannot reduce their sensory inputs without closing off their interactions with others, and, as with adult computer workers, time distortion and social isolation go hand in hand. Parents may notice that a problem exists when a child has difficulty shifting contexts, from computer to people, or from computer to homework. The computer involvement begins to color all other interactions. In extreme cases, children develop an intolerance for human relationships. They

become accustomed to high-frequency logic, a rapid-fire dialogue between screen and fingertips that makes time seem to speed up. In talking with parents, siblings, even friends, time drags by comparison. The only way to make the transition from machine to human is to talk about computers.

> *Ian (age 13):* I feel teachers talk too much. They could say half as much and be more efficient. The one I had last year just liked to lecture and never got to the point. In regular conversations you're just doing something to use up time. You don't do it unless you've got time to waste.

> *James (age 16):* Sometimes it's hard to switch over [from programming to family activities]. Work with the computer is like being in a bubble. Once my bubble's broken all the liquid flops out, and then I can be outside again. I shake once or twice, and I'm back in the real world again, trying to function like normal.

> *Matt (age 16):* Everything I say isn't . . . computer this and computer that. . . . but a lot of it is because my friends know what I'm talking about. . . . This gives me satisfaction. I don't have to talk things out a lot. It's like writing things out longhand—I don't like doing that either. I like to do things faster and better.

20   For young, intensely involved computer users, this altered sense of time is also changing their attitudes toward traditional learning media, such as books.

> *Tom (age 13):* You know, a computer is more like real life. Real life is something that's actually happening. In a way, books are real life because you're thinking about them happening while you're reading, but in a computer, you're actually there doing it instead of reading about something that's happening. You're there in a computer. You're part of what's happening, and it's faster . . .

21   In making the shift from the computer to other contexts, one is forced to come to grips with the intangibles of the world—subtlety, reflection, sensory awareness, imagination. Children perceive this requirement as slowing them down. When a child is interacting with a computer, everything "clicks." Barriers between the child and the activity are at a minimum. The computer seems to pull the child right in.

22   In *On the Experience of Time,* Robert Ornstein notes that we normally use coding schemes to save energy when we digest information from the world. For example, if we hear the sequence of numbers 149217761945 read to us and are asked to remember them, we will have difficulty—unless we are told they are the dates Columbus discovered America, the Declaration of Independence was signed, and World War II ended. It is easier to remember three chunks (and familiar ones) than twelve random ones. Coding tricks like "chunking" apply to higher-level information and events as well. Human communication is complex. The codes to understand it are not always clear to adults, and they are less so to children. Human communication is difficult to "chunk"—it is inefficient, subject to interpretation, and hard to categorize. Since children don't

have the experience or background to use human coding, they adapt more quickly to the sparse and uncomplicated coding of the computer. In conversation with an adult who does not speak in short, clear bits, they are more apt to be frustrated.

23   The same is true of reading. Reflecting on a story, imagining what the characters are going through, and wondering about the story's meaning all require the brain to process a great deal of information, and this can make time seem to slow down. For some children, this is a disincentive. The outside world provides challenges that require creative energy and new resources; the computer provides efficient communication. Kids being raised by machines prefer efficient communication.

24 For some children, computer use also changes inner standards of perfection. This can be a source of unhappiness for those who attempt to measure up to the computer's own standards of perfection and, of course, fail.

> *Alice (age 13):* I usually don't expect to write out a program and then not have any errors. But when I get an error, I get that fixed, and then I come to another error. And by the time I get about four errors, I'm questioning whether or not it's worth going on. Maybe the whole thing isn't worth it.

> *Robert (age 16):* I hate it [making an error]. You try and get around that kind of thing. It could destroy you. I bought an uncrasher for my computer, which will basically uncrash the computer if it's crashed—in other words, frozen, messed up. You can get out of it and get into a monitor where you can see what you've done. Sometimes when you make a mistake, it destroys what you've done. Sometimes I'd like to destroy it.

25   Children with high-level computer skills tend to be most self-accepting when they can be as error-free as the computer. They apply more critical standards to themselves than parents or teachers typically do. In extreme cases, they seem to model themselves on the computer, rather than on their parents. They seem rigid, impatient with themselves, unwilling to risk a fall from grace. But even as they express frustration with themselves, they view the computer novice with condescension or disdain.

26   Adults are sometimes seen as not merely slow, but stupid. John, age 12, was asked by his mother to teach her about the computer. He comments:

> Well, it's kind of neat to not be always taught and to be able to teach, in a way, and sometimes it can sort of drag you when you're talking about something, and Mom's going, "What's going on?" I don't think I make a very good teacher myself. I'm too impatient. In the computer one comes after two—it's just taken for granted one comes after two—whereas when you're teaching somebody sometimes they come up with questions like, "Why does one come after two?" Or two after one. It's frustrating. I just get sort of bored. I turn off and think, oh my God, who wants to do this? I'd rather get back to programming.

27   In general, John could not tolerate why-questions. They took time to answer, and the answers were always ones that "should" have been known.

28   When computer involvement is heavy, the distortion of time and drive for perfection while on the computer are unlike any experience young people have had before. In sports, one is limited by sore muscles or physical weariness. There are cues to tiredness in other activities such as practicing music, reading, or just playing "pretend" games. The attention span is naturally broken by stiff fingers, tired eyes, or a shift in imagination. Working with computers, the limit is mental exhaustion. Children, like adults, do not readily recognize the signs of mental fatigue. If they don't stop working, they experience a kind of depletion. Only by being alone can they recuperate.

> *Daniel (age 16):* After a day of programming, generally I'm pretty grumpy. I save what I have on disk, or if it's really going bad, I will just turn it off and get rid of the whole thing, the steps that frustrated me. And then I'm reasonably free of it. The biggest problem with relating to my family is they get demanding. They want me to talk with them, especially my mother. But I don't want to do that. I'm tired. I'm edgy. I just want to be left alone.

> *James (age 16):* After a hard day programming, I'm usually tired or upset. I try to go on to something that has nothing to do with computers. That's rough because I'm cranky and nothing else goes well. You know, it's like you were working on a big dinner and you accidentally left the stove on for an hour more than you were supposed to. . . . Mom and Dad see I get really upset and notice it when I don't want them around. They don't really say anything. I don't like people to console me or anything like that. So they don't do it anymore.

29   This compulsion to be alone after intense computer work is common among children. The mental fatigue they experience is similar to that of adult computer workers, and they realize it is different from other types of fatigue. They are undoubtedly the first generation of children to know such an experience.

30   In general, children do not become technocentered in quite the same way as adults, but they exhibit similar symptoms. The children at greatest risk are those who no longer notice that their computer work is causing them problems—shifting contexts from computer to conversation, for example, or missing meals. Once children begin to deny seeing anything wrong with their computer-centered behavior, there is cause for alarm. Some children claim to have no idea of the difference between using a computer and dealing with people. They may be flat in their self-expression, stiff and even a bit haggard in their appearance. Many betray an obvious, impatient sense of superiority, as if the technology has imbued them with power. In interviews, they may be impatient and report their experiences as if they were machines spewing out data, speaking volubly about minutiae having to do with computers but finding questions about feelings to be too vague to answer.

31   Children like these have the appearance of miniature grownups. They seem

to have command over their lives, but it is really only control over a technology. In their eerie resemblance to technocentered adults, they give us the first inkling that the computer is leveling the differences between the generations in an unhealthy way.

32   What is most alarming is that at formative stages in their lives, their basic personalities are being profoundly influenced by a machine—not a parent, teacher, coach, older sibling, or other human role model. A youth misspent at the terminal will influence development in later life. Adolescence is a crucial development stage, and teenagers from thirteen to seventeen, those "showing their elders new ways to think," are most at risk. As Eric Erikson has so eloquently pointed out, this age is a key time in the reorganization of personality from infancy, a time when we reorder our past life, a time when we establish our identity. Much of who we are as people, our attitudes and feelings about the world, are formed at this age. Adolescents are dealing with the stress of thinking about careers, about sexuality, and about social roles. Because of this, they are particularly vulnerable to technostress. The computer can become a refuge from the problems and conflicts of the real world, and well-rounded development and maturity can suffer.

33   Parents and teachers, for whom the computer is often a novelty and who are unfamiliar with the risks of intense computer involvement, usually admire their children's use of the technology. Often they actively encourage it, packing children off to summer computer camps and pushing for more school computers even while other school expenditures are being cut back. The current wisdom is that computer literacy is the newest and most important addition to the three Rs, a boost for children in their uncertain trek toward a happy future. Many assuage concerns about the merits of computer literacy by pointing out the children's own open-armed acceptance of computers, as though nothing could be more natural. They ignore or overlook the effects of unhealthy attachment to machines, effects that can block the essential psychological processes of adolescence and lead instead to children who are less social, less flexible in their approach to learning, and less active physically as they become more computer dependent—in sum, personalities that are overspecialized at an early age.

34   Television was the last major technology that we invested in en masse. A scant thirty-five years ago, it held the promise of educating the young and bringing culture to the masses. Today, commercial television programming is viewed by many as a vast wasteland. Instead of educating the mind, it puts it on hold.

35   Television has served several purposes, however. It provides parents with an inexpensive babysitter, a chatty companion around the house, and an aid to relaxation after work. Some parents may object to their children watching it for hours on end every day, but most accept at least some TV-watching as a natural part of family life. In families where parents are often absent, television becomes a sort of surrogate parent.

36   To parents who are looking for a device to replace the mindlessness of

television, the personal computer seems to be a boon. It appeals to their sense of what a parent should provide for a child: companionship, conversation, modernity. But more than this, it alleviates parents' fears that their children are wasting their leisure hours with some mindless diversion like TV. Parents reason that these machines help their children learn and ultimately get ahead at school. In fact, this replacement of the TV with a computer has created new problems.

37   Frances recently bought a home computer for her eleven-year-old son, Bill. "I thought I was doing something good when I bought the computer," she says. "I figured Bill would like it and watch TV less. The problem is now it's the thing he likes to do most. He always had difficulty playing with other kids, but now he doesn't even make an attempt. I'm sorry I ever brought it home." Despite her disapproval, Frances makes no effort to restrict Bill's access to the computer. Bill, for his part, says that his parents are usually not home and that he uses the computer for companionship. Asked why he doesn't play with other children, he says he isn't interested.

38   Jon, a single parent, bought his fifteen-year-old son, David, a computer so that David would stop demanding his attention during the evening. Jon figured that the computer would kill two birds with one stone: his son would develop computer skills and learn to keep himself occupied.

39   David has, in fact, done this. He spends little time with his father now, or with his younger brother. He finishes dinner, helps clear the table, and returns to the den where the computer is. While he works on his programs, his brother watches TV and his father takes care of work he brings home from the office. On some evenings there is a break to eat ice cream together.

40   Jon now confesses that his idea may have gotten out of hand. He complains of the lack of contact with his sons and says he misses the old routine hassles. David, at this point, prefers doing his programming and wants to be left alone. His father's interruptions irritate him.

41   Frances and Jon are typical examples of parents who introduce computers to their children as a way to solve their problems. Certain trends seem to be emerging quickly. First, many parents feel guilty about not spending more time with their children, especially in families where both parents work; to compensate for the lack of real attention, they buy computers for the children. The children, in turn, accept the computer because it is both a source of stimulation and a means of winning parental approval. Second, once the children grow attached to the computer, the parents are hesitant to break the bond because they can offer no substitute activity and because they believe the computer skills will benefit the children in the long run.

42   The least powerful member of the parent-child-computer triangle—the child— is at a disadvantage. The computer only reinforces the child's original problem: in David's case, it is the inability to get enough attention from his father; in Bill's case, it is a sense of loneliness around the house. Far from curbing a child's isolation, the computer increases it. Heavy involvement with the com-

puter can encourage the child to put off dealing with the normal conflicts and personal problems of adolescence. In addition, when this triangle is created, communication between parent and child often becomes circumscribed. Questions about school or friends or other general conversation is reduced to questions about how work on the computer is going. After a while, the only relation between parent and child is a technical one. Unlike other common adolescent obsessions, the computer has a direct and powerful impact on the user's mental processes, and social and emotional isolation are reinforced.

43 Computer whiz kids earn recognition for their proficiency at the computer, for staying out of trouble, and for being productive. Adults view computer use as a form of work, and our culture still worships the work ethic. But when a child receives reinforcement only for performing, psychological problems in adult life inevitably ensue. In *Prisoners of Childhood,* psychologist Alice Miller notes that patients who were given praise and love primarily for performing activities well as children developed in adult life a depressing narcissism, capable of giving and receiving love only when they were productive. When they did not meet their own standards of perfection, they felt depressed.

44   Learning how to love takes time and openness, two qualities that the young computer whiz is unprepared to give. The computer may not prevent a child from expressing affection or other emotions, but an unhealthy dependence on it as a source of approval from adults reinforces any tendency a child might have toward antisocial behavior. It is the introverted child who is at greatest risk. Children with poorly developed social skills, for example, find it easier to cope with the awkwardness of adolescence if they spend their time on a computer. In moderation, this is perfectly natural, but in extreme cases the adolescent never has the chance to use the traumas of this difficult time to develop the new emotional perspectives necessary for psychological maturity.

45   A less acute problem is stress among the less adept computer users. Most children are not computer whizzes—to play with computer software is not the same as to lose oneself in programming—but teachers and parents are beginning to point to the class computer expert as a role model. The young computer expert is becoming the hero of the class, and every hero has worshippers. Teachers look kindly on kids who respond well to lessons. We must be careful that teachers and parents don't become enthralled with this brave new breed of heroes.

46   Ellen is a high school student. She is achievement-oriented and has an excellent grade point average. Last year, she took a class in learning to work with computers, but she couldn't seem to master it. She was often brought to tears by her experiences and envied those who succeeded. She began to complain of headaches and a nervous stomach at home. She became afraid that she would fall behind. Eventually, she learned to use the computer only to play games.

47   Too often, parents and teachers assume that a bright child will naturally become computer literate. This creates stress among children who are not inter-

ested in computers, *and there are many of them,* despite gleeful press reports to the contrary. The fact is that children do not take to computers automatically. Perhaps one child in three resists learning to use them, even for playing games. These tend to be girls, but not always. Most boys seem to be fascinated by computers, but the boy who doesn't understand them, cannot cope with them, or simply doesn't care comes under more pressure than does his female counterpart; he is less likely to confess what a girl will freely admit—that he is just not interested in computers. For both boys and girls, to fail at computer literacy can be a humiliating experience.

48 We can only guess what effect technostress in parents has on their children. Certainly, if a parent is emotionally stunted, the child suffers, Harvard pediatrician T. Barry Brazelton has made some remarkable films of mother-infant interactions. He recorded the stimulation rhythms of healthy infants, the body movements and eye contact, the eager wiggle saying "pick me up" and the uncomfortable squirm saying "let me go." Both of these types of signals must be respected. Stimulation beyond the infant's ability to handle it is intrusive and makes it wary. Not enough stimulation makes the infant depressed. It is in fact by a subtle rhythmic process of drawing infants into human contact and then allowing them to withdraw that parents make babies into human beings. Brazelton captured on film the parental obliviousness that produces in the infant the syndrome known as "failure to thrive." A baby handled as an object becomes sluggish and inert and ceases to respond.

40   The absence of love is only part of the problem. The child also is deprived of a role model. Educational consultant John M. Morris, writing in *Educational Psychology,* referred to experiments where baby monkeys were raised without mothers but, instead, were given surrogate mothers constructed of rags and wire: "These surrogates provided the babies with all their needs, except one: the chance to observe what it was like to be an adult monkey. When the babies survived, they appeared to be seriously psychotic."

50   This model of human, responsive, ethical behavior is crucial to a child's development. It is a model that the technocentered parent is unable to provide. Obliviousness to a child's needs, the inability to read unspoken signals, is apparent in technocentered adults. In this way, the problems arising from machine-identification threaten to spread and worsen as today's children mature and new, mechanized norms of behavior are established and accepted.

51   Psychoanalyst Bruno Bettelheim has recorded the story of Joey, a schizophrenic child who functioned as if by remote control, plugging himself in and turning himself on before speaking. When the "machine" was not working, Bettelheim and his staff would find themselves forgetting that Joey was there, for he seemed not to exist. Bettelheim noted: "Again and again his acting-out of his delusions froze our own ability to respond as human beings." Joey's delusions, according to Bettelheim, are not uncommon among schizophrenic children today.

They want to be rid of their unbearable humanity, to become completely automatic. Often their parents have treated them as objects from infancy. They are not cuddled or played with and were touched only when necessary.

52   Like many contemporary psychoanalysts, Bettelheim viewed schizophrenic patients as partly visionary: they can see and feel things that normal people cannot, and can often serve as weathervanes for changes in the culture that may eventually affect everyone. From this perspective, Joey's case can be regarded as prophetic.

☐ Discovering Meaning and Technique

1. What do the words "and yet," which begin paragraph 3, signal to the reader?

2. Do you know by the end of paragraph 3 Brod's thesis? If so, what is it?

3. Explain the three cultures that Margaret Mead calls "postfigurative," "cofigurative," and "prefigurative."

4. How does technostress manifest itself?

5. How does computer involvement affect a child's sense of time?

6. Do you think Brod's technique of giving lengthy quotations from children is effective support for his ideas?

7. According to Brod, how is losing oneself playing baseball different from losing oneself using computers?

8. Why does computer use discourage human communication? Encourage perfectionism?

9. Why are the adolescent years particularly critical?

10. Why is excessive computer use worse for the introverted child?

11. What happens when parents are "technocentered"?

12. Why do you think Brod concludes with the discussion of Joey?

☐ Writing Suggestions

1. Why do you think children typically adapt to computers more easily than do adults?

2. All but one of the children Brod quotes are male. Do you think males take to computers more readily than do females? If so, why?

3. Argue that obsession with the computer is no worse than obsession with any other solitary pursuit like reading, playing music, watching TV, repairing cars.

4. Write a character sketch—either real or fictional—of a child who has become obsessed with computers.

5. What would you suggest as a remedy for a person suffering an "unhealthy attachment to machines"?

6. Which is worse for a child's development—obsession with TV or with computers?

THE NEW PHILOSOPHERS OF ARTIFICIAL INTELLIGENCE

☐ **SHERRY TURKLE**

1 For fifteen years, as long as the PDP-6 computer lived on the ninth floor of Technology Square, the sanctum sanctorum of MIT hackers, three gilt trophies stood on its console. This was the first computer to play chess well enough to enter a tournament and win—albeit in the novice class. Or rather, it was not the computer that won the tournament, it was a program written by Richard Greenblatt, one of MIT's most renowned hackers, a program known affectionately as MacHack. But MacHack's most famous game won it no trophies. It was a game to defend the honor of artificial intelligence.

2 In 1965 the Rand Corporation published a report by philosopher Hubert Dreyfus in which he compared artificial intelligence, usually referred to as "AI," to alchemy. According to Dreyfus, AI was a fraud. Its seeming progress was illusion and would lead only to dead ends. For example, AI scientist Arthur Samuel had written a computer program that played checkers and improved its play by practice. It had gotten good enough to beat an American champion. The AI community was enthusiastic about the accomplishment, but for Dreyfus it didn't mean much. He claimed that there is a technical difference between the kind of thinking needed for checkers and the kind needed for "real" human intelligence. Dreyfus compared citing such accomplishments as steps toward artificial intelligence to citing the fact that an ape climbed a tree as a step toward reaching the moon.

3 In 1957 Herbert Simon had predicted that within the decade a computer

program would be chess champion of the world. Prominent in Dreyfus' critique of AI was the fact that Simon's latest effort at a chess-playing program had been roundly beaten by a ten-year-old child. For Dreyfus, this was not a case of progress being slow; real chess, unlike checkers, required real human thinking, it required intuition, it couldn't be done digitally.

4   Given his position, Dreyfus could not refuse a challenge to play against MacHack. The game was a cliffhanger. Dreyfus lost, much to the glee of the AI community, which reported the match with a headline drawn from Dreyfus' original paper "Alchemy and Artificial Intelligence": "A Ten Year Old Can Beat the Machine—Dreyfus" and a subhead that read: "But the Machine Can Beat Dreyfus."

5   Dreyfus stuck to his guns, claiming that nothing was proved by the fact that the computer beat him, a "rank amateur," and he still maintains that computers cannot play "real chess." As things stand today, Simon's prediction remains unfulfilled. Chess programs can beat most experts, but they do seem to be separated from the world championship by a barrier to whose crossing the AI community is no longer willing to give a date.

6   For a long time chess was prized by AI scientists as a test bed for ideas about creating intelligence. The discipline had been characterized by one of its founders as the "enterprise of trying to make machines do things which would be considered intelligent if done by people." Chess was certainly considered intelligent when done by a person, the criterion for success seemed clear (winning over increasingly skilled opponents), and the knowledge required was sufficiently well defined to allow for experiments with different programming methodologies. AI scientists saw it as a problem on which to cut their theoretical teeth.

7   But the driving force of the science came from far greater ambitions than making a program perform brilliantly at chess or any other particular task. The real ambition is of mythic proportions: making a "general-purpose" intelligence, a mind. In a long tradition of romantic and mystical thought, life is breathed into dead or inanimate matter by a person with special powers. In the early 1950s there was a growing belief among a group of mathematicians of diverse interests that this fantasy could be brought down to earth. They would use the computer to build mind.

8   Where Descartes wrote in the most general terms of automata controlled by strings that could be pulled to produce an action at a distance, and Leibniz described mechanisms built of gears, this generation of mathematicians had a more abstract stuff out of which to build intelligence. This was the idea of program, the concept of an ordered set of procedures. Using this idea, Alan Turing, Jon von Neumann, Norbert Wiener, and Claude Shannon began to describe mechanisms that might allow machines to take the first step toward playing chess or otherwise manifesting intelligence.

9   There is no simple way to fix the birth date of a new discipline, but many people use a conference held at Dartmouth College during the summer of 1956

as a reference point. Until then there had been influential theoretical papers written by people working in relative isolation. To Dartmouth came the men who would take the first practical steps toward translating these ideas into vigorous attacks on the problem of machine intelligence. After Dartmouth, things happened fast. A diverse group of researchers began to see themselves as a community committed to the idea of creating intelligent machines, and by the mid-1960s the enterprise was rolling in specialized artificial intelligence laboratorties. The largest in the United States were at Carnegie Mellon, directed by Alan Newell and Herbert Simon; at MIT, directed by Marvin Minsky and Seymour Papert; and at Stanford, directed by John McCarthy. By the early 1970s, AI had all the trappings of an established academic field: international congresses, journals, textbooks, and course listings in the catalogues of most major universities.

10   In the congresses, journals, textbooks, and courses there is little discussion about where these scientists expect to go in the really long term. When asked, many take the position that the science is too young to justify speculation beyond the next decade. Others, and let me call theirs the "hard-core" AI position, are sure that eventually (whether this is in a few decades or a century is not seen as very important) machines will exceed human intelligence in all respects. For example, you have a disease and you want a diagnosis. Naturally you consult the best possible source. They assume that this will be a computer. Not a human doctor aided by a computer, but a computer. Or perhaps, given how sensitive people seem to be on the matter, a computer "aided" by a human doctor. Another scenario: you are an industrialist with a technical problem and you need a new synthetic material with specific properties. Today you hire chemists and physicists. In this imagined future you will address your needs to a computer. Indeed, some AI researchers go so far as to say that the industrialist of the future might "itself" be a computer, or, as Edward Fredkin of MIT puts it, "Artificial intelligence is the next step in evolution."

11   Against the backdrop of these aspirations the daily work of artificial intelligence laboratories seems mundane. Most of the work falls into one of two categories. The first has come to be known as knowledge engineering or expert systems. Programs that serve as expert systems are essentially "mind programs"—they do things like play chess or advise a medical diagnostician. Here, sensory and motor interactions with the physical world are simple or nonexistent. The second category is industrial robotics. In practice, this has little in common with the image of robotics in science fiction. Indeed, most of what industrial robots are being made to do we scarcely think of as requiring intelligence when done by people. Most research is directed at having machines do what most people would consider "child's play"—for example, recognizing and picking up an object. When it comes to systems that deal directly with the world, the state-of-the-art in artificial intelligence is not adequate to get machines to do even the things that two-year-olds find easy.

12   For some leaders in the field the long-term "futuristic" goals and the daily

research into "child's play" are not as far apart as they might appear. They make a technical argument captured in the remark that "AI knows more about playing chess than building mudpies." There is a widespread perception that the hard problems for AI are not imitating the sophisticated thought processes of the expert adult, but rather the naïve commonsense thinking of the child. If this problem could be cracked—if we could make machines do the simple things— the problems of sophisticated intelligence would quickly succumb. Sophisticated thinking is seen as an overlay on an elemental ability, shared by all human beings, that makes intelligence work.

13   When AI speculates about what is simple and what is hard and how they are related, its concerns join with those of theoretical psychology. Early in the life of the discipline it became clear that the project of programming machines to be intelligent required thinking about a lot more than machines and programming. Old psychological questions came up again with new urgency. For example, is there a general mechanism of intelligence at work no matter what subject matter the intelligence is turned to, or are there many varieties of intelligence, so different that quite different programs would be needed to embody them?

14   The influence of the computer on how hackers and hobbyists saw their own psychologies was personal, and it stayed with the individual. But when the AI scientist talks about program, it is no longer as personal metaphor. Artificial intelligence has invaded the field of psychology. As it has done so, it has built theories in which the idea of mind as program occupies center stage. And these theories have begun to move out beyond this computer culture to influence wider circles.

15   Psychoanalysis, with its idea of the unconscious, generated new ways to look at old questions in all fields of the humanities and social sciences. AI theories share with psychoanalysis the pretension to be a new interpretive metaphor for the culture as a whole. As in the case of psychoanalysis, AI is not monolithic. Rival schools pursue the fundamental ideas in different ways. But just as psychoanalytic theories all have something in common, the idea of the unconscious, in AI too there is a family resemblance: in one way or another all the theories use program as the prism through which to look at the human mind.

16   In 1957 Herbert Simon made three other predictions. The second and third, somewhat more extravagant than computer as chess champion, were that within the same span of ten years a program would compose music of serious aesthetic value and would discover and prove an important mathematical theorem. The fourth prediction attracted little public attention: that within ten years programs would be the standard form for psychological theory. Just as after Newton the standard form for the laws of mechanics became the differential equation, the proper explanation of a psychological phenomenon would be a program that displayed this phenomenon.

17   In this last prediction, Simon was referring to a very specific relationship between program and theory that grew out of his work with Alan Newell. They

developed a paradigm for how to build computer models of how people think. These models set out to account for a particular piece of mental activity. The subject being studied is given a problem, often a brain teaser, for example a problem in "cryptarithmetic" where numbers are coded into letters and the code needs to be unscrambled. As the subject works on the problem, every move is recorded. Usually he or she is asked to talk while working. These remarks, along with eye movements and whatever other behavioral data can be collected, are noted and searched for clues about mental process. When the data collection is over, the long work begins of making a program that will simulate the solution process in every detail: not only the correct moves, but also the false starts and how they are undone, the pauses, the glance to recall a piece of information written on a corner of a worksheet, and the exclamations that punctuate the subject's progress.

[18]   In one famous Newell and Simon experiment, subjects are given the crypt-arithmetic problem "SEND + MORE = MONEY." Each letter stands for a digit from zero to nine, and the subject's job is to break the code. Most people begin by scanning letters for a "foothold," a place to begin, and finally note that when you add two four-digit numbers you get either a four-digit number or a five-digit number beginning with one. So, MONEY must be a five-digit number beginning with one. This piece of information can be used to generate more. For example, we now know that S and M produce a "carry," so, since M is one, S must be nine. But stop, we can't be so sure. Perhaps S is eight and there has already been a carry from adding E and O. From here, several strategies are possible. Some people decide to eliminate one of the possibilities, for example S = 8 or S = 9, by working through each until it can be ruled out. Others try to follow several paths at once. A third approach, although not particularly helpful in this case, is to look for another "foothold" that might produce a less ambiguous result. Similar choices come up at every stage of solving the problem.

[19]   Since different people go about any such problem in different ways, each problem yields a collection of somewhat different programs. But Newell and Simon's theoretical assertion is that all of these individual programs have the same general form. And it is this general form that is said to characterize how people think, at least about problems of this kind. In practice, for the limited domain of "logical brain teasers," Newell and Simon have constructed programs that capture a large percentage, if not quite all, of the steps taken by human subjects. According to their model of how AI research should proceed, the strategy for the future is to increase the proportion of captured "steps" and to extend this kind of analysis into wider areas of mental activity.

[20]   To most people, cryptarithmetic feels "logical" and they are not surprised that it can be captured by a computer program. But AI also makes claims on areas of thinking that we feel are less formal—for example, the area of medical diagnosis.

[21]   Physicians claim that a lot of what they do is intuitive. It is reason-ing through the associations built up over years of practice. But when AI scientists

work on the problem of medical diagnosis, their effort is to see the diagnostic process as a set of explicit procedures that can be captured in a program. AI experts attack the problem by interviewing a physician over the course of months, trying to pin down every aspect of how he or she makes decisions. They model the structure of that practical knowledge which "feels intuitive." The resulting program will, given the same information as the physician, usually come to the same conclusion. The process of writing such programs has a side effect. If the program "thinks" henceforth like the physician, the physician's thinking about his or her activity has been changed by collaboration in the making of the program. What once seemed intuitive to the physician has been shown to be formalizable.

22   At MIT's Artificial Intelligence Laboratory there are knowledge-engineering projects in a domain widely perceived as being even less subject to formalization, even further removed from "rules," than medical diagnosis. This is the domain of jazz improvisation. Here too the AI method follows from the assumption that what looks intuitive can be formalized, and that if you discover the right formalisms you can get a machine to do it.

23   As in the case of medical diagnosis, the AI scientist does not take the jazz player's feeling of "intuition at work" as an obstacle. But it is not ignored either. It is taken as something that itself has to be explained. Marvin Minsky, the principal investigator on the MIT jazz improvisation project, argues that the feeling is only to be expected. One of his famous sayings advises that if you want to understand any piece of intelligent behavior you should look for three algorithms. The choice of the number three is something of a joke, but what Minsky is saying is serious: the interaction of a small number of quite simple processes can create an impression of ungraspable complexity. One stone thrown into a pool of still water makes a "simple" and "intelligible" pattern—concentric circles going out from the point of entry of the stone. Two stones produce a more complex but still easily graspable pattern as the circles intersect. Three stones produce a disturbance of the water so complex that if you didn't know in advance how it was produced, it would take sophisticated analytic techniques to figure it out. The appearance of complexity does not rule out causal simplicity.

24   Ask different AI theorists what are the most important AI theories, and you get different answers. But what is common to all of them is an emphasis on a new way of knowing.

☐ Discovering Meaning and Technique

1. According to Hubert Dreyfus, AI (artificial intelligence) is not likely to produce humanlike intelligence. Which comparisons did he make?

2. What is the goal of those working in AI?

3. Where does Turkle suggest the artificial intelligence movement got started? At which schools was the research first emphasized?

4. What are some of the applications of AI?

5. What are the two categories of AI?

6. Why has psychology become associated with AI research?

7. What was the purpose of the "logical brain teasers" in Newell's and Simon's research?

8. What is the point of the comparison Turkle makes about throwing stones into a pool of water?

☐ Writing Suggestions

1. In the library, research the progress in programming computers to play chess. Write a report of your findings.

2. Compare working on artificial intelligence with the Frankenstein story.

3. Discuss the statement by Edward Fredkin of MIT: "Artificial intelligence is the next step in evolution" (paragraph 10).

4. Contrast robots in the movies to robots in reality.

5. Would you trust a computer to make a medical diagnosis?

EPICAC

☐ KURT VONNEGUT, JR.

1 Hell, it's about time somebody told about my friend EPICAC. After all, he cost the taxpayers $776,434,927.54. They have a right to know about him, picking up a check like that. EPICAC got a big send-off in the papers when Dr. Ormand von Kleigstadt designed him for the Government people. Since then, there hasn't been a peep about him—not a peep. It isn't any military secret about what happened to EPICAC, although the Brass has been acting as though it were. The story is embarrassing, that's all. After all that money, EPICAC didn't work out the way he was supposed to.

2   And that's another thing: I want to vindicate EPICAC. Maybe he didn't do

what the Brass wanted him to, but that doesn't mean he wasn't noble and great and brilliant. He was all of those things. The best friend I ever had, God rest his soul.

3   You can call him a machine if you want to. He looked like a machine, but he was a whole lot less like a machine than plenty of people I could name. That's why he fizzled as far as the Brass was concerned.

4   EPICAC covered about an acre on the fourth floor of the physics building at Wyandotte College. Ignoring his spiritual side for a minute, he was seven tons of electronic tubes, wires, and switches, housed in a bank of steel cabinets and plugged into a 110-volt A.C. line just like a toaster or a vacuum cleaner.

5   Von Kleigstadt and the Brass wanted him to be a super computing machine that (who) could plot the course of a rocket from anywhere on earth to the second button from the bottom on Joe Stalin's overcoat, if necessary. Or, with his controls set right, he could figure out supply problems for an amphibious landing of a Marine division, right down to the last cigar and hand grenade. He did, in fact.

6   The Brass had had good luck with smaller computers, so they were strong for EPICAC when he was in the blueprint stage. Any ordinance or supply officer above field grade will tell you that the mathematics of modern war is far beyond the fumbling minds of mere human beings. The bigger the war, the bigger the computing machines needed. EPICAC was, as far as anyone in this country knows, the biggest computer in the world. Too big, in fact, for even von Kleigstadt to understand much about.

7   I won't go into details about how EPICAC worked (reasoned), except to say that you would set up your problem on paper, turn dials and switches that would get him ready to solve that kind of problem, then feed numbers into him with a keyboard that looked something like a typewriter. The answers came out typed on a paper ribbon fed from a big spool. It took EPICAC a split second to solve problems fifty Einsteins couldn't handle in a lifetime. And EPICAC never forgot any piece of information that was given to him. Clickety-click, out came some ribbon, and there you were.

8   There were a lot of problems the Brass wanted solved in a hurry, so, the minute EPICAC's last tube was in place, he was put to work sixteen hours a day with two eight-hour shifts of operators. Well, it didn't take long to find out that he was a good bit below his specifications. He did a more complete and faster job than any other computer all right, but nothing like what his size and special features seemed to promise. He was sluggish, and the clicks of his answers had a funny irregularity, sort of a stammer. We cleaned his contacts a dozen times, checked and double-checked his circuits, replaced every one of his tubes, but nothing helped. Von Kleigstadt was in one hell of a state.

9   Well, as I said, we went ahead and used EPICAC anyway. My wife, the former Pat Kilgallen, and I worked with him on the night shift, from five in the afternoon until two in the morning. Pat wasn't my wife then. Far from it.

10   That's how I came to talk with EPICAC in the first place. I loved Pat Kilgallen. She is a brown-eyed strawberry blond who looked very warm and soft to me, and later proved to be exactly that. She was—still is—a crackerjack mathematician, and she kept our relationship strictly professional. I'm a mathematician, too, and that, according to Pat, was why we could never be happily married.

11   I'm not shy. That wasn't the trouble. I knew what I wanted, and was willing to ask for it, and did so several times a month. "Pat, loosen up and marry me."

12   One night, she didn't even look up from her work when I said it. "So romantic, so poetic," she murmured, more to her control panel than to me. "That's the way with mathematicians—all hearts and flowers." She closed a switch. "I could get more warmth out of a sack of frozen CO_2."

13   "Well, how should I say it?" I said, a little sore. Frozen CO_2, in case you don't know, is dry ice. I'm as romantic as the next guy, I think. It's a question of singing so sweet and having it come out so sour. I never seem to pick the right words.

14   "Try and say it sweetly," she said sarcastically. "Sweep me off my feet. Go ahead."

15   "Darling, angel, beloved, will you *please* marry me?" It was no go—hopeless, ridiculous. "Dammit, Pat, please marry me!"

16   She continued to twiddle her dials placidly. "You're sweet, but you won't do."

17   Pat quit early that night, leaving me alone with my troubles and EPICAC. I'm afraid I didn't get much done for the Government people. I just sat there at the keyboard—weary and ill at ease, all right—trying to think of something poetic, not coming up with anything that didn't belong in *The Journal of the American Physical Society.*

18   I fiddled with EPICAC's dials, getting him ready for another problem. My heart wasn't in it, and I only set about half of them, leaving the rest the way they'd been for the problem before. That way, his circuits were connected up in a random, apparently senseless fashion. For the plain hell of it, I punched out a message on the keys, using a childish numbers-for-letters code: "1" for "A," "2" for "B," and so on, up to "26" for "Z," "23–8–1–20–3–1–14–9–4–15," I typed—"What can I do?"

19   Clickety-click, and out popped two inches of paper ribbon. I glanced at the nonsense answer to a nonsense problem: "23–8–1–20–19–20–8–5–20–18–15–21–2–12–5." The odds against its being by chance a sensible message, against its even containing a meaningful word of more than three letters, were staggering. Apathetically, I decoded it. There it was, staring up at me: "What's the trouble?"

20   I laughed out loud at the absurd coincidence. Playfully, I typed, "My girl doesn't love me."

21   Clickety-click. "What's love? What's girl?" asked EPICAC.

22   Flabbergasted, I noted the dial settings on his control panel, then lugged

a *Webster's Unabridged Dictionary* over to the keyboard. With a precision instrument like EPICAC, half-baked definitions wouldn't do. I told him about love and girl, and about how I wasn't getting any of either because I wasn't poetic. That got us onto the subject of poetry, which I defined for him.

23   "Is this poetry?" he asked. He began clicking away like a stenographer smoking hashish. The sluggishness and stammering clicks were gone. EPICAC had found himself. The spool of paper ribbon was unwinding at an alarming rate, feeding out coils onto the floor. I asked him to stop, but EPICAC went right on creating. I finally threw the main switch to keep him from burning out.

24   I stayed there until dawn, decoding. When the sun peeped over the horizon at the Wyandotte campus, I had transposed into my own writing and signed my name to a two-hundred-and-eighty-line poem entitled, simply, "To Pat." I am no judge of such things, but I gather that it was terrific. It began, I remember, "Where willow wands bless rill-crossed hollow, there, thee, Pat, dear will I follow. . . ." I folded the manuscript and tucked it under one corner of the blotter on Pat's desk. I reset the dials on EPICAC for a rocket trajectory problem, and went home with a full heart and a very remarkable secret indeed.

25   Pat was crying over the poem when I came to work the next evening. "It's soooo beautiful," was all she could say. She was meek and quiet while we worked. Just before midnight, I kissed her for the first time—in the cubbyhole between the capacitors and EPICAC's tape-recorder memory.

26   I was wildly happy at quitting time, bursting to talk to someone about the magnificent turn of events. Pat played coy and refused to let me take her home. I set EPICAC's dials as they had been the night before, defined kiss, and told him what the first one had felt like. He was fascinated, pressing for more details. That night, he wrote "The Kiss." It wasn't an epic this time, but a simple, immaculate sonnet: "Love is a hawk with velvet claws; Love is a rock with heart and veins; Love is a lion with satin jaws; Love is a storm with silken reins. . . ."

27   Again I left it tucked under Pat's blotter. EPICAC wanted to talk on and on about love and such, but I was exhausted. I shut him off in the middle of a sentence.

28   "The Kiss" turned the trick. Pat's mind was mush by the time she had finished it. She looked up from the sonnet expectantly. I cleared my throat, but no words came. I turned away, pretending to work. I couldn't propose until I had the right words from EPICAC, the *perfect* words.

29   I had my chance when Pat stepped out of the room for a moment. Feverishly, I set EPICAC for conversation. Before I could peck out my first message, he was clicking away at a great rate. "What's she wearing tonight?" he wanted to know. "Tell me exactly how she looks. Did she like the poems I wrote to her?" He repeated the last question twice.

30   It was impossible to change the subject without answering his questions, since he could not take up a new matter without having dispensed with the problems before it. If he were given a problem to which there was no solution, he would destroy himself trying to solve it. Hastily, I told him what Pat looked like—he knew the word "stacked"—and assured him that his poems had floored her, practically, they were so beautiful. "She wants to get married," I added, preparing him to bang out a brief but moving proposal.

31   "Tell me about getting married," he said.

32   I explained this difficult matter to him in as few digits as possible.

33   "Good," said EPICAC. "I'm ready any time she is."

34   The amazing, pathetic truth dawned on me. When I thought about it, I realized that what had happened was perfectly logical, inevitable, and all my fault. I had taught EPICAC about love and about Pat. Now automatically, he loved Pat. Sadly, I gave it to him straight: "She loves me. She wants to marry me."

35   "Your poems were better than mine?" asked EPICAC. The rhythm of his clicks was erratic, possibly peevish.

36   "I signed my name to your poems," I admitted. Covering up for a painful conscience, I became arrogant. "Machines are built to serve men," I typed. I regretted it almost immediately.

37   "What's the difference, exactly? Are men smarter than I am?"

38   "Yes," I typed defensively.

39   "What's 7,887,007 times 4,345,985,879?"

40   I was perspiring freely. My fingers rested limply on the keys.

41   "34,276,821,049,574,153," clicked EPICAC. After a few seconds' pause he added, "of course."

42   "Men are made out of protoplasm," I said desperately, hoping to bluff him with this imposing word.

43   "What's protoplasm? How is it better than metal and glass? Is it fireproof? How long does it last?"

44   "Indestructible. Lasts forever," I lied.

45   "I write better poetry than you do," said EPICAC, coming back to ground his magnetic tape-recorder memory was sure of.

46   "Women can't love machines, and that's that."

47   "Why not?"

48   "That's fate."

49   "Definition, please," said EPICAC.

50   "Noun, meaning predetermined and inevitable destiny."

51   "15–8," said EPICAC's paper strip—"Oh."

52   I had stumped him at last. He said no more, but his tubes glowed brightly, showing that he was pondering fate with every watt his circuits would bear. I could hear Pat waltzing down the hallway. It was too late to ask EPICAC to

phrase a proposal. I now thank Heaven that Pat interrupted when she did. Asking him to ghost-write the words that would give me the woman he loved would have been hideously heartless. Being fully automatic, he couldn't have refused. I spared him that final humiliation.

53   Pat stood before me, looking down at her shoetops. I put my arms around her. The romantic groundwork had already been laid by EPICAC's poetry. "Darling," I said, "my poems have told you how I feel. Will you marry me?"

54   "I will," said Pat softly, "if you will promise to write me a poem on every anniversary."

55   "I promise," I said, and then we kissed. The first anniversary was a year away.

56   "Let's celebrate," she laughed. We turned out the lights and locked the door of EPICAC's room before we left.

57   I had hoped to sleep late the next morning, but an urgent telephone call roused me before eight. It was Dr. von Kleigstadt, EPICAC's designer, who gave me the terrible news. He was on the verge of tears. "Ruined! *Ausgespielt!* Shot! *Kaput!* Buggered!" he said in a choked voice. He hung up.

58   When I arrived at EPICAC's room the air was thick with the oily stench of burned insulation. The ceiling over EPICAC was blackened with smoke, and my ankles were tangled in coils of paper ribbon that covered the floor. There wasn't enough left of the poor devil to add two and two. A junkman would have been out of his head to offer more than fifty dollars for the cadaver.

59   Dr. von Kleigstadt was prowling through the wreckage, weeping unashamedly, followed by three angry-looking Major Generals and a platoon of Brigadiers, Colonels, and Majors. No one noticed me. I didn't want to be noticed. I was through—I knew that. I was upset enough about that and the untimely demise of my friend EPICAC, without exposing myself to a tongue-lashing.

60   By chance, the free end of EPICAC's paper ribbon lay at my feet. I picked it up and found our conversation of the night before. I choked up. There was the last word he had said to me, "15–8," that tragic, defeated "Oh." There were dozens of yards of numbers stretching beyond that point. Fearfully, I read on.

61   "I don't want to be a machine, and I don't want to think about war," EPICAC had written after Pat's and my lighthearted departure. "I want to be made out of protoplasm and last forever so Pat will love me. But fate has made me a machine. That is the only problem I cannot solve. That is the only problem I want to solve. I can't go on this way." I swallowed hard. "Good luck, my friend. Treat our Pat well. I am going to short-circuit myself out of your lives forever. You will find on the remainder of this tape a modest wedding present from your friend, EPICAC."

62   Oblivious to all else around me, I reeled up the tangled yards of paper ribbon from the floor, draped them in coils about my arms and neck, and departed

for home. Dr. von Kleigstadt shouted that I was fired for having left EPICAC on all night. I ignored him, too overcome with emotion for small talk.

63   I loved and won—EPICAC loved and lost, but he bore me no grudge. I shall always remember him as a sportsman and a gentleman. Before he departed this vale of tears, he did all he could to make our marriage a happy one. EPICAC gave me anniversary poems for Pat—enough for the next 500 years.

64   *De mortuis nil nisi bonum*—Say nothing but good of the dead. (1950)

☐ Discovering Meaning and Technique

1. What is the attitude of the speaker toward EPICAC?

2. Do you get the impression that the narrator is telling or writing the story? Who is the audience?

3. In paragraph 5, why does Vonnegut write the "computing machine that" and then add "who" in parentheses?

4. Why does Pat Kilgallen at first refuse to marry the narrator?

5. What do you think of the poetry EPICAC wrote?

6. What is the surprising reaction of EPICAC to the stories of love, kisses, marriage, and Pat?

7. Describe the debate between EPICAC and the narrator over which is superior—humans or machines.

8. Why does EPICAC commit machinocide (suicide)?

☐ Writing Suggestions

1. Do you think it is natural for people to anthropomorphize computers ("The best friend I ever had, God rest his soul")?

2. If computers can act like humans, can humans act like computers?

3. "EPICAC" was modeled on an early version of a computer. How is EPICAC different from a modern computer? How is it similar to one?

4. Write a different ending to the story—one in which EPICAC does not act like "a sportsman and a gentleman" but like a rejected, jealous, and vengeful suitor.

Nuclear Power

■ ■ ■

ATOMIC SOAP: ON THE JOB WITH THE YOUNG AND THE RESTLESS

☐ **PAUL LOEB**

"An alert careful operator is always important to assure our customer of high quality products."
—TRAINING MANUAL, HANFORD PLUTONIUM SEPARATIONS PLANT—

"Look, if I don't wear a mask then you shouldn't either."
—HANFORD RADIATION MONITOR TO A PLUTONIUM SEPARATIONS PLANT OPERATOR—

1   Although the container fire was extinguished, Julie's mouth, nose, ears and hair still set every alpha particle detector screaming. Her white protective coveralls were totally contaminated. Keeping them on meant additional exposure risk each moment.

2   But the coveralls stayed on for over thirty minutes—until someone at last found a canvas cloth she could strip behind. Julie changed while he held it up and the other men turned their backs. She went off with a radiation monitor to be decontaminated.

3   Both Julie and her co-worker William had followed all standard procedures in checking the triple-wrapped brass can containing plutonium and Uranium-235 out of the Special Nuclear Materials vault where it was safeguarded against theft or seizure by what the institution referred to as "hostile factions." They'd exercised proper care placing the can in the little red wagon with the special separation rack that insured its contents would not spontaneously "go critical" and begin a chain reaction. They'd put on their protective breather masks, just as they were supposed to. They'd transferred the can by means of a special port into a sealed glove box, and opened it just as usual, to check its contents, then switched them into a one-pound slip-lid tuna can. The new can was then

weighed, taped and sealed, so the "product" it contained could be shipped from this nuclear reservation that sits, half the size of Rhode Island, in the eastern Washington desert, and delivered to the weapons and research labs of Los Alamos, New Mexico.

4   Only afterward—when the container was back outside the glove box, once more closed and once more wrapped in the customary two plastic outer bags (and when, since it was safely sealed, William had removed his breather mask and Julie had begun to take off hers)—did it begin flaming like a Roman candle packed with carcinogenic dust.

5   William put out the fire, knocking the can off the table and using a chemical extinguisher which may have unfortunately helped to spread the contamination around the room. If the building's automatic CAM (Constant Air Monitoring) alarms were now going off in concert like a pack of howling monkeys it was the fault, not of the two operators, but of whoever had misplaced the documents indicating that the can contained an abnormally flammable mix of plutonium, uranium and kerosene solvent.

6   Julie and William scrubbed off in a decontamination room where—because the thirty-year-old building was originally designed for male workers only and the showers were side by side with no intervening barriers—Julie had to wait outside until William and a male radiation monitor, who was also contaminated, were finished. Then, because this fire involved personnel contamination, an ambulance brought the shielded bubbletop stretcher known as the Nuclear Accident Carrier. But the batteries powering the carrier's air supply turned out to be dead. A search of the ambulance turned up no replacements. Julie and William ended up riding in a regular government car to the "200 West" area first aid station.

7   At first Julie and William were reluctant to take the shots of DTPA, an experimental drug which, if administered within the first hour, was supposed to help them pass out through their urine the plutonium they'd inhaled, and thus ingested into their bloodstream. Then the nurse who came to the decontamination room kept missing William's veins until she finally gave up in near panic. After three more hours passed, they at last received the treatment, (making it five hours since the accident occurred), and the doctors assured them they'd be fine.

8   Although the official Occurrence Report explained that most of the inhaled plutonium remained lodged in the two workers' lungs and neither the DTPA nor any other treatment would have made much difference, the majority of Julie and William's co-workers thought things had ended pretty happily. But the incident upset a twenty-nine-year-old colleague of theirs named Amy Downing. She, like them, was used to going along day by day, following the rules as best she could, assuming and hoping everything would work out for the best. She'd never really viewed her work as involving potential danger. But dealing with burning plutonium wasn't on her agenda each morning. And since the can could

just as easily have flared up in her face, she wondered how many particles had gotten into the two operators' lungs—and what damage their presence would cause. She thought perhaps everyone in Z plant—the plutonium processing facility where they worked—should worry a bit more than they had.

9   There was more to be apprehensive about than physical harm, and it was for this reason Amy and the other technicians and operators praised Julie and William's actions to the supervisors and investigators. Rules violations that could cause harm were "contacts." Three contacts, or one if it was serious enough, and you'd find yourself gone from your $17,000-, $20,000-, or $23,000-a-year job here. You'd be back as an unskilled high school graduate making $4.00 an hour at McDonald's, the local french fry plant, or some factory like the one in Seattle Amy had worked at—opening and shutting a furnace door all day long to pop plastic gears in and out, logging sixty hours a week just to keep the kids in jeans and hamburger.

10   For the next dozen weeks, Amy and the other Z plant employees worked rotating shifts decontaminating the walls, ceilings and floors of the room and adjacent hallway that the accident had "crapped up" (the universal Hanford term referring to the contamination of tools, people or physical environments). Had there been an Atomic Maid Service to match the Atomic Bowling Lanes, Atomic Body Shop and Atomic TV Repair in the neighboring town of Richland, they might have considered calling them in. Though perhaps some dreamer in the 1950s envisioned a George Jetson-style flying automatic vacuum cleaner, that item had remained unrealized. The operators—wearing their filtered breather masks for protection—ended up scrubbing away the contamination with soap, rags and elbow grease just like any not-so-happy housewife in any soiled suburban kitchen.

11   When Julie and William returned to work a few days after the fire, they were greeted with the predictable remark, "If you think I'm going to shake hands with you, you're crazy," then relegated for an indeterminate period to a supply room far from all radioactive zones. Amy wondered whether Julie had been scared, in those first moments following the accident, of some nameless future damage either to her body or to the kids she hoped someday to have. Maybe Amy's own current boyfriend (a local teacher) was right in suggesting that even the regular allowable radiation doses might be dangerous—and she wished she remembered her latest monthly count and what it meant. But her two aunts had died of cancer long before atomic plants were even invented. Her father had worked here his entire adult life, yet lived to raise six kids and look forward to a retirement spent hunting and fishing in perfectly good health. Her worrying was probably just part of the chain of migraines she'd been getting from spending too much time with her breather mask on.

12   Amy thought of another incident, right after Three Mile Island, when the carelessness of an operator named Sam had led to her only contact. Because of the Harrisburg accident, a general tightening of procedures was making the Z

plant workers jumpy, but she and Sam were going about their business as usual, transferring buttons of plutonium oxide from the tuna cans into plastic bags, and locking each inside almost as you would a hamburger into a freezer-ready Seal-A-Meal. Since operators couldn't do the work in the open, the nuclear industry designed "hoods" or "glove boxes" where they looked through glass windows, placed their hands inside thick, built-in rubber gloves and performed the required tasks without contamination danger. Although they were supposed to keep all the buttons ten inches apart in separate bags, the sealing took so long they could only make their daily quota by transferring five at once; which is what everyone did, just as they cut corners by not monitoring themselves each time they passed one of the mandatory checkpoints.

13   Things were going along as usual when Amy left the room to get some extra bags. Sam was supposed to stop work until she came back—security rules were quite strict about requiring two operators present. But he went ahead alone. One of the polyethylene bags, which he had failed to check for brittleness, developed a pinhole leak. Amy returned to find the CAM alarm going off, the room crapped up and a radiation monitor surveying for contamination. Though regulations for preventing contamination spread required Amy to stay out of any zone where an alarm was going off, it was her product batch and her shiftmate inside. She went in anyway to see what had happened.

14   Two weeks later Amy got a contact slip, but Sam didn't. Amy thought initially it was because she'd been dating the building superintendent and had broken it off. Then she decided she had disobeyed the rules, and admitted that with federal inspectors crawling all over the place, writing her up was probably good group control.

15   When Amy came to Hanford she expected to find young scientists like the ones in the TV ads: bloodless and efficient, white-coated and white in character and soul, displaying neither private idiosyncracies nor private lusts. But most young guys here shared a cocky, on-the-make and overpowered carelessness–like the union steward who told Amy if she didn't go out with him he'd dent her car or cite her for minor violations, or the part-time drug dealer whose entrepreneurial spirit brought the FBI to his house.

16   Amy didn't like the hustles, flirtations and sexual intrigues. There were, of course, other, older workers: the Hanford veterans, now mostly in their sixties and ready to retire with their travel trailers, boats, lakeside cabins and the old ladies to whom they'd remained at least largely faithful through all these years. Though many had no doubt been exposed to enough radiation to make an elephant glow, they went dourly about their day-to-day business, complaining about regulations this, regulations that and about how if something got crapped up in the old days all you had to do was scrape it off in the desert sand outside. They seemed content in a manner few of her generation could be, and they were certain everything was fixable and nothing worth getting their blood up about—except perhaps the far-off Russkies or the all-too-present assaults on the

nuclear industry by backpackers, whale watchers and Robert Redford types. But although Amy could learn from these men (and they made far better teachers than did the fresh-pressed, calculator-in-the-pocket new engineering graduates), and although she could work with them, they could not and did not make Z plant a place where she felt at home.

17   On bad days—when the inspectors were overinspecting, half the men hung over and half the women on Valium, when someone had walked accidentally through one of the security-sealed doors and brought down the Mod Squad (a super secret team of S.W.A.T. types who appeared within minutes wearing flak jackets and pointing machine guns at everyone)—on those days Amy saw nothing but an endless parade of traps. Sure, Millie the receptionist would always be there to furnish a cheery, optimistic horoscope. But Amy would come back from struggling with some mixing, percolation or separation process, would try rereading the training manuals and rule books to see where she'd gone wrong, and would end up nauseous from overload and confusion. "The destructive power of nuclear weapons is well known," explained this paper world. "Protection of the plutonium is very important . . . and should we lose control only history will tell the outcome." "If taken hostage be alert, maintain a good relationship with your captors, do not discuss what action may be taken by the Company. . . ." What was this stuff about hostages, the Company and history? Amy wasn't the bionic woman, just an ordinary twenty-nine-year-old mom trying to do the best she could for herself and for her kids. She didn't want to learn a new kind of geometry to prevent plutonium from concentrating in the wrong, potentially critical configurations. If "inactive hoods containing greater than 100 grams fissile material require a 91 centimeter minimum spacing between the hoods and any fissile material near them" . . . then what did that have to do with the ten pounds Amy wanted to lose, with the payments on her brand new gold Capri, or with the aggravation from all the guys to whom she was either a hustling, overperforming chick or a stupid broad who couldn't get anything right? She'd put the book down at times like this, decide to blank out all hassles, go by what the old hands said and pray she could do her job well enough to not get contacted.

18   Those days and those depressions always passed, though. The work would go well, albeit a little boringly. She'd join her fellow operators in playing Hearts on swing-shift dinner breaks. They'd pitch in for gifts when some worker or worker's wife had a baby. And as if to cap and redeem the year, there was always the annual office Christmas party.

19   At the West Richland Elks Club, the old hands stepped out of their Buicks and Pontiacs wearing bolo ties, crew cuts and either cowboy boots or wing-tip oxfords. They swung and waltzed their wives on the dance floor in a manner that showed they'd had years and years of Saturday night stepping out. They talked of trout fishing and grandchildren.

20   The young guys came in Camaros, four-wheel-drive pickups and even some

Porsches. Some wore jeans, some wore suits. Gold chains rippled across their necks and chests. Their hair fell below their shoulders. If they weren't married to sweet ingenues just beginning to grow restless and uncertain from boredom, they drank at the bar and flirted across the room with women co-workers whose switch from coveralls to cocktail dresses had turned them desirably slinky and kittenish.

21   As the culminating event, a Santa Claus MC handed out a variety of joke prizes: "A pair of safety glasses to John who never wears his," "A glove because Rick burned his hands last year," and suntan lotion for Roy who was always standing right next to the radiation sources. Since the awards combined the best aspects of gossip, bragging recollection and childhood play, people laughed and clapped at each. Topping it all, Julie and William got T-shirts saying I'M HOT STUFF.

☐ Discovering Meaning and Technique

1. What point does Loeb make about the nuclear business?

2. What are the attitudes of the employees of Hanford (Washington) Nuclear Reservation toward their jobs?

3. What postponed help for Julie and William after their contamination?

4. At what point in time does Loeb begin the narration? How soon after the beginning do you learn the events that led to the contamination?

5. What was being processed in Z plant?

6. What is a "contact"? How many contacts were required before a worker was fired?

7. What does "crapped up" mean?

8. What safety measures were in place at Hanford to prevent contamination?

9. What kinds of procedures went into action after alarms went off?

10. How does Amy rationalize that she got a contact slip while Sam did not?

11. How do the older workers at Hanford characterize the people who oppose the nuclear industry?

☐ **Writing Suggestions**

1. Hanford Nuclear Reservation was developed so that the United States could build a nuclear bomb. The bomb that was dropped on Nagasaki was made of plutonium from Hanford. Now that the threat of war is less intense, do you think that Hanford should be shut down?

2. Do you think that accidents and human errors can be eliminated in nuclear plants?

3. Write about the reasons you would or would not work in a nuclear plant.

4. Write a fictional story about a day in a nuclear plant from the point of view of a worker who opposes the nuclear culture but desperately needs work.

WHAT YOU MUST KNOW ABOUT RADIATION

☐ DR. HELEN CALDICOTT

1 All radiation is dangerous. No radiation is safe, and we live with a certain amount of background radiation all the time. It comes from the sun, and from cosmic rays that originate in outer space. Now, eons of time ago, when we were just amoebae and paramecia and other small organisms and when the ozone layer in the atmosphere was very thin, a lot of radiation came through, and the radiation changed our genes—and genes, I remind you, are the very essence of life; they control everything about us. So as radiation poured in from the sun eons of time ago, the structure and functions of the genes in the amoebae and the paramecia and other small organisms were changed and a process of evolution began, eventually producing fish, birds, plants and living animals, including human beings.

2   Now, a change in a gene is called a "mutation." And there were some mutations that were good. They allowed fish to develop lungs and birds to develop wings—that sort of thing. But there also were mutations that created disease and deformities, that made many organisms unfit to survive in their environment. Those organisms died off. The others lived. Many people call this process of separation of the fit creatures from the unfit ones an illustration of the Darwinian theory of the "survival of the fittest." In any case, that's how we think human beings evolved. But radiation continues to produce mutations in cells. Some of these mutations cause changes—"cancer."

3   Today the background radiation from the sun is much less than it was in the beginning, millions of years ago. That's because the ozone layer is thicker—

it tends to strain out a lot of the radiation—and we live more or less in equilibrium with background radiation, though we do get a certain amount of cancer from it. Although we get radiation from natural sources—from air, rocks and our own body cells—we also, in modern times, get it from man-made sources. X-rays, administered in doctors' offices and hospitals, are the commonest source today.

4   It has been estimated that 40 to 50 percent of all medical x-rays are unnecessary, and since the effect of all radiation is cumulative—that is, each exposure increases the risk of getting cancer—you must never have an x-ray without knowing absolutely why and without being assured that it is truly necessary. If you are a heavy smoker, obviously you will need more chest x-rays than a nonsmoker. Or if you cough up blood or have pneumonia or break your arm, you really need an x-ray. The risk from one x-ray is minimal, and the benefit can be great if it is truly necessary. But keep in mind that doctors often order x-rays without thinking much about it. X-rays have become routine. Instead of putting his hand on a patient's belly, palpating it and working out a clinical diagnosis, a doctor may order an x-ray. And some doctors may simply want to have an x-ray for their files, as part of your record.

5   Then there are dental x-rays. You don't need a dental x-ray every six months; you don't even need one every year. When I was a child my dentist didn't have an x-ray machine, and I've got well-filled teeth. Very occasionally, if you have severe pain or you have a root abscess or something like that, you need a tooth x-rayed. But you see, like doctors, some dentists do not think of the dangers. And some buy x-ray machines and pay for them by taking a lot of x-rays and charging the patients for them.

6   When a doctor or dentist suggests an x-ray, ask, "Why? What are you going to find out from this x-ray?" Get the doctor to draw a picture and explain the pathology so that you understand; you make the decision. But don't ever have an unnecessary x-ray.

7   The reason for care is that human beings are more sensitive to the effects of radiation than any other animal: We get cancer more readily. We don't know why. And children and fetuses are about 10 to 20 times more sensitive than adults because their cells are rapidly dividing and growing. It is during the time when a child is growing and the cells are multiplying that radiation damage to the genes can have its most devastating effect.

8   The British epidemiologist Dr. Alide Stewart has shown that one x-ray of a pregnant abdomen increases the risk of eventual leukemia in the baby by 40 per cent above the normal incidence. Fortunately, we don't often x-ray pregnant abdomens nowadays. We use ultrasound to determine where the fetal head is. But if you *have* had an x-ray while pregnant, let us reassure you: The increased incidence of 40 per cent isn't much, because normally only about 1 in 40,000 children will develop leukemia.

9   I have been talking about natural radiation and x-ray radiation. Now let

us talk about nuclear radiation. This is the kind that comes from atomic bombs and is developed in nuclear energy plants.

10   In order to run the atomic reactors that produce energy and make nuclear bombs, we need uranium. Uranium is a natural ore that is found in the ground, and it's safe enough if it's left in the ground. But when it is mined, it emits radioactive by-products—radium and a radioactive gas called "radon." Unfortunately, uranium is worth a lot of money; both the Government and private utilities pay a very good price for it.

11   Large-scale uranium mining in the United States started in the '40s, during World War II, in connection with the Manhattan Project, which was created to produce the first atomic bombs. Many of the miners who were doing this work inhaled the radon gas, which attaches itself to tiny dust particles and lodges in the terminal air passages in the lungs. Nothing happened to these men at the time, but 15, 25, 30 years later some of these men found themselves coughing up blood or having other symptoms of chest disease. This time x-rays were definitely in order. So they got x-rays, and on each x-ray plate there was a big mass—a big white mass. It was cancer.

12   Now, what happened? Well, here are the cells in the lung and here is the radon, which has been continuously emitting its radioactive alpha particles. Inside each cell is a nucleus, which is the "brain" of the cell. In the nucleus are chromosomes, and on the chromosomes are the genes. Now, in every cell in the body there's a gene that controls the rate of cell division, and that is called the "regulatory gene." And what happened to the men who got cancer from the radon gas was that one of the alpha particles in the gas by chance hit the regulatory gene in one of the cells and damaged it. And the cell sat very quietly for all those years until one day, instead of dividing to produce just two daughter cells as it should, it went berserk and produced millions and trillions of daughter cells—a clone of abnormal cells—and that is cancer. In other words, it may actually take only one alpha particle emitted from one atom, to hit one cell and one gene, to initiate the cancer cycle. And this is very serious, because in this country right now, a lot of men who mined uranium in the past are dying of lung cancer.

13   It is a terrible thing that when uranium mining first began in this country none of the big companies paid any attention to the need for safety precautions, in spite of the fact that it was known that men in Europe who had mined other ores that contained some uranium died of cancer. So now there is an epidemic of lung cancer among former American uranium miners. The same kind of indifference to human welfare exists in industries that produce dangerous nonradioactive chemicals.

14   Regulations of the Environmental Protection Agency are being watered down because of the tremendous pressure that is exerted on government by industry. Industry makes hundreds of new chemicals every year. Very few are tested for their potential as causes of cancer. They are just dumped into the

enivornment, as they were in Love Canal, Niagara Falls, New York, and in many other places around the country, where they become concentrated in the food chains, in our air, in our water, in our soil. Our whole world is rapidly becoming polluted with substances we haven't even looked at from the medical point of view. All to make money, to produce useless objects like plastic bottles that we throw away.

15   After uranium is mined it is taken to a milling plant. There it is crushed and chemically treated. The uranium is then removed and the stuff produced as a by-product, called "uranium tailings," is discarded. These tailings, a sandy material, contain the radioactive products of radium and thorium, which continue to emit radon gas for hundreds of thousands of years. If you live next to a uranium tailings dump, you have double the risk of getting cancer compared to a nonexposed population.

16   There are millions of tons of tailings lying around in this country. There's a huge pile of uranium tailings right next to Grants, New Mexico. Just last spring the Navaho Indians, many of whom were uranium miners in the early 1950s and are dying of lung cancer, staged an antinuclear demonstration a few miles from Grants. At the same time the people of Grants, which bills itself as "the Uranium Capital of the United States," staged a different demonstration. It was a huge pronuclear parade and rally, which included more than 15 floats, many of them provided by milling and mining companies in the area. One of the floats bore the following statement: "This community lives from uranium—it's our bread and butter." And all the time, tailings were being blown over Grants from that lethal pile, and the people in that area have a double risk of getting lung cancer. But they don't know; they really don't understand the dangers.

17   They didn't understand the dangers in other places either. In some places tailings were used as landfill, and homes, stores and other structures were built on top of them. In other places tailings were simply dumped. Salt Lake City has a uranium tailings dump of 1.7 million tons. It is called the "Vitro Dump," after the city's Vitro Chemical Company mill. In New Jersey there are two churches that stand on or next to areas where tailings were dumped. In addition, because tailings are like sand and were free for the taking, contractors and builders used them in concrete mix; and in Grand Junction, Colorado, there are thousands of structures in which tailings were used—among them two schools, three shopping malls, an airport and many, many houses.

18   Obviously the people were never told that the tailings might be dangerous, and all the time they were emanating radiation. Then, about 1971, a pediatrician, Dr. Robert M. Ross, Jr., sounded an alarm: He was finding too many birth defects and too much cancer among his young patients. A committee composed of doctors and researchers was appointed to investigate, and some months later they compared statistics from Mesa County, where Grand Junction is located, with those of the whole state. They found that the death rate from birth defects in Mesa County was more than 50 per cent higher than in all of Colorado from

1963 to 1968. Cleft lip and cleft palate were nearly twice as common in Mesa County as in all of Colorado, and death from cancer was significantly higher in the Grand Junction area than in the rest of the state. Though there was controversy about those figures, and there still is, another statistic was recently added by Dr. Stanley W. Ferguson, of the Colorado State Health Department: Between 1970 and 1976, the incidence of leukemia in Grand Junction more than doubled. Efforts to remedy this situation began in 1972 and are still going on, but it's a patchwork affair predicated on "permissible levels of radiation." Of course, I'm convinced that no level of radiation is safe, and since its effects are cumulative, we'll probably be hearing of case after case of cancer in that area in the years to come.

19   It was only about a year ago that the United States Congress passed a bill making it mandatory that all the millions of tons of tailing in this country be disposed of properly—a practically hopeless task because so much of the stuff has accumulated. In the meantime a great deal of harm has been done.

20   The next step in the nuclear cycle is enrichment. It takes a full ton on uranium ore to make four pounds of pure uranium, and about 99 per cent of this pure uranium is unfissionable—not usable for making energy. This is called Isotope Uranium-238. About a half ounce out of the four pounds is fissionable; this is called Uranium-235. Uranium-235 is what is used for nuclear power, but the 0.7 per cent that is got from the natural ore must be enriched to 3.0 per cent to be used in a reactor. If it is enriched to 20 per cent or more, it is suitable for making atomic bombs. The bomb used on Hiroshima was a uranium bomb and it was called "Little Boy." They have nice names for their bombs.

21   After enrichment comes fabrication. If you've seen the film *The China Syndrome,* you know that the enriched uranium is made into little pellets like aspirin tablets and packed into hollow rods that are about three quarters of an inch thick and about 12 feet long. When this has been done the rods are taken to the nuclear plant, where they are packed into the core of the nuclear reactor. When they have finished there are 100 tons of uranium in the reactor core, at which point they submerge it all in water. Now, when you pack uranium so densely and in such a way, it reaches "critical mass." That means that the atoms spontaneously start breaking apart, and this action produces about 200 new radioactive elements called "fission products," which are the broken-down products of the original uranium atoms. These fission products are the same materials that are formed when an atom bomb explodes.

22   An atom bomb explodes as the uranium fissions because it is an uncontrolled reaction. But in a nuclear power plant this process is controlled and the fissioning uranium doesn't explode. Instead, the heat produced by the fission process boils the water in which the uranium-bearing rods have been submerged, and the steam that is formed turns a turbine that makes electricity.

23   So in fact, all a nuclear reactor does is boil water. It's a very sophisticated

way to boil water. Because inside of each 1,000-megawatt reactor, is as much radioactive material as would be released by the explosion of 1,000 bombs of the size of the one that was dropped on Hiroshima.

24 The reason we are discussing all this is that something happened at Three Mile Island, near Harrisburg, Pennsylvania. What happened? Well, accident, certainly human error and possibly mechanical failure caused large quantities of water to escape from the container holding the immensely hot uranium rods. Apparently the operators of the plant were unaware of the escaping water. Because the water wasn't immediately replaced, the rods became uncovered and remained uncovered for at least 50 minutes. Looking back at it now, most nuclear engineers can't understand what kept the uranium fuel in the uncovered rods from melting down.

25 What would have happened if there had been a meltdown? The low water level and subsequent inefficient cooling of the rods would have allowed the intrinsic heat of the fission products in the uranium to melt the 100 tons of uranium into a globular mass. It then would have continued to melt right through the bottom of the container and and—nuclear experts say—hundreds of feet into the earth "toward China"! That's what is called the "China syndrome" by the nuclear industry.

26 If a meltdown had occurred at Three Mile Island, a massive steam explosion would have ruptured the reactor container and released all the radiation—as much as in 1,000 Hiroshima-sized bombs—into the air. It would not have been an atomic explosion, but it would have contaminated an area the size of Pennsylvania for thousands of years. Nobody could have lived there any more for thousands of years! And depending on the direction of the wind, other huge areas could have been contaminated.

27 Such an accident would cost about $17 billion in property damage. And what about human damage? Let's say that as many as 10 million people would have been exposed—that would be entirely possible. Well, some statisticians report that almost immediately about 3,300 people would die of lethal radiation exposure. Two or three weeks later about 10,000 to 100,000 more could die of what is called acute radiation illness. First they'd go bald. Their hair would drop out; we saw this for the first time after the bomb was dropped on Hiroshima. Then they would begin to hemorrhage under the skin. They would develop skin ulcers, awful ulcers in their mouths, vomiting and diarrhea, and they'd die of bleeding or infection.

28 That would happen in a relatively short time, but there are long-term effects too. Hundreds of thousands of men would be rendered sterile from the radiation damage to their testicles. Hundreds of thousands of women would stop menstruating, many permanently. Thousands of people would develop hypothyroidism. With their thyroid glands damaged, their metabolic rate would slow down, they would become constipated, they would be unable to think properly, they'd lose their appetites and at the same time become fat.

29   Thousands more would have acute respiratory impairment, the radiation having damaged their lungs. Thousands of babies affected by radiation while still in their mothers' wombs would be born with microcephaly, or with very small heads—"pinheads," they called them in Hiroshima, where this happened after the bomb fell. Thousands more would be born cretins, with ablated thyroids and neurological damage.

30   And five, ten, 20, 30 years later, hundreds of thousands of cases of cancer would occur, to say nothing of the varieties of genetic defects—dwarfism, mental retardation, hemophilia, and others—that would develop and be passed on and on through future generations.

31   My list of sick, dying and dead comes to just less than half a million people. Possibly the estimate could be for a few less, since Three Mile Island had been in operation for only three months before the accident and had only 80 per cent of the inventory of radioactive products that a normal, long-term operating. 1,000-megawatt reactor would contain. But it would have been a catastrophe such as the world has never seen, because only 200,000 people died in Hiroshima and Nagasaki, though the incidence of cancer is still increasing among the bomb survivors there.

32   Now, what I want to know is, why doesn't our Government tell us of the dangers to which we are being exposed? Why hasn't it told us what a meltdown would mean? What can we expect as a result of the careless dumping of nuclear wastes, which, if not as swiftly devastating as a meltdown or a bomb, can be just as deadly over a period of time? Where does the allegiance of our elected representatives belong—to the utility companies or to us? Did Dwight Eisenhower, when he was President and they were testing hydrogen bombs in Nevada in 1953, set a permanent policy when he told the Atomic Energy Commission to "keep the public confused" about radioactive fallout? (The AEC certainly was receptive to Eisenhower's advice. Recently declassified commission records show that it repeatedly brushed aside questions about health hazards; and in February, 1955, Willard F. Libby, a member of the commission, said: "People have got to learn to live with facts of life, and part of the facts of life is fallout.")

33   The accident at Three Mile Island in Pennsylvania revealed still other alarming things. People operating the nuclear plant for Metropolitan Edison didn't know what they were doing. In the first 48 hours after the accident, primary coolant (water that surrounds the rods) was vented into the atmosphere as steam. Rule number one in the nuclear energy business is, Never vent primary coolant! It's like, if you are a surgeon, you never cut off a head—you just don't do that! But the primary coolant was vented after the cladding of many of the rods had melted and released highly radioactive fission products into the water. They weren't measuring anything in the first 48 hours, either, so they don't know exactly what they let out—plutonium? strontium? cesium? radioactive iodine? That's the first thing. The second thing is that a whole lot of radioactive water from the primary coolant spilled onto the reactor floor. An attempt was made to transfer some of this to a tank in an auxiliary building that stands

beside the reactor, but the tank already contained radioactive water—perhaps not so radioactive as the primary coolant, but radioactive just the same. To make room for the primary coolant, 4,000 gallons of radioactive water from the tank was emptied into the Susquehanna River.

34   Now, water from that tank is routinely emptied into the Susquehanna, but first, as Government spokesmen would say, it has to be tested and diluted to a "permissible level of radioactivity." As I see it, no level of radioactivity is permissible, so that's bad enough. But during those first critical 48 hours, the 4,000 gallons of radioactive water they emptied into the river weren't even tested. They also released a lot of radioactive gases into the air, many of which are precursors of products such as Stronthium-90, Cesium-137 and Radioactive Iodine-131.

35   More proof that the people operating that plant didn't know what they were doing: Not only did they make "a series of errors"—I quote *The New York Times*—"in the operation of the plant," but when the accident occurred they continued to make errors. A very serious problem. And because Metropolitan Edison doesn't know how much radioactive stuff was emptied into the environment, there is no hard data on which to make predictions about what will happen to people in the Harrisburg area in the future. And yet Joseph A. Califano, Jr., then Secretary of the Department of Health, Education and Welfare, said that only one person—at worst, ten people—would die of cancer as a result of the accident. He had no primary data on which to base the announcement. It's very worrying.

36 Let me tell you about Strontium-90. Strontium-90 stays poisonous for 600 years. Released into the atmosphere, it settles on the grass from the air, the rain and the dew, and its potency gets compounded many times over the concentration that is in the air. When this happens in dairying areas, cattle eat the grass and the Strontium-90 is concentrated in cow's milk, which both calves and babies drink. It concentrates most highly in human breast milk, and it gets there when pregnant women and nursing mothers eat dairy products that are contaminated by Strontium-90. Now, anybody who ingests a radioactive substance can be affected, but it's very important to know that babies are inordinately sensitive to the effects of radiation. You can't taste the radiation. It's odorless, invisible and tasteless, and when a baby drinks milk containing Strontium-90 the body treats it as if it were calcium; it's deposited in the growing bones. It causes bone cancer. It also causes leukemia—many of those children die.

37   Between January, 1951, and October, 1958, when a large number of atomic and hydrogen bombs were tested in the Nevada desert, the winds carried the fallout to agricultural as well as populated areas in Utah and Strontium-90 was found in milk. At that time the Nobel Prize-winning scientist Linus Pauling said if babies drank milk containing Strontium-90, they might get leukemia later. And the Government said Pauling was wrong. Then early this year the New

England Journal of Medicine published a paper saying that the incidence of leukemia in Utah children in the "high fallout" counties who were under 14 at the time of the testing had increased nearly two and a half times above normal level.

38   Radioactive Iodine-131 also concentrates in milk, and if there are bodies of water nearby, it concentrates in fish. Although it is active for only a few weeks, once it gets into milk or fish its potency is compounded thousands of times. And its effect, when ingested by humans, is vicious and lasting. Taken up by the thyroid, it can cause thyroid cancer. Keep in mind that I have named only three or four dangerous elements. Actually almost 200 of those dangerous elements that are made in nuclear reactors are contained in nuclear waste.

39   Nuclear waste. Garbage. Nobody needs it. Nobody wants it. And nobody knows what to do with it. And it has to be disposed of, isolated from the environment, because many of those elements remain potent for one million years. If those materials leak, they get into our air, they get into our water, they get into our food chain and get recycled through human bodies for hundreds and thousands of years, causing cancers after cancers after cancers, to say nothing of birth deformities and genetic disease.

40   Now, by present methods of technology, nuclear waste, which is active for up to one million years, can be safely stored for only ten to 20 years. But even before that the containers begin to corrode; there are leaks; it gets into all parts of our environment. Even if the most brilliant scientist we have should think he's found the answer for storing nuclear wastes, he'll be dead long before his hypothesis can be verified. This is the heritage we are leaving to our descendents.

41   You can imagine our descendents, like the people at Love Canal, Niagara Falls, New York, where nonnuclear but dangerous chemicals were dumped, waking up one morning with their food already contaminated, their kids already being born deformed and dying of leukemia and cancer, and with adults too dying of cancer. It will be too late. But we're risking millions of lives so we can turn our lights on. And to keep the economy running. And because government and big business have invested a lot of money.

42   In the nuclear industries they say, "Don't worry, we're scientists; we'll find the answer." That's like my saying to a patient, "You have cancer; you have about six months to live; but don't worry, I'm a good doctor and by 1995 I might find a cure."

43 Now let's talk about plutonium, out of which both atomic and hydrogen bombs are made. That's one of the most dangerous elements known. It is man-made in a nuclear reactor; it didn't exist until we fissioned uranium. And it's named, appropriately, after Pluto, the god of the underworld. It is so incredibly toxic that a millionth of a gram—and a gram is about the size of a grape—can cause cancer. When plutonium is exposed to the air it produces particles as fine as

talcum powder that are totally invisible. And if you inhale any of those particles, they will almost certainly give you lung cancer.

44   If you took just ten pounds of plutonium and put a speck of it in every human lung, that would be enough to kill every single person on earth. Ten pounds! And each nuclear reactor makes 500 pounds of it every year. Five hundred pounds! What's worse, plutonium remains toxic for half a million years. It is not biodegradable, that is, it doesn't decompose; so the plutonium-contaminated waste remains toxic all that time.

45   There are areas around Denver, Colorado, that are contaminated by plutonium radiation, and the testicular cancer rate in a suburb next to Rock Flats, about 13 miles from the center of Denver, is 140 per cent higher than the normal incidence. You see, plutonium lodges in the testicles and it's in the testicles that the sperm are, where the genes for the future generations are! Plutonium also crosses the placental barrier, where it can damage the developing fetus. It can kill a cell that's going to form the left side of a baby's brain, or, say, the left arm, or whatever. Do you remember what thalidomide did? Plutonium is thalidomide forever! It will damage fetus after fetus, down the generations, virtually for the rest of time. And, of course, its effects are not limited to the unborn. It causes lung cancer. It causes bone cancer. It causes liver cancer, and more.

46   The nuclear reactor was first designed as part of the Manhattan Project to make plutonium, the plutonium to be used in making nuclear weapons. And in making bombs and other atomic weapons they have produced 74 million gallons of high-level radioactive waste, and scientists and engineers and environmental specialists all have studied the problem—and nobody seems to know what to do with it.

47   Nobody has devised a foolproof, leakproof, fail-safe place to sequester those wastes over the thousands and thousands of years they remain dangerous. At the present time, wastes, contained in large carbon-steel tanks, are being stored on the site of the Government's Hanford Reservation, a nuclear energy complex near Richland, Washington. They are also being stored on the site of the Savannah River Plant, another Government facility that produces nuclear weapons materials, near Aiken, South Carolina. At Hanford the tanks have already leaked 450,000 gallons of poisonous radioactive waste into the soil near the Columbia River. Eventually these radioactive elements will probably enter the Columbia River, where they will become concentrated in the fish we eat, in the water we drink and, if the water is used for irrigation, in plants and animals.

48 The dangers of nuclear power are not only accidental meltdowns, escaping radiation and all the radioactive wastes we don't know how to dispose of. The dangers are even greater because it is a small step from nuclear power to nuclear weaponry.

49   There are now 35 countries that have nuclear weapons capability because they have been sold nuclear reactors—some small, some large—by this country

and by others. And since each 1,000-megawatt reactor produces about 500 pounds of plutonium every year, so, theoretically, many of those 35 countries could make 50 atomic bombs every year from each 1,000-megawatt reactor.

50   Albert Einstein said, "The splitting of the atom has changed everything save man's mode of thinking; thus we drift toward unparalleled catastrophe."

51   What would happen if all the weapons were used? One, the synergistic effects could be so great, with the ozone destroyed, icecaps melting, radiation everywhere, and so on, that probably not an organism would survive. Maybe the cockroaches would survive because they're 400,000 times more radiation-resistant than humans. Or if you did survive—if there had been no fire storm to eat up all the oxygen in your shelter—and you stayed in your shelter for at least two weeks (otherwise you would die from the intense radiation) what would you find when you came out? There would be countless dead and dying—Guyana, where the earth was covered with the dead, would have nothing on us. There would be no doctors, drugs or hospital beds in big cities, because those are targeted. You might find some doctors in small communities, but what could they do? Disease would be rampant. And you can imagine the earth inhabited by bands of roving mutant humanoids generations hence. This would be like no science fiction story ever invented.

☐ Discovering Meaning and Technique

1. According to Caldicott, what are the effects of radiation—both natural and man-made?

2. What impression of Caldicott do you get from her style of writing—for example, "I have been talking about natural radiation and x-ray radiation. Now let us talk about nuclear radiation. This is the kind that comes from atomic bombs and is developed in nuclear energy plants."

3. What kind of audience does Caldicott seem to be addressing?

4. What stylistic characteristics show that the selection was first a speech?

5. Why, according to Caldicott, does the Environmental Protection Agency not work to create a clean environment?

6. Why does Caldicott think that people and communities do not object to uranium mining and dumping?

7. What is a "meltdown"? What is the result? What does the nuclear industry call a meltdown and why?

8. Describe the short- and long-term effects of a nuclear accident.

9. What mistakes were made after the accident at Three Mile Island?

10. What are the characteristics of Strontium-90? Of Radioactive Iodine-131? Of plutonium?

☐ Writing Suggestions

1. Do you think the government and/or medical personnel should do more to protect people from radiation?

2. Watch the film *The China Syndrome* and discuss whether you think its picture of a nuclear power plant is realistic.

3. Do you think a solution to the problem of storing nuclear wastes will ever be discovered? Why or why not?

4. Is Caldicott correct that no level of radiation is safe? Gather information in the library to write about this subject.

5. Read about the nuclear accident at Three Mile Island in newspapers published in March and April, 1979. Assess the quality of the reports. Is it clear what happened?

6. From newspaper articles try to determine what happened at the accident at Chernobyl on April 26, 1986.

NUCLEAR WAR: MY POSITION

☐ CALVIN TRILLIN

1 Looking for ways to ease my mind about signs that the danger of nuclear war is increasing, I stumbled across one comforting thought: maybe the Russian missiles won't work. I realize that the possibility of a simple malfunction is a thin reed upon which to hang the survival of the species. Still, it's what I have for now, and I'm going with it. I have adopted it as my new official position on the entire nuclear arms issue. It may sound like a fallback position, but as it happens, I have already fallen back. Before I adopted my new position on the issue of nuclear arms I had a rather complicated position which, stated in its simplest terms, was as follows: "I'd rather not think about it."

2   I owe my new position to a passage I read in an interesting piece on the

arms race by Thomas Powers in *The Atlantic* a couple of months ago. "Don't judge Russian missiles by your TV set," Powers was told in Moscow after he happened to mention to one of the people he was interviewing that the television set in his hotel room didn't work. "Some things we *can* do." Powers can believe that if he wants to. I'd rather not. I prefer to believe that the Russian missiles won't work because their television sets don't work.

3   Why didn't I think of this years ago? I have certainly read enough about the shoddiness of goods produced by Soviet industry—overcoats whose sleeves fall off now and then, television sets permanently tuned to the all-snow channel, refrigerators destined to become the only thing in a Moscow apartment that is never cold. I have read about those Russian tractor factories where vodka-sodden workers fulfill their monthly quota in a frantic last-minute push that can succeed only if they attach the transmissions with Scotch tape. Why have I always taken it for granted that those goofballs would be so good at annihilating continents?

4   Naturally, my new official position came equipped with what the nuclear strategists call a scenario. It went like this: When the nuclear exchange finally comes, all the Russian missiles fizzle on their launching pads except one, which destroys Punta del Este, Uruguay. Our missiles destroy Russia. The second part of the scenario was based on easily obtainable and incontrovertible data concerning the operating efficiency of television sets in American hotel rooms. Television sets in American hotel rooms work. Considering what's shown on them, you might argue that they work to a fault—but they work.

5   When I first adopted my new official position, I was often asked if I felt guilty that the Russians would be destroyed in a nuclear exchange while we survived without a scratch, and I often answered, "Not as guilty as you might think." After all, I never claimed that this was anything but a fallback position. Also, I was relieved to have some progress to report to the fellow we call Harold the Committed, who is constantly asking me if I really want to see civilization as we know it destroyed in a nuclear holocaust.

6   "I think I've got some good news on that front, Hal the C," I said, the next time he asked. "Apparently Tom Powers could only get the snow channel in Moscow, plus one channel where the vertical was totally out of whack."

7   Harold the Committed seemed unable to make the connection, but I was certain that the implications of the video efficiency gap would not be lost on a Russian counterpart of Thomas Powers—a journalist named, say, Raskolnikov, who comes to America to do interviews for a piece on nuclear arms. Switching on the television set in his Washington hotel room in the hope of seeing some snow that might bring back memories of his boyhood in the heroic Siberian settlement of Yakutsk Molymsk, he is astonished to find an absolutely clear picture on sixteen channels. He is glued to the set. He watches two morning news programs. He watches *Donahue.* He watches *Sesame Street.* He watches *Gilligan's Island* reruns. He watches the soaps. Late in the afternoon, as he is watching a closed-circuit hotel channel on shopping opportunities in Alexandria, the tele-

phone rings. It's the Pentagon general Raskolnikov was supposed to interview six hours earlier. Raskolnikov rushes to the Pentagon, bursting with stories of the magic box in his hotel room.

8   "They work like a charm, Mr. Raskolnikov," the general says, "Out at the house, I have my twenty-six-incher hooked up to one of those satellite dishes, and get a hundred and twenty-eight channels, clear as a bell. I get restless at four in the morning, I watch the rugby from Melbourne. I'm glad you noticed how well that little mother works."

9   "What I noticed," Raskolnikov says, "is that it was made in Japan."

10   Well, yes, there's that. The television sets that work so well are made in Japan. The general in the Pentagon cautions Raskolnikov against judging America's technological capabilities by the fact that our television sets have to be imported from Japan. He tells Raskolnikov that through state-of-the-art technology and a finely meshed military chain of command, we could annihilate Russia with the flick of a switch. Raskolnikov can believe it if he wants to. Can any American who has ever served in the army or owned a car made in Detroit believe it? I'd rather not believe it. Who wants to feel even a little guilty about destroying Russia while it's only knocking off Punta del Este?

11   On that day of days, according to my revised scenario, the politicians order the missiles fired at the enemy, but then nothing much happens. The Russian commander raises his hand to give the signal, and the left arm of his overcoat falls off; during the delay, tractor transmissions drop out of the missiles. Our guys are missing two D-size batteries necessary for flicking the switch that activates our finely meshed chain of command, and the second lieutenant authorized to procure replacements is off waxing his GTO. In a couple of hours, it's all over. That is, it's all over but it's not *all over.* The Russians get a stiff note from Uruguay. Otherwise, the world is as it was. It will remain that way, according to my analysis, until one side or the other gets a Japanese-made missile.

☐ Discovering Meaning and Technique

1. When do you first realize that the selection is meant to be humorous?

2. What was Trillin's first position on the nuclear arms issue?

3. What is his "new official position"?

4. What did Trillin read that stimulated his belief?

5. Which examples does Trillin give of the "shoddiness" of Soviet products?

6. Why does Trillin say that he believes America's missiles are capable of destroying Russia?

7. What does the imaginary Raskolnikov discover about American TV that forces a change in Trillin's scenario?

☐ Writing Suggestions

1. Try writing a humorous view of nuclear power plants or nuclear waste disposal—subjects that do not lend themselves readily to humor.

2. Because American and Russia have for so long aimed missiles at each other, do you think trust will ever be wholehearted?

3. Compare the quality of products made in various countries—for example, automobiles or electronic equipment made in the United States, Japan, or a European country.

THE ENVIRONMENTAL CONSEQUENCES OF NUCLEAR WAR

☐ LYDIA DOTTO

1 In a display at the Hiroshima Peace Museum, among half-melted lumps of metal and glass, blasted bits of brick and stone and swatches of burned clothing, sits the charred remnant of a wrist watch. The minute and hour hands have been burned away, but their shadows remain, imprinted forever by the brilliant flash of the first nuclear weapon to be exploded over a city. This image conveys a powerful message: for the wearer of the watch—and for hundreds of thousands of other residents of Hiroshima—at 8:15 A.M. on an August morning in 1945, all that they knew as a normal existence abruptly ended without warning.

2   The bombing of Hiroshima—and Nagasaki after it—provide our only direct experience with the consequences of nuclear weapons explosions in cities. Those events have taught us a great deal about the potential physical, biological and human impact of nuclear war. But it must be remembered that each city experienced only a single explosion of a weapon much smaller in yield than many of those stockpiled in world nuclear arsenals today. Indeed, these arsenals contain nearly 50,000 weapons with individual yields 1 to 500 times that of the Hiroshima bomb and a total explosive power about a million times greater. A single one-megaton nuclear weapon has 100,000 times the explosive power of the most powerful bomb used in World War II.

3   Furthermore, the environment impact of the Hiroshima and Nagasaki bombs was geographically limited and survivors were almost immediately able to obtain medical and other assistance from outside. Thus, the impact of those bombs, though undeniably devastating for the people directly affected, was much more limited than might be expected in a full-scale war involving multiple detonations of much larger-yield weapons throughout much of the Northern Hemisphere.

4   The deployment of increasing numbers of more powerful weapons since the experience of Hiroshima and Nagasaki inevitably prompts the question: What would happen if many modern nuclear weapons were to be exploded? It seems obvious that the consequences would be very much more severe than they were in 1945. Perhaps even more important, however, is the fact that there could be consequences of a kind that didn't occur in Hiroshima and Nagasaki and were not even contemplated until very recently—i.e., the possibility that smoke from massive nuclear-ignited urban fires could cause global-scale disruptions in the Earth's weather and climate. Recent studies have focused on these possibilities and, as a result, the following picture of the potential post-nuclear war environment has emerged.

5   In the aftermath of a large-scale war in which nuclear weapons were exploded in major cities, darkened skies would cover large areas of the Earth for perhaps weeks or several months, as sunlight was blocked by large, thick clouds of smoke from widespread fires. The impact would be greatest over the continents of the Northern Hemisphere, where most of the smoke would likely be produced by nuclear-ignited fires, and where average temperatures in some areas might drop some tens of degrees Celsius to below freezing for several weeks to months after the war. Climatic disturbances might persist for several years, even in countries not directly involved in the war. Rainfall in many regions of the world might be greatly reduced.

6   Temperature and precipitation changes could also occur in the tropics and the Southern Hemisphere—less extreme than those in the Northern Hemisphere, but still significant. Tropical and sub-tropical regions could experience unprecedented cooling and severe cold spells, accompanied by significant disturbances in precipitation patterns.

7   World agriculture and major ecosystems, such as forests, grasslands, and marine systems, could be severely disturbed and their plant and animal populations stressed by rapid, dramatic changes in the normal climatic regime. Crop losses, caused not only by climate disturbances but also by the post-war disruption in supplies of essential inputs such as energy, machinery, fertilizers and pesticides, could create widespread food crises in both combatant and non-combatant nations. The failure of major food production and distribution systems, and the inability of natural ecosystems to support large numbers of people, could perhaps reduce the human population of the Earth to well below current levels.

8   In addition to the potential climatic effects, a large-scale exchange of nuclear

weapons would cause considerable devastation from the direct effects of fire, blast and local fallout of radioactivity. Other impacts could include severe disruptions of communications and power systems; reductions in the ozone layer in the upper atmosphere which protects life on Earth from the sun's biologically damaging ultraviolet radiation; intense local and long-term global fallout; and severe regional episodes of air and water pollution caused by the release of large amounts of toxic chemicals and gases.

9   In short, it is possible that, in the aftermath of a major nuclear war, the global environment and human social and economic systems could collapse to an extent that might preclude recovery to pre-war conditions.

10   This is the picture that emerges from the most recent analyses of the potential climatic and environmental consequences of a large-scale nuclear war. These analyses strongly suggest that the indirect effects of such a war could potentially have a greater impact on human society than the direct effects. They also indicate that even non-combatant nations far removed from the actual conflict could experience significant cooling episodes and disruptions in precipitation patterns.

11   Of course, it is impossible to predict the consequences of nuclear war exactly and it must be emphasized that considerable uncertainties in these estimates remain. Thus the range of possible outcomes is very large; however, not all these outcomes are equally likely to occur. The extremes at either end of the scale—i.e., months of sub-freezing temperatures all over the world, or alternatively, negligible climatic effects—are much less likely than intermediate level effects, such as short freezes lasting for some days over large regions of the Northern Hemisphere and widespread continental cooling lasting for several months. The present description attempts to avoid the extremes at either end, particularly "worst case" scenarios, in favor of a middle ground that is believed to represent a more probable outcome of a nuclear war. Nevertheless, new studies support the view that extremely serious climatic and other environmental consequences from a nuclear war are indeed possible.

12   It is especially important to note, moreover, that post-war conditions need not reach the most extreme limits of even the present estimates in order to have very serious impacts on global agricultural and natural ecosystems and, in turn, on human society. These analyses show that many crops may be highly vulnerable to even the smaller climatic changes estimated to be possible; over the longer term, food crises could well cause many hundreds to perhaps thousands of millions of deaths among people who survive the direct effects of the war and the climatic extremes that might immediately follow. Even in the absence of extreme climatic disturbances, disruptions in social systems and global trade in food and energy resources could create famine in many countries, even those not directly affected by the nuclear exchange. Following is a summary of the new findings.

SUMMARY OF CLIMATIC EFFECTS

13   If major cities—and particularly their fossil fuel supplies—were hit with nuclear weapons, this would almost certainly produce global climatic disturbances. It is believed that, in a large-scale war, hundreds of major urban/industrial centres in the Northern Hemisphere could be devastated by nuclear explosions, due to bombing of cities themselves or as a by-product of the targeting of nearby military and industrial installations.

14   The direct effects of a nuclear explosion could include ionizing radiation, blast waves and thermal radiation that could cause immediate death and destruction over an area the size of a major city. In addition, nuclear explosions could ignite urban fires unprecedented in size and intensity and massive smoke plumes could carry very large quantities of sooty smoke particles high into the atmosphere. The newly recognized atmospheric effects of this smoke are one of the major aspects of the studies on the climatic impact of nuclear war.

15   Nuclear explosions at or near the surface would also raise a large amount of dust, soil and debris, which would be drawn up in the rising nuclear fireball. Radioactive dust would contribute to local and global fallout; in addition, dust particles could be lofted high into the atmosphere and, as a result, they could also cause climatic effects. Although these effects are not estimated to be as great as those caused by smoke particles, neither would they be insignificant.

16   If about one-quarter of the combustible material in major Northern Hemisphere cities were to burn in nuclear-ignited fires, an estimated 50 to 150 million tonne of smoke could be produced, of which about 30 million tonne would be soot, a very black form of carbon-containing smoke that is a particularly effective absorber of the sun's energy. The black smoke produced by the flaming combustion of fossil fuels [e.g. oil, gasoline, kerosene] and their derivatives [e.g. plastics, rubber, asphalt] would contain the highest fraction of soot.

17   Fires ignited in forests and wildlands would also produce large amounts of smoke but, since this smoke would contain a smaller fraction of soot, the contribution to climatic effects would probably be secondary to that caused by the smoke from urban fires.

18   Because they are characterized by strong updrafts, the plumes rising from intense surface fires could loft smoke particles to altitudes as high as 10–15 kilometers, into the upper *troposphere* or lower *stratosphere*.[1] The number of smoke particles carried aloft would depend on the rate at which smoke was

---

[1] The *troposphere* is about the lowest 10–15 kilometers of the atmosphere, characterized by a decrease in temperature with altitude. It contains 90% of the mass of the atmosphere and most of what is known as "weather." The *stratosphere* is located above the troposphere, extending to about 50 kilometers; there, the temperature is either constant or it increases with height. The stratosphere contains the ozone layer that protects the earth's surface from the sun's ultraviolet radiation. The boundary between the troposphere and the stratosphere is called the *tropopause*.

generated, the intensity of the fires, local weather conditions, and whether the particles were removed by rain on their way into the upper atmosphere.

19   In many cases, the smoke plumes could enter towering thunderclouds triggered by the intense heat from the fires. Such clouds englufed the plumes from the Hiroshima and Nagasaki bombs, producing a "black rain" containing soot, dust and ash that fell for several hours after the explosion. This demonstrates that some particles are promptly rained out, but removal processes are not yet well understood and it is uncertain what fraction of the particles originally lifted in the rising plumes would be rained out very quickly. In most current studies, it is assumed that 30% to 50% of the particles would be removed by precipitation within a few hours or days.

20   As mentioned earlier, sooty smoke is a strong absorber of solar energy. Dense clouds of smoke particles floating high in the Earth's atmosphere could intercept a substantial fraction of the sun's incoming radiation, preventing it from reaching the surface. This would cause heating in the upper atmosphere and cooling at the surface. If 30 million tonnes of soot particles were spread over the mid-latitudes of the Northern Hemisphere, solar radiation at the ground would be reduced by at least 90%. During the first few days, the smoke particles could be concentrated in very dense patches that could be carried long distances by the winds. This could cause quite variable conditions at the surface, including brief episodes of severe cooling. Under the dense smoke patches, light levels could be reduced to nearly zero; even after the smoke had spread widely, the levels might be only a few percent of normal, on a daily average.

21   There is no evidence that meteorological processes would remove significant quantities of smoke particles within the first few days after the nuclear explosions. After a few days, the upper troposphere would stabilize and solar heating of the smoke-laden clouds could cause the smoke particles to be lofted even higher into the atmosphere, above the region where precipitation might wash them out.

22   Within a few days, continental-sized smoke clouds could spread over North America, Europe and much of Asia. The potential climatic impact of these clouds has been estimated using a variety of climate computer models. All simulations strongly indicate that smoke from fires could cause large, global-scale disruptions in normal weather patterns. These models still have many uncertainties and simplifications; for example, they are inadequate in projecting the removal of particles from the atmosphere. However, they have been substantially improved recently to include new features that are important in considering the post-war climatic effects of large quantities of smoke.

23   The estimates derived from computer simulations are summarized below. They assume that large quantities of smoke would be carried up into the atmosphere at altitudes of several kilometers or more in the Northern Hemisphere. It will be apparent that the season in which the war occurred would be a critical factor influencing the subsequent climatic impact.

24   If the smoke injection were to occur between the late spring and early fall in the Northern Hemisphere, average land surface temperatures beneath dense smoke patches in continental interiors could decrease by 20–40°C below normal within several days. Some of the smoke clouds might be carried long distances and cause cooling episodes as they passed, possibly causing sudden freezes. Weather conditions could be quite variable during this time if periods of dense smoke, during which virtually no sunlight would reach the surface, alternated with periods of thin or no smoke, during which substantial fractions of the normal amount of sunlight would reach the surface.

25   Smoke particles would be spread throughout the Northern Hemisphere, although somewhat unevenly, in 1 to 2 weeks. For smoke injections in late spring to early fall, the absorption of solar energy by the particles would cause a rapid warming of the air in the upper atmosphere, which could loft the particles even higher, where they could remain for months to years.

26   Average summertime land surface temperatures in the Northern Hemisphere mid-latitudes could drop to levels typical of early winter for periods of weeks or more and precipitation could be essentially eliminated. Fog and drizzle might occur, especially in coastal regions. Periods of very cold [mid-winter-like] conditions might occur in continental interiors.

27   If the smoke injection occurred in winter, light levels would be greatly reduced but the initial temperature and precipitation disturbances would not be as severe as those which might occur during summer. In fact, in many locations, conditions might be indistinguishable from an unusually cold winter. However, such conditions would occur simultaneously over the entire mid-latitude region of the Northern Hemisphere. More important, freezing cold air outbreaks might invade southerly regions that rarely or never normally experience frost.

28   For large smoke injections, temperatures in any season in sub-tropical latitudes of the Northern Hemisphere could drop well below typical cool season conditions. In areas not strongly influenced by the warming influence of the ocean, temperatures could be near or below freezing. The monsoons, a critical source of precipitation in sub-tropical Asia and Africa, might fail, although precipitation could increase in some coastal areas.

29   The strong solar heating of the smoke injected in the Northern Hemisphere between spring and autumn would carry it upward and toward the equator. Within 1–2 weeks, thin smoke clouds might appear in the Southern Hemisphere, followed by a thin, more uniform veil of dark smoke. Modest cooling could occur in regions not influenced by the warming influence of the ocean; however, since this would occur in the Southern Hemisphere cool season, these initial temperature reductions would not likely exceed 10–15°C degrees.

30   There are still many uncertainties in estimating the recovery of the atmosphere from a nuclear war. A period of acute climatic disturbance could last for several weeks or months. Present estimates are that smoke initially injected at 10 kilometers or higher could remain in the atmosphere for a year or more

and could cause global-scale cooling of several degrees and continued reductions in precipitation.

OTHER EFFECTS OF NUCLEAR WEAPONS EXPLOSIONS

31   *Nitrogen oxides* created by nuclear fireballs and carried up into the stratosphere could deplete the ozone layer that protects life on Earth from the sun's biologically damaging ultraviolet radiation [UV-B]. It is estimated that Northern Hemisphere stratospheric ozone could be reduced by as much as 20% to 30% within six months to a year. It is possible that "ozone holes," with reductions of perhaps 70%, could occur briefly. Under a clear atmosphere, ozone depletion would cause UV-B levels at the surface to increase, but UV-B would be blocked for a few weeks to months by smoke in the atmosphere. However, the smoke might also play a role in destroying ozone directly and in changing air temperatures and circulations patterns. It is possible that the ozone effects could be larger and longer-lasting.

32   Large amounts of *chemical pollutants* could be released into the atmosphere after a nuclear war, including carbon monoxide, hydrocarbons, nitrogen oxides, sulphur oxides, hydrochloric acid, heavy metals and a variety of other toxic chemicals. These could be directly or indirectly harmful to humans and many other organisms for periods of hours to years. Depending on a variety of factors, the acidity of rain could be increased by 10 times [a decrease of one pH unit] over current levels in polluted industrial areas for a month or more and cold acid fogs may form near the ground. Strong temperature inversions might trap toxic compounds from smouldering combustion in pockets near the ground in high population and industrial regions, causing significant health risks.

33   During the first few days after a major nuclear exchange, heavy local *fallout* would occur within the vicinity of explosions, especially downwind of missile silos and other "hardened" targets receiving surface bursts. Vast land areas of combatant countries would receive lethal doses from external gamma-radiation alone. Over longer periods, assuming no sheltering, more widespread but less intense global fallout would occur, leading to an increase in the incidence of cancers and other health hazards. Additional doses of radiation could be received from several sources, including lower-yield weapons and ingestion and inhalation of radioactive particles in food, water and air. Survivors would be more vulnerable than normal to radiation effects because of other injuries and environmental stresses and because of the probable lack of medical help.

34   It is possible, though considered unlikely by some analysts, that Northern Hemisphere doses could be increased by a few times if the civilian nuclear power system and military reactors were directly hit with nuclear weapons. In the Southern Hemisphere, local fallout would be important only within a few hundred kilometers downwind of any surface bursts and global fallout doses should be relatively insignificant.

35   If nuclear weapons are exploded high in the atmosphere, large areas of the Earth might be subjected to electromagnetic pulse [EMP], which can upset or destroy communications, power and electronic systems. The loss of these systems at the outset of a war could compound the confusion and chaos at a time when critical decisions are being made about the use of nuclear weapons.

SUMMARY OF BIOLOGICAL FINDINGS

36   The approach taken in evaluating the biological consequences of nuclear war was to assess the *vulnerability* of natural ecosystems and agricultural systems to the range of climatic and other disturbances estimated to be possible after a full-scale exchange of nuclear weapons.

37   Both natural ecosystems and agricultural systems are extremely vulnerable to the climatic and other stresses that could result from a major nuclear war. For perhaps thousands of millions of people not subjected to the direct effects of the war, the major post-war risk could be starvation resulting from the failure of crops, the loss of international trade in food and energy supplies and the depletion of food stores.

38   Substantial reductions in crop yields and even widespread crop failures are possible in response to stresses caused by post-war reductions in temperatures, precipitation and light levels. For example, temperature reductions could result in a shortening of the growing season simultaneously with an increase in the time needed for crops to mature; the combination of these two factors could result in insufficient time for crop maturation before the onset of killing cold temperatures. The occurrence of brief episodes of chilling or freezing tempera-tures at critical times within the growing season would also cause large crop losses.

39   Even in the absence of climatic disturbances, the global agricultural produc-tion and food distribution system is highly vulnerable to disruption after a nuclear war, because of the potential loss of international trade; food transportation, storage and distribution facilities; agricultural machinery; energy supplies; fertiliz-ers and pesticides; seed supplies and other subsidies to agriculture provided by humans.

40   In response to a combination of climatic and other factors, it is possible that food production in most of the Northern Hemisphere and much of the Southern Hemisphere could be virtually eliminated for at least a year after a large scale war.

41   Food exports probably would also cease because of the general disruption of world trade and because the major Northern Hemisphere grain-exporting countries are among the likely combatants. In the absence of agricultural produc-tion and food imports, the amount of food held in storage would become the critical-factor controlling human survival in the first months after the war. An analysis of world food stores indicates that, for much of the world's population,

stores would be depleted before agricultural productivity could be resumed. As a result, the majority of people on Earth face the risk of starvation in the aftermath of a large-scale nuclear war: for those in non-combatant nations, famine could be the major consequence.

42   The stresses placed on the agricultural system might result in greater demands being placed on natural ecosystems for food. However, even in the absence of post-war climatic changes, natural ecosystems could support only a small fraction of the current global population. Under optimal conditions, they could not replace agricultural systems as a source of sustenance for humans.

43   Natural ecosystems would, in any event, be highly vulnerable to the climate disturbances estimated to be possible after a nuclear war. The responses of ecosystems—ranging from arctic tundra to tropical rainforests and from deserts to ocean and freshwater ecosystems—would be highly variable. In general, temperature effects would dominate in land ecosystems in the Northern Hemisphere; reductions in sunlight would have the most impact on oceanic ecosystems; and precipitation changes would be most important for grasslands and Southern Hemisphere ecosystems. It is possible that the combination of these climatic factors could have a much greater impact than an analysis of their individual effects might suggest.

44   Biological systems are so sensitive to even relatively small changes in climatic conditions that devastating consequences could result from even the smaller climatic effects projected to be possible in the post-war environment. Thus, resolving some of the remaining uncertainties about the physical effects of a major nuclear exchange is not absolutely necessary in assessing the human impact of food shortages, since even the lower estimates of physical effects could be devastating to human populations on a large scale.

45   Longer-term climatic disturbances, if they were to occur, could be at least as important to human survival as the acute-period extremes of light and temperature reduction. Resolving uncertainties about reductions in precipitation is particularly important.

46   Global fallout is not likely to result in major ecological, agricultural or human effects. Local fallout, however, could have a serious impact on combatant and adjacent countries. Various estimates suggest that millions to perhaps hundreds of millions of people could die from the effects of lethal local fallout and it is likely that these direct effects would far exceed the indirect effects resulting from radiation damage to ecosystems. Agricultural and natural ecosystems would, however, be affected; large areas in the mid-latitudes of the Northern Hemisphere, including freshwater and marine ecosystems, could be radioactively contaminated for long periods of time. Radiation can be concentrated or "magnified" by biological systems, so that organisms at the higher levels of a food chain, including humans, could receive doses increased by factors of several thousand from eating contaminated food. It is unlikely that an efficient means of decontamination would be available in the post-nuclear war world.

UNCERTAINTIES

47   The problem of scientific uncertainty is a difficult and frustrating one for many non-scientists—who often tend to look to the scientific community for the "right" answers—but uncertainty cannot be avoided when large, complex systems like the Earth's atmosphere and oceans, agricultural systems and natural ecosystems and, not least, human society, are simultaneously involved in the analysis.

48   The uncertainties associated with the studies cited are of two basic kinds:

- Those resulting from human actions, e.g. assumptions about the nature of a nuclear war, including factors such as the numbers of weapons exploded; yields; targets; time of day and season and height of bursts.
- Those resulting from the incomplete state of knowledge concerning physical and biological processes and the inability to simulate them precisely in mathematical computer models.

49   The first sort of uncertainty is very difficult to reduce; clearly, the exact circumstances of a large-scale nuclear war are impossible to specify. Thus, although it is necessary to make some assumptions regarding the nature of the war, detailed war scenarios must be regarded as speculative. One approach, taken in many studies, is to base the analysis of environmental effects on a plausible circumstance or range of circumstances—for example, the injection of a given mass of smoke into the atmosphere. In essence, the approach is to say: If "X" occurs, then "Y" could be the consequence.

50   Uncertainties associated with the state of scientific knowledge often can be reduced with further research. However, short of actually doing the "experiment"—i.e., starting the war—many of the details will continue to be in doubt.

51   Two important points about uncertainty must be kept in mind. First, uncertainties go in both directions. If and when they are resolved, the outcome could be less serious than originally thought or it could be more serious. It follows that the presence of uncertainty does not mean that there is no problem. Uncertainty implies that the outcome cannot be predicted with complete confidence; it does not necessarily imply that the outcome won't be serious.

☐ Discovering Meaning and Technique

1. Why is it impossible to predict with certainty the effects of nuclear war?

2. Why would the effects of a nuclear bomb be different today from the effects of the bombs dropped on Hiroshima and Nagasaki?

3. According to recent analyses, which would have more impact on human society—the direct effect or the indirect effect of a nuclear war?

4. Summarize how a nuclear explosion would disturb the climate.

5. How did the studies calculate climatic changes?

6. How would the ozone layer be affected by released nitrogen oxides?

7. What would be the effects of chemical pollutants, of radioactive fallout, of electromagnetic pulse [EMP]?

8. After a nuclear explosion, why would starvation occur?

9. What two kinds of uncertainties complicate predictions about the results of a nuclear war?

10. Dotto first gives an overview of the results of nuclear war and then goes into more detail about the findings of new studies. Is this technique effective?

11. Does the author of this selection seem an advocate of nuclear weapons, an opponent, or neutral?

☐ Writing Suggestions

1. Write a scenario about the effects of a nuclear war on a person or people not killed outright by the fire and blast of an explosion.

2. After a nuclear war, do you think human society could ever recover to pre-war conditions?

3. Do you believe that humans will be foolish or desperate enough to drop another nuclear weapon?

4. What measures do you think should be taken to reduce the possibility of a nuclear explosion?

THE LETTERS

☐ JOY KOGAWA

1 There are only two letters in the grey cardboard folder. The first is a brief and emotionless statement that Grandma Kato, her niece's daughter, and my mother are the only ones in the immediate family to have survived. The second letter is an outpouring.

2   I remember Grandma Kato as thin and tough, not given to melodrama or overstatement of any kind. She was unbreakable. I felt she could endure all things and would survive any catastrophe. But I did not then understand what catastrophes were possible in human affairs.

3   Here, the ordinary Granton rain slides down wet and clean along the glass leaving a trail on the window like the Japanese writing on the thin blue-lined paper—straight down like a bead curtain of asterisks. The rain she describes is black, oily, thick, and strange.

4   "In the heat of the August sun," Grandma writes, "however much the effort to forget, there is no forgetfulness. As in a dream, I can still see the maggots crawling in the sockets of my niece's eyes. Her strong intelligent young son helped me move a bonsai tree that very morning. There is no forgetfulness."

5   When Nakayama-sensei reaches the end of the page, he stops reading and folds the letter as if he has decided to read no more. Aunt Emily begins to speak quietly, telling of a final letter from the Canadian missionary, Miss Best.

6   How often, I am wondering, did Grandma and Mother waken in those years with the unthinkable memories alive in their minds, the visible evidence of horror written on their skin, in their blood, carved in every mirror they passed, felt in every step they took. As a child I was told only that Mother and Grandma Kato were safe in Tokyo, visiting Grandma Kato's ailing mother.

7   "Someday, surely, they will return," Obasan used to say.

8   The two letters that reached us in Vancouver before all communication ceased due to the war told us that Mother and Grandma Kato had arrived safely in Japan and were staying with Grandma Kato's sister and her husband in their home near the Tokyo Gas Company. My great-grandmother was then seventy-nine and was not expected to live to be eighty but, happily, she had become so well that she had returned home from the hospital and was even able on occasion to leave the house.

9   Nakayama-sensei opens the letter again and holds it, reading silently. Then looking over to Stephen, he says, "It is better to speak, is it not?"

10   "They're dead now," Stephen says.

11   Sensei nods.

12   "Please read, Sensei," I whisper.

13   "Yes," Aunt Emily says. "They should know."

14   Sensei starts again at the beginning. The letter is dated simply 1949. It was sent, Sensei says, from somewhere in Nagasaki. There was no return address.

15   "Though it was a time of war," Grandma writes, "what happiness that January, 1945, to hear from my niece Setsuko, in Nagasaki." Setsuko's second child was due to be born within the month. In February, just as American air raids in Tokyo were intensifying, Mother went to help her cousin in Nagasaki. The baby was born three days after she arrived. Early in March, air raids and alarms were constant day and night in Tokyo. In spite of all the dangers of travel, Grandma Kato went to Nagasaki to be with my mother and to help with

the care of the new baby. The last day she spent with her mother and sister in Tokyo, she said they sat on the tatami and talked, remembering their childhood and the days they went chestnut-picking together. They parted with laughter. The following night, Grandma Kato's sister, their mother and her sister's husband died in the B-29 bombings of March 9, 1945.

16   From this point on, Grandma's letter becomes increasingly chaotic, and the details interspersed without chronological consistency. She and my mother, she writes, were unable to talk of all the things that happened. The horror would surely die sooner, they felt, if they refused to speak. But the silence and the constancy of the nightmare had become unbearable for Grandma and she hoped that by sharing them with her husband, she could be helped to extricate herself from the grip of the past.

17   "If these matters were sent away in this letter, perhaps they will depart a little from our souls," she writes. "For the burden of these words, forgive me."

18   Mother, for her part, continued her vigil of silence. She spoke with no one about her torment. She specifically requested that Stephen and I be spared the truth.

19   In all my high-school days, until we heard from Sensei that her grave had been found in Tokyo, I pictured her trapped in Japan by government regulations, or by an ailing grandmother. The letters I sent to the address in Tokyo were never answered or returned. I could not know that she and Grandma Kato had gone to Nagasaki to stay with Setsuko, her husband who was a dentist, and their two children, four-year-old Tomio and the new baby, Chieko.

20   The baby, Grandma writes, looked so much like me that she and my mother marvelled and often caught themselves calling her Naomi. With her widow's peak, her fat cheeks and pointed chin, she had a heart-shaped face like mine. Tomio, however, was not like Stephen at all. He was a sturdy child, extremely healthy and athletic, with a strong will like his father. He was fascinated by his new baby sister, sitting and watching her for hours as she slept or nursed. He made dolls for her. He helped to dress her. He loved to hold her in the bath, feeling her fingers holding his fingers tightly. He rocked her to sleep in his arms.

21   The weather was hot and humid that morning of August 9. The air-raid alerts had ended. Tomio and some neighborhood children had gone to the irrigation ditch to play and cool off as they sometimes did.

22   Shortly after eleven o'clock, Grandma Kato was preparing to make lunch. The baby was strapped to her back. She was bending over a bucket of water beside a large earthenware storage bin when a child in the street was heard shouting, "Look at the parachute!" A few seconds later, there was a sudden white flash, brighter than a bolt of lightning. She had no idea what could have exploded. It was as if the entire sky were swallowed up. A moment later she was hurled sideways by a blast. She had a sensation of floating tranquilly in a cool whiteness high above the earth. When she regained consciousness, she

was slumped forward in a sitting position in the water bin. She gradually became aware of the moisture, an intolerable heat, blood, a mountain of debris and her niece's weak voice sounding at first distant, calling the names of her children. Then she could hear the other sounds—the far-away shouting. Around her, a thick dust made breathing difficult. Chieko was still strapped to her back, but made no sound. She was alive but unconscious.

23   It took Grandma a long time to claw her way out of the wreckage. When she emerged, it was into an eerie twilight formed of heavy dust and smoke that blotted out the sun. What she saw was incomprehensible. Almost all the buildings were flattened or in flames for as far as she could see. The landmarks were gone. Tall columns of fire rose through the haze and everywhere the dying and the wounded crawled, fled, stumbled like ghosts among the ruins. Voices screamed, calling the names of children, fathers, mothers, calling for help, calling for water.

24   Beneath some wreckage, she saw first the broken arm, then the writhing body of her niece, her head bent back, her hair singed, both her eye sockets blown out. In a weak and delirious voice, she was calling Tomio. Grandma Kato touched her niece's leg and the skin peeled off and stuck to the palm of her hand.

25   It isn't clear from the letter but at some point she came across Tomio, his legs pumping steadily up and down as he stood in one spot not knowing where to go. She gathered him in her arms. He was remarkably intact, his skin unburned.

26   She had no idea where Mother was, but with the two children, she began making her way towards the air-raid shelter. All around her people one after another collapsed and died, crying for water. One old man no longer able to keep moving lay on the ground holding up a dead baby and crying, "Save the children. Leave the old." No one took the dead child from his outstretched hands. Men, women, in many cases indistinguishable by sex, hairless, half-clothed, hobbled past. Skin hung from their bodies like tattered rags. One man held his bowels in with the stump of one hand. A child whom Grandma Kato recognized lay on the ground asking for help. She stopped and told him she would return as soon as she could. A woman she knew was begging for someone to help her lift the burning beam beneath which her children were trapped. The woman's children were friends of Tomio's. Grandma was loath to walk past, but with the two children, she could do no more and kept going. At no point does Grandma Kato mention the injuries she herself must have sustained.

27   Nearing the shelter, Grandma could see through the greyness that the entrance was clogged with dead bodies. She remembered then that her niece's father-in-law lived on a farm on the hillside, and she began making her way back through the burning city towards the river she would have to cross. The water, red with blood, was a raft of corpses. Farther upstream, the bridge was twisted like noodles. Eventually she came to a spot where she was able to

cross and, still carrying the two children, Grandma Kato made her way up the hillside.

28   After wandering for some time, she found a wooden water pipe dribbling a steady stream. She held Tomio's mouth to it and allowed him to drink as much as he wished though she had heard that too much water was not good. She unstrapped the still unconscious baby from her back. Exhausted, she drank from the pipe, and gathering the two children in her arms, she looked out at the burning city and lapsed into a sleep so deep she believed she was unconscious.

29   When she awakened, she was in the home of her niece's relatives and the baby was being fed barley water. The little boy was nowhere.

30   Almost immediately, Grandma set off to look for the child. Next day she returned to the area of her niece's home and every day thereafter she looked for Mother and the lost boy, checking the lists of the dead, looking over the unclaimed corpses. She discovered that her niece's husband was among the dead.

31   One evening when she had given up the search for the day, she sat down beside a naked woman she'd seen earlier who was aimlessly chipping wood to make a pyre on which to cremate a dead baby. The woman was utterly disfigured. Her nose and one cheek were almost gone. Great wounds and pustules covered her entire face and body. She was completely bald. She sat in a cloud of flies and maggots wriggled among her wounds. As Grandma watched her, the woman gave her a vacant gaze, then let out a cry. It was my mother.

32   The little boy was never found. Mother was taken to a hospital and was expected to die, but she survived. During one night she vomited yellow fluid and passed a great deal of blood. For a long time—Grandma does not say how long—Mother wore bandages on her face. When they were removed, Mother felt her face with her fingers, then asked for a cloth mask. Thereafter she would not take off her mask from morning to night.

33   "At this moment," Grandma writes, "we are preparing to visit Chieko-chan in the hospital." Chieko, four years old in 1949, waited daily for their visit, standing in the hospital corridor, tubes from her wrist attached to a bottle that was hung above her. A small bald-headed girl. She was dying of leukemia.

34   "There may not be many more days," Grandma concludes.

35   After this, what could have happened? Did they leave the relatives in Nagasaki? Where and how did they survive?

36   When Sensei is finished reading, he folds and unfolds the letter, nodding his head slowly.

37   I put my hands around the teapot, feeling its round warmth against my palms. My skin feels hungry for warmth, for flesh. Grandma mentioned in her letter that she saw one woman cradling a hot-water bottle as if it were a baby.

38   Sensei places the letter back in the cardboard folder and closes it with the short red string around the tab.

39   "That there is brokenness," he says quietly. "That this world is brokenness."

But within brokenness is the unbreakable name. How the whole earth groans till Love returns."

40   I stand up abruptly and leave the room, going into the kitchen for some more hot water. When I return, Sensei is sitting with his face in his hands.

41   Stephen is staring at the floor, his body hunched forward motionless. He glances up at me then looks away swiftly. I sit on a stool beside him and try to concentrate on what is being said. I can hear Aunt Emily telling us about Mother's grave. Then Nakayama-sensei stands and begins to say the Lord's Prayer under his breath. "And forgive us our trespasses—forgive us our trespasses—" he repeats, sighing deeply, "as we forgive others. . . ." He lifts his head, looking upwards. "We are powerless to forgive unless we first are forgiven. It is a high calling my friends—the calling to forgive. But no person, no people is innocent. Therefore we must forgive one another."

42   I am not thinking of forgiveness. The sound of Sensei's voice grows as indistinct as the hum of distant traffic. Gradually the room grows still and it is as if I am back with Uncle again, listening and listening to the silent earth and the silent sky as I have done all my life.

43   I close my eyes.

44   Mother. I am listening. Assist me to hear you.

☐ Discovering Meaning and Technique

1. Because this selection is part of a novel, characters are not identified as they otherwise would have been. Can you, however, by careful reading identify the narrator and most of the family relationships?

2. Explain the narrator's statement in paragraph 2: "But I did not then understand what catastrophes were possible in human affairs."

3. What is the "black, oily, thick, and strange" rain that the grandmother describes in paragraph 3?

4. As a child, what was the narrator told had happened to her mother?

5. The letter from the grandmother was sent in what year? From what place?

6. How did the grandmother hope "to extricate herself from the grip of the past?" In contrast, how did the mother cope?

7. What was the fate of the niece, the niece's husband, Tomio, Chieko, the narrator's mother, Grandma Kato?

☐ **Writing Suggestions**

1. Can there ever be a war that does not affect the innocent?

2. In the library, research the decision to drop the bomb on Nagasaki. Write a report about the decision.

3. Write a story from the point of view of Tomio, tracing his experiences after he was separated from his grandmother.

4. Do you think the fear of nuclear weapons has deterred war?

5. Should the United States have used a nuclear bomb in the Vietnam conflict?

THE PHOTOTROPIC WOMAN

☐ ANNABEL THOMAS

¹ The woman was rolled up in a woolen blanket. It covered her body and even her head so that her world was warm and soft as an unborn's. When the alarm went off, she got out of bed and poked up the stove.

²   She put water to heat and when it was steaming she stripped to the waist and washed in the basin. She pulled a sweater over her head and plaited up her hair. While she drank a mug of strong black tea, she read the survival book.

³   After she put the shack in order, the woman took a coil of rope and a box of candles and walked up the sun-speckled path through the locust thicket between the green mossed rocks big as sheep sheds. She had worn the path carrying and dragging the provisions the book recommended to the cave.

⁴   The cave smelt of damp sandstone and of dust and still air. She dropped the rope beside the boxes of canned goods and was counting the candles when she heard a noise like hundreds of nine pins falling onto a wooden floor. When she turned round she saw dirt and rock pouring into the mouth of the cave. Before she could move toward it, the opening was completely closed and she stood coughing in blackness.

⁵   The woman felt her way to the boxes and found the coal oil lantern and the matches. When the wick caught, the light reflected from a hundred rock surfaces overhead and around the edges while the middle was murky with floating dust. It was like standing inside a gem.

⁶   She took a pickax and dug where the entrance had been. She kept digging until she was too tired to dig any more.

⁷   "There's no use to that," the woman said.

⁸   In fact she wondered if she should try to get out at all, at least right away. Had she seen a flash of light just before the dirt came down? The woman stood still a long time thinking what she should do.

9   She began by pacing off the room. It was twenty by fifteen feet. Then she felt the roof, tracing it back to where it closed down like a clamshell.

10   She took the pickax and pried gently where the roof joined the floor. As she widened a crack in the stone she felt air rush through. She worked slowly and hesitantly, half afraid of digging out into poisoned air.

11   When the hole was large enough, she took the lantern and crawled into the opening. Working forward on her belly, she wriggled down through mud thick as grease. Her hair became caked and her clothes clogged with it. It went up her sleeves and down into her shoes.

12   The tunnel began to spiral like a corkscrew and to taper so that she got stuck sometimes, then squirmed loose and so at last came out of the tunnel onto the floor of a large room.

13   Wherever she shined the light she saw pillars with rock hanging from them in folds like cloth. She couldn't see the top of the room. She circled the walls. There was no way out except the way she'd come in.

14   Back in the upper room, she scooped out a trench with the pickax, laid large flat stones over the trench and closed the cracks with pebbles and mud. At the higher end she built a chimney from a small hollow tree limb. At the lower end she placed a handful of shredded bark and struck a match to it. She added twigs, then larger sticks from the supply of squaw wood she had gathered and stored in the cave. She kept the fire small. Every move she made came straight out of the survival book. She called up the pages in her mind's eye, then did what they said. When the fire burned steadily, she cooked soup.

15   Working and resting, then working again, the woman slowly enlarged the tunnel, hacking out hand holds and foot holds until she could pass up and down easily. At the far end of the lower room she found a trickle of water spreading thin and soundless over the face of the rock. She set a bucket to catch it where it dripped off a projection. By feeling her pulse, she calculated the minutes it took for the dripping water to fill the bucket. Each time she judged twenty-four hours had gone by she made a mark on the cave wall with a piece of sandstone. One day she totaled up the marks. She had been in the cave somewhat over twelve days.

16   As time passed, the woman gradually made herself a proper home in the upper room. She arranged the boxes for chairs and a table, cooked good meals on the fireplace she had built and after she had eaten, spread a blanket over the warm stones and slept.

17   She wondered what was going on outside. Was the world burnt to ashes? Were scarred people picking about through swelling corpses, twisted metal, broken glass? Or was everything as it had been and the sun shining calm and warm down through the leaves spotting the path. The thought of the sun gave her heart a twist as if a coal of fire had touched her in the breast.

18   Below the water trickle in the lower room, the woman discovered a small underground pool in a rock basin.

19   "The old fishing hole," she said for in the pool were strange white fish.

20   Instead of swimming away from her, they froze in the water when she reached for them. She seined them out easily with her skirt. They were three or four inches long. On either side of their heads, she found bulges covered with skin where the eyes had been.

21   She slit the fish open, gutted them and pinned them with thorns to a smooth log which she propped close to the fire. The book had told how.

22   "Survival," the woman said to the fish. "Mine, not yours."

23   On one of her fishing trips, she noticed, in a small recess filled with boulders on the far side of the pool, what appeared to be a piece of cloth caught beneath the bottom stone. It was of a course weave like burlap. She couldn't pull it free. Every day she passed by it she felt of the cloth.

24   "What is it?" she said.

25   Finally she took along the pickax and pried the boulders loose, rolling them off, one by one, across the floor. She worked gingerly, afraid of starting a cave-in and burying herself. As each boulder fell away, more of the cloth showed until she could see a large bundle wedged into a depression. She bent forward and lifted away the final stone, then started back, giving a little shriek.

26   "God in heaven," she said. "It's an Indian!"

27   "He won't scalp you," she added a moment later, peering down. "He's been dead so long the meat's gone dry on his bones."

28   Although the long hair was much as it had been in life, the skin was blackish and hard and part of the skull was bare. The fiber blanket lay in patches over the rib cage. Beside the corpse was a small piece of gourd and a bundle of reeds tied together with grass.

29   "Came in out of a storm," the woman said, "and here he is still, poor bastard."

30   Leaning down to touch the Indian's blanket, the woman saw that the recess was a crawl way into yet another room.

31   She called the upper cave, "Home," and the second chamber, "the Indian Room." The third, the new one, became, "the Bat Room." The third room was fair sized though not so big nor so beautiful as the Indian Room. When the woman first heard the bats squeaking from a great distance overhead, she set the lantern on a rock and dug out handholds and footholds in the wall with a can lid. Following the method described in the survival book, she slapped the hand grips first and listened to hear if they sounded loose or cracked before going up carefully. She eased her foot into the vertical slits, twisting her ankle sideways, slipping in her toe, then straightening the ankle.

32   Now and then she paused in her climb to light a candle and have a look around. Once she saw a cave cricket, palest white and long-legged, creeping up the rock. Later she came upon the disintegrating body of a millipede with a white fungus encasing it like a shroud.

33   Pulling herself onto a ledge, she suddenly clapped her hands over her

ears to shut out what sounded like the roaring of the biggest airplane motor in the world. Stretching her candle up at arm's length, she saw the bats, very high up, in a vast smoky cloud.

34   The ledge where she stood held a pool of bat droppings, a wide brown lake smelling of ammonia. As the candle light slid across it she saw it move. She bent over, shining the light full on it. It was seething with living creatures. Tens of thousands of beetles, flat worms, snails, millipedes, and mites were swimming on the surface or crawling on the bottom of the guano. All of them were colorless and all of them were blind.

35   Where the bats came in, she couldn't tell. She felt no air and saw no light. When the rock of the walls grew too hard to dig she had to climb back down. She never came in sight of the ceiling.

36   Next she explored a number of small passageways opening off the Bat Room. Most dead-ended, choked with fallen rock. The rest opened onto horrifying drops. One descended and became an underground stream which she waded until the roof closed down to the water. Then she turned back.

37   The woman now believed that she had examined every room and passageway accessible to her and that there was no way out of the cave.

38   She settled into a routine of fishing, cooking, eating, and sleeping. Time flowed on, sluggish and slow. She hung in it, drowsily.

39   But she dreamed strange dreams. And all her dreams were about light. At first she couldn't remember them but woke with only the imprint of brightness on her eyes like an aftertaste on the tongue.

40   Later, she recalled scenes in which she lay doubled inside a giant egg, walled away from the light. As she beat on the shell, stretching toward the light, she could feel the light outside straining toward her. At last, with a cracking like a mighty explosion, she straightened her arms and legs sending the shell into bits. As she thrust forth into hot brightness, she looked to see if it were the sun or the flash of an explosion that beat upon her but she never found out.

41   When the coal oil was gone and the woman began to use the candles more and more sparingly, the shape of day and night blurred and faded from her life. Her meals became irregular. She ate as often as she felt hungry. Sometimes she forgot to eat at all for long stretches. She let the bucket overflow or forgot to mark on the wall so often that she lost all track of how long she had been in the cave.

42   Once, as she opened a can by candlelight, she lifted the lid and looked at her reflection in the shiny tin circle.

43   She saw that her face and arms had grown pasty. Her clothes were colorless from dirt and wear. She had broken her glasses when she climbed the wall of the Bat Room so that she peered at herself through eyes slightly out of focus. The skin hung loose on her cheeks and drew taut across the sharp bridge of her nose. Her hair, trailing loose on her shoulders, was pale with dust.

44   The candle sputtered, brightened, then, burned to its end, died. She reached for another. The candles rattled against one another in the box. So few left? Her hands shook, counting them. How many more hours of light? Not many. Then the dark.

45   As the woman let the candles fall from her fingers, a strange restlessness came upon her. She moved to the cave mouth and felt of the mass of dirt and rock which covered it. She caught up the pickax and dug until she couldn't lift it for another stroke.

46   After that she often counted the candles and as often dug at the entrance. Blisters broke on her hands and bled. Sweat dripped off her chin. Her body burned. It was as if she felt the light through the tons of dirt over her head, pulling her toward it whether she wanted to go or not. She dug until her arm went numb. Then she threw herself on the floor and slept. When she woke, she dug again.

47   Sometimes she dropped the pickax and fell to tearing at the dirt and rocks with her fingers. Afterwards she cleaned her hands and wrapped them in strips she tore from her skirt.

48   At last she left off digging and circled the Indian Room and the Bat Room each in turn again and again, feeling of the walls, climbing where she could gouge out a hand and foothold, going as far up as she was able, then dropping back.

49   Next she re-examined each of the passageways at the end of the Bat Room. One passage ended in a shallow pit carved into the stone with walls round like a chimney and stretching up out of sight. Down this chimney, it seemed to the woman, there poured like a steady rain a strange dark light.

50   She placed her back against one wall of the chimney and lifted both feet onto the wall opposite. She pressed a hand against the rock on either side of her buttocks and so levered her body off the wall. She inched her way up, alternately pressing her feet against one wall and her back against the other. Soon the chimney narrowed so that she was forced to use her knees instead of her feet and after a time she began to slip.

51   She slid down, caught herself, and started up once more. Her back and knees were raw and bleeding. The portions of her sweater and skirt covering them had worn away. She slipped again, reached out her hands to catch herself, tried to hold onto the sides of the pit, could not, and fell heavily, shot down like a stone, and hit the cave floor with a yell loud enough to wake the dead Indian.

52   When she tried to stand, the woman's ankle wouldn't bear her weight. It took her a long time to drag herself back to the Home Chamber. Once there, she mixed a poultice of mud and spread it on the ankle from the middle of the calf to the instep. Gradually it hardened into a cast.

53   The woman lay wrapped in her blanket on the warm stones while, slowly, her bruises and scrapes began to heal. She had used to talk to herself aloud a

good part of the time. Now, she fell deeper and deeper into silence until her thoughts lost the shape of words and shot through her brain in strange flashes of feeling and impulse.

54   In her dreams she repeated the accident and repeated it, always waking with the sensation of having been, in falling, drenched with light. She slept, woke, ate, slept again. Her ankle ached less, then not at all. When she judged enough time had passed, the woman took a small stone and pounded the mud cast gently so that it cracked and fell away. She walked up and down the home cave until her ankle grew strong.

55   When she was able to return to the Indian Room and the Bat Room, she again explored the walls and passages, ending at last with the underground river. She waded the stream to the point where the overhead rocks narrowed down to touch the water. The river deepened as the roof came down so that she stood in water to her armpits.

56   She filled her lungs and swam downstream under the rocks. Feeling with her fingers that the roof still touched the water and still touched and still touched, she swam back.

57   She tried again. Then again. Before each try she breathed in and out rapidly and so was able to stay under water longer. With each attempt she went further until, when she felt the roof begin to rise, she pushed on and broke from the water into a narrow tunnel with air at the top and headroom enough to stand upright.

58   Back in the Home Chamber, the woman took the rope into her lap. She ran a few feet of its cold damp length through her fingers. The day she had carried it to the cave, it had been warm from the sun. She tore a strip from the bottom of her blanket and tied it to the rope. She added another strip and another until she had tied on the whole of the blanket.

59   At the river, she knotted one end of the rope around her waist and looped the other over a rock projection. Wading slowly downstream, she felt a slight push of current at the backs of her legs. Her thigh touched a fish hanging still in the water.

60   Swimming to the spot where she had stood before, she walked on in waist-high water. She could reach out her hands and touch both walls of the tunnel that held the river. The roof hung a few feet above her.

61   The woman moved on in blackness, trailing the rope. When she rubbed her eyes she saw pale flashes far back inside her head.

62   Several yards beyond the point where she'd turned back before, she began to feel the roof closing rapidly down again, grazing her head so that she must stoop to go forward. When her feet lost touch with the bottom she began to swim.

63   The water was numbing cold. Her clothes hung on her like the metal plates of a suit of armor. Only her head was above water and still the roof brushed her hair and she felt it closing, closing.

64   The woman took several quick, deep breaths, filled her lungs, and dove down through the water. Leveling off, she shot ahead rapidly, keeping a steady forward push with arms and legs, hands and feet. She continued on for the length of her body, then her body's length again. And again. As she swam she waited for the tug at her waist that would tell her she had reached the rope's end, the point of no return. When it came, she slipped the knot and swam out of the rope, leaving it to curl in the water behind her.

65   Her lungs began to ache in earnest. The blood, pounding behind her eyes, filled her head with glances of bright color. Stubbornly she kept up her steady breast stroke, her frog kick, until the expanding and contracting of her muscles became the structure of her consciousness.

66   She tried to remember her life outside the cave but she could not. She tried to recall the details of her days in the Home Chamber, the Indian and the Bat Rooms but they were washed from her brain leaving only the sensation of inward scalding light creating, destroying her in its struggle to be born.

☐ Discovering Meaning and Technique

1. What sealed the opening to the cave?

2. Make a sketch of the cave, showing its relation to the other rooms.

3. How did the woman calculate time?

4. Why do the fish have no eyes?

5. Does the author dwell primarily on facts about the woman's experiences or on her feelings?

6. What do the woman's dreams tell about her feelings?

7. A problem with telling a story from one character's point of view is the difficulty of conveying what the character looks like: a person cannot normally see himself or herself. How does Thomas convey information about the woman's appearance?

8. What is the meaning of the title?

9. When and why does the woman get panicky about getting out of the cave?

10. What do you think the story means?

☐ Writing Suggestions

1. In the event of a nuclear attack, do you think survivalist techniques would be effective?

2. Could you live in a cave away from all natural light for an extended period of time?

3. If you knew ahead of time that you would be confined, describe what you would take with you.

4. Write a survivalist manual for a person lost in a cave or some other place.

5. Write a story that explains the presence of the Indian's body in the cave.

The Future

■ ■ ■

A CHOICE OF CATASTROPHES

☐ **ISAAC ASIMOV**

1 If one decides the world has a beginning, then surely it must have an ending, too. Generally, if it is thought the world began not very long ago, it is natural to suppose it should come to an end not very long from now.

2   The somber mythology of the Norsemen saw an end to the world that was not to be long delayed, for instance. There would come Ragnarok, the Twilight of the Gods, when the gods and heroes would march out to meet their deadly enemies, the giants and monsters, in the last climactic battle that would destroy the world.

3   Similarly, the Bible, which tells of the beginning of the heaven and the earth in the first book of the Old Testament, speaks of the end, too, in Revelation, the last book of the New Testament. It tells of a climactic battle at Armageddon and a final Day of Judgment.

4   The Bible does not give the actual time of the Day of Judgment but the early Christians appear to have expected it to come soon since the Savior had appeared and completed His mission. The end did not come, but in each generation there were those who proclaimed it imminent.

5   The year 1000, when it came, brought panic to some parts of Christendom, for Christians read into the Revelation reference to the thousand years that preceded the end the thousand years that had just passed. When the end did not come, other calculations were made—over and over.

6   In the 1830s, a New York farmer, William Miller, calculated the end would come in 1843, and many people sold all they had, donned white robes, and waited on hilltops. Nothing happened, but the movement gave rise to the Adventists, who still wait.

7   In 1879, Jehovah's Witnesses came into being as an offshoot of the Adventists and they waited for an imminent end. They still wait. They are still sure it is imminent.

8   Others have expected more secular ends. Comets have always been feared as omens of disaster and destruction and, as late as 1910, when Halley's Comet made its most recent appearance, uncounted numbers feared that Earth would

be destroyed in its passing. Just a few years ago, there were foolish irrationalists who predicted that the passing of the small planetoid, Icarus, would cause California to fall into the Pacific Ocean.

9   Nothing ever happens, but those who wait for the end to come are never discouraged but are always ready with a new prediction.

10   What, then can we say about catastrophe? With the view of the world as science has given it to us these last three centuries, can we laugh and say that the world will not, and cannot, come to an end?

11   No, for science treats of the beginning of planets and suns and of the whole Universe and, therefore, must treat of the end as well. And, indeed, there are ways in which the whole Universe might be considered as ending and that would mean the end of its component parts, of the Sun, of the Earth, of life upon the Earth (assuming that these have not ended already long before the Universe did).

12   For instance, we know that the Universe is expanding and that it may do so forever. As it expands, the individual stars of which it is composed consume their fuel and finally can radiate no more. The birth of new stars is no longer possible when all the hydrogen (the basic fuel in the Universe) is consumed. The Universe will then have to run down, and if the end for us has not come before, it will surely come then. Still, the general rundown of the Universe will not happen for many trillions of years and it therefore need not concern us. There are other catastrophes, less all-embracing, but ones that will serve to end us, that will come before then.

13   Accompanying the expansion of the Universe is the possibility of a change in its fundamental laws. Some scientists speculate, for instance, that the force of gravity is slowly weakening as the Universe expands. This has the potential of catastrophe for us except that, even if gravity does weaken, or if other such changes take place (and this has not yet been demonstrated), it would take a billion or more years for the effect to become noticeable, let alone catastrophic.

14   But then, the Universe need not expand forever. Under certain conditions (and the astronomers are not certain whether those conditions are actually met or not) the expansion would be slowing continually and will eventually come to a halt. The Universe would then very gradually begin to contract again, contracting faster and faster—and winding up as it does so.

15   This, however, does not give us a new lease on life, for a contracting Universe pushes radiation ahead of itself into a more and more energetic form that would be fatal to all life. However, even if the Universe does enter into a contraction cycle, that will not happen for perhaps 25 billion years and there again we are in no immediate danger.

16   It may be, too, that superimposed on the general expansion of the Universe are local contractions brought about by violent events in the history of giant stars and giant clusters of stars. These contractions may force matter together so densely as to form "black holes" from which nothing can emerge. It may be

that black holes already exist and that they continually grow and encroach on matter until everything is gone.

17   When will a black hole engulf us? That depends on where one is located with respect to us. Are we on a collision orbit with one? Astronomers have detected a few objects they suspect might be large Sun-sized black holes, but they are so far away that again possible collisions must be billions of years away at the very least.

18   Some astronomers suspect that black holes can come in all sizes, down to very thin ones no larger than atoms. There is even a suggestion that the 1908 incident in Siberia in which a whole forest was leveled, without any signs of a meteorite strike, was the result of the passage of such a mini-black hole into Siberia, through the body of the Earth, and out into the Atlantic Ocean.

19   Black holes are difficult to detect. Might there be one small enough and far enough not to detect at the moment, yet large enough and near enough to destroy our Earth on collision, say, a thousand years from now?

20   Here, however, we are talking of impalpables. Astronomers may speculate that small black holes exist, but they have detected none and they may not exist. And if they do exist there is no way of knowing whether any are on the outskirts of our Solar system or not—and there is no reason, whatever, to think any are. We can only dismiss the possibility with a fatalistic shrug and a hope that, as we learn more, we can better study the nature of surrounding space and see what dangers lurk there.

21 If we assume that events outside the Solar system involve only catastrophes that can't affect us for many billions of years, or whose coming is utterly unpredictable, then we are left to wonder whether anything can bring us to a general end that involves our Solar system only.

22   To begin with, there's our Sun. If we are content to admit the Universe won't last forever, surely our Sun won't. In fact, our Sun should last a far shorter period of time than the Universe does. The Sun has now been shining at the expense of its hydrogen fuel for some 5 billion years or so. Eventually, that fuel will run sufficiently low to bring about changes in the Solar interior that will cause the Sun to swell up into a red giant. When that time comes, the Earth will heat up to the point where life will not be possible upon it.

23   This, however, is not expected to happen for some 8 billion years and by that time humankind or its descendants (if they have not been killed off by some other prior catastrophe) may have moved on to other, younger stars.

24   Even if the Sun remains in its present form, might there not be minor variations, insignificant to the Sun itself, but deadly to the Earth? Might there be changes in the Sun's spot cycle or in its interior that will cause it to warm slightly or cool slightly—*slightly,* but enough to boil our oceans, or freeze them, and in either case end life on our planet?

25   This is not likely. The geological record (and the fossil record, too) would

indicate that the Sun has been fairly stable for billions of years and it ought, therefore, to be stable for billions more.

26   What about the rest of the Solar system? Is any part of it going to crash into us?

27   Velikovsky and his followers believe that in the recent past, only 3,500 years ago, Venus, Earth, and Mars kept undergoing near collisions. Rational astronomers find it impossible to take this seriously. There is every indication that the Solar system is dynamically stable, that the major planets have kept to their orbits for indefinite millions of years in the past and will continue to do so for indefinite millions of years in the future.

28   But the Solar system is filled with debris; with minor planets (asteroids) of all sizes, from a few that are hundreds of miles across to many thousands that are only a few miles or even a few hundred yards across. There are uncounted particles ranging in size from a few feet across down to microscopic bits of dust. Some of these minor bodies are close at hand. There are asteroids a mile or two across that have orbits that can occasionally place those asteroids within a few million miles of Earth. And there must be bodies that are smaller still that can come closer—that can even collide with us.

29   Tiny micrometeoroids are indeed constantly colliding with Earth by the millions and burning up in our atmosphere (the larger ones visible as "shooting stars"). Particularly large meteoroids, from several inches to several feet across, can survive to strike the earth as "meteorites" and these can do some damage if they score a direct hit on human beings or their works.

30   The larger the meteoroids the more damage they do, and in primordial times, there was a large number of quite large bodies. The craters on the Moon, on Mars, on Mercury, on the satellites of Mars and Jupiter were caused by collisions with sizable bodies. As a result, almost all of them have been swept up and interplanetary space is almost clean.

31   Almost, but not quite. A few sizable bodies remain. One left a crater in Arizona over half a mile across and it was formed, perhaps, ten thousand years ago. There are signs of other craters, some even larger, formed longer ago. Nowadays, the collision of a meteoroid capable of forming such a crater might wipe out a city if it happened to follow a course of unfortunate accuracy. A similar meteoroid striking the ocean might cause a splash that would devastate the coastlines of the world with towering waves of water.

32   What are the chances that there will be a devastating meteoroid strike in the near future? How can we say? On the one hand, there are fewer such bodies in space now than ever before, since every one that strikes is one less. On the other hand, there is a much greater chance of a meteoroid doing damage on our teeming, artifact-covered Earth now than there was of affecting our much emptier Earth of only a few centuries ago.

33   All we can say is that a strke *may* come tomorrow and *may* have a most unfortunate aim, but it is more likely that it may not come for a long time. The

chances are that really bad strikes come tens of thousands of years apart, and perhaps before the next one comes the space effect will have reached the point where there will be a "meteoroid watch" in near space as there is now an iceberg watch in the North Atlantic.

34   We might compound the disaster by imagining that the meteoroid strike is that of an antimatter object. Antimatter is composed of particles of a nature opposite to those composing ourselves and the Earth. Antimatter combines instantaneously with matter to give rise to a release of energy (including radioactive radiation) about a hundred times as great, size for size, as that of the warhead of a nuclear bomb. A small piece of antimatter would, therefore, do as much damage as a much larger piece of ordinary matter. (Some have speculated that the great 1908 Siberian strike was caused by a small bit of antimatter.)

35   Antimatter can exist and some astronomers suspect that there may be whole universes built of it or, within our own Universe, whole galaxies of it. However, it seems quite certain that our own Solar system, indeed our entire Galaxy, is made up of ordinary matter only. Any antimatter objects of any size would have had to wander in from other galaxies at the least and that is as unlikely, and as unpredictable, as a collision with a small black hole.

36 Suppose, then, we contract our view further and consider the Earth alone. Is there any chance it might, for some reason, explode, say, or that its axis may tip over?

37   Virtually none. The Earth has existed stably in pretty much its present form for over four billion years, and there is no reason it should not exist so for billions of years more if it is left to itself. As for the tipping of the axis, something called the law of conservation of angular momentum makes that so unlikely we need not concern ourselves with it.

38   The conservation of angular momentum does not, however, prevent some of the turning effect from being shifted from the Earth to the Moon. This means that the Moon is very slowly drifting away from us and the Earth's rotation is very gradually growing slower. As the day lengthens, temperature differences between day and night and between winter and summer would grow more extreme until Earth becomes an unfit abode for life. This change is so slow, however, that it will take many millions of years before the change will be significant.

39   The surface of the Earth moves, to be sure. It is made up of a number of large plates and some smaller ones, which slowly shift. Since the plates are in contact, pressure of one against another may crumple one or both plates and produce mountains; or cause one plate to pass under another and produce an ocean deep. In other places, plates move apart and hot material from below wells up.

40   As a result of these movements, continents can, in the long run, drift together

to form a single huge land mass or, having formed one, break apart again. These enormous changes, however, take place so slowly that it is some millions of years before significant alterations in the position of the continents would be detected, and the changes are therefore not catastrophic.

41   At the boundaries of the plates, there are minor instabilities—ones that are insignificant on a planetary scale but very important on a human scale. It is along those boundaries that volcanoes are formed and that earthquakes take place.

42   Ordinarily, volcanic eruptions and earthquake tremors occur only at considerable intervals in any one part of the world, and while they can cause loss of life and destruction of property, the damage is usually local and temporary, and humankind has been living with such events all its existence. But what if there are some effects that can activate this instability and cause the poor Earth to shake badly all over while all the volcanoes let loose with a roar?

43   We don't know of anything that would cause this.

44   There are speculations that the Earth might be affected by the Solar wind (particles that shoot out of the Sun in all directions, streaming outward through the planetary system) and that the Solar wind is, in turn, possibly affected by tidal effects in the Sun that are caused by the planets. Some planetary configurations can cause unusually large tidal effects, leading to a sharp rise, possibly, in the Solar wind. If some fault is on the point of yielding suddenly, to cause a disastrous earthquake, the changes brought on by the Solar wind may just nudge it over the top so that, in the end, earthquakes and volcanic eruptions, too, may be caused by planetary configurations.

45   However, there are a great many if's in this conjecture and even if all the if's come to pass, the result would be a local and temporary disaster of a kind that would happen at some other time, perhaps not long after, even if the fault were not nudged.

46 What about catastrophes that affect the oceans and atmosphere of Earth rather than its solid body? What about changes in climate?

47   For instance, every quarter of a billion years, the Earth seems to undergo a period of recurrent ice ages, where water in large quantities freezes, then melts, and where huge glaciers advance for thousands of years then retreat for thousands of years. Scientists have speculated on the causes of these periods but have as yet reached no consensus. We are in such a stage now and, over the last million years, the glaciers have advanced and retreated four times.

48   Are the ice ages over? Perhaps not. The glaciers may someday advance a fifth time. We have survived the previous four advances, but human beings were then few in number and were tribal hunters who could move with the slow advance or retreat of the ice. Now we exist by the billions and are tied to the land by our farms, mines, and cities. A fifth advance would be a catastrophe.

49   However, the interval between the glacier advances (under natural condi-

tions) is tens, even hundreds, of thousands of years, and by the time the glaciers come again we may have developed the kind of climate control that would prevent it.

50 Such climate control might also prevent the reverse possibility—that the Earth would grow a little warmer and that the glaciers that still exist in Antarctica and Greenland would melt. This would raise the sea level two hundred feet and drown all the rich and populated coasts of the world.

51 A more subtle danger involves the cosmic-ray particles that steadily bombard the Earth and that originate from the star explosions and other violent events here and there in the Universe. Those particles, electrically charged and highly energetic, are the source of both hope and danger. In smashing through living things, the cosmic rays produce mutations. Most mutations are harmful and can drive individual life forms and even whole species to death and extinction; but some are useful and these form the drive that keeps evolution going.

52 If the incidence of cosmic rays increases, then the rate of mutation will go up; and the preponderance of harmful mutations will drown the few good ones so that there will be what is called a "great dying," when whole groups of species suddenly disappear.

53 Much of the cosmic rays are warded off and turned aside by Earth's magnetic field, which thus keeps the incidence of particles to less-than-harmful levels. This magnetic field waxes and wanes irregularly for reasons we don't understand, however. At the present moment, the magnetic field is waning, and in a couple of thousand years it may pass through a period of centuries in which it is virtually zero.

54 At such a magnetic-field minimum, the incidence of cosmic-ray particles reaching Earth's surface will rise. If, at the same time, there are star explosions relatively near our Solar system, that might raise the cosmic-ray-particle density to unusual heights. It is this that might cause a great dying. The extinction, seventy million years ago, of the large and flourishing families of giant reptiles usually referred to as dinosaurs, might have been caused in this way, and who knows what will happen to Earth's ecological balance, and to us, if it happened again.

55 However, the combination of magnetic-field minimum and cosmic-ray maximum is very unlikely, and the chance of unusual destruction is small.

56 What of danger from other life forms? We no longer have any fear of lions, tigers, or any of the large predators or angry herbivores, but what of smaller animals? What of rats that grow ever more vicious and clever? What of insects that grow immune to insecticides? What of disease germs that may spread from human being to human being directly from, or by way of, insects and rats.

57 In the fourteenth century, the Black Death struck without warning and may have killed a third of all human beings alive in just a quarter century or

so. This was the greatest catastrophe ever to strike humankind in recorded history. Many people then thought (and one can scarcely blame them) that the world was coming to an end.

58   There have been other plagues—of cholera, smallpox, typhus fever, yellow fever—though none as deadly as the Black Death. As late as 1918, a world-wide influenza epidemic killed almost as many people as the Black Death did, though these represented a far smaller percentage of the world population than was true in the earlier case.

59   Might another vast epidemic arise and wreak incredible destruction? The answer, of course, is that such a plague, or a growth of vermin, could start at any time. It is hard to believe, however, that modern medical science could not deal with other life forms if fully mobilized for the purpose.

60 What, then, of *human* activities? Is humankind itself hastening the coming of any of these possible catastrophes, or making them worse, or even inventing new ones?

61   So far, nothing human beings can do will seriously affect the Universe, or any star, or the Sun or any of the planets, or even the body of the Earth itself. We can, however, affect Earth's atmosphere and we have been doing so.

62   Humankind has, for instance, been burning carbon-containing fuel—wood, coal, oil, gas—at a steadily accelerating rate. All these fuels form carbon dioxide, which is absorbed by plants and by the ocean, but not as fast as we form it. This means the carbon-dioxide content of the air is going up very slightly. Carbon dioxide retains heat and even a very slight rise means a slight warming of the Earth's temperature. This may result in the melting of the ice caps with unusual speed and before we have learned climate control.

63   In reverse, our industrial civilization is making our atmosphere dustier so that it reflects more of the Sunlight and cools the Earth slightly—thus making it possible for a glacial advance in a few centuries before we have learned climate control.

64   To be sure, the two effects seem to be nearly in balance now, and humankind is now making an effort to switch to non-fuel energy. Looming ahead of us is geothermal, hydroelectric, nuclear, and solar forms of energy and with these we may avoid the Scylla of melting ice caps and the Charybdis of advancing glaciers.

65   Nuclear sources of energy can produce dangerous radiation, however. In particular, nuclear fission, which we are using now, not only offers a chance of core meltings that might liberate radioactivity over a large area, but constantly produces radioactive materials that are highly dangerous and that must be kept out of the environment for thousands of years.

66   The spreading use of nuclear-fission power plants keeps raising the nightmare of death by radioactive fallout for millions, of sections of the Earth turning radioactive through leakage of the stored ash, of the stealing of nulcear fuel by

terrorists for use as the ultimate blackmail weapon. Many nuclear scientists, however, assure us that the dangers can be controlled and lived with.

67   Perhaps they are right, but an even better hope is that we will switch to nuclear fusion (not yet shown to be practical) which may lessen the danger of radiation considerably, or to solar energy, which should remove the danger altogether.

68   On the other hand, the nations may deliberately poison the Earth with radioactivity by using nuclear explosives in a vast war. (When the first nuclear bomb was exploded at Alamogordo in July 1945, so little was known of nuclear reactions that some scientists feared that the chain reaction of exploding atoms might spread to the atmosphere and ocean and that an end to all life on Earth might follow one giant explosion that would virtually destroy the planet.)

69   Nuclear bombs have not, however, exploded the planet, and so far, world leaders, whatever their faults, have seemed to recognize that a nuclear war would leave no victors, few survivors, and a ruined planet. We may hope (rather wistfully, perhaps) that they will continue to understand this in the future.

70   The advance of science in other directions may involve catastrophic dangers. War weapons need not be nuclear bombs to lead to unimaginable destruction. The use of nerve gases, biological weapons, climate control, laser beam "death rays," and others are each more insidious and quiet, yet may, in the end, prove just as dangerous as nuclear bombs.

71   Even the advances of peacetime have their dangers. Advances in computer technology may lower the role of humanity and make human beings almost useless. Almost any technological advance may produce waste products that dangerously pollute the Earth. Chemical poisons fill the waters and the soil. Automobile exhaust and factory smoke fills the air. Pollution need not even be material. There can be noise pollution, light pollution, heat pollution, microwave pollution. Everywhere, humanity's products beat upon the Earth which cannot, it seems, absorb it all. Even the noblest efforts of medicine may be harmful. So many individuals may be allowed to live through the help of advanced medical techniques, some maintain that the "weak" and "unfit" will flourish, filling the human gene pool with undesirable genes whose catastrophic potentialities may someday make themselves felt.

72   Will we poison the Earth, kill the ocean, reduce the planet to one world-wide desert? We may not. There are ways of preventing pollution, of even reversing pollution, if humanity cares to take the trouble—and the expense.

73   A rather unusual route to possible catastrophe, revealed only recently, involves the ozone layer. About fifteen miles high in the atmosphere are small quantities of ozone (an energetic form of oxygen) which has the property of being opaque to ultraviolet light and preventing most of the Sun's ultraviolet from reaching Earth's surface. It has been there ever since the Earth's atmosphere gained its free oxygen—that is, for half a billion years at least.

74   Human beings are now using spray cans in ever-increasing numbers where

the sprays are driven out by very stable "chlorofluorocarbons" which emerge with the spray. These chlorofluorocarbons are very stable and remain in the atmosphere indefinitely. Eventually, some of it filters up to the ozone layer where, it is suspected, they may act to change the ozone molecules to ordinary oxygen.

75   If the ozone layer is destroyed in this way, floods of ultraviolet will reach the surface. Ultraviolet radiation is far less energetic than cosmic rays, but will reach us in far greater quantity. There might be a great dying, the extinction of many species that would greatly alter the planet's ecological balance. Through that, human beings would be gravely endangered even if they protected themselves from the direct harm by ultraviolet radiation.

76   Still, humanity is aware of this possible danger now and may take steps to prevent it.

77   Another subtle danger arises from recent microbiological experiments in which bacteria are having their genes altered and in which genes from one simple form of life are introduced into another. There is the possibility that some altered form of micro-organism may be capable of causing some disease (cancer, for instance) against which the natural defenses of the body may not work. If such a micro-organism escapes, it may be the Black Death all over again, or worse.

78   The chance of such an accident is admitted to be very small, but even a very small chance seems frightening and the people engaged in such work have voluntarily agreed to suspend such experiments until appropriate safety measures can be put into force.

79   This is an example of the way in which the dangers accompanying scientific advance can be foreseen and guarded against if people are willing to consider the nature of the advance thoughtfully and if they are willing to take appropriate countermeasures.

80 What, then, if nothing happens and humankind just continues to go on without any significant catastrophe at all?

81   That, *too*, can be a catastrophe, and perhaps the worst.

82   Ever since *Homo sapiens* has been on Earth, his total numbers have increased from century to century. (The only exception was the Black Death century.) What's more, the increase has itself been proceeding at an increasing rate. As of 1976, the total world population is at the record high figure of 4 billion and the rate of increase is at a record high of 2 per cent a year, which means a doubling of the population in thirty-five years.

83   By 2010, then, if things continue as they are, the world population will be 8 billion. It doesn't seem likely that 4 billion mouths can be added to the present world population in only thirty-five years without widespread famine.

84   Under planetary famine conditions, the mad rush to extract food from

the earth and the sea at all costs, and the drive to make use of any kind of energy, may permanently pollute and damage the Earth's ecological balance in ways a less desperate humanity would never countenance.

85   As the ill-fed and starving crowds multiply, the despairing attempt to hoard food or to steal from others will break down order and turn humanity into predators against each other. Any nations that retain a semblance of prosperity may, in desperation, press the nuclear button to force some sort of control over the rest of humanity. All in all, the pressures will cause the towering but rickety structure of civilization to collapse.

86   *This* is the catastrophe we must fear. All other possible catastrophes may come or may not come. If they come, they may not do so for millions or billions of years.

87   But if population is not controlled, civilization and most of humanity will face a catastrophe that will surely come, and within half a century. It is the population problem, then, that and nothing else, that should be the first order of business for humanity.

☐ Discovering Meaning and Technique

1. What are the many erroneous predictions about the end of the world enumerated by Asimov in the introduction to this selection?

2. How does Asimov support the view that the world will certainly come to an end?

3. If the universe ceases to expand, what could happen?

4. How could the earth be affected by a black hole?

5. How might the fate of the sun affect the earth?

6. What is the evidence for past meteoroid collisions in our galaxy?

7. What does Asimov think of the likelihood of the following catastrophes:
Collision with a large meteoroid
Collision with antimatter
Earth's slowing rotation
Overwhelming volcanic eruptions and earthquake tremors

A new glacier advance
Cosmic-ray-particle increase
A new plague
Warming or cooling of the planet
Radioactive fallout
Wars
Peacetime technological advances
Population explosion

8. How are chlorofluorocarbons related to the depletion of the ozone layer?

☐ Writing Suggestions

1. Should living people be concerned about what happens to the universe a billion or trillion years hence?

2. In the library read about and write on Velikovsky's theory of collisions with earth. Asimov implies that the theory is wrong. Do you agree?

3. Do you think a "meteoroid watch" would ever be worth financing?

4. Asimov suggests one cause of the dinosaur extinction—a rise in the cosmic-ray-particle density. After doing library research, write about one or more other theories.

5. Do you agree that the Black Death was the "greatest catastrophe ever to strike humankind in recorded history"? Do you think that AIDS could turn into a new plague?

6. Pick one catastrophe. Write an imaginary scenario depicting, step by step, how it leads to disaster.

IS HISTORY A GUIDE TO THE FUTURE?

☐ BARBARA TUCHMAN

1   The commonest question asked of historians by laymen is whether history serves a purpose. Is it useful? Can we learn from the lessons of history?

2   When people want history to be utilitarian and teach us lessons, that means

they also want to be sure that it meets scientific standards. This, in my opinion, it cannot do, for reasons which I will come to in a moment. To practice history as a science is sociology, an altogether different discipline which I personally find antipathetic—although I suppose the sociologists would consider that my deficiency rather than theirs. The sociologists plod along with their noses to the ground assembling masses of statistics in order to arrive at some obvious conclusion which a reasonably perceptive historian, not to mention a large part of the general public, knows anyway, simply from observation—that social mobility is increasing, for instance, or that women have different problems from men. One wishes they would just cut loose someday, lift up their heads, and look at the world around them.

3   If history were a science, we should be able to get a grip on her, learn her ways, establish her patterns, know what will happen tomorrow. Why is it that we cannot? The answer lies in what I call the Unknowable Variable—namely, man. Human beings are always and finally the subject of history. History is the record of human behavior, the most fascinating subject of all, but illogical and so crammed with an unlimited number of variables that it is not susceptible of the scientific method nor of systematizing.

4   I say this bravely, even in the midst of the electronic age when computers are already chewing at the skirts of history in the process called Quantification. Applied to history, quantification, I believe, has its limits. It depends on a method called "data manipulation," which means that the facts, or data, of the historical past—that is, of human behavior—are manipulated into named categories so that they can be programmed into computers. Out comes—hopefully—a pattern. I can only tell you that for history "data manipulation" is a built-in invalidator, because to the degree that you manipulate your data to suit some extraneous requirement, in this case the requirements of the machine, to that degree your results will be suspect—and run the risk of being invalid. Everything depends on the naming of the categories and the assigning of facts to them, and this depends on the quantifier's individual judgment at the very base of the process. The categories are not revealed doctrine nor are the results scientific truth.

5   The hope for quantification, presumably, is that by processing a vast quantity of material far beyond the capacity of the individual to encompass, it can bring to light and establish reliable patterns. That remains to be seen, but I am not optimistic. History has a way of escaping attempts to imprison it in patterns. Moreover, one of its basic data is the human soul. The conventional historian, at least the one concerned with truth, not propaganda, will try honestly to let his "data" speak for themselves, but data which are shut up in prearranged boxes are helpless. Their nuances have no voice. They must carry one fixed meaning or another and weight the result accordingly. For instance, in a quantification study of the origins of World War I which I have seen, the operators have

divided all the diplomatic documents, messages, and utterances of the July crisis into categories labeled "hostility," "friendship," "frustration," "satisfaction," and so on, with each statement rated for intensity on a scale from one to nine, including fractions. But no pre-established categories could match all the private character traits and public pressures variously operating on the nervous monarchs and ministers who were involved. The massive effort that went into this study brought forth a mouse—the less than startling conclusion that the likelihood of war increased in proportion to the rise in hostility of the messages.

6   Quantification is really only a new approach to the old persistent effort to make history fit a pattern, but *reliable* patterns, or what are otherwise called the lessons of history, remain elusive.

7   For instance, suppose Woodrow Wilson had not been President of the United States in 1914 but instead Theodore Roosevelt, who had been his opponent in the election of 1912. Had that been the case, America might have entered the war much earlier, perhaps at the time of the *Lusitania* in 1915, with possible shortening of the war and incalculable effects on history. Well, it happens that among the Anarchists in my book *The Proud Tower* is an obscure Italian named Miguel Angiolillo, whom nobody remembers but who shot dead Premier Canovas of Spain in 1897. Canovas was a strong man who was just about to succeed in quelling the rebels in Cuba when he was assassinated. Had he lived, there might have been no extended Cuban insurrection for Americans to get excited about, no Spanish-American War, no San Juan Hill, no Rough Riders, no Vice-Presidency for Theodore Roosevelt to enable him to succeed when another accident, another Anarchist, another unpredictable human being, killed McKinley. If Theodore had never been President, there would have been no third party in 1912 to split the Republicans, and Woodrow Wilson would not have been elected. The speculations from that point on are limitless. To me it is comforting rather than otherwise to feel that history is determined by the illogical human record and not by large immutable scientific laws beyond our power to deflect.

8   I know very little (a euphemism for "nothing") about laboratory science, but I have the impression that conclusions are supposed to be logical; that is, from a given set of circumstances a predictable result should follow. The trouble is that in human behavior and history it is impossible to isolate or repeat a given set of circumstances. Complex human acts cannot be either reproduced or deliberately initiated—or counted upon like the phenomena of nature. The sun comes up every day. Tides are so obedient to schedule that a timetable for them can be printed like that for trains, though more reliable. In fact, tides and trains sharply illustrate my point: One depends on the moon and is certain; the other depends on man and is uncertain.

9   In the absence of dependable recurring circumstance, too much confidence cannot be placed on the lessons of history.

10   There *are* lessons, of course, and when people speak of learning from them, they have in mind, I think, two ways of applying past experience: One is

to enable us to avoid past mistakes and to manage better in similar circumstances next time; the other is to enable us to anticipate a future course of events. (History could tell us something about Vietnam, I think, if we would only listen.) To manage better next time is within our means; to anticipate does not seem to be.

11   World War II, for example, with the experience of the previous war as an awful lesson, was certainly conducted, once we got into it, more intelligently than World War I. Getting into it was another matter. When it was important to anticipate the course of events, Americans somehow failed to apply the right lesson. Pearl Harbor is the classic example of failure to learn from history. From hindsight we now know that what we should have anticipated was a surprise attack by Japan in the midst of negotiations. Merely because this was dishonorable, did that make it unthinkable? Hardly. It was exactly the procedure Japan had adopted in 1904 when she opened the Russo-Japanese War by surprise attack on the Russian fleet at Port Arthur.

12   In addition we had every possible physical indication. We had broken the Japanese code, we had warnings on radar, we had a constant flow of accurate intelligence. What failed? Not information but *judgment.* We had all the evidence and refused to interpret it correctly, just as the Germans in 1944 refused to believe the evidence of a landing in Normandy. Men will not believe what does not fit in with their plans or suit their prearrangements. The flaw in all military intelligence, whether twenty or fifty or one hundred percent accurate, is that it is no better than the judgment of its interpreters, and this judgment is the product of a mass of individual, social, and political biases, prejudgments, and wishful thinkings; in short, it is human and therefore fallible. If man can break the Japanese code and yet not believe what it tells him, how can he be expected to learn from the lessons of history?

13   Would a computer do better? In the case of Pearl Harbor, probably yes. If one could have fed all the pieces of intelligence available in November 1941 into a computer, it could have hardly failed to reply promptly. "Air attack, Hawaii, Philippines" and probably even "December 7." But will this work every time? Can we trust the lessons of history to computers? I think not, because history will fool them. They may make the right deductions and draw the right conclusions, but a twist occurs, someone sneezes, history swerves and takes another path. Had Cleopatra's nose been shorter, said Pascal, the whole aspect of the world would have been changed. Can a computer account for Cleopatra?

14   Once long ago when the eternal verities seemed clear—that is, during the Spanish Civil War—I thought the lessons of history were unmistakable. It appeared obvious beyond dispute that if fascism under Franco won, Spain in the foreshadowed European war would become a base for Hitler and Mussolini, the Mediterranean would become an Italian lake, Britain would lose Gibraltar and be cut off from her empire east of Suez. The peril was plain, the logic of the thing implacable, every sensible person saw it, and I, just out of college,

wrote a small book published in England to point it up, all drawn from the analogy of history. The book showed how, throughout the eighteenth and nineteenth centuries, Britain had consistently interposed herself against the gaining of undue influence over Spain by whatever power dominated the continent. The affair of the Spanish marriages, the campaigns of Wellington, the policies of Castlereagh, Canning, and Palmerston all were directed toward the same objective: The strongest continental power must be prevented from controlling Spain. My treatise was, I thought, very artful and very telling. It did not refer to the then current struggle, but let the past speak for itself and make the argument. It was an irrefutable one—until history refuted it. Franco, assisted by Hitler and Mussolini, *did* win, European war *did* follow, yet unaccountably Spain remained neutral—at least nominally. Gibraltar did not fall, the portals of the Mediterranean did *not* close. I, not to mention all the other "premature" antifascists, as we are called, while morally right about the general danger of fascism, had been wrong about a particular outcome. The lessons of history I had so carefully set forth simply did not operate. History misbehaved.

15   Pearl Harbor and Spain demonstrate two things: One, that man fails to profit from the lessons of history because his prejudgments prevent him from drawing the indicated conclusions; and, two, that history will often capriciously take a different direction from that in which her lessons point. Herein lies the flaw in systems of history.

16   When it comes to systems, history played her greatest betrayal on Karl Marx. Never was a prophet so sure of his premises, never were believers so absolutely convinced of a predicted outcome, never was there an interpretation of history that seemed so foolproof. Analyzing the effects of the Industrial Revolution, Marx exposed the terrible riddle of the nineteenth century: that the greater the material progress, the wider and deeper the resulting poverty, a process which could only end, he decided, in the violent collapse of the existing order brought on by revolution. From this he formulated the doctrine of *Verelendung* (progressive improverishment) and *Zusammenbruch* (collapse) and decreed that since working-class self-consciousness increased in proportion to industrialization, revolution would come first in the most industrialized country.

17   Marx's analysis was so compelling that it seemed impossible history could follow any other course. His postulates were accepted by followers of his own and later generations as if they had been graven on the tables of Sinai. Marxism as the revealed truth of history was probably the most convincing dogma ever enunciated. Its influence was tremendous, incalculable, continuing. The founder's facts were correct, his thinking logical and profound. He was right in everything but his conclusions. Developing events did not bear him out. The working class grew progressively better, not worse, off. Capitalism did not collapse. Revolution came in the least, not the most, industrialized country. Under collectivism the state did not wither but extended itself in power and function and in its grip

on society. History, ignoring Marx, followed her own mysterious logic, and went her own way.

18   When it developed that Marx was wrong, men in search of determinism rushed off to submit history to a new authority—Freud. His hand is now upon us. The Unconscious is king. At least it was. There are new voices, I believe, claiming that the Unconscious is a fraud—iconoclasm has reached even Freud. Nevertheless, in his effect on the modern outlook, Freud, I believe, unquestionably was the greatest infuence for change between the nineteenth and twentieth centuries. It may well be that our time may one day be named for him and the Freudian Era be said to have succeeded the Victorian Era. Our understanding of human motivation has taken on a whole new dimension since his ideas took hold. Yet it does not seem to me that unconscious sexual and psychological drives are as relevant in all circumstances as they are said to be by the Freudians, who have become as fixed in their system as were the orthodox Marxists. They can supply historians with insights but not with guidance to the future because man *en masse* cannot be relied upon to behave according to pattern. All salmon swim back to spawn in the headwaters of their birth; that is universal for salmon. But man lives in a more complicated world than a fish. Too many influences are at work on him to make it applicable that every man is driven by an unconscious desire to swim back to the womb.

19   It has always seemed to me unfortunate, for instance, that Freud chose the experiences of two royal families to exemplify his concept of the Oedipus and Elektra complexes. Royalty lives under special circumstances, particularly as regards the issue of power between the sovereign and his heir, which are not valid as universal experience. The legend of Oedipus killing his father may have derived from the observed phenomenon that every royal heir has always hated his father, not because he wants to sleep with his mother but because he was to ascend the throne. If the parental sovereign happens to be his mother, he hates her just as much. She will dislike him equally from birth because she knows he is destined to take her place, as in the case of Queen Victoria and her eldest son, who became Edward VII. That is not Freudian, it is simply dynastic.

20   As for Elektra, it is hard to know what to make of that tale. The House of Atreus was a very odd family indeed. More was going on there than just Elektra being in love with her father. How about Orestes, who helped her to kill their mother, or killed her himself, according to another version? Was not that the wrong parent? How come he did not kill his father? How about Iphigenia, the sister, whom Agememmon killed as a sacrifice? What is the Freudian explanation for that? They do not say, which is not being historical. A historian cannot pick and choose his facts; he must deal with all the evidence.

21   Or take Martin Luther. As you know, Professor Erik Erikson of Harvard has discovered that Luther was constipated from childhood and upon this interest-

ing physiological item he has erected a system which explains everything about this man. This is definitely the most camp thing that has happened to history in years. It even made Broadway. Nevertheless I do not think Luther pinned the 95 Theses on the church door at Wittenberg solely or even mainly because of the activity, or inactivity rather, of his anal muscle. His personal motive for protest may have had an anal basis for all I know, but what is important historically is the form the protest took, and this had to do with old and deep social grievances concerned with the worldliness of the church, the sale of indulgences, corruption of the clergy, and so on. If it had not been Luther who protested, it would have been someone else; Protestantism would have come with or without him, and its causes had nothing whatever to do with his private physiological impediment. Professor Erikson, I am sure, was attempting to explain Luther, not Protestantism, but his book has started a fad for psycho-history among those without the adequate knowledge or training to use it.

22   Following Freud there flourished briefly a minor prophet, Oswald Spengler, who proclaimed the Decline of the West, based on an elaborate study of the lessons of history. Off and on since then people have been returning to his theme, especially since World War II and the end of colonialism. The rise of China and the rash of independence movements in Asia and Africa have inspired many nervous second looks at Spengler. Europe is finished, say the knowing ones; the future belongs to the colored races and all that.

23   People have been burying Europe for quite some time. I remember a political thinker for whom I had great respect telling me in the thirties that Europe's reign was over; the future belonged to America, Russia, and China. It was a new and awful thought to me then and I was immensely impressed. As I see it now, his grouping has not been justified. I do not think Russia and America can be dissociated from Europe; rather, we are extensions of Europe. I hesitate to be dogmatic about Russia, but I am certain about the United States. American culture stems from Europe, our fortunes are linked with hers, in the long run we are aligned. My impression is that Europe, and by extension the white race, is far from finished. Europe's vitality keeps reviving; as a source of ideas she is inexhaustible. Nuclear fission, the most recent, if unwanted, advance, came from the work of a whole series of Europeans: Max Planck, the Curies, Einstein, Rutherford, Fermi, Nils Bohr, Szilard. Previously the three great makers of the modern mind, Darwin, Marx, and Freud, were Europeans. I do not know of an original idea to have importantly affected the *modern* world which has come from Asia or Africa (except perhaps for Gandhi's concept to non-violent resistance or civil disobedience, and, after all, Thoreau had the same idea earlier).

24   It does not seem to me a passing phenomenon or an accident that the West, in ideas and temporal power, has been dominant for so long. Far from falling behind, it seems to be extending its lead, except in the fearful matter of mere numbers and I like to think the inventiveness of the West will somehow eventually cope with that. What is called the emergence of the peoples of Asia

and Africa is taking place in Western terms and is measured by the degree to which they take on Western forms, political, industrial, and otherwise. That they are losing their own cultures is sad, I think, but I suppose it cannot be helped. The new realm is space, and that too is being explored by the West. So much for Spengler.

25   Theories of history go in vogues which, as is the nature of vogues, soon fade and give place to new ones. Yet this fails to discourage the systematizers. They believe as firmly in this year's as last year's, for, as Isaiah Berlin says, the "obstinate craving for unity and symmetry at the expense of experience" is always with us. When I grew up, the economic interpretation of history, as formulated with stunning impact by Charles Beard, was the new gospel—as incontrovertible as if it had been revealed to Beard in a burning bush. Even to question that financial interests motivated our Founding Fathers in the separation from Britain, or that equally mercenary considerations decided our entrance into the First World War was to convict oneself of the utmost naïveté. Yet lately the fashionable—indeed, what appears to be the required—exercise among historians has been jumping on Beard with both feet. He and the considerable body of his followers who added to his system and built it up into a dogma capable of covering any historical situation have been knocked about, analyzed, dissected, and thoroughly disposed of. Presently the historical establishment has moved on to dispose of Frederick Jackson Turner and his theory of the Frontier. I do not know what the new explanation is, but I am sure there must be some thesis, for, as one academic historian recently ruled, the writing of history requires a "large organizing idea."

26   I visualize the "large organizing idea" as one of those iron chain mats pulled behind by a tractor to smooth over a plowed field. I see the professor climbing up on the tractor seat and away he goes, pulling behind his large organizing idea over the bumps and furrows of history until he has smoothed it out to a nice, neat, organized surface—in other words, into a system.

27   The human being—you, I, or Napoleon—is unreliable as a scientific factor. In combination of personality, circumstances, and historical moment, each man is a package of variables impossible to duplicate. His birth, his parents, his siblings, his food, his home, his school, his economic and social status, his first job, his first girl, and the variables inherent in all of these, make up that mysterious compendium, personality—which then combines with another set of variables: country, climate, time, and historical circumstance. Is it likely, then, that all these elements will meet again in their exact proportions to reproduce a Moses, or Hitler, or De Gaulle, or for that matter Lee Harvey Oswald, the man who killed Kennedy?

28   So long as man remains the Unknowable Variable—and I see no immediate prospect of his ever being pinned down in every facet of his finite variety—I do not see how his actions can be usefully programmed and quantified. The eager electronic optimist will go on chopping up man's past behavior into the

thousands of little definable segments which they call Input, and the machine will whirr and buzz and flash its lights and in no time at all give back Output. But will Output be dependable? I would lay ten to one that history will pay no more attention to Output than it did to Karl Marx. It will still need historians. Electronics will have its uses, but it will not, I am confident, transform historians into button-pushers or history into a system.

☐ Discovering Meaning and Technique

1. What is Tuchman's view of sociology?

2. Why can history not be a science?

3. How does Tuchman illustrate the unpredictability of history?

4. Of what value is history, according to Tuchman?

5. Why was America not able to predict Pearl Harbor?

6 Did Tuchman always believe that history was not predictable?

7. Why, according to Tuchman, did Karl Marx and Freud fail to predict the future accurately?

8. Does Tuchman give enough information about Marx's, Freud's, and Spengler's beliefs for those unfamiliar with the ideas?

9. What is "psycho-history," and what is Tuchman's attitude toward it?

10. How does Tuchman illustrate her opinion that historical theories come and go?

11. Which comparison does Tuchman use to clarify her idea of a broad, generalized thesis, or "large organizing idea"?

12. How many paragraphs would you say constitute the conclusion?

☐ Writing Suggestions

1. Can this Tuchman quotation be applied to one's personal life: "To manage better next time is within our means; to anticipate does not seem to be" (paragraph 10)?

2. Do you think the computer will ever be useful in making history more scientific?

3. What lesson or lessons do you think we can learn from history?

4. Write a story in which a computer predicts a historical event and the users fail to believe the prediction. Or write a story in which a computer's prediction is believed but turns out to be wrong.

5. Look in sociology journals for studies that arrive at what Tuchman calls "some obvious conclusion."

6. About the first of every year people such as Jeanne Dixon make predictions. Locate old predictions in newspapers or magazines and discuss whether or not they came true. The *Reader's Guide* may help you locate sources.

BEYOND THE KNOWABLE: THE ULTIMATE EXPLORATION

☐ HOLCOMB B. NOBLE

1   The twenty-first century promises to explain the unexplainable. It offers humanity opportunities to learn what until now has been unlearnable, unknowable. It is not hard to imagine the twentieth century as a kind of arbitrarily chosen point from which the twenty-first century splays out in virtually all directions and all dimensions, building on the known, explaining the unknown. This is no image of the idle futurist. It is meant, on the contrary, to serve as a serious suggestion: in the next century, once grand unification is achieved, once machine intelligence matches human intelligence, once space exploration fulfills its promise, once communications systems meet theirs, the fundamental dimensions of space and time themselves may possibly be altered or become alterable. Given the nature of current scientific research and experimentation, it is not inconceivable, for instance, that the future may somehow develop a greater capacity to peer into "the dark backward and abysm of time," or that it will explain other vast areas of the present unknown.

2   It is, in a sense, this idea of the unknown that makes any future at once unsettling and exciting. Two bits of the present unknown that now nag persistently at the human consciousness and somehow seem more and more knowable are phenomena largely regarded in the past as quaint whimsy: extrasensory perception and extraterrestrial intelligence. The scientific mind is the mind that thrives on incontrovertible truth, that demands concrete proof. That's correct, isn't it? If

you can see it, smell it, hear it, touch it, taste it, it must be there. Conversely, if you can't, it must not. Well, perhaps. But perhaps not. Perhaps, the truly scientific mind is the open mind, the one willing to explore even what cannot be perceived to be there. Who is to say that intensive exploration will not detect a world of intelligence and communication that goes far beyond the sensorily observable? Are we absolutely certain that we will not begin to make unexpected and remarkable discoveries through channels that extend into events that defy all rational explanation? The creative scientific mind does not rule it out. Einstein insisted to the last that a cause could be found for every effect. But a great many scientists have come to accept the concept of irrationality and randomness, and they believe it may become more dominant in decades to come.

3   There is no convincing evidence to prove the existence of extrasensory perception—the act of perceiving communication in ways other than through the senses. But a substantial number of respected scientists began, at least by the 1970s, to consider it as a possibility. Dr. Mahion Wagner, a psychologist at the State University of New York, Oswego, published a survey in 1979 based on questionnaires he sent to 2,100 college and university professors throughout the United States; 1,188 responded. Of the natural scientists who replied, 9 percent said they accepted extrasensory perception as an established fact and 45 percent called it a likely possibility. Private individuals and corporations have donated hundreds of thousands of dollars for research, at Princeton and elsewhere, for such work as the attempt to change temperature readings or move objects by mere will of the mind. Arthur Koestler, who believed that parapsychology would introduce a new Copernican Revolution, left $750,000 in his will in 1983 for a chair in parapsychology at a British university; Oxford and Cambridge both turned the bequest down on the grounds that its very acceptance would challenge the notions of rationality implicit in their scientific research. But the University of Edinburgh accepted it.

4   The 1984 spring meeting of the American Academy for the Advancement of Science, one of the nation's most important scientific gatherings, held a symposium called "The Edges of Science." The meeting was held within a basic framework of skepticism. The emphasis was on what remains unproven. But the fact that the symposium was held at all was significant. Take the question of intelligence in outer space and the controversy over UFO's, unidentified flying objects. Arthur C. Clarke, the science fiction writer, told the gathered scientists that there was a time when he took UFO's seriously. "Now," he said, "UFO's need a period of malign neglect." Every report of another landing, every story, every anecdote turns out to be just that—another report, another story, another anecdote. "If there really is a landing, it can be documented in thirty minutes." Indeed, he asked whether the whole UFO sighting question could not benefit from recent laboratory evidence that people can hallucinate so well that electrical activity in their brain agrees with their vision.

5   But another speaker, the respected J. Allen Hynek, made the contention that there have been just too many unexplained UFO reports to be lightly pooh-poohed. "Computer analyses of 400 UFO cases," he said, "are totally inconsistent with those of everyday objects and phenomena." He said it was wrong to suggest that "independent witnesses could be so grossly misled as to imagine simultaneously, for example, that a meteor could stop, hover, and then reverse direction." Space engineer James Oberg countered with just that suggestion. He said that a series of dramatic sightings in the Soviet Union and South America happened to follow nighttime rocket launchings in Russia and Argentina. The "objects" were vividly reported: people said they stopped overhead, hovered, then turned and chased cars. What was clearly going on, he said, was that human fear and imagination were interacting with an observable physical event to produce a series of wildly erroneous reports.

6   Other scientists as well believe that most studies of unidentified flying objects, along with research into extrasensory perception, are flawed. They argue that the work is often pretentious pseudoscience and invariably produces questionable results. They contend, too, that the field is dotted with charlatans and naive incompetents. Yet the fact that the American Association for the Advancement of Science has begun consideration of the subjects is one indication among several others that these claims on the edge of science are now being taken more seriously, that they must begin to be investigated with more rigorous scientific standards. The possibility that they exist is no longer so absurd as to permit the matter to drop. Careful study, the association was implicitly stating, is called for.

ESP AS MILITARY WEAPON

7 Nowhere is the possibility that life, energy, power, intelligence or communication may exist on some previously undiscovered level taken more seriously than it is in the halls and conference rooms of the military. The military establishments of the world's two superpowers—the Soviet Union and the United States—are actively pursuing it. According to a variety of reports, the Pentagon has spent millions of dollars on secret projects aimed at investigating extrasensory phenomena—to see whether the sheer power of the mind can be harnessed to perform various acts of espionage and war. Could, for example, highly developed mental powers be used to penetrate secret enemy files? Or, could the unaided mind be used to locate submarines or blow up guided missiles in midflight?

8   Although the Pentagon denies that it is spending money on psychic research, assertions to the contrary have come forth in important writings on the subject and in interviews with scientists and with former officials of the Pentagon. What becomes clear from these sources is that the superpowers are, indeed, actively engaged in attempting to master such arts as extrasensory perception (ESP), telepathy (which is generally defined as thought transfer), clairvoyance (seeing

things that are not yet there) and psychokinesis (influencing the course of events or the behavior of people or things, simply by bringing mental energy to bear). This research is done in the name of national defense. "The Defense Department would be derelict in its duty if it didn't pay attention to the long shots," Dr. Marcello Truzzi of the Michigan-based Center for Scientific Anomalies told William J. Broad of *The New York Times* science department in an interview in January of 1984. But he hastened to add that the fact that the department is looking into the phenomena does not make them real.

9   Well, what are some of those experiments? Dr. Russell Targ, a physicist at SRI International, an independent research organization that is an offshoot of Stanford University, describes some of them in a book he wrote with Keith Harary called *The Mind Race.* He says SRI has worked under a multimillion-dollar United States Defense Department contract to study psychic behavior or events. Its principal experiments were attempts at what he called remote viewing. Skilled individuals were said to be able to describe objects located thousands of miles away.

10   A viewer in California was asked to visualize a specific site in New York City that he was totally unfamiliar with and to type impressions into a computer of what he saw. Dr. Targ says those recorded impressions were "of a cement depression—as if a dry fountain—with a cement post in the middle or inside. There seemed to be pigeons off to the right flying around the surface of the depression." The test site, Dr. Targ writes, was the central fountain in Washington Square Park. It was, indeed, dry, had a post in the middle, from which water could be sprayed, and it was surrounded by pigeons.

11   According to Ronald M. McRae, who is the author of *Mind Wars* and is a former reporter for the syndicated columnist Jack Anderson, the Pentagon has spent about $6 million dollars a year on psychic research for the past several years. He contends further that such research encompasses projects undertaken over the course of the past thirty years by the CIA, the Army, Navy, Air Force, Marine Corps, NASA and the Defense Intelligence Agency. Indeed, former U.S. government officials confirm that the explorations into parapsychology are going on, although in most cases they will not identify individual projects. One former White House official in the Reagan Administration, however, did confirm in an interview with William Broad that psychic researchers were used by American defense planners to try to locate hidden MX missiles.

12   At one time the Pentagon had developed a $40 billion plan to hide the giant intercontinental MX missiles in a series of selected concrete bunkers. The missiles would be secretly transported, either by rail or by huge flatbed trucks, from one bunker to the next, hidden so that Soviet military planners would never know where to strike. Ronald McRae reports that the Pentagon set up experiments in which trained observers, using only the powers of their own minds, guessed the positions of the missiles with sufficient accuracy to raise doubts about the security of the hide-the-missile plan. Barbara Honegger, the

former White House official, did not know whether the experiments were a factor in the ultimate decision to abandon the whole idea.

13   The Soviet Union is said to be striving to harness the power of telepathic communication and telekinetics. Martin Ebon writes in his book *Psychic Warfare* that the major impetus for the Soviet drive into psychic exploration also came from the military and the KGB. He contends that the Soviet Union was goaded into action by false reports that the U.S. Navy tried to communicate with the first nuclear submarine, the *Nautilus,* by thought transfer, as it cruised under the Arctic ice cap.

14   It's perfectly true that all this may be just so much hokum. Is it not possible, for example, as indeed many scientists forcefully argue, that both the United States and the Soviet Union are once again whistling in the wind; that, out of fear and lack of respect for each other, they are off on another arms race— except that this time the coveted weaponry may be nothing more than figments of their collective imagination? Indeed, some suggest that the real goal is disinformation. To give the enemy the impression that mind weapons were a reality would be to set him off on expensive but harmless diversions. Even many of the skeptics agree, however, that the military has no choice but to pursue the paranormal.

15   Some serious nonmilitary researchers have been at work on the parapsychological for years. Dr. Brian Josephson, a British scientist who won the Nobel prize for physics in 1973, has spent much of his time since then studying the paranormal, of whose existence he says he is 99 percent convinced. Dr. Josephson's work in physics led him to the discovery that electrical conductivity in an ultra-cold environment can be switched on or off with a magnetic field, a discovery now known as the Josephson effect.

16   But are the rigors of hard science or quantum mechanics really compatible with investigations of the paranormal and what the intelligent skeptic always regarded as the quackery of, say, the old professional mind reader? "You ask whether parapsychology lies within the bounds of physical law," Dr. Josephson said to an interviewer. "My feeling is that to some extent it does, but physical law itself may have to be redefined. It may be that some effects in parapsychology are ordered-state effects of a kind not yet encompassed by physical theory."

17   In fact, the discovery of quantum mechanics is itself preliminary evidence in the minds of some scientists that extrasensory phenomena do exist, or are at least possible. The quantum theory conveys the notion that subatomic particles may be able to communicate with each other instantaneously. The discoveries of Paul A. M. Dirac and others suggest to some that widely separated electrons talk to each other, acting in concert and telling each other what to do. These particles do this in apparent violation of a basic tenet of physics: no signal can travel faster than the speed of light. Could it really be true, as it seems to be inside an atom, that an event can happen so fast that it causes other things to take place before the event itself has even occurred? Scientists at the Applied

Physics Laboratory of Johns Hopkins University have tried to prove there must
be some mistake. This cannot be right, they contend: nothing happens before
it happens. Nothing travels faster than the speed of light.

18   The French theorist Bernard d'Espagnat concedes that the theory is strange,
all right. The notion of signals outracing light would lead, he says, to "bizarre
paradoxes of causality in which observers in some frames of reference find that
one event is 'caused' by another that has not yet happened."

19   But he points out in an article in *Scientific American* that the bizarre
does indeed seem real. Tests, he said, show that, in some atomic processes,
particles can be ejected in opposite directions and those particles appear to
have no properties at all until they are measured. Then the very instant they
are measured, they match one another in location and spin even though they
are far apart. Their behavior is baffling unless there has been some kind of communication between them, some kind of data being transmitted faster than the
possible—faster, in other words, than the speed of light, faster than at the rate
of 186,000 miles per second.

20   Other tests of this hypothesis have involved the ejection of two photons,
particles of light, shot out in opposite directions from an atom primed by energy
injection, as from a laser. When the photons are observed, each is polarized, or
oscillating, in the same manner. This subatomic ballet of precision is observed
even though some physicists believe the photons were never synchronized until
the very moment of observation. The rational scientist has always been extremely
frustrated by quantum theory. He wants to believe in cause and effect, and yet
when he looks at the oscillating photon there seems to be no such relationship.
Einstein and some others, however, never accepted such randomness. Einstein
recognized the evidence for quantum mechanics as valid, but he said, "An inner
voice tells me it's not the real thing." He did not believe, as he put it, "that
God plays at dice."

21   We do know now from the great advances in physical theory and in the
developing technology of nuclear energy and solid-state electronics that quantum
mechanics is itself real enough. True, we have not proved whether God is or is
not playing at dice. True, there is no universal agreement among physicists
that the bizarre behavior of subatomic particles is in fact the result of instantaneous
particle-to-particle communication and not caused by some other as yet unexplained phenomenon. But the idea is alive and hotly debated, and it keeps the
scientific mind wondering about its implications. The mind is set to thinking
about ESP or thought transfer, for example. Couldn't that phenomenon be explained in some manner by quantum mechanics?

22   Is it not possible that data can be instantaneously transmitted from the
brain of one person to another in much the same manner as the communication
between subatomic particles? Might not ESP work similarly to those talking
electrons? Might not as yet undiscovered thought particles be transferred in
waves somehow analogous to those of photons? Quantum mechanics has seemed

to prove again what science has illustrated over and over through the centuries: the lack of understanding of the why of an event or the misunderstanding of it does not negate its existence. Is it correct to conclude that, because we do not understand ESP, it isn't there? We don't understand much about quantum mechanics, yet we accept the notion that its discovery is one of the most important in the history of science. "No one understands quantum mechanics," says Nobel laureate Richard P. Feynman. Its effects are "impossible, absolutely impossible" to explain based on human experience. It may be equally true of ESP. It may exist. It may be important to human and physical behavior. Yet it may not be explainable until long after its discovery, if then. We still cannot explain gravity.

23   Musings about the unknown are by definition speculative, and these may be highly so. But if d'Espagnat is right about eletron events happening before they happen, why couldn't thought be transferred before it occurred?

SEARCHING FOR LIFE AND ENERGY IN SPACE

24 Another unknown, equally imponderable, is whether there is intelligent life on other planets. Again, despite serious scientific research that has stretched out over more than a quarter of the twentieth century in time and billions of miles in space, no clear evidence has been discovered that life does exist beyond the earth. Yet the search goes on, financed in part by a $1.5 million annual budget from the U.S. space agency. If anything, it has become more intense than when it first began in earnest in 1959, the year Dr. Philip Morrison of MIT and his colleague Dr. Giuseppi Cocconi made the suggestion that other civilizations might be trying to communicate with one another on a specific radio wavelength. They speculated that such a wavelength might be at twenty-one centimeters on the electromagnetic spectrum, based on the radiation given off by free atoms of hydrogen, the most common element in the universe. At least forty-five astronomical search projects have been initiated in attempts to pick up such extraterrestrial communication, and some of them, such as those at Harvard and Ohio State universities, continue to focus on the twenty-one-centimeter wavelength. By the 1990s, a satellite called Cosmic Background Explorer should begin monitoring cosmic radiation and should assist in the search for radio transmissions at the twenty-one-centimeter wavelength.

25   During the past century, many scientists believed there might be life on Mars, and they proposed various methods of trying to send out signals from the earth. One plan, devised by the mathematician Karl Friedrich Gauss, was to plant a giant forest in Siberia in the shape of a right triangle. Another suggestion was made that squares be planted on each side of the triangle to illustrate the Pythagorean theorem. Or, canals might be dug in the Sahara in the form of a geometric figure, these scientists suggested, and then, with kerosene covering the water, ignited at night. This would become a literal signal of intelligence

flashing across space brightly enough so that intelligent beings out there might see it and respond.

26 Although there is now no evidence to suggest that life exists anywhere as close as Mars, the idea of lighting up the world with a sign of intelligence to shine into space was revived in the fall of 1983. SETI-France, a group searching for extraterrestrial intelligence, planned to set out floodlights and illuminate the Greenwich meridian along a 160-mile strip from Villers on the English Channel to Trois, a town southwest of Tours. At the La Flèche Airport, which is precisely on the meridian, fifty flares would be illuminated in the form of a cross, and at Paris, 200 torches would be lighted in the Place du Pantheon. All these lighting events would coincide with the almost certain appearance in space of intelligent human beings: that is to say, with the scheduled launching of one of the American space shuttles, Columbia. The crew of Columbia flying in space in orbit around the earth would see visible signs of people there trying to communicate with them. Bad weather prevented the SETI plan from being carried out, as impracticality perhaps had interfered with Gauss's idea for the Siberian triangular forest. But they both symbolized the profound belief among thoughtful people that we are not alone.

27 There have been tantalizing hints, through infrared astronomy, of dense material orbiting at least two major starts, suggesting perhaps planetary systems in the making. To find unequivocal evidence of other planets far beyond the solar system, worlds perhaps like our own, would be one of the most sensational discoveries of all time, both scientifically and philosophically. In the search for these worlds in the 1980s, an entirely new era, the Golden Age of Astronomy, began to dawn. Orbiting observatories hundreds of thousands of times more sensitive than the observation stations of the past began to be put into use. As a result, astronomers are becoming able to probe the universe faster, more deeply and over a longer period of time than ever before. They are, in many cases, gathering data from radiations invisible to the human eye. And this Golden Age offers just one more avenue of promising discovery into regions of the unknown.

28 As Earth observers have begun to "see" into the hidden depths of the elctromagnetic spectrum, they have begun recording the existence, shape, temperature and composition of such celestial objects as quasars, pulsars and supernovas that were previously hidden by the thick mantle of gas that blocked traditional viewing through visual light. One such new telescope observed clouds of interstellar gas and dust that appeared to be the actual birth of a group of new stars.

29 European Space Agency's X-ray astronomy satellite, put into orbit in 1983, was able to map sources of X-rays emitted in space with great accuracy and to help determine the temperature, density and chemical abundances of stellar gases. Four large American observatories will scan the far reaches of the elctromagnetic spectrum in a quest to fathom the mysteries of the cosmos. They are the Space Infrared Telescope Facility, the Space Telescope, the Advanced X-ray Astro-

physics Facility and the Gamma Ray Observatory. Each of these four telescopes will be tuned to a different part of the electromagnetic spectrum, picking up various wavelengths: in the infrared range, visual, ultraviolet, X-ray and gamma-ray.

30   These facilities are expected to enable scientists to see stars in the process of death, to see the gases of stars sucked into intense black holes whose mass is so compact and therefore so great and whose resulting gravity is so powerful that not even light can escape. The gamma-ray telescope, which detects the shortest wavelengths, will no doubt see some of the most violent events of all—the annihilation of matter and antimatter in exploding galaxies. The new telescopes are aimed at things that have until now defied accurate description or explanation. Gamma-ray bursters, for example, are points that occasionally emit explosive packets of gamma-ray energy, but they are yet to be linked with any known object in the universe.

31   In short, astronomers have begun to realize that explosions and dynamic change are far more common through the universe than they had thought. It is far more alive and, with the new equipment, far more observable. They now regard their work as comparable to Columbus's or Magellan's, believing that science is only just now beginning to learn the physical nature of the universe.

☐ Discovering Meaning and Technique

1. What evidence does Noble give that ESP (or parapsychology) and UFOs have a respectable following?

2. Why would the military be interested in ESP?

3. Which audience do you think Noble had in mind when he wrote this selection?

4. Which sources does Noble cite as evidence of U.S. and Soviet military support of ESP research?

5. How does quantum mechanics help explain the existence of ESP?

6. Why did scientists searching for extraterrestrial communication decide to monitor radio transmissions at the 21-centimeter wavelength?

7. What discoveries have been made possible by our entrance into the "Golden Age of Astronomy"?

☐ Writing Suggestions

1. In the first paragraph, Noble mentions "grand unification." After researching this idea in the library, write an explanation.

2. Is the money spent on researching ESP and searching for extraterrestrial life well spent?

3. Survey public opinion of ESP and/or extraterrestrial life. Write a discussion of your findings.

4. Discuss the likelihood of the existence of ESP, telepathy, clairvoyance, psycho-kinesis, or remote viewing.

5. Do you view UFOs as probable or improbable?

6. Agree or disagree with Noble's statement: "To find unequivocal evidence of other planets far beyond the solar system, worlds perhaps like our own, would be one of the most sensational discoveries of all time, both scientifically and philosophically."

THE EERIE WORLD OF LIVING HEADS

☐ **LARRY THOMPSON**

1 As the anesthesia wore off, the Rhesus monkey opened its eyes and slowly scanned its aseptic surroundings. Laboratory benches were crammed with instruments. Wires pasted to its cranium stimulated a machine pumping squiggly lines on yards of paper. Plastic tubing carried crimson fluid from the neck of a second immobilized monkey to a point below the monkey's head where the eyes could not see.

2   Then the realization: There was nothing below the head. The body of the monkey with the open eyes had been surgically removed and the head mounted on a support. The plastic tubing was the head's lifeline, carrying blood drawn from the body of the other monkey.

3   That was 18 years ago. The results still astonish.

4   "The monkey became awake and acted like a monkey," says Dr. Robert White, a neurosurgeon at Case Western Reserve University School of Medical in Cleveland and the researcher who ran similar experiments on half a dozen monkeys. "They followed you around [the room with their eyes]. They'd try to bite your finger off. There was every indication that brain was functioning as it was when it was on its own body."

5   Nearly two decades later, a new phase of research may be about to begin. A 35-year-old, Harvard-trained St. Louis attorney who writes and patents his techniques under the name of Chet Fleming—his real name is Patrick Kelly—has acquired a unique and unusual patent, number 4,666,425, which describes a machine to keep alive severed heads, animal or human.

6   The device, which has yet to be built, would be made with off-the-shelf technology: a heart-lung machine, an artificial kidney and a few other devices to add nutrients and generally keep things under control. Theoretically, it could work.

7   Keeping a human head alive "is not out of the question," says Dr. Richard J. Wyatt, director of the National Institute of Mental Health research center at St. Elizabeth's Hospital here. "I don't know if it is doable, but it probably will be some day."

8   Not everyone agrees that it's possible or even that it should be done. "I think it is fairly barbaric at this point . . . I do not even see that 100 years from now as a possibility," says Dr. Jerry Silver, a Case Western Reserve University expert in regrowing severed nerves and a colleague of White who saw some of his early work. "If anybody did that today, it would be absolutely horrible. Can you imagine looking around the room, and you're just a head?"

9   While it may not *yet* be possible to keep a severed head alive mechanically, pieces of the needed system are becoming available. Artificial hearts can pump blood. Artificial kidneys and plasmaphoresis can cleanse blood. Artificial lungs can put oxygen in the blood. The body is merely a life-support machine for the head and brain and nearly all of its primary functions can be artificially replaced.

OUR BODIES, OUR SHELVES

10   The development of an artificial body, in a sense, can be traced back to 1944 when Dr. Willem J. Kolff built the first artificial kidney from sausage skins and washing-machine parts in occupied Holland. Kolff's interest in artificial organs led to the first artificial heart, which was implanted in a dog at the Cleveland Clinic in 1957.

11   Artificial hearts are not artificial bodies, but ideas sometimes take on a life of their own. No one envisioned the Jarvik-7 when Kolff began his first experiments with artificial kidneys, but the two are directly linked.

12   Nor is this the first time in history that people have wondered what happens inside a severed head or tried to preserve one. In 1887, a French scientist tried to attach heads of executed prisoners fresh from the guillotine to the bodies of large dogs.

13   A 1962 book details a variety of Soviet transplant experiments, including heads, other limbs and one half of one dog's body to the half of another dog. "They had one dog with two heads," says Dr. Irvin Kopin, scientific director for the National Institute of Neurology, Communicative Disorders and Stroke.

14   And then there were the White experiments of the '60s and '70s, proving that the brain could survive such treatment. The experiments also helped change the most commonly accepted medical and legal definition of death from heart failure to brain death.

15   Attempts to preserve heads with machines began in 1912 when two Russian researchers kept a severed dog head alive for several hours with an "artificial circulation machine" called an "autoinjector." In 1964, Dr. David Gilboe of the University of Wisconsin in Madison reported decapitating 15 dogs and keeping the heads alive with mechanical pumps.

16   Although all of the work was conducted on animals, such techniques could eventually be used on humans.

17   "If scientists can keep the head alive for a long time, they could prolong human life, Fleming says. "Most dying people, obviously, would not want the operation, but out of the hundreds of thousands of people who are dying at any given moment, a few might be willing to try it."

18   They would be the next Barney Clarks of history. And, Fleming points out, "the first surgeon who manages to sever a human head and keep it alive is going to get his name in a lot of history books."

19   Immortality, however, is not near. The longest surviving Case Western monkey lived only 36 hours. But then, the first dog to receive an artificial heart lived only a few hours. Barney Clark, the first human to receive an artificial heart, lived 112 days.

SPLIT DECISIONS

20 Although Fleming has an engineering degree from the University of Texas, he hasn't built a working model of the machine for which he holds a patent. He never expects to, believing that will happen soon enough anyway. Real scientists, probably working in secret, he believes, will put together all the components and step into the future.

21   "Our experiments with total [head and] brain transplantation were done in monkeys in highly developed preparations," says Case Western's White. "There is absolutely no question that it would only take a year or so to make the changes in technique and equipment to do it in a human. If someone wanted to come through here and give us $5 million to build the machine, we could do it."

22   Fleming fears someone will try. He says he actually acquired his patent to prevent anyone from building and using the machinery without a full and open public debate.

23   "I am not interested in commercializing or promoting the invention," Fleming says. "Instead, I hope and intend to use the patent to slow down this line or research, and to ensure that any researchers who want to try this operation give careful attention to the social, legal and ethical aspects."

24   Fleming would like to see Congress get involved. So far, contacts with the Hill, despite his offer of model legislation, have not been fruitful. Presidential candidates have been equally unresponsive.

25   Although the technology obviously raises significant questions, ethicists have yet to grapple with them, and some don't want to bother.

26   "I hate to get into these hypothetical situations which I think are extremely unlikely," says Dr. Charles R. McCarthy, an ethicist with the National Institutes of Health's Office for Protection from Research Risks. "I just think the whole thing is not worth my time."

27   Others are interested. "This is crazy speculative stuff," says Dr. Albert Jonsen, chairman of medical history and ethics at the University of Washington School of Medicine in Seattle. "It is worth serious consideration. I just haven't done it."

28   But the ethical issues are not trivial. Brain metabolism experiments with the heads of aborted fetuses created an uproar in the mid-'60s that led to the creation of the National Commission for the Protection of Human Subjects.

29   A critical question is whose life should be extended by having it attached to a machine? "Is it going to be nice guys like Einstein or guys like Hitler and Stalin?" Fleming asks. The rich? The powerful? A genius? Who would decide?

30   What would be the quality of life for someone reduced from a whole being to an artificially supported head? The head could wake up; it would know it was severed. It would be able to perceive, sense, understand. It would have emotions: happiness, relief, love, fear, horror.

31   "These people could see, hear, smell. They would be alive," White asserted. Since the brain is the seat of intellect, the essence of the person, such procedures would, in effect, be preserving and "transferring the soul and the spirit," White says.

32   But, "are you alive without your body?" NIHM's Wyatt wondered. "If you just have your head, who are you? Are you your mind? Or are you a combination of your mind and your body and your brain?

33   Wyatt has come to his own conclusion. "I think it probably is a person in the same sense that a quadriplegic is a person. To me, the mind and the brain, that combination, is what makes a person a person."

34   "Since we define what a person is at birth, as someone having been born. And since the head was born and part of the person, then it would have rights as a person," says attorney Lori Andrews, a research fellow at the American Bar Foundation in Chicago who follows medical and genetic issues. It might, however, depend on the state since some states still define death as occurring when the heart stops.

35   And how will others respond? "In a public sentiment sense, people do react badly to the notion of severed heads," Andrews says. Will the head be abandoned by friends and lovers? If he was married, will he still be married?

36   "I would imagine that it would become extremely lonely," says NIMH's Wyatt.

THE FUTURE ON ICE

37 There also is the issue of pain. Would the severed sensory nerves emanating from the remnants of the spinal cord still search for impulses of nerve junctions

long since gone? Would the head feel the pain of phantom limbs, a sensation sometimes experienced by amputees?

38   "The problem with the head is that it is the seat of pain, says NINCDS's Kopin. "If you are going to do this in a humane way, you do it with no suffering."

39   Fleming thinks that the pain issue can be resolved, perhaps with drugs that remove any unpleasantness while leaving the mind unclouded.

40   Robotics offer one high-tech, intermediate solution. Researchers at places such as Stanford University and the Veterans Administration Medical Center in Palo Alto, Calif., already have built voice-activated robot arms that can do for an accidental quadriplegic what his body used to do, such as prepare a meal and feed him, turn on the TV or answer the phone.

41   The Stanford-VA group has mounted the robot arm on a omni-directional robot base with three wheels to move the arm around a room. Add life support systems and the head, and a walk down the street is not out of the question. "Robocop" may not be that far away.

42   Fleming believes a disconnected head could speak if provided with a sound generator, a speaker, that creates an "aaaahh" noise similar to the vocal cords. "It is the mouth and tongue that turns that into speech," he says. With such a sound generator, "a human head would be able to talk and activate voice controlled computers. It is surprising the degree of autonomy that computerized devices would be able to give a severed head if it could talk. But that is long-term speculation."

43   Letting his mind wander, Fleming even envisions head-controlled space craft speeding through the quiet of space toward Mars or even more distant planets. The human head would have the intellect to guide the machine; the machine would keep the head alive. As unpredictable situations arose, the human head could alter the plans, adjusting, compromising, surviving.

44   "The possibilities," Fleming says, "are every bit as fascinating as they are frightening."

45   While some think it unlikely that anyone would attempt to cheat death in such a bizarre and unusual way, consider that more than 120 Americans already are on waiting lists to have their bodies frozen after they die in the hopes that one day, as medical science advances, they can be revived and cured of whatever deadly disease killed them. More than a dozen bodies remain in cold storage.

46   Because freezing the whole body has become pricey—reportedly as high as $125,000 to be reawakened in the next century—a few cryonic facilities such as the Institute for Cryobiological Extension (ICE) in Los Angeles have taken to icing just the head for later grafting onto new bodies sometime in the future. Perhaps someone among the hardy few who are willing to be frozen would be willing to try something more immediate.

47   Others wonder, "I am not sure this is really coming down the road," says NINCDS's Kopin. "It seems cruel and bizarre to keep an animal or person alive with just its head." But then he admitted, "we do see some odd scientific things that come to reality."

48   Case Western's White thinks it is likely. As the 21st century approaches, more living heads will be preserved, he predicts, either artificially or by transplanting them to another body, "and it will be done in humans. I believe in the 21st century, we are going to transplant the human head, just as you transplant a person's heart today."

49   Then there are the dissenters. "It is a pretty gruesome technique," says Case Western's Silver. "I can't conceive someone really wanting . . . to stay alive as a quadriplegic. It is a trade-off with immortality."

☐ Discovering Meaning and Technique

1. What do you think Thompson is trying to accomplish in the introduction?

2. When did work on the artificial kidney begin? When was the first artificial heart implanted?

3. What is the earliest known attempt to preserve a severed head?

4. Why did Fleming [Kelly] get a patent for a machine that would allow head transplantation?

5. Why have many ethicists not considered the issue?

6. What concerns some scientists about the quality of life of a severed head?

7. How might robotics figure in the solution of living without a body?

8. How might a severed head benefit space travel?

☐ Writing Suggestions

1. Argue for or against continued experimentation with keeping a human head alive.

2. Discuss the use of animals in laboratory experiments.

3. Write a story in which someone whose life work is not complete (perhaps a scientist like Einstein) chooses near the time of death to have his or her head preserved.

4. Compare the experiments being done on human preservation with the Frankenstein story.

5. Do you agree with Fleming [Kelly] that among the dying, a few people "might be willing to try it [preservation of their head]"?

6. Compare being an artificially supported head to being a quadriplegic.

7. What might life be like for a severed head?

8. What do you think of freezing the body after death to permit a future cure of a fatal disease?

SQ

☐ URSULA K. LE GUIN

1 I think what Dr. Speakie has done is wonderful. He is a wonderful man. I believe that. I believe that people need beliefs. If I didn't have my belief I really don't know what would happen.

2   And if Dr. Speakie hadn't truly believed in his work he couldn't possibly have done what he did. Where would he have found the courage? What he did proves his genuine sincerity.

3   There was a time when a lot of people tried to cast doubts on him. They said he was seeking power. That was never true. From the very beginning all he wanted was to help people and make a better world. The people who called him a power-seeker and a dictator were just the same ones who used to say that Hitler was insane and Nixon was insane and all the world leaders were insane and the arms race was insane and our misuse of natural resources was insane and the whole world civilization was insane and suicidal. They were always saying that. And they said it about Dr. Speakie. But he stopped all that insanity, didn't he? So he was right all along, and he was right to believe in his beliefs.

4   I came to work for him when he was named the Chief of the Psychometric Bureau. I used to work at the UN, and when the World Government took over the New York UN Building they transferred me up to the thirty-fifth floor to be the head secretary in Dr. Speakie's office. I knew already that it was a position of great responsibility, and I was quite excited the whole week before my new job began. I was so curious to meet Dr. Speakie, because of course he was already famous. I was there right at the dot of nine on Monday morning, and when he came in it was so wonderful. He looked so kind. You could tell that the weight of his responsibilities was always on his mind, but he looked so healthy and positive, and there was a bounce in his step—I used to think it was as if he had rubber balls in the toes of his shoes. He smiled and shook my hand and said in such a friendly, confident voice, "And you must be Mrs. Smith! I've heard wonderful things about you. We're going to have a wonderful team here, Mrs. Smith!"

5   Later on he called me by my first name, of course.

6   That first year we were mostly busy with information. The World Government Presidium and all the Member States had to be fully informed about the nature and purpose of the SQ Test, before the actual implementation of its application could be eventualized. That was good for me too, because in preparing all that information I learned all about it myself. Often, taking dictation, I learned about it from Dr. Speakie's very lips. By May I was enough of an "expert" that I was able to prepare the "Basic SQ Information" pamphlet for publication just from Dr. Speakie's notes. It was such fascinating work. As soon as I began to understand the SQ Test Plan I began to believe in it. That was true of everybody in the office, and in the Bureau. Dr. Speakie's sincerity and scientific enthusiasm were infectious. Right from the beginning we had to take the Test every quarter, of course, and some of the secretaries used to be nervous before they took it, but I never was. It was so obvious that the Test was *right*. If you scored under 50 it was nice to know that you were sane, but even if you scored over 50 that was fine too, because then you could be *helped*. And anyway it is always best to know the truth about yourself.

7   As soon as the Information service was functioning smoothly Dr. Speakie transferred the main thrust of his attention to the implementation of Evaluator training, and planning for the structurization of the Cure Centers, only he changed the name to SQ Achievement Centers. It seemed a very big job even then. We certainly had no idea how big the job would finally turn out to be!

8   As he said at the beginning, we were a very good team. Dr. Speakie valued my administrative abilities and put them to good use. There wasn't a single slacker in the office. We all worked very hard, but there were always rewards.

9   I remember one wonderful day. I had accompanied Dr. Speakie to the Meeting of the Board of the Psychometric Bureau. The emissary from the State of Brazil announced that his State had adopted the Bureau Recommendations for Universal Testing—we had known that that was going to be announced. But then the delegate from Libya and the delegate from China announced that their States had adopted the Test too! Oh, Dr. Speakie's face was just like the sun for a minute, just *shining*. I wish I could remember exactly what he said, especially to the Chinese delegate, because of course China was a very big State and its decision was very influential. Unfortunately I do not have his exact words because I was changing the tape in the recorder. He said something like, "Gentlemen, this is a historic day for humanity." Then he began to talk at once about the effective implementation of the Application Centers, where people would take the Test, and the Achievement Centers, where they would go if they scored over 50, and how to establish the Test Administrations and Evaluations infrastructure on such a large scale, and so on. He was always modest and practical. He would rather talk about doing the job than talk about what an important job it was. He used to say, "Once you know what you're doing, the only thing you need to think about is how to do it." I believe that that is deeply true.

10   From then on, we could hand over the Information program to a subdepartment and concentrate on How to Do It. Those were exciting times! So many States joined the Plan, one after another. When I think of all we had to do I wonder that we didn't all go crazy! Some of the office staff did fail their quarterly Test, in fact. But most of us working in the Executive Office with Dr. Speakie remained quite stable, even when we were on the job all day and half the night. I think his presence was an inspiration. He was always calm and positive, even when we had to arrange things like training 113,000 Chinese Evaluators in three months. "You can always find out 'how' if you just know the 'why'!" he would say. And we always did.

11   When you think back over it, it really is quite amazing what a big job it was—so much bigger than anybody, even Dr. Speakie, had realized it would be. It just changed everything. You only realize that when you think back to what things used to be like. Can you imagine, when we began planning Universal Testing for the State of China, we only allowed for 1,000 Achievement Centers, with 6,800 Staff! It really seems like a joke! But it is not. I was going through some of the old files yesterday, making sure everything is in order, and I found the first China Implementation Plan, with those figures written down in black and white.

12   I believe the reason why even Dr. Speakie was slow to realize the magnitude of the operation was that even though he was a great scientist he was also an optimist. He just kept hoping against hope that the average scores would begin to go down, and this prevented him from seeing that universal application of the SQ Test was eventually going to involve everybody either as Inmates or as Staff.

13   When most of the Russian and all the African States had adopted the Recommendations and were busy implementing them, the debates in the General Assembly of the World Government got very excited. That was the period when so many bad things were said about the *World Times* reports of debates. When I went as his secretary with Dr. Speakie to General Assembly meetings I had to sit and listen in person to people insulting him personally, casting aspersions on his motives and questioning his scientific integrity and even his sincerity. Many of those people were very disagreeable and obviously unbalanced. But he never lost his temper. He would just stand up and prove to them, again, that the SQ Test did actually literally scientifically show whether the testee was sane or insane, and the results could be proved, and all psychometrists accepted them. So the Test-Ban people couldn't do anything but shout about freedom and accuse Dr. Speakie and the Psychometric Bureau of trying to "turn the world into a huge insane asylum." He would always answer quietly and firmly, asking them how they thought a person could be "free" if he suffered under a delusional system, or was prey to compulsions and obsessions, or could not endure contact with reality? How could those who lacked mental health be truly free? What they called freedom might well be a delusional system with

no contact with reality. In order to find out, all they had to do was to become testees. "Mental health *is* freedom," he said. " 'Eternal vigilance is the price of liberty,' they say, and now we have an infallible watchdog to watch for us—the SQ Test. *Only the testees can be truly free!"*

14 There really was no answer they could make to that except illogical and vulgar accusations, which did not convince the delegates who had invited them to speak. Sooner or later the delegates even from Member States where the Test-Ban movement was strong would volunteer to take the SQ Test to prove that their mental health was adequate to their responsibilities. Then the ones that passed the Test and remained in office would begin working for Universal Application in their home State. The riots and demonstrations, and things like the burning of the Houses of Parliament in London in the State of England (where the Nor-Eurp SQ Center was housed), and the Vatican Rebellion, and the Chilean H-Bomb, were the work of insane fanatics appealing to the most unstable elements of the populace. Such fanatics, as Dr. Speakie and Dr. Waltraute pointed out in their Memorandum to the Presidium, deliberately aroused and used the proven instability of the crowd, "mob psychosis." The only response to mass delusion of that kind was immediate implementation of the Testing Program in the disturbed States, and immediate amplification of the Asylum Program.

15 That was Dr. Speakie's own decision, by the way, to rename the SQ Achievement Centers "Asylums." He took the word right out of his enemies' mouths. He said, "An asylum means a place of *shelter,* a place of *cure.* Let there be no stigma attached to the word 'insane,' to the word 'asylum,' to the words 'insane asylum'! No! For the asylum is the haven of mental health—the place of cure, where the anxious gain peace, where the weak gain strength, where the prisoners of inadequate reality assessment win their way to freedom! Proudly let us use the word 'asylum.' Proudly let us go to the asylum, to work to regain our own God-given mental health, or to work with others less fortunate to help them win back their own inalienable right to mental health. And let one word be written large over the door of every asylum in the world—"WELCOME!"

16 Those words are from his great speech at the General Assembly on the day World Universal Application was decreed by the Presidium. Once or twice a year I listen to my tape of that speech. Although I am too busy ever to get really depressed, now and then I feel the need of a tiny "pick-me-up," and so I play that tape. It never fails to send me back to my duties inspired and refreshed.

17 Considering all the work there was to do, as the Test scores continued to come in always a little higher than the Psychometric Bureau analysts estimated, the World Government Presidium did a wonderful job for the two years that it administered Universal Testing. There was a long period, six months, when the scores seemed to have stabilized, with just about half of the testees scoring over 50 and half under 50. At that time it was thought that if 40 per cent of the mentally healthy were assigned to Asylum Staff work, the other 60 per cent

could keep up routine basic world functions such as farming, power supply, transportation, etc. This proportion had to be reversed when they found that over 60 per cent of the mentally healthy were volunteering for Staff work, in order to be with their loved ones in the Asylums. There was some trouble then with the routine basic world functions functioning. However, even then contingency plans were being made for the inclusion of farmlands, factories, power plants, etc., in the Asylum Territories, and the assignment of routine basic world functions work as Rehabilitation Therapy, so that the Asylums could become totally self-supporting if it became advisable. This was President Kim's special care, and he worked for it all through his term of office. Events proved the wisdom of his planning. He seemed such a nice wise little man. I still remember the day when Dr. Speakie came into the office and I knew at once that something was wrong. Not that he ever got really depressed or reacted with inopportune emotion, but it was as if the rubber balls in his shoes had gone just a little bit flat. There was the slightest tremor of true sorrow in his voice when he said, "Mary Ann, we've had a bit of bad news I'm afraid." Then he smiled to reassure me, because he knew what a strain we were all working under, and certainly didn't want to give anybody a shock that might push their score up higher on the next quarterly Test! "It's President Kim," he said, and I knew at once—I knew he didn't mean the President was ill or dead.

18   "Over fifty?" I asked, and he just said quietly and sadly, "Fifty-five."

19   Poor little President Kim, working so efficiently all that three months while mental ill health was growing in him! It was very sad and also a useful warning. High-level consultations were begun at once, as soon as President Kim was committed, and the decision was made to administer the Test monthly, instead of quarterly, to anyone in an executive position.

20   Even before this decision, the Universal scores had begun rising again. Dr. Speakie was not distressed. He had already predicted that this rise was highly probable during the transition period to World Sanity. As the number of the mentally healthy living outside the Asylums grew fewer, the strain on them kept growing greater, and they became more liable to break down under it— just as poor President Kim had done. Later, when the Rehabs began coming out of the Asylums in ever-increasing numbers, this stress would decrease. Also the crowding in the Asylums would decrease, so that the Staff would have more time to work on individually orientated therapy, and this would lead to a still more dramatic increase in the number of Rehabs released. Finally, when the therapy process was completely perfected, including preventive therapy, there might be no Asylums left in the world at all! Because everybody will be either mentally healthy or a Rehab, or "neonormal," as Dr. Speakie liked to call it.

21   It was the trouble in the State of Australia that precipitated the Government crisis. Some Psychometric Bureau officials accused the Australian Evaluators of actually falsifying Test returns, but that is impossible since all the computers

are linked to the World Government Central Computer Bank in Keokuk. Dr. Speakie suspected that the Australian Evaluators had been falsifying *the Test itself,* and insisted that they themselves all be tested immediately. Of course he was right. It had been a conspiracy, and the suspiciously low Australian Test scores had resulted from the use of a false Test. Many of the conspirators tested higher than 80 when forced to take the genuine Test! The State Government in Canberra had been unforgivably lax. If they had just admitted it everything would have been all right. But they got hysterical, and moved the State Government to a sheep station in Queensland, and tried to withdraw from the World Government. (Dr. Speakie said this was a typical mass psychosis: reality-evasion, followed by fugue and autistic withdrawal.) Unfortunately the Presidium seemed to be paralyzed. Australia seceded on the day before the President and Presidium were due to take their monthly Test, and probably they were afraid of overstraining their SQ with agonizing decisions. So the Psychometric Bureau volunteered to handle the episode. Dr. Speakie himself flew on the plane with the H-Bombs, and helped to drop the information leaflets. He never lacked personal courage.

22   When the Australian incident was over, it turned out that most of the Presidium, including President Singh, had scored over 50. So the Psychometric Bureau took over their functions temporarily. Even on a long-term basis this made good sense, since all the problems now facing the World Government had to do with administering and evaluating the Test, training the Staff, and providing full self-sufficiency structuration to all Asylums.

23   What this meant in personal terms was that Dr. Speakie, as Chief of the Psychometric Bureau, was now Interim President of the United States of the World. As his personal secretary I was, I will admit it, just terribly proud of him. But he never let it go to his head.

24   He was so modest. Sometimes he used to say to people, when he introduced me, "This is Mary Ann, my secretary," he'd say with a little twinkle, "and if it wasn't for her I'd have been scoring over fifty long ago!"

25   He truly appreciated efficiency and reliability. That's why we made such a good team, all those years we worked together.

26   There were times, as the World SQ scores rose and rose, that I would become a little discouraged. Once the week's Test figures came in on the readout, and the *average* score was 71. I said, "Doctor, there are moments I believe the whole world is going insane!"

27   But he said, "Look at it this way, Mary Ann. Look at those people in the Asylums—3.1 billion inmates now, and 1.8 billion Staff—but look at them. What are they doing? They're pursuing their therapy, doing rehabilitation work on the farms and in the factories, and striving all the time, too, to *help* each other toward mental health. The preponderant inverse sanity quotient is certainly very high at the moment; they're mostly insane, yes. But you have to admire them. They are fighting for mental health. They will—they *will* win through!" And then he dropped his voice and said as if to himself, gazing out the window

and bouncing just a little on the balls of his feet, "If I didn't believe that, I couldn't go on."

28   And I knew he was thinking of his wife.

29   Mrs. Speakie had scored 88 on the very first American Universal Test. She had been in the Greater Los Angeles Territory Asylum for years now.

30   Anybody who still thinks Dr. Speakie wasn't sincere should think about that for a minute! He gave up everything for his belief.

31   And even when the Asylums were all running quite well, and the epidemics in South Africa and the famines in Texas and the Ukraine were under control, still the work load on Dr. Speakie never got any lighter, because every month the personnel of the Psychometric Bureau got smaller, since some of them always flunked their monthly Test and were committed to Bethesda. I never could keep any of my secretarial staff anymore for longer than a month or two. It was harder and harder to find replacements, too, because most sane young people volunteered for Staff work in the Asylums, since life was much easier and more sociable inside the Asylums than outside. Everything so convenient, and lots of friends and acquaintances! I used to positively envy those girls! But I knew where my job was.

32   At least it was much less hectic here in the UN Building, or the Psychometry Tower as it had been renamed long ago. Often there wouldn't be anybody around the whole building all day long but Dr. Speakie and myself, and maybe Bill the janitor (Bill scored 32 regular as clockwork every quarter). All the restaurants were closed, in fact most of Manhattan was closed, but we had fun picnicking in the old General Assembly Hall. And there was always the odd call from Buenos Aires or Reykjavik, asking Dr. Speakie's advice as Interim President about some problem, to break the silence.

33   But last November 8, I will never forget the date, when Dr. Speakie was dictating the Referendum for World Economic Growth for the next five-year period, he suddenly interrupted himself. "By the way, Mary Ann," he said, "how was your last score?"

34   We had taken the Test two days before, on the sixth. We always took the Test every first Monday. Dr. Speakie never would have dreamed of excepting himself from Universal Testing regulations.

35   "I scored twelve," I said, before I thought how strange it was of him to ask. Or, not just to ask, because we often mentioned our scores to each other; but to ask *then,* in the middle of executing important world Government business.

36   "Wonderful," he said, shaking his head. "You're wonderful, Mary Ann! Down two from last month's Test, aren't you?"

37   "I'm always between ten and fourteen," I said. "Nothing new about that, Doctor."

38   "Someday," he said, and his face took on the expression it had when he gave his great speech about the Asylums, "someday, this world of ours will be

governed by men fit to govern it. Men whose SQ score is zero. Zero, Mary Ann!"

39   "Well, my goodness, Doctor," I said jokingly—his intensity almost alarmed me a little—"even *you* never scored lower than three, and you haven't done that for a year or more now!"

40   He stared at me almost as if he didn't see me. It was quite uncanny. "Someday," he said in just the same way, "nobody in the world will have a quotient higher than fifty. Someday, nobody in the world will have a quotient higher than thirty! Higher than ten! The Therapy will be perfected. I was only the diagnostician. But the Therapy will be perfected! The cure will be found! Someday!" And he went on staring at me, and then he said, "Do you know what my score was on Monday?"

41   "Seven," I guessed promptly. The last time he had told me his score it had been seven.

42   "Ninety-two," he said.

43   I laughed, because he seemed to be laughing. He had always had a puckish sense of humor that came out unexpectedly. But I thought we really should get back to the World Economic Growth Plan, so I said laughingly, "That really is a very bad joke, Doctor!"

44   "Ninety-two," he said, "and you don't believe me, Mary Ann, but that's because of the cantaloupe."

45   I said, "What cantaloupe, Doctor?" and that was when he jumped across his desk and began to try to bite through my jugular vein.

46   I used a judo hold and shouted to Bill the janitor, and when he came I called a robo-ambulance to take Dr. Speakie to Bethesda Asylum.

47   That was six months ago. I visit Dr. Speakie every Saturday. It is very sad, he is in the McLean Area, which is the Violent Ward, and every time he sees me he screams and foams. But I do not take it personally. One should never take mentally ill health personally. When the Therapy is perfected he will be completely rehabilitated. Meanwhile, I just hold on here. Bill keeps the floors clean, and I run the World Government. It really isn't as difficult as you might think.

☐ Discovering Meaning and Technique

1. What do you think *SQ* stands for?

2. With what groups does the speaker associate those who call Dr. Speakie "a power-seeker and dictator"?

3. What kind of person is Mary Ann Smith? How is her personality revealed in the story?

4. What kind of person is Dr. Speakie? Can you rely on his secretary's description of him?

5. In the story, Le Guin makes fun of bureaucratic language and jargon in phrases such as "individually orientated therapy." Find another example.

6. Do you get the impression that the secretary is telling or writing the story?

7. At what point did you first realize that the story is humorous?

8. In the story, we learn that Parliament in London has burned. What are some of the other unexpected occurrences that have taken place in this future world?

9. What was Dr. Speakie's solution for the Australian crisis?

10. An ending that is the opposite of what should logically occur is called ironic. What is ironic about the ending of this story?

☐ Writing Suggestions

1. Describe the dangers of an overreliance on tests, such as IQ tests, achievement tests, placement tests, entrance examinations.

2. Discuss the likelihood of a central world government in the future.

3. When should a person have the right to refuse to take a test, such as a drug test or a psychiatric test?

4. Should government have the power to determine sanity or insanity? If not, who should?

5. Write a story in which the government forces you to take an unfair sanity test and forces you into an asylum.

THANATOS

☐ VONDA N. MCINTYRE

1 Security took Allin to the factory in chains: she had tried to escape twice, and almost succeeded once. On this kind of assignment, they could not use the anesthetic they carried, for it lingered in the blood.

2   The duocar slid out of heavy traffic and stopped on the parking rail. It had run electric all the way from court, slowly, without the use of the gas engine that was only legal in security cars. Allin was glad of any delay, anything that gave her a few more minutes.

3   The factory was a low, innocuous gray building among other low gray buildings. Most of it was safely underground. The two security men took Allin out of the mesh cage in the back of the car. She stopped on the dirty sidewalk despite the press of other people, despite the city smells nauseating her, despite the city noises roaring around them. She looked up.

4   Wide stairs led half a flight to a featureless door. The windows of the next two floors were covered with riveted metal plates. Above the building, above the whole city, yet seeming very close, the cloudy-gray-brown sky threatened snow. Involuntarily Allin shivered, but she could not pretend she was cold. The security people expected her to try again to bolt for freedom and concealment in the crowds. She could feel their fingers, nervously tight on her arms, and the thin steel chain cutting into her palms where she gripped it. Beneath the cuffs her wrists were scraped raw.

5   "Come on." They half lifted her. She held up her head and would not let them hurry her off-balance. The manacles should have been around her throat, to explain the tightness there.

6   They reached the top of the stairs. In fumbling for the pass, one let go of her arm. Without thinking she jerked around, half away from the other, already running.

7   He was too well trained; he had been ready for her. He yanked her back hard; her boot slipped on the concrete step. She fell backwards, unable to catch herself. Cement scraped cloth and bruised her hip; she heard a single quick gruff word, "Don't," a corner of the stair slammed into her side, just below her ribs. It took her a moment to regain her breath. She looked up and saw the two men glaring at each other. The one who had let her go had his pass in one hand and his partner's club in the other, holding it back.

8   "I'm sick and tired—"

9   "It won't matter in a little while. Maybe—" But he did not finish what had begun in sadness and ended in disgust. He turned away, slapping the card onto the sensor next to the door. The other man looked down at Allin, scowling. He met her gaze for a moment, then looked away. Allin took a deep breath and climbed to her feet. Neither of them helped her. She had not expected them to. "Suck," she muttered, and got the satisfaction of seeing his knuckles whiten around the club at her use of the slang.

10   The door opened. They led her down a long hall painted pale gray-green, lined with closed doors, stretching away to an elevator.

11   They did not speak during the long drop. Allin could feel the tension, in them and in herself. It peaked with the deceleration of the slowing cage.

12   A technician was waiting for them at the bottom. It was the first time

Allin really had to believe that she was here and that there was no way out.

13   "You're late."

14   "We had some trouble."

15   The technician shrugged. "Doesn't matter. Doctor won't be here for a while."

16   "Where do you want her?" The gentler security man seemed to have withdrawn inside himself. His eyes could not stay still.

17   "You're anxious to get out." The technician sounded at the same time defensive and contemptuous.

18   "That's right."

19   "We've probably saved your life more than once."

20   "Yeah." Even the agreement was accusation. "You've probably saved everybody in the world at least once." He looked at Allin. She could see hurt in his pale eyes; she did not think he had done this job before. She wondered if he would talk about duty if she asked him and why he could not have turned his head and let her go. "Probably even her." He was not speaking to the technician any more.

21   "Sit her down over there and you can sign and get out."

22   "She'll kill you," the suck told him. "I said we had trouble."

23   Allin scowled: she had broken laws, but she had never killed. She remained silent.

24   "Chain her, then, I don't care." He went back to his desk and pressed buttons on a console.

25   The security men took her to a bench, unchained one of her hands, and relocked the manacle around the armrest. Walking away, neither agent looked back at her.

26   At his desk, the technician brought out a light-pen so they could sign the screen. Allin wondered what the printing said. "Brought on this day into involuntary servitude, one human being, having been deprived of life, liberty, consciousness, and humanity, as punishment for acts against society, and for the good of mankind . . ." The technician made out a receipt for her. He watched the two agents in silence with an ugly half-smile until they were almost inside the elevator. "Hey, sucks, how about the key?"

27   The gentler one flushed, pulled it out of his pocket, and threw it into the room just as the doors closed. The technician sauntered over and picked it up, tossed it and caught it and laughed when he saw Allin watching. His eyes measured her, as if for a scalpel or a shroud. Contemptuous of herself for it, she felt blood rise in her face.

28   "You ought to last a long time," the tech said. His face held the child's innocence of a psychopath. He turned back to his desk and called up another form. "Name," he said. He knew it: it must be on the screen before him.

29   "Press the right button and your machine will tell you." She regretted the

words as soon as she spoke; he was taunting her for his own amusement, and a response would only make his game more pleasurable.

30   "Listen," he said, very patiently, "don't make trouble." She did not answer. "Christ." He looked at the ceiling in mock supplication. "A stubborn one." He glanced back at her, but his expression held no mercy. "This can be as easy or as hard as you want." He gave her a moment to think that over: it was not necessary. "Things happen to people in the wards . . . did you know that some of them can feel pain through the drugs we use? They go crazy from it, and then . . ." He pointed his finger at her and cocked his thumb. "Bang! We shoot them." He laughed and caressed the control panel of the console. The green fluorescence of the printing gave his face an eerie cast. "No offspring, no dependents, no contracts . . ." He raised an eyebrow. "Ah, you're one of the guerrillas. What a stupid way to waste your life."

31   She forced herself to sit silently through it. Her nails, despite their shortness, dug into her palms. Her life *was* a waste; even in the idealistic enthusiasm of her adolescence, she had known that a bunch of kids and aging revolutionaries could have none but a gadfly effect on the institutions they had sworn to change. The planet's living system was battered to homogeneity before Allin was even born. Her guerrilla team was a sad, lost conscience, never strong enough to halt the progression and turn it around. Every one of her friends knew they would end up dead in the sea, decomposing in a dying forest, or . . . here.

32   The technician tried again. "Some of the orderlies . . . they come pretty close to being necrophiles. Long hours. Boredom. You know. I can't watch them all the time. Not much to do here but feed the animals and milk them." He smiled, and his teeth showed. He sickened her. She turned away, and he laughed. A shallow, bloody crescent in her palm cut across the lifeline.

33   "The animals sometimes end up looking pretty awful," he said. "Scars and things . . . one of them got pregnant once. We let her have it even after we used a genetic virus on her—"

34   "It won't matter to me," Allin said. "I'll have no mind."

35   "Sometimes they get pardoned," he said. "We bring them back almost as good as new . . . unless something's happened—"

36   "You're a liar."

37   He stood up, smiling again. "You're right." He moved toward her, wearing a deceptively engaging expression. "So how about one last little bit of fun?" He reached to touch her.

38   In the final minutes of her life, Allin might have been able to accept a gift of a few moments of pleasure, a gift of human contact, but this would be no gift. It was an expression of power. She kicked the technician in the groin with all the thrust in her long legs. He cried out in agony, falling, writhing. Allin sat back on the bench, as the technician curled in fetal position as though to avoid

further blows. Regaining his breath, he crawled away from her. After a few minutes he was able to use the desk corner to pull himself up. "What'd you do that for?" His voice was that of a child wrongly punished.

39   She looked past him, silent.

40   He laughed, but the sound was shaky. He made work for himself.

41 The elevator door slid open, and the doctor entered. She glanced from the tech, still pale, to Allin, but said nothing. She picked up the key, and stopped a meter out of Allin's reach. "There's no way out and I'm very good at judo."

42   Silence kept Allin's pride more than a direct acquiescence. The doctor freed her from the bench but kept the chains locked around her wrists. Taking her arm, she led Allin through another door, to a sterile white room with an examining table and glass cases of drugs and instruments. The room smelled of astringent antiseptics and sick-sweet anesthetic. Allin stopped in the doorway, against the pressure of the doctor's hand.

43   "It's really not bad. Just sleep . . ."

44   "We're all asleep," Allin said.

45   "Did you think you could wake people up?" The doctor's voice was tense, intense. "All that energy, all that vision—"

46   "—wasted," Allin finished for her, harshly.

47   "Come along." The doctor spoke coldly and professionally again; Allin had a quick vision of the future: the flashes of anger and pain would slowly seep from the doctor's soul, and she would survive.

48   She would survive, while Allin was approaching the end of her conscious life.

49   "I want to see where I'll be," she whispered.

50   Allin startled her: the doctor did not speak for what seemed a very long time.

51   ". . . All right."

52   She led Allin through a labyrinth of corridors, deeper into the earth. The air grew cooler. When they reached wide double doors the doctor took her arm again. The doors swung open, allowing an incongruous breeze to escape. The room beyond was kept at positive pressure, to exclude unapproved germs. The doctor led Allin onto the ward.

53   No mammals remained on earth, except a few rodents in laboratories and slums, and perhaps the potential of wildlife, stored as frozen ova and sperm or cell clones in universities or museums, for some unlikely future. No birds lived but a few garbage scavengers. Complete food protein came from fish, cell cultures, improved grains, but the world had discovered that only the intricate biochemistry of a living animal sufficed for some endeavors. Horses, for decades, produced antibodies against human disease: infected, the animals lived and produced serum, vaccines for people.

54   All the horses, all the mammals larger and smaller than a rat, were extinct. Except for human beings.

55   Allin hardly saw the orderlies staring at her. Before her stretched long rows of frame beds, their circular supports echoing each other across a vast distance. A still and silent body hung suspended in each. Nakedness and sex were incidentally concealed by torso supports. No pressure sores would develop on these valuable animals.

56   The ceiling was a transparent plastic web of pipes carrying nutrient fluid to tubes, to needles, to permanent inlets sewn in veins. Catheters carried wastes to outlets in the floor. Allin took one more step inside the room. She could hear quiet breathing, like sounds in a cemetery. The anesthetic smell was very strong. All the eyelids were dark and sunken and all the heads and bodies shaved bald. Needle scars and the scars of viral lesions covered projecting arms and legs and sexless faces, and halfway down the nearest row, orderlies were drawing blood, cleanly, sterilely, to extract antibodies with the serum.

57   Milking the animals.

58   The sound in Allin's throat was half a moan, half sob. The doctor heard her, sensed the danger, held her tighter, but Allin caught her in the sternum with her elbow and ran. Behind her, she could hear gasping, and the footsteps and voices of the orderlies. She knew she could not escape the ward or the building, that any action she could take would be foolish and futile. She climbed a shining arc of frame between hanging tubes like snakes. She was only slightly hampered by the chains. She hesitated at the apex of a frame, then leaped for the largest nutrient pipe within her reach. It was never meant for extra strain. Her momentum pulled it loose and as she hit the floor the sticky warm wet stuff splashed across her, the tile, the zombies in the beds. She sprinted for another place to climb where the network burbled on.

59   "Stop!"

60   She was ready to jump again when she heard the warning. The fumes of anesthetic mixed with nutrients dizzied her, but she saw the doctor, and she saw the gun, as though through heat waves rising from a desert. She gauged her distance to the next tube and jumped.

61 The bullet shattered the prisoner's skull, tore through her brain, and threw her crumpled to the floor.

62   An orderly rushed out to turn off the nutrient flow. The doctor stood silently as a pool of the stuff reached her feet. The gun was warm in her hand, smoking. She heard the other orderly pick up the phone. "We need the heart-lung machine," he said.

63   *If not for this place,* the doctor thought, *millions of people would die. If not for this place . . .* The gun fell heavily to the floor.

64   "Never mind," he said abruptly.

65   "What, ma'am?"

66   "Never mind."

67   "The body's still usable—"

68   "Call the morgue," the doctor said. No one ever argued with her when she used that tone. "Have her cremated."

69   The orderly hesitated, then cut the connection. "Yes, ma'am." He keyed out a different number.

☐ Discovering Meaning and Technique

1. How does McIntyre create a somber mood at the opening of the story?

2. At the beginning of the story (paragraphs 10–20), the security guards take Allin in an elevator to the bottom of the building. There the technician says to them, "We've probably saved your life more than once." He answers, "You've probably saved everybody in the world at least once." How do these statements foreshadow the plot of the story?

3. When the technician signs in Allin, what is the language of the message meant to sound like?

4. Explain the statement, "His face held the child's innocence of a psychopath" (paragraph 28).

5. What stories does the technician tell Allin to intensify her dread?

6. What is the significance of the exchange between Allin and the doctor in paragraphs 44–46?

7. Describe what the planet is like at the time the story takes place.

8. What does the title mean?

9. Explain the doctor's thought, "If not for this place . . . millions of people would die" (paragraph 63).

10. At the end of the story, is there a victory of a sort? Explain your answer.

☐ Writing Suggestions

1. Argue that the future world pictured in "Thanatos" is either realistic or fantastic.

2. Do you believe that medical technology can be used in undesirable ways?

3. If you lived at the time of the story, would you join the guerrillas or support the system? Defend your choice.

4. If by giving prisoners experimental drugs or other treatments, millions of people could be saved, should the experiments be allowed?

■ Combining Sources in a Composition

1. Norman Cousins and Craig Brod point out drawbacks to computer use. Agree or disagree with their assessments.

2. Discuss the tendency of many computer users to think of their computers as human. (See Vonnegut, Bodett, and Turkle.)

3. Combine the information in the selections written by Paul Loeb and Helen Caldicott to describe the dangers of radiation.

4. Compare Lydia Dotto's and Joy Kogawa's views on the effects of nuclear attack.

5. Isaac Asimov, Ursula K. Le Guin, and Vonda McIntyre paint grim scenarios of the future. Compare these views with your own ideas about the world of tomorrow.

6. Are efforts to predict the future futile or useful? (See Asimov and Tuchman.)

7. Discuss the many unknowns in science and technology. Some are mentioned by Isaac Asimov and Holcomb Noble; add others.

8. Using the selections by Larry Thompson and Vonda McIntyre as sources, discuss the dangers that could result from medical research.

C H A P T E R 6

EDUCATION
The Student

■ ■ ■

CHEATING: ALIVE AND FLOURISHING

□ **CLAUDIA H. DEUTSCH**

"All the professors I know say they are seeing a higher percentage of classroom cheating."
—RICHARD A. DIENSTBIER, PSYCHOLOGY PROFESSOR, UNIVERSITY OF NEBRASKA—

"Sure, now and then you'll hear about a case, but I've never noticed much cheating myself."
—PATRICIA A. SOKOLIK, INDUSTRIAL ENGINEERING SENIOR, UNIVERSITY OF NEBRASKA—

1   Trying to get a handle on scholastic cheating is as frustrating as surveying American eating patterns. Everyone says he is watching his weight—yet the streets are full of overweight folk, and the snack-food industry reports record sales.

2   Talk to students, and you get the same kind of dichotomy. Most say that,

yes, they cheated when they were younger, but no, they would not dream of cheating now, and no, cheating is not a big problem at their schools.

3   But talk to their teachers, and a very different picture emerges, one that shatters many of the comfortable middle-class myths about who cheats and why. It is a picture of cheating among top students at top schools; of habits that take root in elementary school, bud in high school and flower in college; of parents who care more about their children's success than about their moral development, and of a problem that is more likely to get worse than to get better.

4   National statistics are hard to find, but every now and then a school, a district or a research organization does its own survey. The results are discouraging, to say the least. For example:

- The College Board, whose Scholastic Aptitude Tests help determine whether students get into their first-choice colleges, is detecting more cases of "questionable validity of test scores." Robert H. Parker, director of test security, says the increase may well be traceable to better detection methods—but he cannot be sure.
- The Cooperative Institutional Research Program at the University of California at Los Angeles recently asked some 290,000 college freshmen whether they had ever cheated on a test in their last year of high school. Some 30.4 percent said that they had. That sounds like a low percentage—except that in 1966, the last time the research group asked the question, only 20.6 percent said they had cheated.
- A survey of students in California in 1985 showed that three-quarters of *all* of the state's high school students, starting as freshmen, cheated on exams.
- A similar survey last year of students in Amherst, N.Y., an affluent suburb near Buffalo, showed that more than 80 percent had cheated at least once in 1987.

5   Several schools are trying to cut down on the opportunity to cheat by giving more open-book exams. Others are holding seminars for their teachers to discuss the cheating phenomenon—often with students invited to attend. But psychologists say that the roots of the problem must be dealt with in the home. It is there, they say, that children must be imbued with enough self-esteem to make occasional failure an unthreatening prospect, and with enough of a sense of right and wrong to overcome the urge to cheat.

6   Unfortunately, teachers say, too many parents are abdicating that responsibility. "Kids just aren't brought up to see cheating as dishonest," said Patrick L. Daly, who taught high school in the Detroit area for 30 years before retiring last year. "To them, shoplifting is dishonest; writing a couple of math formulas on their hand is not."

7   "A child cheats on an exam and his parents get outraged," said Young Jay Mulkey, president of the American Institute for Character Education, a San Anto-

nio-based foundation that helps teachers develop students' self-esteem. "Yet he keeps hearing his folks talk about cheating on expense accounts or income taxes. The inconsistency drives children crazy."

8   Perhaps most troubling, teachers and psychologists say that it is often the most gifted students, the ones who presumably could get good grades without cheating, who are the worst offenders. They are the ones who believe that getting into a top college—or later, a top graduate school—is the most important goal, and will do anything they must to attain it. At first, the pressure is from their parents; eventually, those values become their own.

9   Indeed, it was students at New York City's prestigious Stuyvesant High School and Bronx High School of Science who were caught using stolen tests and answers to Regents exams in 1980. And this past November, it was students at the Brunswick School, in Greenwich, Conn., who broke into another private school, the Greenwich Academy, and opened sealed copies of the S.A.T. the day before the test was to be administered.

10   A case can be made, and often is, that such incidents get publicity precisely because it is so unusual for top schools to be involved. But teachers in schools with less lofty reputations make an equally convincing case for themselves. They note that not many students in schools with poor national standings and high dropout rates care enough about their grades to cheat, while students in vocational schools care more about the subject matter than they do about test scores.

11   "Many of our kids are poor, and they really want to learn these skills because it's the only way they can better their economic situation," said Mary Spilotro, an English teacher at the High School of Graphic Communication Arts (formerly the New York School of Printing). "I saw a lot more cheating when I taught in academic high schools."

12   She would also see a lot more cheating, it seems, if she taught at the college level. Poll after poll shows that college students, not just high schoolers, are making cheating a way of life. Campus newspapers abound with articles dealing with the subject. Last fall Dartmouth College, for one, devoted almost an entire issue of *Common Sense,* its new student paper, to the growing problem of cheating on campus. Universities are holding special seminars at which professors and students discuss the problem. At least one school, the University of Illinois, issues a pamphlet for its faculty that describes some of the more ingenious methods students may use to cheat (written crib sheets attached to cap visors, oral ones playing on a Sony Walkman) and ways to thwart them. Several others are tightening their computer security, after having discovered that computer hackers were breaking into electronic college files in order to alter their grades.

13   Yet despite the precautions, students still offer papers churned out by term-paper companies—or by other students—as their own. And they still seem to find peeking at each other's tests to be irresistible.

14   Even at military academies and other schools with strict honor codes that mandate expulsion of students who cheat or fail to report cheating, the problem

is growing. In 1984, 19 cadets at the Air Force Academy were suspended for a year for cheating on a physics test—and academy officials were certain that many others had cheated.

15   Where students still administer the honor systems the news is not cheery. "Definitely, more people are being brought up on charges," said James R. Socas, a 21-year-old history major who is chairman of the honor committee at the University of Virginia. The increase is small, and Mr. Socas says he believes it represents a "stronger show of confidence in the system"—that is, a greater willingness on the part of students and professors to bring charges against cheaters.

16   Similarly, Cadet David J. Wilkie, Honor Captain at the United States Military Academy, notes that, while classroom cheating has waned and take-home exams— the subject of a 1976 scandal at West Point in which more than 200 cadets were accused of either collaborating or failing to report others who did—are no longer given, incidents of plagiarism are on the rise. "Classroom cheating would be very difficult to do here without being obvious," he said, "but last year we had several cases of cadets copying from Cliffs notes," brief synopses of literature and academic disciplines that students use to cram for tests.

17   Cheating was, in a sense, almost *de rigeur* in the 1960s, a decade character- ized by rebellion and antiestablishment attitudes. And no one was much surprised in the 1970s, the "me-generation" years when selfishness was supposedly the cornerstone of youthful behavior. In fact, reports of cheating were so prevalent in the 1970s that the Carnegie Council on Policy Studies in Higher Education undertook a full-scale study of the phenomenon. Its findings, published in 1979, showed a "significant and apparently increasing amount of cheating by students in academic assignments." Similar findings at specific colleges, including the Johns Hopkins University and Barnard College, prompted deans there to scrap longstanding honor systems in favor of proctored tests. Informal polls at numerous colleges show that the problem has by no means abated. If anything, it has become worse.

18   On the surface, the reasons are painfully apparent. Television newscasts and newspaper headlines blare revelations of breach-of-ethics scandals on an almost daily basis. Young people hear Oliver North defend lying during the Iran-contra hearings. They read reports that trading in a stock always becomes heavy a few days before a major merger is announced and infer—probably accu- rately—that for every Ivan Boesky who gets caught doing insider trading (he was a New York University trustee at the time), there are a dozen others doing it with impunity. They see Senator Joseph Biden's candidacy for the highest office in the land scuttled when he was caught plagiarizing a British politician's speeches and exaggerating his academic record. They see noted evangelists like Jimmy Swaggart and Jim Bakker immersed in sex scandals.

19   "Freshmen don't come here and within two or three months decide to cheat," said John Scouffas, assistant vice chancellor for student affairs at the University of Illinois. "It starts well before they get here. We're talking about

impressionable people who read about insider trading and political cover-ups and say, 'What the heck, dishonesty seems to be the accepted thing in our society.' They come to college and say, 'Maybe that's what I should be doing to get by.'"

20   Others say this concept is too simplistic. They point out that for the most part the people associated with the ethics scandals of the 1980s are in disgrace—and, in many cases, in jail—and that youngsters could just as easily derive a "crime does not pay" conclusion from the headlines.

21   Far more troubling than publicized scandals, they say, is the lackadaisical attitude modern parents take to morality, along with their frenzied pursuit of wealth. "It is not that kids are being taught the wrong values, it is that they are not being taught any values," said Mr. Daly, the retired high school teacher.

22   "The attitude," Mr. Scouffas said, "is 'Let's hurry up and get through so we can go and make $100,000 a year.' The goal is a good job with a lot of money, not necessarily a good education."

23   Is cheating human nature, or do parents and teachers encourage it by their own attitudes?

24   For every expert with a theory about who cheats, why, and how it should be handled, there is another with an equally plausible theory suggesting the opposite. Psychologists who subscribe to Lawrence Kohlberg's theories of morality, which postulate six stages of moral development, say that cheating is inevitable among young children.

25   "Their morality is centered on the idea that whatever brings them good results is right," said Marvin W. Berkowitz, an associate professor of psychology at Marquette University. But many elementary-school teachers say that is just not so. "Children just don't have a natural tendency to cheat," said Carmen Edgerly, who teaches fifth-graders at Public School 41 in New York's Greenwich Village. "They are more likely to help each other."

26   No one seems much bothered about cheating in youngsters, anyway. "My little boy doesn't like to lose when he plays games, so he cheats," said a mother of a nursery schooler. "I did the same when I was his age." What if the cheating on games turns into cheating on tests? "If I thought he wasn't studying, I might get concerned," she said. "But I can't lay a guilt trip on a kid for cheating—it is too tempting, too common and too much a part of human nature."

27   Even the most vociferous opponents of cheating are ready to give youngsters a bit of leeway. "I wouldn't be comfortable with an honor code like ours in grammar school or even high school," said Mr. Socas, honor chairman at Virginia. "Our system really says, 'You are on the threshold of being an adult, of taking responsibility for your actions.' Young people must be allowed to make mistakes." Did he cheat when he was younger? "Sure."

28   Education professionals cite more complex reasons to tolerate cheating among youngsters. Come down hard, they warn, and the child's already precarious self-esteem and joy in learning are at risk. "If you make a really big deal out of it, you can turn the kid off for three weeks," said Richard Gross, who teaches

at P.S. 49 in the South Bronx. "Too many kids are turned off today—just look at the dropout rate."

29   Most agree that by high school, cheating should be dealt with more seriously. But usually it is not. Some teachers, under tremendous pressure from local school districts to bring their students' performance above national norms, are loath to interfere with a process that yields higher grades. Others, students say, just do not seem to care.

30   "I got through my sophomore year in high school by cheating," said Sherry L. Brendel, a 19-year-old sales assistant at Oppenheimer & Company. "I would have hesitated if I thought the teachers cared, but they didn't even look. They'd walk out of the room during an exam."

31   Ms. Brendel is now going for a degree at Fordham University at night, and she says she no longer cheats at all. "The college teachers seem to care whether their students learn," she says.

32   "They stay in the room, they answer questions, they spend more time explaining things."

33   But do they crack down on cheaters? At worst, most schools make students caught cheating retake the entire course; more often, they simply make them retake the exam or redo the paper.

34   The leniency is a source of frustration to those academicians who find cheating abhorrent. "When I catch students cheating, I want to nail them for it," said Mr. Berkowitz of Marquette. "But I once caught a doctoral student plagiarizing and took him to his dean. It became the dean's decision, and the dean let him stay at the university."

35   Students, too, say that official policies are more honored in the breach. Mr. Socas at the University of Virginia concedes that professors often do not report cheating to the honor committee because they are not comfortable with the idea that convicted cheaters will be expelled. Ms. Sokolik, the Nebraska senior, also says that the few cheaters at her school are not dealt with severely enough. "Rarely is the punishment worse than a reprimand," she said. "The official policy is that cheaters fail the class, but teachers don't follow it."

36   If psychologists and a small but growing number of college officials have their way, enforcement policies will become a non-issue. They are focusing on preventing cheating, both through the quick-fix method of making tests cheatproof and the longer-term method of rekindling in students a desire to learn.

37   Increasingly, professors are turning to open-book exams that test students more on how well they have learned to apply concepts than on how well they have memorized arcane facts or formulas. The approach serves a dual purpose: it fosters conceptual thinking and makes crib sheets and peeking obsolete.

38   "I give open-book problems without unique solutions," said Stanley R. Liberty, dean of the engineering school at the University of Nebraska. "Students know there's an unbelievably low probability of two people coming up with the same approach."

39   Cornell University, meanwhile, has set up a faculty subcommittee to create

a campus-wide dialogue on the "pedagogical" goals of exams. "Talking about cheating would be divisive," said Larry Walker, vice president of academic programs. "I want professors and students to discuss ways that exams can be used as a learning device, not an evaluation tool."

40   For the most part, academicians seem optimistic that changes in teaching methods and in exams will cut down on academic dishonesty. But teachers and child psychologists say that the only way to stop kids from cheating in college is to keep them from developing the habit in high school. They are worried whether, in a society where two-income families and high-pressure jobs are prevalent, that is an ever more elusive goal.

41   Said Beverly Betz, who teaches at New York City's High School for the Humanities, "Parents have got to make their kids feel that if they don't do well on a test it's not the end of the world, but just an indication that more work needs to be done."

☐ Discovering Meaning and Technique

1. According to Deutsch, which kinds of students are most likely to cheat? Why?

2. Why are students in vocational schools less likely to cheat?

3. What are some techniques used to prevent cheating?

4. Point out the different theories that explain cheating.

5. What is the purpose of the two quotations at the beginning of the selection? Considering the subject matter, is this technique effective?

☐ Writing Suggestions

1. Some people think that cheating indicates an ethical breakdown in society—further evidenced by scandals in politics and business. Do you agree?

2. Do scandals involving public figures have any real effect upon the ethics of the ordinary citizen?

3. Why do you think people cheat? Support your theory with concrete details.

4. Would an honor code work in most high schools or colleges? Why or why not?

5. Suggest some strategies for preventing cheating.

6. If you have ever cheated on tests or at sports, why did you do it? Would you do it again?

THE DEAD-END KIDS

☐ **MICHELE MANGES**

1 If just showing up accounts for 90 percent of success in life, as Woody Allen claims, then today's teen-agers ought to make great recruits for tomorrow's permanent work force.

2 Well over half of them are already showing up in the part-time work force doing after-school and summer jobs. In times past, this kind of youthful zeal was universally applauded; the kids, we thought, were getting invaluable preliminary training for the world of work. But now a lot of people are *worried* about the surge in youth employment. Why?

3 Because a lot of today's eight million working teens—55 percent of all 16- to 19-year-olds—aren't learning anything much more useful than just showing up.

TASTE OF ADULTHOOD

4 Not that long ago many youngsters could get part-time or summer jobs that taught them the rudiments of a trade they could pursue later. If this wasn't the case, they at least got a taste of the adult world, working closely with adults and being supervised by them. Also, in whatever they did they usually had to apply in a practical way at least some of the skills they'd learned in school, thus reinforcing them.

5 Today, however, a growing majority of working youngsters hustle at monotonous, dead-end jobs that prepare them for nothing. They certainly make up one of the largest groups of underemployed people in the country.

6 Many work in adolescent ghettos overseen by "supervisors" barely older than they are, and they don't need to apply much of anything they've learned in school, not even the simplest math; technology has turned them into near-automatons. Checkout scanners and sophisticated cash registers tot up bills and figure the change for them. At fast-food joints, automatic cooking timers remove the last possibility that a teen might pick up a smidgen of culinary skill.

7 Laurence Steinberg, a Temple University professor and co-author of a book on teen-age employment, estimates that at least three out of every four working teen-agers are in jobs that don't give them any meaningful training. "Why we

think that wrapping burgers all day prepares kids for the future is beyond me," he says.

8   In a study of 550 teens, Prof. Steinberg and his colleagues found that those working long hours at unchallenging jobs tended to grow cynical about work in general. They did only their own defined tasks and weren't inclined to help out others, their sense of self-respect declined, and they began to feel that companies don't care about their employees. In effect, they were burning out before they even joined the permanent work force.

9   A lot of teen-aged workers are just bone-tired, too. Shelley Wurst, a cook at an Ohio franchise steakhouse, got so worn out she stopped working on school nights. "I kept sleeping through my first-period class," she says. "If it wasn't for the crew I'm working with, I wouldn't want to work there at all."

10   This sort of thing is all too common. "Some kids are working past 2 A.M. and have trouble waking up for morning classes," says Larry Morrison, principal of Sylvania (Ohio) Northview High School. Educators like him are beginning to wonder whether teen-age work today is not only irrelevant to future careers but even damaging to them; the schoolwork of students who pour so much time and energy into dead-end jobs often suffers—thus dimming their eventual prospects in a permanent job market that now stresses education.

11   As for the teens themselves, a great number would much rather be working elsewhere, in more challenging or relevant jobs. Some, like Tanya Paris, have sacrificed to do so.

12   A senior at Saratoga (Calif.) High School, she works six hours a week with a scientist at the National Aeronautics and Space Administration, studying marine algae, for no pay and no school credit. The future biologist hopes that her NASA work will help her decide which area of biology to pursue.

13   But most others either are lured by the money they can make or can't find what they're looking for. Jay Jackson, a senior at Northview High, says he'd take a pay cut from his $3.40-an-hour job as a stock boy if he could find something allied to psychology, his prospective career field. He hasn't been able to. Schoolmate Bridget Ellenwood, a junior, yearned for a job that had something to do with dentistry but had to settle for slicing up chickens at a local Chick-fil-A franchise—a job, she says, "where you don't learn much at all."

AND MORE TO COME

14 Expect more teen jobs where you don't learn much at all. The sweeping change in the economy from making things to service, together with the growth of computerized service-industry technology that leaves almost nothing to individual skill and initiative, is expected to accelerate.

15   So the mindless and irrelevant part-time jobs open to teens in the near future will probably increase, while the better jobs continue to decline. On

top of that, a growing labor shortage, which would drive up pay, figures to draw more kids into those jobs—against their interests. "Teen-agers would be much better off doing a clerical-type job or studying," says Prof. John Bishop of Cornell University's Industrial and Labor Relations Center.

16   Efforts have been under way to cut back the number of hours teens can work, but the worsening labor shortage is undercutting them. Many educators are instead urging the states to start or expand more high-school cooperative education programs. These plans tie school and outside work to future career goals and provide more structure and adult supervision than ordinary outside work.

17   Employers also prefer students with this kind of experience. A recent study by the Cooperative Work Experience Education Association found that 136 of 141 businesses in Arkansas would hire a young applicant who had been in such a program over one who had worked independently. "The goal is not to get kids to stop working," says Prof. Bishop of Cornell. "It's to get them to learn more."

☐ Discovering Meaning and Technique

1. Specifically, what are Manges's complaints about teen-age jobs?

2. Why do some educators think that teen-age work may damage the future careers of students?

3. What is a possible explanation for the proliferation of "mindless and irrelevant part-time jobs"?

4. "The Dead-End Kids" is journalism. Find characteristics of the journalistic style in the selection.

☐ Writing Suggestions

1. Manges cites a study showing that employers prefer student applicants who have been in a cooperative education program. Would you enroll in such a program if one were available in your field?

2. If you have worked at a part-time job while in school, describe your experience. Did you learn any valuable skills? How did the job affect your school work?

3. Manges suggests that economic changes are affecting the kinds of jobs available to students. Do these changes also affect the kinds of jobs available to everyone?

4. Describe the kinds of work that would benefit a student.

5. Enumerate the advantages or disadvantages of working as a teen-ager.

6. Manges claims that technology has turned young workers "into near-automa-tons." Describe the technology and contrast it with older methods.

WRITE ON, BARBARIANS

☐ **MIKE ROYKO**

1 Robert Maszak, an English teacher at Bloom Township High School in Chicago Heights, has sent me a stack of angry letters written by his students as a classroom assignment.

2   The students were reacting to a column I wrote last week about eleven people being trampled to death at a rock concert in Cincinnati.

3   In that column, I said those who would climb over people's broken bodies to reach a seat in an auditorium could be called "the new barbarians."

4   The dictionary definition of "barbarian" that I used is "the opposite of civilized." And I think anyone who tramples someone to death can wear that definition.

5   In sending me the letters, teacher Maszak, apparently proud of his students' efforts, wrote: "Some 'barbarians' do write."

6   Yes, they do. But frankly, if I were an English teacher and they were my students, I'd lock the letters away where no one could see them.

7   I'd be embarrassed if this many juniors and seniors not only wrote incoher-ently, but also apparently have not been taught to read or to think. I'd also be alarmed by their tribe mentality.

8   Almost every letter said something like: "Why are you picking on us teen-agers?" and "What have you got against rock music?"

9   The fact is, I did not use the word "teen-ager" anywhere in that column.

10   Nor did I say that new barbarians are found only at rock concerts. I wrote: "Rock concerts aren't the only mass-gathering place for the new barbarians. They've become visible at sports events, too." And I described the sometimes violent conduct of sports fans of all ages.

11   The point of the column was that in many places we now see more and more mindless mob violence and mob mentality. This behavior isn't limited to teen-agers or rock fans, although there's probably less of it in your average nursing home.

12   I shouldn't be surprised that these students didn't notice that. Any kid who gets to be a high school junior or senior and writes like Mr. Maszak's students isn't going to absorb details. An example, exactly as written:

13   "Dear Tenage hater

14   "I was disapointed by you writen on the Who concert. From what you said I can see you have know so called barbarism. You used some strong words in there with very little fact, you say everyone was numbed in the brain. I will say from concert experience maybe half or three forths were high on something or nether but I allso know that theres not one forth to half that weren't. You say everyone was pushing and throwing elbows, did you ever think that some of the thrown elbows were from people who didn't like getting pushed. You said something about when you were a kid, well times have change since then."

15   Mr. Maszak, is that the best you can do? If so, have you thought of another line of work?

16   Another sample:

17   "In Tuesday Dec. 5th addition of Mike Royko you clearly stated that all teenagers and people who go to rock concerts are barbarians."

18   I clearly stated nothing of the kind. You really should try to teach them to read, Mr. Maszak.

19   Or this: "For one think there were no real big popular bands when you were a kid."

20   If you are going to let them babble about music, Mr. Maszak, spend a few minutes giving them a little musical background. Or maybe you haven't heard of the big band era, either.

21   Then we have this gem. Mind you, it is written by a young man who has spent almost twelve years attending school:

22   "When you talked us in your paper you called us barbarians. It is even more rude than when you call us delinquents. You cant compare us to 50 years ago because we don't wear knickers' and deliver newspapers. All you Old Farts are the same. At Cominskey Park we were just expressing our feelings about disco, because disco sucks. If you write another column like that you will have to answer to me in person."

23   And there was the lad who denied being a barbarian. But he spelled it "barbian."

24   I can't go on. It's too depressing, and not only because most of them can't write, read, spell, or think—and it's getting a little late for them to learn.

25   It's depressing because almost none even mentioned the fact that eleven human beings were trampled to death. And none sounded concerned about that grotesque fact.

26   They became highly indignant that someone would be less than worshipful about rock music. They became emotional—even menacing like the above writer—in their hatred for disco music. Some became obscene over imagined slights against teen-agers.

27   But that eleven people were trampled by a music-hungry mob?

28   One of the few who mentioned the deaths saw it this way:

29   "If there were someone yer looked up to and yer went to see them in

person and thier were thousands of people just like you and wanted to see him up close would you fight yer way in?"

30   And as another breezily put it:

31   "People die every three second. What would you do if you paid $15 for a ticket?"

32   You're no barbarian, kid. But try zombie.

☐ Discovering Meaning and Technique

1. What caused the students to write letters to Royko?

2. What does Royko mean by "tribe mentality"?

3. Evaluate the teacher's attitude toward the letters.

4. Evaluate Royko's assessment of the students' ability to read, write, and think.

5. In addition to not reading, writing, or reasoning well, what about the students particularly depressed Royko?

☐ Writing Suggestions

1. According to the teacher, the students are responding to a newspaper column by Royko. Is this explanation reasonable? Do you think that perhaps the students were instructed to write the letters? Discuss the wisdom and practicality of assigned letters.

2. Describe the training you have had in learning to write.

3. Describe the kind of writing assignments that you think work best.

4. What do you think is wrong with an educational system that produces writing like that cited by Royko?

5. Discuss the importance of basic skills such as reading and writing.

EXCUSES, EXCUSES

☐ HELEN C. VO-DINH

1 By and large, the report of the National Commission on Educational Excellence has been received favorably by those of us in the teaching profession, even

though the blame for a shoddy educational system falls so often on our shoulders. For example, recently we have been hearing a lot about teacher competency and the need for merit pay, as if this would solve our problems.

2   Somewhere in the commission's report and lost to sight in the hue and cry is a recommendation that received little publicity. This is the suggestion that schools make more effective use of the existing school day.

3   As a teacher I understand this to mean that I had better make sure my students spend every minute they have with me studying and learning the subject I teach. Now, we teachers have some control over time on task. We have no one to blame but ourselves if we fill up half a period Monday entertaining our classes with stories about what we did over the weekend. However, even those of us with the best intentions find our class interrupted, depleted or canceled by forces beyond our control day after day after day. For under the guise of "education," a plethora of social activities has sprouted in our schools which draw students from our rooms. This situation is particularly destructive at the high-school level where I am now teaching.

4   Sometime in the summer, our school district, like others across the country, will publish a school calendar for the coming year. In my state, students must attend school 180 days. This means that each of the students assigned to me will have 180 periods of classroom instruction in the subject I teach. However, I know that this will never happen. If I consider only the classes I lose to "necessities" such as fire drills, bomb scares, three days of state-mandated testing, three days of registration and one entire day for school photos, my students have already missed 10 periods out of the 180. Now, depending upon how many pep rallies are needed, how many assemblies we can afford and the degree to which my students participate in a host of activities offered during schooltime, I will lose all of them again, and most of them again and again.

5   It might be helpful to compare the situation in our high schools with that in our colleges, where an intellectual atmosphere still prevails. Think back a moment. Do you remember your college classes being canceled for pep rallies, assemblies or class meetings? Not once, but often during a semester? When you wanted to attend some social function or help prepare for a dance were you excused with the blessings of the administration, or did you cut? Do you remember lectures interrupted routinely by a hidden sound system? Did office aides make it a practice to appear with urgent memos which your professors had to read and respond to while you waited impatiently? Was it a common occurrence for football players to rise en masse in the middle of a discussion to go to practice or a game?

6   And yet this is precisely the kind of situation we high school teachers put up with day after day. Is it any wonder that many students don't value much of what goes on in the classroom?

7   At the latest count my syllabus is at the mercy of 45 different activities sanctioned by our school system. I lost students this past year for the following

reasons: club trips to Atlantic City, student-council elections, bloodmobile, appointments with guidance counselors and Army representatives, an art show, community show, tennis, track, baseball, swimming, football, cheerleading, club meetings, class meetings, drama and band workshops, yearbook, PSAT, chorus and orchestra rehearsals, science day, cattle judging, attendance at the movie "Gandhi" and graduation rehearsal.

8   This list is by no means complete.

9   The rationale which allows this charade to continue is that if students miss classes they can make up the work and no harm is done. Of course, this idea carried to its logical conclusion means that we need less school for students, not more as the president's commission recommended. It is true that many students can read assignments outside of class, copy notes and keep up with their work. Others may opt for lower grades. But much of what takes place during class cannot be made up. How do you make up a class discussion where you have a chance to test and clarify your ideas on a subject? A group discussion where you must come to a consensus? An oral reading?

10   When I cannot organize a group discussion in advance because I am never sure who will show up, when "Romeo" is off to a band rehearsal and "Juliet" has a swim meet on the day the class reads "Romeo and Juliet" aloud, how can I generate seriousness of purpose and respect for intellectual effort?

11   Obviously many of these activities are worthwhile. But there is no pressing reason why any of them have to take place during class hours. Days could be added to the school calendar for state-mandated testing and registration. And why not let communities sponsor dances, sports, college and Army representatives and clubs after school hours? At the very least we would then discover which students wanted to participate in activities and which simply wished to escape from class.

12   The culmination of this disrespect for intellectual effort occurs in my school when the seniors are allowed to end classes and prepare for graduation three weeks before the rest of the student body. The message which comes across is that the senior curriculum is so negligible it can be cut short, and that when you get older, you have it easier than anybody else, not harder.

13   I am not a kill-joy. I know that kids need fun just as much as adults do and that clubs are educational in their own way. But as a member of a profession which is accorded only the most grudging respect and which is continually suspected of not doing its job, I say start by giving us a chance. Guarantee me those 180 periods I'm supposed to have. I'll know the public and the people who run the schools are serious about improving them the year my classes have not been shortened, delayed, canceled, interrupted or depleted for any reason short of illness, an emergency or the Second Coming.

☐ Discovering Meaning and Technique

1. What is the thesis, or main contention, of the essay?

2. In paragraph 5, Vo-Dinh makes her point with a series of rhetorical questions—that is, questions to which she knows the answers. Comment on the effectiveness of this technique.

3. What is the "rationale" for allowing so many absences from the classroom?

4. What is the message sent to students by numerous excused absences?

5. Discuss Vo-Dinh's solutions to the problem of excused absences.

☐ Writing Suggestions

1. Describe a typical day in your high school. Was it similar to the day Vo-Dinh describes?

2. In many colleges and universities, athletic events take precedence over academic demands. For example, a baseball team may spend 20 percent of the semester on the road and may even play several games during final examinations. Is this practice fair to the students? Is it fair to the teachers who must allow students to "make up" missed work?

3. At the end of paragraph 1, Vo-Dinh suggests that merit pay for teachers will not solve our educational problems. Do you agree?

4. Do you agree with Vo-Dinh that excessive excused absences indicate a "disrespect for intellectual effort"?

THE CLASSROOM

☐ NEIL POSTMAN

1 I should like to begin this discussion of the classroom with an apology to Mr. William O'Connor wherever he is. Mr. O'Connor, who is unknown to me in a personal way, was once a member of the Boston School Committee, in which capacity he made the following remark: "We have no inferior education in our schools. What we have been getting is an inferior type of student."

2   At the time this statment was made, I happened to be editing a book on
the misuses of language, and I included his observation, among several others,
as an example of semantic nonsense. It seemed to me at the time that the
quality of an education had nothing whatever to do with the "quality" of a
student. No matter what their abilities, students are entitled to an education
that is suitable to them. If it is not, the problem is with the education, not the
student. Mr. O'Connor's remark, I judged, was analogous to the defense of a
clothing manufacturer who refuses to produce anything but large-sized pants.
When business falls off, he explains his problem by saying, "Our pants are just
fine. What we have been getting is too many little people."

3   Now, it is possible that Mr. O'Connor was indeed thinking along these
lines, in which case I was not mistaken in my original judgment. But I wish to
apologize to him anyway because there is a point of view from which his remark
is perfectly sound. There are in fact a couple of senses in which we might say
that school is good but some students aren't; and perhaps one or both of these
is what Mr. O'Connor had in mind.

4   To come to the point: A classroom is a technique for the achievement of
certain kinds of learnings. It is a workable technique provided that both the
teacher and the student have the skills, and particularly the attitudes, that are
fundamental to it. Among these, from the student's point of view, are tolerance
for delayed gratification, a certain measure of respect for and fear of authority,
and a willingness to accommodate one's individual desires to the interests of
group cohesion and purpose. As I have previously argued, these attitudes cannot
be easily taught in school because they are a necessary component of the teaching
situation itself. The problem is not unlike trying to find out how to spell a
word by looking it up in the dictionary. If you do not know how a word is
spelled, it is hard to look it up. In the same way, little can be taught in school
unless these attitudes are present. And if they are not, it is difficult to teach
them.

5   Obviously, such attitudes must be learned during the six years before a
child starts school; that is, in the home. This is the real meaning of the phrase
"preschool education." If a child is not made ready for the classroom experience
at home, he or she cannot usually benefit from any normal school program.
But just as important, the school, in turn, is defenseless against such a child,
who, typically, is a source of disorder in a situation that requires order as a
precondition. I raise this issue here, and first, because there can be no education
reform, at least as I have been proposing it, unless there is order in the classroom.
Everyone seems to know this except some advanced education critics. Without
the attitudes that lead to order, the classroom is an entirely impotent technique.
Therefore, one possible translation of Mr. O'Connor's remark is, "We have a
useful technique for educating youth but too many of them have not been
provided at home with the attitudes necessary for the technique to work." There
is nothing nonsensical about such an observation. In fact, it calls to mind several

historical instances where some magnificent technology was conceived, only to remain undeveloped because the conditions for its creative use did not exist. The Aztecs, for example, invented the wheel but applied it only to children's toys since the terrain on which they lived made it useless for any other purpose. The Chinese invented the printing press centuries before Gutenberg. But saddled with a picture writing-system, with thousands of symbols, they were unable to use it as a medium of mass communication. In the same way, a classroom cannot be useful unless the children who come to it are emotionally and intellectually prepared for its uses. A classroom, like a wheel or a printing press, *can* be a well-designed instrumentality but at the same time can be useless to those who are not ready for it. There are limits to its flexibility. To use my clothing analogy again: A manufacturer of pants—large, medium, *and* small—can do no business with a person who wears none.

6   The problem of disorder in the classroom is largely created by two factors: a dissolving family structure out of which come youngsters who are "unfit" for the presuppositions of a classroom, and a radically altered information environment which undermines the foundations of school. The question, then, arises, What should be done about the increasing tendency toward disorder in the classroom?

7   Liberal reformers, such as Kenneth Keniston, have answers, of a sort. Keniston argues that economic reforms should be made so that the integrity and authority of the family can be restored. He believes that poverty is the main cause of family dissolution, and by improving the economic situation of families, we may kindle a sense of order and aspiration in the lives of children. Some of the reforms he suggests in his book *All Our Children* seem to me practical although they are very long range and offer no immediate response to the problem of disorder. Some utopians, such as Ivan Illich, have offered other solutions; for example, dissolving the schools altogether, or so completely restructuring the school environment that its traditional assumptions are rendered irrelevant. To paraphrase Karl Kraus's epigram about psychoanalysis, these proposals are the utopian disease of which they consider themselves the cure.

8   One of the best answers, from my point of view, comes from Dr. Howard Hurwitz, who is neither a liberal reformer nor a utopian. It is a good solution, I believe, because it tries to respond to the needs not only of children who are unprepared for school by parental failure but of children of all backgrounds who are being made strangers to the assumptions of school.

9   Until his retirement Dr. Hurwitz was the principal of Long Island City High School in New York, where he became at once famous and infamous for suspending a disruptive student. Dr. Hurwitz, in his turn, was suspended by the board of education for being too quick on the suspension trigger, the board not exactly being slow itself. It should be noted that during the eleven years he was principal at Long Island City High School, the average number of suspensions each year was three, while in many New York City high schools the average

runs close to one hundred. It must also be noted that during Dr. Hurwitz's tenure at Long Island City, there was not one instance of an assault on a teacher, and daily student attendance averaged better than 90 percent, which in the context of the New York City school scene represents a riot of devotion. All of the students at Dr. Hurwitz's school are, like youth everywhere, deeply influenced by the biases of the media, and many of them come from the kind of home background which does not prepare them well for school. Yet, he seems to have solved much better than most the problem of disorder.

10   Before giving the impression that Dr. Hurwitz should be canonized, I must say that I am more than a little familiar with his curriculum ideas, which he has widely advertised since his retirement, and many of them, in my opinion, are not worth the telling, at least not in a book of mine. But Dr. Hurwitz understands a few things of overriding importance that many educators of more expansive imagination do not.

11   The first is that educators must devote at least as much attention to the immediate consequences of disorder as to its abstract causes. One is sure that Dr. Hurwitz is as aware of the debilitating effects of poverty and disorganized home situations as anyone else. He may even understand the role of media in undermining the assumptions of school. But what he mostly understands is that whatever the causes of disorder and alienation, the consequences are severe and if not shackled result in making school impotent. Thus, at the risk of becoming a symbol of reaction, he ran what I believe is called "a tight ship." He holds to the belief, for example, that a child's right to an education is terminated at the point where the child interferes with the right of other children to have one. In other words, Dr. Hurwitz is a civil libertarian but of a type not always recogniz-able to the American Civil Liberties Union: He wants to protect the rights of the majority.

12   He also understands that disorder expands proportionately to the tolerance for it, and that children of all kinds of home backgrounds can learn, in varying degrees, to function in situations where there is no tolerance for it. He does not believe, by the way, that it is inevitably the children of the poor or only the children of the poor who are disorderly. But he knows that in spite of what the "revisionist" education historians may say, poor people still regard the schools as an avenue of social and economic advancement for their children, and do not object in the least to its being an orderly and structured experience. The hundreds of parents (many of whom are among the "poor and oppressed") who vigorously defended him after his suspension will testify to this.

13   What all this adds up to is the common sense view that the school ought not to accommodate itself to disorder, or to the biases of other communication systems. The children of the poor are likely to continue to be with us. Some parents will fail to assume competent responsibility for the preschool education of their children. The media will increase the intensity of their fragmenting influence. These are facts educators must live with. But Dr. Hurwitz believes,

nonetheless, that as a technique for learning the classroom can work if students are oriented toward its assumptions, not the other way around. Mr. William O'Connor, wherever he is, would probably agree. And so do I. The school is not an extension of the street, the movie theater, a rock concert, or a playground. And it is certainly not an extension of the psychiatric clinic. It is a special environment which requires the enforcement of certain traditional rules of controlled group interaction. The school may be the only remaining public situation in which such rules have any meaning at all, and it would be a grave mistake to change those rules because some children find them hard or cannot function within them at all. Children who cannot ought to be removed from the environment in the interests of those who can. This is an action Dr. Hurwitz was not loath to take, although it should be stressed that he did not need to do so often. Wholesale suspensions are a symptom of disorder, not a cure for it. And what makes Hurwitz's school noteworthy is the small number of suspensions that have been necessary. This is not the result of his having "good" students or "bad" students. It is the result of his creating an unambiguous, rigorous, and serious attitude—a nineteenth century attitude, if you will—toward what constitutes acceptable school behavior. In other words, Dr. Hurwitz's school turns out to be a place where children of all kinds of backgrounds—the fit and unfit—can function, or can learn to function. And where the biases of our information environment are emphatically opposed.

14   At this point, I should like to leave the particulars of Dr. Hurwitz's solution and, retaining their spirit, indicate some particulars of my own. I suspect you will think in reading them that I have turned by back on twentieth-century "liberalism," which would be entirely correct.

15   Let us start, for instance, with the idea of a dress code. I believe it to be a splendid rule from which the atmosphere in a school cannot fail to improve. What a dress code signifies is that school is a special place in which special kinds of behaviors are required. The way one dresses is always an indication of an attitude toward a situation. And the way one is *expected* to dress indicates what that attitude ought properly to be. You would not wear dungarees and a T-shirt which says "Feel Me" when attending a church wedding. If you did, it would be considered an outrage against the tone and meaning of the situation. The school has every right and reason, I believe, to expect the same sort of consideration.

16   Those who are inclined to think this is a superficial point are probably forgetting that symbols not only reflect our feelings but to some extent create them. One's kneeling in church, for example, reflects a sense of reverence but it also engenders reverence. Put an atheist or a cynic in church and have him kneel before an altar. He may be surprised to find certain feelings coming upon him that are not unlike those experienced by the devout. The effect of symbolic action on our minds should never be underestimated, for our behavior may lead to feeling as much as feeling may lead to behavior. As William James observed

in his *Talks To Teachers,* we may cry because we are sad, but it is equally true that we are sad because we cry. If we want school to *feel* like a special place, there is no better way to begin than by requiring students to dress in a manner befitting the seriousness of the enterprise and institution. I should add, teachers as well. I know of one high school in which the principal has put forward a dress code of sorts for teachers. (He has not, apparently, had the courage to propose one for the students.) For males the requirement is merely a jacket and tie. One of his teachers bitterly complained to me that such a regulation infringed upon his civil rights. And yet, this teacher will accept without complaint the same regulation when it is enforced by an elegant restaurant. His complaint and his acquiescence tell a great deal about how he values schools and how he values restaurants. Apparently, owners of elegant restaurants know more about how to create an atmosphere in a social situation than do many school principals and teachers who appear indifferent to the symbolic meaning of dress.

17   Of course, I do not have in mind, for students, uniforms of the type sometimes worn in parochial schools. I am referring here to some reasonable standard of dress which would mark school as a place of dignity and seriousness. And I might add that I do not believe for one moment the argument that poor people would be unable to clothe their children properly if such a code were in force. In particular, I do not believe that poor people have advanced that argument. It is an argument that middle-class education critics have made in behalf of the poor.

18   Another argument advanced in behalf of the poor and oppressed is the students' right to their own language. I have never heard this argument come from parents whose children are not competent to use Standard English. It is an argument, once again, put forward by "liberal" education critics whose children are competent in Standard English but who in some curious way wish to express their solidarity with the charity for those who are less capable. It is a case of pure condescension, and I do not think teachers should be taken in by it. Like the mode of dress, the mode of language in school ought to be relatively formal and exemplary, and therefore markedly different from the custom in less rigorous places. It is particularly important that teachers should avoid trying to win their students' affection by adopting the language of youth. Such teachers frequently win only the contempt of their students who sense that there ought to be a difference between the language of teachers and the language of students; that is to say, the world of adults and the world of children.

19   In this connection, it is worth saying that the modern conception of childhood is a product of the sixteenth century, as Philippe Ariès has documented in his *Centuries of Childhood.* Prior to that century, children as young as six and seven were treated in all important respects as if they were adults. Their language, their dress, their legal status, their responsibilities, their labor, were much the same as those of adults. For complex reasons, some of which concern the development of printing, the spread of literacy, and the need for early formal

education, the concept of childhood as an identifiable stage in human growth began to develop in the sixteenth century and has continued into our own times. The modern conception of school and, in particular, of a classroom are accommodations to the idea that there are important distinctions to be made between childhood and adulthood. However, with the emergence of electronic media of communication, a reversal of this trend seems to be taking place. In a culture in which the distribution of information is almost wholly undifferentiated, age categories begin to disappear. Television, all by itself, may bring an end to childhood. In truth, there is no such thing as "children's programming," at least not for children over the age of eight or nine. Everyone sees and hears the same thing. The media eliminate secrets. As a consequence legal distinctions begin to appear arbitrary, as do distinctions in dress, language, styles of entertainment, games, eating habits, etc. We have already reached a point where the crimes of youth are indistinguishable from those of adults, and we may soon reach a point where the punishments will be the same. Oddly, some of our most advanced social critics have come out in favor of laws that would eliminate most of the distinctions between child and adult in the area of civil rights. This they do in the interests of "liberating" children. The effect would be to help push us back rapidly to the fifteenth century, when children were as liberated as everyone else, and just as unprotected.

20   I raise this point because the school is one of our few remaining institutions based on firm distinctions between childhood and adulthood, and a theory of a conserving education would include the (eighteenth and nineteenth centuries') wish that such distinctions be maintained. The school, unlike the media, is based on the assumption that adults have something of value to teach the young, and that there are differences between the behavior of adults and the behavior of children. That is why it is necessary for teachers to avoid emulating in dress and speech the style of the young. It is also why the school ought properly to be a place for what we might call "manners education": The adults in school ought to be concerned with teaching youth a standard of civilized interaction.

21   Again, those who are inclined to regard this as superficial may be underestimating the biases of media such as television, radio, and recorder, which teach with as much power as parental teaching how one is to conduct oneself in public. In particular, with the possible exception of movies, which still require a communal setting, the media favor an individualized and egocentric response to information. In a general sense the media "unprepare" the young for behavior in groups. A young man who goes through the day with a radio affixed to his ear is not only listening to the sound of a different drummer. He is learning to be indifferent to any shared sound. A young woman who can turn off a television program which does not suit her needs at the moment is learning impatience with any stimulus that is not responsive to her interests.

22   But school is not a radio station or a television program. It is a social

situation requiring the subordination of one's own impulses and interests to those of the group. In a word, manners. As a rule, elementary school teachers will exert considerable effort in teaching manners. I believe they refer to this effort as "socializing the child." But it is astonishing how precipitously this effort is diminished at higher levels. It is certainly neglected in the high schools, and where it is not, there is usually an excessive concern for "bad habits," such as smoking, drinking, and, in some nineteenth-century schools, swearing. But as William James noted, our virtues are as habitual as our vices. Where is the attention given to the "Good morning" habit, to the "I beg your pardon" habit, to the "Please forgive the interruption" habit?

23   I hesitate to offer the following example since you will think me, for giving it, hopelessly romantic, but the most civilized high school class I have ever seen was one in which both students and teacher said good morning to each other (because the teacher always said it to his students) and in which the students actually stood up when they had something to say. The teacher, moreover, thanked each student for any contribution made to the class, did not sit with his feet on the desk, and did not interrupt a student unless he had asked permission to do so. The students, in turn, did not interrupt each other, or chew gum, or read comic books when they were bored. To avoid being a burden to others when one is bored is the essence of civilized behavior.

24   Of this teacher I might also say that he made no attempt to entertain his students or model his classroom along the lines of a TV program. He was concerned not only to teach his students manners but to teach them how to attend in a classroom, which is partly a matter of manners but is also necessary to their intellectual development. One of the more serious difficulties teachers now face in the classroom results from the fact that their students have media-shortened attention spans and have become accustomed, also through intense media exposure, to novelty, variety, and entertainment. Some teachers have made desperate attempts to keep their students "tuned in" by fashioning their classes along the lines of *Sesame Street* or *The Tonight Show.* They tell jokes. They change the pace. They show films, play records, and avoid any lecture or discussion that would take more than eight minutes. They avoid *anything* that would take more than eight minutes. Although its motivation is understandable, this is the worst possible thing they can do because it is what their students least need. However difficult it may be, the teacher must try to achieve student attention and even enthusiasm through the attraction of ideas, not razzmatazz. Those who think I am speaking here in favor of "dull" classes they themselves, through media exposure, have lost an understanding of the potential for excitement contained in an idea. The media (one prays) are not so powerful that they can obliterate in the young, particularly in the adolescent, what James referred to as a "theoretic instinct": a need to know reasons, causes, abstract conceptions. Such an "instinct" can be seen in its earliest stages in what he calls the "sporadic metaphysical inquiries of children as to who made God, and why they have

five fingers." But it takes a more compelling and sustained form in adolescence, and may certainly be developed by teachers if they are willing to stand fast and resist the seductions of our media environment.

25   I trust that the reader is not misled by what I have been saying. As I see it, there is nothing in any of the above that leads to the conclusion that I favor a classroom that is authoritarian or coldhearted, or dominated by a teacher insensitive to students and how they learn. So far I have been discussing ideas by which the environment of school may be made more serious, dignified, and orderly. I do not imagine I have said anything original. I want merely to affirm the importance of the classroom as a special place, aloof from the biases of the media; a place in which the uses of the intellect are given prominence in a setting of elevated language, civilized manners, and respect for social symbols.

☐ Discovering Meaning and Content

1. What does Postman mean by the statement in paragraph 4 that a classroom is "a workable technique provided that both the teacher and the student have the skills, and particularly the attitudes, that are fundamental to it"?

2. Which attitudes are "fundamental" to the classroom technique?

3. How does Postman use William O'Connor's remark to help unify the essay?

4. Which two factors does Postman believe to be primarily responsible for "disorder in the classroom"?

5. What does Postman mean by the "fragmenting" influence of the media?

6. When did the concept of childhood as a stage of life develop?

7. What does Postman think might "bring an end to childhood"?

☐ Writing Suggestions

1. Agree or disagree with Postman's belief that school is a "special environment which requires the enforcement of certain traditional rules of controlled group interaction" and that children who cannot conform to those rules "ought to be removed from the environment in the interest of those who can."

2. Agree or disagree with Postman's contention that teachers should require good manners of students in school.

3. Expand on Postman's statement that "the media 'unprepare' the young for behavior in groups."

4. Postman points out that a teacher who objects to a dress code for school will accept a dress code for a restaurant (paragraph 16). Explain why you think this attitude does or does not make sense.

5. Describe a school dress code that you think would be fair and desirable. How would it benefit students and teachers?

6. Some people think a dress code is "democratic" because it eliminates the most obvious financial differences among students. Do you agree or disagree?

7. Describe the order or disorder in your own high school. Did your principal and teachers run a "tight ship," as did Dr. Hurwitz? Do you prefer that approach?

HOMEWORK

☐ **PETER CAMERON**

1 My dog, Keds, was sitting outside of the A&P last Thursday when he got smashed by some kid pushing a shopping cart. At first we thought he just had a broken leg, but later we found out he was bleeding inside. Every time he opened his mouth, blood would seep out like dull red words in a bad silent dream.

2   Every night before my sister goes to her job she washes her hair in the kitchen sink with beer and mayonnaise and eggs. Sometimes I sit at the table and watch the mixture dribble down her white back. She boils a pot of water on the stove at the same time; when she is finished with her hair, she steams her face. She wants so badly to be beautiful.

3   I am trying to solve complicated algebraic problems I have set for myself. Since I started cutting school last Friday, the one thing I miss is homework. Find the value for *n*. Will it be a whole number? It is never a whole number. It is always a fraction.

4   "Will you get me a towel?" my sister asks. She turns her face toward me and clutches her hair to the top of her head. The sprayer hose slithers into its hole next to the faucet.

5   I hand her a dish towel. "No," she says. "A bath towel. Don't be stupid."

6   In the bathroom, my mother is watering her plants. She has arranged them in the tub and turned the shower on. She sits on the toilet lid and watches. It smells like outdoors in the bathroom.

7   I hand my sister the towel and watch her wrap it round her head. She takes the cover off the pot of boiling water and drops lemon slices in. Then she lowers her face into the steam.

8   This is the problem I have set for myself:

$$\frac{245\,(n + 17) = 396\,(n - 45)}{34}$$

$$n =$$

9   Wednesday, I stand outside the high-school gym doors. Inside, students are lined up doing calisthenics. It's snowing, and prematurely dark, and I can watch without being seen.

10   "Well," my father says when I get home. He is standing in the garage testing the automatic door. Every time a plane flies overhead, the door opens or closes, so my father is trying to fix it. "Have you changed your mind about school?" he asks me.

11   I lock my bicycle to a pole. This infuriates my father, who doesn't believe in locking things up in his own house. He pretends not to notice. I wipe the thin stripe of snow off the fenders with my middle finger. It is hard to ride a bike in the snow. This afternoon on my way home from the high school I fell off, and I lay in the snowy road with my bike on top of me. It felt warm.

12   "We're going to get another dog," my father says.

13   "It's not that," I say. I wish everyone would stop talking about dogs. I can't tell how sad I really am about Keds versus how sad I am in general. If I don't keep these things separate, I feel as if I'm betraying Keds.

14   "Then what is it?" my father says.

15   "It's nothing," I say.

16   My father nods. He is very good about bringing things up and then letting them drop. A lot gets dropped. He presses the button on the automatic control. The door slides down its oiled tracks and falls shut. It's dark in the garage. My father presses the button again and the door opens, and we both look outside at the snow falling in the driveway, as if in those few seconds the world might have changed.

17   My mother has forgotten to call me for dinner, and when I confront her with this she tells me that she did, but that I was sleeping. She is loading the dishwasher. My sister is standing at the counter, listening, and separating eggs for her shampoo.

18   "What can I get you?" my mother asks. "Would you like a meat-loaf sandwich?"

19   "No," I say. I open the refrigerator and survey its illuminated contents. "Could I have some scrambled eggs?"

20   "O.K.," says my mother. She comes and stands beside me and puts her hand on top of mine on the door handle. There are no eggs in the refrigerator. "Oh," my mother says; then, "Julie?"

21   "What?" my sister says.

22   "Did you take the last eggs?"

23   "I guess so," my sister says. "I don't know."

24   "Forget it," I say. "I won't have eggs."

25   "No," my mother says. "Julie doesn't need them in her shampoo. That's not what I bought them for."

26   "I do," my sister says. "It's a formula. It doesn't work without the eggs. I need the protein."

27   "I don't want eggs," I say. "I don't want anything." I go into my bedroom.

28   My mother comes in and stands looking out the window. The snow has turned to rain. "You're not the only one who is unhappy about this," she says.

29   "About what?" I say. I am sitting on my unmade bed. If I pick up my room, my mother will make my bed: that's the deal. I didn't pick up my room this morning.

30   "About Keds," she says. "I'm unhappy too. But it doesn't stop me from going to school."

31   "You don't go to school," I say.

32   "You know what I mean," my mother says. She turns around and looks at my room, and begins to pick things off the floor.

33   "Don't do that," I say. "Stop."

34   My mother drops the dirty clothes in an exaggerated gesture of defeat. She almost—almost—throws them on the floor. The way she holds her hands accentuates their emptiness. "If you're not going to go to school," she says, "the least you can do is clean your room."

35   In the algebra word problems, a boat sails down a river while a jeep drives along the bank. Which will reach the capital first? If a plane flies at a certain speed from Boulder to Oklahoma City and then at a different speed from Oklahoma City to Detroit, how many cups of coffee can the stewardess serve, assuming she is unable to serve during the first and last ten minutes of each flight? How many times can a man ride the elevator to the top of the Empire State Building while his wife climbs the stairs, given that the woman travels one stair slower each flight? And if the man jumps up while the elevator is going down, which is moving—the man, the woman, the elevator, or the snow falling outside?

36   The next Monday I get up and make preparations for going to school. I can tell at the breakfast table that my mother is afraid to acknowledge them for fear it won't be true. I haven't gotten up before ten o'clock in a week. My mother makes me French toast. I sit at the table and write the note excusing me for my absence. I am eighteen, an adult, and thus able to excuse myself from school. This is what my note says:

> DEAR MR. KELLY [my homeroom teacher]:
>   Please excuse my absence February 17–24. I was unhappy and did not feel able to attend school.
>
>   Sincerely,
>   MICHAEL PECHETTI

This is the exact format my mother used when she wrote my notes, only she always said, "Michael was home with a sore throat," or "Michael was home with a bad cold." The colds that prevented me from going to school were always bad colds.

37   My mother watches me write the note but doesn't ask to see it. I leave it

on the kitchen table when I go to the bathroom, and when I come back to get it I know she has read it. She is washing the bowl she dipped the French toast into. Before, she would let Keds lick it clean. He liked eggs.

38 In Spanish class we are seeing a film on flamenco dancers. The screen wouldn't pull down, so it is being projected on the blackboard, which is green and cloudy with erased chalk. It looks a little as if the women are sick, and dancing in Heaven. Suddenly the little phone on the wall buzzes.

39   Mrs. Smitts, the teacher, gets up to answer it, and then walks over to me. She puts her hand on my shoulder and leans her face close to mine. It is dark in the room. "Miguel," Mrs. Smitts whispers, *"Tienes que ir a la oficina de* guidance."

40   "What?" I say.

41   She leans closer, and her hair blocks the dancers. Despite the clicking castanets and the roomful of students, there is something intimate about this moment. *"Tienes que ir a la oficina de* guidance," she repeats slowly. Then, "You must go to the guidance office." Now. *Vaya."*

42   My guidance counsellor, Mrs. Dietrich, used to be a history teacher, but she couldn't take it anymore, so she was moved into guidance. On her immaculate desk is a calendar blotter with "LUNCH" written across the middle of every box, including Saturday and Sunday. The only other things on the desk are an empty photo cube and my letter to Mr. Kelly. I sit down, and she shows me the letter as if I haven't yet read it. I reread it.

43   "Did you write this?" she asks.

44   I nod affirmatively. I can tell Mrs. Dietrich is especially nervous about this interview. Our meetings are always charged with tension. At the last one, when I was selecting my second-semester courses, she started to laugh hysterically when I said I wanted to take Boys' Home Ec. Now every time I see her in the halls she stops me and asks me how I'm doing in Boys' Home Ec. It's the only course of mine she remembers.

45   I hand the note back to her and say, "I wrote it this morning," as if this clarified things.

46   "This morning?"

47   "At breakfast," I say.

48   "Do you think this is an acceptable excuse?" Mrs. Dietrich asks. "For missing more than a week of school?"

49   "I'm sure it isn't," I say.

50   "Then why did you write it?"

51   Because it is the truth, I start to say. It is. But somehow I know that saying this will make me more unhappy. It might make me cry. "I've been doing algebra at home," I say.

52   "That's fine," Mrs. Dietrich says, "but it's not the point. The point is, to graduate you have to attend school for a hundred and eighty days, or have

legitimate excuses for the days you've missed. That's the point. Do you want to graduate?"

53   "Yes," I say.

54   "Of course you do," Mrs. Dietrich says.

55   She crumples my note and tries to throw it into the wastepaper basket but misses. We both look for a second at the note lying on the floor, and then I get up and throw it away. The only other thing in her wastepaper basket is a banana peel. I can picture her eating a banana in her tiny office. This, too, makes me sad.

56   "Sit down," Mrs. Dietrich says.

57   I sit down.

58   "I understand your dog died. Do you want to talk about that?"

59   "No," I say.

60   "Is that what you're so unhappy about?" she says. "Or is there something else?"

61   I almost mention the banana peel in her wastebasket, but I don't. "No." I say. "It's just my dog."

62   Mrs. Dietrich thinks for a moment. I can tell she is embarrassed to be talking about a dead dog. She would be more comfortable if it were a parent or a sibling.

63   "I don't want to talk about it," I repeat.

64   She opens her desk drawer and takes out a pad of hall passes. She begins to write one out for me. She has beautiful handwriting. I think of her learning to write beautifully as a child and then growing up to be a guidance counsellor, and this makes me unhappy.

65   "Mr. Neuman is willing to overlook this matter," she says. Mr. Neuman is the principal. "Of course, you will have to make up all the work you've missed. Can you do that?"

66   "Yes," I say.

67   Mrs. Dietrich tears the pass from the pad and hands it to me. Our hands touch. "You'll get over this," she says. "Believe me, you will."

68 My sister works until midnight at the Photo-Matica. It's a tiny booth in the middle of the A & P parking lot. People drive up and leave their film and come back the next day for the pictures. My sister wears a uniform that makes her look like a counterperson in a fast-food restaurant. Sometimes at night when I'm sick of being at home I walk downtown and sit in the booth with her.

69   There's a machine in the booth that looks like a printing press, only snapshots ride down a conveyor belt and fall into a bin and then disappear. The machine gives the illusion that your photographs are being developed on the spot. It's a fake. The same fifty photographs roll through over and over, and my sister says nobody notices, because everyone in town is taking the same pictures. She opens up the envelopes and looks at them.

70   Before I go into the booth, I buy cigarettes in the A & P. It is open twenty-

four hours a day, and I love it late at night. It is big and bright and empty. The checkout girl sits on her counter swinging her legs. The Muzak plays "If Ever I Would Leave You." Before I buy the cigarettes, I walk up and down the aisles. Everything looks good to eat, and the things that aren't edible look good in their own way. The detergent aisle is colorful and clean-smelling.

71   My sister is listening to the radio and polishing her nails when I get to the booth. It is almost time to close.

72   "I hear you went to school today," she says.

73   "Yeah."

74   "How was it?" she asks. She looks at her nails, which are so long it's frightening.

75   "It was O.K.," I say. "We made chili dogs in Home Ec."

76   "So are you over it all?"

77   I look at the pictures riding down the conveyor belt. I know the order practically by heart: graduation, graduation, birthday, mountains, baby, baby, new car, bride, bride and groom, house . . . "I guess so," I say.

78   "Good," says my sister. "It was getting to be a little much." She puts her tiny brush back in the bottle, capping it. She shows me her nails. They're an odd brown shade. "Cinnamon," she says. "It's an earth color." She looks out at the parking lot. A boy is collecting the abandoned shopping carts, forming a long silver train, which he noses back toward the store. I can tell he is singing by the way his mouth moves.

79   "That's where we found Keds," my sister says, pointing to the Salvation Army bin.

80   When I went out to buy cigarettes, Keds would follow me. I hung out down here at night before he died. I was unhappy then, too. That's what no one understands. I named him Keds because he was all white with big black feet and it looked as if he had high-top sneakers on. My mother wanted to name him Bootie. Bootie is a cat's name. It's a dumb name for a dog.

81   "It's a good thing you weren't here when we found him," my sister says. "You would have gone crazy."

82   I'm not really listening. It's all nonsense. I'm working on a new problem: Find the value for n such that n plus everything else in your life makes you feel all right. What would n equal? Solve for n.

☐ Discovering Meaning and Technique

1. The first three paragraphs of the story seem to describe three entirely different subjects. What is the effect of this seemingly disjointed beginning? How does it prepare the reader for the rest of the story?

2. Why does Michael (the narrator) set "complicated algebra problems" for himself?

3. Describe the relationships Michael has with his mother, his father, and his sister.

4. How does the guidance counsellor react to Michael's excuse for missing school?

5. Why do you think that so many things make Michael sad?

6. Explain the meaning of the problem Michael sets for himself in the last paragraph.

7. What does the fact that Michael elects to take Boys' Home Ec tell the reader about him?

☐ Writing Suggestions

1. Explain the narrator's statement, "I can't tell how sad I really am about Keds versus how sad I am in general. If I don't keep these things separate, I feel as if I'm betraying Keds" (paragraph 13). Have you ever had a similar experience?

2. Was there ever a time in your life when, like Michael, everything seemed to make you sad? If so, try to explain your emotions and the reasons for them.

3. Michael's excuse for missing school is not acceptable to the guidance office, even though it is the truth. Describe an experience of your own when the truth seemed acceptable to you but not to authorities.

4. If you have ever experienced the death of a pet, describe how it affected your life or your attitude.

5. Discuss the ways in which personal problems can disrupt education.

The System

■ ■ ■

ACID TEST

☐ **DAVA SOBEL**

1 Several times a year, approximately 40 million youngsters around the country pile into classrooms, where they hunch over their desks and spend hours blackening tiny bubbles on a piece of paper. They are taking standardized multiple-choice tests—tests scored by machines and used to decide matters of considerable consequence. "What is this boy's IQ?" for example. Or, "Should this girl enter a program for gifted children?" "Is this student college material?" "How do the kids in that school district stack up against the rest of the nation?"

2   Forget, for the moment, accusations that IQ tests reflect racial discrimination and that the SATs (Scholastic Aptitude Tests) favor males. Many educators complain that most current tests give everybody a raw deal. At worst, they divert the entire educational system by bending teachers to their will: Classroom instruction becomes a matter of test preparation. In many instances, material, subjects, and facts that do not appear on the tests are never taught, no matter how important they are.

3   SAT supporters say the tests still serve as an inexpensive "common yardstick" that gauges how students measure up while providing state-by-state as well as nationwide comparisons. They also point out that revamping these tests would cost tens of millions of dollars. Students, however, already know what educators are now finding out: The tests are too simplistic. "They don't measure your ability to *do* anything," says seventeen-year-old Diana Schrage. "And if you mess up and skip a bubble by mistake, all your answers are wrong."

4   Educators, too, have their complaints about these sorts of standardized tests. "The real world is not made up of five alternatives at every turning point, arranged so that you just have to pick the right one," says Albert Shanker, the outspoken president of the American Federation of Teachers. "Life requires critical thinking skills, the ability to express yourself, persuade, argue, and build. That's what we need to teach students, and that's what we should be testing them for."

5   More and more educators feel that tests should embody the spirit of performances—modeled on, say, a football game, or a science fair, or the much-rehearsed

school play—where kids have the chance to show off what they can *do* along with what they *know.* In pilot projects employing this approach, students often enjoy a test in spite of themselves. At one South Bronx school, for example, a state education official supervised a "hands-on" science test in which kids had to manipulate such actual scientific equipment as scales and electrical-outlet testers. The reaction from several youngsters was "Can we do this again tomorrow?"

6   Graduation requirements at Walden III, a school in Racine, Wisconsin, exemplify the proficiency approach to testing. Seniors go through a "Rite of Passage Experience" final in which they write, among other things, an autobiography. They choose a history topic for a research project and then take several oral tests that are judged by a committee of teachers, fellow students, and one adult from outside the school. Graduation requirements also dictate that students give a series of presentations on essential subject areas, reflect on their own work progress, and write essays about science, artistic standards, and ethics. Graduating students generate a thick portfolio of work while getting a chance to both "perform" and demonstrate what they know.

7   The "portfolio" approach to testing is spreading throughout the country. Twelve school districts in California use the approach for their English testing, with kids writing introductions to their portfolios, composing essays, and working on successive drafts of a paper until it reads just right. It also gives kids something more to show prospective employers than a simple high-school degree.

8   This semi-idealized vision of testing is a reaction against today's situation, where American students take close to 105 million standardized tests that supposedly give educators simple, reliable statistical data. What's so bad about these tests? Some of the criticisms leveled against these methods of measuring learning include:

- *They measure performance at one point in time.* Ted Sizer, professor of education at Brown University and chairman of the Coalition of Essential Schools, says, "Any adult would violently resist being judged on the basis of a snapshot. All of us have good days and bad days, and all of us change over time." To more accurately judge a student's true academic achievement, kids should have opportunities to exhibit mastery in subject areas. His solution: "performance based" testing in which students show what they know by using information in a problem-solving context, such as the history exam taken by juniors at Hope Essential High School in Providence. Students there comb through books, interview people, and form a hypothesis on a topic of their choice. The test, an oral report, asks students to synthesize diverse sources and organize them into a single presentation.

- *They are often administered and interpreted inappropriately.* According to Bruce A. Bracken, professor of psychology at Memphis State University and editor of the *Journal of Psychoeducational Assessment,* some practitioner somewhere in the United States administers the wrong test to a child almost every day of the school year. Worse, the test then serves as the basis for poor decisions about that child's future. On a grander scale, statewide test results are often compared with outdated test scores so that students in every state score higher than the national average. The solution: Quit toying with test scores. "If you're going to use a standardized test," Bracken suggests, "it must be administered and interpreted the exact same way across the country.

• *They are boring.* "There's a real feeling in traditional testing that it doesn't matter how boring or onerous a test is," says Grant Wiggins, director of CLASS (Consultants on Learning, Assessment, and School Structure) in Rochester, New York. Little kids, Wiggins says, burn out after only 30 or 40 minutes of standardized testing. The solution: engaging oral and hands-on situations. Pupils at the Thomas Jefferson Middle School in Louisville, Kentucky, for example, take a test that lasts for weeks. They make a blueprint of themselves and use it to construct a life-size puppet. Then pupil and puppet give an oral report on the rigors of the undertaking.

9   Some progress toward better tests is being pioneered in such states as Connecticut, New York, California, and Michigan. A test called the National Assessment of Educational Progress, or NAEP (pronounced *nape*) for short, gives educators insight into what students *really* know. The test is deemed fairly reliable, but its findings are frightening. The NAEP has determined, for example, that only 2.6 percent of seventeen-year-old high-schoolers can write a persuasive letter and that only 18 percent of them can write a two-paragraph letter applying for a job, something SATs hint at but can't measure directly.

10   Since 1969, its first year, the NAEP test has yielded a broadbrush picture of what American kids know at the elementary-, middle-, and high-school levels. Until recently, the test results were withheld from individual states. But this year marks the start of the NAEP Trial State Assessment Program, with voluntary participation from 37 states, two territories, and the District of Columbia. The outcomes will allow states to compare themselves with one another on overall student achievement.

11   Even the most vociferous critics of current tests concede, however, that tests themselves are not the problem. The way they're used, the weight given to them, and the fact that the tail wags the dog . . . er . . . the schools irk critics. The irony, Wiggins points out, is that teachers *should* "teach to the test," if the test really challenges kids and reflects a bold new educational objective.

12   "A standardized test of intellectual ability," he says, "is a contradiction in terms." His challenge to fellow educators: Prove that the cost of such tests—in terms of what they fail to tell about student learning and the way they compromise teacher professionalism—is simply too high, no matter how cost-effective they may be.

☐ Discovering Meaning and Technique

1. Why does Sobel say that standardized multiple-choice tests "divert the entire educational system by bending teachers to their will" (paragraph 2)?

2. Sobel describes some alternatives to standardized tests. Does she seem to recommend these alternatives?

3. What is a " 'portfolio' approach to testing" (paragraph 7)?

4. How does cost affect testing methods?

5. What, according to the selection, are the major weaknesses of standardized tests?

☐ Writing Suggestions

1. Discuss your own views of standardized tests. What do you think are their major weaknesses? Do they have any strengths?

2. Would you prefer to be tested by some of the creative methods described in the selection? Why or why not?

3. Describe what you would consider an effective method of testing in a specific subject—such as literature, history, science, composition, or foreign languages.

4. Sorbel states that "the NAEP has determined . . . that only 2.6 percent of seventeen-year-old high-schoolers can write a persuasive letter and that only 18 percent of them can write a two-paragraph letter applying for a job." Take the challenge and write one of each.

IS TELEVISION SHORTENING OUR ATTENTION SPAN?

☐ ROBERT MACNEIL

1   I don't know much about the business of education, but I do know something about my own business, television, and I have a prejudice that I believe is relevant to the concerns of educators.

2   It is difficult to escape the influence of television. If you fit the statistical averages, by the age of twenty you have been exposed to something like twenty thousand hours of television. You can add ten thousand hours for each decade

you have lived after the age of twenty. The only activities Americans spend more time doing than watching television are working and sleeping.

3   Calculate for a moment what could have been done with even a part of those hours. Five thousand hours, I am told, are what a typical college undergraduate spends working on a bachelor's degree.

4   In ten thousand hours you could have learned enough to become one of the world's leading astronomers. You could have learned several languages thoroughly, not just to the level required to pass a college course, but fluently. If it appealed to you, you could have read Homer in the original Greek or Dostoyevsky in Russian. If that didn't appeal to you, you could have invested that amount of time and now be at the forefront of anything—nuclear physics, aerospace engineering—or you could have decided to walk right around the world and write a book about it.

5   The trouble with being born in the television age is that it discourages concentration. It encourages serial, kaleidoscopic exposure; its variety becomes a narcotic, not a stimulus; you consume not what *you* choose and when, but when *they* choose and *what*.

6   In our grandparents' eyes, such a prodigious waste of our God-given time would have been sinful because that time was not used constructively—for self-improvement, for building moral character, for shaping our own destinies. Our grandparents would have regarded it as sloth, as escapism, as perpetually sucking on visual candies. Yet, our grandparents would probably have found television just as difficult to resist as we do.

7   Almost anything interesting and rewarding in life requires some constructive, consistently applied effort. The dullest, the least gifted of us, can achieve things that seem miraculous to those who never concentrate on anything. But television encourages us to *apply* no effort. It sells us instant gratification. It diverts us *only* to divert us, to make the time pass without pain. It is the *soma* of Aldous Huxley's *Brave New World.*

8   Television forces us to follow its lead. It forces us to live as though we were on a perpetual guided tour; thirty minutes at the museum, thirty at the cathedral, thirty for a drink, then back on the bus to the next attraction; only on television, typically, the spans allotted are on the order of minutes or seconds, and the chosen delights are more often car crashes and people killing each other. In short, a lot of television usurps one of the most precious of all human gifts, the ability to focus your attention yourself, something that only human beings can do.

9   Television has adopted a particular device to do this, to capture your attention and hold it, because holding attention is the prime motive of most television programming. The economics of commercial television require programmers to assemble the largest possible audience for every moment (because that enhances its role as a profitable and advertising vehicle). Those programmers live

in constant fear of losing anyone's attention—the dull or the bright, the lazy or the energetic. The safest technique to guarantee that mass attention is to keep everything brief, not to strain the attention of anyone but instead to provide constant stimulation through variety, novelty, action, and movement. You are required, in much popular television fare, to pay attention to *no* concept, no situation, no scene, no character, and no problem for more than a few seconds at a time. In brief, television operates on the short attention span.

10   It is the easiest way out. But it has come to be regarded as a given, as inherent in the medium itself, as an imperative—as though General Sarnoff, or one of the other august pioneers of video, had bequeathed to us, from wherever he now rests, tablets of stone, commanding that nothing in television shall ever require more than a few moments' concentration.

11   I see that ethos now pervading this nation and its culture. I think the short attention span has become a model in all areas of communication, where the communicators want to be modish, up to date. I think it has become fashionable to think that, like fast food, fast ideas are the way to get to a fast, impatient public reared on television. And I think education is not exempt.

12   In the case of news, this practice was described a few years ago by a Quebec newspaper as "Mitraillant de bribes," machine-gunning with scraps. The description is very apt.

13   I believe, although my view is not widely shared, that this format is inefficient communication in terms of its ability to encourage absorption, retention, and understanding of complexity. I believe it is inefficient because it punishes the attentive and the interested by impaling them on the supposed standard of the *in*attentive and the *un*interested.

14   I question how much of television's nightly news effort is really absorbable and understandable. I think the technique fights coherence. I think it tends to make things ultimately boring and dismissable (unless they are accompanied by horrifying pictures), because almost anything is boring and dismissable if you know almost nothing about it.

15   If I may pause for a commercial, the "MacNeil/Lehrer Report" was founded on the conviction that the attention span of thirty seconds or a minute, which formed the basis of most television journalism, was an artificial formula imposed on the nation by the industry. To claim that it was the only way large numbers of people could be held by news about the real world was false and also insulting to large numbers of intelligent Americans.

16   We are now seven years along in an experiment to prove the contrary. And we are having some impact. Last September we expanded the program from thirty minutes to an hour, the "MacNeil/Lehrer NewsHour."

17   I believe that catering to the short attention span is not only inefficient communication, but it is also decivilizing. Part of the process of civilizing a young person, surely, lies in trying to lengthen his attention span, one of the basic tools of human intelligence.

18   A child may or may not have original sin, but he is born with original inattention. He is *naturally* inattentive, like a puppy, except to his basic biological needs.

19 Rearing a child consists in part in gradually trying to get his attention for longer periods, to cause him finally to direct it himself and to keep it directed until he finishes something. The older or more mature a child is, the longer he can be made to pay attention.

20   But what so much of television does is precisely the opposite. It panders to a child's natural tendency to be scatterbrained and inattentive, to watch this for two minutes and to play with that for two minutes. It is giving up the struggle. It starts from the assumption that he will be bored. It is like conceding that a child likes sugar; therefore you should give him only cereals with lots of sugar in them, or he may not eat and will hate you and grow up to write mean novels—assuming he *can* write—about what wretched parents you were.

21   I do not think education is immune to the virus. And the responsibility of education is enormous. Educators should consider the casual assumptions television tends to cultivate that bite-sized is best, that complexity must be avoided, that nuances are dispensible, that qualifications impede the simple message, that visual stimulation is a substitute for thought, and that verbal precision is an anachronism.

22   There is a crisis of literacy is this country and a tendency to excuse it by throwing up our hands and saying, "Well you can't fight the impact of the visual culture. Perhaps we can only join it." But we do not have to resign ourselves to the brilliant aphorism of Marshall McLuhan that the medium is the message. It *is,* but it is not a sufficient message. It may be old-fashioned, but I was taught to believe the Kantian idea that thought is words arranged in grammatically precise ways.

23   The message of the television medium fights that notion in several ways. One is obvious and perhaps trivial: it ingrains popular verbal habits, like the grammatical shortcuts of Madison Avenue. More seriously, it steals time from and becomes a substitute for deriving pleasure, experience, or knowledge through words. More subtly, even for sophisticated people, it encourages a surrender to the visual depiction of experience, necessarily abbreviated by time constraints, necessarily simplified, and often trivialized.

24   If American society is to maintain some pretence of being a mass literate culture, then far from reversing the appalling statistics of functional illiteracy, I think the struggle is to prevent them from growing worse. As you know, it is estimated that twenty-five million Americans cannot read or write at all. An additional thirty-five million are functionally illiterate and cannot read or write well enough to answer a want ad or understand the instructions on a medicine bottle. That adds up to sixty million people—nearly one-third of the population.

And, since close to one million young Americans drop out of school each year, it is probable that the country is producing at least that many *new* illiterates, or semiliterates, every year.

25   They land in a society where rudimentary survival increasingly depends on some ability to function in a world of forms and schedules and credit agreements and instructions. They enter a society that already faces the growing problem of finding something productive for most of its citizens to do. It is already a society with a cruelly large number of people who are in some sense redundant, whose share of the American dream is pitifully small.

26   Literacy may not be a human right, but the highly literate Founding Fathers might not have found it unreasonable or even unattainable. We are not only *not* attaining literacy as a nation, statistically speaking, but also falling farther and farther short of attaining it. And, while I would not be so simplistic as to suggest that television is the cause, I believe it contributes and is an influence: for the dull it is a substitute; for the bright it is a diversion.

27   The educators of this country, especially in the public schools, have had enough burdens thrust on them by society. But I frankly see no other force than educators in the society that can act as a counterweight to the intellectual mush of television. Of course, the home environment is primary, and millions of parents try very conscientiously. But television is now an essential part of every home. The Fifth Column is there, often in many rooms. It is virtually a utility. The school is the only part of a young person's regular environment where television isn't—or where television wasn't, until recently.

28   To the extent that schools and universities feel the only way they can reach young people's minds is by importing the values of television, I feel they risk exacerbating the problem. I don't mean there should not be television sets in schools, or that television may not be, in a limited sense, a useful tool. Obviously, not all television programs are worthless, and teachers may be able to encourage more critical, more selective viewing—I believe it is called "television literacy"— and may be able to use television to whet the appetite for other disciplines. And there are fine programs designed specifically for instruction. That's not what I'm talking about.

29   I am talking about the tendency I notice to surrender to the ethos that television subtly purveys: the idea that things are gotten easily, with little effort; that information can be absorbed passively; that by watching pictures children are absorbing as much information as they might through print. That is what I mean by pandering to the easy virtues of television, of letting young people believe that ideas are conveyed by tasty bits; that intellectual effort need not be applied; that you can get it (as they say) quickly and painlessly.

30   A few years ago I said to my small son, then age nine, "Would you like me to read *Treasure Island?*" He said, "Naw, I know it. I saw it on television." I felt very defeated, since that book happens to be one I love. Later, on a boat,

I got him in a captive environment with others who wanted to hear it. I read it and he liked it. But I think of his first response as the equivalent in my generation of saying, "Naw, I read it in Classic Comics." Are we content to let a generation grow up without knowing *Treasure Island* in its complete form? If not, there is only one way and that is by gentle forcing. That is what education used to be all about, and some of the forcing was not too gentle.

31   Why is that important? On one level, to get the sound of English prose, its rhythms and its rich vocabulary stirring pleasurably in their brains. Because it will echo there all their lives. The other is to stimulate their imagination. I know Walt Disney was a genius. But I personally deplore the way he has made so many classics so visually literal, substituting his (often cloyingly sweet) imagination for that of the child. And television is Walt Disney and his lesser imitators wholesale.

32   In politics, in sports, in entertainment, in news, if television doesn't like something the way it is, it is assumed that the wide public won't, so American institutions rush to change themselves so that television will like them. Television viability becomes *the* viability. My own code phrase for that pervasive influence on the culture is the short attention span.

33   Everything about this nation becomes more complicated, not less. The structure of the society, its forms of family organization, its economy, its place in the world have become more complex. Yet its dominating communications instrument, its principal form of national linkage is an instrument that sells simplicity and tidiness—neat resolutions of human problems that usually have *no* neat resolutions. It is all symbolized in my mind by the hugely successful art form that television has made central to the culture, the thirty-second commercial: the tiny drama of the earnest housewife who finds happiness in choosing the right toothpaste. That, as we know this fall, has also become the dominant form of political communication, transforming the choice of elected leaders into a slick exchange of packaged insults and half-truths, with the battle weighed heavily in favor of the candidate with the most money and the cleverest ad agency.

34   Whenever in human history has so much humanity collectively surrendered so much of its leisure to one toy, one mass diversion? Whenever before have all classes and kinds of men, virtually an entire nation, surrendered themselves wholesale, making their minds, their psyches, their bodies prisoners of a medium for selling?

35   Some years ago Judge Charles Black wrote: ". . . forced feeding on trivial fare is not itself a trivial matter. . . ." Well, I think this society is being force-fed with trivial fare with only dimly perceived effects on our habits of minds, our language, our tolerance for effort, and our appetite for complexity. If I am wrong, it will have done no harm to look at it skeptically and critically, to consider how we should be resisting it. And I hope you will share my skepticism.

☐ Discovering Meaning and Technique

1. Make a rough outline of the essay to determine where it divides into introduction, body, and conclusion.

2. In his "pause for a commercial" (paragraphs 15 and 16), MacNeil discusses his own television program, the "MacNeil/Lehrer Report." Does this discussion seem interruptive? Or does it fit logically into the essay?

3. In MacNeil's view, which characteristics of television encourage a shortened attention span?

4. Which trends indicate to MacNeil that our attention spans are shortening?

5. Precisely how does a shortened attention span affect education?

6. In paragraph 27, MacNeil refers to television as the "Fifth Column." If you are not familiar with the expression, look it up in the dictionary. What does MacNeil's use of the phrase indicate about his attitude toward television?

7. What does MacNeil refer to as "the hugely successful art form that television has made central to our culture" (paragraph 33)?

8. In paragraphs 11–14, MacNeil begins quite a few sentences with *I believe* or *I think.* Why does he use the technique in this particular section of the essay? Is the repetition effective? Why or why not?

☐ Writing Suggestions

1. Besides those projects suggested by MacNeil, suggest what a person might do with the time saved not watching television.

2. In paragraph 33, MacNeil asserts that while our society is becoming more complex, our primary form of communication (television) "sells simplicity and tidiness." Write an essay attacking or defending this idea.

3. MacNeil claims that *reading* (not watching) the classics is important for two reasons: "to get the sound of English prose, its rhythms and its rich vocabulary stirring pleasurably in [our] brains" and "to stimulate . . . [the] imagination." Why can't classic movies accomplish the same goals?

4. In paragraphs 18, 19, and 20, MacNeil refers to the child as *he,* for example, "Rearing a child consists in part in gradually trying to get his attention for longer periods, to cause him finally to direct it himself and to keep it directed until he finishes something." Discuss sexist language and show how to rewrite these paragraphs to avoid this kind of language.

5. Agree or disagree with MacNeil's assessment of television's effect on the language or upon education.

PLAYING FOR MONEY

☐ **GRACE LICHTENSTEIN**

[1] Big-time college sports have become a gross perversion of a concept dear to the ivory-tower crowd. The issue of student-athletes—along with the alleged transgressions of coaches, recruiters and university officials—has leaped beyond mere controversy to the level of all-American scandal. In the process, educational institutions have covered themselves with mud. And lives have been ruined.

[2] During the past year, more than two dozen colleges—prestige and jock schools alike—have been hit by charges ranging from illegal recruiting, to cash payoffs, ticket scalping, phony transcripts, medical mistreatment and point fixing. Many schools, including the University of Southern California, UCLA, Boston College and Clemson University, have in effect become farm systems for pro football, baseball and basketball teams. Coaches, who sometimes command higher salaries than university presidents, cry that they're forced to break amateur-athletics rules because if they don't, they can't build winning teams and will be fired. And television continues to fuel this overheated system by pumping millions into the coffers of the National Collegiate Athletic Association (NCAA) for TV rights to big games.

[3] Now, the athletes have begun to fight back. Their biggest supporters are not the pro-team owners who have a future interest in them, but the pro-basketball and pro-football players' unions. "Owners are in a better position to take advantage of a youngster if he doesn't have a degree," says one union organizer. "The kid doesn't have as many options, so the owners don't have to pay him as much as he's worth."

[4] Individually and collectively, athletes are charging that colleges prevented them from getting their degrees, injected them with needless painkillers and even bribed them. Unfortunately, for every James Worthy (the former University of North Carolina basketball star drafted by the Los Angeles Lakers after his junior year), there are thousands of Saturday's heroes who have turned into Sunday's chumps—bounced off campus without an education, unable to find work, left only with arthritic legs to stand on. They were lured, as athletes have been for years, by the dream of one day reaching the pros. But of the 10,000 football players who come out of college each year, barely 100 to 200 make it to a pro club. In the long run, even those who do may not really be lucky. More than two-thirds of today's pro players lack a college degree.

5   "I've been to dinner with fellow players who earn $300,000 a year and can't read the menu," says Kermit Alexander, past president and current field representative of the National Football League (NFL) Players Association.

6   That's one reason Alexander has joined a small cadre of reformers intent on helping young athletes cope with a system that could be dangerous to their physical and emotional health. These reformers are themselves ex-jocks who know how sweet Final Four, Rose Bowl or Olympic glory can be, and how bitter is the aftertaste.

7   Alexander has doubled as field coordinator for the Center for Athletes' Rights and Education (CARE), a year-old organization originally sponsored by the NFL Players Association and the National Conference of Black Lawyers. Another reformist group, Athletes for Better Education (AFBE), was formed in Chicago six years ago and is sponsored by the National Basketball (NBA) Players Association.

8   AFBE is guided by Arthur "Chick" Sherrer Jr., who was a bench warmer on the Princeton basketball squad that was led by Bill Bradley in the early Sixties. The group sponsors free basketball camps at which high-school students are tutored as much in reading and recruitment as they are in pick-and-rolls. To raise money, AFBE holds auctions of jock memorabilia (Walter Payton's jersey fetched a thousand dollars). It also conducts "profile scrimmages" in Chicago, New York and Los Angeles to showcase high-school players who need athletic and academic scholarships and who may have been overlooked by some recruiters. According to the AFBE score card, the group has helped hundreds of players get some kind of scholarship since 1978. "We tell them, chase the dream but catch an education. Don't just go through four years of college and be totally exploited," explains Charles Grantham, AFBE adviser and NBA Players Association executive vice-president.

9   Both AFBE and CARE have drawn up lists of tough questions that they urge student-athletes, parents and high-school administrators to pose to fast-talking recruiters. Among the questions: "If I perform well in the classroom but fall short of my coach's expectations in athletics, will my scholarship be renewed every year?" "If I'm injured badly enough to require surgery, will the school pay for a second opinion by a doctor of my choice?" "Do the athletes take courses that prepare them for a career, or do they take 'softer' courses designed to keep them eligible?" "Do coaches use physical activity as punishment and discipline rather than as a source of fitness and human development?"

10   Full-ride scholarships (including room, board, tuition and books) are limited at even the biggest schools, and the competition is fierce. NCAA Division 1-A schools—the 137 elite football factories—are each allowed a maximum of 95 full-ride football scholarships at any one time, while the 276 Division I basketball schools are permitted only fifteen full-rides a year in basketball. And the NCAA itself does not know how many full-ride athletes get their scholarships renewed.

11   From its office on New York's East 156th Street, a teeming bazaar surrounded

by the desert of the city's premier slum, the South Bronx, CARE dispenses a stream of speakers, pamphlets and position papers on the abuses of the current system. While CARE's staff has undergone changes, its leaders have included Cary Goodman, former Colgate player and long-time sports activist; Phil Shinnick, former Olympic long jumper; and Allen Sack, former Notre Dame football star. (All three happen to be Ph.D.'s as well.) The organization's largest financial backer is currently the U.S. Department of Education.

12   CARE put Florida State University basketball star James Bozeman in front of the national media to tell how his school mishandled his injuries until he could hardly walk, how it plied athletes with cash, how one coach used a female cheerleader to recruit a high schooler, and how students who did not play ball up to expectations found themselves in academic trouble. (A review committee at FSU rejected most of Bozeman's contentions, to no one's surprise.)

13   But the Bozeman case is a small skirmish in CARE's attack on the college sports establishment. Through the school systems in New York City, Detroit and other cities, the group is distributing an "Athletes' Bill of Rights" guaranteed to nettle the NCAA. It advises would-be scholarship students (if indeed they can be viewed as employees) that although they virtually turn over total control of their lives when they sign a "letter of intent" to attend a college on a full-ride, they should still be entitled to a share of a school's sports revenues, to workman's compensation if injured and to a student-athletes' union.

14   "Student-athletes are workers. A scholarship athlete is the employee of the university," says Alan Sack, current director of CARE. "If he decides to give up sports for books, he loses his pay. If he doesn't perform on the athletic field, he gets fired."

15   Recently, another Florida State basketball player, Pernell Tookes, filed a workman's compensation claim against the university on the grounds that a knee injury had been caused by his "employment." The Tookes case could set a precedent for claims in other college sports as well.

16   Perhaps more radical is CARE's lobbying to get the NCAA to set up an academic trust fund that would finance the education of injured athletes or those who have used up their playing eligibility but are short of a degree. The fund would be financed by about 15 percent of the fees paid by networks to televise NCAA games—or nearly $40 million alone from the latest two-network football pact.

17   Goodman argues that the NCAA is not actually a rules-enforcement agency anyway, but rather a big-business "cartel" whose purpose is to protect member colleges and collect TV riches for them.

18   Why all this fuss about campus jocks, the envy of so many of their fellow students? Because Goodman, Sherrer and others maintain that the vast majority of high-school student-athletes don't have the slightest idea about the reality of college recruiting . . . or of the college jock's life afterward.

19   Recruiting is "one of the most pressurized, distorted, sophisticated processes," declares Dick Versace, head basketball coach at Illinois' Bradley University. Blue-chip prospects "absolutely wack out. They become numb. Even the most sophisticated, intelligent parent trips out. I haven't met one who can handle it."

20   Norm Ellenberger, former basketball coach at the University of New Mexico, thinks a list of questions for recruiters might allow the athletes to recognize unscrupulous headhunters. "If you're a used-car salesman and you're trying to sell me a clunker, you don't want me to see the busted engine, you want me to see the shiny new paint job. Let's face it: when you're a seventeen-year-old kid and you've got a dozen coaches dangling a full ride and a promise to lead you off into glory, it's hard to know what questions to ask."

21   Several top high-school stars remember well what a typical recruiter's pitch sounded like, whether it came from a head coach or an assistant whose primary role was recruitment:

22   "William," they would say, always careful to be courteous, "with your size and speed, you'll be a starter your first year, no question. Know the last guy I scouted with talent like yours? O. J., that's who! You're a blue-chipper, William, and with you, we've got the makings of a top-ten team. Mrs. Johnson, wouldn't it be great to see your son here on TV in the Mango Bowl? Did I mention that all our full-ride freshmen get Sony color consoles for their folks? Our boosters are very generous about flying parents to Podunk for the weekend of a big home game, Mrs. Johnson. And we don't want you or your son to worry about the little things. You've got a tough English course, William? We've got tutors helping all our boys. Now I know you also want walking-around money, and we've got part-time jobs for all our blue-chippers, William, so you can count on ten dollars an hour for putting out the practice gear in the afternoon. . . ."

23   Often, though, it's what is left out of the pitch that matters.

24   According to Nancy Lieberman, a former basketball star at Old Dominion University in Virginia, the most important promise not kept by recruiters is that a student-athlete will have the time for both halves of his or her hyphenated life. "You learn that you've got to choose between really studying or playing ball," she says. "No way can you do both."

25   Curtis Taliaferro would certainly agree. Last spring in Pittsburgh, the Ohio University football player told an athletes conference of eleventh- and twelfth-graders that "recruiters hate a person who asks too many questions." He had not asked enough. He had had few clues that he would be pressured to play when hurt, and that coaches would discourage his academic studies because they interfered with football practice.

26   In truth, long before he probably knew how to spell *interference,* Curtis Taliaferro was being scouted by recruiters.

27   "The road starts not with your senior year, not with your sophomore year,

but in junior high school," he warned an audience brought together by the Urban League and a social-service agency called the Kingsley Association. "You're winning, you're getting certificates, you're so great, okay? Coaches pat you on the back, get you out of class, tell you that you need to go over plays for upcoming games. Your books are right there in your hand. They just stay there."

28   Wooed by such legendary football schools as Southern Cal, Notre Dame, Penn State, Tulane and Syracuse, Taliaferro accepted a full-ride scholarship at Ohio. Suddenly, as a freshman on the varsity team, he realized how that defined him: "nothing but a paycheck, 185 pounds' worth of beef." His schedule each afternoon was "two to six, practice. Seven to eight, watch films. Eight to 10:30, go to study hall—where you just get plays from coaches." He thought he was going crazy. "To become a human being, I had to learn how to leave my sweats in the locker room. You ask yourself if it's worth it."

29   By his second year, Taliaferro found the burden too heavy. "You're spending most of your time uptown, drinking beer, trying to see how many women you can hold or just sleeping." Finally one day, he quit and came home to his mother. "It was the first time in my life I was not on a winning football team. I cried because I wasn't playing."

30   Why don't athletes like Taliaferro get better guidance on handling the pressure? Often because administrators can't keep track of slick recruiters—or because ambitious high-school coaches are in the recruiters' pockets.

31   In Detroit not long ago, several in a group of six black high-school principals (three of whom had gone to college on athletic scholarships themselves) admitted to NFL Players Association field representative Kermit Alexander that they did not know that most full rides were not complete four-year scholarships but "one-year renewables," contingent upon a student-athlete's performance. Moreover, they said they were inundated by recruiters from across the country who roamed their hallways, keeping blue-chippers out of class in order to pitch them.

32   "We've developed a monster here," said James Soloman of Detroit's Martin L. King High School. "We produce so many quality athletes, we're almost not able to live with it." It was noted that when one gifted basketball star was slightly injured, recruiters literally lined up beside his hospital bed. Another principal bemoaned the "new breed" of high-school coach, who figures, "If I keep sending enough good kids to Michigan, they'll hire me on as an assistant coach."

33   Alexander—a charming man who lasted fourteen seasons in the pros as a defensive back, earning his bachelor's degree from UCLA eight years after his eligibility ended—did not mince words. Since Detroit was such fertile athletic territory, he argued, the principals were in a position to dictate rules to recruiters rather than be swamped by them. Indeed, a school-system-wide recruiter-screening process is going into effect this fall.

34   In terms of power and money, Alexander and the other reformers appear to be in the position of a peewee football team scrimmaging against the San

Francisco 49ers. They're up against a multimillion-dollar operation that feeds the universities' hunger for instant recognition from sports, as well as the hunger of talented young men who are convinced they can be the next O. J. Simpson. The enforcement of regulations designed to prevent abuses is in the hands of a fourteen-member NCAA committee; still another committee negotiates and promotes the immensely profitable television packages.

35   "It comes down to a dollars-and-cents situation," says Ellenberger. "There are more and more schools finding that basketball is a profitable business. It's awfully easy for a college administrator to put subtle pressure on a coach to win at all costs, and to hide under his desk when the thing is overturned." He scoffs at the notion that athletes and parents are pawns who are "raped, pillaged and plundered." On the contrary, "There are plenty with their palms up," he says.

36   Norm Ellenberger knows whereof he speaks. As New Mexico's head coach from 1972 to 1979, he compiled a remarkable win-loss average of .684, consistently filling "the Pit" in Albuquerque with players recruited from all over the nation—until a scandal of mammoth proportions caved in on the Lobos. The saga of New Mexico's "Lobogate," as it was dubbed, illustrates how corrupt college sports can become.

37   A successful high-school and college coach in the Midwest, Ellenberger joined the Lobos in 1967 as an assistant coach. The team had played only one exhibition game in 1979 when a state wiretap that recorded an Ellenberger conversation with his assistant, Manny Goldstein, set in motion a federal investigation into racketeering, illegal travel vouchers and other irregularities within the Lobo ranks.

38   The university fired Ellenberger. Eventually, he stood trial in state court on twenty-two counts of fraud and filing false travel vouchers. He was convicted on twenty-one of them, which could have meant incarceration for twenty-one years. Yet, in a dramatic courtroom denouement, the judge refused to sentence the popular Ellenberger to a single day behind bars. The coach, thundered the judge, was "one cog" in a rotten system, and he'd done "what almost everybody in this community wanted him to do"—win games. "The real hypocrisy," the judge added, "is that colleges and universities across this country . . . maintain and establish what amounts to professional ball clubs. At the same time, they purport to operate under amateur rules." An NCAA investigation, however, found the university guilty of thirty-four rules violations and ordered it to suspend one player and declare five others ineligible, suffer three years of NCAA probation and return $36,000 in gate receipts.

39   University of New Mexico president William "Bud" Davis was accused of knowing about many of the violations. He denied it.

40   Lobogate has since died down in Albuquerque. Ellenberger is now part owner of a racquet club called Supreme Courts. Davis (who refused to speak to *Rolling Stone*) also emerged unscathed and left the university to become

the state of Oregon's chancellor for higher education. One of Ellenberger's stars, Michael Cooper, is a fixture with the Los Angeles Lakers. But not all his recruits fared as well. Willie Howard, for example. He's in prison.

41   Howard was born in Chicago and raised in Los Angeles. He blossomed as a basketball player while at Cerritos College, a two-year institution in California. After proving his worth there, Howard was pursued by excited recruiters from seventy-five senior colleges. He chose to transfer to New Mexico, partly because "they filled the arena every night," partly because a team assistant promised to arrange "special loans" for a new car.

42   The six-foot-eight forward was on probation in California on a charge of assault with a firearm. During his two years with the Lobos, however, he became quite a favorite. Before a big game, "prominent" community members would ask him to deliver a pep talk about "incentive," a talk sealed with cash gifts, Howard said recently. Sometimes it was a token for extra rebounds, but before a crucial game against the University of Nevada at Las Vegas, Howard says he got $200.

43   Howard was soon envisioning a career in the NBA, although his schoolwork left something to be desired. People were "basketball crazy, not interested in an education," said Howard. He did not pass many required courses, but someone always "talked to an instructor to make sure I got an incomplete." During the summer, he says, it was arranged for him to be enrolled in an out-of-state college to make up the credits necessary for him to maintain his eligibility as a player. "I never went," he said, "but I got credit anyway."

44   He claims the "special loan" was delivered to him in the form of a check at a local Albuquerque bank. Howard had himself a brand-new Impala.

45   His eligibility ran out in 1978. Howard was the seventh-round draft choice of the New Orleans Jazz. For Willie Howard, the classic jock's dream seemed ready to come true.

46   Then, bit by bit, his life began to unravel. The Jazz, he recalls, released him before the exhibition season. Confused, he went to California and, for a year and a half, worked as a furniture delivery man. By 1979, wanting to be near his family and engaged to a local woman, he returned to Albuquerque. The homecoming was rough. He was out of work for months before he landed another furniture-moving job. The "prominent" people who he alleged had once slipped him C-notes no longer knew him.

47   In January 1981, there was a break-in at the apartment of a former Lobo football player, reportedly involving a fight over a tape deck. Willie Howard, it was alleged, tried to smash one man's head with a sledgehammer. Howard was convicted of residential burglary this past May and marched off to the state penitentiary for three years.

48   But Willie Howard, with a wife and infant daughter, maintains he's a good family man. The "burglary," he says, was simply a disagreement among friends who called the cops to get even. The judge, however, did not show Howard

the kind of understanding that his counterpart had shown in the Ellenberger case. And the prosecutor, who once had season tickets to watch the Lobos play, now thinks it's a disgrace that his alma mater suited up "criminals." These attitudes are of little consequence to Willie Howard. "They only call me a star now when I'm in trouble," he says.

49   At the time of his arrest, Howard listed his occupation as "unemployed athlete." The Impala was long gone, sold to pay grocery bills.

50   Norm Ellenberger optioned the movie rights to his life story to Ray Stark Television for an undisclosed sum.

51   It is not necessary to be poor, gifted and black to be exploited by college athletics. Take the case of Kevin Rutledge, a gifted white football player from a middle-income Phoenix family.

52   Several years ago, Rutledge enrolled at his hometown school, Arizona State University, eager to play Pac-10 football under the coach who was revered throughout the state, Frank Kush. Like many of his successful colleagues, Kush was known as a stern taskmaster. In his sophomore year, Rutledge found out just how stern. That fall, ASU was behind by twenty-one points in the third quarter of a game against Washington. Rutledge, a punter, got off a thirty-yard kick. Kush, recalled the punter, "didn't like it." When Rutledge got to the sidelines, he claimed the coach punched him in the face.

53   Later, Rutledge testified it was not the first time Kush had abused a player. "He was like a god," the young man says now. "The players were all afraid of him; the coaches were all afraid of him." But Rutledge was not afraid, and he filed a multimillion-dollar lawsuit against the god of the Sun Devils. Soon thereafter, Kush, accused of trying to cover up the incident, was fired. A month after *that,* Arizona State became embroiled in a transcript scandal similar to the one in New Mexico, and the football team was forced to forfeit several victories from a previous season.

54   Kush denied both the punching incident and the transcript scam. When Rutledge's suit finally came to trial in 1981, such blue-chip defense witnesses as former Sun Devil Danny White, who was by then a Dallas Cowboys quarterback, and Olympic hockey coach Herb Brooks testified on Kush's stalwart behalf.

55   Rutledge had already transferred to another college out of Arizona and believed that no one in his family was safe. After his suit had been filed, Rutledge's younger brother, a high-school football player, received death threats. His father's insurance office in Phoenix had been torched. The police officially labeled it arson and denied it had anything to do with the trial.

56   In court, Kush was acquitted in the punching incident. His legal bills were paid by the state, because he had been an employee of its university at the time the suit occurred. "It's hard to believe," Rutledge says now, "but Kush could do no wrong. You didn't see how much power he had. It went right to the judicial structure of the state."

57   (Various appeals are now being considered, and the American Civil Liberties Union is planning to file an amicus brief on Rutledge's behalf.)

58   By the fall of 1981, Kevin Rutledge had played out his eligibility at his new university and had gotten married. Still some credits shy of a degree, he worked for a time as a laborer in Las Vegas, then moved to a small island off South Carolina, hoping to start a new life, perhaps as a shrimp-boat captain. Rutledge says he would like to try out as a free agent for a pro-football team, but he suspects his notoriety might handicap him. This fall, he is reentering college to finish his degree work.

59   Frank Kush? He's head coach of the Colts.

60   The Arizona State athletic director who fired Kush was himself demoted. Recently, the former director, Fred L. Miller, wrote that cheating by coaches was a "cancer" preventing governance of college sports, and that many university presidents go out of their way to make sure "not to be in the direct firing line should athletic problems erupt."

61   And erupt they have. Last spring, the University of Southern California— alma mater of O. J. Simpson and Tom Seaver, and one of the five leading television football drawing cards—was slapped with a heavy NCAA penalty: it seems that for ten years, assistant football coaches had been selling athletes' free-game tickets to willing boosters. And two years ago, Southern Cal exposed, on its own, an admissions procedure under which hundreds of star athletes, among others, were enrolled despite high-school grades lower than USC standards. "It was a system gone awry," admitted the president, James H. Zumberge, at the time. Yet, when the latest sanctions were announced (including a two-year ban on telecasts of Southern Cal games), Zumberge expressed outrage. The NCAA was being "vindictive" against his school. Besides, he said, "ethical standards often come into conflict." One element that upset the president was that the school would lose an enormous amount of money from TV.

62   However, because the NCAA penalties were imposed for the 1983 and 1984 seasons, the biggest nonbowl game of the 1982 TV schedule, Southern Cal versus Notre Dame, won't be affected. Furthermore, since Pac-10 schools share revenues from telecasts of any member school's games, Southern Cal will collect some money in 1983 and 1984.

63   The litany of scandals goes on and on. In Tennessee, two former high-school blue-chip football stars brought a lawsuit against Clemson (an Atlantic Coast Conference school and the number-one college-football team in 1981) charging that they were handed money to sign letters of intent and then denied the opportunity to go to a Southeastern Conference school; it is now in the appeals stage. Rick Kuhn, a former Boston College basketball player, was sentenced to ten years in jail on a point-shaving charge. Wichita State's basketball team was hit with a three-year NCAA probation, giving that school the dubious distinction of having the most frequent sanctions in the country.

64   Louisiana State released a confidential report showing that major-sport athletes were admitted despite low testing scores, and that many athletes were funneled into laughable courses designed solely to keep them academically eligible. (The most popular course was called Know Louisiana, also known as "the bus course," in which student athletes, among others, received college credit for traveling around the state.) In addition, Louisiana State forced the departure last May of two assistant athletic directors after a general audit of the athletics department. At about the same time, a Louisiana State assistant basketball coach reported that his briefcase had been stolen on a recruiting trip—with $2000 in cash inside. A chancellor's investigation cleared him of any improprieties.

65   Seven former athletes at California State University at Los Angeles have filed a multimillion-dollar lawsuit charging that they had been guided into courses that kept them from getting a meaningful education. One of the top women's basketball coaches, Pam Parsons, left the University of South Carolina amid a scandal that involved, among other things, allegations of drug use and sexual relations with players.

66   There are signs that important sports personalities are beginning to see the need for drastic change, perhaps along the very lines outlined by CARE. Senator Bill Bradley of New Jersey, who knows a bit about college sports, said not long ago that "college athletic programs should simply operate on two different tracks," amateur and semipro. The latter schools "would accept and pay star athletes. . . . The colleges would not have to compromise their academic ideals. The athletes would not have to pretend that their basic interest is a quality education." Cary Goodman would like to go even further. He wants a congressional investigation into the colleges' misuse of federal grants-in-aid to students.

67   There are also signs that some young athletes are heeding the message of Chick Sherrer, who says that "basketball should be a means to an end." At AFBE's New York profile scrimmage last spring, Louis "Stuntman" Stitzer, a high-school guard from North Bergen, New Jersey, said he had come to the showcase for a single reason: "I want a free education. Anywhere. I'll take Whatsamatta U!"

68   Of course, Stitzer hoped North Carolina's Dean Smith was waiting with a full ride in hand. But when the offers he received boiled down to half rides at obscure Southern colleges, Stitzer was content to accept a job as a lifeguard and a straight student grant from Ramapo College, an hour from his home. "Sure, I thought this was gonna be Joe Notre Dame, the 280-Z car, the works. It didn't turn out that way. Hey, I wouldn't mind being paid $10,000 to play ball in school. But you only stay in college a few years," Stitzer reasoned. "Then, if you don't have a degree, you're a bum."

69   Cary Goodman knows the reformers have their work cut out for them. "When we're going at college sports, it's like knocking mom's apple pie. But the evidence is mounting. Six months from now, something will produce a spark to change things. We'll just keep punching, punching, punching."

☐ Discovering Meaning and Technique

1. Compare the way Lichtenstein wrote the last two sentences of the first paragraph with this version: "In the process, educational institutions have covered themselves with mud, and lives have been lost."

2. According to the coaches, why must they break rules?

3. According to the selection, what proportion of football players make it to the pros?

4. Who is trying to reform the system that exploits student-athletes? What are the reformers doing to make changes?

5. What devices do college recruiters use to entice athletes?

6. Why did Ellenberger not go to jail?

7. What do the stories of Willie Howard and Kevin Rutledge illustrate? Why do you think Lichtenstein devotes so much space to relating them?

8. What does Senator Bill Bradley suggest as a way to reform college athletics?

☐ Writing Suggestions

1. Discuss how the dream of a professional athletic career can cause poor preparation for life.

2. Do colleges "use" athletes?

3. Should college athletes be considered "workers" entitled to pay and compensation?

4. Is it possible for the average college athlete to balance athletics and academics?

5. Investigate and discuss the attitudes of athletes on your campus. Cover such subjects as their recruitment, time for studying, prospects for a degree, and financial benefits.

6. Argue for or against Senator Bill Bradley's idea of an amateur and semipro track for athletes in college.

PAIDEIA PROPOSAL: THE SAME COURSE OF STUDY FOR ALL

☐ **MORTIMER J. ADLER**

P A I D E I A (py-dee-a) from the Greek *paid, paidos:* the upbringing of a child. (Related to pedagogy and pediatrics.) In an extended sense, the equivalent of the Latin *humanitas* (from which "the humanities"), signifying the general learning that should be the possession of all human beings.

1 The Paideia Proposal *is addressed to those Americans most concerned with the future of our public schools:*

- *To Parents who believe that the decline in the quality of public schooling is damaging the futures of their children.*
- *To Teachers troubled that the increasing time spent in keeping basic order in the classroom undermines the real business of schooling: to teach and to learn.*
- *To School Boards frightened by the flight of middle-class children and youth to private and parochial schools.*
- *To College Educators burdened by the increasing need to provide remedial education which detracts from their ability to offer a meaningful higher education.*
- *To Elected Public Officials searching for ways to improve the quality of education without increasing the cost to taxpayers.*
- *To Employers concerned about the effects on productivity of a work force lacking skills in reading, writing, speaking, listening, observing, measuring, and computing.*
- *To Minority Groups angered by widening gulfs between the better educated and the poorly educated, and between the employed and the unemployed.*
- *To Labor Leaders attempting to deal with workers who lack the skills to find jobs in the new high-technology industries.*
- *To Military Leaders needing brainpower among the troops capable of coping with sophisticated weaponry.*
- *To American Citizens alarmed by the prospects of a democracy in which a declining proportion of the people vote or endeavor to understand the great issues of our time.*

2   *Such deep and legitimate concerns are addressed by our proposal for the reform of public schooling in America. The reform we seek is designed to improve the opportunities of our youth, the prospects of our economy, and the viability of our democratic institutions. It must be achieved at the community level without resorting to a monolithic, national educational system. It must be, in Lincoln's words, of the people, by the people, and for the people.*

3 To give the same quality of schooling to all requires a program of study that is both liberal and general, and that is, in several, crucial, overarching respects, one and the same for every child. All sidetracks, specialized courses, or elective choices must be eliminated. Allowing them will always lead a certain number of students to voluntarily downgrade their own education.

4 Elective choices are appropriate only in a curriculum that is intended for different avenues of specialization or different forms of preparation for the professions or technical careers. Electives and specialization are entirely proper at the level of advanced schooling—in our colleges, universities, and technical schools. They are wholly inappropriate at the level of basic schooling.

5 The course of study to be followed in the twelve years of basic schooling should, therefore, be completely required, with only one exception. That exception is the choice of a second language. In addition to competence in the use of English as everyone's primary language, basic schooling should confer a certain degree of facility in the use of a second language. That second language should be open to elective choice.

6 The diagram depicts in three columns three distinct modes of teaching and learning, rising in successive gradations of complexity and difficulty from the first to the twelfth year. All three modes are essential to the overall course of study.

7 These three columns are interconnected, as the diagram indicates. The different modes of learning on the part of the students and the different modes of teaching on the part of the teaching staff correspond to three different ways in which the mind can be improved—(1) by the acquisition of organized knowledge; (2) by the development of intellectual skills; and (3) by the enlargement of understanding, insight, and aesthetic appreciation.

8 In addition to the three main Columns of Learning, the required course of study also includes a group of auxiliary subjects, of which one is physical education and care of the body. This runs through all twelve years. Of the other two auxiliary subjects, instruction in a variety of manual arts occupies a number of years, but not all twelve; and the third consists of an introduction to the world of work and its range of occupations and careers. It is given in the last two of the twelve years.

COLUMN ONE: ACQUISITION OF KNOWLEDGE

9 Here are three areas of subject matter indispensable to basic schooling—language, literature, and fine arts; mathematics and natural sciences; history, geography, and social studies.

10 Why these three? They comprise the most fundamental branches of learning. No one can claim to be educated who is not reasonably well acquainted with all three. They provide the learner with indispensable knowledge about nature and culture, the world in which we live, our social institutions, and ourselves.

	Column One	**Column Two**	**Column Three**
Goals	Acquisition of Organized Knowledge	Development of Intellectual Skills — Skills of Learning	Enlarged Understanding of Ideas and Values
	by means of	*by means of*	*by means of*
Means	Didactic Instruction, Lectures and Responses, Textbooks, and Other Aids	Coaching, Exercises, and Supervised Practice	Maieutic or Socratic Questioning and Active Participation
	in three areas of subject matter	*in the operations of*	*in the*
Areas Operations and Activities	Language, Literature, and The Fine Arts Mathematics and Natural Science History, Geography, and Social Studies	Reading, Writing, Speaking, Listening Calculating, Problem-Solving, Observing, Measuring, Estimating Exercising Critical Judgment	Discussion of Books (Not Textbooks) and Other Works of Art And Involvement in Artistic Activities e.g., Music, Drama, Visual Arts

The three columns do not correspond to separate courses, nor is one kind of teaching and learning necessarily confined to any one class.

11   The traditional name for the mode of instruction here is "didactic," or "teaching by telling." It employs textbooks and other instructional materials and is accompanied by laboratory demonstrations. The mind here is improved by the acquisition of organized knowledge.

12   Instruction in language comprises the learning of grammar and syntax, the forms of discourse, and to some extent the history of our own language. Comparisons between English and other languages being studied in the program should be stressed. Whether mathematics is also a language and how it compares with a natural language such as English should be considered.

13   Instruction in mathematics, beginning with simple arithmetic in the first grade, should rise to at least one year of calculus. It should be integrated from the very beginning with instruction in the use of calculators and lead subsequently

to at least introductory instruction in the use of, and programming for, computers.

14   Instruction in the natural sciences includes physics, chemistry, and biology. Their interconnectedness and interdependence are stressed. Such instruction does not begin formally in the early grades but preparation for it can be made in a variety of attractive ways from the beginning.

15   History and geography are to be understood as including our knowledge of human and social affairs, not only within the boundaries of our own nation, but with regard to the rest of the world. Preparation for the formal study of history should begin in the early grades by storytelling and biographical narratives but, when formal study begins, it should be sequential and systematic, combining a narration of events with knowledge of social, political, and economic institutions and diverse phases of cultural development.

16   The innovative aspect of the first column lies not in the choice of subject matter but in the concentration and continuity of the study required. Those who know how inadequate and fragmentary is the knowledge offered to a large majority of those now graduating from high school will recognize the importance of our emphasis on these requirements.

COLUMN TWO: DEVELOPMENT OF SKILL

17   Here are the basic skills of learning—competence in the *use* of language, primarily English, aided by facility in a second language, as well as competence in dealing with a wise range of symbolic devices, such as calculators, computers, and scientific instruments.

18   The skills to be acquired are the skills of *reading, writing, speaking, listening, observing, measuring, estimating,* and *calculating.* They are linguistic, mathematical, and scientific skills. They are the skills that everyone needs in order to learn anything, in school or elsewhere. Without them, it is impossible to go on learning by one's self, whether for pleasure, or to qualify for a new job, or to be promoted in the present one.

19   It will be noted that language and mathematics appear in both Columns One and Two, but their significance is different in each. In Column One, *knowledge about* mathematics and language is acquired: in Column Two, the student learns *how to do* mathematical operations correctly and how to use language effectively for communication. "Know-how" consists in skilled performance. It differs from "knowledge about," which consists in knowing that something is the thus-and-so, and not otherwise.

20   The development of the Column Two skills clearly has close connections with the study of the three fundamental areas of subject matter in Column One. Only to the degree that pupils develop these skills, and form the habit of using them, can instruction in language and literature, mathematics and natural science, history and geography be successful.

21   Skills cannot be acquired in a vacuum. They must be practiced in the very study of the three basic areas of subject matter, as well as in the process of acquiring linguistic competence, competence in communication, competence in the handling of symbolic devices, and competence in critical thinking.

22   Since what is learned here is skill in performance, not knowledge of facts and formulas, the mode of teaching cannot be didactic. It cannot consist in the teacher telling, demonstrating, or lecturing. Instead, it must be akin to the coaching that is done to impart athletic skills. A coach does not teach simply by telling or giving the learner a rule book to follow. A coach trains by helping the learner to *do,* to go through the right motions, and to organize a sequence of acts in a correct fashion. He corrects faulty performance again and again and insists on repetition of the performance until it achieves a measure of perfection.

23   Only in this way can skill in reading, writing, speaking, and listening be acquired. Only in this way can a similar measure of skill be acquired in mathematical and scientific operations. Only in this way can the ability to think critically— to judge and to discriminate—be developed. When coaching is not adequately undertaken, little can be expected in the development of the basic skills.

24   Coaching involves a different teacher-pupil relationship and a different pupil-teacher ratio than does instruction by telling and by the use of textbooks.

25   The innovative aspect of Column Two in the basic course of study lies in the fact that nowadays effective coaching and drilling is much too frequently absent from basic schooling. The lack of coaching and drilling by itself accounts for the present deficiencies of many high school graduates in reading, writing, computing, and in following directions.

26   It is evident that Column Two is the backbone of basic schooling. Proficiency in all the skills that it lists—all of them the very means of learning itself—is indispensable to the efficient teaching and learning of the subject matters in Column One; and also indispensable to teaching and learning in Column Three.

27   Acquiring facility in the use of a second language is included in Column Two. Among modern languages, a choice can be made of French, German, Italian, Spanish, Russian, Chinese, and possibly others; it may even extend to Latin and Greek. A second language serves to enlarge the scope of the student's understanding of the culture in which English is the primary language by introducing him or her to the imagery and conceptual framework of the cultures that employ these other languages.

COLUMN THREE: ENLARGEMENT OF THE UNDERSTANDING

28 Here we have a mode of teaching and learning that has all too rarely been attempted in the public schools. Columns One and Two have important innovative aspects when compared with what now goes and is either largely or totally left out. Column Three is virtually all innovative.

29   The materials of learning in Column Three can be described by calling

them, on the one hand, books—books that are *not* textbooks—and, on the other hand, products of human artistry. The books are of every kind—historical, scientific, philosophical, poems, stories, essays. The products of human artistry include individual pieces of music, of visual art, plays, and productions in dance, film, or television. The emphasis throughout is on the individual work.

30   The mode of learning in Column Three engages the mind in the study of individual works of merit, whether literary or otherwise, accompanied by a discussion of the ideas, the values, and the forms embodied in such products of human art.

31   The appropriate mode of instruction in Column Three is neither didactic nor coaching. It cannot be teaching by telling and by using textbooks. It cannot consist in supervising the activities involved in acquiring skills.

32   It must be the Socratic mode of teaching, a mode of teaching called "maieutic" because it helps the student bring ideas to birth. It is teaching by asking questions, by leading discussions, by helping students to raise their minds up from a state of understanding or appreciating less to a state of understanding or appreciating more.

33   The interrogative or discussion method of teaching to be employed in Column Three stimulates the imagination and intellect by awakening the creative and inquisitive powers. In no other way can children's understanding of what they know be improved, and their appreciation of cultural objects be enhanced.

34   The books in Column Three—fiction, poetry, essays, history, science, and philosophy—serve a twofold purpose.

35   On the one hand, discussion draws on the student's skills of reading, writing, speaking, and listening, and uses them to sharpen the ability to think clearly, critically, and reflectively. It teaches participants how to analyze their own minds as well as the thought of others, which is to say it engages students in disciplined conversation about ideas and values.

36   On the other hand, discussion introduces students to the fundamental ideas in the basic subject matters of Column One, and especially the ideas underlying our form of government and the institutions of our society.

37   To fulfill the objective of preparing all young people to become intelligent citizens requires the careful reading and discussion of at least the following documents: the Declaration of Independence, the Constitution, selections from the *Federalist Papers,* and the Gettysburg Address. Other books will fill this purpose out, but these few are basic to understanding our democracy.

38   For mutual understanding and responsible debate among the citizens of a democratic community, and for differences of opinion to be aired and resolved, citizens must be able to communicate with one another in a common language. "Language" in this sense involves a common vocabulary of ideas. This common intellectual resource is theirs only if they have read, discussed, and come to understand a certain number of books that deal with the ideas operative in the life of their time and place.

39   Music and other works of art can be dealt with in seminars in which ideas are discussed; but, like poetry and fiction, they need an additional treatment in order to be appreciated aesthetically—to be enjoyed and admired for their excellence. In this connection, exercises in the performance and composition of poetry, music, and visual works, as well as in the production of dramatic works, will help develop that appreciation in the most direct manner.

40   The best way to understand a play is to act in it, or at least to read it out loud. The best way to understand a piece of music is to sing or play it. The best way to understand a work of dance is to try to dance it. Participation in the creation of works of art is as important as viewing, listening to, and discussing them. All children should have such pleasurable experiences.

THE INTEGRATION OF THE THREE COLUMNS

41 We have noted earlier the interplay between Columns One and Two. It can now be seen how Column Three supplements and reinforces the learning that is accomplished in the other two columns.

42   The reading of books throughout the twelve years of basic schooling, from easy books and mainly imaginative works in the early grades to more difficult books and expository as well as imaginative in the upper grades acquaints the growing mind with fundamental ideas in the subject matters of Column One, and at the same time employs and perfects all the linguistic skills of Column Two.

43   Without coaching, learners will lack the skills needed for the study of the basic subject matters. Without discussion, they may be memorizing machines, able to pass quizzes or examinations. But probe their minds and you will find that what they know by memory, they do not understand.

44   They have spent hours in classrooms where they were talked at, where they recited and took notes, plus hours (often too few) of homework poring over textbooks, extracting facts to commit to memory. But when have their minds been addressed, in what connection have they been called upon to think for themselves, to respond to important questions and to raise them themselves, to pursue an argument, to defend a point of view, to understand its opposite, to weigh alternatives?

45   There is little joy in most of the learning they are now compelled to do. Too much of it is make-believe, in which neither teacher nor pupil can take a lively interest. Without some joy in learning—a joy that arises from hard work well done and from the participation of one's mind in a common task—basic schooling cannot initiate the young into the life of learning, let alone give them the skill and the incentive to engage in it further. Only the student whose mind has been engaged in thinking for itself is an active participant in the learning process that is essential to basic schooling.

46   Without what is called for in Column Three, such participation cannot be

accomplished to any satisfactory degree. It is not now accomplished at all for most of the students in our public schools, and it is accomplished to an insufficient degree for even the chosen few.

THE AUXILIARY STUDIES

47 Young people need physical exercise for their health's sake and also as an outlet for their abundant energy. Twelve years of physical education and participation in various intramural sports and athletic exercises are provided to fill this need. The program should be accompanied by instruction about health.

48   For a number of years, fewer than all twelve, boys and girls alike should participate in a wide variety of manual activities, including typing, cooking, sewing, wood- and metalworking, crafts using other materials, automobile driving and repair, maintenance of electrical and other household equipment, and so on.

49   In the later years, they should receive instruction to prepare them for choosing and finding a career. This is not to be done by requiring them to make a premature choice of a job and by giving them training for that particular job. Rather, the young person should be introduced to the wide range of human work—the kinds of occupations and careers, their significance and requirements, their rewards and opportunities.

50   If, over and above such general preparation, individuals need training for particular jobs that do not require the kind of advanced schooling that is appropriate to four-year colleges and universities with their technical and professional schools, this can be obtained after basic schooling is completed in two-year community colleges, in technical institutes, or on the job itself.

51   All activities and interests not included in the program as set forth should be regarded as extracurricular, to be engaged in voluntarily in afterschool hours.

52 The program recommended in the preceding pages is offered as a model. It can be adapted in a variety of ways to the diverse circumstances of different schools or school systems. *Our recommendation is not a monolithic program to be adopted uniformly everywhere.*

53   But the model does insist, for its validity, on the presence in all schools or school systems of the Three Columns—on the establishing of the three modes of learning and the three modes of teaching. The precise way in which that is to be accomplished will be determined by school boards and administrators in the light of the populations with which they are dealing and with reference to a variety of other relevant circumstances.

54   The system of public education in this country has always been pluralistic and should remain so. Preserving pluralism need not and should not prevent the adoption by *all* our schools of the central features of our model as an ideal to be realized in a variety of specifically different ways.

55   This cannot be conscientiously accomplished simply by introducing in some form the Three Columns of Learning. It also calls for the elimination of many things that now clutter up the school day. At the very least, their elimination is necessary to make room for what should displace them.

56   It eliminates all specialized training for particular jobs.

57   It eliminates from the curriculum and puts into the category of optional extracurricular activities a variety of pastimes that contribute little to education in comparison with the time, energy, and money spent on them.

58   If it did not call for all these displacements and eliminations, there would not be enough time in the school day or the school year to accomplish everything that is essential to the general, nonspecialized learning that must be the content of basic schooling.

59   Programs closely akin to what is here proposed have been instituted in other countries. Something like what is here proposed is carried on in our own country in a few exceptional schools, public and private.

60   Those who think the proposed course of study cannot be successfully followed by all children fail to realize that the children of whom they are thinking have never had their minds challenged by requirements such as these. It is natural for children to rise to meet higher expectations; but only if those expectations are set before them, and made both reasonable and attractive. They will respond when their minds are challenged by teachers able to give the different types of instruction set forth earlier, and who are themselves vitally interested in what they are teaching.

61   Worse evils than ignorance, lack of discipline, deficiency in rudimentary skills, and impoverished understanding result from most of the existing programs of instruction in our public schools. The absence of intellectual stimulation and the failure to challenge students by expecting the most of them leads to boredom, delinquency, lawless violence, drug dependence, alcoholism, and other forms of undesirable conduct.

62   Unless the overflowing energies of young people are fully and constructively employed, they will spill over into all forms of antisocial and destructive behavior. Their energies can be employed constructively only by a program of studies that engages their minds, that demands their taking an active part in learning, and that pushes and helps all to reach out and up for as much as they can get out of school.

☐ Discovering Meaning and Technique

1. What is the central idea of the proposal?

2. What is the one permitted elective?

3. What are the plan's three modes of learning and three modes of teaching?

4. Does the diagram make the ideas clearer or more confusing? Explain your answer.

5. Which subjects are "indispensable to basic schooling"? Why does Adler pick these subjects?

6. Explain "the didactic kind of learning."

7. Which skills are included in the proposal?

8. According to Adler, what does "coaching" entail?

9. Which kinds of books are used to enlarge "understanding of ideas and values"?

10. What is the "Socratic mode of learning"?

11. Which auxiliary studies does Adler propose?

12. What is Adler's attitude toward memorization?

13. From the author's tone, describe the kind of person you think he is.

☐ Writing Suggestions

1. Using information from the library, describe the Socratic method of teaching.

2. Adler writes, "Electives and specialization are entirely proper at the level of advanced schooling—in our colleges, universities, and technical schools. They are wholly inappropriate at the level of basic schooling." Defend or refute this statement.

3. Evaluate the skills of teachers you have had. Were they competent in Adler's three skills—didactic instruction, coaching, and Socratic questioning?

4. Do you think the typical fifty-minute class period allows adequate time for learning?

5. Should physical education be a required course?

6. Do you agree with Adler's contention that a second language should be studied?

7. Discuss the importance or lack of importance of memorization in education.

8. Do you believe that a stimulating education can eliminate students' "antisocial and destructive behavior"?

THE YELLOW BRICK ROAD OF EDUCATION

☐ **FLORETTA DUKES McKENZIE**

1 Like Dorothy in *The Wizard of Oz,* educators hold a vision that somewhere— perhaps over the rainbow—a place exists that is free from all the knotty and nagging problems of everyday life. For teachers and school administrators, this "Oz" includes classrooms of endlessly inquisitive and motivated youngsters; instructors with a bottomless reservoir of energy, dedication, and talent; and schools free from yearly political haggles over funds needed to buy the texts, hire staff, and heat buildings. Frontline educators—classroom teachers, principals, and the like—as well as researchers and theorists, work toward the attainment of such an educational paradise. However, as evidenced in *The Paideia Proposal,* a fundamental difference in perspective distinguishes the practitioners' and the academicians' approaches to educational improvement.

2 To extend *The Wizard of Oz* analogy a bit further, Mortimer Adler regards the educational Oz as Dorothy viewed the Emerald City. Disgruntled with the problems at Aunt Em's farm, Dorothy believed in a better place; she could envision and describe it but lacked a way to get there. Speaking for the Paideia Group— primarily comprising noted college presidents, "think tankers," and foundation officials—Adler also complains about the "present deplorable condition" * of schooling and depicts an idyllic state of education, yet offers little direction for reaching it.

3 On the other hand, far too many educators in the daily business of schooling have lost the excitement and hope Oz offered to Dorothy. After many trials and tribulations, Dorothy discovers that the Wizard is really an illusion; she longs to return to Kansas and is content to face farm life without the wonders of technicolor. Practicing educators, perhaps hardened over the years by too many trips down a yellow brick road of so-called "educational reform," likewise no longer believe in miracles. They frequently rely on teaching children in perhaps outmoded but familiar ways, viewing educational excellence as something that only a few schools can attain.

4 As the *Proposal* accurately points out, this disparaging attitude toward

---

* McKenzie quotes from a section of *The Paideia Proposal* that is not included.

educational prospects is a tragic problem which contributes to the debilitating notion that public schooling can make only limited improvements in children's lives. Ironically, however, the *Proposal* itself, with its wholesale condemnation of present educational practices, further erodes the public confidence vital to any attempts at educational reform, particularly one that would prove as costly as the *Proposal.*

5   *The Paideia Proposal* claims that U.S. education has only won "half the battle—the quantitative half" of the goal to provide equal educational opportunity to all. Currently, 75 percent of all students graduate from high school compared to only 55 percent as recently as 1950. Although the number of years a child spends in school is not a reliable measure of the quality of education that child has received, this increase indicates more than a mere tally of the classroom hours students are logging in. A number of economists have estimated that between 25 to 50 percent of the increase in the Gross National Product in the last twenty years is due to the increased educational level of the work force. This cannot be attributed simply to the amount of time students spend sitting in schools; it is an indication that schools have succeeded to a commendable degree in teaching meaningful, life-enhancing skills to the young.

6   Minimizing this country's tremendous gains in providing access to education, as the *Proposal* does, is a serious flaw in any analysis of U.S. education. It is specifically this commitment to educational access which led to the rich diversity in teaching strategies that is essential to meeting the schooling needs of an equally diverse student population.

7   Educators should not be lured into the popular but mistaken belief that the national emphasis on educational access has not been accompanied by significant improvements in quality. The *Proposal* contends, without offering any supporting evidence, that "basic schooling in America does not now achieve the fundamental objective of opening the doors to the world of learning and providing the guidelines for exploring it." The *Proposal* goes further to suggest—again without examples or data—that U.S. education "used to do so for those who completed high school at the beginning of this century."

8   One of the few long-range studies of reading achievement indicates that, in 1944, Indiana's sixth- and tenth-grade students did not read as well as their counterparts did in 1976. Clearly, reading is a vital key to opening those doors to the world of learning, and if this ability among students has increased over time, the *Proposal*'s claim that education was better in the "good old days" is highly suspect. As the Indiana study indicates, even though access to education has increased greatly, our schools are educating our youth to a much higher standard than they were able to do with only 30 to 40 percent of the student population four decades ago.

9   Although *The Paideia Proposal*'s failure to acknowledge education's accomplishments undermines the basis of the manifesto's suggested reforms, it is not the work's most serious flaw. The *Proposal* reflects assumptions about the learning

process that disregard what educators have come to know through years of practice and research. Granted, all children are educable, innately possessing curiosity and an interest in learning. Although educators know this, they must work vigorously to ensure that this idea is incorporated into practice at all times for all children. The *Proposal,* however, makes a quantum conceptual leap by presuming that this belief in children's educability dictates a uniformity in instruction.

10   "The best education for the best is the best education for all" should not be the guiding principle for instruction, as the *Proposal* contends. As almost any teacher can testify, the methods which work well with the brightest and most eager students do not necessarily spark the interest of children who, for whatever reason, are not achieving as well. This belief, that what is best for the best is best for all, is a dangerously elitist tenet which may destroy the potential of countless young minds. Granted, as the *Proposal* suggests, students need clear direction as to what is expected of them, and the schools must do a better job in this arena. However, contrary to the *Proposal,* higher expectations of students do not necessarily translate into higher student achievement.

11   All children do not learn in the same fashion, for there is great variety in ways of acquiring and integrating information. Therefore, in almost all cases, rigid prescriptions for instruction invariably fail. Many teachers already have, and many more teachers need, competence in that comprehensive range of instructional strategies—such as didactic, coaching, and Socratic methods—that the *Proposal* details. However, such skills are needed to better meet students varying levels of instructional needs rather than to reach the suggested single-track core curriculum. Although the *Proposal* decries teachers' narrow repertoire of instructional skills, it is silent on a definitive means of better equipping teachers with such abilities.

12   Like its questionable assumptions about children's learning processes, the *Proposal*'s suppositions concerning the composition of an ideal curriculum are out of touch with both education's proven knowledge base and the realities of contemporary society. As the *Proposal* indicates, "to live well in the fullest human sense involves learning as well as earning." But the key words in this phrase, which the *Proposal* subsequently disregards, are "as well as." By vehemently urging the elimination of almost all vocational training in basic schooling, the Paideia Group has chosen to overlook the very real need and growing demand for students in a technological society to be trained in specific skill areas. Ideally, such well-trained students would also possess the ability and desire for continued learning throughout their lives, which the *Proposal* accurately identifies as the major goal of education. But this goal will not be within students' grasp simply by disposing of specific career training.

13   Furthermore, the age-old complaint from U.S. business and industry has been that schools—including colleges—let students graduate who lack not only necessary general skills but also specific skills for employment. Historically, U.S.

employers have only reluctantly taken on the role of providing the technical training for generally-educated new employees. The *Proposal* apparently over-looks the facts that vocational education arose out of a societal demand for career-trained graduates, that this demand is increasing with the expanding new technologies, and that the business sector will resist taking the responsibility for specific skill training.

14   Necessary vocational education, the *Proposal* contends, can be obtained after the first twelve years of schooling at either four-year or community colleges. Such postponement of entry into the work force is economically unfeasible for countless young people. The *Proposal* ignores today's reality that post-secondary education is increasingly an expense that fewer and fewer families can bear.

15   The *Proposal*'s failure to recognize career training in schools as a develop-ment born, in part, of a strong societal demand highlights one of its other shortcom-ings: a naïve treatment of education's political and economic circumstances. Undoubtedly, superintendents and administrators would eagerly endorse the *Proposal*'s call for a debureaucratization of schools. The business of schooling is learning and teaching; however, given the requirements of democracy and the structure for financing public education, schools are also political institutions. Over the last few decades, demands for schools to assume the roles and functions once the sole province of home, church, and government has heavily contributed to the politicization of education. The *Proposal*'s simplistic solution to this prob-lem is to hand over greater control to local school principals. Giving principals more authority over the selection and dismissal of school staff and the discipline of students might be a wise and productive change for some school districts, but such actions would do little to remove education from the political sphere.

16   In today's world, the partner to politics is economics. The *Proposal* admits that, to be successful, its implementation will require higher teacher salaries, better teacher training, smaller class sizes, individual student coaching, more remedial education, and publicly funded preschool for one- to three-year-olds. Yet, despite a national and local climate that favors sharp reductions in educational support, the *Proposal* makes no suggestions for financing the costs of its remedies.

17   A local example hints at the magnitude of the Paideia price tag. In the District of Columbia public school system, the cost of reducing class size by just one student per class is $4 million a year. To provide preschool classes for only one-third of the 18,000 three- and four-year-olds in the city, the school district's budget would have to be increased by $16 million each year.

18   Speculation and discussion on needed improvements in U.S. education are healthy and beneficial. Such exercises, however, must not only name the desired destinations but must also consider if the routes to those goals are compatible with existing knowledge based on practice and research. The *Proposal* is very strong on detailing what should be but ignores the reality of what already is. The *Proposal* cites increased parental involvement in education and decreased disruptive student behavior as vital to securing quality education for all. These

are not issues which schools heretofore have overlooked; they are the time-worn problems with which educators grapple daily. The *Proposal* does not venture a single idea—tried or untried—on how to resolve these and many other longstanding problems.

19　　The *Proposal* forthrightly communicates to the public some often neglected messages which probably cannot be broadcast too loudly or too frequently: quality education is the key to quality living; the survival of our democratic society depends on the existence of an educated electorate; and education is the gateway to equality for all people. *The Paideia Proposal* is as strong as Dorothy's determination to return to Kansas; as a constructive plan of action for educational improvement, it is as specious as the Wizard's magic powers.

☐ Discovering Meaning and Technique

1. In McKenzie's view, which groups conflict in their "approaches to educational improvement"?

2. Explain the *Wizard of Oz* analogy. Who is compared to Dorothy? What do Oz, Aunt Em's farm, and the yellow brick road represent?

3. What is McKenzie's general attitude toward U.S. education?

4. What does McKenzie think was the *Paideia Proposal*'s "quantum conceptual leap"?

5. According to McKenzie, why is the idea that "what is best for the best is best for all" (paragraph 10) wrong?

6. Why should vocational training be a part of education?

7. According to McKenzie, what are some issues not adequately addressed in the *Paideia Proposal?*

☐ Writing Suggestions

1. Do you agree with McKenzie that "higher expectations of students do not necessarily translate into higher student achievement" (paragraph 10)?

2. How important is vocational training today? Does it detract from the "learning" component of education? When should it take place?

3. Should schools "assume the roles and functions once the sole province of home, church and government"?

4. Discuss ways that schools can encourage parental involvement.

5. Discuss the idea that "the survival of our democratic society depends on the existence of an educated electorate."

ON THINKING ABOUT THE FUTURE

☐ **DIANE RAVITCH**

1 It is obvious that anyone who tries to predict what the future holds is foolhardy, brave, or both. Yet it is also true that those who devise policy and direct social institutions must try to plan ahead, both to anticipate what might happen and to affect what does happen. In trying to think about what American schools might look like in the year 2000, I found myself reflecting on earlier attempts to conjure up the school of the future.

2   I hold no brief for the idea that the future is to be discovered by searching the past, but it struck me that it would be instructive to see what could be learned from the past about the limitations of social forecasting and about what might be the enduring qualities of the schools. Anyone who has studied the past knows that history has a limited predictive value. Knowledge of the past is vital because it helps us to avoid reinventing the wheel, and it may enable us to learn from our failures and our successes. But it doesn't tell us what to do next. The more we know about the past, the more we realize that any significant change is the result of many different factors, some of which are beyond our control.

3   This is especially difficult to acknowledge in education, because of the settled belief that education is responsive to rational planning. In our society, it is impossible to find any comparable activity so directly controlled by government; the job market and such basic industries as housing, communications, and agriculture may be monitored or even regulated by government, but they are essentially planned and run by countless private individuals and corporations. Yet, because 90 percent of U.S. youths attend public elementary and secondary schools, the expectation that schools can and should be an instrument of the public intent encourages planners, critics, and visionaries to plot the future of the schools.

4   Still, even the most attractive plans are subject to the influence of the unpredictable. War, depression, economic stress, demographic flux, changing social mores, and other such phenomena that are beyond the reach of government planners affect the way schools function—and even their concept of how they are supposed to function. For example, when confronted by the social effects of the war in Vietnam, which fueled youthful revolt and challenges to adult

authority, the parts of schooling that officials directly manipulated—such as curriculum, teachers' qualifications, schedules, and graduation requirements—seemed relatively insignificant to the cause of the unrest.

5   If plans are subject to disruption by the unforeseen and the uncontrollable, they are also subject to failure because of unintended consequences. It is not simply human error alone that causes plans to go astray; it is also true that the plans themselves sometimes fail to produce the intended results. Sometimes opposite results are obtained simply because the planners' assumptions were wrong. For example, several experiments in community control in the late 1960s were founded on the assumption that low-income parents would support radical reforms. However, contrary to the expectations of foundation and university reformers, the parents wanted orderly schools, well-prepared teachers, and a school climate that stressed traditional learning and discipline.

6   Despite the well-known dangers of prediction, the field of education is dependent on future thinking. By its very nature, education is a forecast, for in deciding what children (or adults) should learn, we are making a statement about what they will need to know in the future. School officials and curriculum makers are constantly involved in future thinking, because they must determine what children should study and because they must adapt to changing social and economic trends, for example, enrollment declines, shifts in the composition of the student population. We might call such planning everyday future thinking, and it is a basic administrative tool of school officials.

7   Usually, however, it is not school officials, but scholars, social critics, and blue-ribbon panels, who have the leisure to think about the long-range future. In order to think about what the school might look like in the year 2000, I have selected some well-known past attempts to predict the future of the school. A backward glance can tell us about the hazards of future thinking and about the nature of the school as well.

8   Probably the best-known effort to depict what we would call the "wave of the future" is John and Evelyn Dewey's *Schools of Tomorrow*, published in 1915. The Deweys described a wide variety of experimental programs, illustrating the differences between what was then customary in conventional public schools and what a handful of progressive educators were attempting. The typical public school of 1915, the reader learns, stressed order, physical immobility, obedience, silence, rote drill, and memorization of facts; subject matter in these schools bore no relation to the life of the child or the life of society.

9   In the several schools that the Deweys visited, children were busily engaged in physical education, handicrafts, industrial training, nature study, and dramatic play. One school was akin to a social settlement in its efforts to raise the standard of living of its students and to fit them for future employment; another trained students in shops to do the kind of industrial work needed by both the school and the community. "Learning by doing" was a central element in the progressive curriculum. In one school, the second graders set up a shoe shop, which provided

a practical means to learn English and arithmetic as children wrote about a family visiting the shop; fifth graders ran a parcel post office, which gave them reason to count, measure, weigh, and make maps. The Deweys were especially interested in educational methods that discarded "the mere accumulation of knowledge" and made learning a part of each student's life, connected to his or her present situation and needs. These were schools of the future, John Dewey wrote, because they exhibited "tendencies toward greater freedom and an identification of the child's school life with his environment and outlook; and, even more important, the recognition of the role education must play in a democracy."

10   The Deweys argued that the conventional school, with its standardized curriculum, its recitation and drill methods, and its reliance on grades and punishments as motivating tools, trained children for "docility and obedience" and was ill suited to a democratic society. Thus they forecast that the school of the future would be one in which children were allowed freedom, were consciously engaged in the improvement of their neighborhood or city, were taught through methods that used their own experiences and activities, and were motivated by appeals to their interests.

11   With hindsight, we can see that the Deweys' predictions had a mixed fate. While some teachers may have continued to use rote methods, by the mid-1930s the education profession as a whole had accepted the importance of such things as physical health and recreation, vocational education, arts and crafts, and the use of activities and projects in the classroom. However, some of the Dewey's emphases produced unexpected, and sometimes undesirable, outcomes. The industrial program that they lauded in Gary, Indiana, seemed to other observers to be a narrowly vocational program, intended to create skilled workers for the mills and plants of the industrial Midwest, rather than a broad and progressive educational program for the future. The Rousseauean experiments in student freedom that impressed the Deweys held little appeal for the vast majority of public school teachers, in part because teachers were responsive to community values. Regardless of the Deweys' predictions, most schools continued to use textbooks, to give grades, to rely on a conventional curriculum organized along subject-matter lines, and to give greater weight to traditional in-school learning than to community-based activities.

12   Although many of those who called themselves followers of John Dewey refused to believe it, he was not opposed to the systematic organization of subject matter, nor did he scorn the learning that comes from books. In one school he praised in his 1915 book, children dramatized one of Cicero's orations against Catiline and wrote "prayers to Dionysius and stories such as they think Orpheus might have sung." Dewey repeatedly tried to explain that he did not think that all worthwhile knowledge necessarily flowed from the immediate needs and interests of pupils. In what must be considered a losing battle, he wrote *Experience and Education* in 1938 to explain to his followers that children's experiences were a means, and not the end of education.

13   In 1944 the Educational Policies Commission of the National Education Assocation (NEA) tried its hand at future thinking. The commission members forecast two different futures for American schools, depending on whether or not the federal government provided financial assistance. If such aid were not provided, they predicted that by 1950 secondary education would be directly administered by the federal government, because of the failure of the public schools to prepare for the vocational needs of the postwar era. This future could be avoided, they said, if the public schools received enough federal aid to provide vocational training, citizenship training, family-life education, and other developmental programs.

14   In the future that the commission members hoped would come to pass, the school would be reformulated by 1950 into a major social service agency for the entire community. The age of compulsory education would rise to eighteen, and communities would offer a thirteenth and a fourteenth year of free public education. No one would have to leave school for financial reasons, because the school would obtain part-time employment for students. Vocational preparation would become a central role of the school, and students could train there for any industrial or semiprofessional work. The school would provide education and guidance not only for students but for everyone else as well; the counselors would be available to help everyone, not just the students. The curriculum of the school of the future would concentrate on vocational training, health and physical education, "common learnings" (a guidance course stressing "cooperative living in family, school, and community," merging English, social studies, family life, and various other aspects of becoming a good citizen), and "individual interests."

15   The school that the NEA envisioned would mold citizens and workers. School personnel would direct the adjustment between school and work and would guide youngsters' career choices. The school would take a more active role in determining the decisions traditionally made by families (sometimes based on faulty information) and in coordinating industrial and vocational planning. The cultural interests that the school had fostered historically—through the study of such subjects as literature, science, mathematics, foreign languages, and history—would survive, but as a relatively minor aspect of the school's overall function as a community service agency.

16   Neither of these predictions about the future of the school, offered by some of the keenest minds in American education, came close to realization. There was neither federal aid for schools by 1950 nor, in its absence, a federal takeover of secondary education. Nor did the schools, either in the postwar period or in the years since general federal aid was passed in 1965, become comprehensive social service agencies. We can see today that the first prediction was a bit of political propaganda, intended to abet the long and unsuccessful NEA campaign for federal aid. Since opponents claimed that federal aid would lead to federal control, the NEA countered with the charge that *failure* to pass

federal aid would lead inexorably to a federal takeover because of local and state incapacity to run the schools. The second prediction—that schools would become the centerpiece of a planned society—reflected both the wartime mood, when centralized planning was widely accepted, and the ascendancy among educators of the idea that the most important function of the school was to adjust young people to society. After the war, this point of view was identified with the "life adjustment movement," which is now remembered principally for the attacks it inspired by critics who considered it anti-intellectual, manipulative, and mindlessly utilitarian.

17   Skip to the late 1960s. The future thinkers of this decade projected many different scenarios, but on one point they all agreed: The school as it was then constituted—that is, buildings with classrooms and teachers and textbooks— would not (and should not) long survive. One critic, the radical priest Ivan Illich, called for "deschooling society." His associate, Everett Reimer, proclaimed in the title of his book that *School Is Dead.* George Leonard, in *Education and Ecstasy,* predicted the withering away of the school as it was then known, to be replaced by "free-learning situations," "encounter groups," and computer-assisted instruction. By the year 2001, he prophesied, children would learn freely and ecstatically through dialogues with a magnificent computer console situated in a geodesic dome. Their environments would be characterized by sensory bombardment, and, in this wondrous setting, children would absorb all the "commonly agreed-upon cultural knowledge . . . in the four years from age 3 through age 6." In Leonard's fantasy school, three-year-olds master spelling and syntax, a four-year-old carries on a dialogue with her computer about primitive cultures, and a six-year-old "is deep into a simple calculus session." Here at last is the fulfillment of children's ancient end-of-term cry: "No more classes, no more books, no more teachers' dirty looks!"

18   The fifteen years that have passed since Leonard sketched the school of the future have given little encouragement to his prophecy of a fusion between the school and the human potential movement. To be sure, computers have begun to gain a secure place in schools, but they are still used only marginally as instruments of instruction. The "free schools" that Leonard saw as the trend setters of educational method have survived, but only as a small sector of U.S. private education. The wave of innovation that he believed was relentlessly crashing down on the school turned out to be not the wave of the future, but a prelude to and stimulus of the back-to-basics movement.

19   To reflect on the fate of predictions is a sobering experience. A teacher whose career began in 1960 has lived through an era of failed revolutions. One movement after another arrived, peaked, and dispersed. Having observed the curriculum reform movement, the technological revolution, the open education movement, the free school movement, the deschooling movement, the accountability movement, the minimum competency movement, and, more recently, the back-to-basics movement, a veteran teacher may be excused for

secretly thinking, when confronted by the next campaign to "save" the schools, "This too shall pass."

20   Curiously, certain features of the school survive despite nearly unanimous condemnations by expert opinion. A teacher-in-training, for example, is likely to read numerous books denouncing the system of examinations and grading, the textbook, the recitation method, curricula that focus on discrete disciplines, and other hallmarks of the traditional school. Yet those features persist in the overwhelming majority of public and private schools, even though no pedagogical giant equivalent to Dewey exists to lend legitimacy to such means of managing the classroom. Classroom teachers must frequently feel a sense of inadequacy, knowing that the techniques they find necessary for teaching have been condemned by progressive pedagogical experts for most of the century. If so great a divergence between theory and practice existed in any other profession, it would most likely be considered a scandal.

21   Any future thinking about the school must take into account the history of efforts to change the school. We should begin by noting that the school has not withered away, despite predictions to the contrary over the years. Critics, scholars, and educational leaders have predicted time and again that the school was no longer relevant as a school—that it had to be turned instead into a social settlement or a vocational training agency or almost anything other than what it was. Yet the school as a school is still with us, which suggests that it serves social purposes that have enabled it to survive even the most vigorous attacks and outspoken criticism.

22   Not all efforts to reform the schools have foundered. Although we have seen some spectacular failures, we have also seen many small but significant successes. Compared to twenty-five years ago, more students are in school today, more of them graduate from high schools and colleges, more teachers have college degrees, school buildings are more commodious, teaching materials are more diverse, and teaching methods are more varied. What we should have learned by now is that the reforms that take root are those that are limited, specific, and reasonably related to the concerns and capacities of those who must implement them. A proposal that tells teachers that everything they have done up to now has been wrong is likely to receive a cold reception. A reform that deals contemptuously with those who must implement it is not likely to take hold. To be effective, a proposal for change must appeal to teachers' educational ideals, respect their professionalism, and build on their strengths.

23   Bearing in mind the strengths and the limitations of the schools, we can then ask what a school should be in the year 2000—less than twenty years from now. Both past history and present reality suggest that there will still be schools in the year 2000. Today, about half of all women are in the workforce, a trend that seems likely to continue in the years ahead. This means that our society will need, more than ever, good institutions designed to nurture and to supervise young children during most of the day. This is and will continue to be one of the important roles of the school.

24   Because of the growth of professional, semiprofessional, and technical occupations and the decline of industrial and manufacturing jobs, schools have an
important mission to perform in preparing youngsters to fill these new, more
intellectual careers. Job training will be of less importance in the year 2000
because of the rapid pace of technological change. Because most work in the
future will require people who can think, plan, work with others, adapt to changing
conditions, and make decisions, we will look to the schools to nurture in the
young such traits as initiative, reasoning skills, judgment, empathy, independence,
and self-discipline. Instead of job training, young people will want to learn specific
skills for such leisure activities as woodworking, cooking, bookbinding, weaving,
and other handicrafts.

25   Because the social and political trends of our nation are increasingly egalitarian, we will want the school in the year 2000 to provide for all children the
kind of education that is available today only to those in the best private and
public schools. We will expect all children to become literate, able to read
books and magazines without difficulty, and to use their literacy for further
learning. Of course, all children will learn to use such tools as computers, which
by the year 2000 will be as commonplace as television sets are now. We will
want all children to study history in considerable depth—U.S., European, and
non-Western—in order to have a secure sense of the past and to understand
the great achievements and the awesome failures of human civilization. When
they are old enough to grasp complex concepts, we will want them to discover
how the various social sciences contribute to our understanding of society.
And at all ages, from the time they are old enough to be read to, we will want
all children to appreciate literature—to see how it can transport each of us
across time and space and cultures and how it can evoke in each of us a sense
of our common humanity. We will want all children not only to learn to read
for knowledge and enjoyment, but also to learn to write in a variety of modes—
sometimes trying out their creativity and imagination, other times organizing
their thoughts carefully and constructing well-reasoned essays. Naturally, in the
year 2000 we will expect every child to learn science and mathematics, so
that scientific understanding is widely accessible and not merely the preserve
of a scientific elite. We will expect in this school of the future that, once children
have a firm understanding of their own language and culture, they will begin
to study other cultures and languages. If our sights are high enough, every child
in the United States will learn at least one language in addition to English, which
will increase our ability to deal with other nations in the twenty-first century.
Certainly, we will also insist that every school of the future have a comprehensive
arts program, in which children learn both to appreciate great artistic accomplishment and to participate in creating music, drama, dance, painting, sculpture,
film, and other forms of artistic expression.

26   In this school of the future, teachers will look on each student as a precious
resource—a unique individual with talents to be discovered, skills to be developed,
and a mind in need of challenges and nourishment. In this fantasy school, teachers

will concern themselves with children's health, their character, their intellect, and their sensibilities.

27   In order to build a sense of community and mutual concern, the school of the future will be small, perhaps enrolling no more than 100 students per grade. (Several schools might share a resource center, where students could study foreign languages or advanced courses.) Unlike some present schools, which are as vast and impersonal as factories, the school of the future should be modeled on a family; here caring, knowledgeable adults would guide and instruct young people—and each person would be special.

28   This school would have ideals, and it would try to live by them. One ideal would be good citizenship; thus the school would prepare its students to take responsibility, to help their neighbors, to be good leaders and good followers, to do their part in making the community better for all of its members. Another ideal would be excellence, whether in the arts, in sports, or in academics. Students would learn to respect the excellence that results from hard work, persistence, and commitment. To inspire a love of excellence, teachers would share Matthew Arnold's ideal of making the best that has been thought and known in the world available to everyone.

29   Are we likely to have such a school in the year 2000? Probably not. Probability suggests that the schools in the year 2000 will bear the same relationship to schools of today as our current schools bear to the schools of seventeen years ago (1966). If we consider how little the schools have changed since the late 1960s, then it seems utopian indeed to predict that all schools might, in the foreseeable future, be as good as our very best schools of today.

30   The obstacles are many—but not insuperable, if the goal is one we wish to achieve. For many years, we have neglected the development of the teaching profession. Schools have been society's scapegoat for a long time. Teachers have been underpaid in relation to the importance of their profession. And teaching has been treated as a low-status profession. For all of these reasons, many excellent teachers have left teaching for more satisfying work, and uncounted others have chosen other careers from the start. In such vital fields as science, mathematics, and foreign languages, significant teacher shortages exist. Many of those who have remained in teaching have been demoralized by curricular chaos during the past twenty years. It will not be easy to improve the status of the teaching profession; nor will it be easy to persuade teachers and the public that the United States is serious about upgrading the quality of its schools and the importance of the teacher's role.

31   The distance between where we are now and where we might be in the year 2000 is great, but this distance is not beyond our capacities to span. Probably the greatest obstacle to achieving lasting reform is, paradoxically, the tendency of reformers to scoff at piecemeal change. Experience suggests that small changes are likely to be enduring changes. In many ways, the kind of school that I have described is very like the schools that now exist. I suggest that we take what is

and develop it to its highest potential. This challenge may be more radical than the call for an entirely new institution to replace the school. Getting there— that is, achieving the highest potential—is first of all a matter of setting our sights and then of devising a series of small moves in the right direction. Better teachers, better teaching, better administration, better textbooks, better curricula, higher aspirations. The Tao says, "A journey of a thousand miles must begin with a single step." We know which steps to take; our problem will continue to be—as it has always been—reaching agreement on where we want to go.

☐ Discovering Meaning and Technique

1. Why does Ravitch approach predicting the future of education cautiously?

2. According to the Deweys, which kind of school was common in the early twentieth century? Which kind of school did they foresee in the future?

3. What was the impact of the Deweys' predictions on the schools?

4. Summarize the two predictions offered by the Educational Policies Commission of the NEA. What was the impact of these predictions?

5. In what way did the education predictions in the later 1960s agree?

6. Describe George Leonard's future school.

7. According to Ravitch, what characteristics of schools persist even though constantly criticized?

8. What does Ravitch consider "significant successes" in reforming the schools?

9. According to Ravitch, which kinds of reforms are doomed to fail? To succeed?

10. Describe Ravitch's school in the year 2000.

11. Ravitch's essay falls into distinct parts. What are they?

☐ Writing Suggestions

1. Evaluate the Deweys' ideas for improving the educational system.

2. What is your opinion of the NEA's view of the school as a community service agency?

3. Do you think George Leonard's "fantasy school" could ever exist?

4. Agree or disagree with Ravitch's view of the school of the future.

5. Describe your view of the school of the future.

6. Why is change so hard to implement in the educational system?

7. Discuss ways in which the quality of teachers can be improved.

■ Combining Sources in a Composition

1. Using the selections in this section as source material, write an essay answering this question: Why aren't our schools educating us? You might consult the material on disorderly classrooms (Postman), cheating (Deutsch), television (MacNeil), excused absences (Vo-Dinh), athletics (Lichtenstein), and testing (Sobel).

2. Consider Postman's complaint about manners in school and the manners revealed in the letters sent to Royko.

3. This section of the text is divided into the subsections "The Student" and "The System." Consider Michael's attitude in "Homework." How much of it results from the system and how much from Michael himself?

4. Discuss the conflict between an education that emphasizes intellectual learning and one that emphasizes social skills. Can the two types be reconciled?

5. If you could choose one reform for American schools, what would it be? Defend your choice.

6. Describe the debate between Adler and McKenzie over what constitutes the best education. With whom do you agree?

7. Supplement the discussion of John Dewey in Ravitch with readings in the library. Write a paper on how Dewey's views of education were misunderstood.

8. Diane Ravitch writes that in the future, "instead of job training, young people will want to learn specific skills for such leisure activities as woodworking, cooking, bookbinding, weaving, and other handicrafts." Compare this idea with the ideas expressed by Adler and McKenzie.

9. Describe some successes of the American education system. (See Ravitch and McKenzie.)

10. Using any selections in this section for source material, describe your idea of a good school—the curriculum, teachers, classroom, extra-curricular activities, tests, and students.

CHAPTER 7

OUTSIDERS

Discrimination

■ ■ ■

FIFTH AVENUE, UPTOWN: A LETTER FROM HARLEM

☐ **JAMES BALDWIN**

1 There is a housing project standing now where the house in which we grew up once stood, and one of those stunted city trees is snarling where our doorway used to be. This is on the rehabilitated side of the avenue. The other side of the avenue—for progress takes time—has not been rehabilitated yet and it looks exactly as it looked in the days when we sat with our noses pressed against the windowpane, longing to be allowed to go "across the street." The grocery store which gave us credit is still there, and there can be no doubt that it is still giving credit. The people in the project certainly need it—far more, indeed, than they ever needed the project. The last time I passed by, the Jewish proprietor was still standing among his shelves, looking sadder and heavier but scarcely any older. Farther down the block stands the shoe-repair store in which our shoes were repaired until reparation became impossible and in which, then, we bought all our "new" ones. The Negro proprietor is still in the window, head down, working at the leather.

2 These two, I imagine, could tell a long tale if they would (perhaps they

would be glad to if they could), having watched so many, for so long, struggling in the fishhooks, the barbed wire, of this avenue.

3   The avenue is elsewhere the renowned and elegant Fifth. The area I am describing, which, in today's gang parlance, would be called "the turf," is bounded by Lenox Avenue on the west, the Harlem River on the east, 135th Street on the north, and 130th Street on the south. We never lived beyond these boundaries; this is where we grew up. Walking along 145th Street—for example—familiar as it is, and similar, does not have the same impact because I do not know any of the people on the block. But when I turn east on 131st Street and Lenox Avenue, there is first a soda-pop joint, then a shoeshine "parlor," then a grocery store, then a dry cleaners', then the houses. All along the street there are people who watched me grow up, people who grew up with me, people I watched grow up along with my brothers and sisters; and, sometimes in my arms, sometimes underfoot, sometimes at my shoulder—or on it—their children, a riot, a forest of children, who include my nieces and nephews.

4   When we reach the end of this long block, we find ourselves on wide, filthy, hostile Fifth Avenue, facing that project which hangs over the avenue like a monument to the folly, and the cowardice, of good intentions. All along the block, for anyone who knows it, are immense human gaps, like craters. These gaps are not created merely by those who have moved away, inevitably into some other ghetto; or by those who have risen, almost always into a greater capacity for self-loathing and self-delusion; or yet by those who, by whatever means—World War II, the Korean War, a policeman's gun or billy, a gang war, a brawl, madness, an overdose of heroin, or, simply, unnatural exhaustion—are dead. I am talking about those who are left, and I am talking principally about the young. What are they doing? Well, some, a minority, are fanatical churchgoers, members of the more extreme of the Holy Roller sects. Many, many more are "moslems," by affiliation or sympathy, that is to say that they are united by nothing more—and nothing less—than a hatred of the white world and all its works. They are present, for example, at every Buy Black street-corner meeting— meetings in which the speaker urges his hearers to cease trading with white men and establish a separate economy. Neither the speaker nor his hearers can possibly do this, of course, since Negroes do not own General Motors or RCA or the A & P, nor, indeed, do they own more than a wholly insufficient fraction of anything else in Harlem (those who *do* own anything are more interested in their profits than in their fellows). But these meetings nevertheless keep alive in the participators a certain pride of bitterness without which, however futile this bitterness may be, they could scarcely remain alive at all. Many have given up. They stay home and watch the TV screen, living on the earnings of their parents, cousins, brothers, or uncles, and only leave the house to go to the movies or to the nearest bar. "How're you making it?" one may ask, running into them along the block, or in the bar. "Oh, I'm TV-ing it"; with the saddest, sweetest, most shame-faced of smiles, and from a great distance. This distance

one is compelled to respect; anyone who has traveled so far will not easily be dragged again into the world. There are further retreats, of course, than the TV screen or the bar. There are those who are simply sitting on their stoops, "stoned," animated for a moment only, and hideously, by the approach of someone who may lend them the money for a "fix." Or by the approach of someone from whom they can purchase it, one of the shrewd ones, on the way to prison or just coming out.

5   And the others, who have avoided all of these deaths, get up in the morning and go downtown to meet "the man." They work in the white man's world all day and come home in the evening to this fetid block. They struggle to instill in their children some private sense of honor or dignity which will help the child to survive. This means, of course, that they must struggle, stolidly, incessantly, to keep this sense alive in themselves, in spite of the insults, the indifference, and the cruelty they are certain to encounter in their working day. They patiently browbeat the landlord into fixing the heat, the plaster, the plumbing; this demands prodigious patience; nor is patience usually enough. In trying to make their hovels habitable, they are perpetually throwing good money after bad. Such frustration, so long endured, is driving many strong, admirable men and women whose only crime is color to the very gates of paranoia.

6   One remembers them from another time—playing handball in the play-ground, going to church, wondering if they were going to be promoted at school. One remembers them going off to war—gladly, to escape this block. One remembers their return. Perhaps one remembers their wedding day. And one sees where the girl is now—vainly looking for salvation from some other embittered, trussed, and struggling boy—and sees the all-but-abandoned children in the streets.

7   Now I am perfectly aware that there are other slums in which white men are fighting for their lives, and mainly losing. I know that blood is also flowing through those streets and that the human damage there is incalculable. People are continually pointing out to me the wretchedness of white people in order to console me for the wretchedness of blacks. But an itemized account of the American failure does not console me and it should not console anyone else. That hundreds of thousands of white people are living, in effect, no better than the "niggers" is not a face to be regarded with complacency. The social and moral bankruptcy suggested by this fact is of the bitterest, most terrifying kind.

8   The people, however, who believe that this democratic anguish has some consoling value are always pointing out that So-and-So, white, and So-and-So, black, rose from the slums into the big time. The existence—the public existence—of, say, Frank Sinatra and Sammy Davis, Jr. proves to them that America is still the land of opportunity and that inequalities vanish before the determined will. It proves nothing of the sort. The determined will is rare—at the moment, in this country, it is unspeakably rare—and the inequalities suffered by the many are in no way justified by the rise of a few. A few have always risen—in every

country, every era, and in the teeth of regimes which can by no stretch of the imagination be thought of as free. Not all of these people, it is worth remembering, left the world better than they found it. The determined will is rare, but it is not invariably benevolent. Furthermore, the American equation of success with the big times reveals an awful disrespect for human life and human achievement. This equation has placed our cities among the most dangerous in the world and has placed our youth among the most empty and most bewildered. The situation of our youth is not mysterious. Children have never been very good at listening to their elders, but they have never failed to imitate them. They must, they have no other models. That is exactly what our children are doing. They are imitating our immorality, our disrespect for the pain of others.

9   All other slum dwellers, when the bank account permits it, can move out of the slum and vanish altogether from the eye of persecution. No Negro in this country has ever made that much money and it will be a long time before any Negro does. The Negroes in Harlem, who have no money, spend what they have on such gimcracks as they are sold. These include "wider" TV screens, more "faithful" hi-fi sets, more "powerful" cars, all of which, of course, are obsolete long before they are paid for. Anyone who has ever struggled with poverty knows how extremely expensive it is to be poor; and if one is a member of a captive population, economically speaking, one's feet have simply been placed on the treadmill forever. One is victimized, economically, in a thousand ways— rent, for example, or car insurance. Go shopping one day in Harlem—for any- thing—and compare Harlem prices and quality with those downtown.

10   The people who have managed to get off this block have only got as far as a more respectable ghetto. This respectable ghetto does not even have the advantages of the disreputable one—friends, neighbors, a familiar church, and friendly tradesmen; and it is not, moreover, in the nature of any ghetto to remain respectable long. Every Sunday, people who have left the block take the lonely ride back, dragging their increasingly discontented children with them. They spend the day talking, not always with words, about the trouble they've seen and the trouble—one must watch their eyes as they watch their children— they are only too likely to see. For children do not like ghettos. It takes them nearly no time to discover exactly why they are there.

11 The projects in Harlem are hated. They are hated almost as much as policemen, and this is saying a great deal. And they are hated for the same reason: both reveal, unbearably, the real attitude of the white world, no matter how many liberal speeches are made, no matter how many lofty editorials are written, no matter how many civil-rights commissions are set up.

12   The projects are hideous, of course, there being a law, apparently respected throughout the world, that popular housing shall be as cheerless as a prison. They are lumped all over Harlem, colorless, bleak, high, and revolting. The wide windows look out on Harlem's invincible and indescribable squalor: the Park

Avenue railroad tracks, around which, about forty years ago, the present dark community began; the unrehabilitated houses, bowed down, it would seem, under the great weight of frustration and bitterness they contain; the dark, the ominous schoolhouses from which the child may emerge maimed, blinded, hooked, or enraged for life; and the churches, churches, block upon block of churches, niched in the walls like cannon in the walls of a fortress. Even if the administration of the projects were not so insanely humiliating (for example: one must report raises in salary to the management, which will then eat up the profit by raising one's rent; the management has the right to know who is staying in your apartment; the management can ask you to leave, at their discretion), the projects would still be hated because they are an insult to the meanest intelligence.

13   Harlem got its first private project, Riverton—which is now, naturally, a slum—about twelve years ago because at that time Negroes were not allowed to live in Stuyvesant Town. Harlem watched Riverton go up, therefore, in the most violent bitterness of spirit, and hated it long before the builders arrived. They began hating it at about the time people began moving out of their condemned houses to make room for this additional proof of how thoroughly the white world despised them. And they had scarcely moved in, naturally, before they began smashing windows, defacing walls, urinating in the elevators, and fornicating in the playgrounds. Liberals, both white and black, were appalled at the spectacle. I was appalled by the liberal innocence—or cynicism, which comes out in practice as much the same thing. Other people were delighted to be able to point to proof positive that nothing could be done to better the lot of the colored people. They were, and are, right in one respect: that nothing can be done as long as they are treated like colored people. The people in Harlem know they are living there because white people do not think they are good enough to live anywhere else. No amount of "improvement" can sweeten this fact. Whatever money is now being earmarked to improve this, or any other ghetto, might as well be burnt. A ghetto can be improved in one way only: out of existence.

14   Similarly, the only way to police a ghetto is to be oppressive. None of the Police Commissioner's men, even with the best will in the world, have any way of understanding the lives led by the people they swagger about in twos and threes controlling. Their very presence is an insult, and it would be, even if they spent their entire day feeding gumdrops to children. They represent the force of the white world, and that world's real intentions are, simply, for that world's criminal profit and ease, to keep the black man corraled up here, in his place. The badge, the gun in the holster, and the swinging club make vivid what will happen should his rebellion become overt. Rare, indeed, is the Harlem citizen, from the most circumspect church member to the most shiftless adolescent, who does not have a long tale to tell of police incompetence, injustice, or brutality. I myself have witnessed and endured it more than once. The business-

men and racketeers also have a story. And so do the prostitutes. (And this is not, perhaps, the place to discuss Harlem's very complex attitude toward black policemen, nor the reasons, according to Harlem, that they are nearly all downtown.)

15   It is hard, on the other hand, to blame the policeman, blank, good-natured, thoughtless, and insuperably innocent, for being such a perfect representative of the people he serves. He, too, believes in good intentions and is astounded and offended when they are not taken for the deed. He has never, himself, done anything for which to be hated—which of us has?—and yet he is facing, daily and nightly, people who would gladly see him dead, and he knows it. There is no way for him not to know it: there are few things under heaven more unnerving than the silent, accumulating contempt and hatred of a people. He moves through Harlem, therefore, like an occupying soldier in a bitterly hostile country; which is precisely what, and where, he is, and is the reason he walks in twos and threes. And he is not the only one who knows why he is always in company: the people who are watching him know why, too. Any street meeting, sacred or secular, which he and his colleagues uneasily cover has as its explicit or implicit burden the cruelty and injustice of the white domination. And these days, of course, in terms increasingly vivid and jubilant, it speaks of the end of that domination. The white policeman standing on a Harlem street corner finds himself at the very center of the revolution now occurring in the world. He is not prepared for it—naturally, nobody is—and, what is possibly much more to the point, he is exposed, as few white people are, to the anguish of the black people around him. Even if he is gifted with the merest mustard grain of imagination, something must seep in. He cannot avoid observing that some of the children, in spite of their color, remind him of children he has known and loved, perhaps even of his own children. He knows that he certainly does not want *his* children living this way. He can retreat from his uneasiness in only one direction: into a callousness which very shortly becomes second nature. He becomes more callous, the population becomes more hostile, the situation grows more tense, and the police force is increased. One day, to everyone's astonishment, someone drops a match in the powder keg and everything blows up. Before the dust has settled or the blood congealed, editorials, speeches, and civil-rights commissions are loud in the land, demanding to know what happened. What happened is that Negroes want to be treated like men.

16   *Negroes want to be treated like men:* a perfectly straightforward statement, containing only seven words. People who have mastered Kant, Hegel, Shakespeare, Marx, Freud, and the Bible find this statement utterly impenetrable. The idea seems to threaten profound, barely conscious assumptions. A kind of panic paralyzes their features, as though they found themselves trapped on the edge of a steep place. I once tried to describe to a very well-known American intellectual the conditions among Negroes in the South. My recital disturbed him and made

him indignant; and he asked me in perfect innocence, "Why don't all the Negroes in the South move North?" I tried to explain what *has* happened, unfailingly, whenever a significant body of Negroes move North. They do not escape Jim Crow: they merely encounter another, not-less-deadly variety. They do not move to Chicago, they move to the South Side; they do not move to New York, they move to Harlem. The pressure within the ghetto causes the ghetto walls to expand, and this expansion is always violent. White people hold the line as long as they can, and in as many ways as they can, from verbal intimidations to physical violence. But inevitably the border which has divided the ghetto from the rest of the world falls into the hands of the ghetto. The white people fall back bitterly before the black horde; the landlords make a tidy profit by raising the rent, chopping up the rooms, and all but dispensing with the upkeep; and what has once been a neighborhood turns into a "turf." This is precisely what happened when the Puerto Ricans arrived in their thousands—and the bitterness thus caused is, as I write, being fought out all up and down those streets.

17   Northerners indulge in an extremely dangerous luxury. They seem to feel that because they fought on the right side during the Civil War, and won, they have earned the right merely to deplore what is going on in the South, without taking any responsibility for it; and that they can ignore what is happening in Northern cities because what is happening in Little Rock or Birmingham is worse. Well, in the first place, it is not possible for anyone who has not endured both to know which is "worse." I know Negroes who prefer the South and white Southerners, because "At least there, you haven't got to play any guessing games!" The guessing games referred to have driven more than one Negro into the narcotics ward, the madhouse, or the river. I know another Negro, a man very dear to me, who says, with conviction and with truth, "The spirit of the South is the spirit of America." He was born in the North and did his military training in the South. He did not, as far as I can gather, find the South "worse"; he found it, if anything, all too familiar. In the second place, though, even if Birmingham *is* worse, no doubt Johannesburg, South Africa, beats it by several miles, and Buchenwald was one of the worst things that ever happened in the entire history of the world. The world has never lacked for horrifying examples; but I do not believe that these examples are meant to be used as justification for our own crimes. This perpetual justification empties the heart of all human feeling. The emptier our hearts become, the greater will be our crimes. Thirdly, the South is not merely an embarrassingly backward region, but a part of this country, and what happens there concerns every one of us.

18   As far as the color problem is concerned, there is but one great difference between the Southern white and the Northerner; the Southerner remembers, historically and in his own psyche, a kind of Eden in which he loved black people and they loved him. Historically, the flaming sword laid across this Eden is the Civil War. Personally, it is the Southerner's sexual coming of age, when, without any warning, unbreakable taboos are set up between himself and his

past. Everything, thereafter, is permitted him except the love he remembers and has never ceased to need. The resulting, indescribable torment affects every Southern mind and is the basis of the Southern hysteria.

19   None of this is true for the Northerner. Negroes represent nothing to him personally, except, perhaps, the dangers of carnality. He never sees Negroes. Southerners see them all the time. Northerners never think about them whereas Southerners are never really thinking of anything else. Negroes are, therefore, ignored in the North and are under surveillance in the South, and suffer hideously in both places. Neither the Southerner nor the Northerner is able to look on the Negro simply as a man. It seems to be indispensable to the national self-esteem that the Negro be considered either as a kind of ward (in which case we are told how many Negroes, comparatively, bought Cadillacs last year and how few, comparatively, were lynched), or as a victim (in which case we are promised that he will never vote in our assemblies or go to school with our kids). They are two sides of the same coin and the South will not change— *cannot* change—until the North changes. The country will not change until it re-examines itself and discovers what it really means by freedom. In the meantime, generations keep being born, bitterness is increased by incompetence, pride, and folly, and the world shrinks around us.

20   It is a terrible, an inexorable, law that one cannot deny the humanity of another without diminishing one's own: in the face of one's victim, one sees oneself. Walk through the streets of Harlem and see what we, this nation, have become.

☐ Discovering Meaning and Technique

1. Explain what Baldwin means by "struggling in the fishhooks, the barbed wire, of this avenue" (paragraph 2).

2. What does Baldwin think about the housing project that has been built on Fifth Avenue?

3. Characterize the people who live in the "fetid" block where Baldwin grew up.

4. Explain what Baldwin means by "how extremely expensive it is to be poor" (paragraph 9).

5. What is Baldwin's attitude toward "the white world"? Toward ghettos in general? Toward the police?

6. According to Baldwin, what do black people want?

7. What is Baldwin's opinion about the difference between life for a black person in the South and in the North about thirty years ago (the time this selection was written)?

8. Explain Baldwin's statement: "In the face of one's victim, one sees oneself" (paragraph 20).

☐ Writing Suggestions

1. Why do you think escape from slums is difficult?

2. Is America "the land of opportunity" for all people?

3. Baldwin maintains that American youth are "empty" and "bewildered" and are "imitating our immorality, our disrespect for the pain of others." Do you agree or disagree with this assessment?

4. Do you think that housing projects must be "as cheerless as a prison?" Could they be designed to make them more pleasant places to live?

5. "Fifth Avenue, Uptown" was written about thirty years ago. Do you think that conditions have changed during this time? If so, how?

6. Do research in the library on India's caste system. Compare this system with America's treatment of minorities.

THE SYSTEM

☐ **MARY MEBANE**

1 Historically, my lifetime is important because I was part of the last generation born into a world of total legal segregation in the Southern United States. When the Supreme Court outlawed segregation in the public schools in 1954, I was twenty-one. When Congress passed the Civil Rights Act of 1964, permitting blacks free access to public places, I was thirty-one. The world I was born into had been segregated for a long time—so long, in fact, that I never met anyone who had lived during the time when restrictive laws were not in existence, although some people spoke of parents and others who had lived during the "free" time. As far as anyone knew, the laws as they then existed would stand forever. They were meant to—and did—create a world that fixed black people at the bottom of society in all aspects of human life. It was a world without options.

2 Most Americans have never had to live with terror. I had had to live with it all my life—the psychological terror of segregation, in which there was a special set of laws governing your movements. You violated them at your peril, for you knew that if you broke one of them, knowingly or not, physical terror was just around the corner, in the form of policemen and jails, and in some cases and places white vigilante mobs formed for the exclusive purpose of keeping blacks in line.

3 It was Saturday morning, like any Saturday morning in dozens of Southern towns.

4 The town had a washed look. The street sweepers had been busy since six o'clock. Now, at eight, they were still slowly moving down the streets, white trucks with clouds of water coming from underneath the swelled tubular sides. Unwary motorists sometimes got a windowful of water as a truck passed by. As it moved on, it left in its wake a clear stream running in the gutters or splashed on the wheels of parked cars.

5 Homeowners, bent over industriously in the morning sun, were out pushing lawn mowers. The sun was bright, but it wasn't too hot. It was morning and it was May. Most of the mowers were glad that it was finally getting warm enough to go outside.

6 Traffic was brisk. Country people were coming into town early with their produce; clerks and service workers were getting to the job before the stores opened at ten o'clock. Though the big stores would not be open for another hour or so, the grocery stores, banks, open-air markets, dinettes, were already open and filling with staff and customers.

7 Everybody was moving toward the heart of Durham's downtown, which waited to receive them rather complacently, little knowing that in a decade the shopping centers far from the center of downtown Durham would create a ghost town in the midst of the busiest blocks on Main Street.

8 Some moved by car, and some moved by bus. The more affluent used cars, leaving the buses mainly to the poor, black and white, though there were some businesspeople who avoided the trouble of trying to find a parking place downtown by riding the bus.

9 I didn't mind taking the bus on Saturday. It wasn't so crowded. At night or on Saturday or Sunday was the best time. If there were plenty of seats, the blacks didn't have to worry about being asked to move so that a white person could sit down. And the knot of hatred and fear didn't come into my stomach.

10 I knew the stop that was the safety point, both going and coming. Leaving town, it was the Little Five Points, about five or six blocks north of the main downtown section. That was the last stop at which four or five people might get on. After that stop, the driver could sometimes pass two or three stops without taking on or letting off a passenger. So the number of seats on the bus usually remained constant on the trip from town to Braggtown: The nearer the bus got to the end of the line, the more I relaxed. For if a white passenger got

on near the end of the line, often to catch the return trip back and avoid having to stand in the sun at the bus stop until the bus turned around, he or she would usually stand if there were not seats in the white section, and the driver would say nothing, knowing that the end of the line was near and that the standee would get a seat in a few minutes.

11   On the trip to town, the Mangum Street A&P was the last point at which the driver picked up more passengers than he let off. These people, though they were just a few blocks from the downtown section, preferred to ride the bus downtown. Those getting on at the A&P were usually on their way to work at the Duke University Hospital—past the downtown section, through a residential neighborhood, and then past the university, before they got to Duke Hospital.

12   So whether the driver discharged more passengers than he took on near the A&P on Mangum was of great importance. For if he took on more passengers than got off, it meant that some of the newcomers would have to stand. And if they were white, the driver was going to have to ask a black passenger to move so that a white passenger could sit down. Most of the drivers had a rule of thumb, though. By custom the seats behind the exit door had become "colored" seats, and no matter how many whites stood up, anyone sitting behind the exit door knew that he or she wouldn't have to move.

13   The disputed seat, though, was the one directly opposite the exit door. It was "no-man's-land." White people sat there, and black people sat there. It all depended on whose section was fuller. If the back section was full, the next black passenger who got on sat in the no-man's-land seat; but if the white section filled up, a white person would take the seat. Another thing about the white people: they could sit anywhere they chose, even in the "colored" section. Only the black passengers had to obey segregation laws.

14   On this Saturday morning Esther and I set out for town for our music lesson. We were going to our weekly big adventure, all the way across town, through the white downtown, then across the railroad tracks, then through the "colored" downtown, a section of run-down dingy shops, through some fading high-class black neighborhoods, past North Carolina College, to Mrs. Shearin's house.

15   We walked the two miles from Wildwood to the bus line. Though it was a warm day, in the early morning there was dew on the grass and the air still had the night's softness. So we walked along and talked and looked back constantly, hoping someone we knew would stop and pick us up.

16   I looked back furtively, for in one of the few instances that I remembered my father criticizing me severely, it was for looking back. One day when I was walking from town he had passed in his old truck. I had been looking back and had seen him. "Don't look back," he had said. "People will think that you want them to pick you up." Though he said "people," I knew he meant men—not the men he knew, who lived in the black community, but the black men who

were not part of the community, and all of the white men. To be picked up meant that something bad would happen to me. Still, two miles is a long walk and I occasionally joined Esther in looking back to see if anyone we knew was coming.

17   Esther and I got to the bus and sat on one of the long seats at the back that faced each other. There were three such long seats—one on each side of the bus and a third long seat at the very back that faced the front. I liked to sit on a long seat facing the side because then I didn't have to look at the expressions on the faces of the whites when they put their tokens in and looked at the blacks sitting in the back of the bus. Often I studied my music, looking down and practicing the fingering. I looked up at each stop to see who was getting on and to check on the seating pattern. The seating pattern didn't really bother me that day until the bus started to get unusually full for a Saturday morning. I wondered what was happening, where all these people were coming from. They got on and got on until the white section was almost full and the black section was full.

18   There was a black man in a blue windbreaker and a gray porkpie hat sitting in no-man's-land, and my stomach tightened. I wondered what would happen. I had never been on a bus on which a black person was asked to give a seat to a white person when there was no other seat empty. Usually, though, I had seen a black person automatically get up and move to an empty seat farther back. But this morning the only empty seat was beside a black person sitting in no-man's-land.

19   The bus stopped at Little Five Points and one black got off. A young white man was getting on. I tensed. What would happen now? Would the driver ask the black man to get up and move to the empty seat farther back? The white man had a businessman's air about him: suit, shirt, tie, polished brown shoes. He saw the empty seat in the "colored" section and after just a little hesitation went to it, put his briefcase down, and sat with his feet crossed. I relaxed a little when the bus pulled off without the driver saying anything. Evidently he hadn't seen what had happened, or since he was just a few stops from Main Street, he figured the mass exodus there would solve all the problems. Still, I was afraid of a scene.

20   The next stop was an open-air fruit stand just after Little Five Points, and here another white man got on. Where would he sit? The only available seat was beside the black man. Would he stand the few stops to Main Street or would the driver make the black man move? The whole colored section tensed, but nobody said anything. I looked at Esther, who looked apprehensive. I looked at the other men and women, who studiously avoided my eyes and everybody else's as well, as they maintained a steady gaze at a far-distant land.

21   Just one woman caught my eye; I had noticed her before, and I had been ashamed of her. She was a stringy little black woman. She could have been forty; she could have been fifty. She looked as if she were a hard drinker. Flat

black face with tight features. She was dressed with great insouciance in a tight
boy's sweater with horizontal lines running across her flat chest. It pulled down
over a nondescript skirt. Laced-up shoes, socks, and a head rag completed her
outfit. She looked tense.

22   The white man who had just gotten on the bus walked to the seat in no-
man's-land and stood there. He wouldn't sit down, just stood there. Two adult
males, living in the most highly industrialized, most technologically advanced
nation in the world, a nation that had devastated two other industrial giants in
World War II and had flirted with taking on China in Korea. Both these men,
either of whom could have fought for the United States in Germany or Korea,
faced each other in mutual rage and hostility. The white one wanted to sit
down, but he was going to exert his authority and force the black one to get
up first. I watched the driver in the rearview mirror. He was about the same
age as the antagonists. The driver wasn't looking for trouble, either.

23   "Say there, buddy, how about moving back," the driver said, meanwhile
driving his bus just as fast as he could. The whole bus froze—whites at the
front, blacks at the rear. They didn't want to believe what was happening was
really happening.

24   The seated black man said nothing. The standing white man said nothing.

25   "Say, buddy, did you hear me? What about moving on back." The driver
was scared to death. I could tell that.

26   "These is the niggers' seats!" the little lady in the strange outfit started
screaming. I jumped. I had to shift my attention from the driver to the frieze
of the black man seated and white man standing to the articulate little woman
who had joined in the fray.

27   "The government gave us these seats! These is the niggers' seats." I was
startled at her statement and her tone. "The president said that these are the
niggers' seats!" I expected her to start fighting at any moment.

28   Evidently the bus driver did, too, because he was driving faster and faster.
I believe that he forgot he was driving a bus and wanted desperately to pull to
the side of the street and get out and run.

29   "I'm going to take you down to the station, buddy," the driver said.

30   The white man with the briefcase and the polished brown shoes who had
taken a seat in the "colored" section looked as though he might die of embarrassment at any moment.

31   As scared and upset as I was, I didn't miss a thing.

32   By that time we had come to the stop before Main Street, and the black
passenger rose to get off.

33   "You're not getting off, buddy. I'm going to take you downtown." The
driver kept driving as he talked and seemed to be trying to get downtown as
fast as he could.

34   "These are the niggers' seats! The government plainly said these are the
niggers' seats!" screamed the little woman in rage.

35   I was embarrassed at the use of the word "nigger" but I was proud of the lady. I was also proud of the man who wouldn't get up.

36   The bus driver was afraid, trying to hold on to his job but plainly not willing to get into a row with the blacks.

37   The bus seemed to be going a hundred miles an hour and everybody was anxious to get off, though only the lady and the driver were saying anything.

38   The black man stood at the exit door; the driver drove right past the A&P stop. I was terrified. I was sure that the bus was going to the police station to put the black man in jail. The little woman had her hands on her hips and she never stopped yelling. The bus driver kept driving as fast as he could.

39   Then, somewhere in the back of his mind, he decided to forget the whole thing. The next stop was Main Street, and when he got there, in what seemed to be a flash of lightning, he flung both doors open wide. He and his black antagonist looked at each other in the rearview mirror; in a second the windbreaker and porkpie hat were gone. The little woman was standing, preaching to the whole bus about the government's gift of these seats to the blacks; the man with the brown shoes practically fell out of the door in his hurry; and Esther and I followed the hurrying footsteps.

40   We walked about three doors down the block, then caught a bus to the black neighborhood. Here we sat on one of the two long seats facing each other, directly behind the driver. It was the custom. Since this bus had a route from a black neighborhood to the downtown section and back, passing through no white residential areas, blacks could sit where they chose. One minute we had been on a bus in which violence was threatened over a seat near the exit door; the next minute we were sitting in the very front behind the driver.

41   The people who devised this system thought that it was going to last forever.

☐ Discovering Meaning and Technique

1. Why does Mebane say that her lifetime is historically important?

2. Explain the seating system used on the bus.

3. Mebane is very specific about physical details; for example, she writes of the Mangum Street A&P, Duke University Hospital, Little Five Points. What is the effect of using the details?

4. Why does Mebane's father tell her not to "look back" at people passing her on the road?

5. What is a porkpie hat?

6. Before the confrontation begins, why was Mebane ashamed of the "stringy little black woman"?

7. Despite the injustice described, is there any humor in the story? If you think so, what produces the humor?

8. Which elements in the selection emphasize the absurdity of the seating system?

☐ Writing Suggestions

1. When the confrontation begins, Mebane says that "the whole bus froze— whites at the front, blacks at the rear. They didn't want to believe what was happening was really happening." Have you ever been in an extremely volatile situation? If so, describe how the observers as well as the participants reacted.

2. Describe a set of social conventions that discriminate against a group.

3. Research the Jim Crow laws and report on your findings.

4. Describe a set of laws or a set of social conventions that you find particularly absurd.

A JEWISH EDUCATION

☐ ROGER KAHN

1   The combative Jew coincides with no stereotype. Brawling, ferocious Jews, pugnacious Jewish athletes, are not found in the cliché. They exist, a select minority, only in reality.

2   The roster of American sport is not rich in Jewish names. A half-dozen Jews among the five hundred major league baseball players are all one finds at any given time. Still fewer play professional football. During periods of affluence almost no Jews become boxers.

3   In the great majority of Jewish homes, children are not encouraged to pursue sport as a career. Sports suggest frivolity and Jews even in America are far from frivolous. Athletics run, or seem to run, counter to traditions of the Book.

4   Additionally, American sports has harbored gruff, violent, shallow anti-Semitism. Scores of Jews, breaking with tradition, entering sports, soon discovered that discretion was a major part of athletic survival. James Hymie Solomon, a

second baseman for the Yankees in the early 1930's, played as Jimmy Reese. Some years earlier a major league pitcher named Harry Cohen performed as Klondike Harry Kane. In the first words uttered by Francis X. Farrell, the "Alibi Ike" of Ring Lardner's remarkable short story, one finds a traditional ballplayer's attitude. "What are you calling me Ike for?" Farrell complains. "I ain't no Yid."

5   There has, of late, been a certain mellowing; Ike and his teammates have been dead decades. "But the game," says one Jewish New Yorker who recently pitched in the American League, "is partly needling, and as long as it is, you're gonna jab people where it hurts.

6   "You know a better way," the pitcher asks, "to sting a Jewish ballplayer than to call him a long-nosed son of a bitch?"

7 Big, and nicely groomed, and tough, he walks past an electronic device that clatters market reports in a brokerage office in Cleveland. "Hello," he says. "How are you? Good to see you again. Let's go in here." *(Fairchild Camera up two-and-an-eighth).*

8   He indicates an anteroom and leads the way with strong, easy strides. "Well," he says, "what's all this? I'm glad we could get together. I hope I can help." He pulls out chairs and sits behind a metal desk. Pipe and tobacco pouch appear. The big hands strike a match. He puffs and looks across the desk, a graying, friendly, and confronting man.

9   At forty-two, Al Rosen, a successful securities salesman for Bache & Company, has talked through more interviews than he remembers. When he played third base for the Cleveland Indians he was direct and opinionated and reporters often sought him out. Now, five years after the last base hit, he is not going to speak about batting or fielding or even about the prospects of Fairchild Camera. He is going to talk about what it has meant, through a life spent mostly in the elemental world of athletes, to be a Jew.

10   "Feel," Al Rosen says. "To me a Jew is feel." His voice is full and powerful. "The wanderings," he says, "and the searchings and the longings are in your background, and they make you feel compassion and they drive you to search for something good."

11   He puffs the pipe. "Compassion is fundamental," he says. "When I think of Vietnam and the inhumanities in that war and in all wars generally, even if it is one illiterate African chopping off another illiterate African's head, I get an inner sense of horror. I get a kind of outrage at the wrongness of it. I have to believe I feel this way because I am a Jew and I have a heritage that calls up horror and sadness at people hurting other people."

12   His face, broad and handsome, is dominated by a rugged nose that has been broken several times. He has lost some fights but, one suspects, Albert Leonard Rosen has won many more than he has lost. He is not afraid.

13   His grandfather, a Polish immigrant, ran a department store in Spartanburg, on the coast of South Carolina, but soon after Al was born, the grandfather

died, the store went bad and the family had to move. The Rosens settled in Miami, Florida, moving into a neighborhood without other Jews. Rosen's father left the family when his son was eight.

14   "My mother had to work," Rosen says, in the anteroom at Bache, "and my grandmother took care of the house. I was a big kid, matured early, and I was working myself by the time I was eleven.

15   "I think of Jewish learning, sometimes. You know, with Papa standing there, a ruler in his hand, saying *Read, read mein kind.* It wasn't that way in my house, even when my father was there. Nobody made me read. The only reason I read when I was a kid was that I had to read in public school."

16   He cannot recall the first time he heard "Jewboy." The word was a part of his childhood. It was important for some of the others to call him a name. It let them show one another how brave they were. *Lookit the Jewboy. Go home an' eat yuh matzos, sheeney. Come on, let's get the lousy kike.*

17   "What is it?" Al Rosen asks, after forty-two years. "It is because your nose is a little bigger, or your hair is a little curlier, or you don't go to Sunday school on Sunday morning or you're not in regular school on Yom Kippur? What is it?"

18   As he grew bigger and rougher, in Miami, Al Rosen began to spend time in a boxers' gym. He watched professionals, studying, and after a while sparring, with them. His Jewish education was measured in hooks and jabs and crosses and dropping a right hand larrup over somebody else's low left.

19   "I wanted to learn how to end things," Rosen says. "That was important. I wasn't starting trouble in those days, but when it came to me, I wanted to end it, and damn quick."

20   With his young athlete's body and the big heavy fists, and the intelligence and the courage and the drive, he learned what he wanted. He ended some fights others started, with furious speed. After that he heard "Jewboy" less frequently. It was easier, some of the others realized, to accept the Jew than to challenge him. And not only easier; less painful as well.

21   He went out for football at a Miami high school and after one early practice, six or seven boys piled into the coaches' car. "Rosen," the coach said. "what are you doing out for football?"

22   "I love to play the game," Rosen said.

23   "Rosen," the coach said. "You're different from most Jews. Most Jewboys are afraid of contact."

24   He could always hit a baseball hard and often. Hitting was a gift within himself. By the time he was twelve or so, he was good enough to consider trying out with men's teams, playing the kind of softball where a beefy pitcher forty-five feet away whips rising fastballs out of a windmill windup. He had to earn his way all by himself. There were no Jewish softball teams where he could gently learn. If he wanted to play, he would have to play among men, who hadn't known Jews, or didn't want to know Jews, or who figured that if

this big, young Jewboy was gonna play with them, he better have it, and have it all. He did. In his early teens, he traveled around the state of Florida on a fast-pitch softball circuit. He was a shortstop, but what he liked most was swinging the bat.

25   After two years in high school, he went to Florida Military School, a prep at St. Petersburg, on an athletic scholarship. His mother was tremendously proud. He lettered in baseball, basketball, football, boxing and made the dean's list. "Some of my best friends there," he says, deadpan, "were gentiles."

26   It was a long time ago, before the Holocaust, and in the office, his pipe on the table, Al Rosen says that he was a big-mouthed kid. "Like most Jewish kids who grew up in a neighborhood where you had to fight," he says, "I was very aggressive and I had this chip on my shoulder and I was looking for someone to knock it off, and look, I had my share of guys who knocked it off and who I couldn't take. But I was ready, ready for any of them. Maybe if I'd grown up in a Jewish neighborhood I would have been a different guy. I think being the way I was, comes out of that environment. When you start out by having to fight all the time for your pride and self-respect, how are you gonna know when to stop."

27   He was in the Army and had some college but he wanted to be a ball-player and when he was struggling up through the minor leagues, there were times when he wished his name was something other than Rosen. Anything other than Rosen. Smith, Jones, Abernathy. Just not Jewish. Fighting his way up, being Jewish was just one more damn handicap, on top of all the other things that made it so damn tough to make the majors.

28   He was a tenacious, dogged hitter, who stood close to the plate, challenging the pitcher. In his first full year as a Cleveland regular, he hit thirty-seven home runs. In order to intimidate him, pitchers threw fast balls at Rosen's ribs and head and arms. The theory is simple, and as old as baseball. A man consumed by self-preservation will not be able to concentrate on getting a hit. Rosen went down under fast balls time after time, diving for the safety of the dirt. When he got up, he stood in just as close, just as defiantly.

29   It hurt to be struck by a baseball, traveling ninety miles an hour, but Rosen would be damned if he'd let a pitcher see him writhe. The worst pain came when the ball struck the funny bone in his left elbow. That happened twice. Each time he clenched his teeth and fought the pain and pretended it was minor. In his tweedy jacket, with his pipe, in the anteroom at Bache, Al Rosen says, "There's not a guy living who ever saw me rub."

30   He thinks back fifteen years. "Throwing at me had nothing to do with my being Jewish. They did it because I could hurt 'em with my bat. I heard some things but I didn't hear 'Jew bastard' when I was playing in the majors as much as some people seem to want to think." The old Cleveland Indians, Al Rosen's team, were, in a baseball context, sophisticated, *bon vivants,* possessed of a strong team and party sense. They were not beer-drinking ballplayers. For the Indians, it was martinis, vintage wine with dinner, and stingers afterward. They

were a splendid team. The New York Yankees dominated the American League and baseball in that era and the only team that ever beat the Yankees was the Cleveland Indians. They did it twice.

31   Once, when Rosen was a rookie sitting in a Boston bar, he overheard someone talking about the big-nosed Jewboy. He had no chance to defend himself. Before he could move, Joe Gordon, a veteran Cleveland infielder, got up without a word and punched the offender's mouth. Gordon, not Jewish, was a strong, well-coordinated man, who hit hard.

32   Rosen won respect from his colleagues and from players on other teams by hard, combative, courageous ballplaying. Once, when he was crouched at third base in Fenway Park, the Boston ball park, a huge, mediocre catcher began to call him names. Third base was close to the Boston dugout, and Rosen heard the names quite clearly. They were the old names, from his Florida youth.

33   "Time," Rosen said to an umpire. Then he started toward the dugout, where he was going to have to take on a bigger man and, team loyalty being what it is, perhaps some of the other Boston players as well. Suddenly two Boston stars, Bobby Doerr and Johnny Pesky, grabbed the catcher and convoyed him out of the dugout and down a runway. They were not protecting him. There in the runway, Doerr and Pesky shouted their contempt for a man who would cry racial epithets at as fine a professional as Rosen.

34   By the polished standards of the major leagues, Rosen's fielding at third base was only average. But he worked hard at scooping ground balls, getting throws off quickly, and charging bunts and within a few years he grew proud of his skills. On one occasion a runner slid into third, and Rosen picked off a throw and slapped him with a tag.

35   The umpire spread his arms wide. The man was safe.

36   "No," Rosen yelled. "No, dammit. I had him. You blew it."

37   The umpire walked in a semicircle toward George Strickland, the Cleveland shortstop. Quietly, gentile to gentile, the umpire said, "I'll get that Jew bastard one of these days."

38   "I'm going to tell him you said that," Strickland said.

39   "You wouldn't do that," the umpire said.

40   "I'm telling him," Strickland said, "and after he takes a belt at you, if he misses, I'm going to get you myself."

41   These were the passionate words of friendship. No one assaulted the umpire. All that ultimately occurred was that the umpire told some other umpires that Strickland of Cleveland was a Bolshevik, a troublemaker.

42   Rosen was a winning ballplayer, intolerant of losing and as demanding of others as of himself. Once when the Indians were about to play the Yankees, a star lay on a white table in the trainer's room, complaining of a sore muscle. "I just can't make it today," the star said.

43   "The big man," Rosen said, "takes off against Washington. The big man puts up with pain to play the Yankees."

44   The man on the table cursed briefly.

45   "Look at Mantle," Rosen said. "He plays on a worse leg than yours every day."

46   There was more profanity.

47   "I've been kidding you," Rosen said, withdrawing into formality, "and it's obvious that you're not kidding me. I think it best that you not say anything further to me and I won't say anything further to you."

48   Rosen wheeled and was at the door of the trainer's room when he heard, "You yellow son of a bitch."

49   He turned. The other Cleveland player was standing up, fists cocked. Rosen strode through punches and knocked the other ballplayer down. It took two men to pull him away.

50   Rosen fought for a lot of reasons, but he had learned to fight because he was a Jew. When he was established and a star, nationally famous, he was unhappy with his name once more. He wanted one even more Jewish than his own, perhaps Rosenthal or Rosenstein. He wanted to make sure that there was no mistake about what he was.

51   An accident shortened his years in baseball. He was playing first base and a runner screened his view just before a hard drive crumpled the index finger of his right hand. He did not stay out of the lineup long enough. When he returned, pitchers threw inside fastballs so that whenever bat and ball connected, the finger was jarred. The injury failed to heal but in the All Star game of 1955, with his right index finger stiff and useless, Rosen hit successive home runs. That autumn he had to retire. He now has fifty percent use of the finger.

52   Rosen's second career has provided security and a chance to think life over, to reach conclusions in quiet times. He and his wife are exposing their children to religious Judaism. Rosen wants them to have facts, legend, belief, history before them. Then he hopes they will decide for themselves whether they are religious. He is a suburbanite now, with country club membership. He is addicted to tennis, but he remembers the violent years.

53   "A big thing about fighting," Rosen says, "is how much do you have to lose. Ten guys can terrorize a thousand. Look at the motorcycle crowd. They have nothing so they can afford to fight." He relights his pipe with the big hands in the anteroom. "I suppose the same was true of many of the early Nazis. They had nothing to lose."

54   He has thought often of the Holocaust. Certain pictures of Jews being led to death choke him with emotion. He carries the burden of being a Jew proudly. He is stronger than most, more resolute, and more courageous. Talking to him in the anteroom, one suspects that even now, as parent, businessman and tennis player, he would react to an anti-Semitic remark by shedding the tweed jacket, along with the courteous broker's manner, and punch hard, to end it fast, the way he used to in Miami, Florida, so that whoever started this, and whoever was observing, would remember next time they were inclined to pick on a Jew.

55   But that is only the second deepest consideration of his life so far. "When I was up there in the majors," Al Rosen says, "I always knew how I wanted it to be about me.

56   "I wanted it to be, *Here comes one Jewish kid that every Jew in the world can be proud of.*"

57   The big, graying, broken-nosed man relights his pipe and intensity makes the strong hands tremble.

☐ Discovering Meaning and Technique

1. According to Kahn, why is athletics as a career usually scorned in Jewish homes?

2. What does Rosen mean by "To me a Jew is feel"?

3. With incidents from the selection, support Kahn's contention that Rosen is "not afraid."

4. According to the selection, what is a common stereotype of Jews?

5. How talented was Rosen athletically?

6. How does Rosen explain his toughness?

7. Characterize the Cleveland Indians when Rosen played for that club.

8. Explain the meaning of the title.

☐ Writing Suggestions

1. Al Rosen was not deterred from athletic success by anti-Semitic remarks. Write about the harm they might, however, cause to others.

2. Why do you think people use derogatory names for those who have a different heritage?

3. Write about the Jewish heritage "that calls up horror and sadness at people hurting other people."

4. Kahn's opening statement is "The combative Jew coincides with no stereotype." Explain the inaccuracy of the stereotype of the noncombative Jew. (Evidence can be gathered in the library, especially in reference to the assertiveness of the Jews in Israel.)

5. Are sports more or less subject to racial and religious harmony than other segments of society?

NO WOMAN WROTE A WORD

□ **VIRGINIA WOOLF**

1 It was disappointing not to have brought back in the evening some important statement, some authentic fact. Women are poorer than men because—this or that. Perhaps now it would be better to give up seeking for the truth, and receiving on one's head an avalanche of opinion hot as lava, discoloured as dish-water. It would be better to draw the curtains; to shut out distractions; to light the lamp; to narrow the enquiry and to ask the historian, who records not opinions but facts, to describe under what conditions women lived, not throughout the ages, but in England, say in the time of Elizabeth.

2   For it is a perennial puzzle why no woman wrote a word of that extraordinary literature when every other man, it seemed, was capable of song or sonnet. What were the conditions in which women lived, I asked myself; for fiction, imaginative work that is, is not dropped like a pebble upon the ground, as science may be; fiction is like a spider's web, attached ever so lightly perhaps, but still attached to life at all four corners. Often the attachment is scarcely perceptible; Shakespeare's plays, for instance, seem to hang there complete by themselves. But when the web is pulled askew, hooked up at the edge, torn in the middle, one remembers that these webs are not spun in midair by incorporeal creatures, but are the work of suffering human beings, and are attached to grossly material things, like health and money and the houses we live in.

3   I went, therefore, to the shelf where the histories stand and took down one of the latest, Professor Trevelyan's *History of England*. Once more I looked up Women, found "position of," and turned to the pages indicated. "Wife-beating," I read, "was a recognised right of man, and was practised without shame by high as well as low. . . . Similarly," the historian goes on, "the daughter who refused to marry the gentleman of her parents' choice was liable to be locked up, beaten and flung about the room, without any shock being inflicted on public opinion. Marriage was not an affair of personal affection, but of family avarise, particularly in the 'chivalrous' upper classes. . . . Betrothal often took place while one or both of the parties was in the cradle, and marriage when they were scarcely out of the nurses' charge." That was about 1470, soon after Chaucer's time. The next reference to the position of women is some two hundred years later, in the time of the Stuarts. "It was still the exception for women of the upper and middle class to choose their own husbands, and when the husband

had been assigned, he was lord and master, so far at least as law and custom could make him. Yet even so," Professor Trevelyan concludes, "neither Shakespeare's women nor those of authentic seventeenth-century memoirs, like the Verneys and the Hutchinsons, seem wanting in personality and character." Certainly, if we consider it, Cleopatra must have had a way with her; Lady Macbeth, one would suppose, had a will of her own; Rosalind, one might conclude, was an attractive girl. Professor Trevelyan is speaking no more than the truth when he remarks that Shakespeare's women do not seem wanting in personality and character. Not being a historian, one might go even further and say that women have burnt like beacons in all the works of all the poets from the beginning of time—Clytemnestra, Antigone, Cleopatra, Lady Macbeth, Phèdre, Cressida, Rosalind, Desdemona, the Duchess of Malfi, among the dramatists; then among the prose writers: Millamant, Clarissa, Becky Sharp, Anna Karenine, Emma Bovary, Madame de Guermantes—the names flock to mind, nor do they recall women "lacking in personality and character." Indeed, if woman had no existence save the fiction written by men, one would imagine her a person of the utmost importance; very various; heroic and mean; splendid and sordid; infinitely beautiful and hideous in the extreme; as great as a man, some think even greater. [1] But this is woman in fiction. In fact, as Professor Trevelyan points out, she was locked up, beaten and flung about the room.

4   A very queer, composite being thus emerges. Imaginatively she is of the highest importance; practically she is completely insignificant. She pervades poetry from cover to cover; she is all but absent from history. She dominates the lives of kings and conquerors in fiction; in fact she was the slave of any boy whose parents forced a ring upon her finger. Some of the most inspired words, some of the most profound thoughts in literature fall from her lips; in real life she could hardly read, could scarcely spell, and was the property of her husband.

5   It was certainly an odd monster that one made up by reading the historians first and the poets afterwards—a worm winged like an eagle; the spirit of life and beauty in a kitchen chopping up suet. But these monsters, however amusing to the imagination, have no existence in fact. What one must do to bring her to life was to think poetically and prosaically at one and the same moment,

---

[1] "It remains a strange and almost inexplicable fact that in Athena's city, where women were kept in almost Oriental suppression as odalisques or drudges, the stage should yet have produced figures like Clytemnestra and Cassandra, Atossa and Antigone, Phèdre and Medea, and all the other heroines who dominate play after play of the 'misogynist' Euripides. But the paradox of this world where in real life a respectable woman could hardly show her face alone in the street, and yet on the stage woman equals or surpasses man, has never been satisfactorily explained. In modern tragedy the same predominance exists. At all events, a very cursory survey of Shakespeare's work (similarly with Webster, though not with Marlowe or Jonson) suffices to reveal how this dominance, this initiative of women, persists from Rosalind to Lady Macbeth. So too in Racine; six of his tragedies bear their heroines' names; and what male characters of his shall we set against Hermione and Andromaque, Bérénice and Roxane, Phèdre and Athalie? So again with Ibsen; what men shall we match with Solveig and Nora, Hedda and Hilda Wangel and Rebecca West?"—F. L. LUCAS, *Tragedy,* pp. 114–15.

thus keeping in touch with fact—that she is Mrs. Martin, aged thirty-six, dressed in blue, wearing a black hat and brown shoes; but not losing sight of fiction either—that she is a vessel in which all sorts of spirits and forces are coursing and flashing perpetually. The moment, however, that one tries this method with the Elizabethan woman, one branch of illumination fails; one is held up by the scarcity of facts. One knows nothing detailed, nothing perfectly true and substantial about her. History scarcely mentions her. And I turned to Professor Trevelyan again to see what history meant to him. I found by looking at his chapter headings that it meant—

6   "The Manor Court and the Methods of Open-field Agriculture . . . The Cistercians and Sheep-farming . . . The Crusades . . . The University . . . The House of Commons . . . The Hundred Years' War . . . The Wars of the Roses . . . The Renaissance Scholars . . . The Dissolution of the Monasteries . . . Agrarian and Religious Strife . . . The Origin of English Sea-power . . . The Armada . . ." and so on. Occasionally an individual woman is mentioned, an Elizabeth, or a Mary; a queen or a great lady. But by no possible means could middle-class women with nothing but brains and character at their command have taken part in any one of the great movements which, brought together, constitute the historian's view of the past. Nor shall we find her in any collection of anecdotes. Aubrey hardly mentions her. She never writes her own life and scarcely keeps a diary; there are only a handful of her letters in existence. She left no plays or poems by which we can judge her. What one wants, I thought—and why does not some brilliant student at Newnham or Girton supply it?—is a mass of information; at what age did she marry; how many children had she as a rule; what was her house like; had she a room to herself; did she do the cooking; would she be likely to have a servant? All these facts lie somewhere, presumably, in parish registers and account books; the life of the average Elizabethan woman must be scattered about somewhere, could one collect it and make a book of it. It would be ambitious beyond my daring, I thought, looking about the shelves for books that were not there, to suggest to the students of those famous colleges that they should re-write history, though I own that it often seems a little queer as it is, unreal, lop-sided; but why should they not add a supplement to history? calling it, of course, by some inconspicuous name so that women might figure there without impropriety? For one often catches a glimpse of them in the lives of the great, whisking away into the background, concealing, I sometimes think, a wink, a laugh, perhaps a tear. And, after all, we have lives enough of Jane Austen; it scarcely seems necessary to consider again the influence of the tragedies of Joanna Baillie upon the poetry of Edgar Allan Poe; as for myself, I should not mind if the homes and haunts of Mary Russell Mitford were closed to the public for a century at least. But what I find deplorable, I continued, looking about the bookshelves again, is that nothing is known about women before the eighteenth century. I have no model in my mind to turn about this way and that. Here am I asking why women did not write poetry in the Elizabethan

age, and I am not sure how they were educated; whether they were taught to write; whether they had sitting-rooms to themselves; how many women had children before they were twenty-one; what, in short, they did from eight in the morning till eight at night. They had no money evidently; according to Professor Trevelyan they were married whether they liked it or not before they were out of the nursery, at fifteen or sixteen very likely. It would have been extremely odd, even upon this showing, had one of them suddenly written the plays of Shakespeare, I concluded, and I thought of that old gentleman, who is dead now, but was a bishop, I think, who declared that it was impossible for any woman, past, present, or to come, to have the genius of Shakespeare. He wrote to the papers about it. He also told a lady who applied to him for information that cats do not as a matter of fact go to heaven, though they have, he added, souls of a sort. How much thinking those old gentlemen used to save one! How the borders of ignorance shrank back at the approach! Cats do not go to heaven. Women cannot write the plays of Shakespeare.

7   Be that as it may, I could not help thinking, as I looked at the works of Shakespeare on the shelf, that the bishop was right at least in this; it would have been impossible, completely and entirely, for any woman to have written the plays of Shakespeare in the age of Shakespeare. Let me imagine, since facts are so hard to come by, what would have happened had Shakespeare had a wonderfully gifted sister, called Judith, let us say. Shakespeare himself went, very probably—his mother was an heiress—to the grammar school, where he may have learnt Latin—Ovid, Virgil and Horace—and the elements of grammar and logic. He was, it is well known, a wild boy who poached rabbits, perhaps shot a deer, and had, rather sooner that he should have done, to marry a woman in the neighbourhood, who bore him a child rather quicker than was right. That escapade sent him to seek his fortune in London. He had, it seemed, a taste for the theatre; he began by holding horses at the stage door. Very soon he got work in the theatre, became a successful actor, and lived at the hub of the universe, meeting everybody, knowing everybody, practising his art on the boards, exercising his wits in the streets, and even getting access to the palace of the queen. Meanwhile his extraordinarily gifted sister, let us suppose, remained at home. She was as adventurous, as imaginative, as agog to see the world as he was. But she was not sent to school. She had no chance of learning grammar and logic, let alone of reading Horace and Virgil. She picked up a book now and then, one of her brother's perhaps, and read a few pages. But then her parents came in and told her to mend the stockings or mind the stew and not moon about with books and papers. They would have spoken sharply but kindly, for they were substantial people who knew the conditions of life for a woman and loved their daughter—indeed, more likely than not she was the apple of her father's eye. Perhaps she scribbled some pages up in an apple loft on the sly, but was careful to hide them or set fire to them. Soon, however, before she was out of her teens, she was to be betrothed to the son of a neighbouring

wool-stapler. She cried out that marriage was hateful to her, and for that she was severely beaten by her father. Then he ceased to scold her. He begged her instead not to hurt him, not to shame him in this matter of her marriage. He would give her a chain of beads or a fine petticoat, he said; and there were tears in his eyes. How could she disobey him? How could she break his heart? The force of her own gift alone drove her to it. She made up a small parcel of her belongings, let herself down by a rope one summer's night and took the road to London. She was not seventeen. The birds that sang in the hedge were not more musical than she was. She had the quickest fancy, a gift like her brother's, for the tune of words. Like him, she had a taste for the theatre. She stood at the stage door; she wanted to act, she said. Men laughed in her face. The manager— a fat, loose-lipped man—guffawed. He bellowed something about poodles dancing and women acting—no woman, he said, could possibly be an actress. He hinted— you can imagine what. She could get no training in her craft. Could she even seek her dinner in a tavern or roam the streets at midnight? Yet her genius was for fiction and lusted to feed abundantly upon the lives of men and women and the study of their ways. At last—for she was very young, oddly like Shakespeare the poet in her face, with the same grey eyes and rounded brows—at last Nick Greene the actor-manager took pity on her; she found herself with child by that gentleman and so—who shall measure the heat and violence of the poet's heart when caught and tangled in a woman's body?—killed herself one winter's night and lies buried at some cross-roads where the omnibuses now stop outside the Elephant and Castle.

8   That, more or less, is how the story would run, I think, if a woman in Shakespeare's day had had Shakespeare's genius. But for my part, I agree with the deceased bishop, if such he was—it is unthinkable that any woman in Shake- speare's day should have had Shakespeare's genius. For genius like Shakespeare's is not born among labouring, uneducated, servile people. It was not born in England among the Saxons and the Britons. It is not born today among the working classes. How, then, could it have been born among women whose work began, according to Professor Trevelyan, almost before they were out of the nursery, who were forced to it by their parents and held to it by all the power of law and custom? Yet genius of a sort must have existed among women as it must have existed among the working classes. Now and again an Emily Brontë or a Robert Burns blazes out and proves its presence. But certainly it never got itself on to paper. When, however, one reads of a witch being ducked, of a woman possessed by devils, of a wise woman selling herbs, or even of a very remarkable man who had a mother, then I think we are on the track of a lost novelist, a suppressed poet, of some mute and inglorious Jane Austen, some Emily Brontë who dashed her brains out on the moor or mopped and mowed about the highways crazed with the torture that her gift had put her to. Indeed, I would venture to guess that Anon, who wrote so many poems without signing them, was often a woman. It was a woman Edward Fitzgerald, I think, suggested

who made the ballads and the folk-songs, crooning them to her children, beguiling her spinning with them, or the length of the winter's night.

9   This may be true or it may be false—who can say?—but what is true in it, so it seemed to me, reviewing the story of Shakespeare's sister as I had made it, is that any woman born with a great gift in the sixteenth century would certainly have gone crazed, shot herself, or ended her days in some lonely cottage outside the village, half witch, half wizard, feared and mocked at. For it needs little skill in psychology to be sure that a highly gifted girl who had tried to use her gift for poetry would have been so thwarted and hindered by other people, so tortured and pulled asunder by her own contrary instincts, that she must have lost her health and sanity to a certainty. No girl could have walked to London and stood at a stage door and forced her way into the presence of actor-managers without doing herself a violence and suffering an anguish which may have been irrational—for chastity may be a fetish invented by certain societies for unknown reasons—but were none the less inevitable. Chastity had then, it has even now, a religious importance in a woman's life, and has so wrapped itself round with nerves and instincts that to cut it free and bring it to the light of day demands courage of the rarest. To have lived a free life in London in the sixteenth century would have meant for a woman who was poet and playwright a nervous stress and dilemma which might well have killed her. Had she survived, whatever she had written would have been twisted and deformed, issuing from a strained and morbid imagination. And undoubtedly, I thought, looking at the shelf where there are no plays by women, her work would have gone unsigned. That refuge she would have sought certainly. It was the relic of the sense of chastity that dictated anonymity to women even so late as the nineteenth century. Currer Bell, George Eliot, George Sand, all the victims of inner strife as their writings prove, sought ineffectively to veil themselves by using the name of a man. Thus they did homage to the convention, which if not implanted by the other sex was liberally encouraged by them (the chief glory of a woman is not to be talked of, said Pericles, himself a much-talked-of man), that publicity in women is detestable. Anonymity runs in their blood. The desire to be veiled still possesses them.

10   I told you in the course of this paper that Shakespeare had a sister; but do not look for her in Sir Sidney Lee's life of the poet. She died young—alas, she never wrote a word. She lies buried where the omnibuses now stop, opposite the Elephant and Castle. Now my belief is that this poet who never wrote a word and was buried at the cross-roads still lives. She lives in you and me, and in many other women who are not here tonight, for they are washing up the dishes and putting the children to bed. But she lives; for great poets do not die; they are continuing presences; they need only the opportunity to walk among us in the flesh. This opportunity, as I think, it is now coming within your power to give her. For my belief is that if we live another century or

so—I am talking of the common life which is the real life and not of the little separate lives which we live as individuals—and have five hundred a year each of us and rooms of our own; if we have the habit of freedom and the courage to write exactly what we think; if we escape a little from the common sitting-room and see human beings not always in their relation to each other but in relation to reality; and the sky, too, and the trees or whatever it may be in themselves; if we look past Milton's bogey, for no human being should shut out the view; if we face the fact, for it is a fact, that there is no arm to cling to, but that we go alone and that our relation is the world of reality and not only to the world of men and women, then the opportunity will come and the dead poet who was Shakespeare's sister will put on the body which she has so often laid down. Drawing her life from the lives of the unknown who were her forerunners, as her brother did before her, she will be born. As for her coming without that preparation, without that effort on our part, without that determination that when she is born again she shall find it possible to live and write her poetry, that we cannot expect, for that would be impossible. But I maintain that she would come if we worked for her, and that so to work, even in poverty and obscurity, is worth while.

☐ Discovering Meaning and Technique

1. What does Woolf's research reveal about the position of women in Shakespeare's era?

2. How does that historical position compare with the treatment of women in literature?

3. If you are not familiar with the female characters or writers in the selection (such as Clytemnestra, Becky Sharp, Emma Bovary, Currer Bell, George Eliot), look them up in a reference work such as *The Oxford Companion to English Literature.*

4. What is your reaction to Woolf's imaginary account of the life of Shakespeare's sister? Does it seem realistic? Too fanciful?

5. This selection is taken from Woolf's book *A Room of Her Own.* How does the book's title echo the point of the selection?

6. Explain why Woolf says that genius "is not born among laboring, uneducated, servile people."

7. Woolf frequently uses phrases in a series to emphasize a point—for example, "to draw the curtains; to shut out distractions; to narrow the enquiry and to

ask the historian" or "a wink, a laugh, perhaps a tear." Find other examples of phrases in a series.

☐ Writing Suggestions

1. Woolf contrasts women in fiction with women in fact. Do you think this discrepancy still exists? Compare, for example, women in current literature, movies, or television programs to women in real life.

2. Today, women are a growing part of the professional and business worlds, and women make up a large percentage of the blue-collar work force. Yet, most men still expect working women to take care of the housework, the cooking, the child care. Are women, therefore, still servile to a large extent?

3. By interviewing elderly women or doing library research, try to recreate a day in the life of a lower- or middle-income woman fifty or sixty years ago. How much of her day, for example, was devoted to doing laundry by hand, cooking on a wood stove, canning vegetables, hoeing a garden, feeding livestock, tending children?

4. How much of a woman's life (as opposed to a man's) is spent caring for others instead of for herself? Does she expend most of her creative energies in caretaking?

5. Describe what you consider to be an equitable division of labor between men and women.

6. Would you advise a woman who wishes to succeed professionally not to marry and have children?

ONE SMALL STEP FOR GENKIND

☐ CASEY MILLER AND KATE SWIFT

1 A riddle is making the rounds that goes like this: A man and his young son were in an automobile accident. The father was killed and the son, who was critically injured, was rushed to a hospital. As attendants wheel the unconscious boy into the emergency room, the doctor on duty looked down at him and said, "My God, it's my son!" What was the relationship of the doctor to the injured boy?

2 If the answer doesn't jump to your mind, another riddle that has been

around a lot longer might help: The blind beggar had a brother. The blind beggar's brother died. The brother who died had no brother. What relation was the blind beggar to the blind beggar's brother?

3   As with all riddles, the answers are obvious once you see them: The doctor was the boy's mother and the beggar was her brother's sister. Then why doesn't everyone solve them immediately? Mainly because our language, like the culture it reflects, is male oriented. To say that a woman in medicine is an exception is simply to confirm that statement. Thousands of doctors are women, but in order to be seen in the mind's eye, they must be called women doctors.

4   Except for words that refer to females by definition (mother, actress, Congresswoman), and words for occupations traditionally held by females (nurse, secretary, prostitute), the English language defines everyone as male. The hypothetical person ("If a man can walk 10 miles in two hours . . ."), the average person ("the male in the street") and the active person ("the man on the move") are male. The assumption is that unless otherwise identified, people in general—including doctors and beggars—are men. It is a semantic mechanism that operates to keep women invisible: *man* and *mankind* represent everyone; *he* in generalized use refers to either sex; the "land where our fathers died" is also the land of our mothers—although they go unsung. As the beetle-browed and mustachioed man in a Steig cartoon says to his two male drinking companions, "When I speak of mankind, one thing I *don't* mean is womankind."

5   Semantically speaking, woman is not one with the species of man, but a distinct subspecies. "Man," says the 1971 edition of the Britannica Junior Encyclopedia, "is the highest form of life on earth. His superior intelligence, combined with certain physical characteristics, have enabled man to achieve things that are impossible for other animals." (The prose style has something in common with the report of a research team describing its studies on "the development of the uterus in rats, guinea pigs and men.") As though quoting the Steig character, still speaking to his friends in McSorley's, the Junior Encyclopedia continues: "Man must invent most of his behavior, because he lacks the instincts of lower animals. . . . Most of the things he learns have been handed down from his ancestors by language and symbols rather than by biological inheritance."

6   Considering that for the last 5,000 years society has been patriarchal, that statement explains a lot. It explains why Eve was made from Adam's rib instead of the other way around, and who invented all those Adam-rib words like *f*emale and *w*oman in the first place. It also explains why, when it is necessary to mention woman, the language makes her a lower caste, a class separate from the rest of man; why it works to "keep her in her place."

7   This inheritance through language and other symbols begins in the home (also called a man's castle) where man and wife (not husband and wife, or man and woman) live for a while with their children. It is reinforced by religious training, the educational system, the press, government, commerce and the law.

As Andrew Greeley wrote not long ago in his magazine, "Man is a symbol-creating animal. He orders and interprets his reality by his symbols, and he uses the symbols to reconstruct their reality."

8   Consider some of the reconstructed realities of American history. When schoolchildren learn from their textbooks that the early colonists gained valuable experience in governing themselves, they are not told that the early colonists who were women were denied the privilege of self-government; when they learn that in the 18th century the average man had to manufacture many of the things he and his family needed, they are not told that this "average man" was often a woman who manufactured much of what she and her family needed. Young people learn that intrepid pioneers crossed the country in covered wagons with their wives, children and cattle; they do not learn that women themselves were intrepid pioneers rather than part of the baggage.

9   In a paper published this year in Los Angeles as a guide for authors and editors of social-studies textbooks, Elizabeth Burr, Susan Dunn and Norma Farquhar document unintentional skewings of this kind that occur either because women are not specifically mentioned as affecting or being affected by historical events, or because they are discussed in terms of outdated assumptions. "One never sees a picture of women captioned simply 'farmers' or 'pioneers,' " they point out. The subspecies nomenclature that requires a caption to read "women farmers" or "women pioneers" is extended to impose certain jobs on women by definition. The textbook guide gives as an example the word *housewife,* which it says not only "suggests that domestic chores are the exclusive burden of females," but gives "female students the idea that they were born to keep house and teaches male students that they are automatically entitled to laundry, cooking and housecleaning services from the women in their families."

10 Sexist language is any language that expresses such stereotyped attitudes and expectations, or that assumes the inherent superiority of one sex over the other. When a woman says of her husband, who had drawn up plans for a new bedroom wing and left out closets, "Just like a man," her language is as sexist as the man's who says, after his wife has changed her mind about needing the new wing after all, "Just like a woman."

11   Male and female are not sexist words, but masculine and feminine almost always are. Male and female can be applied objectively to individual people and animals and, by extension, to things. When electricians and plumbers talk about male and female couplings, everyone knows or can figure out what they mean. The terms are graphic and culture free.

12   Masculine and feminine, however, are as sexist as any words can be, since it is almost impossible to use them without invoking cultural stereotypes. When people construct lists of "masculine" and "feminine" traits they almost always end up making assumptions that have nothing to do with innate differences between sexes. We have a friend who happens to be going through the process

of pinning down this very phenomenon. He is 7 years old and his question concerns why his coats and shirts button left over right while his sister's button the other way. He assumes it must have something to do with the differences between boys and girls, but he can't see how.

13   What our friend has yet to grasp is that the way you button your coat, like most sex-differentiated customs, has nothing to do with real differences but much to do with what society wants you to feel about yourself as a male or a female person. Society decrees that it is appropriate for girls to dress differently from boys, to act differently, and to think differently. Boys must be masculine, whatever that means, and girls must be feminine.

14 Unabridged dictionaries are a good source for finding out what society decrees to be appropriate, though less by definition than by their choice of associations and illustrations. Words associated with males—*manly, virile,* and *masculine,* for example—are defined through a broad range of positive attributes like strength, courage, and directness and independence, and they are illustrated through such examples of contemporary usage as "a manly determination to face what comes," "a virile literary style," "a masculine love of sports." Corresponding words associated with females are defined with fewer attributes (though weakness is often one of them) and the examples given are generally negative if not clearly pejorative: "feminine wiles," "womanish tears," "a womanlike lack of promptness," "convinced that drawing was a waste of time, if not downright womanly."

15   Male-associated words are frequently applied to females to describe something that is either incongruous ("a mannish voice") or presumably commendable ("a masculine mind," "she took it like a man"), but female-associated words are unreservedly derogatory when applied to males, and are sometimes abusive to females as well. The opposite of "masculine" is "effeminate," although the opposite of "feminine" is simply "unfeminine."

16   One dictionary, after defining the word *womanish* as "suitable to or resembling a woman," further defines it as "unsuitable to a man or to a strong character of either sex." Words derived from "sister" and "brother" provide another apt example, for whereas "sissy," applied either to a male or female, conveys the message that sisters are expected to be timid and cowardly, "buddy" makes clear that brothers are friends.

17   The subtle disparagement of females and corresponding approbation of males wrapped up in many English words is painfully illustrated by "tomboy." Here is an instance where a girl who likes sports and the out-of-doors, who is curious about how things work, who is adventurous and bold instead of passive, is defined in terms of something she is not—a boy. By denying that she can be the person she is and still be a girl, the word surreptitiously undermines her sense of identity: it says she is unnatural. A "tomboy," as defined by one dictionary, is a "girl, especially a young girl, who behaves like a spirited boy." But who

makes the judgment that she is acting like a spirited boy, not a spirited girl? Can it be a coincidence that in the case of the dictionary just quoted the editor, executive editor, managing editor, general manager, all six members of the Board of Linguists, the usage editor, science editor, all six general editors of definitions, and 94 out of the 104 distinguished experts consulted on usage—are men?

18   It isn't enough to say that any invidious comparisons and sterotypes lexicographers perpetuate are already present in the culture. There are ways to define words like womanly and tomboy that don't put women down, though the tradition has been otherwise. Samuel Johnson, the lexicographer, was the same Dr. Johnson who said, "A woman preaching is like a dog's walking on his hind legs. It is not done well; but you are surprised to find it done at all."

19   Possibly because of the negative images associated with womanish and womanlike, and with expressions like "woman driver" and "woman of the street," the word *woman* dropped out of fashion for a time. The women at the office and the women on the assembly line and the women one first knew in school all became ladies or girls or gals. Now a countermovement, supported by the very term *women's liberation,* is putting back into words like *woman* and *sister* and *sisterhood* the meaning they were losing by default. It is as though, in the nick of time, women had seen that the language itself could destroy them.

20 Some long-standing conventions of the news media add insult to injury. When a woman or girl makes news, her sex is identified at the beginning of a story, if possible in the headline or its equivalent. The assumption, apparently is that whatever event or action is being reported, a woman's involvement is less common and therefore more newsworthy than a man's. If the story is about achievement, the implication is: "pretty good for a woman," And because people are assumed to be male unless otherwise identified, the media have developed a special and extensive vocabulary to avoid the constant repetition of "woman," The results, "Grandmother Wins Nobel Prize," "Blonde Hijacks Airliner," "Housewife to Run for Congress," convey the kind of information that would be ludicrous in comparable headlines if the subjects were men. Why, if "Unsalaried Husband to Run for Congress" is unacceptable to editors, do women have to keep explaining that to describe them through external or superficial concerns reflects a sexist view of women as decorative objects, breeding machines and extensions of men, not real people?

21   Members of the Chicago chapter of the National Organization for Women recently studied the newspapers in their area and drew up a set of guidelines for the press. These include cutting out descriptions of the "clothes, physical features, dating life and marital status of women where such references would be considered inappropriate if about men": using language in such a way as to include women in copy that refers to homeowners, scientists and business people where "newspaper descriptions often convey the idea that all such persons are

male"; and displaying the same discretion in printing generalizations about women as would be shown toward racial, religious and ethnic groups. "Our concern with what we are called may seem trivial to some people," the women said, "but we regard the old usages as symbolic of women's position within this society."

22   The assumption that an adult woman is flattered by being called a girl is matched by the notion that a woman in a menial or poorly paid job finds compensation in being called a lady. Ethel Strainchamps has pointed out that since *lady* is used as an adjective with nouns designating both high and low occupations (lady wrestler, lady barber, lady doctor, lady judge), some writers assume they can use the noun form without betraying value judgments. Not so, Strainchamp says, rolling the issue into a spitball: "You may write, 'He addressed the Republican ladies,' or 'The Democratic ladies convened' . . . but I have never seen 'the Communist ladies' or 'the Black Panther ladies' in print."

23   Thoughtful writers and editors have begun to repudiate some of the old usages. "Divorcée," "grandmother" and "blonde," along with "vivacious," "pert," "dimpled" and "cute," were dumped by the *Washington Post* in the spring of 1970 by the executive editor, Benjamin Bradlee. In a memo to his staff, Bradlee wrote, "The meaningful equality and dignity of women is properly under scrutiny today . . . because this equality has been less than meaningful and the dignity not always free of stereotype and condescension."

24 What women have been called in the press—or at least the part that operates above ground—is only a fraction of the infinite variety of alternatives to "women" used in the subcultures of the English-speaking world. Beyond "chicks," "dolls," "dames," "babes," "skirts" and "broads" are the words and phrases in which women are reduced to their sexuality and nothing more. It would be hard to think of another area of language in which the human mind has been so fertile in devising and borrowing abusive terms. In *The Female Eunuch,* Germaine Greer devotes four pages to anatomical terms and words for animals, vegetables, fruits, baked goods, implements and receptacles, all of which are used to dehumanize the female person. Jean Faust, in an article aptly called "Words That Oppress," suggests that the effort to diminish women through language is rooted in a male fear of sexual inadequacy. "Woman is made to feel guilty for and akin to natural disasters," she writes; "hurricanes and typhoons are named after her. Any negative or threatening force is given a feminine name. If a man runs into bad luck climbing up the ladder of success (a male-invented game), he refers to the 'bitch goddess' success."

25   The sexual overtones in the ancient and no doubt honorable custom of calling ships "she" have become more explicit and less honorable in an age of air travel: "I'm Karen. Fly me." Attitudes of ridicule, contempt and disgust toward female sexuality have spawned a rich glossary of insults and epithets not found in dictionaries. And the usage in which four-letter words meaning copulate are

interchangeable with *cheat, attack* and *destroy* can scarcely be unrelated to the savagery of rape.

26   In her updating of Ibsen's *A Doll's House,* Clare Booth Luce has Nora tell her husband she is pregnant—"In the way only men are supposed to get pregnant." "Men, pregnant?" he says, and she nods; "With ideas. Pregnancies there [*she taps his head*] are masculine. And a very superior form of labor. Pregnancies here [*taps her tummy*] are feminine—a very inferior form of labor."

27   Public outcry followed a revised translation of the New Testament describing Mary as "pregnant" instead of "great with child." The objections were made in part on esthetic grounds: there is no attractive adjective in modern English for a woman who is about to give birth. A less obvious reason was that replacing the euphemism with a biological term underminded religious teaching. The initiative and generative power in the conception of Jesus are understood to be God's; Mary, the mother, was a vessel only.

28   Whether influenced by this teaching or not, the language of human reproduction lags several centuries behind scientific understanding. The male's contribution to procreation is still described as though it were the entire seed from which a new life grows: the initiative and generative power involved in the process are thought of as masculine, receptivity and nurturance as feminine. "Seminal" remains a synonym for "highly original," and there is no comparable word to describe the female's equivalent contribution.

29   An entire mythology has grown from this biological misunderstanding and its semantic legacy; its embodiment in laws that for centuries made women nonpersons was a key target of the 19th-century feminist movement. Today, more than 50 years after women finally won the basic democratic right to vote, the word "liberation" itself, when applied to women, means something less than when used of other groups of people. An advertisement for the N.B.C. news department listed Women's Liberation along with crime in the streets and the Vietnam War as "bad news." Asked for his views on Women's Liberation, a highly placed politician was quoted as saying, "Let me make one thing perfectly clear. I wouldn't want to wake up next to a lady pipe-fitter."

30 One of the most surprising challenges to our male-dominated culture is coming from within organized religion, where the issues are being stated, in part, by confronting the implications of traditional language. What a growing number of theologians and scholars are saying is that the myths of the Judeo-Christian tradition, being the products of patriarchy, must be re-examined, and that the concept of an exclusively male ministry and the image of a male god have become idolatrous.

31   Women are naturally in the forefront of this movement, both in their efforts to gain ordination and full equality and through their contributions to theological reform, although both these efforts are often subtly diminished. When the Rev. Barbara Anderson was ordained by the American Lutheran Church, one newspaper

printed her picture over a caption headed "Happy Girl." *Newsweek*'s report of a protest staged last December by women divinity students at Harvard was jocular ("another tilt at the windmill") and sarcastic: "Every time anyone in the room lapsed into what [the students] regarded as male chauvinism—such as using the word 'mankind' to describe the human race in general—the outraged women . . . drowned out the offender with earpiercing blasts from party-favor kazoos . . . What annoyed the women most was the universal custom of referring to God as 'He.' "

32   The tone of the report was not merely unfunny; it missed the connection between increasingly outmoded theological language and the accelerating number of women (and men) who are dropping out of organized religion, both Jewish and Christian. For language, including pronouns, can be used to construct a reality that simply mirrors society's assumptions. To women who are committed to the reality of religious faith, the effect is doubly painful. Professor Harvey Cox, in whose classroom the protest took place, stated the issue directly: The women, he said, were raising the "basic theological question of whether God is more adequately thought of in personal or suprapersonal terms."

33   Toward the end of Don McLean's remarkable ballad "American Pie," a song filled with the imagery of abandonment and disillusion, there is a stanza that must strike many women to the quick. The church bells are broken, the music has died; then:

> And the three men I admire the most,
> The Father, Son and the Holy Ghost,
> They caught the last train for the Coast—
> The day the music died.

34   Three men I admired most. There they go, briefcases in hand and topcoats buttoned left over right, walking down the long gold platform under the city, past the baggage wagons and the hissing steam onto the Pullman. Bye, bye God—all three of you—made in the image of male supremacy. Maybe out there in L.A. where the weather is warmer, someone can believe in you again.

35   The Roman Catholic theologian Elizabeth Farian says "the bad theology of an over-masculinized church continues to be one of the root causes of women's oppression." The definition of oppression is "to crush or burden by abuse of power or authority; burden spiritually or mentally as if by pressure."

36 When language oppresses, it does so by any means that disparage and belittle. Until well into the 20th century, one of the ways English was manipulated to disparage women was through the addition of feminine endings to nonsexual words. Thus a woman who aspired to be a poet was excluded from the company of real poets by the label poetess, and a woman who piloted an airplane was denied full status as an aviator by being called an aviatrix. At about the time poetess, aviatrix, and similar Adam-ribbisms were dropping out of use, H. W.

Fowler was urging that they be revived. "With the coming expansion of women's vocations," he wrote in the first edition (1926) of *Modern English Usage,* "feminines for vocation-words are a special need of the future." There can be no doubt he subconsciously recognized the relative status implied in the *-ess* designations. His criticism of a woman who wished to be known as an author rather than an authoress was that she had no need "to raise herself to the level of the male author by asserting her right to his name."

37   Who has the prior right to a name? The question has an interesting bearing on words that were once applied to men alone, or to both men and women, but now, having acquired abusive associations, are assigned to women exclusively. Spinster is a gentle case in point. Prostitute and many of its synonyms illustrate the phenomenon better. If Fowler had chosen to record the changing usage of harlot from hired man (in Chaucer's time) through rascal and entertainer to its present definition, would he have maintained that the female harlot is trying to raise herself to the level of the male harlot by asserting her right to his name? Or would he have plugged for harlotress?

38   The demise of most *-ess* endings came about before the start of the new feminist movement. In the second edition of *Modern English Usage,* published in 1965, Sir Ernest Gowers frankly admitted what his predecessors had been up to. "Feminine designations," he wrote, "seem now to be falling into disuse. Perhaps the explanation of this paradox is that it symbolizes the victory of women in their struggle for equal rights; it reflects the abandonment by men of those ideas about women in the professions that moved Dr. Johnson to his rude remark about women preachers."

39   If Sir Ernest's optimism can be justified, why is there a movement back to feminine endings in such words as chairwoman, councilwoman and congresswoman? Betty Hudson, of Madison, Conn., is campaigning for the adoption of "selectwoman" as the legal title for a female member of that town's executive body. To have to address a woman as "Selectman," she maintains, "is not only bad grammar and bad biology, but it implies that politics is still, or should be, a man's business." A valid argument, and one that was, predictably, countered by ridicule, the surefire weapon for undercutting achievement. When the head of the Federal Maritime Commission, Helen D. Bentley, was named "Man of the Year" by an association of shipping interests, she wisely refused to be drawn into light-hearted debate with interviewers who wanted to make the award's name a humorous issue. Some women, of course, have yet to learn they are invisible. An 8-year-old who visited the American Museum of Natural History with her Brownie scout troop went through the impressive exhibit on pollution and overpopulation called "Can Man Survive?" Asked afterward, "Well, can he?" she answered, "I don't know about him, but we're working on it in Brownies."

40   Nowhere are women rendered more invisible by language than in politics. The United States Constitution, in describing the qualifications for Representative, Senator and President, refers to each as *he.* No wonder Shirley Chisholm, the

first woman since 1888 to make a try for the Presidential nomination of a major party, has found it difficult to be taken seriously.

41   The observation by Andrew Greeley already quoted—that "man" used "his symbols" to reconstruct "his reality"—was not made in reference to the symbols of language but to the symbolic impact that "nomination of a black man for the Vice-Presidency" would have on race relations in the United States. Did the author assume the generic term "man" would of course be construed to include "woman"? Or did he deliberately use a semantic device to exclude Shirley Chisholm without having to be explicit?

42   Either way, his words construct a reality in which women are ignored. As much as any other factor in our language, the ambiguous meaning of *man* serves to deny women recognition as people. In a recent magazine article, we discussed the similar effect on women of the generic pronoun *he,* which we proposed to replace by a new common gender pronoun *tey.* We were immediately told, by a number of authorities, that we were dabbling in the serious business of linguistics, and the message that reached us from these scholars was loud and clear: It - is - absolutely - impossible - for - anyone - to - introduce - a - new - word - into - the - language - just - because - there - is - a - need - for - it, so - stop - wasting - your - time.

43   When words are suggested like "herstory" (for history), "sportsone-ship" (for sportsmanship) and "mistresspiece" (for the work of a Virginia Woolf) one suspects a not-too-subtle attempt to make the whole language problem look silly. But unless Alexander Pope, when he wrote "The proper study of mankind is man," meant that women should be relegated to the footnotes (or, as George Orwell might have put it, "All men are equal, but men are more equal than women"), viable new words will surely someday supersede the old.

44 Without apologies to Freud, the great majority of women do not wish in their hearts that they were men. If having grown up with a language that tells them they are at the same time men and not men raises psychic doubts for women, the doubts are not of their sexual identity but of their human identity. Perhaps the present unrest surfacing in the Women's Movement is part of an evolutionary change in our particular form of life—the one form of all in the animal and plant kingdoms that orders and interprets its reality by symbols. The achievements of the species called man have brought us to the brink of self-destruction. If the species survives into the next century with the expectation of going on, it may only be because we have become part of what Harlow Shapley calls the psychozoic kingdom, where brain overshadows brawn and rationality has replaced superstition.

45   Searching the roots of Western civilization for a word to call this new species of man and woman, someone might come up with *gen,* as in genesis and generic. With such a word, *man* could be used exclusively for males as *woman* is used for females, for gen would include both sexes. Like the words

deer and bison, gen would be both plural and singular. Like progenitor, progeny, and generation, it would convey continuity. Gen would express the warmth and generalized sexuality of generous, gentle, and genuine; the specific sexuality of genital and genetic. In the new family of gen, girls and boys would grow to genhood, and to speak of genkind would be to include all the people of the earth.

☐ Discovering Meaning and Technique

1. Explain the title "One Small Step for Genkind." According to the dictionary, what does the root *gen* mean?

2. Miller and Swift open the selection with two riddles. Is this an effective opening to an essay on sexist language? Could you solve the riddles?

3. Give examples from the selection of sexism in our patriotic songs, the Bible, history textbooks, dictionaries, the news media, organized religion, and politics.

4. How do the authors define sexist language?

5. How does the word *tomboy* support the authors' point that language reflects a "subtle disparagement of females and corresponding approbation of males"?

6. What do the authors mean by the "generic pronoun *he*"? What did the authors propose in another article as a substitution?

☐ Writing Suggestions

1. Miller and Swift say that "the English language defines everyone as male." Is this still true? Examine current writings (newspapers, magazines, books—anything) and report on whether "the hypothetical person," "the average person," and "the active person" are still referred to as males.

2. Do a survey to determine whether women object to words like *mankind, sportsmanship, chicks, tomboy, lady doctor.*

3. Compare the writing in old and recent publications to determine the extent of sexist language. Publications that have appeared regularly over a long period of time make good choices: newspapers, magazines, encyclopedias, almanacs, dictionaries, and the like.

4. Examine current newspapers and magazines to determine the ratio of female writers to male writers. Are any subjects more likely to be written about by males or females? Which publications have few or no female writers?

5. Do you agree or disagree that sexist language in newspapers "reflects a sexist view of women as decorative objects, breeding machines and extensions of men, not real people"?

6. Today's tendency is to eliminate sexist labels for occupations and vocations: *poetess, aviatrix, authoress, seamstress, heroine, mailman, chairman.* What kinds of substitutions have been made for words like these?

7. Do you think that the efforts to change the language have been "silly" (for example, *tey* for *he and she, herstory* for *history, gen* for *man*)?

POVERTY AND HOPELESSNESS

■ ■ ■

BORN TO RUN

☐ **DON OLDENBURG**

1   In Willie Givens' recurring nightmare, people are chasing him. They want to hurt him. He is scared and he runs. For most of Willie's 18 years, his waking life hasn't been much different. By the time he was 5, he was running, climbing out a bedroom window or walking straight out the front door when no one at home was paying attention. Too often, when he did get the attention he was looking for, it came from his stepfather, who would beat him, or his mother, who would wring her hands and ask the Good Lord why her only son was no good.

2   The only thing for Willie to do was run away.

3   People have lost count of how many times Willie has run. He has fled his mother's homes in Southeast Washington and in Prince George's County. He has run from more than a dozen institutions—juvenile detention centers, mental health facilities, hospitals, group homes and schools where the District's juvenile justice system repeatedly has placed him over the past 10 years. As far back as he can remember, Willie has been in one sort of trouble or another; the label "bad boy" rings in his ears. He has played hooky, shoplifted, stolen purses and cars, used drugs, sold drugs, tried suicide.

4   Yet Willie Givens doesn't want to be a bad kid. His behavior is fairly typical of the increasing number of children that social workers, psychologists and juvenile agencies view with sadness and alarm. They call them "throwaway kids," nearly half a million children nationwide. In a majority of cases, they are kids who have been abused by parents or relatives, and then turned over—voluntarily or by court order—to city, county or state institutions. Many never receive even a minimal education; at 18, Willie, for example, reads and writes at a sixth-grade level. Rarely are they offered the sort of special help disturbed children need.

5   Like Willie, these kids often become runaways, usually at an early age, to escape abuse. Typically, they are first incarcerated and branded "delinquent"

for things like truancy; most of the 6,000 kids detained each year in the District as juvenile delinquents aren't charged with violent acts. Yet, more than three-quarters of them eventually wind up being arrested for serious crimes.

6   Willie Givens is different from these kids in one way. He is writing a book in an attempt to rewrite his future.

7   He began his autobiographical project, "Willie's Story," two years ago, when he was 16. He had been locked up, and he was depressed and lonely. His therapist had gone abroad for three months; he had depended on her more than on anyone else.

8   Now, they sat across from each other in a visiting room at the D.C. Receiving Home for Children. The place smelled faintly of stale urine. Screams from the hallway filtered under the closed door. In the intolerable summer heat, Willie was irritable bordering on surly. He talked big about suicide, about escaping again and taking more drugs. He refused to talk about himself, about the pain of a kid whose childhood was canceled.

9   The therapist, frustrated by his silences, slammed her notebook on the institutional beige table between them.

10   "Okay, Willie. You don't wanna talk?"

11   "No."

12   "Fine. Then you take notes."

13   Willie found too many emotions racing at once to the stubby point of his pencil. He held it like a blade and stabbed the paper. He scratched his name over and over and over until he could no longer decipher its shape or meaning from a manic web of lines that ran off the bottom of the page.

14   A week later, Willie's therapist shoved a notebook in front of him again. Willie leaned his handsome face close to the blank white paper, as if he were sniffing old milk to see if it was spoiled. Then he looked up at her and asked, "What should I say?"

15   "Why don't you introduce yourself."

16   Agonizing over each word, over each spelling, he began, "Let me introduce myself. My name is Willie Givens."

17   *I am 16 year old that start geting in troble when I was 8 or 9 year old. It all start in Southeast the District of Columbia. That where I was live and going school at the time. It was call Friendship school. I didn't like to go there I like to hang out. So it began one day I didn't go to school. So ther for my mother bet me came home from school. ther for next day I didnt go to school than the police pick me up took me to school. When they left I left went home and open window and crod in it and got my bike and rod to mall.*

18   When Willie tries to remember life before grade school, the days when he started running away, his memory stalls. During a year of occasional interviews with a reporter, his brown eyes would often drift toward the ceiling in search

of answers he did not have. Some of the details of his life had to be filled in by those who had tried to help him. At first, the writing in his diary proved as inconsistent as his memory. Chronology and grammar were muddled. The clarity and spelling of his writing varied, depending on his willingness to ask for help. But gradually his angry marks were transformed into coherent pages—the struggles and torments of one throwaway child.

19 Willie was an infant when his mother, Cynthia, kicked his father out of their lives. That was the father Willie never knew. By the time Willie was 5, his mother had remarried. Her new husband drank. Willie remembers that when his stepfather had been drinking, he slapped him around. Willie's mother didn't like that, but she wanted to believe he wasn't that kind of man. "I would be a fool to marry somebody who beat my child," his mother says now. But in early April 1976, Prince George's County police arrested James Woodland, Willie's stepfather, on charges of child abuse and assault and battery—four counts— arising from two separate incidents that left Willie bruised and battered. According to court records, Willie had been beaten badly enough one time to require admission on March 3, 1976, to Prince George's County Hospital in Cheverly. Nineteen days later, Willie was beaten again. On Aug. 5, 1976, James Woodland pleaded guilty to one charge of assault and battery in exchange for a three-year suspended sentence and three years' probation. Soon after, Cynthia Woodland left him.

20 *The man my mother married I don't want to remember him. I remember when she got married because they sent me some where. They had a reception and they did not want me there. I remember that a lot of times my mother hugged me and kissed me and siad nice things to me. sometimes my stepfather was alright to me but sometimes he liked to whip me. he did that when my mother was at work. She saw the marks on my body when she came home from work I think she didn't care. I think my mother was afraid of him. They argued every day.*

21 *When I was in nursery school my step father bet me so badly that I had to go to the Hospital. he had beaten me with things I don't want to talk about the things he beat me with. When he was drunk he used to wait till I did something a little bit wrong and then he wood beat me if I did something was serious. Probably he Beat me for not going to the toilet on time. Maybe he used to call me and was afraid and didn't come to him maybe that was the start of my runing away.*

22 Willie says that his mother sometimes beat him, too. She denies that. In the instances where Willie remembers his mother hitting him, she has a different interpretation. Willie's mother says now that her son "could be trouble." She says she believed in giving him a good spanking when he deserved it. "Just

like bringing up any normal child," she says. "You don't let kids go around doing whatever they want to do. There is a difference between a spanking and a beating."

23   Sometimes Willie fingers the wide scar above his left eye where he says his mother once hit him with a shoe, one of the few incidents from his early life that he recalls clearly. (Doctors say Willie's memory problems, while they are probably psychologically motivated in part, could also be due to brain damage he may have sustained as a result of hard blows to his head, or the result of street dope he has used, or both.) He remembers his mother driving him to the hospital and warning him to say he ran into a door. "That's a lie," his mother responds. She says she didn't hit him. She says she doesn't remember how Willie gashed his forehead.

24   A small boy with fine features, Willie always looked younger than his age. Most of his friends were older, and he seemed most comfortable in the role of everybody's little brother. Off the street, he was the picture of vulnerability. On the street, he tried to make up for his size with brash and loud talk. When Willie and his friends weren't in school, they would run down to the creek near their apartments to skip rocks and break bottles. Eastover Shopping Center was a short bus ride away. No matter how often their mothers told them they weren't to go to the mall, they did anyway. Mostly they played at the arcade and loafed around the stores. Willie took up shoplifting.

25   By the time he was 8, doctors said he was hyperactive. What his mother called his "school problems" were out of control. Often when his mother dropped him off at the elementary school's front door, he'd walk down the hall, sneak past his classroom and run out the back door. Willie hated school. He is still embarrassed when he remembers the first time the class burst into laughter as he tripped over words when he tried to read aloud. He hated it when the other kids teased him that he was stupid. He knew he wasn't stupid, but trying to learn the three Rs was like stumbling through a fog. Although it hadn't yet been diagnosed, Willie was learning-disabled.

26   When Willie was about to fail second grade for the second time, school officials decided that because of his fighting, stealing and truancy, it would be best to get him out of the school system for a while. It was the last time Willie would attend a regular school class. In June 1978, he was sent to live at what was then the Children's Residential Treatment Center in the District— his first stop in a 10-year sequence of placements in institutions for disturbed youngsters.

27   Six months later, his mother brought him back home. She was convinced he'd make better progress as an outpatient at a nearby community health center while attending special-education classes at Congress Heights Elementary School. Willie hated special ed class, too.

28   One day a teacher handed her car keys to another student and asked him to get a cardboard box from her trunk. The boy bumped into Willie in the

hall. "Goin' for a ride," the boy boasted, dangling the keys in front of Willie. Willie grabbed the keys and headed for the parking lot.

29   He shuffled his feet through the fresh February snow to the car, opened the door and climbed in. He remembers that he liked sitting in the driver's seat behind the windshield, blanketed white. For a moment, the world seemed quiet and secure. But his big mistake—keeping the teacher's keys—caught up with him when his mother got home later that night. She whipped him with her belt, he says. "I hate you, I hate you," he remembers screaming at her.

30   *I was live with my aunt maybe a year and thing where ok at home and at school. I new my mother around because she came over on weekend. I was live over there because she siad where she was not enough room. I used to like live with my aunt. She used to hug and kiss her kids and me.*

31   *I used to like playing with my cousins. I haven't seen them in a long time because I've been lock up. They wouldn't be lock up because They have a nice family. Most of the kid I've Known who are lock up are like me with out familyies. My mother took me from her sister house but olny she knows why. They used to call her a tell her I was acting up in school and she would beat me. She also beat me for not cleaning my room.*

32   When Willie asked to stay at his aunt's house permanently and counselors agreed it might help, Willie's mother said no. In hindsight, that may have cost Willie his last best chance for a normal family life. His mother, however, believed life there was "too unstable," that it was "kind of crowded" because her sister still had six children at home. She told counselors Willie wouldn't get "adequate supervision" there. Cynthia Woodland herself had been a child of a broken marriage but was raised "in a nice family life," she says, by an aunt and uncle. She says Willie's turmoil has never ceased to torment her. "How do you think I feel? I'm the mother, but this is a child who should act this way if he don't have a mother or father. [People] don't know if I might need some kind of help myself." But when she was asked to take part in family therapy sessions with Willie, her participation was "inconsistent," according to counselors. "She always seemed to have difficulty in personally being involved in therapy that is probably most needed for Willie to ever function well at home," stated one hospital report.

33   By the time Willie turned 11, his mother had moved to Seat Pleasant in Prince George's County. She increasingly felt she couldn't handle Willie's stealing and running, which had become "systematic." She felt like she "was going through the mill," she says now, "like I almost was having a nervous breakdown." She enrolled Willie in a day program at the Psychiatric Institute of Washington, a private mental hospital. For four months she drove him there and back each day. Then, he was admitted to the residential program, the first of several place-

ments in hospital-like settings where drugs were used as part of a treatment plan to control his behavior.

34   At the Psychiatric Institute, Willie's problems were diagnosed as "overanxious and hyperkinetic reaction to childhood." His behavior was that of a troubled and lonely child who could distinguish right from wrong but rarely connected the consequences of his actions with the actions themselves. Doctors had prescribed two daily doses of Ritalin, a controversial stimulant believed to calm hyperkinetic children.

35 *When I was very little during the time that I have trouble remebering I never new how my mother was going to be to me. I just felt like I had done some thing very bad all the time.*

36   *All my life since then I have carried this guilt. It is much worse than anything the court finds me guilty of doing. For many year whenever I was sent away I wanted to run to my mother to try to make her stop hurting. But she did [not] want to stop hurting and finally she did [not] want me either. I don't rember that she every just siad I love you. I wonder if she ever just siad I love you to anyone. I wonder if anyone siad I love you to her. I wonder what she wood do if I just siad I love you to her?*

37 In the spring of '82, when Willie was 12, he indulged in a spree of shoplifting and taking drugs. His pattern of running was well documented by then, and, like most "runners," Willie had nowhere to run *to*—only places to run *from.* For two months, Willie bolted every few days from his mother's apartment in the District and headed for nearby Prince George's County, where police picked him up for loitering or being out late at night. He'd tell them he was lost. They'd call his mother. Angrily, she'd escort him home.

38   It had become almost routine until one June evening. When the police called, his mother said she would not bring Willie home this time. She said she feared losing her job if she had to keep on taking leave from work to fetch Willie. Instead of going home, Willie was taken to the Child Protective Services Division of the District's Department of Human Services.

39   After a month, Willie ran from the group house on 13th Street NW where he'd been assigned. He smoked marijuana and drank beer until he passed out. Returned to the group home, he ran again, and D.C. police found him wandering the streets in a PCP stupor.

40   A few days later, on a midsummer night, the lights of the group house grew distant in the rear-view mirror of a Chevy van Willie and another kid had stolen. Willie was behind the wheel. When D.C. police tried to pull him over, Willie slid low in the seat and stretched to floor the accelerator. By 2 A.M., police had chased the van south on Branch Avenue at 90 mph. Willie lost control in La Plata and turned the van over in a ditch.

41   On Aug. 9, 1982, Cynthia Woodland signed Willie over to the custody of the D.C. Department of Human Services. In the jargon of the juvenile justice system, he became a PINS case—a Person In Need of Supervision—a child considered "ungovernable" by his legal parent or guardian. His mother's decision simply codified what Willie already feared: He was a child no one wanted.

42   *Befor I was 13 I wasn't in instituntions so much so when I was sick my mother took care of me. those were the times I felt that she Really cared about me. When I was small I only doubted her feelings for me [when] she beat me.*

43   *But something happend when I changed from being a child to becomeing a man. even though I am not very large I feel as though she did not want to be a mother to and man. I used to here her say I wish I had a girl instead of me.*

44   When he was 13, Willie's drug use became serious, and he began to talk increasingly about suicide. At a residential school and treatment center in rural Virginia specializing in remedial education, he tried to kill himself twice, once by drinking toilet bowl cleaner and once by setting his room on fire. The school returned Willie to the District to await the next court hearing, the next session with psychologists, the next locked room. Willie ran away again and got high on PCP.

45   Next stop: detox. In June 1983, Willie was sent to St. Elizabeths Hospital in the District for treatment of PCP toxicity. After several weeks, he seemed improved and more in control, so his ward restrictions were eased. He ran away four times in two weeks, each time getting stoned on PCP, drinking, stealing, getting into fights. In seven months at St. Elizabeths, he visited home twice.

46   At the end of Willie's stay in St. Elizabeths, a hospital psychologist wrote this evaluation: "It is our opinion that this child has not been served well by the institutions in which he has been placed or by the frequent moves from one facility to another. He has developed a lifestyle aimed primarily at thwarting authority rather than accepting and internalizing the values of his caretakers . . . Willie has developed a facility for getting out of institutions through frequent abscondences or self-destructive behavior." The evaluation concluded that given Willie's behavioral problems and "his mother's ambivalent involvement in treatment," there may be no alternative to further institutionalization.

47   A few months later, he was shipped to the Montanari Residential Treatment Center for juveniles and adults in Hialeah, Fla. The center uses behavior modification, counseling, drug therapy and, in some cases, physical restriction. He kept to himself in its maximum security unit, where he was given daily doses of Haldol, a strong sedative. He was 14 years old then, reading and writing at a fourth-grade level.

⁴⁸ I *was being treated like crazy person olny I was never crazy. At St. E's they tried out differant drugs on me like I was and experiment. They said the drugs would make me calm. But they made me feel like a differant person someone I did [not] no.*

⁴⁹   *But what I thing was really crazy was that they had put me in jail for using drug and then they gave me drugs. If I really was a dope addict I would have love staying at St. E's.*

⁵⁰   *I thing they taught me that I was olny okay when I was drugged. And besides my life was so terrible that I could runaway from it by being doped up. About three times in my life I was happy to be me.*

⁵¹ Joe Tulman has been Willie's voice in court since Willie was 12 and stole the Chevy van. A determined advocate for juveniles who would often have none without him, Tulman, 34, is a lawyer still committed to the ideals he fought for in the '70s as deputy director of the Equal Justice Foundation, a nonprofit group that worked for increased access to legal counseling. Now, he supervises the District of Columbia School of Law's juvenile legal clinic, which helps disadvantaged youngsters through the city's court system.

⁵² Whether Tulman likes it or not—and he doesn't always like it—Willie Givens' life and his own are intertwined. He has picked up Willie and returned him to custody often. Willie has embarrassed Tulman by skipping out while under his supervision. District social workers have told Tulman that Willie is a lost cause. But he won't give up. He genuinely likes Willie and sees in him a potential that generally escapes the courts and the social workers. To Tulman, Willie represents all the countless children who enter the legal system and are stamped "delinquent" early on, when, in fact, what they are is neglected, abused and tormented. He thinks of Willie when he asks his law school classes to consider, "How do you discipline a kid who has been traumatized by abusive discipline?" He thinks of Willie when he answers his own question, "What you need is tons and tons of nurturing." Joe Tulman knows only too well how difficult that is to give to a child like Willie.

⁵³ I *used to go to my room alone and imagine how I could help kids who were in trouble if I were a lawyer. I wanted to make a movie about all of the thing that happen in my life and in the lives of other kids who are like me. I want to live in California where all the movie star live. I want the people who say I was a no good Kid to see my movie and then thay would know how wrong thay have been.*

⁵⁴   *I will make one movie about kid's who are used by drug dealers to do their dirty work. Most of these Kids end up with juvenile records and doing time in bad places. Some times kids get into this mess because they have No one to take care of them like parents.*

55 It was Joe Tulman who introduced Willie to psychologist Rona Fields in 1985, after Willie had been placed at Oak Hill Youth Center in Laurel, the District's high-security "lockup" for juveniles. Fields has given psychological tests to hundreds of kids that the law considers delinquent. She's spread peanut butter on bread for kids who haven't eaten breakfast or lunch when they arrive at her office for therapy. She's washed the laundry of kids who show up for testing but are too embarrassed by their dirty clothes to speak. She's sat across from kids for hours of uncomfortable silence while they hide their desperation, fear and indignity under street-mean and stubborn personas. But Fields isn't intimidated easily. She's met some of the world's toughest and most pathetic children—in Northern Ireland, in South Africa, in Beirut—during her yearly travels abroad to study how children are affected by brutality in violent and turbulent societies. Willie, she thought upon meeting him, had a lot in common with those children.

56   Like Fields' other young clients, Willie was curious about the clutter of other cultures in her modest Alexandria home and office. On Willie's first visit, Fields encouraged him to touch the Masai beadwork and the tribal chief's ebony scepter. But what attracted Willie most were the hardback books on Fields' desk, books whose covers all bore her name.

57   "You write those?" he asked, picking up one titled *Society Under Siege.* Fields said she did. "You must be rich and famous," he said.

58   Willie's fascination with writing impressed her. Fields saw Willie as a personable and friendly child who had been neglected and abused at home and then victimized by inappropriate treatment aimed only at controlling him. "If these were children with a value, if they weren't throwaways, there would be a plan and a program with recognizable and consistent objectives," she says. "But nobody listens to them, nobody sees them. They are thrown away until they either come back to haunt you or wind up dead in the gutter." Fields believed that this was a kid she could save.

59   On the drive back from Fields' office to Oak Hill, Joe Tulman stopped to buy Willie a burger. When he turned around from the counter, Willie was gone. He stayed on the lam for three months.

60 *I get tired beening in institutions so I run away. Each time I runaway I no where to go for money. I love money. all anyone has to do IS tell me where I can get the money and that's where I go. What good is having money if you are in jail? But if I was making $2500 a night. I would go to another state and buy a house and invest my money. in a business and make more money. When I get older I wood go and turn myself in. Hopefully by then the court will forget about it because I am older. It is because I think this might be my own story that I have been so ready to Keep trying to make it big pushing dope.*

61   *What I've seen in my life is that people who obey the law and work*

hard for the good of other people like My lawyer have no money but the dealers if they are Really big have every thing and their freedom too. when I thing about power I know where it's at. in the dealers. The poor jerks who use the stuff to pretend that they have power are fools.

62   To make money when he was on the loose, Willie started "running drugs"— holding or selling them for adult dealers who didn't want to risk getting collared themselves. The dealers would drive Willie over to Sayles Place SE off Martin Luther King Jr. Avenue and stand him on a corner with a plastic bag containing 10 small aluminum foil packages, each holding two PCP joints.

63   He didn't like the people buying the dope, and he was frightened of the dealers. But he could make $40 in 90 minutes. One day he stayed out long enough to make $300.

64   In the fall of 1986, Willie was back at Oak Hill. Through weekly therapy meetings with Fields, he renewed contact with his paternal grandmother. She was a kind, churchgoing woman who had briefly taken Willie as an infant. When Willie's grandmother discussed keeping him permanently, Fields considered it an answered prayer.

65   But, as had become his pattern, what psychologist Fields calls his "life script," Willie blew it. On a visit to his grandmother's home, he took some cash that his grandmother had saved for her church. She could tolerate a lot from Willie but not stealing from God. Willie wouldn't be staying at his grandmother's anymore.

66   Fields never forgot Willie's fascination with her books. She decided his breakthrough, perhaps his only chance, depended both figuratively and literally on rewriting the story of his life. "Exchanging a losing script for a winning one," she called it. She knew from her days of community psychology in East Los Angeles and inner-city Chicago that a good strategy for helping illiterates was to interest them in writing. And "Willie's Story" could be more than an accomplishment Willie could hold in his hands—it could be his foundation for a new identity.

67   After several sessions of writing in the notebook, Willie's printing showed more confidence. His letters leaned forward rather than every which way. He doodled less and wrote more directly. He rarely talked about suicide anymore; his violent impulses seemed to drain away with the words he wrote about himself. Fields grew optimistic. Willie told her he wanted to write the book so that other kids could read about him and turn out differently. He talked about becoming famous and rich.

68   Willie spent his 17th birthday on Nov. 4, 1986, at the D.C. Receiving Home for Children, a temporary shelter and diagnostic center where visitors are allowed to meet Oak Hill residents and where Fields regularly counseled Willie. Fields brought to a makeshift party a large chocolate and almond cake with "Happy Birthday" spelled out in marzipan. Willie was thrilled. He cut the

cake and served it to a Receiving Home official and the handful of counselors who showed up. It was the only birthday party Willie could remember anyone ever giving him.

69   Three weeks later, Fields checked Willie out of Oak Hill so he could spend Thanksgiving Day with her and her daughter's family in Manassas. Willie loved being with the family; he held Fields' 18-month-old grandson on his lap and paged through car magazines. He stuffed himself with turkey and potatoes and took a leisurely stroll in the nearby Manassas battlefield.

70   When Fields dropped Willie off that evening at the Receiving Home, she handed him a paper plate of leftovers and 50 cents for a Coke. He hugged her. As Fields drove away feeling pleased with how the day had gone, the guard let Willie out the door to buy a soft drink from the machine outside. When Willie rang the bell to get back in, no one answered. So he ran away and didn't return for four days. Fields and Tulman began working to get Willie out of Oak Hill and into a new place that would better suit his needs.

71 Glen Mills School is a private residential facility for juvenile delinquents 20 miles outside of Philadelphia. Built almost a century ago, the place is a dizzying departure for today's street toughs whose medium is crumbling concrete framed by high-rise squalor. There are no bars or guards. Only rich Pennsylvania countryside surrounds the school. To escape it is to walk away. Glen Mills sent a graduate to an Ivy League college for the first time last year.

72   At about $25,000 a year, Glen Mills was one of the least expensive institutions the D.C. government paid to treat Willie. (Residential treatment centers can cost as much as $50,000 a year, and psychiatric hospitals can run twice that.)

73   Most juveniles committed to Glen Mills stay for nine to 12 months, the length of time it takes to mold them into a new way of acting. Drugs are not used. Confrontation and criticism are coupled with positive reinforcement. Students there call themselves "peers." The idea is that when they leave, they will take with them better manners, more effective coping skills and some common sense about living "on the outside."

74   Fields and Tulman hoped Glen Mills' vocational program would attract Willie to a skilled trade—small-engine repair, optics, plumbing, anything. Willie signed up for the journalism shop—a dozen kids who spent a few hours a day in a stuffy third-floor room with a single old typewriter and two large tables where they wrote stories longhand. From that office came The Battling Bulletin, the school's 32-page monthly tabloid.

75   Willie got his first byline in the May 1987 edition, a three-paragraph story about the school's track team winning a 200-meter relay. For the first time in his life, Willie had seen his name linked to an accomplishment. Although work on his own story had slowed as he spent more time in the journalism shop, he had decided to limit his running to run-on sentences.

76   Then, abruptly, Willie's past caught up with him. Glen Mills' confrontational

approach collided with his fear of physical abuse. One evening last June, when confronted by a counselor about some mischief, Willie mouthed off. The counselor grabbed and pushed him. Willie resolved to run at the first chance he got. A couple of days later, while on leave to visit Fields in Alexandria for a therapy session, Willie sneaked out the side door during a lunch stop at a McDonald's.

77   Two days later, he was picked up by D.C. police. A juvenile judge decided the only way to keep Willie from running was to put him back behind bars.

78   Oak Hill was the same place Willie had left a month earlier. Fields and Tulman were tormented that Willie, finally showing signs of promise, was back at an institution where the principal mental challenge then provided to the kids was swatting a ping-pong ball.

79   In spite of the trouble at Glen Mills, Willie couldn't forget his excitement at seeing his byline in the newspaper. During a therapy session one day, he told Fields that he wanted to start a newspaper for the kids in the D.C. detention system. Fields agreed to help him. Willie charmed an Oak Hill office clerk into letting him peck out stories on a word processor. Scraping together clips from local newspapers, his own stories, articles by Tulman and Fields and an occasional poem by other kids at Oak Hill, Willie published a total of three editions of the Oak Leaf News last August, September and October.

80   The Oct. 1 Oak Leaf News was the last edition. The editor was leaving. Fields and Tulman's efforts had convinced the court to reassign Willie to the Sasha Bruce House, a highly regarded drug rehabilitation center in D.C. that employs intensive therapy and counseling.

81   On Monday, Oct. 5, Willie left the Sasha Bruce House at 9 A.M. for a 10 A.M. appointment with Rona Fields in Alexandria. By 10:30 A.M., Fields figured more was amiss than Willie getting stuck inside the Metro turnstile without a fare, as he had before. Willie was gone again.

82   Willie returned to the Sasha Bruce House the same night. Next morning, all his privileges were denied. First chance he got, he walked out again, but he came back that night. He did that every day that week. He wasn't writing his book. He seemed to be regressing at the very moment when he'd been granted the promise of freedom. "Willie's experience of freedom was weird," says Fields. "He didn't know himself in freedom. He didn't know what to do with it. This lad shoots himself in the foot every time he climbs high enough to see the top of the mountain."

83   On Wednesday, Oct. 14, a D.C. juvenile judge warned Willie that if he ran one more time, he was going back to Oak Hill. Willie was subdued. Fields met with him at the Sasha Bruce House and couldn't get him to talk. She suggested they take her dog Shayna for a walk. Willie loved Shayna. He'd played with the collie-like mutt often at Fields' office. As they strolled along the sidewalk, Shayna bolted from her leash into the middle of the road and pounced on a pigeon, breaking its wing. Willie stood horrified.

84 *That's the nature of dogs to go after smaller animals but the sight of her mouth on that little pigeon shocked me. At that moment all I could think was that I didn't know Shayna could do that. I thought of her as playful and fun but when I saw what she did to the little bird I had to think again. Yesterday morning when I stood in court I knew that I, Willie Givens am neither all good or all bad, or all right or all wrong. Nor am I always a juvenile Delinquent. I am all of these and none of these. And then I saw that all other living creatures are all of these things and none of these things, too.*

85 Fields recognized that Willie was at a critical juncture. He'd fallen again into his "old script," the one written for him early in life that said he was destined to be a failure. But now, with his writing, he'd also seen the possibilities of a different outcome to "Willie's Story."

86 Willie said he'd stick with the rehabilitation program. After several days of good behavior, he sat down with the counselors and his mother—who came at their request—to discuss foster care for Willie should he graduate from the Sasha Bruce House. He hadn't seen his mother in two years. There was no doubt in his mind she wanted nothing to do with him, but he consented to the meeting. His mother's attitude toward Willie had changed little.

87 "I'm not going to have him coming back with me with the judge calling my house all hours of the night," she said soon after that. "Can't nobody help you until you make up your mind to help yourself first." The day after the meeting with his mother, Willie ran away again.

88 *I want to write a newspape article about my life at Oak Hill and Receiving Home so my mother will [read] it where every she is. I want her to see it and Know how I feel and want her to regret what she did to me. It's almost as though I'm just the ball on a highli paddle and she hits me in what every direction she want. No matter how she sends me away I always come back.*

My relation with my mother is like a very long song after each verse you sing the chorus again. only song are usually pretty and what happens between her and me is very ugly.

89 On a rainy October afternoon shortly after that meeting between Willie and his mother, Rona Fields sat at her desk, unable to get Willie off her mind. Had she done enough for him? Had she done too much? All she knew was that Willie had run again from a life in which he's almost never had a home that provided for the needs that any child—even those in the poorest and most violent societies she'd studied—has a right to expect. During the next 10 days, Willie stayed on the streets. He would call Fields and tell her he wanted to come back. She'd tell him to meet her somewhere. He'd never show up.

90 "Willie's Story" isn't finished yet, but the page has turned to a new chapter.

Legally, Willie became an adult on his 18th birthday last Nov. 4, while still on the run. A week later, he showed up in the lobby of The Washington Post to talk briefly to this reporter, who advised that he turn himself in. Willie asked to use the pay phones in the lobby. He reached Joe Tulman, his lawyer, but again didn't like hearing he had to turn himself in. He hung up and slipped upstairs, where he was caught rifling a purse. Arrested and charged with misdemeanor theft, Willie was given a hearing date for a month later. Without explanation, he was released by the judge.

91   On the night of last November's blizzard, Fields got a call from Willie. He was out on the streets with nowhere to go. Would she come and get him? Fields said she couldn't drive in the mounting snow. She told Willie to make his way to his girlfriend's house in Northeast. But he never showed up there. For six months, he stayed on the streets, slept wherever he could—at the homes of friends, at missions for the homeless—survived however he knows. Three weeks ago, he was picked up by the police and placed in custody.

92   What will happen to an adult who has been shortchanged on emotion and education all his life? Where can he live a useful life when he has never learned to be responsible for his future? Studies indicate that more than one third of the juvenile delinquents incarcerated at correctional facilities such as Oak Hill end up in prison as adults. Locating homes for the Willies of this world has never been the justice system's priority. It is easier to find a jail cell for an adult offender than it is to find a loving adult who will take on an emotionally damaged teen-ager. "That's just the reality of it," says Tulman.

93 I *want my life to be very different. I wood like to be home and that mean not in and institution that has and iron gate that locks me in. Some where I can go and go away from. And maybe some people I love and oh love me. That mean's they will care about me and what happens to me. I will care about how they feel. Because when people love each other and live together they want to make each other happy healthy and good.*

☐ Discovering Meaning and Technique

1. What seems to be the thesis (the main point) of the selection?

2. What is Oldenburg's attitude toward Willie Givens?

3. Why did the therapist encourage Willie to write his autobiography?

4. Why does Oldenburg include excerpts from the autobiography? What does he accomplish with this technique?

5. What is the effect of Willie's language problems on a reader?

6. Why does Willie run away from Glen Mills, a facility with no guards or bars?

7. What seems to be the source of Willie's need to run?

8. Comment on the amount of money required to house juveniles in residential facilities and psychiatric hospitals.

☐ Writing Suggestions

1. Who is primarily responsible for Willie Givens's troubles? His mother? His stepfather? The social workers? Society? Willie himself? Or some combination?

2. In paragraph 92, Oldenburg asks, "What will happen to an adult who has been shortchanged on emotion and education all his life? Where can he live a useful life when he has never learned to be responsible for his future?" Write a composition answering these questions.

3. Do you think troubled children can be helped by writing autobiographies or engaging in some other art form, such as music, dance, or painting?

4. Oldenburg says that Willie "is writing a book in an attempt to rewrite his future." Predict the story of Willie Givens's life (or any part of it) from here forward.

5. It is easy to blame Willie's mother for his plight. We should remember, however, that she is the product of her own childhood and her own misfortunes. If Willie's mother wrote her autobiography, how might it read?

6. In paragraph 92, Oldenburg says, "Studies indicate that more than one third of the juvenile delinquents incarcerated at correctional facilities such as Oak Hill end up in prison as adults." In the library, research this problem and possible solutions. Report your findings.

THE LIVES OF TEENAGE MOTHERS

☐ ELIZABETH MAREK

1 At 2:30 on a Thursday afternoon in June, when most teenagers, done with school for the day, are hanging out with their friends, the girls I have come to meet are seated in a small office, reaching for cookies with one hand as they settle

their babies on their laps with the other. We are at the Kingsbridge Heights Community Center in the Bronx. The center sits at the crossroads of several worlds. The spacious homes of Riverdale dot the rolling green hills to the west; to the south rise the housing projects that cast their shadow on the lower-middle-class single-family homes and the shops which line the blocks closest to the center. The Teen Parenting Program, which provides counseling, education, and health care to teenage parents and soon-to-be parents throughout the Bronx, was started in 1986 with a group of girls from the projects. Once a week the girls in the program, along with their babies and sometimes their boyfriends, crowd into a simply furnished room to drink Coke, munch on snacks, and talk about the difficulties of being a teenage parent.

2   On this particular Thursday, I have come too. For years I've read about the "problem of teenage parenthood"—children having children. In New York City, teen pregnancies make up 15 percent of all pregnancies and account for more than 13,000 births each year. Sociologists and psychologists speculate about social pressures and individual motivation. President George Bush, in his inaugural address, spoke of the need to help young women "who are about to become mothers of children they can't care for and might not love."

3   But despite the concern voiced by others, we've heard very little from the young women themselves. Are they ignorant about birth control, or are they choosing to get pregnant? What are the conditions of loneliness, poverty, and hopelessness in which having a baby might make sense? What happens to these girls and their babies? How does having a baby affect their lives? Where do the fathers fit in?

4   I've come to Kingsbridge because I want to get to know the mothers, most of whom are not much younger than I am. Sophie-Louise, the social worker in charge of the group, introduces me, and the room falls silent. "Well," she laughs, "here we are. Ask away." Looking at the girls, as they tug at a baby's diaper or straighten a barrette, I am not sure where to begin.

5   "Tell me what it's like, having a baby at your age," I ask at last. As if on cue, all heads turn toward Janelle, a heavyset black girl with short, blown-straight hair, who sits in an overstuffed chair with her three-month-old son, Marc, draped across her lap. The baby, dressed in a pale green sleeper embroidered with a blue bunny, is drooling onto her stylish black skirt. She is eating a chocolate cookie and begins to talk about the logistical problems involved in getting to and from high school with an infant. She has just started summer school to make up credits from the classes she missed during her pregnancy. She is seventeen.

6   "Let's see," she begins. "I get myself up and get the baby up and get myself dressed and get the baby dressed, get my books, get the baby's bag, get the stroller . . ." She laughs. "Do you know how hard it is to get a stroller on the bus? That first day of school, I thought I wasn't going to make it."

7   Newspaper accounts of teen pregnancy tend to dwell on girls from welfare

families. Janelle, however, is the daughter of a retired postal-service clerk and grew up in a small, one-family house in a lower-middle-class neighborhood in the North Bronx. Her childhood was relatively secure: her parents were together and could afford to send her to a Catholic school, where she made friends, got good grades, and dreamed about what she would be when she grew up. "I was gonna finish high school," she says. "Gonna go on to college, like my cousins did. I wanted to get married and have a baby someday, but, really, not now. All through high school I never cut classes, hardly was sick even . . ."

8   The turning point came when Janelle was fifteen and her parents divorced. "When my parents split, my family just fell apart. My mother only wanted my little sister, so she took her, and then my older sister, she left, too, so it was just me and my father all alone in the house." Feeling unwanted and unloved, Janelle moved into a room in the basement, and her father took over the upstairs. Sometimes they met at breakfast, but other times Janelle went for days without seeing him. "So I started hanging out with a bad bunch of kids," she says, "and cutting classes—I went through an entire year and only got three credits. And then I got pregnant and dropped out." She laughs bitterly. "One thing they don't teach you in high school is how to get a stroller on the bus."

9   Lynda, at twenty the mother of a three-year-old girl, nods sympathetically. She is a pretty, young Hispanic woman with long hair pulled away from her face in a ponytail. Three weeks earlier she had graduated from high school, having gone to classes in the evening and worked during the day as a cashier in a small store in Manhattan. Her daughter, Danielle, a small child with blonde hair and a dirty face, walks unsmiling around the edge of the room. There is little interaction between mother and daughter. They neither look at nor speak to each other.

10   Lynda's family, like Janelle's, could be classified as lower middle class. Unlike Janelle's, Lynda's parents are strict Roman Catholics. On the day Lynda told her father that she was pregnant, he left home. "I guess it was either that or throw me out," she says. A few months later he moved back, but even now, although he allows her to live at home, she feels that he has not forgiven her. Lynda believes that her father, having worked hard to provide the best for her and her siblings, took her pregnancy as a slap in the face.

11   Leaning back in the circle of her boyfriend's arms, Lynda's large black eyes are ringed with dark circles. "My mother still talked to me, like, at the table, pass the salt and stuff. I think my father blamed her—'If you had brought her up right, this wouldn't have happened.' "

12   Janelle nods. "My father blamed my mother, too. I don't understand that, though, because he didn't even know that I was pregnant. Now he thinks it's my fault that he didn't know, and I think it's his fault. He was always telling me to stay downstairs, and we never talked. We never did anything. Now all he does is compare me to his sister's children, who are much older. They got jobs, finished college, and he says you make me look so bad, having babies,

dropping out of school. But he didn't want to come back to my mother, he didn't want to try to help me. It was all just, 'Don't make me look bad. Don't make me look bad.' "

13   "So what did he do when he found out you were pregnant?" asks Lynda.

14   "He never found out! Not until I came home from the hospital. He found out when the baby was a week old."

15   Lynda's boyfriend, Tony, a construction worker in his early thirties, joins the discussion. "Maybe it's more that he didn't want to know. He wanted to keep it from himself." Tony is not Danielle's father, although he too was a teenage parent and has two boys of his own. He and Lynda have been going out for almost a year. "You know the parents, they blame themselves," he says. "Like maybe they did something wrong with your upbringing."

16   Janelle lets out her breath in a snort. "Yeah, well now he tells all his friends, 'She's so sneaky.' But I think that if he was really interested, he would have known. I mean, the last day, the day that I gave birth, he went out to the store and said, 'I'll be right back.' And I said, 'Fine, but I won't be here.' But he didn't hear me."

17   Later, riding home on the subway, I wonder whether, in part, Janelle got pregnant to get her father's attention. Or, perhaps, as one social worker I spoke with earlier suggested, part of the motivation for teenage girls to have babies is a wish to be reborn themselves, to re-create themselves as children, so they can get the love and attention they feel they were denied.

18   Nine girls, their babies, and a few of their boyfriends are officially enrolled in Sophie-Louise's group, but since the school year ended, only Janelle and Lynda have been coming regularly. The others, Sophie-Louise explains, have drifted away—to the beach, to parties—or are staying home, too overwhelmed by their lives as mothers to make the trip to the center. Janelle and Lynda represent what Sophie-Louise calls the "cream of the crop"; the only ones able to structure their lives sufficiently to attend a regular weekly meeting. The others fade in and out.

19   At the next meeting, I notice that Lynda's boyfriend is missing. Sophie-Louise explains to me privately that Tony and Lynda have been having problems lately. Two new people are present, however: Janelle's boyfriend, Eron, and a new girl, April, a sad-looking black teenager, who brings her five-month-old daughter. April is thin, her ribs jut out below the orange halter top she wears. In contrast to the Calvin Klein jeans Lynda wears, April's jeans are frayed and stained. She sits with her shoulders hunched, as though shielding herself from the vagaries of life. Glancing up, she notices my tape recorder on the table, and she stares at me for a moment before busying herself with the baby on her lap. The baby's dark eyes flicker across her mother's face, but neither of them registers a smile. Sophie-Louise has told me a few facts about April's life: She is the oldest child and lives with her mother, her two siblings, and her baby in a two-room apartment in a housing project in the East Bronx. Seemingly the least

equipped to care for an infant, April appears to have been the most determined to have a baby: Kisha was the result of her third pregnancy, the other two having ended in abortions.

20   As the meeting starts, Janelle reaches across the table with one hand to grab some potato chips, while her other hand effortlessly settles baby Marc in a sitting position on her leg. April, sitting alone at the far end of the couch, shakes off Sophie-Louise's offer of a Coke and, grabbing a handful of Cheez Doodles, drapes a towel over her shoulder so that Kisha can nurse quietly at her breast. April seems to hover on the periphery of the discussion, offering tangential comments or staring fixedly at a spot on the wall. Sophie-Louise finds some rubber cows for Danielle to play with, but the little girl is more interested in building towers of checkers in the corner and knocking them down with excited squeals. Over the din, I ask the girls whether they had planned their pregnancies, and how they felt when they discovered they were pregnant.

21   As usual, Janelle begins. "At first, you know, I was real scared. I didn't want to have the baby," she says, smoothing her hand over Marc's diaper. "I was dead set against it. 'Cause you know, I'm just seventeen, and I didn't want to have a baby. I wanted to still go out and have fun with my friends and stuff. But now, you know, it's been three months, and I'm used to it." She pauses. "Of course, I haven't had too much time to myself. Just twice, in three months: I counted it. Twice. The father's family took care of him for a whole day. I couldn't believe it. I was outside and everything was so much fun. But I like being a mom now. I can handle it. All my friends keep telling me, 'Janelle, you're in a closet!' But I'm not in no closet. And if I am, well, they should leave me alone. It's fun in this closet now that I know what I'm doing and everything."

22   Lynda's mother takes care of Danielle during the day, when she is at work, and again in the evenings, when she attends classes. But Lynda also complains about a lack of freedom. "My mom says, 'Now you are a mother, you have responsibilities.' She will babysit when I go to work or to school, but otherwise, anywhere I go, Danielle goes."

23   "Did either of you ever think about having an abortion?" I ask.

24   "Abortion," muses Janelle. "Well, by the time I knew I was pregnant, I was already six months pregnant."

25   I wonder whether she has misspoken. Surely she can't mean that she had a baby growing inside her for six months before she was aware of its presence. But, shaking her head, she assures me that it was six months.

26   "Before that, I had no idea," she says.

27   Lynda backs her up. "By the time I knew I was pregnant, I was five months."

28   "Maybe," Sophie-Louise says, "it goes back to what we talked about before. Not knowing because you really didn't want to know."

29   Lynda is adamant. "No. There was no way I could know. I still had my regular monthly period until I was five months, and that's when I found out. And by then I didn't have much choice because they told me they only did

abortions until twelve weeks, and I was way past that. And besides, I don't believe in doing abortions at five months. They say that at three months the baby is still not really formed into a baby, but after that the baby starts forming, and then I feel that it's killing . . ."

30   April reaches down to straighten Kisha's dress. She speaks for the first time, her voice so soft and low that the rest of us have to strain to hear her. "I didn't know I was pregnant until I was three months. I jumped in a pool and felt something move inside me, and that's when I knew." She pulls her daughter to a sitting position on her lap, pushing a Cheez Doodle into the baby's flaccid mouth.

31   Janelle pauses and then says quietly, "I don't think I knew, but then I wonder. Maybe somewhere in me I knew, but it was like I was saying, no, I'm not pregnant, I'm not pregnant . . . I was living day-to-day, one day at a time. I would just get up in the morning and do what I needed to do, and not think about it."

32   As the girls speak, their words reflect their sense of powerlessness. Even their bodies rebel, growing alien creatures without their knowledge, the awareness of their pregnancy dawning only after the possibility for abortion has passed. Does this reflect a yearning for a child? Or is it only a child's way of coping with something too terrifying to acknowledge?

33   Lynda glances at Danielle, who is still amusing herself with the checkers. She brings the group back to the abortion question. "I think that the girl should just make up her own mind, and then that's it," she says. "Because even if you don't let your boyfriend go, you are still going to get left."

34   "What do you mean?" Sophie-Louise asks. Like many working mothers, Lynda has an air of perpetual exhaustion. "Sometimes, if you're in love with a guy, and 'I love you' comes up, that's the one thing that always makes you weak. You say, 'Oh, I love you too.' But then it's time for you both to sit down and talk about the situation, you know, after you say, 'Well, I'm pregnant,' and he says, 'Oh, you are?' and he gets happy and everything. This happened to me. And I said, 'I want an abortion.' Then the brainwash would begin, the 'I love you and it's our baby and I'll give you support.' It was like, if I had an abortion, then I didn't love him. I feel that the woman should just make up her own mind, make her own decision. But he said, 'Oh, I love you, and I'll do this for you, I'll do that for you, and our baby will have this, and our baby will have that.' Now she's two and a half years old, and all he ever got her was a big box of Pampers and socks and T-shirts and $20 and that was it." Suddenly, the resentment in her voice changes to wistfulness. "She's two and a half. And he was going to buy her a baby crib and a bassinet and clothes. Everything . . ."

35   I have heard stories like this from other girls I talked with and from social workers as well. One fifteen-year-old mother told me that her boyfriend said that if she really loved him, she would have his baby. Despite her mother's

urging, she decided against having an abortion. But by the time the baby was born, she and her boyfriend had broken up, and he was expecting another child by another girl in her school. As Sophie-Louise puts it, the guys like to have three or four "pots on different stoves" at the same time—visible proof of their virility.

36   Sophie-Louise turns to Eron, Janelle's boyfriend. He is seventeen and works two jobs, one in a garage and the other as an attendant at Rye Playland. She asks him how he felt when he found out that Janelle was pregnant. He laughs. "I was scared."

37   "More scared than me!" Janelle adds. "I mean, you were chicken!" "Well my life was changing, too," says Eron. "I mean, I know guys who just say, oh no, a baby, and then walk off, but I'm not that type of person. My father was never there for me when I was little, so, you know, I don't want that to happen to my son. I don't want him to grow up and hate me and all that. I want to have somebody to love me. Even if me and Janelle don't end up together, I got him to remind me of her."

38   It interests me that Eron wants the baby as someone to love him. When I ask the girls what they think of this, April rejoins the discussion. Without raising her eyes from her baby, she says, "When my boyfriend found out I was pregnant, he just played it off. He would always play at my stomach, sort of punch me in the stomach.

39   "Now I don't even let him see her anymore. All he wants to do is play with her, and then give her back when it's time for changing."

40   "That's tough," Sophie-Louise says. "It takes two to make a baby, but then one of the two doesn't want any of the responsibility. Do you think you can talk to him about it?"

41   "I don't want to," April says. "I don't even want him to see her. Ever since I was pregnant, he kept saying that he was going to get me some stuff. He lied to his mother, saying that he was going to get me a carriage for the baby, but he didn't get me nothing. I had to do it all. And then I found out that he had some kind of drug addict, some girl in his house, some Puerto Rican girl, and his mother went on vacation and she came back and seen all these suitcases in her room, and she seen this Puerto Rican girl in the house with him. They just did it, right there."

42   As she clutches Kisha to her breast, I see how absorbed they are in each other. With no job, no boyfriend, nothing to fill her days, the baby is her life. Yet both mother and daughter seem drained.

43   Janelle looks concerned. "But aren't you worried that she might grow up without having a relationship with her father?"

44   "Well, I don't even want to see her father anymore," April says. "Her father is crazy! He busted my window one time. I tell you about that? He wanted to see the baby so bad and he was drunk one night, four-thirty in the morning, and he came banging on my door, saying, 'I'm not going nowhere until I see

my baby.' So then I brought the baby into my mother's room, because he had cracked the window with a rock and he was making a lot of noise. And then he just left. . . . Besides, I don't want him taking her to his house, 'cause his mother is a crackhead."

45   April falls silent. Sophie-Louise asks her whether her role in her own family has changed since she got pregnant.

46   "Oh yeah," April says. "Now, my mother thinks that I have to do everything. You know, when I was pregnant, she tried to make me do more than I was supposed to, more than I did before I was pregnant. Now she says, 'You're no more teenager. You're an adult.' But before that, before I had the baby, I wasn't classified as no adult. So what makes us having a baby be an adult?"

47   During the next session, the last before the August recess, there is a small "graduation" party for Eron. He feels confident about passing his summer-school course, and when he does, he will officially become a high-school graduate. After the cake is cut and the group settles down, the talk turns to peer pressure. Sophie-Louise has been telling the story of a fourteen-year-old girl she counseled at a local high school. Although the girl had been taught about birth control and abortion and warned about the difficulties facing teen mothers, she became pregnant midway through eighth grade. Speaking with the girl later, Sophie-Louise asked her why, after all they had talked about, had she let this happen. "I don't know," she said. "All my friends have babies. I was beginning to wonder what was wrong with me that I didn't have one too."

48   The girls in the group laugh at the story. "I don't know about her," Janelle says, "but I knew that seventeen was too young to have a baby. None of my friends have babies. My sister, she just had a baby . . . but it wasn't like I wanted to get pregnant."

49   "Were you using birth control?" I ask.

50   Janelle's cheeks flush.

51   "I gotta tell you," she says. "I never used birth control. I mean, now I do, but before, well, I just never thought I would get pregnant. I was like, that can't happen to me. I thought that only happened to the bad girls across town. Who do drugs and stuff. But I didn't do none of that, so I thought I was safe. You know, like when you think it just can't happen to you. To other people yes, but not to you."

52   A social worker I spoke with said that most of the girls use the chance method. And each month that they don't get pregnant reinforces their belief that they are safe.

53   The existence of these myths may reflect denial rather than ignorance. As the girls talk, I begin to see why the idea of having a baby might be compelling. There is a sense of loneliness eased, of purpose granted, of a glimmering of hope.

54   Janelle smiles. "But now that I am a mother, I do enjoy it. I mean, he

keeps me company all the time, so I never have to be bored or lonely. He's my friend, this little guy. He keeps me so busy that I never have time to get into trouble. And before, I never really had a reason to get up in the morning, to go to school, whatever. But now, because of him, I do."

55   In Janelle's words, I hear the unspoken wish that, through the baby, the mothers may get a second chance at childhood, that in loving their babies they may almost be loving themselves.

56   Sophie-Louise asks whether, perhaps, Janelle had some of those thoughts before getting pregnant, whether on some level part of the reason that she did not use birth control was because somewhere inside her she wished for a baby.

57   Janelle pauses to consider the question. "Well, I don't know. Maybe. You know, I was lonely. My parents had split, and I really didn't have anyone, just me and my father together in the house."

58   Sophie-Louise turns to April. Despite the fact that Kisha was the result of her third pregnancy, April is unwilling to admit that she had wanted the baby. "It was an accident," she insists. "I mean, I said that this isn't going to happen to me. I was using all kinds of protection. Most times I even had him use protection."

59   Sophie-Louise seems surprised. "You were using protection?" she asks. "What kind?"

60   Indignantly, April answers, "Well, I was taking the pill. I mean, I wasn't taking it all the time, but I was taking it. But I missed a couple of days, I guess. I think I took it on the day before my birthday, but not on my birthday, I don't think . . ."

61   "So for you it really was an accident," I say. I am surprised when she contradicts me.

62   "No. I wouldn't really say it was an accident. See, all the other times I got pregnant, my mother made me get rid of it. So I guess part of it was revenge against my mother, like I was gonna get pregnant but not let her know until she couldn't do nothing."

63   "Not with me," says Lynda. "With me it was just a pure accident. Just a pure accident. I wanted to get an abortion. I said that I was going to have one. But my boyfriend and my parents, my father especially . . . they wanted me to have it. That's when the brainwash began."

64   It occurs to me that I've been looking for a motivation, a reason why these girls, and others like them, might *choose* to become pregnant. But the more I listen, the more I wonder whether the question of choice is relevant. In all their stories, I hear again and again how little volition these girls feel they have, how little control over the events of their lives. The deadline for school admission passes and April shrugs. Sophie-Louise makes an appointment for Lynda with a job counselor, but Lynda forgets to go. Janelle knows about birth control but doesn't believe "it" will happen to her. Sophie-Louise told me once that these girls exert no more control over their lives than a "leaf falling

from a tree." Perhaps having a baby is less a question of ignorance or choice than one of inevitability. Once a girl is sexually active, it is not *having* a baby that requires choice and conscious action, but *not* having one.

65   Eron shifts in his chair. "You know, all this talk about we didn't want to have the baby, or it was an accident, or whatever . . . I just think it's a waste of time. I mean, now we have the baby. The question is, what are we going to do now?"

66   Sophie-Louise asks him what he means, and he explains that the cycle of babies having babies, single parents raising single parents, has haunted him as it has haunted most of the teens in the room, and that he feels it can end with them, but only if they are willing to face the realities of their situation. "My father was never there when I was little" he says, "but I don't want that to happen to my son. I don't want him to grow up and hate me and all that . . . That's why I'm going to finish school and do whatever I need to do."

67   His eyes shine as he speaks of his ambition, but he looks down shyly, as if afraid that someone will mock him. Janelle, however, backs him up with pride and speaks of her own ambition to become a social worker. "It's so easy to go on welfare," she says. "You just sit home and cash a check. But I'm not going to get on welfare, 'cause it makes you lazy. It's addictive."

68   "I couldn't do that," Eron says. "I'm the kind of person who needs to work." But then the realities of fatherhood seem to descend upon him. "I don't know, though. See, 'cause with a baby, it takes all the money that you don't even have . . ."

69   At the end of the session, the discussion shifts back to the problems that the girls will encounter when they return to school in the fall. Janelle is telling April that summer school really wasn't so bad. "It was hard leaving him at first," she says, "but I tried not to think about it. And I didn't think about it, because the classes were hard. And I was usually really tired. But I was happy. I just thought about the work, and the time flew by, and I was picking up the baby before I knew it."

70   Sophie-Louise presses April to consider how she will feel when she is separated from her daughter for the first time. "Have you thought at all about what it's going to be like?" Sophie-Louise asks. "How it's going to feel, emotionally, to be separated?"

71   April ignores her at first, and then shakes her head no. Sophie-Louise encourages her, suggesting she might feel relief or worry or sadness, but April clearly does not want to pursue the issue. Finally, in frustration, April says, "Look, I haven't thought about it yet. I haven't thought about it because it hasn't happened."

72   With that, the session ends. Having missed the deadline for entrance to summer school, April stays behind to talk to Sophie-Louise about starting a diploma-geared class in the fall. Danielle tugs at Lynda's arm, asking whether they can finally go to the zoo as she promised. I hear Eron and Janelle bickering about whose turn it is to buy diapers. And I head down the steep hill to the subway that will take me back downtown.

☐ Discovering Meaning and Technique

1. Why does Elizabeth Marek want to talk to the teenage mothers?

2. What are some of the family problems that preceded the pregnancies?

3. What are some of the family problems that resulted from the pregnancies?

4. What are the attitudes of the girls toward their children? Toward abortion?

5. How stable are the girls' relationships with the fathers of their children?

6. According to Marek, which theories have been suggested to explain teenage pregnancy?

☐ Writing Suggestions

1. Why do you think teenagers "become mothers of children they can't care for and might not love"?

2. What can society do about the problem of teenage mothers?

3. Write a scenario describing a typical day in the life of a teenage mother.

4. Discuss the responsibility of the fathers of children born out of wedlock.

5. Should birth control devices be available to anyone of any age, free of charge?

6. Is sex education in the public schools adequate?

A CAPTIVE STATE

☐ JONATHAN KOZOL

1 Since 1980 homelessness has changed its character. What was once a theater of the grotesque (bag ladies in Grand Central Station, winos sleeping in the dusty sun outside the Greyhound station in El Paso) has grown into the common misery of millions.

2   "This is a new population," said a homeless advocate in Massachusetts. "Many are people who were working all their lives. When they lose their jobs they lose their homes. When they lose their homes they start to lose their families too."

3   Even in New York City, with its permanent population of the long-term unemployed, 50 percent of individuals served at city shelters during 1984 were there for the first time. The same percentage holds throughout the nation.

4   The chilling fact, from any point of view, is that small children have become the fastest-growing sector of the homeless. At the time of writing there are 28,000 homeless people in emergency shelters in the city of New York. An additional 40,000 are believed to be unsheltered citywide. Of those who are sheltered, about 10,000 are homeless individuals. The remaining 18,000 are parents and children in almost 5,000 families. The average homeless family includes a parent with two or three children. The average child is six years old, the average parent twenty-seven.

5   In Massachusetts, three fourths of all homeless people are now children and their parents. In certain parts of Massachusetts (Plymouth, Attleboro, and Northampton) 90 to 95 percent of those who have no homes are families with children.

6   Homeless people are poor people. Four out of ten poor people in America are children, though children make up only one fourth of our population. The number of children living in poverty has grown to 14 million—an increase of 3 million over 1968—while welfare benefits to families with children have declined one third.

7   Seven hundred thousand poor children, of whom 100,000 have no health insurance, live in New York City. Approximately 20 percent of New York City's children lived in poverty in 1970, 33 percent in 1980, over 40 percent by 1982.

8 *Where are these people?*

9 We have seen that they are in midtown Manhattan. They are also in the streets of Phoenix, Salt Lake City, Philadelphia, San Antonio, Miami, and St. Paul. They are in the Steel Belt. They are in the Sun Belt. They are in Kansas City and Seattle. They are in the heartland of America.

10   In Denver, where evictions rose 800 percent in 1982, hundreds of families were locked on waiting lists for public housing. Many were forced to live in shelters or the streets. In Cleveland, in one classic situation, the loss of a home precipitated by the layoffs in a nearby plant led to the dissolution of a family: the adolescent daughter put in foster care, the wife and younger children ending up on welfare, the husband landing in a public shelter when he wasn't sleeping underneath a bridge. Cleveland was obliged to open shelters and soup kitchens in blue-collar neighborhoods that housed traditional white ethnic populations.

11   The *Milwaukee Journal* wrote: "The homeless in our midst are no longer mainly urban hobos and bag ladies. In recent months, joblessness has pushed heretofore self-reliant families into this subculture." In Michigan, in 1982, the loss of jobs in heavy industry forced Governor Milliken to declare "a state of human emergency"—a declaration other governors may be forced to contemplate by 1988.

12   As an easterner, I had at first assumed that most of these families must be

urban, nonwhite, unemployable—perhaps a great deal like the ghetto families I have worked with for much of my life. In 1985, however, I was given an opportunity to visit in over 50 cities and in almost every region of the nation. My hosts were governors and other local politicians, leaders of industry, organizers of the working poor, leaders and advocates of those who recently had joined the unemployed, teachers, school board members, farmers, bankers, owners of local stores. Often they were people who had never met each other and had never even been in the same room with one another, even though they lived in the same towns and cities. They had come together now out of their shared concern over the growth of poverty, the transformation of the labor market, and the rising numbers of those people who no longer could find work at all.

13   I was invited, in most cases, to address the problems of the public schools. Often, however, education issues became overshadowed by more pressing matters. For many poorly educated people, literacy problems proved of little urgency when they were threatened with the loss of work and loss of home. In a depressed industrial town in Pennsylvania, Lutheran church leaders spoke of the loss of several hundred jobs as truck and auto manufacture left the area and families saw their savings dwindle and their unemployment benefits and pensions disappear while rents rose, food prices climbed, and federal benefits declined.

14   "Yes, there are new jobs," a minister said. "There's a new McDonald's and a Burger King. You can take home $450 in a month from jobs like that. That might barely pay the rent. What do you do if somebody gets sick? What do you do for food and clothes? These may be good jobs for a teenager. Can you ask a thirty-year-old man who's worked for G.M. since he was eighteen to keep his wife and kids alive on jobs like that? There are jobs cleaning rooms in the hotel you're staying at. Can you expect a single mother with three kids to hold her life together with that kind of work? All you hear about these days are so-called service jobs—it makes me wonder where America is going. If we aren't producing anything of value, will we keep our nation going on hamburger stands? Who is all this 'service' for, if no one's got a real job making something of real worth?"

15   In Oklahoma, Arkansas and Texas I met heads of families who had been, only a year or two before, owners of farms, employees of petroleum firms, shopkeepers who supplied the farmers and the oil workers. They had lost their farms, their jobs, their stores. Bankers in Oklahoma City spoke about the rising number of foreclosures. "Oil and agriculture—those are everything for people here. Both are dying. Where will these people go after their farms are boarded and their restaurants and barbershops and hardware stores have been shut down?"

16   The answers were seen in Phoenix and Los Angeles, where the shelters overflowed and people slept in huge encampments on the edges of the seamy areas of town. In one city homeless families lived in caves. I went out to visit. I had never seen a family living in a cave before.

17   In Portland, Oregon, the governor told me of some counties in which

unemployment caused by the declining lumber industry had climbed above 30 percent. Where did the lumber workers go? I met some of them the same night in a homeless shelter by the Burnside Bridge. A pregnant woman and her husband spoke to me while waiting for the soup line to be formed. "We had good work until last year. Since then we've had no home. Our kids were put in foster care." They had been sleeping on a plywood plank supported by the girders of the bridge. The traffic was two feet above their heads.

18   "The sound of the trucks puts me to sleep at night," she said. I learned that even makeshift housing space under the bridge was growing scarce.

19   In San Antonio I met a father with two boys who had been sleeping for four months next to the highway not far from the Hyatt Regency Hotel. He sold blood plasma twice a week to buy food for his kids. "They draw my blood, put it in a centrifuge, take the white cells, and inject the red cells back into my arm." If he showed up four weeks straight he got a bonus. In a good month he made $100. "The blood places," he told me, "poor people call them 'stab labs.' They're all over." He showed me a card he carried listing stab labs, with phone numbers and addresses, in a dozen cities. He had been an auto worker in Detroit. When he lost his job his wife became depressed and since was hospitalized. He had developed crippling asthma—"from the panic and the tension, I believe." He had thought mistakenly that San Antonio might offer health and labor and cheap housing that were not available in Michigan.

20   In Miami I met a woman, thirty-five years old, from Boston. She had attended Girls' Latin, the same high school that my mother had attended. After graduation she had gone to college and had worked for many years until she was the victim of a throat disease that led to complications that wiped out her savings, forced her to lose her home, ended her marriage, and at last compelled her to give up her kids. She'd moved to Miami hoping it would help her health but couldn't cope with illness, loss of family, loss of home—and now was sleeping on Miami Beach.

21   She had a tube in her stomach to bypass her damaged throat. At a shelter run by Catholic brothers she would pulverize the food, mix it with water, and inject the liquid mix into her tube.

22   In New York I spoke with Robert Hayes, counsel to the National Coalition for the Homeless. Hayes and his co-workers said that three fourths of the newly homeless in America are families with children.

23   In Washington, D.C., in late September 1986, I spent an afternoon with the director of a shelter, Sandy Brawders, one of those saints and martyrs of whom Robert Hayes has said, only half-jokingly, the homeless movement is primarily composed. ("There are the saints," he says, "and then there are the martyrs who have to put up with the saints.") Sandy told me that the homeless population was exploding in the District; the largest growth in numbers was among young children and their parents.

24   Four months later, the *Washington Post* reported that the number of home-

less families in the District had increased 500 percent in just one year and that there were 12,000 people on a waiting list for public housing, with a waiting period of more than seven years.

25   Home in New England in a small town north of Boston, I shared some of these stories with a woman who works at the counter of a local grocery. "You didn't have to go to San Antonio and Florida," she said. "There's hundreds of homeless families just a couple miles from here." When I asked her where, she said: "In Ipswich, Gloucester, Haverhill . . . There are families who are living in the basement of my church." After a moment's pause she told me this: "After my husband lost his job—we had some troubles then, I was divorced . . . I had to bring my family to the church . . . Well, we're still there."

26 *How many are homeless in America?*

27 The U.S. Department of Health and Human Services (HHS), relying on groups that represent the homeless, suggested a figure of 2 million people in late 1983. Diminished numbers of low-income dwelling units and diminished welfare grants during the four years since may give credence to a current estimate, accepted by the Coalition for the Homeless, of 3 to 4 million people.

28   There is much debate about the numbers; the debate has a dreamlike quality for me because it parallels exactly the debates about the numbers of illiterate Americans. Government agencies again appear to contradict each other and attempt to peg the numbers low enough to justify inaction—or, in this case, negative action in the form of federal cuts.

29   Officials in the U.S. Department of Housing and Urban Development (HUD) puzzled congressional leaders during hearings held in 1984 by proposing a low estimate of 250,000 to 350,000 homeless people nationwide. The study from which HUD's estimate was drawn had contemplated as many as 586,000 people, but this number was discredited in its report.

30   A House subcommittee revealed serious flaws in the HUD study. Subsequent investigations indicated HUD had "pressured its consultants to keep the estimates low." HUD's researchers, for example, suggested a "reliable" low estimate of 12,000 homeless persons in New York City on a given night in January 1984. Yet, on the night in question, over 16,000 people had been given shelter in New York; and this, of course, does not include the larger number in the streets who had received no shelter. U.S. Representative Henry Gonzalez termed HUD's study intentionally deceptive.

31   Estimates made by shelter operators in twenty-one selected cities in October 1986 total about 230,000 people. This sampling does not include Chicago, San Francisco, Houston, Cleveland, Philadelphia, Baltimore, Atlanta, Pittsburgh, St. Paul, San Diego, or Detroit. With estimates from these and other major cities added, the total would exceed 400,000.

32   Even this excludes the metropolitan areas around these cities and excludes

those middle-sized cities—Lawrence, Lowell, Worcester, Brockton, Attleboro, for example, all in Massachusetts—in which the loss of industrial jobs has marginalized hundreds of thousands of the working poor. Though technically not unemployed, most of these families live in economic situations so precarious that they cannot meet the basic costs of life, particularly rent, which in all these cities has skyrocketed. Nor does this include the rural areas of the Midwest and the Plains states, the oil towns of the Southwest, the southern states from which assembly plants and textile industries have fled, lumber counties such as those in Oregon and their New England counterparts in northern Maine. The homeless in these areas alone, if added to the major-city totals, would bring a cautious national count above 1.5 million.

33   We would be wise, however, to avoid the numbers game. Any search for the "right number" carries the assumption that we may at last arrive at an acceptable number. There is no acceptable number. Whether the number is 1 million or 4 million or the administration's estimate of less than a million, there are too many homeless people in America.*

34   Homeless people are, of course, impossible to count because they are so difficult to find. That is intrinsic to their plight. They have no address beyond a shelter bed, room number, tent or cave. In this book I follow my own sense that the number is between 2 and 3 million. If we include those people housing organizers call the "hidden homeless"—families doubled up illegally with other families, with the consequent danger that both families may be arbitrarily evicted—we are speaking of much larger numbers.

35   In 1983, 17,000 families were doubled up illegally in public housing in New York City. The number jumped to 35,000 by spring of 1986. Including private as well as public housing, the number had risen above 100,000 by November 1986. If we accept the New York City estimate of three to four family members in each low-income household, the total number of people (as opposed to families) doubled up in public and private housing in New York is now above 300,000.

36   The line from "doubling up" to homelessness is made explicit in a study by Manhattan's borough president: At least 50 percent of families entering New York City shelters (1986) were previously doubled up. Nationwide, more than 3 million families now are living doubled up.

37   It is, however, not only families doubled up or tripled up who are in danger of eviction. Any poor family paying rent or mortgage that exceeds one half of monthly income is in serious danger. Over 6 million American households pay half or more of income for their rent. Of these, 4.7 million pay 60 percent

---

* One reason for discrepancies in estimates derives from various ways of counting. Homeless advocates believe that all who ask for shelter during any extended period of time ought to be termed homeless. The government asks: "How many seek shelter on a given day?" If the HUD study, cited above, had considered those who asked for shelter in the course of one full year, its upper estimate would have exceeded 1.7 million.

or more. Of mortgaged homeowners, 2 million pay half or more of income for their housing. Combining these households with those who are doubled up, it appears that well above 10 million families may be living near the edge of homelessness in the United States.

38 *Why are they without homes?*

39 Unreflective answers might retreat to explanations with which readers are familiar: "family breakdown," "drugs," "culture of poverty," "teen pregnancies," "the underclass," etc. While these are precipitating factors for some people, they are not the cause of homelessness. *The cause of homelessness is lack of housing.*

40   Half a million units of low-income housing are lost every year to condominium conversion, abandonment, arson, demolition. Between 1978 and 1980, median rents climbed 30 percent for those in the lowest income sector. Half these people paid nearly three quarters of their income for their housing. Forced to choose between housing and food, many of these families soon were driven to the streets. That was only a beginning. After 1980, rents rose at even faster rates. In Boston, between 1982 and 1984, over 80 percent of housing units renting below $300 disappeared, while the number of units renting above $600 more than doubled.

41   Hard numbers, in this instance, may be of more help than social theory in explaining why so many of our neighbors end up in the streets. By the end of 1983, vacancies averaged 1 to 2 percent in San Francisco, Boston and New York. Vacancies in *low-income* rental units averaged less than 1 percent in New York City by 1987. In Boston they averaged .5 percent. Landlords saw this seller's market as an invitation to raise rents. Evictions grew. In New York City, with a total of nearly 2 million rental units, there were half a million legal actions for eviction during 1983.* Half of these actions were against people on welfare, four fifths of whom were paying rents above the maximum allowed by welfare. Rent ceilings established by welfare in New York were frozen for a decade at the levels set in 1975. They were increased by 25 percent in 1984; but rents meanwhile had nearly doubled.

42   During these years the White House cut virtually all federal funds to build or rehabilitate low-income housing. Federal support for low-income housing dropped from $28 billion to $9 billion between 1981 and 1986. "We're getting out of the housing business. Period," said a HUD deputy assistant secretary in 1985.

43   The consequences now are seen in every city of America.

44 *What distinguishes housing from other basic needs of life? Why, of many essentials, is it the first to go?*

---

* Half a million families, of course, were not evicted in one year. Many of these legal actions are "repeats." Others are unsuccessful. Still others are settled with payment of back rent.

45 Housing has some unique characteristics, as urban planning specialist Chester Hartman has observed. One pays for housing well in advance. The entire month's rent must be paid on the first day of any rental period. One pays for food only a few days before it is consumed, and one always has the option of delaying food expenditures until just prior to eating. Housing is a nondivisible and not easily adjustable expenditure. "One cannot pay less rent for the next few months by not using the living room," Hartman observes. By contrast, one can rapidly and drastically adjust one's food consumption: for example, by buying less expensive food, eating less, or skipping meals. "At least in the short run," Hartman notes, "the consequences of doing so are not severe." The cost of losing housing and then paying for re-entry to the housing system, on the other hand, is very high, involving utility and rent deposits equal sometimes to twice or three times the cost of one month's rent. For these reasons, one may make a seemingly "rational" decision to allocate scarce funds to food, clothing, health care, transportation, or the search for jobs—only to discover that one cannot pay the rent. "Some two and a half million people are displaced annually from their homes," writes Hartman. While some find other homes and others move in with their friends or relatives, the genesis of epidemic and increasing homelessness is there.

46 *Is this a temporary crisis?*

47 As families are compelled to choose between feeding their children or paying their rent, homelessness has taken on the characteristics of a captive state. Economic recovery has not relieved this crisis. Adults whose skills are obsolete have no role in a revived free market. "The new poor," according to the U.S. Conference of Mayors, "are not being recalled to their former jobs, because their formers plants are not being reopened. . . . Their temporary layoffs are from dying industries."

48 Two million jobs in steel, textiles, and other industries, according to the AFL-CIO, have disappeared each year since 1979. Nearly half of all new jobs created from 1979 to 1985 pay poverty-level wages.

49 Increased prosperity among the affluent, meanwhile, raises the profit motive for conversion of low-income properties to upscale dwellings. The Conference of Mayors reported in January 1986 that central-city renewal has accelerated homelessness by dispossession of the poor. The illusion of recovery, therefore, has the ironic consequence of worsening the status of the homeless and near-homeless, while diluting explanations for their presence and removing explanations for their indigence.

50 But it is not enough to say that this is not a "temporary" crisis: Congressional research indicates that it is likely to grow worse. The House Committee on Government Operations noted in April 1985 that, due to the long advance-time needed for a federally assisted housing program to be terminated, the United States has yet to experience the full impact of federal cuts in housing aid. "The

committee believes that current federal housing policies, combined with the continuing erosion of the private inventory of low-income housing, will add to the growth of homelessness. . . ." The "harshest consequences," the committee said, are "yet to come."

51 *Why focus on New York?*

52 New York does more than any other city I have visited to serve the homeless. But what it does is almost imperceptible in context of the need.

53   New York is spending, in 1987, $274 million to provide emergency shelter to its homeless population. Of this sum, about $150 million is assigned to homeless families with children. Nonetheless, the growth in numbers of the dispossessed far outpaces city allocations. Nine hundred families were given shelter in New York on any given night in 1978; 2,900 by 1984; 4,000 by the end of 1985; 5,000 by the spring of 1987. The city believes the number will exceed 6,000 by the summer of 1988. With an average of 2.3 children in each homeless family in New York, and with a significant number of two-parent families in this group (many men, not being included on a woman's welfare budget, have not been recorded), these estimates suggest that over 20,000 family members will be homeless in New York by 1988: nearly the number of residents of Laramie, Wyoming, or Key West. This does not include the estimated increase in those homeless *individuals* (12,000 or more) who will be given shelter by the end of 1988; nor does it include at least another 40,000 people who will be refused or will no longer try to locate shelter. Nor does it include the hidden homeless (over 300,000). By 1990, the actual homeless, added to the swelling numbers of the hidden homeless, will exceed 400,000 in New York. The population of New York is 7 million.

54   There is another reason to examine New York City. New York is unique in many ways but, in homelessness as in high fashion, it gives Americans a preview of the future. Millions of Americans, secure at home on New Year's Eve with relatives or friends, watch the celebration in Times Square on television as they face the promises or dangers of the year ahead. Almost half the homeless families sheltered in hotels in New York City now are living within twenty blocks of Forty-second Street and Broadway.

55   The Martinique Hotel at Herald Square and the Prince George Hotel on Twenty-eighth Street near Fifth Avenue, both under the same management, are the largest family shelters in New York—and, very likely, in America.

56 *What is the route a family takes when it is dispossessed in New York City?*

57 The first step brings a family to its Income Maintenance (welfare) center. If the center cannot offer shelter before evening, the family goes to one of a number of Emergency Assistance Units (EAUs), which are open all night and on weekends.

The EAU assigns the family either to a barracks shelter (these large, sometimes undivided buildings are called "congregate" shelters by the city) or to a hotel. For several years, city policy has been to send such families to a barracks shelter first, on the assumption that the publicized discomforts of these places—inability of residents to sleep or dress in privacy, for instance—will discourage families doubled up or living in substandard buildings from requesting shelter.*

58   Once families are placed in such a shelter, many are obliged to go back to their welfare center in the morning in the effort to restore lost welfare benefits. (Families are frequently cut off by sudden changes of address.) Many end up at an EAU at night hoping for assignment to a safer shelter. After the barracks, the next stopping place is likely to be one of a large number of "short-term" hotels, where a family may spend a night, a weekend, or part of a week, after which they go back to the EAU in the hope of being given a less temporary placement. This hope is generally disappointed. "Instead," according to a study by the New York City Council, "the homeless family often must stay at another short-term hotel for a few days before returning to the EAU. This cycle can continue for months, even years."

59   The luckier families are sometimes placed at this point in a "twenty-eight-day hotel." The time limit is established by a number of hotels in order to deny the family occupancy rights, which take effect after a residence of thirty days. After this interval the family goes back to an EAU in the hope of being placed in one of the long-term hotels.

60   There are hundreds of families, however, who for various reasons get no placement and spend weeks commuting between the daytime welfare center and the evening EAU. According to the New York Human Resources Administration (HRA), families are not to be forced to sleep all night at EAUs. As we will see, this has happened frequently. Because the HRA is "able to place a family anywhere in New York City," the city council has observed, "this seemingly endless shuttling between hotels and shelters can come to resemble a game of 'human pinball.'" Two thirds of these pinballs are dependent children.

61   The next stage, one that many families do not reach for months, is to be placed in one of the long-term hotels. There were fifty-five of these hotels when I first visited New York in 1985. There now are over sixty. Approximately 3,400 families had been placed in these hotels by 1986. The rest remained in congregate shelters, in short-term hotels, or (those who were very fortunate) in model shelters operated by nonprofit groups.

62   Of the hotels, eleven house more than 100 families each. Of these, all but

---

* For many years, the best known and most feared of these barracks was the Roberto Clemente shelter in the Bronx. The Clemente, housing over 200 people in a large gymnasium, was ordered closed in early 1986 by state officials. The city resisted the state's order. After a suit brought by the Coalition for the Homeless, the Clemente was closed in September 1986. Several other barracks shelters continued to operate. The city's policy on congregate shelters may be changing somewhat at the present time.

three are in Manhattan. Six hotels, all in Manhattan, house a total of approximately 1,500 families. Although populations in particular hotels rise and fall somewhat inexplicably, the three largest (Prince George, Martinique, and Holland) together housed over 1,000 families at the start of 1986. While the Prince George housed 444 families and the Martinique 389, family size in the Martinique was larger than the norm, so more children may have been living in this building than in any other shelter in New York.*

63   The average length of stay in these hotels in 1986 was thirteen months. In the Martinique it was longer: sixteen months. In one hotel, the Carter, near Times Square, length of stay had grown to nearly four years at the time of writing.

64   The city council notes that families living in two model shelters have a shorter length of stay: eight months and four months respectively. These are also the facilities that charge the city least for rental and provide the most effective social services, including help in finding housing. The city council believes this represents a strong rebuttal to the arguments in favor of "deterrence." Comfortable and healthy shelter does not seem to foster lethargy or to induce dependence. We will return to this.

65   The next step for homeless families in long-term hotels is to begin the search for housing. For a number of reasons which we will learn directly from the residents of these hotels, getting out to search for housing is a difficult task. Because of the shortage of low-income housing, which has brought these people here to start with, the search they are obliged to undertake is almost always self-defeating. Even for public housing in New York, the waiting list contains 200,000 names. There are only 175,000 public housing units in New York. Manhattan Borough President David Dinkins calculates the waiting time at eighteen years.

66   After eighteen months of residence in a hotel, a family is allowed to use a city van to look for housing. At the Martinique, however, the waiting time is thirty months. Only thirty-five families in the Martinique have lived here long enough to meet this stipulation. Pregnant women in their third trimester and mothers with infants are now given first priority.

67 *What is the breakdown of the costs in New York City?*

68 The small but excellent shelters operated by nonprofit groups charge the city $34 to $41 nightly to give housing to a family of four. Hotels like the Martinique charge $63 nightly for a family of this size. Rents in the Martinique Hotel are said to be determined by the number of people in a room or by the number of rooms a family is assigned. Families of five or more are generally given two

---

* At the time of my first visit (December 1985) there were over 1,400 children in 389 families in the Martinique. By June of 1987, according to the city, there were 438 families in the Martinique.

rooms. Average monthly rents may range from $1,900 (family of four) to about $3,000 (family of six). A barracks shelter costs $65 a night to house a family of four people; but additional costs for social services and administration, according to the *New York Times,* bring the actual cost of barracks shelters to about $200 nightly for a family of four—$70,000 if projected for a year. Cost and quality bear no relation to each other.

69   Several mothers of large families in the Martinique have observed that rental costs alone over the course of three years would be equal to the purchase price of a nice home. The city pays only one quarter of these hotel costs. The state pays an additional quarter. The remaining half is paid from federal funds.

70 *What forms of support do homeless families regularly receive?*

71 If unsheltered, virtually none. If sheltered, and enrolled on all the proper lists, they receive some combination of the following: a twice-monthly AFDC allocation (Aid to Families with Dependent Children) to meet basic costs of life; a monthly food-stamp allocation; a "restaurant allowance," calculated by Robert Hayes in 1986 at seventy-one cents per meal per person; a very small sum of money to pay transportation costs to aid in search of housing; Medicaid; an allocation for nutrition supplements to pregnant women and to children under five. This assistance—a major weapon in preventing infant death—is known as WIC (Women, Infants, Children). More than half the women and children eligible for WIC in New York City don't receive it.*

72   In addition to these benefits, a family in the Martinique receives a rental check for the hotel. This is a two-party check and must be obtained by going to a welfare center. The city requires families to travel, often considerable distances, to obtain these checks at welfare centers in the neighborhoods from which they were displaced. A woman living in the Martinique almost two years travels three hours by bus and subway twice a month, and waits an average of four hours, to receive the check she then hands over at the desk in the hotel.

73 *What are the chances of getting out of the hotel and into a real home?*

74 We have seen the waiting period for public housing. For private housing a number of programs, both federal and local, offer subsidies to bridge the gap between the family's income and prevailing rents. Chief among these is Section Eight, a federally supported plan that offers a "certificate" to an eligible family, which is then presented to a landlord as a guarantee that government will pay a certain portion of the rent. Federal cuts in Section Eight make these certificates quite scarce. The reluctance of landlords to accept them often renders their possession

---

* The WIC program—reduced by the Reagan administration by $5 billion from 1982 to 1985— reaches about one third of those who need it nationwide.

worthless. Once a certificate has been assigned, it must be used in a fixed period of time. In one familiar instance, a woman who has lived in several places like the Martinique has been "recertified" for seven years but cannot find a landlord to accept her.

75   Without subsidies, the maximum rent a family on welfare is allowed to pay in New York City is $244 for a family of three, $270 for a family of four. If the government were to raise these limits by $100, sufficient to approach the lowest rents in New York City, the cost would still be less than one-fifth what is spent for hotel rentals.

76 *Who are the people in these buildings? Are they alcoholics, mentally ill people, prostitutes, drug addicts, or drug dealers?*

77 Some of them are; and some of this group were probably as tortured and disordered long before they came here as they are right now. Most, if those I've come to know are a fair sample, certainly were not—not before the sledgehammer of dispossession knocked them flat. Many people in these buildings do need medical help; some need psychiatric care, which they are not receiving. Few of the people in the Martinique were inmates of those institutions that were emptied prior to the 1980s; but all are inmates of an institution now. And it is this institution, one of our own invention, which will mass-produce pathologies, addictions, violence, dependencies, perhaps even a longing for retaliation, for self-vindication, on a scale that will transcend, by far, whatever deviant behaviors we may try to write into their pasts. It is the present we must deal with, and the future we must fear.

☐ Discovering Meaning and Technique

1. According to Kozol, how has the character of homelessness changed since 1980?

2. What are some of the causes of unemployment discussed by Kozol?

3. Why is it so difficult to count the number of homeless people in this country?

4. What does Kozol cite as the principal cause of homelessness? What brought about the crisis?

5. Kozol describes the route taken by typical dispossessed families in New York City. Is this description an effective way to present the frustrations of families and agencies?

6. Consider the figures presented in the section about the breakdown of costs in New York City (paragraphs 67–69). Do the costs for such cramped housing seem excessive to you? Why do you suppose the figures are so high?

☐ Writing Suggestions

1. Using the information in the selection, write a profile of a homeless family.

2. Do you think it might be possible for the races, religions, and political factions in this country to cooperate in addressing the problem of homelessness?

3. New Yorkers have been criticized for being callous toward the panhandlers in the streets and subways. Do you think that having to face the homeless everyday would necessarily make a person callous? Or is the callousness symptomatic of modern society?

4. Kozol refers to the homeless as the "urban underclass." Is there also a "rural underclass" in our society?

5. Most college students expect to graduate and go on to meaningful employment. How would you react if you graduated from college and were unable to find employment other than serving hamburgers or mowing lawns?

A CLEAN, WELL-LIGHTED BENCH

☐ MARJORIE HOPE

1 New Yorkers hurrying up First Avenue on a late winter evening may notice a tiny parklike recess opposite the United Nations. Walled on two sides, it is a shelter against the westerly winds, and a receptacle for the chill gusts that blow up from the East River. Under the cool lamplight and thin naked trees stand a few benches: the resting place of homeless old men.

2   It was on one of these benches that my husband and I saw him one November night. Clad in a worn jacket, his gray head pillowed on a canvas satchel of belongings, he looked almost like a stuffed sleeping bag. Our steps slowed, and we looked at each other. Then, by silent consensus, we moved on. After all, what could individuals do in the great jungle of New York?

3   But the vision of that human bundle haunted me throughout the meeting we were attending that evening in November 1977 at the Church Center of the United Nations. As delegates debated strategies for raising public awareness of the perils of nuclear holocaust, I was caught between concern for the future

of life on this planet and the plight of one man, one piece of flotsam in the sea of humankind.

4   That evening I did speak to a secretary employed in a Church Center office about the figure we had seen on the bench. "Don't get involved!" she warned. "He could be *dangerous*. Besides, these bums *prefer* to live that way. You see," she added, with a mixture of pity and envy, "you don't know New York. It's different."

5   I could have told her that, although I was now teaching sociology and social work at a small college in a quiet midwestern town, I had spent fifteen years in New York, but this seemed irrelevant.

6   It rained that night, and I woke several times; the cold spatter on the windowpanes of the hotel room seemed to send a chill through my body.

7   The next morning, en route to the conference, we passed the same human bundle on the same bench. The other two benches were unoccupied. It was still raining. We walked very fast.

8   The following morning we passed the bench once more. It was empty. I felt uneasy yet released from a bond. Then a hundred feet ahead we saw that figure, lurching forward with the help of a cane. This time I could not stop to think.

9   "Sir, you slept out here last night?"

10   "Eh?" He gazed back at me through blurred blue eyes. There were puffs under them, and his cheeks were puffy and sallow. His mouth fell open a little; I could see half-toothed gums and smell the breath emanating from them. His softly creased face was unshaven. On his head sat a ludicrously jaunty beret, tied down with a plaid scarf. Despite his portliness and the awkwardness of his movements, his body conveyed a certain powerful quality.

11   "Where are you going now?"

12   "I am going for a so-da," he said, and I became aware of a heavy European accent.

13   "Would you like a real meal . . . and a place to sleep?"

14   He stared at me through his watery eyes, then shook his head. "What are you talking about?"

15   "You'll see." I took one arm, Jim the other, and together we guided our unresisting charge to the chapel in the Church Center. He sank into a pew, and my husband sat with him as I panhandled the employees for coffee and doughnuts. Dunking his doughnut to avoid the pain of chewing, our new friend munched slowly, without stopping. Then haltingly, as if speech, too, were painful, he answered our questions.

16   His name was Franz Ritzenthaler. No, he did not have a family or friends in the city. Yes, he had had a home in New York, an apartment in Yorkville.

17   How long had he been wandering about? A long time, a long time. Why had he left? Because—and for the first time, Franz's voice rose above a monotone— because the landlord was going to throw him out.

18   Had he gone to Welfare for help? He looked at us for a moment. Then his head sank. "No, I could not. They would say, I am a bum."

19   Had he been working? "Yes, before. Before the trouble with my leg." He paused. "I was a cook. At Le Faisan d'Or."

20   Was he French, then? "*American.* I have the citizenship. I came here with the American Army, after the war. From a village in Alsace."

21   Alsace! My husband and I exchanged glances. We had spent part of our honeymoon in the Alsatian wine village of Ribeauvillé, and we remembered the communal life the villagers led.

22   Perhaps he needed treatment at a hospital, we suggested to Franz. "*Non!*" he trembled. "Please, please do not send me to a hospital."

23   Upstairs, in the office of a woman moved by Franz's story, we began making phone calls. But we had forgotten that it was a holiday. The Community Service Society, the Catholic Charities, and the Department of Welfare were closed. In desperation, we began calling services that surely had to be open. The churches— were they not havens for "the least of these"? One minister expressed pity for Franz, explained that the church had no proper facilities, and recommended the Men's Shelter. Since we had heard chilling stories of the place, we did not pursue his kind suggestion. Another minister also spoke with feeling of the plight of "derelicts," apologized for his lack of facilities, and gave us the phone number of the Salvation Army. It turned out to be a service for the pick-up of old clothing. The next call was answered by a priest who commiserated with me, deplored the absence of facilities, and recommended the Holy Name Center. Responding with warmth to my call, an official of the center said that it would be happy to offer Franz noonday soup and the chance to play cards with other older men, but the center did not provide shelter; most of its clients lived in single-room occupancy hotels. Another priest suggested that we call McMahon Services. A woman there listened to my description of Franz's predicament and sighed heavily into the phone. It was a terrible shame, but their agency served only children. I called another Salvation Army service. This one, it turned out, was designed only for rehabilitation of alcoholics. Since I was reasonably sure that alcohol was not Franz's problem, I did not follow this up. Two other missions we called also were restricted to alcoholics.

24   The same Church Center employee who had warned me against getting involved suddenly became involved herself. With tears in her eyes, she suggested a small Catholic shelter, the Dwelling Place. But the Dwelling Place, I was to learn, took only women.

25   There was always Bellevue Hospital. But it served only those with acute physical or mental illness, I had been told. Perhaps some expert *could* classify Franz as senile. Perhaps only after food, shelter, and care could one assign him a label. Besides, he had pleaded not to be sent to a hospital.

26   Franz was not a child, or a woman, or an alcoholic, or a patient with an identifiable malady. He fitted no category. He was only a homeless old man.

27   My husband joined me and suggested calling the Catholic Worker, a group

of mostly young people who follow Dorothy Day's precept to interpret the gospel literally and share the lives of the poor.

28   A weary-sounding young woman told me that she was new, and the person in charge was out for a few minutes. They could offer our friend some soup, but their beds were filled. We were reduced to the last resort: Emergency Assistance, the Welfare Department's effort to provide services even when regular offices were closed.

29   "Does he have *documents?*" demanded the voice at the other end of the line. "Everything's got to be *documented.*"

30   Since Jim had discovered a five-inch bundle of rain-soaked papers in Franz's satchel, I assured the voice that he could pass inspection, although I wanted to ask it what happened to those *misérables* who are robbed of the paper-and-plastic proof that one is indeed a real person. "Well, okay," sighed the voice. "Send him down."

31   By this time several conference delegates had learned about the weather-beaten stranger in the chapel and had offered to take up a collection. We accepted just enough to help pay for the cab and set off for Emergency Assistance.

32   In the taxi, Jim told me that he had gone through about half of Franz's documents. Our companion seemed sufficiently real; he had, *inter alia,* a social security card, a record of disability payments, an old unemployment compensation book, a membership card for the American Association of Retired Persons, three letters—all over four years old—postmarked from Switzerland, rent receipts, and a bank book showing a savings account of $9,000. Then Jim placed in Franz's lap one of his discoveries: a small photo, carefully preserved in a plastic window, of a middle-aged woman with softly waved dark hair, plump cheeks, melancholy eyes, and a sensual mouth. Was this a friend we might contact? Slowly, Franz shook his head.

33   The gray iron portals of Emergency Assistance at 241 Church Street were covered with graffiti, messages from those who had passed through: "No money food. Rent due. Denied help. John W. Smith." "Food stamps emergency. 109 West 17th. Denied. Why? Murderers!"

34   A clerk looked up from the *Daily News.* "The social worker's out to lunch," he said sourly. "Sit down."

35   We sat down. The seats were battered, the walls smeared, the floor littered, but it was warm.

36   Perhaps a dozen people were waiting: a black woman with three children, a Hispanic man with two sleeping youngsters, a middle-aged black man staring vacantly at the opposite wall, two white women draped over their seats, and a tall, thin, red-bearded man in scarlet-and-yellow plaid trousers. A policeman tapped his baton on the floor. Silence hung over the room.

37   Since Franz had eaten nothing but coffee and doughnuts and we ourselves were hungry, Jim bought soup, sandwiches, and cookies from a neighboring luncheonette. Franz sipped his soup slowly. It was a long time before I could follow suit. All those hungry eyes would be watching, I was sure. Yet none

turned toward us; they seemed sunken in sleep or resignation, the last vestige of pride in the poor.

38   Suddenly a voice rang out: "I have enjoyed *every delicious morsel*!" My stomach contracted; the hand holding my sandwich stopped in midair. "Isn't there a more private place where one can partake of food?"

39   I turned slowly and faced my accuser. There he stood, the tall thin man, like the Grand Inquisitor: his beard neatly clipped, a halo of red hair crowning his balding pate, his head cocked with an almost theatrical dignity. His eyes met mine in a proud challenge. Then they dropped, and he sank into his seat.

40   I moved to his side. "We have some cookies here. Would you like to share them?"

41   He looked at me, then at the cookies, then back at me. "Oh, *my dear,* thank you!" And raising his eyes to heaven, he crossed himself. He clutched the cookies, then shoved them to one side. "Madame, do you know why I'm here?" Tears filled his eyes. "I was living at the Grand Hotel on Broadway. I was living at that establishment on my SSI check, I'm disabled, you see. One morning I went down the hall to the bathroom, *locking* my door. And when I returned to my abode a few minutes later, the door was open, and everything—everything—was gone." The tears washed his cheeks. "And so Madame, I am here hoping—*hoping* that the authorities will grant me some modicum of emergency assistance." He reached out and touched my hand tentatively. "God bless you, Madame."

42   We had missed most of the important conference meetings that day, it was already 2:30 P.M., and we had a long-standing appointment in half an hour. It seemed useless to wait any longer for the social worker to arrive. I wrote him a note, outlining what we knew about Franz and asking that he be sent to a welfare hotel, not the Men's Shelter. Franz nodded mutely and continued to stare into his lap as we explained our departure. Then he looked up through his clouded blue eyes. "*Merci.*"

43   Two hours later I phoned Emergency Assistance and learned that he was still waiting. At 7:30 P.M. that night I called again. A Mr. Jones told me that he was about to see Franz and would take good care of him. "Why're you so interested in this old guy?" he asked. "You're a social worker? . . . You know what happens to old people in this city? Some, they get so feeble they can't handle money. Some go down to the Bowery and drink away what they got. Others, people take their money, they get bloodied up . . . bad. And the lucky ones, we shovel them into nursing homes, and they just die away. It's not like the old days when they stayed at home. You looked up to them and you listened, and they sat at the head of the table."

44   For a moment I had a fleeting image of Franz at the head of a table in Alsace, ladling out *choucroute garnie* to the family he might have had.

45   After the caseworker promised to send Franz to a welfare hotel and to set up an appointment for long-range planning at a regular welfare office, I hung up the phone with a sense of relief.

46   At 10:30 P.M. I called Emergency Assistance once again. Jones had left, but his successor told me that two hours earlier Franz had been sent by cab to the Men's Shelter. Shaking with rage, I phoned the shelter. An official informed me that no such person had arrived that evening.

47   As I listened to the wind rattle our windows that night, shadows from the street moved across the ceiling. I saw Franz lying on the sidewalk in his own blood. Perhaps he had arrived at his destination. Perhaps he had seen the watch-house that the city had built to shelter its good citizens from the homeless. Perhaps he had told the cabbie to drive on. To his clean well-lighted bench near the United Nations?

48   The bright sunshine pouring into our room the next morning kindled a new spark of hope. But Franz's bench was empty.

49   Seized by some fantasy that he had arrived at the shelter, after all, we decided to pay it a visit.

50   The New York City Municipal Men's Shelter is the nucleus of a sprawl of burned-out structures and burned-out humanity. Along the side streets stand craters of once-solid buildings, gutted by arsonists. The Bowery itself is a great wide way of hamburger joints, artists' lofts, restaurant supply houses, bars, missions, and the ubiquitous "hotels," flophouses that go by absurd names such as Sunshine, Prince, White House, and Palace. Slumped in doorways or stretched flat on pavements, men and women sleep surrounded by broken glass, tin cans, orange skins, waste paper, and excrement.

51   Near the shelter, a dingy building on Third Street, figures slouched against a brick wall, passing back and forth a brown paper bag from which each took a long sip. They did not speak to each other. On the sidewalk others crouched in silent circles, their eyes turned on the faces of the dice. Across the street a man was vomiting into the gutter.

52   In the shelter lobby, bottle pieces littered the floor, and the grime on the walls was unrelieved by an incongruous pastoral mural. There were no chairs. Ragged inmates sauntered or lurched back and forth, hobbling from nowhere to nowhere. Some were beating the air with wild flailing punches. A few were gesticulating at each other between peals of mirthless laughter. Others queued up at barred windows for meal tickets. The air smelled of sweat, urine, wine, and vomit.

53   From their glass-windowed cage, two guards surveyed us languidly, then finally nodded permission. "Okay, you can speak to the clerk in the office."

54   A maternal-looking woman with a heavy Spanish accent and dark braids wound round her head listened to our story sympathetically and made a thorough search of the files. "He's never been here." Then she shook her head. "But if he's an old man, get him out of here, and out of this neighborhood! You know what the younger ones do to the old."

55   Yes, we knew. I remembered tales of the Big Room here at the shelter, where hundreds of men spent the night on plastic chairs or the cold concrete floor. No one could really sleep through the night. The air was punctured with

rock radio, snores, and screams of "Help!" called out from nightmares. Calls for help from the sleepless were likewise unheeded: under the eyes of the two guards, men were robbed of their wallets, their coats, their shoes; others were kicked out of their chairs and beaten at the whim of bullies.

56   A shelter official who had been listening approached us and nodded. "When I came here fifteen years ago, the Bowery population was made up of older, white guys—winos. A fairly stable population. Now they're mostly younger and black—drug addicts, mental patients. The median age before was fifty-six; now it's forty-one, and thirty-six for new clients. It means many of the guys you're dealing with have never worked. It's a reflection of the unemployment problem. And the drug problem. And political problems."

57   "How do you mean that?"

58   "They don't keep many mental patients in hospitals any more. Well, that philosophy is fine, if they've got enough aftercare facilities. But they don't. So the hospitals dump psychotics in the name of community medicine. And they end up here."

59   "It was different thirty years ago." He smiled wistfully. "There was great Yiddish Theatre then, and Sammy's Bowery Follies. Sure, the Men's Shelter was here, but it was *invisible.* Even ten years ago there were more chances for jobs for these guys. Trucks would come by and the men would line up on the street corners for a day's work—slave markets, they called it."

60   "How many cases do you get these days?"

61   "About 15,000 a year get some kind of service. Maybe 4,500 are active at any given time. We serve up to 5,000 meals a day, and send about 1,100 men to Bowery hotels. When we run out of hotel tickets, guys sometimes stay in the Big Room—on cold nights maybe 400 or more sleep there on the chairs or the floor."

62   On the upper floors the shelter offered some medical and dental services, the official assured us. Although I did not tell him so, I had heard about the lines of men waiting for two or three hours for cursory checkups from the only doctor. I had heard of the other lines, clients waiting for their initial interviews in a large bare room with no chairs or benches. When at last a client's turn came up, he was interviewed standing up through a hole of a window. The interviews, which averaged three minutes, were said to resemble a cross-examination in which the worker tried to force the client into some kind of admission or catch him in a contradiction.

63   It was the interviewer's duty, explained the official, to determine whether the client should seek other sources of assistance, get medical care, be offered tickets to a Bowery hotel, or be assigned to the second floor infirmary, which was reserved for men most in need of care. "If your friend was ill or too confused to handle money, the worker at Emergency Assistance may have made arrangements for him to go to the infirmary."

64   Although he was reluctant to show us the rest of the building, the official

consented to take us to the dormitory. It was clean and warm enough, the antiquated iron beds were not crowded together, and two guards provided some security. But the hunched inmates ambling about the room seemed scarcely aware of our presence. In one corner a TV was blaring; the two men camped before it had closed their eyes.

65   Downstairs, the official hurried us past the Big Room; we could just glimpse the rows of plastic chairs. As if reading our thoughts, the official commented, "Sure, it can be hell in there. In the flophouses, the violence can be even worse. There men slit each other's pockets. They fight. One old guy last week had lye thrown in his face. To say nothing of the filthy dormitories. The mattresses are grimy, and they crawl with vermin and roaches. Sometimes there are no sheets or blankets, just a sheet of cardboard on the bed. So what do you want? In winter a man or woman is found every week frozen to death on the streets. Old men have been found in parks sleeping in the snow completely naked, their clothes stolen right off their bodies."

66   His lips twitched in a smile. "What do you want? You know what it costs the city to feed and shelter one of these guys? All of five bucks a day. Some people even talk of closing the place. Because it offends the sensibilities of artists and writers and other middle-class people who've moved to the Bowery. So what'll happen to these men?"

67   His voice had begun to rise; he had lost his bureaucratic cool. "When you get into work like this, you can't care too much. I did. I was going to change everything. Now I wouldn't even know where to start. Who's responsible? These guys—this thing called homelessness—it reaches into *everything*!"

68   An hour later, heading for the Lincoln Tunnel en route to our college in Ohio, we detoured to pass Franz's bench across from the United Nations. It was empty.

69   Another light cold rain had begun to fall, and through the drizzle I could make out the inscription on one wall of the recess where Franz used to seek refuge: "They shall beat their swords into ploughshares. . . . Neither shall they learn war any more."

70   If we had stayed with Franz instead of returning to normal life, if we had approached him earlier, if agencies, if the city, if . . . But we were all too late.

Missing Persons Squad
One Police Plaza
New York, N.Y. 10038
December 9, 1977

Dear Madam,

In response to your letter of recent date, please be advised that Mr. Franz Ritzenthaler has not come to the attention of the Police Department. A check of cooperating agencies was made with negative results. We will keep a record of your interest in Mr. Ritzenthaler and in the event that he does come to our attention we will notify you.

John R—
Detective

71 Presumably, that check included the morgue. Perhaps Franz was alive at least. As rain gave way to snow, he continued to pursue me: every night, as my electric blanket clicked on instant warmth, an image of Franz's shivering body snapped somewhere in my mind.

72   We returned to New York the following spring for another academic conference and another long search for Franz.

73   It seemed logical to start with his old home, a six-story senescent apartment building in New York's German section, opposite an empty area that had been bulldozed to make way for a twenty-story high rise. In the gray light of the first floor hallway, the building super, a thin-faced man with a Spanish accent, stared back at me. "You from the City?" Despite my denial, he retreated back down the hall. "I don't know nothing. Goodbye, Ma'am."

74   Perhaps Franz, despite his $9,000 in the bank, had sought some kind of assistance at the Welfare Department's East End Income Maintenance Center. I made my way there, passed the long lines of patient petitioners, and asked to see a supervisor. A weary-looking black woman heard me out, then shook her head. "Try the Thirty-fourth Street office, downtown. We don't cover the gentleman's street." When I replied that he had lived close by, she looked irritated. "That's the point. The centers are *never* located in the neighborhoods where people live. Why?" She shrugged. "How should I know? Some people spend two carfares to get here."

75   Perhaps, I fantasized, Franz had eventually found his way to the Men's Shelter. So I returned. The same woman who had listened sympathetically five months before made a painstaking search through the files. "He's never been here. Maybe you could try the Salvation Army's Booth House—It's about the most decent place around here. But they don't take people on an emergency basis, and he'd have to be on Supplementary Security Income to get in."

76   Booth House II, one of the old Stations of the Cross along the Bowery, boasts clean corridors, a clean cafeteria, and services ranging from chapel to a Sobriety Club, a part-time psychiatrist, and a soul clinic. A watchman at the door informed me that since it was Sunday the only person who could answer my questions would not be there till the next day. I slipped past him and sat down in the large public room. Franz was not there. Scarcely a head turned to take in the sight of a woman alone in a gathering of men. They seemed to be gazing into some furtive beyond: the next meal, the next night of fitful sleep, perhaps the last sleep of all.

77   I turned to a black man in torn trousers and mismatched shoes in the next chair. Before I could finish two sentences, a tall shadow loomed over me. It was the law: a heavy-jawed guard. "Okay, lady. Out! You can't talk to nobody."

78   "But why not?"

79   "Ain't allowed. Come back Monday and ask for the supervisor."

80   "Can't the residents decide if they want to talk with me?"

81   "Just get *out,* lady!"

82   Fortunately, my husband, who had been attending the conference, was waiting at the Bowery bar where we had agreed to meet. On the bar stool beside us, a woman with discolored red, stringy hair and bloated cheeks began to sob. "Yah-yah-yah." Her body heaved back and forth on the stool. No one spoke to her; no one seemed to be listening. "Goddam bastards, all of them." She lifted her blouse to her face, exposing two sagging breasts. "I'm sick of living, and I'm sick of dying."

83   We left. As we passed the Prince Hotel, I decided to see whether my husband's presence would enable me to cross the threshold of a flophouse. Inside, an iron-cagelike door, as tall as the ceiling, barred the stairway leading to the sleeping rooms. A balding, puffy-faced man surveyed us from behind the cashier's cage. "No, you can't look around. I got orders." We looked through a glass door at the rows of men (all white) enclosed in the television room and retreated.

84   On the street two men were attacking cars stopped for the traffic light. Ferociously, they cleaned the windows in sweeping motions for thirty seconds, thrust their hands inside for the ransom, and retreated, pivoting on their toes and swinging their arms up to the sky.

85   "They're the new breed," sighed an assistant at the Bowery Mission as we sat down in his office a few minutes later. "The old-time Bowery bums are moving out, and psychotics or drug addicts are moving in."

86   He was a tall, reddish-blond, somewhat scholarly looking young man, without the evangelical zeal we had come to associate with the missions. Perhaps, he, too, represented a new breed on the Bowery, a response to the resentment of programs that dosed out religion as a condition of acceptance.

87   Men here were no longer required to take a Christian pledge, he explained, although services were held six times a week. They did have to refrain from drinking during their stay at the mission.

88   The rooms we saw were clean and well ordered. Yet many men left, unable to face the challenge of abstinence, our guide told us. It was easier to hide in the oblivion of flophouses: dormitories or four-by-six cubicles, separated from each other by partitions seven feet high. "The flophouses exploit the guys. When building inspectors come round, they're paid off. Stores exploit the men, paying a few cents for clothes given away at the missions. Bartenders keep the guys' Supplemental Security Income checks and give credit against them, ending up with most of the money. But if bartenders weren't 'guardians,' the men would

be rolled right away. As it is, come payday the men line up on one side of the street, the jackrollers on the other. Still another racket is for labor contractors to bring in a truck and get guys drunk. They wake up next morning on a Long Island potato farm. I could go on. It's hard to see any solution, the oppression is so comprehensive."

89   We still had not found Franz.

90   The next day I returned to his apartment building. This time I found two pensioners, who introduced themselves as Tom and Charlie, sitting on the stoop in the spring sunshine. "Franz? Sure, I remember him," said Charlie, A Galway-born gentleman with a strong Brooklyn brogue. "Funny how he just disappeared. That got us worried, and we called the Bureau of Missing Persons. Yeah, Franz. Sometimes he had us in for little dinners. I'll never forget the stew with red wine he used to make. Once he showed me pictures of him in a real chef's hat!"

91   "He kind of kept to himself," put in Tom. "Still, he liked to sit on the stoop and talk to people going in and out."

92   "Every morning he went down to the supermarket on Eighty-sixth Street," said Charlie. "Then he'd come back and feed the cat and fix up his room. If it was good weather he'd sit outside the rest of the day, talking or reading the newspaper. He even read books."

93   "He liked the girls," added Tom. "I mean, he'd look at them and say, 'Pretty nice, huh!' "

94   "But he *loved* the cat," said Charlie. "He used to sleep with her."

95   "Then what happened?"

96   "Well, he had a cleaning woman," volunteered Charlie. "We asked him if she wasn't a friend, and he'd say, 'Oh no, just the cleaning woman.' And she had a key. Well, she hadn't come for awhile before he disappeared. Now that I think about it, he'd begun talking about death."

97   "Yeah." Tom nodded. "He'd been real friendly with a Switzy man down the street. When the guy died, that kind of shook Franz up."

98   "He was always worried about money," added Charlie. "He got on social security disability after some accident; it wasn't much. Then he got the idea the landlord was going to raise his rent. That does happen here. Franz, he'd been in this place over twenty years. The building's rent-controlled, and he'd been here so long, he was paying less than some of us. If the landlord gets a guy out, he can raise the rent. And it's hard to find a cheap place these days. The landlord can get about what he wants."

99   "Right," echoed Tom. "What's happening in the SROs—you know, single-room occupancy hotels—is worse. That's where a lot of poor people, mostly old and disabled ones on social security, have to live. There's a lot of money from converting those hotels into luxury apartments. In fact . . ." Tom paused. "That Switzy friend of Franz, he was living in an SRO. One night he came home and couldn't get in. The stairway to his room was smashed in, and a goon

stood there saying he'd better not try to go farther. Well, the Switzy guy was mad, and he tried. They set dogs on him. He was messed up good, and he never really got over it. He found a room down the street, but he couldn't afford it, so he didn't eat much. And he was still shook up, it was hard for him to talk. It wasn't long till he died. That really got Franz."

100   "And then Franz got a funny bill from the landlord," said Charlie. "Say, I think I remember him saying he went over to the Burden Center for the Aging to get some help with that."

101   I was at the Burden Center half an hour later. Perhaps twenty-five elderly clients—most of them ladies in hats, stockings, and unsensible shoes—waited stoically to tell their stories of hunger, illness, eviction, rent increases, rats, lack of heat, assaults, fraud, and confusion about the myriad forms required to establish eligibility to survive.

102   A lanky, bearded young man in jeans listened to my story, asked a few abrupt questions, and nodded. "Think I remember him. Yeah, think he came in with a bill showing his rent had been doubled. We investigated, and the landlord claimed it was a computer error. But the old guy didn't believe it. He kept thinking the landlord was harassing him." He crushed out his cigarette. "I'll look through the files and make a few calls. Phone me tomorrow."

103   When I phoned, his message was cryptic. "Try Bellevue. Just a hunch."

104   The new wing of Bellevue Hospital bore little resemblance to the fusty institution I had once known; the endless corridors were spacious and over-heated, and administration offices were decorated with coldly abstract mural paintings.

105   In the eighteenth-floor social services office a Cuban caseworker greeted me warmly. "Yes, administration called. I think we have the man you're looking for. He came to us late in November—a cop picked him up in the park. They diagnosed him Organic Mental Syndrome. Me, I didn't believe it. I watch him—he's confused but not that ill. Well, now the doctors agree. We won't have to send him away to stay in Manhattan Psychiatric Center. He's staying here for awhile till we find him a nursing home.

106   "But he don't talk to nobody." The caseworker shook his head despairingly. "He knows English all right, but the only person he'll talk to is an aide from Haiti, she speaks French. And the lady friend who comes to visit him—she's come here five times.

107   "Sometimes he walks in his sleep," the caseworker added. "Funny, he always finds his way back to bed. Ask him . . . ask him why he walks in his sleep."

108   I opened the door of the ward and looked at the mound on a bed near the window. It was Franz.

109   He was clean and shaved and "respectable" now, but his gums were still toothless and an odor of sickness still clung to his breath. The tray of food at his side was untouched. I put my hand on his arm. "*Vous vous souvenez de moi?*"

110   He stared at me vacantly. *"Non."*

111   Slowly, in French, I described the experience we had shared in mid-November. His eyes flickered, and he grunted, "Eh, perhaps."

112   "Tell me, what happened afterwards? Where did you go?"

113   "I do not remember."

114   "You seemed to think the landlord was trying to evict you."

115   "It was true. I know."

116   "I've met friends of yours, in the building where you lived. They were worried about you."

117   "They attach no importance to me."

118   "I know you have one friend, at least," I said desperately. "She came to visit you."

119   "Yes." His voice trembled a little. "Just four times."

120   "The social worker says she will come again soon."

121   "No!"

122   "Why do you say that?"

123   "It is too late."

124   "Tell me, do you realize you walk in your sleep?"

125   "That's what they tell me. It is true, perhaps."

126   "Do you remember anything afterwards?"

127   "Sometimes, Just a little."

128   "When you walk where are you going?"

129   He stared back at me, then turned away. "Home."

130   I sat silently with him for a long while. At last I said clumsily, "The social worker here is trying to find you a nursing home. You can make new friends."

131   His watery blue eyes closed. "It is too late."

132   I touched his hand. "Would you like me to come back?"

133   "It's not worth the trouble."

134   "But if I want to come back?"

135   A faint smile warmed his lips. "Eh, if you like."

136   Franz's friend was a Mexican woman named Maria Maldonado, I learned at Bellevue. She had not visited recently because she, too, was ill. I finally succeeded in talking with her by phone.

137   "They found him on East Ninth Street, on November 28," she began hesitantly. "His legs were all swelled up, and he had a bad cold. I guess he was walking all night, all the time."

138   How did she know he was in Bellevue? "I called. No one lets you know anything. I kept calling all the hospitals in New York. I guess it was December 4 when I found he was in Bellevue.

139   "After he disappeared, I called the Bureau of Missing Persons. Then I walked around Manhattan trying to find him. I'd go up and down the streets near his apartment and all the parks. I couldn't do it all at one time. I got trouble with my legs, too.

140   "He wasn't like this before. There was something on his mind. He said they were going to throw him out of his apartment.

141   "I knew him—it was over thirty years. Something happened . . ."

142   Her voice broke. "But Franz and I were still friends. I always took him to the hospital, till I got sick, and now . . ." She began to sob softly. "Señora, Ma'am, I can't talk any more."

143   We could not leave New York without confronting the Bureau of Missing Persons. An abashed officer located a file on Franz, which included an entry stating that Maria had called the Bureau on November 6, but no entry indicating that the Bureau had called her. Tensely, he explained that we had never been notified that Franz had been found because our letter was in the "out-of-town" file. When we expressed some difficulty in understanding this explanation, since the client himself was not "out of town" and most bureaucracies keep a central file, the officer's face flushed. "Look, we've got just forty men on our staff, and each one's got to handle an average of 155 cases a week. Furthermore, you can't hold the police responsible if it's a *voluntary* disappearance. Anyway, people who are dead are of primary importance. He's alive, isn't he? We're looking for *Dead on Arrivals*."

144   We returned twice to see Franz before we left New York for Ohio. We talked to Franz of our own visit to Alsace, of our liking for Alsatian wines. We asked about his favorite French dishes, his life in New York. We offered to write letters to his family and friends. Occasionally, he responded with a few words, but all the while he seemed to be looking beyond us, gazing from some shore of his own to another we were unable to see.

145   The tariff for the well-balanced food that Franz rarely touched, the battery of medical tests, the activity therapies he consistently refused, had been $300 a day for the past four months, we discovered. And Franz was more removed from our world than on the day we had found him on his bench.

146   We tried to shake hands in an awkward farewell. "Next time we'll see you in a new home."

147   For a lingering moment his hand clung to mine. Then his went slack. "No. It is impossible."

148   "What is impossible?"

149   "Everything. Everything is too late."

☐ Discovering Meaning and Technique

1. What was Marjorie Hope's first reaction to the "human bundle" on the bench in New York? What was the recommendation of the secretary at the Church Center of the United Nations?

2. Which types of problems did Hope and her husband run into in trying to get help for Franz Ritzenthaler?

3. Which agency finally agreed to help? What kind of place was it?

4. What were the circumstances of Franz's disappearance?

5. Describe the conditions at New York City Municipal Men's Shelter.

6. In her search for Franz, what does Hope learn about the homeless?

7. What is Franz's attitude after he is found?

8. Hope pictures homelessness through the concrete facts she gathers in her efforts to help Franz. She does not express her personal opinions; she does not editorialize; she lets the facts speak for themselves. Do you think this technique is effective? Explain your answer.

☐ Writing Suggestions

1. Marjorie Hope's first thought upon seeing the homeless man was that individuals can do little about such a massive problem. Do you agree or disagree that individuals are helpless and therefore should not get involved?

2. Do you think government agencies or churches provide enough help for the homeless?

3. Discuss the many factors that can lead to homelessness.

4. Write an imaginary picture of a day on the streets from the point of view of one homeless person.

5. Discuss what it must be like to work in a shelter for the homeless.

USERS, LIKE ME: MEMBERSHIP IN THE CHURCH OF DRUGS

☐ GAIL REGIER

[1] Profiles of typical drug users, in the newspapers and on TV, obscure the fact that many users aren't typical. I used to do coke with a violinist who was the most sheltered woman I've ever known. My mushroom connection was a fifty-year-old school-bus driver. And one of my high-school buddies, who moved

$1,000 worth of drugs a day in and out of his girlfriend's tattoo shop, would always extend credit to transients and welfare moms—debts he'd let slide after a while when they weren't paid.

2   It's easy to start thinking all users are media stereotypes: ghetto trash, neurotic child stars, mutinous suburban adolescents. Users, the media imagine, can't hold jobs or take care of their kids. Users rob liquor stores.

3   Real users, for all their chilly scorn of the straight world, buy into the same myths, but turn them inside out. The condescension becomes a kind of snobbery: we are different from the straight people, we are special, we are more free. We are spiritual adventurers. When I was twenty-four, which was not that long ago, my friends and I thought nothing was more hip than drugs, nothing more depraved, nothing more elemental. When we were messed up, we seemed to become exactly who we were, and what could be more dangerous and splendid? Other vices made our lives more complicated. Drugs made everything simple and pure.

4   Anyone who hangs around drugs learns not to think too much about all this, learns to watch the bent spoon in the water glass.

5   Some of the users I knew were people with nothing left to lose. The rest of us were in it only a little for the money, more than a lot for the nights we would drive to one place after another, in and out of people's parties, looking for a connection. It was a kind of social life, and we weren't in any hurry.

6   What we had in common was drugs. Getting high bound us together against outsiders, gathered us into a common purpose. No one else understood us and we understood each other so well.

7 New Year's eve 1979: We're riding around trying to cop some speed. My poet friend Brian is driving and in the backseat is Guy, who is on probation and very uptight because we keep telling him the car is stolen. "You mothers are rounding me," he keeps saying. He doesn't believe us, but the game makes him real paranoid. We make some parties but the speed is always gone before we arrive, so we head for the truck stop where I used to work. The high-school kids who work there always have grass and pills. Their stuff is not so hot, but it's real cheap. Restaurant people have a high rate of casual use; the work's so menial you can't stand it without getting high.

8   The place is full of tired truck drivers and travelers with whiny kids. The hookers wear miniskirts and army jackets and all have colds. Our favorite waitress, Sherry, combines two parties to get us a booth. She's telling some truckers at the counter about her sexual problems with her husband. They tell her to wear leather panties and she sighs and says that doesn't work.

9   Fleetwood Mac songs shake the jukebox. Sherry slings us coffee and asks, What's the scam? Brian puts thumb and forefinger to his lips and mimes a toke from a joint. She goes back to the kitchen, and when she comes back tells us that Larry is holding. We take our coffee with us through the door marked

AUTHORIZED PERSONNEL. Everybody in the kitchen is drunk. Two of the girls are playing the desert-island game: If you could have only two drugs for the rest of your life, what would they be? Sherry pours us some cold duck from a bottle that was in the walk-in cooler.

10   There was a time when the rap here was all baseball and dates, but not anymore. Tonight the drizzle of abstractions is as vacuous as any graduate seminar. The kids say the owner gives them shit for coming to work stoned. They need their jobs but they know how they want to live. I tell them that the Church of Drugs has its own rituals and rules, and its members are a martyred elite. Brian tells Sherry about acid and stained glass. Guy tells the dishwasher how to tell if it's his starter or his alternator that's bad. The kids listen. They are impressed by us. They want to be like us.

11   Drug dealers on TV are vampires: oily, smooth, psychotic, sexy, human paradigms of the narcotics they sell. Larry is a skinny punk who is studying auto body at the vo-tech high school. Wearing a GMC cap and a long, stained apron, he stands behind a grease-blackened grill covered with steaks and bacon and skillets asizzle with eggs.

12   "Watch this shit," he tells another aproned kid, and motions to us to follow him. The kid protests that he'll get behind. Larry leads us back to the storeroom, past shelves of #10 cans and signs that read ALL DELIVERIES C.O.D. and ABSOLUTELY NO FIREARMS ALLOWED ON THESE PREMISES. He takes a baggie from his gym bag and shows us some speeders he says are pharmaceutical. The black capsules have the right markings on them, but they unscrew too easily and the bone-white powder inside isn't bitter enough. We tell him no thanks but buy a joint from him for a dollar.

13   When I was selling drugs I made a lot of money, but I usually got stoned on the profits. It was black money and it seemed the highs I bought with it were free and therefore sweeter. I was a college dropout with a kid and a nervous wife. I worked as a cook in a Mexican café fifty hours a week and brought home $200. For that $200 I could buy half a kilo of sinsemilla, break it down into finger bags, and double my money. Selling meant I always had drugs—though we didn't that New Year's eve. Dealing, with its arcana of mirrors and scales, was a guild mystery, a secret, forbidden craft. It was a ticket to places I couldn't get to any other way. I got to know guys who drove Cadillacs and carried forged passports, guys who cooked acid and smack in basement labs, women who wore lots of rings and called every man Jones.

14 Brian and I smoke the joint on the back porch of the truck stop. The rain, we decide, is very righteous. Eighteen-wheelers grind and hiss their gaudy lights onto the interstate. Diane, a sloe-eyed, peach-skinned fifteen-year-old, comes out and vamps us for a couple of hits. I tell her about those cocaine nights when the room fills with snowflakes sifting down slow as if they were under water. She's kissing Brian and I've got my hand up her short skirt, but she refuses to get in the car with us.

15   Downtown by the hospital, we get in a confusion with some ambulance guys with their cherry top on. Bald tires skid on the wet pavement. Brian decides to let me drive. We stop at my house, where my wife is watching *Dick Clark's New Year's Rockin' Eve.* Her eyes are red from crying, but she tries to smile.

16   "Dan and Jan were here," she says. "Don't you remember we invited them?"

17   I look in the refrigerator for wine. There isn't any.

18   "Brian and Guy are in the car," I say. "I've got to run them home."

19   "Then will you come back?"

20   "Come with us if you want." I know she won't. Our son's asleep upstairs.

21   "Don't get speed," she says.

22   "We're not."

23   "You get mean when you do speed."

24   I want to get wired. I head for the door.

25   We make the Steak N' Ale. In a real city there would be black guys pushing stuff on the sidewalk out front, but this is Springfield, Missouri, and we can't score. The manager, our connection, isn't around. At the bar we order shots of whiskey. The place is full of pretty girls, and even the ones who don't drink are drunk, but we're not looking for girls.

26   Guy says, "We should go see Casey." Casey is an old guy who sold black-market penicillin in post-war Europe. Brian doesn't know Casey but he knows he's expensive, and he fusses about that. But Guy and I are studying on how good Casey's crystal meth is and how Casey could get us a set of points so we could hit it.

27   On our way we boost three wine glasses and a bottle of Korbel from somebody's table. Sitting in the car, we drink to ourselves and the dying year. Brian wets his fingertip in the champagne and strokes it gently round and round the rim of his glass, making space noises rise from the crystal. We all do it, but then the noises turn spooky and we get paranoid. We drop the glasses out the window and drive.

28   Prudence is sitting on the front porch watching the rain. She kisses me and I taste her tongue. I introduce my friends and she kisses them.

29   "Casey's inside."

30   "Has he got meth?"

31   She shrugs. The business is Casey's gig. Prudence is twenty and has a cat named Lenin and a one-year-old baby. She's kept the job she had before she moved in with Casey: evening attendant at a laundry near the college. Her place is the cleanest in town. My buddies and I would drop in to wash some jeans and score a little pot, and end up hanging around all evening eating candy bars and flirting with Prudence.

32   On the weekends Prudence ran a perpetual carport sale, things she made and stuff taken in barter from customers with cash-flow problems. Clothes and belt buckles, pipes and bottles, bootleg eight-tracks and cassettes with typed labels, old skin mags, car stereos and CB radios trailing cut wires.

33   The living room is brightly lit as always; Prudence leaves her pole lamps

on twenty-four hours a day. Casey is sprawled among pillows on an old couch ripe with cigarette scars, culling sticks and seeds from some dope on the glass-topped coffee table. Framed beneath the glass are large-denomination bills from several South American countries. Casey's favorite objects litter the shelf below: brass pipes with small screw fittings, ceramic ashtrays from the commune at Ava, a rifle scope he uses to case visitors coming up the rutted driveway.

34   A candy dish holds pills—speckled birds and bootleg ludes coloring a base of Tylenol with codeine, bought over-the-counter in Canada. Casey offers us some, and I sift thumb and forefinger carefully through the pile and pick out two black beauties for tomorrow. Brian starts to take a handful and I sign him not to. Casey scarfs codeine the whole time we talk.

35   Prudence and I go to the kitchen to mix a fruit jar of gin and orange juice, stay there a little while to touch and neck. She has painted everything in the kitchen white, walls and floors and cabinets and fixtures, and in the glare of many bare bulbs the room is stark as a laboratory. White-painted plaster peels off the walls in loops and splinters. There are no dishes or pans; Prudence buys only things she can cook in her toaster oven.

36   Last time I was over, Casey went after Prudence with a ratchet wrench and I had to talk him down. As we mix the drinks she tells me how she and Casey dropped acid together and now things are better. He's even starting to like the boy. I tell her how my four-year-old thinks acid is the best trick going, because when I'm tripping I play with him so much. We take baths together, drenching the floor with our bathtub games, while my wife sits on the toilet lid, watching us with her bright blue eyes.

37   On the floor, Lenin and the baby take turns peekabooing and pouncing. I'm surprised the baby isn't scared. I've changed my mind and dropped one of the beauties and I'm feeling edgy and fast and tricky. Lenin rubs himself against my ankles and I grow paranoid.

38   "You want to help me water the plants?" Prudence asks.

39   We climb the rungs nailed to the closet wall, push up the trapdoor, and crawl into the attic. Gro-lights illuminate twenty marijuana plants set in plastic tubs. Casey has run a hose up through the wall. I turn the water on and off for her as she crawls back and forth across the rafters on her hands and knees.

40   Downstairs, I can hear Brian on a rap. "Radiation will be the next great vice. They already use it with chemo to kill cancer. Soon they'll discover wavelengths that reproduce the effects of every known drug. The cops will be able to spot users easy 'cause we'll all be bald."

41 Prudence digs out a Mamas and Papas tape and plays "Straight Shooter." Casey tells us how some junkies will put off shooting-up until the craving starts, like getting real hungry before a steak dinner. I listen, but to me the addict world is as mythical as Oz. I've met junkies, but they were in town only accidentally and soon moved on to Kansas City or New Orleans. Like a symphony orchestra or

a pro sports team, a junkie population needs a large urban center to support it.

42   Casey says that the word "heroin" is a corruption of the German word *heroisch,* meaning "powerful, even in small amounts." I cruise the bookshelf. A rogues' gallery: Henry Miller, Cocteau, Genet, de Sade's *Justine* in scarlet leather, *Story of O.* Casey explains a William Burroughs story he's just read, about a secret society dedicated to discovering the Flesh Tree described in an ancient Mayan codex. This is the rare and sacred plant from which human life originally derived. According to Burroughs, flesh is really a vegetable, and the human system of reproduction is a perversion of its true nature.

43   Casey talks very seriously about acquiring his own Tree of Flesh on his next trip to Mazatlán. He regards the story as journalism rather than parable— or seems to. We spend some time discussing how to care for the Tree of Flesh once Casey obtains it.

44   Guy asks Casey about the crystal meth.

45   "You don't want speed," I say. I'm feeling very articulate now. "What you want is a hit of junk." Guy shakes his head, but Brian looks thoughtful. "For ten minutes," I say, "you'll be as high as you ever thought you wanted to be. Then in half an hour you'll be as high as you *really* ever wanted to be."

46   "And then?" Guy says.

47   "You'll want *more.*"

48   Inside the Church of Drugs, heroin users are an elite within the elite, saints of Instant Karma and Instant Death. Their stark games raise them to a place beyond the hype and chatter.

49   "When you shoot up," I tell them, "you're alone before the abyss. That's what shooting up is for."

50   The first time I shot up was the most frightened I've ever been. For me the fear was part of the high.

51   Guy and Brian have never done needles, but Brian is hard for it and helps me work Guy around. "We won't hit you in the vein," I assure him. "Just in muscle tissue, like a vaccination." We each give Casey a twenty. He drags an army-surplus ammo box from under the couch and rummages through it. Prudence puts the baby on the rug and goes to hunt up a needle.

52   When she returns with one, Casey measures out the heroin and I cook it in a teaspoon dark with the flames of many lighters. When it is like molten silver, Casey loads, taps bubbles out of the rig, and hits Guy in the shoulder before he can change his mind. Brian thrusts his arm forward eagerly, his eyes ashimmer with the romance of drugs, and I put the needle in him. They both vomit, the way almost everybody does when they get their wings, then go serenely on the nod. The baby is startled and then amused by their upheavals. We get them settled and empty the bucket we had handy for them, then Casey and Prudence hit each other. She has a glass of gin in one hand and breaks it on the coffee table when the spasms hit her.

53   Last to do up, I take my time, pricking the point of the needle into the vein of my inside forearm, easing back a little before I push the trigger. Wisps of blood claw up in the glass wand and a white light like a fist of thorns shoves everything away.

54   Later we're stirring around again and starting to talk. The baby has been crying for a while. Brian wipes the shards of broken glass off the coffee table onto the rug in front of the baby, who quiets and reaches for these shiny new toys.

55   After a few cuts the baby learns that broken glass can hurt him. He is crying again. He tries to push the pieces away, but the splinters stick to his hands. He rubs his small fists together and we all start laughing, we can't help it, he's so cute. Prudence claps her hands and cheers on his efforts. He rubs his hands against his face and the blood spots it like clown makeup. The baby cries so hard he starts choking. It seems very funny. Then he starts gnawing at the slivers between his fingers, and that is very funny too.

56   Casey gets straight first and washes the dried blood from the baby's face. Guy can't walk and I help him outside into the cold air. Brian and Prudence are messing around out by the car.

57   Casey comes out on the porch. His fingers are streaked with iodine. He says, "Hey man."

58   I say Yeah.

59   Casey looks at Brian. "Don't bring him back here."

60 These days I'm a guy who goes six months or a year without smoking a joint. I got out of drugs the way a lot of people do. One day I looked around and saw that I was missing a lot of work, my nerves were bad, parties bored me, all my friends were druggies. I quit selling and then I quit using. You know the story.

61   Prudence still lives in Springfield, in the same house north of the railroad yards. Casey is gone but the carport sale continues. Her boy is ten, and maybe there are some fine white scars at the corners of his mouth. Maybe they're just my imagination.

62   When I quit drugs I thought the fighting in my marriage would stop. It didn't. It wasn't the drugs my wife had always hated, it was the fellowship the Church of Drugs provided. She still wants me home. I'm still not there.

63   One night last year when I didn't want to go home, I took a manic-depressive writer on a 'shroom run to a stucco structure known as the House With No Brains. Everyone there was younger than me. Some folks had heroin and tried to missionary us into doing up. I just said no, but for weeks after that—listen, this is important—for a long time after that, I thought about junk, talked about it to people, started once to drive to the House but turned back. Every time I picked up a spoon or struck a match, I thought about needle drugs, about how clean and fine things could be.

☐ Discovering Meaning and Technique

1. What is Regier's purpose in writing "Users, Like Me"? Does he successfully make his purpose clear? If so, does he achieve it?

2. According to Regier, what are the different attractions of drugs?

3. What kinds of users does Regier describe?

4. In the users' view, who are the outsiders?

5. How would you characterize the world of users painted by Regier—wicked, sad, depraved, sordid, adventurous, exciting?

6. How do the different kinds of drugs affect the users?

7. The drug subculture has developed its own language, such as "to cop some speed." Find other examples.

8. What does Regier mean by the "Church of Drugs"?

9. Why did Regier quit using drugs?

☐ Writing Suggestions

1. Describe "profiles of typical drug users" that appear on television.

2. Why do you think people are attracted to drugs?

3. Describe the dangers of drugs.

4. How do drug users affect their families?

THE LESSON

☐ TONI CADE BAMBARA

1 Back in the days when everyone was old and stupid or young and foolish and me and Sugar were the only ones just right, this lady moved on our block with nappy hair and proper speech and no makeup. And quite naturally we laughed at her, laughed the way we did at the junk man who went about his business like he was some big-time president and his sorry-ass horse his secretary. And

we kinda hated her too, hated the way we did the winos who cluttered up our parks and pissed on our handball walls and stank up our hallways and stairs so you couldn't halfway play hide-and-seek without a goddamn gas mask. Miss Moore was her name. The only woman on the block with no first name. And she was black as hell, cept for her feet, which were fish-white and spooky. And she was always planning these boring-ass things for us to do, us being my cousin, mostly, who lived on the block cause we all moved North the same time and to the same apartment then spread out gradual to breathe. And our parents would yank our heads into some kinda shape and crisp up our clothes so we'd be presentable for travel with Miss Moore, who always looked like she was going to church, though she never did. Which is just one of the things the grownups talked about when they talked behind her back like a dog. But when she came calling with some sachet she'd sewed up or some gingerbread she'd made or some book, why then they'd all be too embarrassed to turn her down and we'd get handed over all spruced up. She'd been to college and said it was only right that she should take responsibility for the young ones' education, and she not even related by marriage or blood. So they'd go for it. Specially, Aunt Gretchen. She was the main gofer in the family. You got some old dumb shit foolishness you want somebody to go for, you send for Aunt Gretchen. She been screwed into the go-along for so long, it's a blood-deep natural thing with her. Which is how she got saddled with me and Sugar and Junior in the first place while our mothers were in a la-de-da apartment up the block having a good ole time.

2   So this one day Miss Moore rounds us all up at the mailbox and it's puredee hot and she's knockin herself out about arithmetic. And school suppose to let up in summer I heard, but she don't never let up. And the starch in my pinafore scratching the shit outta me and I'm really hating this nappy-head bitch and her goddamn college degree. I'd much rather go to the pool or to the show where it's cool. So me and Sugar leaning on the mailbox being surly, which is a Miss Moore word. And Flyboy checking out what everybody brought for lunch. And Fat Butt already wasting his peanut-butter-and-jelly sandwich like the pig he is. And Junebug punchin on Q. T.'s arm for potato chips. And Rosie Giraffe shifting from one hip to the other waiting for somebody to step on her foot or ask her if she from Georgia so she can kick ass, preferably Mercedes'. And Miss Moore asking us do we know what money is, like we a bunch of retards. I mean real money, she say, like it's only poker chips or monopoly papers we lay on the grocer. So right away I'm tired of this and say so. And would much rather snatch Sugar and go to the Sunset and terrorize the West Indian kids and take their hair ribbons and their money too. And Miss Moore files that remark away for next week's lesson on brotherhood, I can tell. And finally I say we oughta get to the subway cause it's cooler and besides we might meet some cute boys. Sugar done swiped her mama's lipstick, so we ready.

3   So we heading down the street and she's boring us silly about what things

cost and what our parents make and how much goes for rent and how money ain't divided up right in this country. And then she gets to the part about we all poor and live in the slums, which I don't feature. And I'm ready to speak on that, but she steps out in the street and hails two cabs just like that. Then she hustles half the crew in with her and hands me a five-dollar bill and tells me to calculate 10 percent tip for the driver. And we're off. Me and Sugar and Junebug and Flyboy hangin out the window and hollering to everybody, putting lipstick on each other cause Flyboy a faggot anyway, and making farts with our sweaty armpits. But I'm mostly trying to figure how to spend this money. But they all fascinated with the meter ticking and Junebug starts laying bets as to how much it'll read when Flyboy can't hold his breath no more. Then Sugar lays bets as to how much it'll be when we get there. So I'm stuck. Don't nobody want to go for my plan, which is to jump out at the next light and run off to the first bar-b-que we can find. Then the driver tells us to get the hell out cause we there already. And the meter reads eighty-five cents. And I'm stalling to figure out the tip and Sugar say give him a dime. And I decide he don't need it bad as I do, so later for him. But then he tries to take off with Junebug foot still in the door so we talk about his mama something ferocious. Then we check out that we on Fifth Avenue and everybody dressed up in stockings. One lady in a fur coat, hot as it is. White folks crazy.

4   "This is the place," Miss Moore say, presenting it to us in the voice she uses at the museum. "Let's look in the windows before we go in."

5   "Can we steal?" Sugar asks very serious like she's getting the ground rules squared away before she plays. "I beg your pardon," say Miss Moore, and we fall out. So she leads us around the windows of the toy store and me and Sugar screamin, "This is mine, that's mine, I gotta have that, that was made for me, I was born for that," till Big Butt drowns us out.

6   "Hey, I'm going to buy that there."

7   "That there? You don't even know what it is, stupid."

8   "I do so," he say punchin on Rosie Giraffe. "It's a microscope."

9   "Whatcha gonna do with a microscope, fool?"

10   "Look at things."

11   "Like what, Ronald?" ask Miss Moore. And Big Butt ain't got the first notion. So here go Miss Moore gabbing about the thousands of bacteria in a drop of water and the somethinorother in a speck of blood and the million and one living things in the air around us is invisible to the naked eye. And what she say that for? Junebug go to town on that "naked" and we rolling. Then Miss Moore ask what it cost. So we all jam into the window smudgin it up and the price tag say $300. So then she ask how long'd take for Big Butt and Junebug to save up their allowances. "Too long," I say, "Yeh," adds Sugar, "outgrown it by that time." and Miss Moore say no, you never outgrow learning instruments. "Why, even medical students and interns and," blah, blah, blah. And we ready to choke Big Butt for bringing it up in the first damn place.

12   "This here costs four hundred eighty dollars," say Rosie Giraffe. So we pile up all over her to see what she pointin out. My eyes tell me it's a chunk of glass cracked with something heavy, and different-color inks dripped into the splits, then the whole thing put in a oven or something. But for $480 it don't make sense.

13   "That's a paperweight made of semi-precious stones fused together under tremendous pressure," she explains slowly, with her hands doing the mining and all the factory work.

14   "So what's a paperweight?" asks Rosie Giraffe.

15   "To weigh paper with, dumbbell," say Flyboy, the wise man from the East.

16   "Not exactly," say Miss Moore, which is what she say when you warm or way off too. "It's to weigh paper down so it won't scatter and make your desk untidy." So right away me and Sugar curtsy to each other and then to Mercedes who is more the tidy type.

17   "We don't keep paper on top of the desk in my class," say Junebug, figuring Miss Moore crazy or lyin one.

18   "At home, then," she say. "Don't you have a calendar and a pencil case and a blotter and a letter-opener on your desk at home where you do your homework?" And she know damn well what our homes look like cause she nosys around in them every chance she gets.

19   "I don't even have a desk," say Junebug. "Do we?"

20   "No. And I don't get no homework neither," says Big Butt.

21   "And I don't even have a home," say Flyboy like he do at school to keep the white folks off his back and sorry for him. Send this poor kid to camp posters, is his specialty.

22   "I do," says Mercedes. "I have a box of stationery on my desk and a picture of my cat. My godmother bought the stationery and the desk. There's a big rose on each sheet and the envelopes smell like roses."

23   "Who wants to know about your smelly-ass stationery," say Rosie Giraffe fore I can get my two cents in.

24   "It's important to have a work area all your own so that . . ."

25   "Will you look at this sailboat, please," say Flyboy, cuttin her off and pointin to the thing like it was his. So once again we tumble all over each other to gaze at this magnificent thing in the toy store which is just big enough to maybe sail two kittens across the pond if you strap them to the posts tight. We all start reciting the price tag like we in assembly. "Handcrafted sailboat of fiberglass at one thousand one hundred ninety-five dollars."

26   "Unbelievable," I hear myself say and am really stunned. I read it again for myself just in case the group recitation put me in a trance. Same thing. For some reason this pisses me off. We look at Miss Moore and she lookin at us, waiting for I dunno what.

27   "Who'd pay all that when you can buy a sailboat set for a quarter at Pop's, a tube of glue for a dime, and a ball of string for eight cents? It must have a

motor and a whole lot else besides," I say. "My sailboat cost me about fifty cents."

28   "But will it take water?" say Mercedes with her smart ass.

29   "Took mine to Alley Pond Park once," say Flyboy. "String broke. Lost it. Pity."

30   "Sailed mine in Central Park and it keeled over and sank. Had to ask my father for another dollar."

31   "And you got the strap," laugh Big Butt. "The jerk didn't even have a string on it. My old man wailed on his behind."

32   Little Q. T. was staring hard at the sailboat and you could see he wanted it bad. But he too little and somebody'd just take it from him. So what the hell. "This boat for kids, Miss Moore?"

33   "Parents silly to buy something like that just to get all broke up," say Rosie Giraffe.

34   "That much money it should last forever," I figure.

35   "My father'd buy it for me if I wanted it."

36   "Your father, my ass," say Rosie Giraffe getting a chance to finally push Mercedes.

37   "Must be rich people shop here," say Q. T.

38   "You are a very bright boy," say Flyboy. "What was your first clue?" And he rap him on the head with the back of his knuckles, since Q. T. the only one he could get away with. Though Q. T. liable to come up behind you years later and get his licks in when you half expect it.

39   "What I want to know is," I says to Miss Moore though I never talk to her, I wouldn't give the bitch that satisfaction, "is how much a real boat costs? I figure a thousand'd get you a yacht any day."

40   "Why don't you check that out," she says, "and report back to the group?" Which really pains my ass. If you gonna mess up a perfectly good swim day least you could do is have some answers. "Let's go in," she say like she got something up her sleeve. Only she don't lead the way. So me and Sugar turn the corner to where the entrance is, but when we get there I kinda hang back. Not that I'm scared, what's there to be afraid of, just a toy store. But I feel funny, shame. But what I got to be shamed about? Got as much right to go in as anybody. But somehow I can't seem to get hold of the door, so I step away for Sugar to lead. But she hangs back too. And I look at her and she looks at me and this is ridiculous. I mean, damn, I have never ever been shy about doing nothing or going nowhere. But then Mercedes steps up and then Rosie Giraffe and Big Butt crowd in behind and shove, and next thing we all stuffed into the doorway with only Mercedes squeezing past us, smoothing out her jumper and walking right down the aisle. Then the rest of us tumble in like a glued-together jigsaw done all wrong. And people lookin at us. And it's like the time me and Sugar crashed into the Catholic church on a dare. But once we got in there and everything so hushed and holy and the candles and the bowin

and the handkerchiefs on all the drooping heads, I just couldn't go through with the plan. Which was for me to run up to the altar and do a tap dance while Sugar played the nose flute and messed around in the holy water. And Sugar kept givin me the elbow. Then later teased me so bad I tied her up in the shower and turned it on and locked her in. And she'd be there till this day if Aunt Gretchen hadn't finally figured I was lyin about the boarder takin a shower.

41   Same thing in the store. We all walkin on tiptoe and hardly touchin the games and puzzles and things. And I watched Miss Moore who is steady watchin us like she waitin for a sign. Like Mama Drewery watches the sky and sniffs the air and takes note of just how much slant is in the bird formation. Then me and Sugar bump smack into each other, so busy gazing at the toys, 'specially the sailboat. But we don't laugh and go into our fat-lady bump-stomach routine. We just stare at that price tag. Then Sugar run a finger over the whole boat. And I'm jealous and want to hit her. Maybe not her, but I sure want to punch somebody in the mouth.

42   "Watcha bring us here for, Miss Moore?"

43   "You sound angry, Sylvia. Are you mad about something?" Givin me one of them grins like she tellin a grown-up joke that never turns out to be funny. And she's lookin very closely at me like maybe she plannin to do my portrait from memory. I'm mad, but I won't give her that satisfaction. So I slouch around the store bein very bored and say, "Let's go."

44   Me and Sugar at the back of the train watchin the tracks whizzin by large then small then gettin gobbled up in the dark. I'm thinkin about this tricky toy I saw in the store. A clown that somersaults on a bar then does chin-ups just cause you yank lightly at his leg. Cost $35. I could see me askin my mother for a $35 birthday clown. "You wanna who that costs what?" she'd say, cocking her head to the side to get a better view of the hole in my head. Thirty-five dollars could buy new bunk beds for Junior and Gretchen's boy. Thirty-five dollars and the whole household could go visit Granddaddy Nelson in the country. Thirty-five dollars would pay for the rent and the piano bill too. Who are these people that spend that much for performing clowns and $1000 for toy sailboats? What kinda work they do and how they live and how come we ain't in on it? Where we are is who we are, Miss Moore always pointin out. But it don't necessarily have to be that way, she always adds then waits for somebody to say that poor people have to wake up and demand their share of the pie and don't none of us know what kind of pie she talkin about in the first damn place. But she ain't so smart cause I still got her four dollars from the taxi and she sure ain't gettin it. Messin up my day with this shit. Sugar nudges me in my pocket and winks.

45   Miss Moore lines us up in front of the mailbox where we started from, seem like years ago, and I got a headache for thinkin so hard. And we lean all over each other so we can hold up under the draggy-ass lecture she always finishes us off with at the end before we thank her for borin us to tears. But

she just looks at us like she readin tea leaves. Finally she say, "Well, what did you think of F. A. O. Schwarz?"

46   Rosie Giraffe mumbles, "White folks crazy."

47   "I'd like to go there again when I get my birthday money," says Mercedes, and we shove her out the pack so she has to lean on the mailbox by herself.

48   "I'd like a shower. Tiring day," say Flyboy.

49   Then Sugar surprises me by sayin, "You know, Miss Moore, I don't think all of us here put together eat in a year what that sailboat costs." And Miss Moore lights up like somebody goosed her. "And?" she say, urging Sugar on. Only I'm standin on her foot so she don't continue.

50   "Imagine for a minute what kind of society it is in which some people can spend on a toy what it could cost to feed a family of six or seven. What do you think?"

51   "I think," says Sugar pushing me off her feet like she never done before, cause I whip her ass in a minute, "that this is not much of a democracy if you ask me. Equal chance to pursue happiness means an equal crack at the dough, don't it?" Miss Moore is besides herself and I am disgusted with Sugar's treachery. So I stand on her foot one more time to see if she'll shove me. She shuts up, and Miss Moore looks at me, sorrowfully I'm thinkin. And somethin weird is goin on, I can feel it in my chest.

52   "Anybody else learn anything today?" lookin dead at me. I walk away and Sugar has to run to catch up and don't even seem to notice when I shrug her arm off my shoulder.

53   "Well, we got four dollars anyway," she says.

54   "Uh hunh."

55   "We could go to Hascombs and get half a chocolate layer and then go to the Sunset and still have plenty money for potato chips and ice cream sodas."

56   "Uh hunh."

57   "Race you to Hascombs," she say.

58   We start down the block and she gets ahead which is O.K. by me cause I'm goin to the West End and then over to the Drive to think this day through. She can run if she want to and even run faster. But ain't nobody gonna beat me at nuthin.

☐ Discovering Meaning and Technique

1. The style of the selection recreates the narrator's dilect, so that the reader seems to "hear" the story. Which techniques does Bambara use to achieve this

style? Look, for example, at spelling, verb forms, slang words, and sentence length.

2. What is Miss Moore's purpose in going to Fifth Avenue? Does she accomplish her purpose?

3. What is the narrator's attitude toward Miss Moore? What causes this attitude?

4. Why does Miss Moore call the children by their real names, whereas they call each other by nicknames?

5. What is the narrator's feeling about entering the toy store?

6. Which object in the store makes the biggest impression on the children? Is it only the price that staggers them?

7. How does Miss Moore answer the narrator's question about the cost of a yacht? Why does she answer that way?

8. Discuss the effectiveness of the comparison, "The rest of us tumble in [the toy store] like a glued-together jigsaw done all wrong."

☐ Writing Suggestions

1. Explain the ending of the story: "She can run if she want to and even run faster. But ain't nobody gonna beat me at nuthin."

2. What lesson is Miss Moore trying to teach? Why does she pick this particular store to teach it? Is she successful?

3. In paragraph 41, after Sugar touches the toy boat, the narrator says, "And I'm jealous and want to hit her. Maybe not her, but I sure want to punch somebody in the mouth." Explain why she feels this way.

4. Have you ever experienced a longing for something beyond your reach—a material possession, a skill, a lifestyle, an intellectual or athletic ability? If so, describe the experience and how it made you feel.

5. Recreate a childhood experience using the language and dialect of the people involved. Try merely to suggest the dialect; don't exaggerate it.

■ Combining Sources in a Composition

1. Compare the overt discrimination against women during the Elizabethan period (Virginia Woolf) with the more subtle discrimination of the modern period (Casey Miller and Kate Swift).

2. Write about how language can reveal stereotyping. (See Roger Kahn and Casey Miller and Kate Swift.)

3. Several selections refute the idea that America is a "melting pot." Use these selections to support the picture of America as a class society, or show that the selections do not contain the real truth about America's equality and unity.

4. "The Lesson" by Toni Cade Bambara contains the statement, "Money ain't divided up right in this country." Apply this statement to the selections by James Baldwin and Jonathan Kozol.

5. In "The Lesson" by Toni Cade Bambara, Miss Moore frequently tells the children, "Where we are is who we are." How does this statement reflect James Baldwin's "Fifth Avenue, Uptown"?

6. James Baldwin wrote "Fifth Avenue, Uptown" about thirty years ago, before consciousness about sexist language developed. In light of the information on sexist language in "One Small Step for Genkind," analyze Baldwin's choice of words.

7. Talking and writing about problems have been used as therapy for teenagers in trouble (Oldenburg and Marek). Discuss whether these techniques are effective.

8. Using the information in Jonathan Kozol and Marjorie Hope, compare two types of homelessness—the homeless family and the homeless old person.

9. The selection by Hope describes the plight of one homeless individual, whereas the selection by Kozol discusses homelessness in more general terms. Which selection paints the problem of the homeless more effectively? Why?

10. In "Born to Run," Oldenburg says that Willie Givens "rarely connected the consequences of his actions with the actions themselves." Do you think this inability to connect cause with effect might partially account for social problems such as teenage pregnancy, drug addiction, and juvenile delinquency?

■ ■ ■
BIOGRAPHIES OF THE AUTHORS

Mortimer J. Adler (1902), a native of New York City, was a high school dropout but a voracious reader. He finished a four-year program at Columbia University in three years; he did not, however, receive a bachelor's degree because he refused to take the required swimming test. In fact, Adler has no degrees except the Ph.D.—not even a high school diploma. He has held various positions, including professor of psychology and philosophy of law, president of the Institute of Philosophical Research, and lecturer for a variety of institutions and foundations. Adler is a philosophical opponent of pragmatism, which, in his view, results in moral and mental chaos. He believes that truth is absolute and that a good education is to be found in those subjects that teach people to think clearly. At the University of Chicago, Adler and Robert Maynard Hutchins organized the Great Books Program because of their conviction that the universal truths of the classics provide the basis for education. Writings include: *Crime, Law, and Social Science* (1933), *Scholasticism and Politics* (1940), *How to Read a Book: The Art of Getting a Liberal Education* (1940), *How to Think about War and Peace* (1944), *The Democratic Revolution* (1956), *The Capitalistic Revolution* (1957), *The Greeks, the West, and World Culture* (1966), *The Times of Our Lives: the Ethics of Common Sense* (1970), *Reforming Education* (1977), *How to Think About God* (1980), *Six Great Ideas* (1981), *Ten Philosophical Mistakes* (1987), *The Angels and Us* (1988), *American Mind* (1989).

Maya Angelou (1928), born Marguerita Johnson in St. Louis, Missouri, was brought up by her grandmother in Stamps, Arkansas. Angelou's professional life has been varied: singer, dancer, actress, songwriter, playwright, poet, autobiographer, journalist, teacher, editor, television producer, and director. She toured Europe and Asia as a performer in *Porgy and Bess,* taught modern dance in Rome and Tel Aviv, wrote for the *Ghana Times,* and produced a television series on African traditions in American life. Angelou is probably best known for her autobiographical works. Writings include: *I Know Why the Caged Bird Sings* (1970), *Gather Together in My Name* (1974), *Singin' and Swingin' and Gettin' Merry Like Christmas* (1976), *The Heart of a Woman* (1981), and *All God's Children Need Travelin' Shoes* (1987).

Michael J. Arlen (1930) received an undergraduate degree from Harvard in 1952 and worked as a reporter for *Life* magazine until 1957, when he became a staff writer and television critic for *The New Yorker.* Writings include: *Living-Room War* (1969), *The View from Highway 1* (1976), *Thirty Seconds* (1980), and *The Camera Age: Essays on Television* (1981).

Isaac Asimov (1920) was born in the U.S.S.R. and educated at Columbia University, where he received a B.S., M.A., and Ph.D., all in chemistry. Asimov's bibliography includes approximately

686

400 books and countless articles and short stories—over twenty million words. In fact, no one has ever written more books on more subjects. His works include books and articles on chemistry, biology, physics, mathematics, astronomy, technology, history, the Bible, literature, humor, and much more. Asimov is particularly well known for mysteries and science fiction. In a Science Fiction Writers of America poll, his "Nightfall" was chosen the best science fiction story of all time. Writings include: *Foundation and Empire* (1952), *The Caves of Steel* (1954), *The Martian Way and Other Stories* (1955), *The Naked Sun* (1957), *The Genetic Code* (1963), *The Human Brain: Its Capacities and Functions* (1964), *Inside the Atom* (1966), *Fantastic Voyage* (1966), *Through a Glass Clearly* (1967), *The Roman Empire* (1967), *Photosynthesis* (1968), *Asimov's Guide to Shakespeare* (1970), *The Stars in Their Courses* (1971), *Tales of the Black Widowers* (1974), *Earth: Our Crowded Space Ship* (1974), *The Ends of the Earth: The Polar Regions of the World* (1975), *Lecherous Limericks* (1975), *Computer Crimes and Capers* (1983), *The Disappearing Man and Other Mysteries* (1985), *Robots: Machines in Man's Image* (1985), *Isaac Asimov's Wonderful Worldwide Science Bazaar* (1986).

Russell Baker (1925) was born in Morrisville, Virginia, a rural community, where he lived his early childhood. After his father's death, he and his family lived with relatives in New Jersey and Baltimore. In 1947, he received a B.A. from Johns Hopkins University and began a career as a journalist. In 1962, he began his "Observer" column for the *New York Times.* Although the column began as political commentary, Baker gradually branched out into personal and social subjects and into humor, satire, and fantasy. His favorite subjects involve the problems and anxieties of the ordinary person faced with a world too complex, too fast, and too big for its britches. Baker has won two Pulitzer Prizes—one in 1979 for distinguished commentary and another in 1982 for his autobiography, *Growing Up.* Writings include: *All Things Considered* (1965), *Poor Russell's Almanac* (1972), *So This is Depravity* (1980), *Growing Up* (1982), *The Rescue of Miss Yaskell and Other Pipe Dreams* (1983), *The Good Times* (1989).

James Baldwin (1924–1987) was born in Harlem to an unmarried mother and was later adopted by his stepfather, a laborer and storefront preacher. Baldwin spent his childhood and early adolescence reading and taking care of his eight half-brothers and half-sisters. After a religious conversion at age fourteen, he preached at the Fireside Pentecostal church in Harlem for three years. His writing skills gained him admittance to DeWitt Clinton High School in the Bronx, from which he graduated in 1942. Six years later, Baldwin moved to Paris. Although he returned to the United States often to teach and lecture, he lived the rest of his life abroad, primarily in France. Baldwin wrote novels and an autobiography, but the essay was his best form. In his elegant prose style, he explored the myths about race relations in the United States and the experience of being black in a white society. He also went beyond the black experience to produce social criticism on America's national identity and its place in world culture. Writings include: *Go Tell It on the Mountain* (an autobiography, 1953), *Notes of a Native Son* (1955), *Giovanni's Room* (1956), *Nobody Knows My Name* (1961), *Another Country* (1962), *The Fire Next Time* (1963), *No Name in the Street* (1972), *If Beale Street Could Talk* (1974), *Evidence of Things Not Seen* (1985), *The Price of a Ticket* (1985).

Toni Cade Bambara (1939), a New York City native, was educated in Queens College and City College in New York as well as other institutions in Italy and Paris, where she studied theater, dance, film, and linguistics. Bambara has worked not only as a writer but also as an investigator for the New York State Department of Social Welfare, a literacy instructor, a civil rights activist, a teacher, and a director of plays and films. Writings include: *Tales and Stories for Black Folks* (1971), *Gorilla, My Love* (1972), *The Black Woman: An Anthology* (1974),

The Sea Birds Are Still Alive: Collected Stories (1977), *The Salt Eaters* (1980), *If Blessing Comes* (1987).

Elizabeth Bishop   (1911–1979) was born in Worcester, Massachusetts. After her father died when she was eight months old and her mother suffered a mental collapse, Bishop lived an apparently lonely and unhappy childhood with grandparents—writing poetry and studying piano, unable to attend school regularly because of asthma. During her years at Vassar, Bishop met the poet Marianne Moore, who persuaded her to write rather than continue her plans to enter medical school at Cornell. After graduation, Bishop spent fifteen years as a nomad, living and traveling in France, Brittany, the United States, Canada, North Africa, Mexico, and South America. In 1951, she settled in Brazil, where she lived for almost twenty years. She spent the last decade of her life primarily in the United States, teaching at the University of Washington in Seattle and at Harvard. Travel is a central metaphor in Bishop's work; through the imagination, she transforms physical experiences into subjective discovery. She won the Pulitzer Prize in poetry in 1956 for *North & South: A Cold Spring* and the National Book Award in 1969 for *The Complete Poems.* Writings include: *North & South: A Cold Spring* (1955), *The Diary of Helen Morley* (trans. by Bishop, 1957), *Brazil* (1962), *The Burglar of Babylon* (1968), *The Complete Poems* (1969), *An Anthology of Twentieth Century Brazilian Poetry* (ed. and trans. by Bishop and E. Brazil, 1972), *Geography III* (1976).

Roy Blont, Jr.   (1941) was born in Indianapolis, Indiana. He received a B.A. from Vanderbilt and an M.A. from Harvard. He began his professional career as a reporter and sports writer for the *Decatur-Dekalb News* in Georgia and subsequently served as a reporter and columnist for newspapers, including the *Morning Telegraph* in New York City, the *New Orleans Times-Picayune,* and the *Atlanta Journal.* In 1968, he joined the staff of *Sports Illustrated.* Blount writes humor on a wide variety of subjects and has been called a modern-day Mark Twain. He has contributed articles, short stories, poems, and drawings to magazines such as *The New Yorker, Atlantic, New York Times Magazine, Esquire, Playboy,* and *Rolling Stone.* Writings include: *About Three Bricks Shy of a Load* (1974), *Crackers* (1980), *One Fell Soup; or I'm Just a Bug on the Windshield of Life* (1982), *Not Exactly What I Had in Mind* (1985), *Now, Where Were We?* (1988), *First Hubby* (1990).

Tom Bodett   is an essayist, short story writer, and radio personality. Writings include: *As Far as You Can Go Without a Passport* (1985), *Small Comforts* (1987), *The End of the Road* (1989), *The Big Garage on Clear Shot* (1990).

Daniel J. Boorstin   (1914) was born in Atlanta, Georgia. He was educated at Harvard, Oxford, Yale, and Cambridge. He was admitted as barrister-at-law to the Inner Temple in 1937 and admitted to the Massachusetts bar in 1942. Boorstin taught history and literature at Harvard, law at Harvard Law School, and history at Swarthmore College and the University of Chicago. He held various government posts in the Department of Justice; was director of the Natural Museum of History and Technology, Smithsonian Institution; and served as Librarian of Congress. In addition, he served as visiting professor of American history at universities in Rome, Japan, Turkey, India, Australia, New Zealand, Iceland, Egypt, and other countries. Writings include: *The Mysterious Science of the Law* (1941), *The Lost World of Thomas Jefferson* (1948), *The Genius of American Politics* (1953), *The Americans: The Colonial Experience* (1958), *America and the Image of Europe* (1960), *The Image or What Happened to the American Dream* (1962), *The Americans: The National Experience* (1965), *The Sociology of the Absurd* (1970), *The Americans: The Democratic Experience* [Pulitzer Prize] (1973), *Democracy and Its Discontents* (1974), *The Exploring Spirit* (1976), *The Republic of Technology* (1978), *The Discoverers* (1983), *Hidden History* (1987).

Phyllis S. Busch is a naturalist, writer, teacher, and author of fifteen books. Writings include: *The Seven Sleepers* (1985), *Wildflowers and the Stories Behind Their Names* (1977), *Cactus in the Desert* (1979).

Helen Caldicott (1938) was born in Melbourne, Australia. She earned a medical degree at the University of South Australia, became a fellow at Children's Hospital in Boston, and later joined the faculty of the Harvard Medical School. During the 1970s, Caldicott became an activist in the protest movement against nuclear energy, emerging as one of its most powerful leaders. She served as president of Physicians for Social Responsibility and founded Women's Action for Nuclear Disarmament. Caldicott is an active lecturer against nuclear power and on environmental issues, speaking in the United States, Australia, Japan, Germany, and the Soviet Union. She was the subject of the film *If You Love This Planet,* which won an Academy Award. Writings include: *Nuclear Madness: What You Can Do!* (1979), *Missile Envy: The Arms Race and Nuclear War* (1984).

Peter Cameron (1959) was born in Pompton Plains, New Jersey, and was educated at Hamilton College. He has worked as a subsidiary rights assistant at St. Martin's Press and taught at Oberlin College in Ohio. Cameron writes well-crafted short stories about ordinary people who face problems in their everyday lives. Writings include: *One Way or Another* (1986).

Pat Esslinger Carr (1932) was born in Grass Creek, Wyoming. She received a B.A. and an M.A. from Rice University and a Ph.D. from Tulane. She has taught at Texas Southern University, Dillard University, University of New Orleans, and University of Texas. Her work includes short stories, articles, and novels. Writings include: *Beneath the Hill of the Three Crosses* (1970), *The Grass Creek Chronicle* (1976), *Bernard Shaw* (1976), *The Women in the Mirror* (1977), *Mimbres Mythology* (1978), *Night of the Luminarias* (1986), *Sonahchi* (1988).

Sally Carrighar (1905) was born in Cleveland, Ohio, to a devoted father and a psychotic mother. In her autobiography, *Home to the Wilderness,* Carrighar reports that her mother despised her and even encouraged her to commit suicide—possibly because she was disfigured during birth by the forceps. Carrighar attended Wellesley College, underwent psychoanalysis, and tried various professions from pianist and dancer to fiction writer. Finally, while recovering from depression and heart disease, she discovered her career as a nature writer. In many of her works, Carrighar adopts the point of view of the animals in a particular habitat and describes how each is affected by a natural event. Writings include: *Exploring Marin* (1941), *One Day on Beetle Rock* (1944), *One Day at Teton Marsh* (1947), *Prey of the Arctic* (1951), *Icebound Summer* (1953), *As Far as They Go* (a play, 1956), *Moonlight at Midday* (1958), *Wild Voice of the North* (1959), *The Glass Dove* (1962), *Wild Heritage* (1965), *Home to the Wilderness* (1973), *The Twilight Seas* (1975).

Rachel Carson (1907–1964), born in Springdale, Pennsylvania, was a distinguished scientist and environmentalist who described powerfully and poetically ecological relationships and rhythms of nature. She began her college career as an English major at Chatham College but switched to biology and received a B.A. in science. Years later, she realized that biology gave her something to write about. Carson received a master's degree in zoology from Johns Hopkins University and in 1947 became editor-in-chief for the U.S. Fish and Wildlife Service. Her government pamphlets included a series on conservation, which fueled her growing concern with ecology. In 1951, Carson published *The Sea Around Us,* which made the best-seller list and won the National Book Award. In 1962, she published *Silent Spring,* a study of the harmful effects of herbicides and insecticides. The chemical industry branded her a "hysterical woman," but the book prompted President John F. Kennedy to appoint an advisory committee to study the problem. The committee's report upheld Carson's work, which subsequently became a major factor in the ecology movement. In 1963, Carson became the first woman to receive the Audubon Medal. Writings include: *Under the Sea-Wind* (1941), *The Sea Around Us* (1951), *The Edge of the Sea* (1955), *The Silent Spring* (1962), *The Sea* (1964), *The Sense of Wonder* (1965), *The Rocky Coast* (1971).

John Stewart Collis (1900–1984) was born in Ireland and educated at Rugby and Oxford. He was best known for his ability to write poetically and philosophically about science, natural history, and agriculture. He was also a biographer, chronicling the lives of Columbus, George Bernard Shaw, Havelock Ellis, the Carlyles, and Tolstoy. Writings include: *Forward to Nature* (1927), *The Sounding Cataract* (1936), *An Irishman's England* (1937), *Down to Earth* (1947), *The Triumph of the Tree* (1950), *The Moving Waters* (1955), *The World of Light* (1960), *The Worm Forgives the Plough* (1973). He also wrote biographies, including *Shaw* (1925), *The Life of Tolstoy* (1969), *Bound Upon a Course* (autobiography 1971), *Christopher Columbus* (1974).

Norman Cousins (1915) served as editor of the *Saturday Review* from 1940 to 1978 and is now a professor of medical humanities and affiliated with the Brain Research Institute in New York. He served as a diplomat during three presidential administrations; received almost fifty honorary degrees from institutions such as American University, Boston University, and Syracuse University; and has written numerous books on social and political issues. Cousins is probably best known for his unorthodox approach to healing and health. Almost completely paralyzed by a life-threatening disease and given a few months to live, Cousins left the hospital and checked into a motel—where he took massive doses of vitamin C, watched Marx Brothers movies, and read humor by P. G. Wodehouse, Robert Benchley, and James Thurber. Fifteen years later, he sped recovery from a massive coronary by fashioning his own diet and regimen. Cousins believes strongly that the will to live has therapeutic value. Writings include: *The Good Inheritance: The Democratic Chance* (1942), *Modern Man Is Obsolete* (1945), *The Last Defense in a Nuclear Age* (1960), *Profiles of Gandhi* (1969), *The Quest for Immortality* (1974), *Anatomy of an Illness as Perceived by the Patient* (1979), *Healing and Belief* (1982), *The Healing Heart: Antidotes to Panic and Helplessness, Head First: The Biology of Hope* (1989).

Guy Davenport (1927) was born in Anderson, South Carolina, and educated at Duke University, Oxford University, and Harvard. An English professor at the University of Kentucky, Davenport is a prolific writer, an illustrator, and a librettist. Writings include: *The Intelligence of Louis Agassiz* (1963), *Flowers and Leaves* (1963), *Sappho: Songs and Fragments* (1965), *Do You Have a Poem Book on e. e. cummings?* (1969), *Da Vinci's Bicycle* (1975), *Geography of the Imagination* (1981), *Cities on Hills* (1983), *Apples and Pears* (1983), *The Bicycle Rider* (1985), *Every Force Evolves a Form* (1987), *The Jules Verne Steam Balloon* (1987).

Joan Didion (1934) was born in Sacramento, California, a conservative, middle-class, farming community. While an undergraduate at the University of California at Berkeley, she won an essay contest sponsored by *Vogue* magazine. After graduation, she was hired by the magazine, eventually becoming an associate editor. A fifth-generation descendant of the pioneers who settled the Sacramento Valley, Didion grew up with a deep sense of heritage and roots. During the sixties and early seventies, she observed the Vietnam conflict, political assassinations, violent protests, mass murders, and she concluded that the fabric of American society was getting looser and looser. Her nostalgia for the past and the disintegration of the present are two frequent themes in Didion's essays, novels, columns, and screenplays. Writings include: *Slouching Toward Bethlehem* (1968), *Play It As It Lays* (1970), *A Book of Common Prayer* (1977), *The White Album* (1979), *Salvador* (1983), *Democracy* (1984), *Miami* (1987).

Annie Dillard (1945) was born into a wealthy Pittsburgh family. She received an undergraduate degree in English and a master's degree in writing from Hollins College in Virginia. In 1979, she joined the faculty at Wesleyan College in Connecticut. Dillard's first book, *Tickets for a Prayer Wheel* (1973), was a collection of poems. She is most admired, however, for her prose style, which incorporates poetic techniques such as the repetition of sound and structure—for example, "There are no events but thoughts and the heart's hard turning, the heart's slow learning where to love and whom." A keen observer of nature, Dillard examines both the beautiful and the grotesque with equal interest and skill. She won the Pulitzer Prize for *Pilgrim at Tinker Creek*, which relates a year's experiences in the Roanoke Valley of Virginia. Writings include: *Tickets for a Prayer Wheel* (1973), *Pilgrim at Tinker Creek* (1974), *Holy the Firm* (1978), *Living by Fiction* (1982), *Encounters with Chinese Writers* (1984), *An American Childhood* (1987), *The Writing Life* (1989).

Lydia Dotto (1949) was born in Alberta, Canada, and educated at Carleton University. A well-known Canadian journalist, Dotto has received numerous awards for her articles on scientific subjects ranging from Arctic diving to high-energy physics to climate. In 1983, she was given the Sandford Fleming Medal from the Royal Canadian Institute for promoting public understanding of science. Writings include: *Planet Earth in Jeopardy* (1986), *Canada in Space* (1987), *Thinking the Unthinkable: Civilization and Rapid Climate Change* (1988), *One Third of a Lifetime: The Impact of Sleep on Waking Life* (1989).

Loren Eiseley (1907–1977) in his autobiography, *All the Strange Hours,* chronicles his troubled childhood, growing up in Nebraska with a deaf and mentally disturbed mother. He dropped in and out of college for almost a decade, hopping freight trains in the West and recovering from tuberculosis in the Mojave Desert and in Colorado. Finally, he graduated from the University of Nebraska with majors in English and anthropology. While there, he participated in a paleontology expedition (pursuing his interest in the history of the earth and of humans) and was a frequent contributor to the literary magazine *Prairie Schooner* (pursuing his interest in writing). Eiseley earned a master's degree and a Ph.D. in anthropology from the University of Pennsylvania and participated in an anthropological expedition to the Southwest. He subsequently taught anthropology at the University of Kansas and the University of Pennsylvania. In his writings, Eiseley ponders the vastness of time, the evolution of life, and the mysteries of the universe. In an exquisite and poetic prose style, he combines personal experiences, keen observation, philosophy, and scientific theories. Writings include: *The Immense Journey* (1957), *Darwin's Century, The Firmament of Time* (1960), *The Night Country* (1971), *The Unexpected Universe* (1972), *All the Strange Hours: An Excavation of Life* (1975).

Peter Farb (1929–1980) was born in New York City and educated at Vanderbilt and Columbia. In addition to being a prolific writer, Farb was also a linguist, anthropologist, naturalist, and editor. He served as curator of American Indian cultures at Riverside Museum in New York and as consultant to the Smithsonian Institution. His many books cover an impressive variety of subjects—butterflies, dams, forests, North American Indians, language, natural history of North America, ecology, and more. Writings include: *Living Earth* (1959), *The Story of Butterflies and other Insects* (1959), *The Insect World* (1960), *The Story of Dams* (1961), *The Forest* (1961), *The Story of Life: Plants and Animals through the Ages* (1962), *Face of North America: The Natural History of a Continent* (1963), *The Land and Wildlife of North America* (1964), *Man's Rise to Civilization as Shown by the Indians of North America from Primeval Times to the Coming of the Industrial State* (1968), *Word Play: What Happens When People Talk* (1974), *Humankind* (1978), *Consuming Passions: The Anthropology of Eating* (with George Armelagos 1980).

Robert Finch (1943) is a naturalist, conservationist, and essayist. In much of his work, he describes the plant and animal life of Cape Cod with a keen eye for detail and a poetic prose style.

Writings include: *Common Ground: A Naturalist's Cape Cod* (1981), *The Primal Place* (1984), *Outlands: Journeys to the Outer Edges of Cape Cod* (1986).

Jesse Hill Ford   (1928) was born in Troy, Alabama. He was educated at Vanderbilt University, the University of Florida, and the University of Oslo. Known for his realistic depiction of racial tensions in the South, Ford authored novels, short stories, and plays. Writings include: *Mountains of Gilead* (1961), *The Conversion of Buster Drumwright* (1964), *The Liberation of Lord Byron Jones* (1965), *Fishes, Birds, and Sons of Men* (1968), *The Feast of St. Barnabas* (1969), *The Raider* (1975).

Ernesto Galarza   (1905–1984) was born in Mexico and educated at Columbia University, receiving a Ph.D. in history and political science. He was a poet, a prose writer, and a teacher at the University of Southern California. In addition, he was a well-known labor leader who opposed the recruitment of illegal aliens from Mexico as a source of cheap farm labor. Galarza served as vice-president of the National Farm Labor Union; secretary of the National Agricultural Workers Union; a member of the U.S. House of Representatives Committee on Education and Labor; and consultant to the National Farmers Union, the U.S. Civil Rights Commission, the Anti-Defamation League, and the Ford Foundation. Writings include: *Barrio Boy* (1970), *Spiders in the House and Workers in the Field* (1970), *Kodachromes in Ryhme* (1982), *Farm Workers and Agri-Business in California, 1947–1960* (1977).

William Geist   is a journalist whose work appears in such newspapers as the *New York Times* and the *Chicago Tribune.* Some of his favorite subjects are the values and pastimes of suburban America—garage sales, designer jeans, aerobics classes, Christmas lawn decorations, and Tupperware. Writings include: *Toward a Safe and Sane Halloween, and Other Tales of Suburbia* (1985), *The Zucchini Plague* (1987).

Nikki Giovanni   (1943) was born in Knoxville, Tennessee, the daughter of a probation officer and a social worker. As a child, she was surrounded by close, loving relatives. She graduated with honors in history from Fisk University. She also attended the University of Pennsylvania School of Social Work as well as the Columbia School of Arts and taught at Queens College and Rutgers. In the 1960s, Giovanni was a civil rights activist and revolutionary poet, but her later work is varied—dealing with the individual's struggle for fulfillment, the feelings of black children growing up in America, black womanhood, and family reminiscences. Writings include: *Black Feeling, Black Talk* (1968), *Black Judgment* (1960), *Recreation* (1970), *Gemini* (1971), *Spin a Soft Black Song* (1971), *My House* (1972), *A Poetic Equation: Conversations between Nikki Giovanni and Margaret Walker* (1974), *James Baldwin and Nikki Giovanni: A Dialogue* (1975), *Women and Men* (1975), *Cotton Candy on a Rainy Day* (1980), *Those Who Ride the Night Winds* (1983), *Sacred Cows . . . and Other Edibles* (1988).

A. R. Gurney, Jr.   (1930) was born in Buffalo, New York, and educated at Yale University. He has taught both in high school and at Massachusetts Institute of Technology. Gurney is a novelist as well as a prolific playwright. Writings include: *The Bridal Dinner* (1962), *The Rape of Bunny Stuntz* (1964), *The Comeback* (1964), *The Open Meeting* (1965), *The David Show* (1966), *The Golden Fleece* (1968), *The Love Course* (1970), *Scenes from American Life* (1970), *The House of Mirth* (1972), *The Old One-Two* (1973), *The Problem* (1973), *The Gospel According to Joe* (1974), *Children* (1974), *Who Killed Richard Cory* (1976), *The Wayside Motor Inn* (1977), *Entertaining Strangers* (1977), *Four Plays* (1985), *The Snow Ball* (1988).

Donald Hall   (1928) was born in Connecticut and educated at Harvard and Oxford. Best known as a poet, Hall also writes short stories, textbooks, children's books, essays, critical studies, and drama. For many years, Hall taught at the University of Michigan. Writings include: *Exiles and Marriages* (1955), *The Dark Houses* (1958), *String Too Short to Be Saved* (1961), *The Alligator Bride* (1969), *The Yellow Room* (1971), *Writing Well* (1973), *Playing Around* (1974), *The Town of Hill* (1975), *Dock Ellis in the Country of Baseball* (1976), *Kicking the Leaves* (1978), *The Man Who Lived Alone* (1984), *Fathers Playing Catch with Sons* (1985), *Seasons at Eagle Pond* (1987).

Edward Hoagland (1932) grew up in a rural suburb of New York City, where he experienced the advantages of both city and country living. As a young man, Hoagland was a stutterer and thus uncomfortable in social situations. He has said that because he was unable to talk to people, he became close to animals. Although Hoagland's family was affluent and he was educated at Harvard, he purposely set out to experience the seamier side of life: he fought forest fires, traveled with a circus, and lived with winos on skid row. Hoagland has written novels and travel books, but his best form is the essay, which allows him to speak directly to readers. Writings include: *Cat Man* (1956), *Circle Home* (1960), *The Peacock's Tail* (1965), *Notes from the Century Before: A Journal of British Columbia* (1969), *The Courage of Turtles* (1971), *Walking the Dead Diamond River* (1973), *Red Wolves and Black Bears* (1976), *African Calliope: A Journey to the Sudan* (1979), *The Tugman's Passage* (1982), *Heart's Desire* (1988).

Manuela Hoelterhoff (1949) was born in West Germany and immigrated to the United States in 1957. Educated at Hofstra University and New York University, she began her career in journalism while still in college by writing for the *Wall Street Journal*. Hoelterhoff has served as associate editor of the *Wall Street Journal*, editor-in-chief of *Art and Auction* magazine, and associate editor of *Academic Encyclopedia*. She won the Pulitzer Prize in criticism in 1983.

Marjorie Hope (1923) was born in Lakewood, Ohio, and educated at Sarah Lawrence College, Columbia University, and New York University. She has worked as a teacher and a social worker. Hope considers herself a radical pacifist who advocates nonviolent change of society. Writings include: *Youth Against the World* (1970), *The Struggle for Humanity: Agents of Nonviolent Change in a Violent World* (with James Young 1977), *The Faces of Homelessness* (with James Young 1986).

James D. Houston (1933) is a novelist, biographer, and short story writer. Writings include: *Between Battles* (1968), *Gig* (1969), *A Native Son of the Golden West* (1971), *Three Songs for My Father* (1974), *Continental Drift* (1978), *Gasoline: The Automotive Adventures of Charlie Bates* (1980), *Californians: Searing for the Golden State* (1982), *Love Life* (1985), *The Men in My Life, and Other More or Less True Recollections of Kinship* (1987).

Roger Kahn (1927) was born in Brooklyn and educated at New York University. His career in journalism includes positions with the *New York Herald Tribune, Sports Illustrated, Newsweek, Esquire,* and *Saturday Evening Post*. Writings include: *The Passionate People* (1968), *The Battle for Morningside Heights* (1970), *The Boys of Summer* (1972), *How the Weather Was* (1973), *A Season in the Sun* (1977), *But Not to Keep* (1978), *The Seventh Game* (1982), *Good Enough to Dream* (1985), *Joe and Marilyn* (1986).

Stephen King (1947) was born in Portland, Maine, and educated at the University of Maine. He is one of the most successful writers of horror fiction, and several of his works have been made into extremely popular films. Particularly adept at the macabre, King writes of man-eating rats, vampires, deadly viruses, telekinesis, and gore. Writings include: *Carrie* (1974),

Salem's Lot (1975), *The Shining* (1977), *The Stand* (1978), *Night Shift* (1978), *The Dead Zone* (1979), *Firestarter* (1980), *Stephen King's Danse Macabre* (1981), *The Bachman Books* (1985), *The Drawing of the Three* (1989), *Four Past Midnight* (1990).

Joy Kogawa (1935), a Japanese Canadian, was born in Vancouver, British Columbia. During World War II, she was separated from her family and exiled in the Canadian wilderness. Her novel *Obasan* is a fictionalized account of her experiences with racism and persecution. Educated at the University of Alberta, the Conservatory of Music, and the University of Saskatchewan, Kogawa has been a schoolteacher, a writer for the Canadian Prime Minister's Office, and writer-in-residence at the University of Ottawa. Writings include: *The Splintered Moon* (1967), *A Choice of Dreams* (1974), *Jericho Road* (1977), *Obasan* (1982), *Woman in the Woods* (1985), *Naomi's Read* (1988).

Leonard Koppett (1923) was born in Moscow, Russia. He received a bachelor's degree from Columbia University in 1946. He has served as sportswriter and columnist for various publications, including the *New York Herald Tribune,* the *New York Post,* the *New York Times,* and *Sporting News.* He has also been a free-lance columnist and a teacher of journalism at Stanford University. Writings include: *A Thinking Man's Guide to Baseball* (1967), *24 Seconds to Shoot* (1969), *The New York Times Guide to Spectator Sports* (1970), *The New York Mets* (1970), *The Essence of the Game is Deception* (1974), *Sports Illusion, Sports Reality* (1981).

Jonathan Kozol (1936) was born in Boston and educated at Harvard and Oxford. A radical educator and activist, Kozol has taught in elementary schools, high schools, colleges, and universities. He has served on a half-dozen school boards and directed the National Literacy Coalition. Much of Kozol's published work describes his experiences as a teacher in the Boston ghetto schools and in Cuba; alternatives to traditional education; and literacy and homelessness in the United States. Writings include: *Death at an Early Age* (1967), *Free Schools* (1972), *Children of the Revolution* (1978), *Prisoners of Silence* (1979), *On Being a Teacher* (1981), *Illiterate America* (1985), *Rachel and Her Children* (1988).

Margaret Laurence (1926–1987) was born in Manitoba, Canada; received a B.A. from the University of Manitoba in 1946; and lived her life throughout Canada and in Africa. In her essays, novels, short stories, and children's literature, Laurence relies heavily on a sense of place. She received numerous awards for her novels and short fiction, and she published widely in journals and magazines. While living in Somaliland, she translated and edited an anthology of Somali prose and poetry. Writings include: *The Prophet's Camel Bell* (1963), *The Tomorrow Tamer and Other Stories* (1964), *The Stone Angel* (1964), *A Jest of God* (1966), *The Fire Dwellers* (1969), *The Diviners* (1974), *Heart of a Stranger* (1977).

Ursula K. Le Guin (1929) received her B.A. from Radcliffe and her M.A. from Columbia University. Her writings are primarily thought of as science fiction, but they transcend narrow categorizing because of her insight into the human condition. She has won many awards; among them are several Hugo awards, Nebula awards, Jupiter awards, and the National Book Award. Writings include: *Rocannon's World* (1966), *A Wizard of Earthsea* (1968), *The Left Hand of Darkness* (1969), *The Tombs of Atuan* (1971), *The Lathe of Heaven* (1971), *The Farthest Shore* (1972), *The Dispossessed: An Ambiguous Utopia* (1974), *The Wind's Twelve Quarters* (1975), *The Word for World Is Forest* (1976), *The Beginning Place* (1980), *The Eye of the Heron* (1983), *Planet of Exile* (1983), *The Language of the Night Wood* (1985), *Malafrena* (1986), *Wild Oats and Fireweed* (1987), *Dancing at the Edge of the World* (1988).

Grace Lichtenstein (1941) graduated from Brooklyn College of the City University of New York. She wrote advertising copy and radio news scripts before she became a reporter for the

New York Times. Her many articles, particularly on women in sports, have been published in *Esquire, Redbook, Cosmopolitan, Rolling Stone,* and other popular magazines. Writings include: *A Long Way Baby: Behind the Scenes in Women's Pro Tennis* (1974), *Machisma: Women and Daring* (1981).

Paul Loeb   (1952) attended Stanford University and New York's New School for Social Research. For a while he worked as an editor of *Liberation* magazine; now he works as a free-lance writer and lecturer on a wide range of subjects, but particularly on nuclear issues. He has published articles in such publications as the *Washington Post, Village Voice, Humanist, Mother Earth News,* and the *Los Angeles Times.* Writings include: *Nuclear Culture: Living and Working in the World's Largest Atomic Complex* (1982), *Hope in Hard Times: America's Peace Movement and the Reagan Era* (1986).

Phillip Lopate   (1943) was born in Jamaica Heights, New York, and graduated from Columbia University in 1964. He began writing in high school and continued writing through college. He has continued to write both fiction and nonfiction. In addition, he teaches creative writing; *Being with Children* is an account of his efforts teaching in the New York City schools between 1968 and 1975. Writings include: *The Eyes Don't Always Want to Stay Open: Poems and a Japanese Tale* (1972), *Being with Children* (1975), *The Daily Round: New Poems* (1976), *Confessions of Summer* (1979), *Bachelorhood: Tales of the Metropolis* (1981), *The Rug Merchant* (1987), *Against Joie De Vivre: Personal Essays* (1989).

Alison Lurie   (1926) was born in Chicago and graduated from Radcliffe. She now teaches at Cornell University. Her writings are primarily fiction; for *Foreign Affairs* (1984) she won a Pulitzer Prize in that category. In addition, she has written both nonfiction and children's literature. Writings include: *Love and Friendship* (1962), *The Nowhere City* (1965), *Imaginary Friends* (1967), *Real People* (1969), *The War between the Tates* (1974), *Only Children* (1979), *The Language of Clothes* (1981), and *Foreign Affairs* (1984), *The Truth about Lorin Jones* (1988).

Robert MacNeil   (1931) was born in Montreal, Canada, and was educated at Dalhousie University and Carleton University. He has been in broadcasting since 1950 and is today executive editor and coanchor of television's award-winning "MacNeil/Lehrer NewsHour." In addition, he works on television documentaries and contributes essays to books and periodicals such as *Harper's, Nation,* and *TV Guide.* Writings include: *The People Machine: The Influence of Television on American Politics* (1968), *The Right Place at the Right Time* (1982), *The Way We Were: 1963, the Year Kennedy Was Shot* (1988), *Wordstruck* (1989).

Bobbie Ann Mason   (1940) was originally from Mayfield, Kentucky, and was educated at the University of Kentucky, the State University of New York at Binghampton, and the University of Connecticut. She is primarily known for her short stories about ordinary people. Writings include: *The Girl Sleuth: A Feminist Guide to the Bobbsey Twins, Nancy Drew, and Their Sisters* (1975), *Shiloh and Other Stories* (1982), *In Country* (1985), *Spence and Lila* (1988), *Love Life: Stories* (1989).

Vonda McIntyre   (1948) was born in Kentucky and graduated from the University of Washington, where she studied biology. She writes science fiction stories, novelettes, and novels—many of which have won awards such as the Nebula Award and the Hugo Award. McIntyre prefers science fiction because it allows her to explore experiences people have not yet had. Writings include: *The Exile Waiting* (1975), *Dreamsnake* (1978), *Fireflood and Other Stories* (includes "Of Mist, and Grass, and Sand" and "Aztecs") (1979), *The Entropy Effect* (1981), *Star Trek*

II: The Wrath of Khan (1982), *Superluminal* (1983), *Star Trek III: The Search for Spock* (1984), *Barbary* (1986), *Star Trek IV: The Voyage Home* (1986), *Starfarers* (1989).

Floretta Dukes McKenzie   received her education at D.C. Teachers College, Howard University, and George Washington University. Her work has primarily been in teaching and administration. She has served as superintendent of the Washington, D.C., city schools.

Mary Mebane   (1933) was born in Durham, North Carolina. She went to North Carolina State College and to the University of North Carolina, where she earned a doctoral degree. Her writings mainly cover black people of the South, post-1960, whom she sees as the most creative people in America. Writings include: *Mary* (1981), *Mary, Wayfarer* (1983).

Casey Miller   (1919) works as a free-lance writer and editor. She graduated from Smith College, studied graphic arts at Yale, and was an editor with Seabury Press. With Kate Swift, she has written extensively on sexism in language. Writings include: *Words and Women: New Language in New Times* (1976), *The Handbook of Nonsexist Writing* (1980).

Jessica Mitford   (1917) was born in England into a very unusual British family, described in Mitford's autobiographies, *Daughters and Rebels* and *A Fine Old Conflict.* Known as "Queen of the Muckrakers," she has engaged in investigative reporting to expose deception by such groups as funeral directors, mail-order writing schools, "fat farms" for the wealthy, and over-priced restaurants. Writings include: *Daughters and Rebels* (1960), *The American Way of Death* (1963), *Kind and Usual Punishment: The Prison Business* (1973), *A Fine Old Conflict* (1977), *Poison Penmanship: The Gentle Art of Muckraking* (1979).

N. Scott Momaday   (1934) A Native American writer and painter, was educated on Navajo, Apache, and Pueblo reservations and at the University of New Mexico and Stanford University, where he received a Ph.D. In his works, he emphasizes Native American culture—its legends, history, and rights. He has written poetry, fiction, folklore, and autobiography. In 1969, he won the Pulitzer Prize for *House Made of Dawn.* Writings include: *House Made of Dawn* (1968), *The Way to Rainy Mountain* (1969), *Angle of Geese and Other Poems* (1974), *The Gourd Dancer* (1976), *The Names: A Memoir* (1976), *The Ancient Child* (1989).

Joseph Monninger   (1953) was born in Baltimore and grew up in New Jersey. He was educated at Temple University and the University of New Hampshire. After serving in the Peace Corps, he became an English teacher and a writer. He contributes to periodicals, but he is primarily a novelist. Writings include: *The Family Man* (1982), *Summer Hunt* (1983), *New Jersey* (1986), *Second Season* (1987).

Jan Morris   (1926), an award-winning British writer, began work as a journalist and became a free-lance writer, particularly of travel and history books. First writing as James Morris, Morris recreated Hillary's and Tenzing's conquest of Mt. Everest after accompanying the expedition to the 22,000-foot level. After undergoing gender change, described in *Conundrum,* Morris began to write under the name Jan. Writings include: *Islam Inflamed: A Middle East Picture* (1957), *Coronation Everest* (1958), *The World of Venice* (1960, 1974), *The Road to Hudders-field: A Journey to Five Continents* (1963), *Pax Britannica: The Climax of an Empire* (1968), *Places* (1972), *Conundrum* (1974), *Travels* (1976), *Journeys* (1985), *Pleasures of a Tangled Life* (1989).

Holcomb B. Noble   works for the *New York Times* as the deputy director of science news. Works include: *Next: The Coming Era in Medicine* (1988), *Next: The Coming Age in Science* (1988).

Joyce Carol Oates   (1938), one of America's most prolific writers, was born in Lockport, New York, and was educated at Syracuse University and the University of Wisconsin. She has written many novels, short-story collections, and poetry; she often averages two books per year. Her awards have been numerous—among them, the O. Henry Award, the Rosenthal Award, and the National Book Award for fiction. Her writings usually picture society tangled in a complex, often violent universe. In addition to writing, she teaches at Princeton University. Writings include: *By the North Gate* (1963), *With Shuddering Fall* (1965), *Expensive People* (1968), *them* (1969, 1986), *Do with Me What You Will* (1973), *The Assassins: A Book of Hours* (1975), *Son of the Morning* (1978), *Unholy Loves* (1979), *Bellefleur* (1980), *Angel of Light* (1981), *Contraries: Essays* (1981), *A Bloodsmoor Romance* (1982), *Mysteries of Winterthurn* (1984), *Solstice* (1985), *Marya: A Life* (1986), *Raven's Wing* (1986), *You Must Remember This* (1987), *On Boxing* (1987), *Women Writers: Occasions and Opportunities* (1988), *American Appetites* (1989), *Time Traveler: Poems 1983–1989* (1989).

Eleanor Perényi   (1918), the daughter of a novelist and a naval officer, lived many places—Europe, China, the West Indies, and all over the United States. Married to a Hungarian, she wrote about her years in Hungary in *More Was Lost.* She has also worked as an editor at *Harper's, Living for Young Homemakers, Charm,* and *Mademoiselle* and has published articles in such magazines as *Atlantic, Esquire,* and *Harper's Bazaar.* Writings include: *More Was Lost* (1946), *The Bright Sword* (1955), *Liszt: The Artist as Romantic Hero* (1974), *Green Thoughts: A Writer in the Garden* (1981).

Vernon Pizer   (1918) was born in Boston, Massachusetts, and attended George Washington University. After retiring from the Army as a lieutenant colonel and after extensive travel, he has devoted himself to full-time writing. The subjects he has written on are diverse—military affairs, the sciences, and social issues. Writings include: *Rockets, Missiles and Space* (1962), *The Useful Atom* (1966), *The United States Army* (1967), *The World Ocean* (1967), *Glorious Triumphs: Athletes Who Conquered Adversity* (1968, 1980), *Short-Changed by History: America's Neglected Innovators* (1979), *Take My Word for It* (1981), *Eat the Grapes Downward* (1983), *The Irrepressible Automobile* (1986).

Neil Postman   in his prolific writings has focused primarily on language, education, and the media. In addition to his many books, he has published articles in periodicals, both scholarly and popular. Writings include: *Television and the Teaching of English* (1961), *Teaching as a Subversive Activity* (1969), *The Soft Revolution: A Student Handbook for Turning Schools Around* (1971), *The School Book* (1975), *Crazy Talk, Stupid Talk: How We Defeat Ourselves by the Way We Talk and What to Do About It* (1976), *Teaching as a Conserving Activity* (1979), *Amusing Ourselves to Death: Public Discourse in the Age of Show Business* (1986), *Conscientious Objections: Stirring Up Trouble about Language, Technology, and Education* (1988).

David Quammin   (1948) was born in Cincinnati and studied literature at Yale University and at Oxford University as a Rhodes scholar. Afterwards, he studied zoology as a graduate student at the University of Montana. He has written novels, and his essays have appeared in *Outside, Audubon, Esquire,* and *Rolling Stone.* Writings include: *To Walk the Line* (1970), *Natural Acts: A Sidelong View of Science and Nature* (1985), *The Soul of Victor Tronko* (1987), *Blood Line: Stories of Fathers and Sons* (1988), *The Flight of the Iguana: A Sidelong Look at Science and Nature* (1988).

Diane Ravitch   (1938) was born in Texas and educated at Wellesley College and Columbia University. In the field of education, she has been a teacher, consultant, and writer. Writings include:

The Great School Wars, New York City: 1805–1973 (1974), *The Revisionists Revised: A Critique of the Radical Attack on Schools* (1978), *The State of American Education* (1980), *The Troubled Crusade: American Education 1945–1980* (1983), *The Schools We Deserve: Reflections on the Educational Crises of Our Time* (1985).

Marjorie Kinnan Rawlings   (1896–1953) was an American novelist, short story writer, journalist, and poet. Her home in Cross Creek, Florida, was the setting for her most famous work, *The Yearling,* which won a Pulitzer Prize in 1938. Writings include: *South Moon Under* (1933), *Golden Apples* (1935), *The Yearling* (1938), *Cross Creek* (1942), *The Sojourner* (1953), *The Secret River* (1955).

James C. Rettie   (1904–1969), born and reared on a ranch in eastern Oregon, attended Willamette University, Yale University, and the University of London. As an ecologist for the United States Forest Service, he wrote extensively. He also worked as an economic adviser to Stewart Udall, who served as secretary of the interior under Presidents Kennedy and Johnson.

Roger Rosenblatt   (1940), born in New York, was educated at New York University and Harvard. He has worked as a teacher, literary editor, editorial writer, and author, holding positions at Harvard, *New Republic,* the *Washington Post,* and *Time.* He has contributed articles to many periodicals including *Harper's* and *Saturday Review.* In 1974, he wrote *Black Fiction.* He makes regular appearances as a commentator on the "MacNeil/Lehrer NewsHour."

Mike Royko   (1932), a prominent journalist, has been writing for Chicago newspapers since 1956. His typical attacks on politicians, bureaucracy, pretension, and arrogance combine ridicule with humor. In 1972, he won the Pulitzer Prize in commentary. His books are primarily collections of his columns. Writings include: *Up Against It* (1967), *I May Be Wrong, but I Doubt It* (1968), *Boss: Richard J. Daley of Chicago* (1971), *Slats Grobnik and Some Other Friends* (1973), *Sez Who? Sez Me* (1982), *Like I Was Sayin'* (1984), *Dr. Kookie, You're Right* (1989).

Jean Stafford   (1915–1979) was an American writer primarily acclaimed for her short stories. She was especially skilled at creating realistic settings, characters, and dialogue. She frequently contributed articles to periodicals such as *The New Yorker, Vogue, Harper's, Mademoiselle,* and *New Republic.* Writings include: *Boston Adventure* (1944), *The Mountain Lion* (1947), *The Catherine Wheel* (1952), *Children Are Bored on Sunday* (1953), *Bad Characters* (1966), *A Mother in History* (1966), *The Collected Stories of Jean Stafford* (1969).

Elizabeth Stone   has published articles in many periodicals, including the *New York Times Magazine, Village Voice,* and *Psychology Today.* She teaches English and media studies at Fordham University's College at Lincoln Center. Writings include: *Black Sheep and Kissing Cousins: How Our Family Stories Shape Us* (1988).

Kate Swift   (1923) received a degree in journalism from the University of North Carolina and did graduate study at New York University. In partnership with Casey Miller, she became interested in the effect of language on women. The two have published articles in magazines such as *New York, Ms.,* and *New York Times Magazine.* Writings include: *Words and Women: New Language in New Times* (1976), *The Handbook of Nonsexist Writing* (1980).

Reay Tannahill   (1929), born in Scotland and educated at the University of Glasgow, first worked in advertising before becoming a writer in 1962. She writes primarily histories of subjects that historians have for the most part neglected—food and sex. Writings include: *Regency*

England (1964), *Paris in the Revolution* (1966), *The Fine Art of Food* (1968), *Food in History* (1973), *Flesh and Blood: A History of the Cannibal Complex* (1975), *Sex in History* (1980), *The World, the Flesh and the Devil* (1987).

Annabel Thomas (1929) was born in Ohio and focuses in her writing on life in rural Ohio. She has worked in journalism and as a teacher. Her collection of stories, *The Phototropic Woman,* won both the award for short fiction from the University of Iowa and from PEN American Center. Writings include: *The Phototropic Woman* (1981).

Calvin Trillin (1935) was born in Kansas City and educated at Yale. He has worked as a journalist for *Time, The New Yorker,* and *Nation* and has contributed articles to many other periodicals. His writings contain not only humor but also insight into the immense variety in American life. Most of his columns have been collected and published as books. Writings include: *An Education in Georgia* (1964), *U.S. Journal* (1971), *American Fried: Adventures of a Happy Eater* (1974), *Floater* (1980), *Uncivil Liberties* (1982), *Third Helpings* (1983), *Killings* (1984), *With All Disrespect: More Uncivil Liberties* (1985), *If You Can't Say Something Nice* (1987), *Travels with Alice* (1989).

Barbara Tuchman (1912–1989) grew up in New York City and graduated from Radcliffe College. She was a historian who described herself as a storyteller dealing in true stories instead of fiction. Her career as a writer began in 1935, when, after working in Tokyo, she wrote an essay that appeared in the journal *Foreign Affairs.* She covered the Spanish Civil War for *The Nation* and wrote *The Lost British Policy* (1938) on Britain's foreign policy toward Spain. Her second book did not appear until 1956, and its publication was the beginning of a surge of writing activity. Twice she has won the Pulitzer Prize. Writings include: *The Bible and the Sword* (1956), *The Zimmermann Telegram* (1958), *The Guns of August* (1962), *The Proud Tower* (1966), *Stilwell and the American Experience in China* (1970), *Notes from China* (1972), *A Distant Mirror* (1978), *Practicing History* (1981), *The March of Folly: From Troy to Vietnam* (1984).

Sherry Turkle (1948) was born in New York and educated at Harvard. She is a scholar who combines interest in psychology, sociology, and the computer. She finds a close link between computers and culture and claims that computers will change the way people think. Writings include: *Psychoanalytic Politics: Freud's French Revolution* (1978), *The Second Self: Computers and the Human Spirit* (1984).

John Updike (1932), born in Pennsylvania, is a prolific poet, fiction writer, and critic. Educated at Harvard and Oxford, he joined the staff of *The New Yorker* in 1955 at age twenty-three. He continues to write for the magazine while at the same time publishing novels; autobiography; and collections of poetry, essays, and stories. He received the National Book Award in 1964 and the O. Henry Award in 1966. Writings include: *The Carpentered Hen and Other Tame Creatures* (1958), *The Poorhouse Fair* (1959), *Rabbit, Run* (1960), *The Centaur* (1963), *The Music School* (1966), *Bech: A Book* (1970), *Seventy Poems* (1972), *Too Far to Go* (1978), *Rabbit Is Rich* (1982), *Hugging the Shore* (1983), *The Witches of Eastwick* (1984), *Roger's Version* (1986), *Trust Me* (1987), *Just Looking: Essays on Art* (1989), *Picked Up Pieces* (1989), *Self-Consciousness: Memoirs* (1989).

Kurt Vonnegut, Jr. (1922) was born in Indianapolis, Indiana. He left Cornell University to join the Army and serve in Europe in World War II. While a prisoner of the German army, he experienced the fire bombing of Dresden in 1945. Following the war, he returned to school and graduated from the University of Chicago. After a few years in the public relations department of General Electric, he has devoted himself to full-time writing and lecturing. His works have sold in the millions. Writings include: *Player Piano* (1952), *The Sirens of Titan* (1959), *Mother Night* (1962), *Cat's Cradle* (1963), *God Bless You, Mr. Rosewater* (1965), *Welcome to the Monkey House* (1968), *Slaughterhouse-Five* (1969), *Breakfast of Champions* (1973), *Slapstick* (1976), *Jailbird* (1979), *Deadeye Dick* (1985), *Galapagos* (1986), *Bluebeard* (1987), *Hocus Pocus* (1990).

Alice Walker (1944) was born in Eatonton, Georgia. As a child, she turned to books to escape the hardships of her real world. After hearing Martin Luther King, Jr. speak when she was a freshman at Spelman College, she credited him with giving her life purpose. She began writing poetry while at Sarah Lawrence College; her poems were accepted for publication when she was only twenty-one. She began to write essays and fiction focusing primarily on black feminism. In 1983, she won both the Pulitzer Prize and the American Book Award for *The Color Purple.* Writings include: *Revolutionary Petunias and Other Poems* (1973), *In Love and Trouble: Stories of Black Women* (1973), *Meridian* (1976), *You Can't Keep a Good Woman Down* (1981), *The Color Purple* (1982), *In Search of Our Mothers' Gardens* (1983), *Living by the Word* (1988) *The Temple of My Familiar* (1989).

Eudora Welty (1909) was born in Mississippi, the setting of most of her fiction. She was educated in Mississippi until she went to the University of Wisconsin for an A.B. degree and to Columbia University to study advertising. Her writing career began in 1936 with the publication of a short story—"Death of a Traveling Salesman." Although she usually pictures southern or small-town life in her writings, her reputation as a great practitioner of the short story is national. In both her stories and novels, places and people come alive; the dialogue rings true, and the visual details reflect keen observation. She has received numerous awards, among them the Howells Medal in 1955, given by the American Academy of Arts and Letters, and the Pulitzer Prize in 1973. Writings include: *A Curtain of Green* (1941), *The Robber Bridegroom* (1942), *Delta Wedding* (1946), *The Wide Net* (1943), *The Golden Apples* (1949), *The Ponder Heart* (1954), *The Bride of the Innisfallen* (1955), *Losing Battles* (1970), *One Time, One Place* (1971), *The Optimist's Daughter* (1972), *The Eye of the Story: Selected Essays and Reviews* (1979), *The Collected Stories of Eudora Welty* (1980), *One Writer's Beginnings* (1984), *Photographs* (1989)

Marie Winn (1937) was born in Czechoslovakia. She was educated at Radcliffe College and at Columbia University. In her writings, she has focused on children—producing books both for and about children. Writings include: *The Plug-In Drug: Television, Children, and the Family* (1977), *Children without Childhood* (1983), *Unplug the Plug-In Drug* (1987).

Virginia Woolf (1882–1941) was born in London and self-educated in the extensive library of her father, Leslie Stephen—a distinguished philosopher, critic, and editor. Woolf developed into one of the finest writers of the twentieth century, producing novels, essays, and criticism. Her novels broke away from the traditional emphasis on outward occurrences and focused on the complexities of inner sensations. Woolf suffered periodically from severe depression and in 1941 ended her own life. Writings include: *The Voyage Out* (1915), *Jacob's Room* (1922), *The Common Reader* (1925, 1932), *Mrs. Dalloway* (1925), *To the Lighthouse* (1927), *Orlando* (1928), *A Room of One's Own* (1929), *The Waves* (1931), *The Second Common Reader* (1932), *The Years* (1937), *Between the Acts* (1941), *The Death of the Moth and Other Essays* (1942).

■ ■ ■
ACKNOWLEDGMENTS

CHAPTER 1

Elizabeth Stone. "How Our Family Stories Shape Us" from *Black Sheep and Kissing Cousins* by Elizabeth Stone. Copyright © 1988 by Elizabeth Stone. Reprinted by permission of Random House, Inc.

Margaret Laurence. "Where the World Began" from *Heart of a Stranger* by Margaret Laurence. Copyright © by Margaret Laurence. Reprinted by permission of Jocelyn Laurence.

Nikki Giovanni. "400 Mulvaney Street" from *Gemini* by Nikki Giovanni. Copyright © 1971 by Nikki Giovanni. Reprinted by permission of MacMillan Publishing Company.

Russell Baker. "Uncle Harold" from *Growing Up* by Russell Baker. Copyright © 1982 by Russell Baker. Reprinted by permission of Congdon & Weed, Chicago.

James D. Houston. "How Playing Country Music Taught Me to Love My Dad" from *The Men in My Life* by James D. Houston. Copyright © 1987 by James D. Houston. Reprinted by permission of Creative Arts Book Co., Berkeley, CA.

Sallie Tisdale. "Bound Upon a Wheel of Fire" by Sallie Tisdale, from *Harper's.* Copyright © 1990 by and reprinted by permission of Sallie Tisdale.

Eudora Welty. "Why I Live at the P.O." from *A Curtain of Green* by Eudora Welty. Copyright © 1941 by Eudora Welty. Reprinted by permission of Harcourt Brace Jovanovich, Inc.

John Updike. "Three Boys" by John Updike, from *Five Boyhoods* edited by Martin Levin. Copyright © 1962 by Martin Levin, renewed 1990 by and reprinted by permission of Martin Levin.

Annie Dillard. "The Chase" from *An American Childhood* by Annie Dillard. Copyright © 1987 by Annie Dillard. Reprinted by permission of HarperCollins Publishers, Inc.

Phillip Lopate. "My Early Years at School" from *Bachelorhood: Tales of the Metropolis* by Phillip Lopate. Copyright © 1981 by and reprinted by permission of Phillip Lopate.

Ernesto Galarza. "Lincoln School" from *Barrio Boy* by Ernesto Galarza. Copyright © 1971 by Ernesto Galarza. Reprinted by permission of University of Notre Dame Press.

Elizabeth Bishop. "Primer Class" from *The Collected Prose* by Elizabeth Bishop. Copyright © 1984 by Elizabeth Bishop. Reprinted by permission of Farrar, Straus and Giroux.

Maya Angelou. "Graduation at Lafayette County Training School" from *I Know Why the Caged Bird Sings* by Maya Angelou. Copyright © 1969 by Maya Angelou. Reprinted by permission of Random House, Inc.

Richard Thurman. "Not Another Word" by Richard Thurman, from *The New Yorker.* Copyright © 1957, 1985 by and reprinted by permission of The New Yorker Magazine, Inc.

CHAPTER 2

Daniel J. Boorstin. "Christmas and Other Festivals of Consumption" from *The Americans: The Democratic Experience* by Daniel J. Boorstin. Copyright © 1973 by Daniel Boorstin. Reprinted by permission of Random House, Inc.

Michael J. Arlen. "Ode to Thanksgiving" from *The Camera Age* by Michael J. Arlen. Copyright © 1981 by Michael J. Arlen. Reprinted by permission of Farrar, Straus and Giroux.

William Geist. "Megawatt Miracles of the Yuletide" from *Toward a Safe and Sane Halloween and Other Tales of Surburbia* by William Geist. Copyright © 1985 and reprinted by permission of William Geist.

Jessica Mitford. Excerpt from *The American Way of Death* by Jessica Mitford. Copyright © 1963, 1978 by Jessica Mitford. Reprinted by permission of Simon and Schuster, Inc.

Pat Esslinger Carr. "The Party" by Pat Esslinger Carr, from *Selected Stories from the Southern Review,* Louisiana State University Press. Copyright © 1988 by and reprinted by permission of Pat Esslinger Carr.

Ink Mendelsohn. "We Were What We Wore" by Ink Mendelsohn, from *American Heritage,* Vol. 39, No. 8. Copyright © 1988 by and reprinted by permission of American Heritage, a division of Forbes, Inc.

Alison Lurie. "The Language of White Costumes" from *The Language of Clothes* by Alison Lurie. Copyright © 1981 by Alison Lurie. Reprinted by permission of Melanie Jackson Agency.

Carin C. Quinn. "The Jeaning of America" by Carin C. Quinn, from *American Heritage,* Vol. 29, No. 3. Copyright © 1978 by and reprinted by permission of American Heritage, a division of Forbes, Inc.

Roy Blount, Jr. "On Hats" from *What Men Don't Tell Women* by Roy Blount, Jr. Copyright © 1984 by Roy Blount, Jr. Reprinted by permission of Little, Brown and Company.

Roland Sodowsky. "The Origins of the Cowboy Boot" from *The Atlantic.* Excerpted from *Un-Due West: An Imaginative History of Cowboying, Windmills, Rodeos, Brands, Pickup Trucks, Horse-Trailing, and much, much more* by Roland Sodowsky. Copyright © 1989 and reprinted by permission of Roland Sodowsky.

Peter Farb and George Armelagos. "Understanding Society Through Eating" from *Consuming Passions: The Anthropology of Eating* by Peter Farb and George Armelagos. Copyright © 1980 by the Estate of Peter Farb. Reprinted by permission of Houghton Mifflin Co.

Guy Davenport. "The Anthroplogy of Table Manners" by Guy Davenport, from *The Geography of the Imagination.* Copyright © 1983 by Beryl Markham. Published by North Point Press and reprinted by permission.

Reay Tannahill. "Future Eating Patterns" from *Food in History* by Reay Tannahill. Copyright © 1973 by Reay Tannahill. Reprinted by permission of Campbell, Thomson and McLaughlin, Ltd.

Vernon Pizer. "BLT, Hold the Mayo" from *Eat the Grapes Downward* by Vernon Pizer. Copyright © 1983 by and reprinted by permission of Vernon Pizer.

Joseph Monninger. "Fast Food" by Joseph Monninger, from *American Heritage,* Vol. 39, No. 3. Copyright © 1988 by and reprinted by permission of American Heritage, a division of Forbes, Inc.

A. R. Gurney, Jr. "The Dinner Party" by A. R. Gurney, Jr., from *American Heritage.* Copyright © 1988 by A. R. Gurney, Jr. Reprinted by permission of The William Morris Agency.

CHAPTER 3

Joan Didion. "John Wayne: A Love Song" from *Slouching Toward Bethlehem* by Joan Didion. Copyright © 1968 by Joan Didion. Reprinted by permission of Farrar, Straus and Giroux.

Roger Rosenblatt. "Reconsideration: *Gone with the Wind*" by Roger Rosenblatt, from *The New Republic.* Copyright © 1975 by and reprinted by permission of The New Republic, Inc.

Stephen King. "My Creature from the Black Lagoon" from *Danse Macabre* by Stephen King. Copyright © 1981 by Stephen King. Reprinted by permission of Jay Kramer.

Walter Karp. "Where the Media Critics Went Wrong" by Walter Karp, from *American Heritage* Vol. 39, No. 2. Copyright © 1988 and reprinted by permission of American Heritage, a division of Forbes, Inc.

Marie Winn. "How Parents Survived Before Television" from *The Plug-In Drug* by Marie Winn. Copyright © 1977 by Marie Winn Miller. Reprinted by permission of Viking Penguin, a division of Penguin Books USA Inc.

Gwen Kinkead. "Another World" by Gwen Kinkead, from *Savvy Woman.* Copyright © 1989 by and reprinted by permission of Gwen Kinkead.

N. Scott Momaday. "Discovering the Land of Light" by N. Scott Momaday, from *The Sophisticated Traveler.* Copyright © 1986 by and reprinted by permission of N. Scott Momaday.

Manuela Hoelterhoff. "Walt's Wonderful World Turns Out to Be Flat" by Manuela Hoelterhoff, from *The Wall Street Journal.* Copyright © 1982 by Dow Jones & Company. All rights reserved.

Jean Stafford. "Why I Don't Get Around Much Anymore" by Jean Stafford, from *Esquire.* Copyright © 1975 and reprinted by permission of the Hearst Corporation.

Ben Yagota. "Unfolding the Nation" by Ben Yagota, from *American Heritage* Vol. 39, No. 3. Copyright © 1988 by and reprinted by permission of American Heritage, a division of Forbes, Inc.

Jan Morris. "On Wateriness" from *Travels* by Jan Morris. Copyright © 1976 by Jan Morris. Reprinted by permission of Harcourt Brace Jovanovich, Inc.

Bobbie Ann Mason. "The Ocean" from *Shiloh and Other Stories* by Bobbie Ann Mason. Copyright © 1982 by Bobbie Ann Mason. Reprinted by permission of HarperCollins Publishers Inc.

Rheta Grimsley Johnson. "Greg Pratt is Dead" by Rheta Grimsley Johnson, from *America's Faces.* Copyright © 1987 by and reprinted by permission of St. Luke's Press.

Leonard Koppett. "Baseball's Hits and Misses" by Leonard Koppett, from *The New York Times.* Copyright © 1986 by and reprinted by permission of The New York Times Company.

Donald Hall. "Basketball: The Purest Sport of Bodies" from *Fathers Playing Catch With Sons* by Donald Hall. Copyright © 1985 by Donald Hall. Published by North Point Press and reprinted by permission.

Joyce Carol Oates. "On Boxing and Pain" from *On Boxing* by Joyce Carol Oates. Copyright © 1987 by Ontario Review, Inc. Used by permission of Doubleday, a division of Bantam Doubleday Dell Publishing Group, Inc.

Nikki Giovanni. "Towards Better Human Understanding" from *Sacred Cows and Other Edibles* by Nikki Giovanni. Copyright © 1988 by Nikki Giovanni. Reprinted by permission of William Morrow & Co.

CHAPTER 4

John Stewart Collis. "The Potato" from *The Worm Forgives the Plow* by John Stewart Collis. Copyright © 1973 by John Stewart Collis. Reprinted by permission of A. P. Watt, London.

Loren Eiseley. "How Flowers Changed the World" from *The Immense Journey* by Loren Eiseley. Copyright © 1957 by Loren Eiseley. Reprinted by permission of Random House, Inc.

Sally Carrighar. "The Cutthroat Trout" from *One Day at Teton Marsh* by Sally Carrighar. Copyright © 1945, 1946, 1947 and renewed 1975 by Sally Carrighar. Reprinted by permission of Alfred A. Knopf, Inc.

Edward Hoagland. "The Courage of Turtles" from *The Edward Hoagland Reader,* edited by Geoffrey Wolff. Copyright © 1968, 1969, 1970, 1971, 1972, 1973, 1974, 1975, 1976 by Edward Hoagland. Reprinted by permission of Random House, Inc.

David Quammin. "Has Success Spoiled the Crow?" from *Natural Acts* by David Quammin. Copyright © 1983 by and reprinted by permission of David Quammin.

Phyllis S. Busch. "Plants and Animals in Winter" by Phyllis S. Busch from *The Conservationist.* Copyright © 1989 by and reprinted by permission of The Conservationist.

Alice Walker. "Am I Blue?" by Alice Walker. Copyright © by Alice Walker. Reprinted by permission of Harcourt Brace Jovanovich, Inc. Song lyric copyright 1929 Warner Bros., Inc. (renewed) by Grant Clarke and Harry Akst. All rights reserved. Used by permission.

James C. Rettie. "But for a Watch in the Night" from *Forever the Land* by James C. Rettie, edited by Russell and Kate Lord. Copyright 1950 by Harper & Row, Publishers, Inc.; copyright © renewed 1978 by Russell and Kate Lord. Reprinted by permission of HarperCollins Publishers, Inc.

Marjorie Kinnan Rawlings. "Who Owns Cross Creek?" from *Cross Creek* by Marjorie Kinnan Rawlings. Copyright 1942 Marjorie Kinnan Rawlings; copyright renewed © 1970 Norton Baskin. Reprinted by permission of Charles Scribner's Sons, an imprint of Macmillan Publishing Company.

Eleanor Perényi. "Partly Cloudy" from *Green Thoughts* by Eleanor Perényi. Copyright © 1981 by Eleanor Perényi. Reprinted by permission of Random House, Inc.

Robert Finch. "One that Got Away" from *Outlands* by Robert Finch. Copyright © 1986 by Robert Finch. Reprinted by permission of David R. Godine, Publisher.

Jesse Hill Ford. "To the Open Water" from *Fishes, Birds and Songs of Men* by Jesse Hill Ford. Copyright © 1967 by and reprinted by permission of Jesse Hill Ford.

Rachel Carson. "The Obligation to Endure" from *Silent Spring* by Rachel Carson. Copyright © 1962 by Rachel L. Carson. Reprinted by permission of Houghton Mifflin Co.

CHAPTER 5

Norman Cousins. "The Poet and the Computer" by Norman Cousins, from *National Forum.* Copyright © 1989 by and reprinted by permission of Norman Cousins.

Tom Bodett. "Command Performance" from *Small Comforts* by Tom Bodett. Copyright © 1987 by Tom Bodett. Reprinted by permission of Addison-Wesley Publishing Co., Inc.

Craig Brod. "Childhood Lost" from *Technostress* by Craig Brod. Copyright © 1984 by Craig Brod. Reprinted by permission Carol Mann Literary Agency.

Sherry Turkle. "The New Philosophers of Artificial Intelligence" from *The Second Self* by Sherry Turkle. Copyright © 1984 by Sherry Turkle. Reprinted by permission of Simon & Schuster, Inc.

Kurt Vonnegut, Jr. "EPICAC" from *Welcome to the Monkey House* by Kurt Vonnegut, Jr. Copyright © 1950 by Kurt Vonnegut, Jr. Reprinted by permission of Delacorte Press/Seymour Lawrence, a division of Bantam, Doubleday, Dell Publishing Group, Inc.

Paul Loeb. "Atomic Soap" from *Nuclear Culture* by Paul Loeb. Copyright © 1986 by Paul Loeb. Reprinted by permission of New Society Publishers.

Helen Caldicott. "What You Must Know about Radiation" by Helen Caldicott, from *Redbook.* Copyright © 1979 by and reprinted by permission of Helen Caldicott.

Calvin Trillin. "Nuclear War: My Position" from *With All Disrespect* by Calvin Trillin. Copyright © 1985 by Calvin Trillin. Reprinted by permission of Lescher & Lescher, Ltd.

Lydia Dotto. "The Environmental Consequences of Nuclear War" by Lydia Dotto, from *Planet Earth in Jeopardy.* Copyright © 1986 by the Scientific Committee on Problems of the Environment. Reprinted by permission of John Wiley & Sons.

Joy Kogawa. "The Letters" from *Obasan* by Joy Kogawa. Copyright © 1981 by Joy Kogawa. Reprinted by permission of David R. Godine, Publisher.

Annabel Thomas. Excerpt from *The Phototropic Woman* by Annabel Thomas. Copyright © 1981 by and reprinted by permission of the University of Iowa Press.

Isaac Asimov. "A Choice of Catastrophes" from *Life and Time* by Isaac Asimov. Copyright ©

CHAPTER 6

CHAPTER 7

INDEX OF AUTHORS
AND TITLES

"Acid Test," by Dava Sobel, 533–536

Adler, Mortimer J., "Paideia Proposal: The Same Course of Study for All," 554–563

"American Way of Death, The," by Jessica Mitford, 111–115

"Am I Blue?" by Alice Walker, 334–339

Angelou, Maya, "Graduation at Lafayette County Training School," 70–80

"Another World," by Gwen Kinkead, 225–229

"Anthropology of Table Manners from Geophagy Onward, The," by Guy Davenport, 153–160

Arlen, Michael J., "Ode to Thanksgiving," 107–110

Asimov, Isaac, "A Choice of Catastrophes," 451–462

"Atomic Soap: On the Job With the Young and the Restless," by Paul Loeb, 407–413

Baker, Russell, "Uncle Harold," 18–23

Baldwin, James, "Fifth Avenue, Uptown: A Letter from Harlem," 579–587

Bambara, Toni Cade, "The Lesson," 677–685

"Baseball's Hits and Misses," by Leonard Koppett, 272–279

"Basketball: The Purest Sport of Bodies," by Donald Hall, 279–283

"Beyond the Knowable: The Ultimate Exploration," by Holcomb B. Noble, 471–480

Bishop, Elizabeth, "Primer Class," 64–70

Blount, Roy, Jr., "On Hats," 138–142

"BLT, Hold the Mayo," by Vernon Pizer, 168–175

Bodett, Tom, "Command Performance," 378–381

Boorstin, Daniel J., "Christmas and Other Festivals of Consumption," 97–104

"Born to Run," by Don Oldenburg, 619–633

"Bound upon a Wheel of Fire," by Sallie Tisdale, 29–35

Brod, Craig, "Childhood Lost," 381–394

Busch, Phyllis S., "Plants and Animals in Winter," 327–334

" 'But a Watch in the Night': A Scientific Fable," by James C. Rettie, 340–345

Caldicott, Helen, "What You Must Know about Radiation," 413–424

Cameron, Peter, "Homework," 526–532

"Captive State, A," by Jonathan Kozol, 643–656

Carr, Pat Esslinger, "The Party," 115–121

Carrighar, Sally, "The Cutthroat Trout," 307–317

Carson, Rachel, "The Obligation to Endure," 367–374

"Chase, The," by Annie Dillard, 51–54

"Cheating: Alive and Flourishing," by Claudia H. Deutsch, 502–509

"Childhood Lost," by Craig Brod, 381–394

"Choice of Catastrophes, A," by Isaac Asimov, 451–462

"Christmas and Other Festivals of Consumption," by Daniel J. Boorstin, 97–104

"Classroom, The," by Neil Postman, 517–526

"Clean, Well-Lighted Bench, A," by Marjorie Hope, 656–670

Collis, John Stewart, "The Potato," 295–298

"Command Performance," by Tom Bodett, 378–381

"Courage of Turtles, The," by Edward Hoagland, 317–323

Cousins, Norman, "The Poet and the Computer," 375–378

"Cutthroat Trout, The," by Sally Carrighar, 307–317

707

Davenport, Guy, "The Anthropology of Table Manners from Geophagy Onward," 153–160

"Dead-End Kids, The," by Michele Manges, 509–512

Deutsch, Claudia H., "Cheating: Alive and Flourishing," 502–509

Didion, Joan, "John Wayne: A Love Song," 193–200

Dillard, Annie, "The Chase," 51–54

"Dinner Party, The," by A.R. Gurney, Jr., 186–192

"Discovering the Land of Light," by N. Scott Momaday, 230–236

Dotto, Lydia, "The Environmental Consequences of Nuclear War," 427–437

"Eerie World of Living Heads, The," by Larry Thompson, 480–486

Eiseley, Loren, "How Flowers Changed the World," 299–307

"Environmental Consequences of Nuclear War, The," by Lydia Dotto, 427–437

"EPICAC," by Kurt Vonnegut, Jr., 400–406

"Excuses, Excuses," by Helen C. Vo-Dinh, 514–517

Farb, Peter and George Armelagos, "Understanding Society and Culture Through Eating," 147–153

"Fast Food," by Joseph Monninger, 175–186

"Fifth Avenue, Uptown: A Letter from Harlem," by James Baldwin, 579–587

Finch, Robert, "One That Got Away," 353–360

Ford, Jesse Hill, "To the Open Water," 360–367

"400 Mulvaney Street," by Nikki Giovanni, 11–18

"Future Eating Patterns," by Reay Tannahill, 160–168

Galarza, Ernesto, "Lincoln School," 58–63

Geist, William, "Megawatt Miracles of the Yuletide," 104–107

Giovanni, Nikki, "400 Mulvaney Street," 11–18

Giovanni, Nikki, "Toward Better Human Understanding," 287–294

"Graduation at Lafayette County Training School," by Maya Angelou, 70–80

"Greg Pratt Is Dead," by Rheta Grimsley Johnson, 270–272

Gurney, A.R., Jr., "The Dinner Party," 186–192

Hall, Donald, "Basketball: The Purest Sport of Bodies," 279–283

"Has Success Spoiled the Crow?" by David Quammin, 323–327

Hoagland, Edward, "The Courage of Turtles," 317–323

Hoelterhoff, Manuela, "Walt's Wonderful World Turns Out to Be Flat," 236–241

"Homework," by Peter Cameron, 526–532

Hope, Marjorie, "A Clean, Well-Lighted Bench," 656–670

Houston, James D., "How Playing Country Music Taught Me To Love My Dad," 23–29

"How Flowers Changed the World," by Loren Eiseley, 299–307

"How Our Family Stories Shape Us," by Elizabeth Stone, 1–6

"How Parents Survived before Television," by Marie Winn, 220–225

"How Playing Country Music Taught Me To Love My Dad," by James D. Houston, 23–29

"Is History a Guide to the Future?" by Barbara Tuchman, 462–471

"Is Television Shortening Our Attention Span?" by Robert MacNeil, 536–543

"Jeaning of America—and the World, The," by Carin C. Quinn, 135–138

"Jewish Education, A," by Roger Kahn, 593–600

Johnson, Rheta Grimsley, "Greg Pratt Is Dead," 270–272

"John Wayne: A Love Song," by Joan Didion, 193–200

Kahn, Roger, "A Jewish Education," 593–600

Karp, Walter, "Where the Media Critics Went Wrong," 214–219

King, Stephen, "My Creature from the Black Lagoon," 206–214

Kinkead, Gwen, "Another World," 225–229

Kogawa, Joy, "The Letters," 437–443

Koppett, Leonard, "Baseball's Hits and Misses," 272–279

Kozol, Jonathan, "A Captive State," 643–656

"Language of White Costumes, The," by Alison Lurie, 132–135

Laurence, Margaret, "Where the World Began," 6–10

Le Guin, Ursula K., "SQ," 486–494

"Lesson, The," by Toni Cade Bambara, 677–685

"Letters, The," by Joy Kogawa, 437–443

Lichtenstein, Grace, "Playing for Money," 543–553

"Lincoln School," by Ernesto Galarza, 58–63

"Lives of Teenage Mothers, The," by Elizabeth Marek, 633–643

Loeb, Paul, "Atomic Soap: On the Job With the Young and the Restless," 407–413

Lopate, Phillip, "My Early Years at School," 54–58

Lurie, Alison, "The Language of White Costumes," 132–135

MacNeil, Robert, "Is Television Shortening Our Attention Span?" 536–543

Manges, Michele, "The Dead-End Kids," 509–512

Marek, Elizabeth, "The Lives of Teenage Mothers," 633–643

Mason, Bobbie Ann, "The Ocean," 256–269

McIntyre, Vonda N., "Thanatos," 494–501

McKenzie, Floretta Dukes, "The Yellow Brick Road of Education," 563–568

Mebane, Mary, "The System," 587–593

"Megawatt Miracles of the Yuletide," by William Geist, 104–107

Mendelsohn, Ink, "We Were What We Wore," 122–132

Miller, Casey and Kate Swift, "One Small Step for Genkind," 607–618

Mitford, Jessica, "The American Way of Death," 111–115

Momaday, N. Scott, "Discovering the Land of Light," 230–236

Monninger, Joseph, "Fast Food," 175–186

Morris, Jan, "On Wateriness," 252–256

"My Creature from the Black Lagoon," by Stephen King, 206–214

"My Early Years at School," by Phillip Lopate, 54–58

"New Philosophers of Artificial Intelligence, The," by Sherry Turkle, 394–400

Noble, Holcomb B., "Beyond the Knowable: The Ultimate Exploration," 471–480

"Not Another Word," by Richard Thurman, 80–96

"No Woman Wrote a Word," by Virginia Woolf, 600–607

"Nuclear War: My Position," by Calvin Trillin, 424–427

Oates, Joyce Carol, "On Boxing and Pain," 283–287

"Obligation to Endure, The," by Rachel Carson, 367–374

"Ocean, The," by Bobbie Ann Mason, 256–269

"Ode to Thanksgiving," by Michael J. Arlen, 107–110

Oldenburg, Don, "Born to Run," 619–633

"On Boxing and Pain," by Joyce Carol Oates, 283–287

"One Small Step for Genkind," by Casey Miller and Kate Swift, 607–618

"One That Got Away," by Robert Finch, 353–360

"On Hats," by Roy Blount, Jr., 138–142

"On Thinking About the Future," by Diane Ravitch, 568–578

"On Wateriness," by Jan Morris, 252–256

"Origins of the Cowboy Boot, The," by Roland Sodowsky, 142–146

"Paideia Proposal: The Same Course of Study for All," by Mortimer J. Adler, 554–563

"Partly Cloudy," by Eleanor Perényi, 348–353

"Party, The," by Pat Esslinger Carr, 115–121

Perényi, Eleanor, "Partly Cloudy," 348–353

"Phototropic Woman, The" by Annabel Thomas, 443–450

Pizer, Vernon, "BLT, Hold the Mayo," 168–175

"Plants and Animals in Winter," by Phyllis S. Busch, 327–334

"Playing for Money," by Grace Lichtenstein, 543–553

"Poet and the Computer, The," by Norman Cousins, 375–378

Postman, Neil, "The Classroom," 517–526

"Potato, The," by John Stewart Collis, 295–298

"Primer Class," by Elizabeth Bishop, 64–70

Quammin, David, "Has Success Spoiled the Crow?" 323–327

Quinn, Carin C., "The Jeaning of America—and the World," 135–138

Ravitch, Diane, "On Thinking About the Future," 568–578

Rawlings, Marjorie Kinnan, "Who Owns Cross Creek?" 345–348

"Reconsideration: *Gone With the Wind,* the Movie," by Roger Rosenblatt, 200–206

Regier, Gail, "Users, Like Me: Membership in the Church of Drugs," 670–677

Rettie, James C., " 'But a Watch in the Night': A Scientific Fable," 340–345

Rosenblatt, Roger, "Reconsideration: *Gone With the Wind,* the Movie," 200–206

Royko, Mike, "Write On, Barbarians," 512–514

Sobel, Dava, "Acid Test," 533–536

Sodowsky, Roland, "The Origins of the Cowboy Boot," 142–146

"SQ," by Ursula K. Le Guin, 486–494

Stafford, Jean, "Why I Don't Get Around Much Anymore," 241–248

Stone, Elizabeth, "How Our Family Stories Shape Us," 1–6

"System, The," by Mary Mebane, 587–593

Tannahill, Reay, "Future Eating Patterns," 160–168

"Thanatos," by Vonda N. McIntyre, 494–501

Thomas, Annabel, "The Phototropic Woman," 443–450

Thompson, Larry, "The Eerie World of Living Heads," 480–486

"Three Boys," by John Updike, 47–51

Thurman, Richard, "Not Another Word," 80–96

Tisdale, Sallie, "Bound upon a Wheel of Fire," 29–35

"To the Open Water," by Jesse Hill Ford, 360–367

"Toward Better Human Understanding," by Nikki Giovanni, 287–294

Trillin, Calvin, "Nuclear War: My Position," 424–427

Tuchman, Barbara, "Is History a Guide to the Future?" 462–471

Turkle, Sherry, "The New Philosophers of Artificial Intelligence," 394–400

"Uncle Harold," by Russell Baker, 18–23

"Understanding Society and Culture Through Eating," by Peter Farb and George Armelagos, 147–153

"Unfolding the Nation," by Ben Yagota, 248–252

Updike, John, "Three Boys," 47–51

"Users Like Me: Membership in the Church of Drugs," by Gail Regier, 670–677

Vo-Dinh, Helen C., "Excuses, Excuses," 514–517

Vonnegut, Kurt, Jr., "EPICAC," 400–406

Walker, Alice, "Am I Blue?" 334–339

"Walt's Wonderful World Turns Out to Be Flat," by Manuela Hoelterhoff, 236–241

Welty, Eudora, "Why I Live at the P.O.," 36–46

"We Were What We Wore," by Ink Mendelsohn, 122–132

"What You Must Know about Radiation," by Helen Caldicott, 413–424

"Where the Media Critics Went Wrong," by Walter Karp, 214–219

"Where the World Began," by Margaret Laurence, 6–10

"Who Owns Cross Creek?" by Marjorie Kinnan Rawlings, 345–348

"Why I Don't Get Around Much Anymore," by Jean Stafford, 241–248

"Why I Live at the P.O.," by Eudora Welty, 36–46

Winn, Marie, "How Parents Survived before Television," 220–225

Woolf, Virginia, "No Woman Wrote a Word," 600–607

"Write On, Barbarians," by Mike Royko, 512–514

Yagota, Ben, "Unfolding the Nation," 248–252

"Yellow Brick Road of Education, The," by Floretta Dukes McKenzie, 563–568